STATE AND LOCAL
GOVERNMENT

VAN NOSTRAND POLITICAL SCIENCE SERIES

Editor

FRANKLIN L. BURDETTE
University of Maryland

HARWOOD L. CHILDS—*Public Opinion*

RUSSELL W. MADDOX, JR.—*Issues in State and Local Government: Selected Readings*

MARTIN C. NEEDLER—*Political Systems of Latin America*

HAROLD and MARGARET SPROUT—*Foundations of International Politics*

WILLIAM G. ANDREWS—*European Political Institutions*

H. B. SHARABI—*Governments and Politics of the Middle East in the Twentieth Century*

RUSSELL W. MADDOX, JR., and ROBERT F. FUQUAY—*State and Local Government*, 2nd Ed.

GUY B. HATHORN, HOWARD R. PENNIMAN, and MARK F. FERBER—*Government and Politics in the United States*, 2nd Ed.

SAMUEL HENDEL—*The Soviet Crucible: The Soviet System in Theory and Practice*, 2nd Ed.

HAROLD ZINK—*Modern Governments*

HAROLD ZINK, HOWARD R. PENNIMAN, and GUY B. HATHORN—*American Government and Politics: National, State, and Local*

CONLEY H. DILLON, CARL LEIDEN, and PAUL D. STEWART—*Introduction to Political Science*

BENJAMIN BAKER—*Urban Government*

WILLIS G. SWARTZ—*American Governmental Problems*, 2nd Ed.

WILLIAM GOODMAN—*The Two-Party System in the United States*, 3rd Ed.

P. M. A. LINEBARGER, C. DJANG, and A. W. BURKS—*Far Eastern Governments and Politics—China and Japan*, 2nd Ed.

ELMER PLISCHKE—*International Relations: Basic Documents*, 2nd Ed.

M. JORRIN—*Governments of Latin America*

LANE W. LANCASTER—*Government in Rural America*, 2nd Ed.

R. G. DIXON, JR., and ELMER PLISCHKE—*American Government: Basic Documents and Materials*

ELMER PLISCHKE—*Conduct of American Diplomacy*, 2nd Ed.

STATE AND LOCAL GOVERNMENT

RUSSELL W. MADDOX

AND

ROBERT F. FUQUAY

Department of Political Science
Oregon State University

SECOND EDITION

D. VAN NOSTRAND COMPANY, INC.

PRINCETON, NEW JERSEY

TORONTO   LONDON

NEW YORK

D. VAN NOSTRAND COMPANY, INC.
120 Alexander St., Princeton, New Jersey (*Principal office*)
24 West 40 Street, New York 18, New York

D. VAN NOSTRAND COMPANY, LTD.
358, Kensington High Street, London, W.14, England

D. VAN NOSTRAND COMPANY (Canada), LTD.
25 Hollinger Road, Toronto 16, Canada

First Published, January 1962
*Reprinted November 1962,
June 1963*
Second Edition, January 1966

PRINTED IN THE UNITED STATES OF AMERICA

Preface to the Second Edition

Since the first edition of this volume was prepared, a relatively short period of time, many changes have occurred in the field of state and local government. Some of these changes have been of fundamental importance. The reapportionment controversy, for example, has made it necessary to reexamine many of the basic postulates of the political system. Significant developments in such areas as judicial organization, approaches to welfare, suffrage qualifications, expenditures, sources of income, and the government of metropolitan areas have also occurred. In the present edition we have attempted to incorporate and consider these and other developments without disturbing the basic organizational framework or the general approach of the first edition.

One of our principal aims in preparing this volume has been to make available to the beginning student a text that he can handle with a minimum of instructional guidance, yet one which will provide him with a comprehensive familiarity with the principles, processes, and functions of government at the state and local levels. If this can be accomplished by textual material, the classroom instructor will be freer to deal with matters of current interest and importance. It would be presumptuous to assert that we have achieved this goal in every particular, but the response from both students and instructors to date has been such as to convince us that there are many who believe that we have contributed significantly to this endeavor.

We wish to express our gratitude to the many individuals who have willingly given us their aid and counsel in the preparation of both editions of this text. Our colleagues, friends, and students have been helpful; and especially, the many public officials and employees in all fifty states who responded to our numerous requests for information deserve particular thanks.

R.W.M.

R.F.F.

Contents

CHAPTER 1

From Colonies into States

Civil government in British North America had its beginnings at Jamestown, Virginia, the first permanent settlement planted by the English on the North American continent. In 1607 three ships of the London Company, a trading enterprise acting under a royal grant to develop the Virginia territory, landed 120 men near the mouth of the James River. Under the direction of a seven-man council a fort was built, a town laid out, and general preparations for community life made.

The settlers were poorly equipped to meet the hardships of colonial living, and the necessity for strong leadership soon resulted in the concentration of all governmental authority in a governor selected by the Company. Still, progress was slow and profits few. Consequently, in the belief that self-government would contribute to prosperous development, a liberal group within the Company obtained the adoption of a plan of government giving to the colonists a measure of control over local affairs. Effective in 1619, an assembly was created to include representatives elected by the people. A council was provided to share the executive duties of the governor and to act with him as a high court of justice. This arrangement, continued after Virginia became a royal colony in 1624, set the basic governmental pattern for other English colonies.

Shortly after the Jamestown venture other settlements were undertaken. One after another, colonies were organized along the Atlantic Coast from the Carolinas to the northern areas of present-day Maine. The inland boundaries were indefinite, but for all practical purposes they extended to the chains of eastern mountains. By 1732, when the colony of Georgia was formed, the colonies destined to become the thirteen original states were in existence.

The prevailing governmental ideas and institutions throughout the colonial period were distinctly English in character. Writings by theorists such as Rousseau, Montesquieu, and Locke had their effect

1

as did the colonial environment. In some areas where settlements were populated in large measure by colonists from countries other than England, deviations from English patterns existed. In general, however, English modes predominated.

THE COLONIAL GOVERNMENTS

Although governments in the colonies were by no means identical, they followed the same general outlines. Throughout the colonial period the governments underwent constant change. They may be classified, however, into three general categories according to the type of charter under which they existed.

Royal Colonies. As implied by the name, the royal colonies were those over which the British monarch exercised the highest degree of direct control. The pattern of government in royal colonies involved appointment by the King of a *royal governor* for each colony. The King also chose a council that served as adviser to the governor and as the "upper house" of the legislature. A "lower house" or assembly was composed of representatives elected by property owners qualified to vote. There were courts, but the council acted as the highest court of appeals. From time to time instructions for the government of the colonies were transmitted from London; and the governors, the most powerful figures in the royal colonies, were responsible for seeing that these were carried out.

At the time of the Revolution there were eight royal colonies: Georgia, Massachusetts, New Hampshire, New Jersey, New York, North Carolina, South Carolina, and Virginia. Of these, Virginia was the first, having been designated a royal colony in 1624. Massachusetts in 1691 and Georgia in 1732 were the last to join the list. It was in these colonies, frequently ruled by stern governors, that much of the agitation leading to the Revolution occurred.

Proprietary Colonies. On Independence Day in 1776 there were three proprietary colonies: Delaware, Maryland, and Pennsylvania. Their governmental system was much the same as that in the royal colonies, with the important difference that the authority to govern flowed directly from a *proprietor* instead of the King. The proprietor was an individual to whom the King had granted lands to be settled and developed. The monarch exercised general supervision, but the proprietor appointed the governor and provided for the other organs of government.

Charter Colonies. Only Connecticut and Rhode Island enjoyed the status of charter, or corporate, colonies at the time of the Revolution. The structure of government was much like that in the royal and proprietary colonies, but the character of government was radically different. A charter colony functioned much as a corporation under a charter granted by the King. According to these charters, property owners in each colony elected a governor and council as well as members of the assembly. The charters, however, were subject to revocation by the King. Massachusetts, long a charter colony but with a record of resistance to the Crown, had its charter revoked in 1684 and seven years later was made a royal colony. The Connecticut charter of 1662 and the Rhode Island charter of 1633 remained in force as constitutions, with only slight changes occasioned by the Revolution, until well into the nineteenth century.

PRELUDE TO REVOLUTION

British administration of the American colonies was poorly organized and without clearly determined goals. Parliament showed a great deal of interest in the regulation of colonial trade, but it was content to leave colonial administration to the King. In turn, the King permitted various governmental agencies to look after such colonial interests as he considered within their competence or jurisdiction. There was no central English colonial office in the colonies. As far as London was concerned, each of the thirteen American colonies was to be treated as a separate, individual entity.

This sort of supervision, without plan or preconceived goals, contributed to the development of a desire for self-government in the colonies. The lack of an over-all plan for colonial development, compounded by the isolation wrought by a 3,000-mile-wide ocean, literally forced the colonies to assume a large measure of self-government. When British colonial policies became more firm after George III ascended the throne in 1760, disagreements were inevitable. It was this basic conflict—the local desire for colonial autonomy versus increased control from the seat of British government—that eventually brought on the Revolution. The many incidents that followed were merely sparks that kindled the fire of rebellion.

During the 1760's Parliament enacted a series of tax and trade laws that stirred deep resentment among the colonials. Duties on imports from the West Indies were raised; the number of British troops garrisoned in the colonies was increased; and in 1765 the well-known Stamp Act was passed. The law required that tax stamps be affixed to all legal documents, newspapers, and recorded business agreements. Colonial reaction was immediate. Within months delegates from nine of the colonies assembled in New York as the Stamp Act Congress. A Declaration of Rights and Grievances was adopted in protest against the recent policies. The Stamp Act was repealed, but colonial resentment remained. Evasion of the laws, boycotts, discontent, and open violence were common.

The events of the next few years led directly to open hostilities. In 1770, British soldiers stationed in Boston were goaded by a jeering mob into opening fire, resulting in the deaths of five colonials—an incident now known as the Boston Massacre. Three years later, local residents disguised as Indians boarded British ships anchored in Boston harbor and threw their cargoes of tea overboard. In retaliation the port was ordered closed. The Virginia Assembly proclaimed a day of mourning for the closing of the port and was summarily dissolved by the royal governor. In September, 1774, all of the colonies except Georgia sent delegates to Philadelphia to participate in the First Continental Congress. That assemblage sent formal protests to the King and openly encouraged the colonies to resist English trade policies. Before the Second Continental Congress could convene in May of the following year, hostilities between English troops and colonial revolutionists had occurred. On April 19, 1775, the battles of Lexington and Concord were fought.

Six weeks after Congress convened, this time with all the colonies represented, provision was made for a continental army. George Washington of Virginia was installed as Commander-in-Chief. Hostilities continued, but it was not until a year later, on June 7, 1776, that Richard Henry Lee of the Virginia delegation proposed that Congress take the stand:

> *Resolved,* That these United States are, and of right ought to be, free and independent states, that they are absolved from all allegiance to the British Crown, and that all political connection between them and the State of Great Britain is, and ought to be, totally dissolved.

Delegates who felt that reconciliation might yet be accomplished succeeded only in delaying adoption of the resolution, and on July 2 it was unanimously passed. Two days later the Declaration of Independence was adopted and announced.

The break with England was, in the colonial view, complete. Not until the war was won, however, could anyone say that independence was actually accomplished. That day came in 1781 when the British were defeated on the fields of Yorktown, Virginia, and General Cornwallis surrendered. Peace was formalized by the treaty concluded in Paris in 1783.

THE NEW STATES

The changeover from colonial status to independent sovereign existence was not accompanied by a rash of governmental changes. There were some modifications, highly important in some cases; but the basic ideas and concepts of governmental form, processes, and relations to the citizen underwent little alteration. The new state governments were, in effect, the old colonial governments operating in a different context.

Each of the states adopted a written constitution. Connecticut and Rhode Island simply deleted references to the English monarch from their charters, but the remainder of the states framed new instruments. In so doing, the states broke from their English heritage and departed from European custom. The concept of a written constitution setting forth the basic, organic law was reaffirmed and became a fixed part of the pattern of government in the American system.

The state constitutions were characterized by a number of concepts that reflected sentiments long held by the revolutionary element. *Popular sovereignty*, the recognition of the people as the source of all political power, was a premise upon which the new governments rested. *Limited government*, the idea that government may exercise only those powers granted by the people, was also apparent in each of the new state documents. As an added precaution each of the new constitutions contained guarantees of the fundamental civil rights of individuals, with separate Bills of Rights appearing in seven of the new instruments.

Fear of oppression and desire to prevent the recurrence of the strict governmental controls exercised by the former royal governors occasioned a substantial reduction in the powers of the governors of the new states. Much of the power formerly wielded by governors was placed in the hands of the legislatures, resulting in governments characterized by legislative supremacy. Still there was actual *separation of powers* with the executive, legislative, and judicial branches exercising *checks and balances* over each other. It was not until several decades after the Revolution, however, with the adoption of amendments and the framing of new constitutions, that the executive and judicial branches of state governments began to approach levels of authority comparable to that of the legislatures.

THE ARTICLES OF CONFEDERATION

Even though there was no constitutional basis for it, a central government composed solely of the Second Continental Congress came into existence in 1775. This Congress represented an informal union cemented by the need for collective action during the Revolutionary War. On that basis the Congress waged war, issued currency, loaned and borrowed money, sent and received ambassadors, and performed other acts ordinarily undertaken only by the governments of independent, sovereign states.

Congress was unable to agree upon a plan of union until 1777. In November of that year it adopted the Articles of Confederation, a document intended, in its own words, to establish a "perpetual Union between the States" in the nature of "a firm league of friendship." Eleven states approved the Articles during the following year, but Delaware withheld assent until 1779, and ratification in Maryland was not obtained until 1781. The Articles of Confederation, in fact, were not legally in effect until six months before the British surrender at Yorktown.

In retrospect, it is not difficult to see that the union under the Articles was doomed to failure. As soon as the war was over, England was no longer an immediate threat to the security of the states. Only in matters of foreign affairs was the central government empowered to act, all other aspects of governmental activity being left to the discretion of the individual states. The return of peace with each state in virtually complete control of its own affairs saw the rise, or at least the emphasis, of interstate jealousies. Each state sought to protect its own interests, often at the expense of its neighbors. Relief through amendments to the Articles was thwarted in every instance due to the requirement that any change had to receive unanimous approval by the states.

The central government was powerless to help. Without authority to tax or to regulate commerce among the states, its credit exhausted, and its requisitions for funds ignored by the states, the Congress was little more than a debating forum. The situation worsened rapidly. In January, 1786, the Virginia Assembly called for a meeting to be held at Annapolis the following September. It was hoped that delegates from the various states would consider and possibly reach some agreement on "a federal plan for regulating commerce." Only five states—New York, New Jersey, Pennsylvania, Delaware, and Virginia—were represented at the Annapolis Convention. Although the lack of numbers defeated their original purpose, the delegates proposed that another meeting be held in Philadelphia in May, 1787, to devise provisions "necessary to render the constitution of the Federal Government adequate to the exigencies of the Union."

At its next session the Confederate Congress considered the possibilities of a convention as suggested at the Annapolis meeting. Spurred perhaps by the fact that seven states had already selected delegates, Congress, on February 17, 1787, called for a convention to be held in Philadelphia in May "for the sole purpose of revising the Articles of Confederation" in order that they be "adequate to the exigencies of Government and the preservation of the Union."

UNION UNDER THE CONSTITUTION

On Friday, May 25, 1787, the Constitutional Convention began its labors. Throughout the summer and until September 17, the delegates met in secret sessions during which an entirely new document was drafted in preference to a revised version of the Articles of Confederation. Of the seventy-four delegates originally named, fifty-five were present at one time or another. On the final day of the convention forty-two delegates were in attendance, and all but three affixed their signatures to the proposed new constitution.

The Constitution drafted by the Convention was much more than a revision of the Articles of Confederation. It provided for a true central government operating directly upon the people rather than upon the states. It called for a substantial surrender of power by the states and provided for a Union that in designated spheres of activity was superior to the states. Consequently, the course of ratification was stormy. Only after bitter argument and extended controversy in some states did the document win the favor of the popularly elected ratifying conventions. According to the terms of the Constitution itself, it was to take effect upon approval by nine states. The necessary number was achieved with ratification by the New Hampshire convention on June 21, 1788. But not until Virginia and New York, the tenth and eleventh states to approve the Constitution, formally entered the Union was the legal effect meaningful. In September, 1788, the Confederate Congress provided for the election of officials, and by the following spring the new government was in operation.

THE CONSTITUTION AND AFTER

Looking backward through a century and three quarters of United States history, the Constitutional Convention of 1787 stands out as a monumental event. There is no doubt that the accomplishments of that assemblage ranks high, if not at the top, in the list of American political achievements. The wisdom exhibited by the leaders of the Convention in understanding the problems facing the states and providing adequate means for meeting and solving them is impressive.

Even so, careful note must be taken of a number of facts often ignored. The actions of the delegates were profoundly influenced, if not in fact dictated, by the circumstances of the prevailing situation. In order to relieve the economic ills of the day, real central authority had to be effected. At the same time, a transfer of total power from the states to a central government was out of the question. The solution, therefore, lay in an arrangement whereby the powers necessary for adequate national controls could be achieved without undue sacrifice of state authority. The genius of the delegates was demonstrated in their ability to recognize the range of action open to them and in their skill in providing for a workable government within such limitations.

An examination of the Constitution reveals that the basic principles of government which underlay the governments of the states were preserved. The principles of popular sovereignty, limited government, separation of powers, and checks and balances were as much a part of the national system as they were of the various state governments. Individual political and civil rights were not viewed in any different light with the birth of the new Union. In short, except for the idea of federalism established by the new document, the basic concepts upon which the Constitution rested were neither new nor untested.

The adoption of the Constitution and formation of the Union did not automatically solve the problems of the day. The means for solution were provided, but the cooperation of the states was still necessary. Acting alone, or against the efforts of the states, the infant national government would have been hard-pressed indeed to enforce its laws and decisions. The assistance of the states, or at least their acquiescence, was essential to any measure of national success during the early years of union.

Even the firm establishment of a federal union did not provide a solution of all governmental problems. While national regulation of commerce between the states brought chaotic trade conditions under control, there were still many other problems to be met. The states remained highly competitive and jealous of each other. The very existence of a true national government opened whole new areas of concern. Questions of states' rights versus national power began to unfold. Many phases of interstate relations remained as vexatious as before. Future development was bound to create new problems and in some cases to compound the old.

Government in the United States has undergone many changes since the days of the Jamestown settlement. Some alterations have been fundamental in nature, others superficial. Some have been accompanied by social, economic, and political upheavals; others have occurred almost unnoticed. Through all these changes certain concepts have remained constant, embedded in basic American political theory. It is to the description and analysis of these many areas of governmental concern and involvement that the chapters which follow are devoted.

BIBLIOGRAPHICAL NOTE

Following Chapters 2 through 28 are lists of selected books and articles. These materials are suggested reading for students who desire broader understanding of, and further information on, various topics discussed in the text. In order to avoid needless repetition, general sources containing data applicable to several chapters, or even the entire range of subject matter in the text, are noted here.

Among the most valuable sources are the publications of the Council of State Governments. The *Book of the States,* which appears biennially, is a collection of articles and tabular material on virtually all aspects of state government. *State Government,* a quarterly periodical, contains articles and news items on problems of interest to the states. *State Government News,* a pamphlet which notes recent developments, is issued monthly.

The International City Managers' Association publishes an annual compendium of data on local government, entitled *Municipal Yearbook.* A wide variety of tabular information on all governments in America is contained in the *Statistical Abstract of the United States,* a volume which is issued yearly by the U.S. Bureau of the Census. Other general publications of the Bureau that are of special interest are the *County and City Data Book* (1956) and *Historical Statistics of the United States: Colonial Times to 1957* (1960).

Bibliographies listing important materials on a state-by-state basis include W. Brooke Graves, Norman J. Small, and E. Foster Dowell, *American State Government and Administration: A State by State Bibliography,* Council of State Governments, Chicago, 1949; Dorothy C. Tompkins, *State Government and Administration: A Bibliography,* University of California Bureau of Public Administration, Berkeley, 1954; and Council of State Governments, *State Government: An Annotated Bibliography,* Chicago, 1959.

Volumes devoted to general description and analysis of individual states are now appearing in increasing numbers. Coverage now includes about half the states, and many others are treated in regional studies. Included in this group of sources are the following:

Aumann, Francis R., and Walker, Harvey, *The Government and Administration of Ohio,* T. Y. Crowell Co., New York, 1956.

Caldwell, Lynton K., *The Government and Administration of New York,* T. Y. Crowell Co., New York, 1954.

Crouch, Winston W., and McHenry, Dean E., *State and Local Government in California,* 2nd ed., University of California Press, Berkeley, 1949.

Dolan, Paul, *The Government and Administration of Delaware,* T. Y. Crowell Co., New York, 1956.

Donnelly, Thomas C., *The Government of New Mexico,* University of New Mexico Press, Albuquerque, 1947.

Doyle, Wilson K., Laird, Angus M., and Weiss, S. Sherman, *The Government and Administration of Florida,* T. Y. Crowell Co., New York, 1954.

Garvey, Neil F., *The Government and Administration of Illinois,* T. Y. Crowell Co., New York, 1958.

Gosnell, Cullen B., and Anderson, D. C. *The Government and Administration of Georgia,* T. Y. Crowell Co., New York, 1956.

Highsaw, Robert B., and Fortenberry, C. N., *The Government and Administration of Mississippi,* T. Y. Crowell Co., New York, 1954.

Karsch, Robert F., *Essentials of Missouri Government,* Lucas Brothers, Columbia, Mo., 1953.

Key, V. O., and Heard, Alexander, *Southern Politics,* Alfred A. Knopf, New York, 1949.

Lambert, O. D., *West Virginia and Its Government,* D. C. Heath, Boston, 1951.

MacCorkle, Stuart A., and Smith, Dick, *Texas Government,* 3rd ed., McGraw-Hill, New York, 1956.

Rankin, Robert S., *The Government and Administration of North Carolina,* T. Y. Crowell Co., New York, 1955.

Renne, R. R., *The Government and Administration of Montana,* T. Y. Crowell Co., New York, 1958.

Rich, Bennett M., *The Government and Administration of New Jersey,* T. Y. Crowell Co., New York, 1957.

Ross, Russell M., *The Government and Administration of Iowa,* T. Y. Crowell Co., New York, 1957.

Sikes, Pressly S., *Indiana State and Local Government,* revised ed., Principia Press, Bloomington, 1946.

Tanger, Jacob, et al., *Pennsylvania's Government: State and Local,* 3rd ed., Penns Valley Publishers, University Park, Pa., 1950.

Trachsel, Herman H., and Wade, Ralph M., *The Government and Administration of Wyoming,* T. Y. Crowell Co., New York, 1956.

Turner, Henry A., and Vieg, John A., *The Government and Politics of California,* McGraw-Hill, New York, 1960.

Webster, Donald H., et al., *Washington State Government,* University of Washington Press, Seattle, 1956.

CHAPTER 2

Intergovernmental Relations: The Nation and the States

Within the American governmental system there are more than 90,000 units of government ranging from the national government centered in Washington, D.C., to thousands of small, specialized local units. Each of them has a legally prescribed jurisdiction. Each of them has legally prescribed powers. Yet none of them can be considered islands in the sea of government. The affairs of each unit of government are to some degree related to those of many or all of the others.

The complexity of twentieth-century American society is reflected in the numerous problems that either ignore or strain the boundaries, both geographical and intangible, between governments. Problems that in earlier decades could be solved locally now command state or national attention. Matters formerly of state concern now demand national consideration. As society matures, new problems arise that governments of one type or another must handle, and in many instances several governments must join efforts in the search for solutions. As these developments take place they add to an already complicated system of intergovernmental relations erected by the Constitution, statutes, compacts, and voluntary, informal agreements.

The pattern of intergovernmental relations in the United States encompasses all levels and types of governments. Although all levels may be involved in some areas of concern, consideration of intergovernmental relations can be divided into four general categories: national-state relations; the relations among states; state-local relations; and national-local associations. It is with the first two categories that this chapter is concerned.[1]

---

[1] State-local and national-local relations are treated in Chapter 23, "The Local Governments: Their Role in Intergovernmental Affairs."

FEDERALISM

The Nature of Federalism. The governments of independent, sovereign countries in the world today can be regarded as either unitary or federal in form. The basic criterion for identification of both types is the manner of allocation of governmental authority. In unitary nations, which are by far in the majority, all power rests ultimately in the central government. The exercise of authority by local units of government is wholly determined by the central unit. Federal governments, on the other hand, are based upon a division of powers between the central government and the constituent units.[2]

Most simply defined, a federal state is one in which governmental powers are divided "so that the general and regional governments are each, within a sphere, coordinate and independent."[3] This statement, however, conveys only a general understanding. A more specific characterization may be found in the view that federalism means a "division of powers between central and local governments by an authority superior to both and in a way that cannot be changed by the action of either the local or central unit acting alone."[4]

In the American system the superior authority is the Constitution, and the means of formally changing that document is the amending process. The central government, through Congress, proposes amendments; and the states decide whether to approve or reject the proposed alterations.

Allocation of Powers. By definition, a federal system is composed of two constitutionally recognized levels of government. In the United States the central level is known as the national or federal government; the local level is composed of a group of governmental units called states.[5] The powers of each level of government are

---

[2] On the basis of these criteria, true federal systems are found in Australia, Canada, Switzerland, the United States, and the West German Republic. Mexico is organized on the federal principle, but controls exercised by the central government suggest the unitary pattern. According to William H. Riker, *Federalism,* Little, Brown, and Company, Boston, 1964, other countries which today have "described themselves as federalisms" include Austria, Argentina, Brazil, the Congolese Federation, Ethiopia, India, Malaysia, Nigeria, Pakistan, the U.S.S.R., Venezuela, and Yugoslavia.

[3] K. C. Wheare, *Federal Government,* Oxford University Press, New York, 1947, p. 11.

[4] John M. Swarthout and Ernest R. Bartley, *Principles and Problems of American National Government,* 2nd ed., Oxford University Press, New York, 1955, p. 89.

[5] A common misconception of American federalism is the notion that there are *three* levels of government—national, state, and local. Confusion in the matter can be dispelled when it is understood that in the legal sense local governments, such as coun-

determined by the Constitution in accordance with the Tenth Amendment which provides that "The powers not delegated to the United States by the Constitution, nor prohibited by it to the States, are reserved to the States respectively, or to the people."

Delegated Powers. With the exception of the inherent powers discussed below, the national government may exercise only those powers granted to it by the Constitution. Thus it may be said that the national government is a government of delegated powers. Throughout the seven articles and twenty-four amendments to the Constitution, specific enumerations of authority are made. Each of the three branches of the national government—legislative, executive, and judicial--is empowered to exercise designated powers.

Of great importance to the national government are those powers implied from specific grants of authority. The Constitution itself does not mention implied authority. Rather, the *doctrine of implied powers* was announced in 1819 by the United States Supreme Court in *McCulloch* v. *Maryland*.[6] Chief Justice John Marshall ruled that Congress had the implied authority to charter a national bank. Application of the doctrine to other delegated powers has broadened the scope of national power to an almost immeasurable extent.

Closely akin to implied authority are grants known as *resultant* powers. These powers cannot be implied from any single enumerated power but instead result from several of them. The power to punish violators of national laws, for example, logically results from the authority of Congress to exercise its enumerated powers. The power to issue paper money results from the expressed powers to borrow and to coin money.[7]

Concurrent Powers. Not all powers delegated to the national government are exercised exclusively by that unit. Only those which are, by their nature, not susceptible to local exercise are the exclusive prerogatives of the central government. Thus the states as well as the national government may tax, borrow money, charter corporations, and exercise the power of eminent domain. Also frequently

---

ties, cities, towns, townships, and special districts, are in reality "creatures of the state." From the legal standpoint, such units are part of the state level of government. The confusion is due largely to the fact that in carrying out many administrative duties, local governments do in fact operate in a manner largely independent of the states. For further clarification of the legal position of local governments, see Chapter 18.

[6] 4 Wheaton 316.

[7] See *Legal Tender Cases,* 12 Wall. 457 (1871).

included in this category is the authority of states to act in other fields not preempted or regulated completely by Congress. Consequently, states have at times been active with regard to bankruptcy laws, fixing standards of weights and measures, and some areas of interstate commerce.

Inherent Powers. In the field of foreign relations many powers of the national government may be said to be inherent. They are powers that inhere in the sovereign state as a member of the family of nations. While such powers as the ability to declare war, make treaties, and maintain diplomatic relations are treated in the Constitution, they are powers which, even "if they had never been mentioned in the Constitution, would have vested in the Federal Government as necessary concomitants of nationality. . . ."[8]

Reserved Powers. At the time the United States Constitution was drafted, virtually all governmental powers were vested in the states. The central government under the Articles of Confederation was limited primarily to the conduct of foreign affairs. Thus the creation of the national government under the Constitution involved the transfer, or delegation, to the national government of powers formerly wielded by the states. The powers not delegated were retained by, or reserved to, the states. Consequently, the reserved powers are not listed in the Constitution, nor, with few exceptions, are they set forth in state constitutions. In general, if a power may be exercised by government and is neither constitutionally granted to the national government nor denied to the states, it is a reserved power.[9]

Growth and Expansion of Governmental Power. Today it is obvious to even the most casual observer that the powers of the federal government have been expanded at a more rapid pace than those of the states. The word "government" itself is, in the mind of the ordinary citizen, practically synonymous with "national government." Hardly an aspect of daily life is unaffected, either directly or indirectly, by policies and programs emanating from Washington, D.C. It is significant that, at the same time national powers have expanded so greatly, the powers and functions of state and local government have also increased. Yet, even though expansion at the state

---

[8] *U.S.* v. *Curtiss Wright Export Corporation,* 229 U.S. 304 (1936).

[9] For discussion of the types of reserved powers, see pp. 153–157, and appropriate subject matter entries in the index.

and local level has been notable, it has not kept abreast of the development and growth of federal authority.

The most important single factor contributing to enlargement of the federal sphere of action has been the doctrine of implied powers. By means of liberal interpretation of the enumerated powers, the national government is now empowered to enter or regulate numerous areas of activity not apparent in the letter of the Constitution. Under the power to regulate interstate commerce, for example, the national government punishes kidnapers, white slavers, and those who transport stolen automobiles across state lines. The same power permits federal regulation of railroads, trucking companies, air lines, labor standards, sales of stocks, agricultural commodities exchanges, radio, television, and many other activities. Other enumerated powers have been interpreted in much the same fashion.

Another important factor in the significant growth of national authority, especially since World War I, has been the use of the grant-in-aid.[10] It has proved particularly useful, from the national viewpoint, in instances where constitutional authority to act is doubtful or direct federal action would be inadequate or politically inadvisable. In a few instances, minor expansion of federal power has been realized through reciprocal law enforcement and cooperative research programs.

ADMISSION OF STATES

The power to admit states is vested in Congress. Under the terms of the Constitution, "New States may be admitted by the Congress into this Union . . ."[11] The meaning of this brief phrase is clear: only Congress, in its discretion, is empowered to recognize the existence of a new state. Qualifications upon this power include the constitutional provisions that ". . . no new State shall be formed or erected within the jurisdiction of any other State; nor any State be formed by the junction of two or more States, or parts of States, without the consent of the legislatures of the States concerned as well as of the Congress."[12] In addition, acts of admission are subject to presidential action in the same manner as other laws.

There is no fixed procedure that a prospective state must follow

---

[10] Grants-in-aid are discussed at length in a later section of this chapter.
[11] Article IV, Section 3.
[12] *Loc. cit.*

in order to gain admission to the Union. Usually an area achieves the status of a territory of the United States before taking steps to attain statehood. The first step involves sending a petition to Congress. Next, Congress passes an *enabling act* granting permission to the people of the prospective state to draft a constitution acceptable to them. This step is not absolutely necessary, for the people of a territory may already have drawn up such a document. The third major step in achieving statehood is congressional and presidential approval of the draft constitution. Should objectionable provisions be found, Congress may refuse to approve it until changes acceptable to Congress, the President, and the territorial residents have been made. When all differences are resolved, Congress enacts a resolution admitting the new state into the Union. It is possible for a statehood bill to require that further conditions be met. For example, statehood was conferred on both Alaska and Hawaii only after the residents of the territories approved the respective acts of admission at special elections.

Only slightly more than half of the states have actually gone through the phases noted above. The thirteen original states, of course, entered the Union merely by ratifying the Constitution. Five states were formed from the territories of other states. Texas was an independent, sovereign country at the time of admission. Altogether, eight states, excluding the original thirteen, have not passed through the stage of territory before admission into the Union.

THE STATES: ADMISSION AND POPULATION

Order of Admission	Territorial Status	Admission to Statehood	Population (1960)
ORIGINAL STATES*			
Delaware		Dec. 7, 1787	446,292
Pennsylvania		Dec. 12, 1787	11,319,366
New Jersey		Dec. 18, 1787	6,066,782
Georgia		Jan. 2, 1788	3,943,116
Connecticut		Jan. 9, 1788	2,535,234
Massachusetts		Feb. 6, 1788	5,148,578
Maryland		Apr. 28, 1788	3,100,689
South Carolina		May 23, 1788	2,382,594
New Hampshire		June 21, 1788	606,921
Virginia		June 25, 1788	3,966,949
New York		July 26, 1788	16,782,304
North Carolina		Nov. 21, 1789	4,556,155
Rhode Island		May 29, 1790	859,488

THE STATES: ADMISSION AND POPULATION (*Continued*)

Order of Admission	Territorial Status	Admission to Statehood	Population (*1960*)
ADMITTED TO STATEHOOD			
Vermont		Feb. 18, 1791	389,881
Kentucky		June 1, 1792	3,038,156
Tennessee		June 1, 1796	3,567,089
Ohio	July 13, 1787**	Mar. 1, 1803	9,706,397
Louisiana	Mar. 24, 1804	Apr. 30, 1812	3,257,022
Indiana	May 7, 1800	Dec. 11, 1816	4,662,498
Mississippi	Apr. 17, 1798	Dec. 10, 1817	2,178,141
Illinois	Feb. 3, 1809	Dec. 3, 1818	10,081,158
Alabama	Mar. 3, 1817	Dec. 14, 1819	3,266,740
Maine		Mar. 15, 1820	969,265
Missouri	June 4, 1812	Aug. 10, 1821	4,319,813
Arkansas	Mar. 2, 1819	June 15, 1836	1,786,272
Michigan	Jan. 11, 1805	Jan. 26, 1837	7,823,194
Florida	Mar. 30, 1822	Mar. 3, 1845	4,951,560
Texas		Dec. 29, 1845	9,579,677
Iowa	June 12, 1838	Dec. 28, 1846	2,757,537
Wisconsin	Apr. 20, 1836	May 29, 1848	3,951,777
California		Sept. 9, 1850	15,717,204
Minnesota	Mar. 3, 1849	May 11, 1858	3,413,864
Oregon	Aug. 14, 1848	Feb. 14, 1859	1,768,687
Kansas	May 30, 1854	Jan. 29, 1861	2,178,611
West Virginia		June 19, 1863	1,860,421
Nevada	Mar. 2, 1861	Oct. 31, 1864	285,278
Nebraska	May 30, 1854	Mar. 1, 1867	1,411,330
Colorado	Feb. 28, 1861	Aug. 1, 1876	1,753,947
South Dakota	Mar. 2, 1861	Nov. 2, 1889	680,514
North Dakota	Mar. 2, 1861	Nov. 2, 1889	632,446
Montana	May 26, 1864	Nov. 8, 1889	674,767
Washington	Mar. 2, 1853	Nov. 11, 1889	2,853,214
Idaho	Mar. 3, 1863	July 3, 1890	667,191
Wyoming	July 25, 1868	July 10, 1890	330,066
Utah	Sept. 9, 1850	Jan. 4, 1896	890,627
Oklahoma	May 2, 1890	Nov. 16, 1907	2,328,284
New Mexico	Sept. 9, 1850	Jan. 6, 1912	951,023
Arizona	Feb. 24, 1863	Feb. 14, 1912	1,302,161
Alaska	Aug. 24, 1912	Jan. 3, 1959	226,167
Hawaii	June 14, 1900	Aug. 21, 1959	632,772

* Ratified United States Constitution on dates indicated.
** Date of Ordinance creating government for the Northwest Territory.

Equality of the States. Once admitted to the Union a state is upon a plane of equality with all other states. No state has more privileges or fewer obligations than any other. Nevertheless, questions have arisen with regard to the equality of newly admitted states in view of conditions placed upon admission. The rule governing such conditions is basically that states may be bound only if the conditions do not interfere with or attempt to control matters recognized as within the domain of state authority. In other words, if Congress or the President should require a prospective state to agree to certain terms before admission is granted, the agreement must be observed by the state only if conformity does not compromise the equality of the state with those already in the Union. For example, Oklahoma, admitted in 1907, was forced, by the terms of the enabling act of 1906, to agree to maintain its capital at Guthrie until 1913. The United States Supreme Court, however, upheld the right of Oklahoma to move the capital to Oklahoma City in 1910, declaring that the state had merely exercised powers that were "essentially and peculiarly state powers."[13] Similarly, Arizona was required to alter its draft constitution to eliminate a provision permitting the recall of judges, but once admitted as a state, Arizona promptly amended its organic law to restore the deleted clauses.

On the other hand, agreements that do not infringe upon essential state powers may be enforced as binding contracts. For example, Minnesota was compelled to refrain from taxing certain national lands in conformity with a condition accepted at the time of admission.[14] In the same way New Mexico was forbidden to use funds from the sale of lands granted by the national government to the state for any purpose not listed in the act of admission.[15]

Constitutional Restrictions upon the States

Among the most important clauses in the Constitution are those that specifically restrict state authority. Through them two basic purposes are served. Areas of national power are more clearly discerned and individual rights and privileges are accorded the protection of constitutional provisions.

Restrictions in Support of National Authority. Article I, Section 10, of the Constitution is composed almost entirely of a list of limitations aimed at preventing state assumption of authority in various areas of national power. These prohibitions may be considered under four general categories—foreign affairs, military and war powers, taxation and commerce, and contracts.

---

[13] *Coyle* v. *Smith*, 221 U.S. 559 (1911).
[14] *Stearns* v. *Minnesota*, 179 U.S. 223 (1900).
[15] *Ervien* v. *United States*, 251 U.S. 41 (1919).

Foreign Affairs. The Constitution unqualifiedly forbids the states to "enter into any treaty, alliance, or confederation." The utility of such a clause is obvious. If it were possible for a state to conclude pacts with foreign countries, not only would a unified national foreign policy be impossible, but the Union itself would be in constant danger of "international" strife and possible dissolution. The states are permitted to make compacts, however, subject to the approval of Congress.[16]

Military and War Powers. The power of the national government to control the military affairs of the Union is effectively guaranteed by provisions in the Constitution that permit the states to maintain armed forces or to engage in war only with the consent of Congress.[17] Only if actually invaded or in imminent danger may a state do so without congressional permission. Under present legislation, states contribute to the maintenance of National Guard units that serve as state troops. These military units are subject to close national regulation, however, and may be incorporated into the national forces.

Taxation and Commerce. In the interest of maintaining a uniform monetary system, the Constitution denies the states authority to coin money, emit bills of credit, or make anything but gold and silver legal tender. Despite these provisions state banks issued paper currency until the mid-nineteenth century. This practice was ended, however, by the simple expedient of a prohibitive national tax upon such notes in 1866.

State taxation of imports and exports is also constitutionally prohibited without specific congressional authorization. The only concession made by the Constitution in this regard is that states may exact fees in amounts sufficient to offset the costs of inspection of items being imported or exported. Tonnage taxes, or levies based upon the holding capacities of ships, are also forbidden except in pursuance of congressional permission.

Contracts. State authority to control the terms of contracts is severely restricted by the Obligation of Contracts Clause found in Article I, Section 10. Under its terms no state may enact any "law

---

[16] For discussion of the nature and use of compacts, see pages 36–37.

[17] Article I, Section 10, also prohibits states from issuing "letters of marque and reprisal." Such letters were authorizations granted by warring states to private individuals permitting them to carry on hostile actions at sea. The clause is now virtually a dead letter of the Constitution.

impairing the obligation of contracts." To be sure, a state may establish the conditions under which a contract may be made, but according to the literal provisions of the Constitution, a valid contract, once concluded, cannot be altered by subsequent legislation. The United States Supreme Court interpreted the clause strictly when it held, in 1819, that the state of New Hampshire could not, in violation of the school's charter, convert Dartmouth College into a public institution.[18] Later rulings have relaxed this interpretation, however, to the extent that charters are subject to legislation designed to protect the public health, safety, welfare, and morals. Further, the Supreme Court decision upholding the legality of moratoria, or suspensions for stated periods of time, on meeting mortgage payments during the depression of the 1930's indicates even greater relaxation of the apparent strictness of the Obligation of Contracts Clause.

Rights and Privileges. Individual rights and privileges are protected by a variety of constitutional provisions. The safeguards erected by the Constitution were designed to prevent arbitrary state action. Thus each provision is a denial of state authority.

Included in Article I, Section 10, are clauses prohibiting the states from granting titles of nobility and passing either bills of attainder or ex post facto laws.[19] The denial of power to establish a nobility of persons makes it impossible for a specially privileged class to be created on that basis. Legislatures may not, because of the attainder clause, enact legislation finding designated persons guilty of criminal acts and prescribing punishment. The Ex Post Facto Clause prevents state legislative bodies from passing criminal laws that operate retroactively to the disadvantage of any person who stands accused or has been convicted of a crime.

Freedom from slavery and involuntary servitude, not only against the states but the national government and private individuals as well, is affirmed by the Thirteenth Amendment. The only exception permitted by the letter of the Constitution is in regard to persons convicted of crimes. The Supreme Court has ruled that service in the armed forces as a result of being drafted and the obligation of fulfilling terms of service in the merchant marine are not forms of involuntary servitude.

---

[18] *Dartmouth College* v. *Woodward*, 4 Wheaton 518.

[19] Article I, Section 9, contains similar restrictions against the national government.

State authority to fix voting qualifications is restricted by several constitutional provisions. Article I, Section 2, and the Seventeenth Amendment provide that representatives and senators shall be chosen by voters who "shall have the qualifications requisite for electors of the most numerous branch of the state legislature." The Fifteenth Amendment disallows qualifications based on "race, color, or previous condition of servitude." The Nineteenth Amendment bars restrictions based on sex, and the Twenty-fourth Amendment prohibits poll taxes as a voting qualification in federal elections.

The most generally stated yet most extensive restrictions upon state action are found in the Fourteenth Amendment. Section 1 of that Amendment declares:

> No State shall make or enforce any law which shall abridge the privileges or immunities of citizens of the United States; nor shall any State deprive any person of life, liberty, or property, without due process of law; nor deny to any person within its jurisdiction the equal protection of the laws.[21]

The vagueness of these limitations has necessitated a great deal of definition and interpretation. The function of imparting specific meanings has been performed largely by the federal judiciary, especially the United States Supreme Court.

"Due process of law" has been defined by the Supreme Court in various decisions as relating primarily to procedure on the one hand and the substance of the law on the other. Hence the Court has developed dual concepts: procedural due process of law and substantive due process of law. Procedural due process obviously refers to the fairness of procedures involved in governmental contacts with individuals. Whether the relationships involve proceedings in courts or before administrative agencies, the individual must be dealt with in such a way that all steps taken by the state are fair to the individual. Because there is no constitutional list of the procedures states must follow, the task of designating fair procedure within the framework of the due process clause is accomplished by federal courts.

---

[20] The Fifteenth Amendment has not eliminated discrimination in regard to the suffrage. Where registration or election officials desire to do so, discrimination can be accomplished in the administration of a valid voting qualification. See Chapter 10, "Nature and Functions of the Electorate."

[21] Discussion of the privileges and immunities of citizens is deferred to a later section of this chapter.

The meaning of substantive due process of law depends upon the character of the right and the statute involved. In general, a statute denies due process of law on substantive grounds when its effect is such that a reasonable exercise of a right is thwarted. For example, a law that seeks to prevent the publication of newspapers or magazines that are openly critical of governmental officers and agencies by making them subject to court orders directing cessation of publication may be in violation of substantive due process. All procedures necessary to conform to the concept of procedural due process of law may be observed, yet the fact would remain that the statute itself might reduce freedom of the press to the point that it would consist of little more than freedom to praise. In other words, the *substance* of the right would be seriously reduced.

A literal application of the Equal Protection of the Laws Clause would mean that every person must be treated identically under all laws. Such a rigid interpretation would mean that minors and adults, natural persons and corporations, the insane and mentally sound would be required to conform to valid laws in exactly the same way. A less severe interpretation obviously is in order. Accordingly, states resort to classification in determining the application of various laws. Thus all bus companies, all banks, all professional boxers, or all motorists may be obliged to conform to statutes not applicable to the public as such. It is only when classifications are unreasonable, such as all Negroes, or all Chinese laundries, that the Equal Protection Clause of the Fourteenth Amendment is violated.[22]

Extra-Constitutional Relations

The Grant-in-Aid. One of the most important aspects of national-state relations is the large number of grants-in-aid made available by the national government to the states. The earliest grants involved transfers of land, but since the turn of the present century they have been, with few exceptions, in the form of money. They are usually offered to the states as an inducement to initiate or expand some service such as slum clearance, construction of local airports, or school construction in federally affected areas—programs which the national government may not, or chooses not to, conduct. The stimulus may stem from a national desire to promote state action in areas of na-

---

[22] The development, application, and abandonment of the well-known "separate but equal doctrine" are discussed in Chapter 26.

tional interest, or the grant-in-aid may be used because it is politically expedient.

A grant-in-aid is a gift of money from one level of government to another—provided the recipient government agrees to meet certain conditions. Over the years "the grant has become a fully matured device of cooperative government. Its elements are well established: the objectives are defined; apportionment and matching formulas are laid down; conditions, minimum standards, and sanctions are prescribed; and provisions are made for administrative supervision."[23]

The extent to which the grant-in-aid is used today is significant. Billions of dollars are made available annually for national grant-in-aid programs. The utility of the device, or at least its success as an instrument in the promotion of national-state relations, is attested by the fact that federal funds expended through grant-in-aid programs in 1915 totaled only five and one-half millions, a minor fraction of the amounts spent in recent years. According to the United States Bureau of the Census, the states received $7.8 billion during the fiscal year of 1963, a figure which, it is estimated, will exceed $10.5 billion in fiscal 1965. It is interesting to note that although there are many federally aided programs, almost ninety per cent of these funds are earmarked for expenditure in the areas of public welfare assistance, public highways, and public education.[24]

Increasing use of the grant-in-aid has stimulated spirited discussion of its merits. The chief protests reflect the fear that through the extended use of grants-in-aid the states are being weakened and the federal system slowly destroyed. Opponents of such aid have pointed out that the national government has found it possible, through conditions placed on grants, to invade fields reserved by the Constitution to the states. The power of Congress to encroach even further into the realm of state activity by means of optional grants is buttressed

---

[23] Commission on Intergovernmental Relations, *Report to the President,* GPO, Washington, 1955, p. 120. Other publications of the Commission concerning grants-in-aid, issued by the same agency and at the same time, include *A Description of Twenty-five Federal Grant-In-Aid Programs, The Administrative and Fiscal Impact of Federal Grants-In-Aid,* and *The Impact of Federal Grants-In-Aid on the Structure and Functions of State and Local Governments.* These documents contain many analyses of the effects of grants-in-aid in individual states. Other valuable sources on the grant-in-aid are Council of State Governments, *Federal Grants-In-Aid,* Chicago, 1949; V. O. Key, *Administration of Federal Grants-In-Aid,* Public Administration Service, Chicago, 1939; and Henry J. Bitterman, *State and Federal Grants-In-Aid,* Mentzer, Bush and Co., Chicago, 1938.

[24] Bureau of the Census, *State Government Finances in 1963,* Washington, D.C., 1964. See Table 8, pp. 14–15.

by the decision of the Supreme Court that neither a private citizen nor a state may question the spending power of Congress.[25] It is contended that the federal government actually controls state decisions on public policy through its power to attach conditions to grants.[26] Or again, the national government has been accused of "coercing" unwise state action by offering attractive sums of money not otherwise available, thus luring states into programs they cannot afford.

Supporters of the grant-in-aid respond to the various objections by pointing out that participation in grant-in-aid programs is wholly voluntary on the part of the states. No state can be forced to accept funds from the national government. The allegation that the vitality of federalism is sapped by the grant-in-aid is met by the argument that state governments are strengthened as a result of federal insistence upon acceptable standards of performance, adequate reporting systems, and adherence to the merit principle in selection of personnel participating in grant-in-aid programs. Further, proponents argue that the grant-in-aid has made possible a level of services and national minimum standards that could not have been achieved by the states acting individually.

Whatever position one may take with respect to the advantages and disadvantages of the grant-in-aid, several conclusions are obvious. The grant-in-aid technique has become firmly established in the complex of national-state relations. The goals of grant-in-aid programs have been achieved to a significant degree. And, on the basis of the tendency of the national government to rely more and more upon aid programs, their extended use in the future seems assured.

National-State Tax Relations. Since both the national and state governments operate directly upon the people, and both levels exercise the power to tax, it would be strange indeed if conflicts did not arise. In actuality, sharp differences between the national and state governments have occurred, but in all instances solutions have been reached. Out of those differences a definite pattern of intergovern-

---

[25] *Massachusetts* v. *Mellon, Frothingham* v. *Mellon,* 262 U.S. 447 (1923).

[26] This is the basis of resistance to expanded aid to education. Opponents of such aid fear that, in return for financial assistance in the construction of school plants and payment of other heavy costs, the federal government may exercise undue control over such things as teacher certification, school administration, and content of course instruction.

mental tax relations has taken form, a pattern existing within the context of constitutional restrictions upon state taxing power.

The status of government instrumentalities represents an area of conflict and adjustment developed over the course of a full century. The question of whether one level of government may tax the instrumentalities of the other has been answered in the negative. The power to do so would, as Chief Justice John Marshall put it, involve the power to destroy.[27] Under this concept, even the salaries of government employees were exempt from income taxes levied by other than the employing government. In *Graves* v. *People of New York ex rel. O'Keefe,* this rule was overturned on the ground that the employing government was not burdened by the tax.[28]

Inheritance tax laws, in the 1920's, caused a national-state tax skirmish. Florida, in order to attract wealthy residents, levied no inheritance tax. With a view toward achieving national uniformity, Congress enacted an inheritance tax law in 1926 with a provision to the effect that similar taxes paid to a state might be used to offset up to eighty per cent of the federal tax. Florida brought suit to have the act set aside as an unconstitutional interference in state affairs, but was met with an adverse decision.[29] In view of the ruling, Florida enacted a law designed to take advantage of the tax credit feature of the federal act. Today Nevada alone does not have an inheritance tax.

National unemployment legislation also incorporates a tax credit feature fashioned to stimulate state passage of similar laws. Only a handful of states had enacted any form of unemployment compensation prior to the depression of the 1930's. In the Social Security Act of 1935, Congress levied a payroll tax of three per cent upon employers but permitted ninety per cent of the federal tax to be offset by payments to the state if a similar state law were enacted. Since the tax revenues were to be collected in any event, unemployment compensation laws were soon placed upon the statute books of all states.

Voluntary Cooperation. In American federalism it is axiomatic that within the framework of the Constitution the national and state governments are separate legal entities. As such, each level may function in its proper sphere of authority without interference from

---

[27] *McCulloch* v. *Maryland,* 4 Wheaton 316 (1819).

[28] 306 U.S. 466 (1939).

[29] *Florida* v. *Mellon,* 273 U.S. 12 (1927).

the other. Despite allocations of authority, however, some problems are of such nature that adequate solutions require the attention and cooperation of both levels of government. Over the years national-state relations have increasingly involved voluntary cooperative efforts of the national government and the states—a development often termed "cooperative federalism."

Intergovernmental cooperation may be effected by means of formal agreements set down in written contracts, by informal understanding, or on the basis of offers of assistance. A broad range of matters is included. For example, personnel of the national Public Health Service may be detailed to state agencies to assist in research with a subsequent sharing of information. The Atomic Energy Commission has made isotopes available to state institutions for research purposes. Numerous federal agencies have entered into contracts with state colleges and universities for the purpose of inquiring into common problems. The Federal Bureau of Investigation maintains a school at which state and local law enforcement officials may receive instructions in techniques and methods. State and local personnel or agencies participate in the administration of such areas of federal interest as selective service, agricultural extension, conservation, elections, and education. Many similar examples could be cited, but they would serve only to illustrate further the observation that intergovernmental cooperation exists on a broad and ever-increasing scale.

INTERGOVERNMENTAL OBLIGATIONS

Just as the Constitution provides for a division of governmental powers and prohibits various types of governmental actions, it imposes a number of obligations upon the national and state governments. These duties, most of which are found in Article IV of the Constitution, include national obligations to the states, duties of the states for the benefit of the nation, and responsibilities of the states to each other.

National Obligations to the States: *Republican Form of Government.* Article IV, Section 4, of the Constitution provides that "The United States shall guarantee to every State in this Union a republican form of government. . . ." The exact meaning of this provision has never been determined. The United States Supreme Court has refused to impart precise meaning to the clause, ruling instead that the issue is a *political question* to be decided in nonjudicial fashion.

In a case growing out of Dorr's Rebellion in Rhode Island in 1841–1842 an attempt was made to draw from the Court a decision as to which of two factions was the legitimate government of the state. The Court declined to rule on the question, characterizing it as political in nature.[30] Again in 1912 the Supreme Court refused to rule on the meaning of the clause. In the case of *Pacific States Telephone and Telegraph Co.* v. *Oregon*, the company argued that a republican form of government was one which was representative, and on that basis a tax levied by means of the initiative was in violation of the Constitution.[31] The Supreme Court repeated its earlier view that a political question was involved.

The closest the Supreme Court came to defining the guarantee was simply to suggest that the question of whether Oregon had a republican form of government had been settled by the admission to membership by Congress of the state's senators and representatives. Today, in fact, about the only test applied by students of government is reference to the action of Congress in receiving new members. Even so, there is also the possibility that the President, through his military powers, may affect any decision respecting the republican character of a state government.

Territorial Integrity of the States. Although the power to admit states is vested in Congress, it is subject to various limitations. Article IV, Section 3, provides that "no new State shall be formed or erected within the jurisdiction of any other State; nor any State be formed by the juncture of two or more States, or parts of States, without the consent of the legislatures of the States concerned as well as of the Congress." From these phrases it is clear that Congress is obliged to respect the territorial integrity of all states—that is, it may not alter the geographical boundaries or area of a state unless the legislature of the state so affected gives specific approval.

Throughout the history of the Union very little difficulty has been encountered with respect to this obligation. Five states have been formed from the territory of other states. In the cases of Vermont, Kentucky, Tennessee, and Maine, all constitutional pre-

---

[30] *Luther* v. *Borden,* 7 Howard 1 (1849).
[31] 223 U.S. 118.

requisites were complied with. Only the admission of West Virginia in 1863, during the Civil War, may be construed as possibly violative of constitutional restrictions. In that instance forty western counties of Virginia refused to comply with the declaration of secession adopted by the legislature and subsequently established a governmental organization of their own. Their successful petition for statehood was based, at least in part, upon congressional acceptance of the "consent" of that portion of the Virginia legislature that represented the western counties. It is interesting to note that in 1869 the Supreme Court, in a case not involving West Virginia, held that secession was constitutionally impossible.[32] If in fact none of the rebellious states had ever been out of the Union, the admission of West Virginia, it may be contended, was not in accord with the Constitution. Yet, after admission, West Virginia was entitled to equality with all other states. The incident is now merely of historical interest, but it is obvious that the spirit, if not the letter, of the Constitution was violated.

Protection and Assistance. Since control of the armed forces is vested primarily in the national government, the Constitution provides, in Article IV, Section 4, that the states are entitled to federal protection.[33] Inasmuch as the states are forbidden to maintain armed forces without congressional consent, and the territory of a state is also part of the nation, imposition of such a duty upon the national government is logical. There have been few instances when the obligation has been implemented for the purpose of combatting invaders, for with the exception of the War of 1812, the American states have not been invaded by the troops of a hostile power. Necessary protection has been extended, of course, during all wars in which the United States has been a belligerent.

Requests for national assistance in cases of domestic violence have not been uncommon. Ordinarily the governor has sought the aid, since state legislatures are in session for such short periods that they cannot usually be convened in special session rapidly enough in true emergency situations. In any event the President decides whether federal assistance will be granted.

In the 1906 San Francisco earthquake and fire and the 1961 floods

---

[32] *Texas* v. *White,* 7 Wallace 700.

[33] "The United States . . . shall protect each of them against invasion; and on application of the legislature, or of the executive (when the legislature cannot be convened) against domestic violence."

in the Midwest, federal troops were quickly dispatched to assist local authorities. President Harding once refused to send aid to quell violence during a miners' strike in West Virginia. Assistance may be rendered over the objection of state authorities. In 1894, despite the protest of Illinois' Governor Altgeld, President Cleveland used federal troops to maintain order in Chicago during the Pullman Strike. The President justified his action on the grounds that the strike obstructed performance of the national postal function. In such situations, however, as in the Little Rock, Arkansas, or Oxford, Mississippi, incidents, there is involvement of federal law upon which intervention can be legally based. Thus, under the Constitution, it appears that the obligation of the national government to extend assistance covers almost any situation in which violence of any type is involved—and the initiative lies as much with the national authorities as with those of the states.

Obligations of the States to the Nation: *Election of Federal Officials.* The national government does not hold elections. Members of the United States Senate and House of Representatives and presidential electors are chosen by the people in elections conducted under state authority, administered by state and local officers, and paid for by state and local governments. Article I, Section 4, of the Constitution specifically empowers state legislatures to fix the "times, places, and manner" of election of senators and representatives. Congress has authority, under the same provision, to alter most state laws thus enacted, and it has prescribed the first Tuesday after the first Monday in November of even-numbered years as the day for such elections.

There is no constitutional clause under which a state may be forced to fulfill its obligations in respect to elections. None is necessary. Any state that fails to perform its electoral duties would lose its voice in the Congress and forego any part in the selection of the President and Vice President.

Consideration of Amendments. The Constitution contains no provision that compels the states to ratify or reject amendments. However, the manner prescribed for making changes in the basic document is such that the part played by the states is absolutely essential. The initiation of amendments takes place at the national level, but they must be approved by the states before becoming a part of the Constitution.[34] The vital character of state participation implies a role that is obligatory in nature.

Interstate Obligations: *Full Faith and Credit.* Article IV, Section 1, provides that "Full faith and credit shall be given in each State to the public acts, records, and judicial proceedings of every other State." The need for such a provision in a federal system is obvious. Without it each state could regard all other states virtually as foreign countries. Moreover, each state would become a haven for anyone who wished to escape or avoid his duties and responsibilities under the laws of any other state.

The coverage of the Full Faith and Credit Clause is quite broad. "Public acts" refer to civil laws passed by state legislatures. "Records" include such things as mortgages, deeds, leases, birth certificates, or any other document that legally fixes, establishes, or determines an obligation, privilege, right, or fact. "Judicial proceedings" comprise decisions made by the courts of a state in all civil affairs *over which they have jurisdiction.* Matters of a criminal nature are not covered by the Full Faith and Credit Clause, for the United States Supreme Court has held that no state is obliged to enforce the criminal laws of another.[35]

The effect of the Full Faith and Credit Clause is best understood by illustration. Assume, for example, that Smith and Jones enter into a valid contract in the state of Texas, and Jones later moves to Iowa where he attempts to escape fulfilling his obligations under the agreement. If Smith, or his agent, brings suit in an Iowa court to force Jones to honor the contract, the Iowa court will enforce the agreement according to Texas contract law. This would be true even if the contract failed to conform to the provisions of Iowa law relating to such documents.

Currently, one of the most confusing problems in regard to full faith and credit is the question of whether a state is compelled to recognize all divorces granted by another state. No question arises when a divorce involves persons who are bona fide residents of the state in which the decree was obtained. But what of the divorce action in which one or both principals have been in a state only long enough to establish residence for divorce purposes? In 1945 the United

---

[34] The various methods of amending the United States Constitution are discussed in Chapter 3.

[35] *Wisconsin* v. *Pelican Insurance Co.,* 127 U.S. 265 (1888).

States Supreme Court ruled that North Carolina was not required to recognize a Nevada divorce decree awarded to a resident of North Carolina who had resided in Nevada six weeks—the period of residence required by that state before a person may enter a suit for divorce.[36] Even though the Nevada requirements had been met, it was held that no domicile, or true residence, had been established. Consequently, the validity of numerous similar divorces was placed in doubt. Three years later the Court stated that if both parties to a divorce action were represented and the question of whether the court had jurisdiction to grant the divorce was not raised during the proceedings, the question could not be raised at a later time.[37] While this ruling clarified the steps that could be taken to avoid difficulties raised by the question of valid domicile, the *Williams* decision was not overruled. The extent to which divorce decrees granted to individuals who have resided in a state barely long enough to meet minimum residence requirements are entitled to full faith and credit is uncertain.

Interstate Rendition. While no state has the responsibility of enforcing the criminal law of any other state, Article IV, Section 2, ostensibly obligates states to return fugitives to the states from which they flee. In the language of the Constitution,

> A person charged in any state with treason, felony, or other crime, who shall flee from justice, and be found in another State, shall on demand of the executive authority of the State from which he fled, be delivered up, to be removed to the State having jurisdiction of the crime.

The purpose of this provision—the "rendition clause"—is obvious. Since the states are essentially independent of each other, some means is necessary to prevent the frustration of criminal laws by the simple act of stepping over a state border.

The apparently mandatory character of the rendition clause is illusory. Its meaning has been softened considerably through Supreme Court interpretation. In the case of *Kentucky* v. *Dennison*[38] the Court was asked to order the governor of Ohio to surrender a fugitive. There was reason to believe the Ohio executive would have

---

[36] *Williams* v. *North Carolina,* 325 U.S. 226.
[37] *Sherrer* v. *Sherrer,* 334 U.S. 343 (1948).
[38] 24 Howard 66 (1861).

refused to obey, so the Supreme Court, without power to coerce obedience, construed the clause as a statement of "moral duty." In other words, a governor who is requested to return a fugitive is morally obligated to do so, but there is no legal requirement that compels him to honor the request.

Although rendition, or "extradition" as it is more commonly called, is not compulsory, it is performed as a matter of course in the vast majority of cases. Once in a while a governor refuses to send a fugitive back to a state. Such instances involve a belief that the ends of justice would, in some way, not be served if the fugitive were extradited.

Privileges and Immunities. The framers of the Constitution were well aware of the fact that when citizens of one state traveled to another state they might encounter discriminatory treatment. A citizen of New York, for example, might find himself treated as an alien in Pennsylvania or New Jersey. Consequently, a clause was included in the organic law to provide that the "Citizens of each state shall be entitled to all the privileges and immunities of citizens of the several states."[39] Inclusive as the provision may appear, it does not protect corporations or aliens, as they are not citizens.

There is no complete list of the privileges and immunities protected by the Constitution. According to judicial interpretation, however, citizens are entitled to

> Protection by the government; the enjoyment of life and liberty, with the right to acquire and possess property of every kind, and to pursue and obtain happiness and safety; subject nevertheless to such restraints as the government may justly prescribe for the general good of the whole. The right of a citizen of one state to pass through, or to reside in any other state, for purposes of trade, agriculture, professional pursuits, or otherwise; to claim the benefit of the writ of habeas corpus; to institute and maintain actions of any kind in the courts of the state; to take, hold, and dispose of property, either real or personal; and an exemption from higher taxes or impositions than are paid by the other citizens of the state; . . .[40]

On the other hand, many of the privileges deriving from the use and enjoyment of the facilities, resources, and political processes of a state

---

[39] Article IV, Section 2.
[40] *Corfield* v. *Coryell,* 4 Wash. C.C. 371 (1825).

may be legally withheld from nonresidents. Most important of these is the privilege of voting. Others include the denial of permission to practice professions such as medicine or law, exclusion from institutions of higher education, and refusal of the privilege to hunt, fish, or trap within the state. Except for voting, however, states may extend privileges otherwise denied to nonresidents upon certain conditions, commonly the payment of fees higher than those charged its own citizens.

Some eighty years after the Constitution was drafted, a clause was added, as part of the Fourteenth Amendment, that prohibited states from abridging the rights and privileges that accrue as a result of national citizenship. Here again, no complete list of such privileges has been compiled. Nevertheless, the right of qualified persons to vote for members of Congress, as set forth in Article I, Section 2, and the Seventeenth Amendment, must be included. Traveling to and from the national capital, use of the navigable waters of the United States, and national protection while traveling abroad are further privileges of United States citizenship. The original intent of the clause—to protect the newly freed Negro—has never been fully realized.

CONFLICT AND COOPERATION AMONG THE STATES

Problem Areas. The character of American state and local government has undergone far-reaching changes since the Union was formed over 175 years ago. The philosophical bases of governmental institutions have not been dislodged, but as the social, economic, and to some extent, political environments have changed, so also has the role of government. Constant change in virtually all fields has produced a society that is highly interdependent, a society in which individual self-sufficiency is minimized. Consequently government—national, state, and local—today performs many more services and exercises more extensive regulatory powers than in former years.

Difficulties are almost certain to arise in any association of governments existing side by side upon a plane of equality. In the American federal system travel, trade, and transportation have become increasingly national in character. As a result, new problems and new complications must be added to the list of conflicts occurring between states.

Because each state is a separate entity, it is free to enact any valid law it chooses. With each state exercising its prerogatives in this respect, it is not unusual to find a great—and sometimes discouraging—diversity among state statutes dealing with the same subject. Trade barriers are erected in the form of quarantines, excessive license fees, and discriminatory taxes. Conflicts develop with respect to interstate problems such as use of the water of river systems, stream pollution, flood control, conservation, and construction of interstate bridges. Jurisdictional disputes and quarrels over the location of state boundaries have contributed to interstate troubles.

Voluntary Cooperation. Despite the fact that in past years there have been episodes involving discriminatory actions and reactions among the states, particularly in regard to trade barriers, the record of voluntary cooperation on an interstate basis is good. In many instances conflicts are kept under control by the informal cooperation of administrators. Private organizations devoted to the study and improvement of government have assisted in the solution of interstate problems. Also, conferences of both temporary and permanent character have contributed to greater cooperation among states.

Numerous organizations and agencies are dedicated to the improvement of state and local government. The National Municipal League, for example, has devoted years of research into the problems of government. Its *Model State Constitution* is generally regarded as particularly well adapted to the requirements of the American states. Since 1892 the National Conference of Commissioners on Uniform State Laws has devoted its efforts to the preparation of model statutes recommended for adoption or imitation by all states. Over one hundred such laws have been drafted, but only about ten per cent have been adopted by thirty or more states. Restatement of the common law in effect throughout the states has been the chosen task of the American Law Institute since 1923. The work of the Institute is accomplished through the cooperative efforts of judges, lawyers, and legal scholars from every state.

Probably the best known of the agencies concerned with problems of state government is the Council of State Governments. The Council is composed primarily of commissions on interstate cooperation from the various states and maintains a permanent headquarters and staff in Chicago. While it performs chiefly as a research agency and clearing house, publishing reports on special problems as well as the quarterly magazine *State Government* and the biennial reference *Book of the States,* the Council also serves as a secretariat for a number of organizations. Among them are such groups as the Governors' Conference, National Association of Secretaries of State, National Association of Attorneys General, Conference of Chief Justices, and the National Association of State Budget Officers.

Interstate Compacts. The principal formal device used in the settlement of interstate disputes is the interstate compact. Compacts are written agreements voluntarily entered into by two or more signatories. As the term "interstate compact" suggests, the signatories are usually states although the United States government or foreign countries may also become participating parties.

According to the Constitution, all compacts must be approved by Congress.[41] When such approval is formally given, Congress simply enacts the compact in the form of a national statute, an action that may be taken either before or after the compact is concluded. In some cases Congress may fail to take action, yet the compact in question may have full legal force and effect.[42] However, compacts that tend to increase state authority or encroach upon national power almost certainly would require formal congressional approval.

Until the last thirty years interstate compacts were rarely used for anything other than the settlement of boundary disputes. In fact, before the year 1900, Congress had given approval to only nineteen compacts, each of which involved only two states. Since the turn of the century, and particularly since the mid-1930's, the total number of compacts submitted to Congress has soared and in many instances the agreements have been multistate in character.

The Interstate Parole and Probation Compact of 1934 is the agreement to which the highest number of states have become parties. Under its terms all states have consented to establish systems for supervision of out-of-state parolees and probationers. One of the most successful compacts established the Port of New York Authority, an agency created in 1921 by the joint action of New York and New Jersey. The Authority regulates the use and, to a considerable degree, the development of the harbor and connecting facilities of the New York City harbor area. Examples of other successful agreements, each

---

[41] Article I, Section 10.
[42] See *Virginia* v. *Tennessee,* 148 U.S. 503 (1893).

involving at least a half-dozen states, include the compacts on conservation and production of oil, allocation of the water of the Colorado River system, civil defense, river pollution, regional education, and marine fisheries.

Despite the recent popularity and successful application of the interstate compact, the device is not without shortcomings. It takes a great deal of time and negotiation to complete a multistate agreement. When haste is essential, the compact is not a satisfactory method of cooperation. The effectiveness of any compact is dependent upon the full, voluntary cooperation of member states. Thus any event that threatens the interests of a signatory state may well threaten the success of the compact.

Suits between States. Frequently, states find themselves unable to resolve their differences by any of the methods discussed above. When such a stalemate occurs, and one of the states feels that its legal rights are compromised, a lawsuit may result. Suits between states are heard in the United States Supreme Court, the only court in the country in which one state may sue another.

States have hailed each other before the Supreme Court for a variety of reasons. Frequently the location of a boundary line has been the point of conflict. The use of water from rivers or river systems that involve the geographical area of several states has been the basis of many suits. Other litigation has arisen over disagreement as to the financial obligations of one state to another. Many similar illustrations could be cited, for the records of the Supreme Court contain numerous interstate suits.

SELECTED REFERENCES

Books:

Anderson, William, *Intergovernmental Relations in Review,* University of Minnesota Press, Minneapolis, 1960.

———, *The Nation and the States: Rivals or Partners?* University of Minnesota Press, Minneapolis, 1955.

Commission on Intergovernmental Relations, *Report to the President,* Government Printing Office, Washington, D.C., 1955.

Council of State Governments, *Interstate Compacts, 1783–1956,* Chicago, 1956.

Goldwin, Robert A., editor, *A Nation of States,* Rand, McNalley and Company, Chicago, 1963.

Graves, W. Brooke, *American Intergovernmental Relations,* Charles Scribner's Sons, New York, 1964.

Leach, Richard H., and Sugg, Redding S., Jr., *The Administration of Interstate Compacts,* Louisiana State University Press, Baton Rouge, 1959.

Maass, A., editor, *Area and Power: A Theory of Local Government,* The Free Press, Glencoe, 1959.

Riker, William H., *Federalism: Origin, Operation, Significance,* Little, Brown and Company, Boston, 1964.

Sady, Emil J., *Research in Federal-State Relations,* Brookings Institution, Washington, D.C., 1957.

Wheare, K. C., *Federal Government,* 4th edition, Oxford University Press, New York, 1964.

Articles:

Anderson, William, "The Commission on Intergovernmental Relations and the United States Federal System," *Journal of Politics,* May 1956.

Bebout, John E., "The States' Best Friend," *National Civic Review,* February 1964.

Celebrezze, Anthony J., "Cooperative Federalism for an Advancing America," *State Government,* Summer 1964.

Dwinell, Lane, "The States and the American Federal System," *State Government,* April 1958.

Huard, Leo Albert, "State Sovereignty and Federal Subsidies," *Georgetown Law Journal,* Spring 1958.

Kestnbaum, Meyer, "To Strengthen Our Federal System," *State Government,* August 1955.

Leach, Richard H., "The Status of Interstate Compacts Today," *State Government,* Spring 1959.

Muskie, Edmund S., "$ and ¢ of Federalism," *National Civic Review,* May 1964.

Shuford, William A., "Federal Encroachment on State Rights," *American Bar Association Journal,* October 1959.

"State Responsibility in a Federal System," Symposium, *New York University Law Review,* June 1959.

Wechsler, Herbert, "The Political Safeguards of Federalism: The Role of the States in the Composition and Selection of the National Government," *Columbia Law Review,* April 1954.

CHAPTER 3

The Basic Law—State Constitutions

Throughout United States history the basic law of each state, as well as that of the national government, has been set forth in a written constitution. While the constitutions in America today are highly similar, still each document is unique. The United States Constitution stands apart as the organic, supreme law of the country as a whole. The constitution of each state is distinguishable in that it reflects local ideas, conditions, and problems.

The position of a state constitution in the hierarchy of law in the United States is determined by the principle of supremacy of national law.[1] Thus state constitutions are subordinate to all national law. When conflicts occur between national law and a provision of a state organic document, or for that matter any type of state law, the national law takes precedence. At the same time, there is no higher state law than the constitution of a state.

In general terms a constitution is intended to accomplish two broad objectives. First, it defines and creates the principal organs of government. Second, it outlines the relations of these governmental organs with each other and with the people. Whether a constitution achieves these goals in a satisfactory, lasting manner depends upon many things. Foremost is the requirement that a stable system of government be established, but established in a way that permits necessary adaptation and change. There is no set pattern which must be followed to achieve these goals. All state constitutions, however, utilize the same basic approach even though there is wide variation as to detail.

---

[1] Article VI, Section 2, of the United States Constitution provides that "This Constitution, and the laws of the United States which shall be made in pursuance thereof; and all treaties made, or which shall be made, under the authority of the United States, shall be the supreme law of the land; and the judges in every state shall be bound thereby, anything in the constitution or laws of any state to the contrary notwithstanding."

THE ORIGINAL STATE CONSTITUTIONS

The middle decades of the eighteenth century were troubled times in the American colonies. The colonies were British territories. As British subjects the colonists owed allegiance to the King. In the British view the colonies were primarily sources of raw materials and markets for goods produced in the mother country. Accordingly, British rule was conducted in a manner designed to benefit England.

Because of the great distance between Britain and the American continent and the resulting slowness of communications, government in the colonies took on an independent character. Despite the close legal controls held by the King, local problems could not be handled effectively from London. As a result, in actual practice the colonial governments exercised a large measure of control over their own affairs.

In retrospect it is not surprising that conflicts developed between the colonies and the King. Measures emanating from London designed to maintain or tighten control over colonial areas engendered colonial resistance, which in turn brought sterner measures from the British seat of government. In April, 1775, open hostilities flared up at Lexington and Concord—and the colonies had reached a critical point of decision. They had to choose either to continue as a part of the British system or to make a bid for independence.

Adoption of the First Constitutions. New Hampshire led the colonies in the adoption of constitutions by framing a temporary document in January, 1776.[2] Within two months South Carolina followed suit. The Continental Congress adopted a resolution in May encouraging the colonies to adopt "such governments as shall, in the opinions of the representatives of the people, best conduce to the happiness and safety of their constituents in particular and America in general" and proclaimed the Declaration of Independence in July. During the remainder of the year fundamental documents were framed in Virginia, New Jersey, Delaware, Pennsylvania, Maryland, and North Carolina. In 1777 Georgia and New York were

---

[2] Copies of the Charters and Constitutions in effect in the various colonies and states to the turn of the present century have been collected in Francis N. Thorpe, *The Federal and State Constitutions*, 7 vols., 1909, printed as House of Representatives Document No. 357, 59th Congress, 2nd session.

added to the list. The two charter colonies—Connecticut and Rhode Island—already enjoying established systems of self-government, merely deleted references to the King in their charters and did not adopt new constitutions until 1818 and 1843, respectively. Massachusetts' constitution was also a revised charter, but frankly recognized as a stop-gap instrument.

None of the constitutions adopted during 1776 and 1777 was submitted to the people for approval. While conventions were used, except in South Carolina, to draft the documents, they were merely the legislative bodies sitting as conventions. In all instances the constitutions depended, in one way or another, upon legislative approval before taking effect. A major role in selecting the membership of conventions and exercising the power to accept or reject constitutions was first exercised by the people of Massachusetts in 1780. The procedures used in Massachusetts, and soon thereafter in New Hampshire, set the general pattern subsequently followed in all states.[3]

Characteristics. In comparison with state constitutions today, the early documents were notable examples of brevity. Covering only a few printed pages, they were for the most part confined to truly fundamental matters. Relatively few provisions of temporary application or significance were inserted in the early constitutions.

Popular sovereignty—the principle that recognizes the people as the source of all political power—characterized each of the first state constitutions. Reaction to the arbitrary controls exercised by England during the colonial days was thus expressed in the basic laws of the new states. Limited government, the companion principle of popular sovereignty, was made apparent in many provisions. The revolutionary view of government was principally one of distrust. Hence the freedom of action of public officials was severely restricted. In seven states a bill of rights was written into the Constitution, and in the remainder the civil rights of the people were protected through random clauses guaranteeing specific rights coupled with reliance upon the common law in effect at the time.

The distrust and suspicion of strong government that marked the revolutionary outlook was evidenced by the principles of separation

---

[3] For a full historical review of the period during which the first state constitutions were drafted, see Allan Nevins, *The American States During and After the Revolution,* The Macmillan Co., New York, 1924, Chapter 4, "The Writing of the State Constitutions."

of powers and checks and balances characteristic of the early constitutions. While fewer than half of the documents espoused the principles in so many words, each was careful to segregate legislative, executive, and judicial powers. Separate branches of government were established and their powers delineated. Each was vested, in theory at least, with powers that would tend to control the actions of the other branches.

In actual practice the theory of separation of powers was weakened in that the popularly elected legislatures were given far more authority than either the executive or judicial branches. Experience under royal colonial governors resulted in an organizational pattern in which the governor was reduced to a mere figurehead. He was generally limited to a one-year term, was chosen by the legislature in all states but New York and Massachusetts, and exercised the power of veto only in South Carolina and Massachusetts. State courts were also subordinate to the legislature since the early constitutions created a judicial framework, leaving the task of completing judicial organization and determining jurisdiction to legislative action. Thus the first years of government under the original state constitutions may correctly be described as a time of legislative supremacy.

Reaction to the policies enforced by British monarchs in colonial days and concern with individual rights during and after the Revolution create an impression that the early constitutions were truly democratic instruments. And for their time they were indeed. However, many of them contained provisions that are now considered thoroughly undemocratic. For example, none of the original documents guaranteed complete freedom of religion. Also, property owners were given preferred status. Holding public office or casting ballots was commonly contingent upon a person's religious convictions and the amount of property he owned.

State Constitutions Today

As already noted, today's constitutions are similar, yet individual in character. Each establishes a framework of government very much like that in every other state. The principles upon which these documents rest are very nearly uniform, but each assumes unique characteristics because of problems peculiar to a state.

Age. Viewed from the standpoint of age alone, American state constitutions are a mixture of contrasts and similarities. The youngest document is that of Michigan, approved on April 1, 1963, while the oldest is that of Massachusetts, adopted in 1780. Thirteen are products of the present century, and fourteen have been in effect for more than one hundred years. On the other hand, all but eight are more than fifty years old, with twenty-four of them having been adopted more than eighty years ago. Of the state constitutions now in effect, thirty were adopted during the last half of the nineteenth century. The average age of the state fundamental documents today is approximately eighty-three years.

While the age of a constitution must certainly be considered in the determination of its character, it can be misleading. Many of the older constitutions have been subjected to frequent amendment, resulting in the inclusion of much recent material. Then, too, interpretation over the years by executive, legislative, and judicial branches can change the precise meanings of various provisions. Thus age is merely one criterion of the suitability of a constitution.

Length. Just as state constitutions vary widely in age, they also differ greatly in length. The Louisiana constitution contains about a quarter of a million words—a bit longer than a 300-page novel. California's basic law is second longest with about 85,000 words. At the other extreme are Connecticut and Rhode Island with constitutions containing less than 7,000 words, while Indiana, Kansas, Iowa, and Vermont have documents of less than 10,000 words. Most state constitutions are somewhere between these two extremes with an average length of about 25,000 words.

Much criticism has been leveled at the modern trend toward longer state constitutions. Too often, it has been said, matters that should be taken care of by means of statute are placed on the same basis as truly fundamental law, resulting in inflexible documents that require frequent amendment. This criticism is probably justified in the case of constitutional provisions which, for example, fix interest rates that may be charged on private loans,[4] establish a minimum sale price of ten dollars per acre on state university lands,[5] prescribe detailed procedures for granting loans and scholarships to medical

---

[4] Constitution of California, Article XX, Section 22.
[5] Constitution of Idaho, Article IX, Section 10.

State and Local Government

THE STATE CONSTITUTIONS

State	Date Admitted	No. of Constns.	Dates Adopted	Effective Date of Present Constn.	Age	Times[1] Amended
Alabama	1819	6	1819, 1861, 1865, 1867, 1875, 1901	1901	64	212
Alaska	1959	1	1956	1959	6	0
Arizona	1912	1	1911	1912	53	50
Arkansas	1836	5	1836, 1861, 1864, 1868, 1874	1874	91	59
California	1850	2	1849, 1879	1879	86	350
Colorado	1876	1	1876	1876	89	64
Connecticut[2]	1788	1	1818	1818	147	57
Delaware	1788	4	1776, 1792, 1831, 1897	1897	68	80[3]
Florida	1845	5	1838, 1861, 1865, 1868, 1886	1887	78	117
Georgia	1788	8	1777, 1789, 1798, 1861, 1865, 1868, 1877, 1945	1945	20	26[3]
Hawaii	1959	1	1950	1959	6	5
Idaho	1890	1	1889	1890	75	68
Illinois	1818	2	1818, 1870	1870	95	13
Indiana	1816	2	1816, 1851	1851	114	20
Iowa	1845	2	1846, 1857	1857	108	21
Kansas	1861	1	1859	1861	104	45
Kentucky	1792	4	1792, 1799, 1850, 1891	1891	74	18
Louisiana	1812	10	1812, 1845, 1852, 1861, 1864, 1868, 1879, 1898, 1913, 1921	1921	44	439
Maine	1820	1	1819	1820	145	89
Maryland	1788	4	1776, 1851, 1864, 1867	1867	98	108
Massachusetts	1788	1	1780	1780	185	81
Michigan	1837	4	1835, 1850, 1908, 1963	1964	2	0
Minnesota	1858	1	1857	1858	107	90
Mississippi	1817	4	1817, 1832, 1868, 1890	1890	75	35
Missouri	1821	4	1820, 1865, 1875, 1945	1945	20	13
Montana	1889	1	1889	1889	76	30
Nebraska	1867	2	1866, 1875	1875	90	94
Nevada	1864	1	1864	1864	101	56
New Hampshire	1788	2	1776, 1783	1784	181	41
New Jersey	1788	3	1776, 1844, 1947	1948	17	6
New Mexico	1912	1	1911	1912	53	55
New York	1788	5	1777, 1822, 1846, 1894, 1938	1939	26	133[4]
North Carolina	1789	4	1776, 1861, 1868, 1876	1876	89	(NA)[5]
North Dakota	1889	1	1889	1889	76	76
Ohio	1803	2	1802, 1851	1851	114	88

THE STATE CONSTITUTIONS (*Continued*)

State	Date Admitted	No. of Constns.	Dates Adopted	Effective Date of Present Constn.	Age	Times1 Amended
Oklahoma	1907	1	1907	1907	58	49
Oregon	1859	1	1857	1859	106	111
Pennsylvania	1788	4	1776, 1790, 1838, 1873	1874	91	62
Rhode Island2	1790	1	1842	1843	112	36
South Carolina	1788	7	1776, 1778, 1790, 1861, 1865, 1868, 1895	1895	70	251
South Dakota	1889	1	1889	1889	76	71
Tennessee	1796	3	1796, 1835, 1870	1870	95	10
Texas	1845	5	1845, 1861, 1866, 1868, 1876	1876	89	154
Utah	1896	1	1895	1896	69	33
Vermont	1791	2	1786, 1793	1793	172	44
Virginia	1788	7	1776, 1830, 1851, 1861, 1864, 1869, 1902	1902	63	92
Washington	1889	1	1889	1889	76	39
West Virginia	1863	2	1862, 1872	1872	93	36
Wisconsin	1848	1	1848	1848	117	66
Wyoming	1890	1	1889	1890	75	25

[1] Adapted from *Book of the States,* 1964–65.
[2] Used modified colonial charter until effective date of first constitution.
[3] Does not include amendments having local effect only.
[4] Includes amendments since 1895.
[5] Data not available.

students,[6] and regulate the way in which warehouses may be operated.[7] When it is recalled that the United States Constitution, the oldest written national constitution in effect in the world today, covers only a few printed pages, it would appear that state constitutions are unnecessarily lengthy.

Even though state constitutions may be considered excessively long, it is not always easy to decide which provisions are not of fundamental importance. What is and what is not fundamental may depend almost entirely upon the peculiarities of a particular state. For example, in states where water is in short supply, constitutions may properly contain provisions relating to the allocation of that resource. A state whose economy depends heavily upon tourism may be justified in devoting space in its fundamental document to a motor

[6] Constitution of Georgia, Article VII, Section 1.
[7] Constitution of Illinois, Article XIII, Sections 1–7.

vehicles fuel tax. Or a state where forestry, mining, or other such activity is of major importance may consider constitutional references to such activities as fundamental.

Nature and Contents. State constitutions deal with a broad range of matters. Each document contains much that is unique, but all constitutions contain provisions that may be considered under several broad categories.

Principles of Government. In no respect are state constitutions more alike than in the governmental principles upon which they are based. It is necessary only to compare the basic structure and processes of a few states to realize that all have been cast from the same general mold. All state constitutions, as they historically have done, espouse the doctrine of *popular sovereignty,* recognizing the people as the source of political power and that government exists through popular consent. *Limited government,* the doctrine that government must operate within defined bounds, is implied if not actually stated in every state constitution. The fact that the powers of every state government are apportioned among legislative, executive and judicial branches, each with certain powers over the others, illustrates the universal acceptance of the doctrines of *separation of powers* and *checks and balances.* As in the case of the national constitution, the fundamental instruments of the states assume the existence of *judicial reveiw,* whereby courts are empowered to adjudge the constitutionality of statutes. Finally, all state constitutions exist within the framework of the American federal system. While none expresses the principle as such, the implicit acceptance of federalism is obvious.

Governmental Organization. Providing a framework of government is a basic task of a constitution, and while the same general technique is used in every state there is great variation in detail. All state constitutions contain individual articles establishing and describing the legislative, executive and judicial branches. In addition, whole articles or scattered provisions outline, with varying degrees of detail, the organization of local governmental units.

The principal differences among state constitutions in regard to providing for the form of governments relate to the inclusion of detail. A few documents follow the national pattern in providing only broad outlines of organization. More often, however, not only is the general system of government described, but intricate details of administrative structure are set forth. Without exception, state constitutional provisions relating to the establishment of governmental framework go far beyond the essentials as set forth in the national Constitution.

The Processes of Government. After delineating the form of government, a constitution must prescribe the basic processes of government. The relations of government to citizens, intergovernmental relations, and the relative positions of component parts of the state organization must be described. In regard to these matters state constitutions are widely divergent.

Every constitution contains statements relating to the powers, limitations, duties, and obligations of the various elements of government. A Bill of Rights is found in each document; provisions for the initiative, referendum, and recall are contained in many; all provide for systems of taxation and finance; and public education, military affairs, corporate activity, and a variety of other governmental activities are dealt with. Some documents are extensively detailed, others are less so; some are highly restrictive, others liberal; and processes are regulated or described in some constitutions and not mentioned in others. Because of this wide variation, the question of whether a particular constitution is "good" or "bad" with respect to its treatment of governmental processes depends largely upon individual evaluation.

Protection of Civil Rights. Each constitution contains, usually in the first article, a list of individual rights. Called Bills of Rights or Declarations of Rights, they contain guarantees similar to those of the first ten amendments of the national Constitution. These lists are much longer than the national Bill of Rights. In addition to guarantees of freedom of speech, press, religion, assembly, petition, security from unreasonable searches and seizures, and the procedural rights of accused persons, state constitutions may list many others. In one constitution or another, for example, are found the rights to self-government, to alter or change the government, to be secure from imprisonment for debt, to emigrate from the state, to organize labor unions, to bargain collectively, to recover damages in suits at law, and even to fish in public waters!

State Bills of Rights frequently contain materials that might better be treated in other parts of the document or in statutes. One Bill of Rights prescribes death as the punishment for first degree murder; another contains a ban on lotteries. Others regulate the sale of liquor, fix state boundaries, direct that "safe and comfortable" prisons be provided, designate population as the sole criterion for legislative reapportionment, order the enactment of workmen's compensation legislation, and prohibit monopolies.

Provision for Constitutional Change. Since constitutions are man-made, none is perfect. Sooner or later, for one reason or another, changes become necessary. Some documents have proved more durable than others, but all of the documents now in effect, except those of Alaska and Michigan, have been altered. Each constitution contains provisions setting forth the manner of formal change. These methods, termed "revision" and "amendment," are discussed at length below.

Miscellaneous Provisions. There are usually several portions of a state constitution that have little or no utility or application. Best known of these is the preamble which precedes the body of a constitution. A preamble has no legal effect whatever and is nothing more than a statement of goals and intentions. Constitutions also include "schedules," that is, articles that prescribe the conditions under which the document takes effect. Once the constitution is in force, the schedule serves no further purpose. Finally, all constitutions contain provisions of the "dead letter" variety, which for some reason have no current application. A section, for example, that determines the composition of the legislature until apportionment can be accomplished or one that relates to a specific bond issue soon becomes outdated. More frequently, however, ineffective provisions result from judicial decisions that render them unenforceable.

ADOPTING AND CHANGING CONSTITUTIONS

Broadly viewed, a written constitution is a document that sets forth the rules of governance in a society. At the time a constitution is adopted and becomes law, it reflects the ideas and concepts held by its framers and the people who approve it. But society is dynamic and constantly changing, with the result that constitutions become outdated, lagging behind inevitable changes in outlooks, attitudes, and institutions.

Some state constitutions have outlasted others. They are usually the ones which were written in such a way that they could grow and expand without sacrificing the basic principles that form the bedrock of American democracy. Other documents which included many detailed, inflexible provisions that permitted little if any adaptation were soon in need of formal change. As a result, some constitutions have been amended repeatedly and others replaced after relatively short periods.

The Initial Constitution. A constitution is not put together as the result of theoretical reflections by a group of framers. Rather, it is the formal recognition of an already existing and generally accepted collection of principles and concepts adhered to by the people. Those ideas are the accepted basic law and are given force and effect by governmental organization of some sort. In short, a written constitution is preceded by organized government.

Prior to its entry into the Union, each of the American states possessed an established government. The thirteen original states were first colonies, and after severing political ties with England they became independent. Some states were formed from lands that were part of, or were claimed by, other states, but in each instance a prospective new state was already governmentally organized. Texas was an independent nation, and California had been a province of Mexico. Slightly more than half of the states had organized territorial governments prior to admission.

Today the generally accepted method of writing and adopting a constitution is through a popularly elected convention followed by ratification by popular vote. A glance through the pages of history discloses that less democratic methods have been used. The constitutions of the original thirteen states were legislative products that were not submitted to the people. Massachusetts, Rhode Island, and Connecticut originally operated with basic laws consisting of legislatively revised colonial charters. In a few instances original constitutions were drafted and proclaimed by conventions without referral to the people.[8]

CONSTITUTIONAL GROWTH AND CHANGE

Constitutions are subject to change by informal and formal means. Informal change is manifested through growth by *custom and usage*,[9]

---

[8] Alabama (1802), Arkansas (1836), Illinois (1818), Indiana (1816), Kentucky (1792), Missouri (1820), and Ohio (1802).

[9] A *custom* is a general practice which by common consent has acquired the force of law. A *usage*, technically, is of local application and does not require a long period of application before it becomes established. Generally, however, the terms are used synonymously and no attempt is made here to distinguish them.

or alteration by means of common acceptance of an established way of doing things; and by *interpretation,* or development through the construction and definition of constitutional provisions by public bodies and officials. Changes by these methods are likely to be gradual, often barely perceptible. Only when a constitutional clause is subjected to extensive redefinition, usually by a court, does general public awareness of the change result.

Formal changes are accomplished by means of *amendment* or *revision.* In the former, only a portion of the constitution, usually an article or a section, is altered. Revision, on the other hand, entails a general overhaul of the basic document. As indicated below, a new constitution usually results from the revision process.

Custom and Usage. A custom may be as strong as though it were set forth in the basic law. Since customs are not buttressed by written law, they do not, technically, have to be observed. However, a custom may become so fixed in the minds of the people and public officials, that to violate it would be tantamount to violating the constitution. Thus customs, while not actual parts of a state constitution, are very real parts of the *constitutional system.*

The force of custom is well illustrated by the requirement that in the absence of written law or judicial direction constitutional conventions must be called by state legislatures. In three-fourths of the states adequate constitutional provision is made for the legislative prerogative, but in the remaining states the constitution is silent. In the absence of any written legal directives, legislatures by custom have assumed the power. It is also by custom that political parties are recognized as an integral part of the governmental process. By the same token, presiding officers in most state legislative houses are required to be members of the bodies over which they preside, although state constitutions usually provide simply that "each house shall choose its own officers."

Interpretation. The courts of each state are often called upon in deciding cases to explain the meaning of constitutional provisions. In this way a clause or section may be construed as permitting actions previously thought to be forbidden, or conversely, as prohibiting others considered permissible. The legislative and executive branches are also extremely important instruments of constitutional interpretation. All laws enacted by the legislature and all acts of the governor or his administrative officers must conform to constitutional requirements. Since this is true, it is obvious that their actions are the result of their interpretations of powers available to them under the constitution.

Interpretations of state constitutions have not resulted in appreciable expansion of state authority, reflecting a difference in character between the national Constitution and those of the states. Inasmuch as the national government is essentially a government of delegated powers, its every action must be authorized by the United States Constitution. Hence the doctrine of *implied powers,* according to which authority may be implied from expressed powers, has resulted in tremendous expansion of federal activity. On the other hand, the powers of the states, with few exceptions, are not listed in state constitutions. A power not delegated to the national government nor prohibited to the states is automatically a state power. Thus at the state level there is no doctrine of implied powers—a doctrine particularly adapted to delineation through interpretation of positive grants of authority. As a result, interpretation of state constitutional pro-

METHODS OF AMENDING STATE CONSTITUTIONS

Initiation	Ratification	States
Constitutional Initiative	(See table on page 56)	Arizona, Arkansas, California, Colorado, Massachusetts, Michigan, Missouri, Nebraska, Nevada, North Dakota, Ohio, Oklahoma, Oregon
Majority of each house	Majority at election	Minnesota
Majority of each house; two successive sessions	Majority on amendment	Hawaii [1]
Two-thirds of each house	Majority on amendment	Alaska, Hawaii,[1] Maine, Mississippi
Three-fifths of each house	Majority on amendment	North Carolina
Majority of members elected	Majority on amendment	Arizona, Missouri, New Mexico, North Dakota, Oregon, South Dakota
	Majority at election	Arkansas, Oklahoma

METHODS OF AMENDING STATE CONSTITUTIONS (*Continued*)

Initiation	Ratification	States
Majority of members elected; two successive sessions	Majority on amendment	Indiana, Iowa, Massachusetts,[2] Nevada, New Jersey,[3] New York, Pennsylvania, Virginia, Wisconsin
	Three-fifths of votes on amendment	Rhode Island
Two-thirds of members elected	Majority on amendment	California, Colorado, Georgia, Idaho, Kansas, Louisiana, Michigan, Montana, Texas, Utah, Washington, West Virginia
	Majority at election	Illinois,[4] Wyoming
	Majority on amendment plus approval of next assembly	South Carolina
Two-thirds of members elected; two successive sessions	No popular ratification	Delaware
Three-fifths of members elected.	Majority on amendment	Alabama, Florida, Kentucky, Maryland, Nebraska,[5] New Jersey,[3] Ohio
	Two-thirds of votes on amendment	New Hampshire
Other		Connecticut,[6] Tennessee,[7] Vermont[8]

[1] Either method may be used. Majority must equal or exceed 35% of total votes cast; if at special election, majority must equal or exceed 35% of registered voters.

[2] Initiation by legislative body sitting in joint session.

[3] Either method may be used.

[4] Or two-thirds of vote cast on amendment.

[5] Majority for ratification must equal or exceed 35% of total votes cast at election.

[6] Majority of lower house; two-thirds of each house at next session. Ratification by majority voting on amendment.

[7] Majority of members elected; two-thirds of members elected at next session. Ratification by majority of votes cast for governor.

[8] Two-thirds majority in Senate, majority in House; majority of members elected at next session. Ratification by majority voting on amendment.

visions is for the most part a matter of judging whether an action is within the broad area of the reserved powers of the states.

Amendment. Formal changes in state constitutions are accomplished most frequently through the process of amendment. Two steps are involved: *initiation* of the suggested change and *ratification*, or approval, of the initiated alteration.[10] Initiation requires fulfillment of legal steps specified by the constitution, ordinarily approval by designated majorities in the legislative houses, or in the case of the initiative process, approval by a specified number of voters. Ratification in all states except Delaware is secured at elections, at which time the voters exercise their prerogative to approve or reject amendments.

Amending procedures prescribed by the national Constitution are not typical of those used in the states. Under the terms of that document initiation is complete when two-thirds of those present and voting in both the Senate and House of Representatives approve a proposed amendment.[11] Then, at the option of Congress, an initiated amendment is subject to ratification by three-fourths of the state legislatures, or by special ratifying conventions called in the states.[12] At no time do the people participate directly, either in initiation or in ratification, reflecting a major difference between federal and state practices.

Amendment by Legislative Action. Only in Delaware can a constitutional amendment be adopted without formal action by the people at some stage. According to the Delaware Constitution, a favorable vote by two-thirds of all members elected to both houses of the legislature at two successive sessions is necessary for adoption of a constitutional amendment.[13] It would appear that this requirement of successive extraordinary majorities would tend to inhibit severely the number of alterations in the state's organic law. This is not the case, however, for the rate at which amendments have been adopted in Delaware exceeds that of two-thirds of the states.

[10] Use of the term "proposed amendment" as synonymous with "initiated amendment," as is done in some state constitutions and statutes, may cause semantic confusion. To avoid this difficulty, the discussion above considers a "proposed" amendment as one which has been suggested, but has not met the legal requirements making it subject to the ratification process. By the same token a proposal which has met those conditions is regarded as having been "initiated."

[11] An as yet unused alternative method of initiating amendments is available. Should two-thirds of the state legislatures petition Congress, a convention "shall" be called by Congress for the purpose of initiating amendments. Since this method has never been used, the exact procedures that would be employed have not been determined.

[12] Of the twenty-four amendments to the United States Constitution only the Twenty-first Amendment, which repealed prohibition as provided for in the Eighteenth Amendment, was ratified by the convention method.

[13] Constitution of Delaware, Article XVI, Section 1.

Although participation in the formal steps of amendment is not available to the electors of Delaware, they are not altogether excluded. The entire membership of the House of Representatives and approximately half of the Senators are subject to election every two years. Aspirants to these legislative positions must be sensitive to the views of the people—including their attitudes on pending amendments. Obviously, opposition to a proposal by a large or important segment of voters will be reflected in the actions of the newly elected, or re-elected, leglislators.

Initiation by Convention. The method least used for the initiation of constitutional amendments has been the convention. A slow and cumbersome procedure, its use has been limited to those situations where it was the only method available,[14] was considered to be the last resort, or was chosen as the most politically expedient method. For example, the Tennessee Constitution, adopted in 1870, proved so difficult to amend through the regular method that it went unchanged until 1953. In that year the people voted to call a convention for the initiation of amendments. Eight were initiated and subsequently approved by the people at a special election. The New York convention held in 1938 extensively revised that state's 1895 constitution and submitted proposals for change to the people as nine different amendments, of which only six were approved. Consequently, the document presently in effect contains many provisions unchanged from the earlier constitution. Therefore, the present New York Constitution, which took effect in 1939, is sometimes regarded as an amended version of the 1895 document.

The constitutions of many other states provide for conventions for the initiation of amendments. In Oregon, conventions have the power to "amend or propose amendments . . . or to propose a new Constitution."[15] Conventions in Ohio may "revise, amend, or change" the basic law.[16] In Oklahoma, constitutional "alterations, revisions, or amendments" may be accomplished by convention.[17] Nebraska conventions may "revise, amend, or change" the constitu-

---

[14] Prior to 1964 amendments to the New Hampshire Constitution could be initiated only by conventions which could be held no oftener that once every seven years. At the general election in November 1964 an amendment was adopted which provides that the leglislature may initiate such alterations.

[15] Article XVII, Section 1.

[16] Article XVI, Section 2.

[17] Article XXIV, Section 2.

tion of that state.[18] Even though available as an amending device, conventions are seldom used for that purpose. The great expense involved, the time necessarily consumed in the convention process, and the fact that regular amending procedures are easier to use, all militate against wide use of the convention for amending purposes.

Legislative Initiation. In each of the fifty states the legislature has authority to initiate constitutional amendments. In practically all states the power is shared equally by the two houses of the legislature. Nebraska, of course, is the most obvious exception since its legislature is unicameral. Amendments to the Connecticut Constitution are proposed in the House of Representatives, but are not initiated until two-thirds of both houses approve at the next legislative session. Two-thirds of the Vermont Senate makes original proposals which, if concurred in by a majority of the House, are held over for approval by a majority of both houses at the next biennial session.

Other variations among the states, as indicated by the table on pages 51–52, are numerous. About one-fourth of the state constitutions stipulate that amendments may be initiated only after favorable action by two successive sessions of the legislature. Majorities required for approval also vary widely, ranging from simple majorities of those present and voting, to three-fifths of the members elected. In some instances, further barriers are placed in the path of amendment. The Kansas Constitution, for example, states that no more than three propositions to amend may be submitted to the voters at any one election. At one election Colorado legislators may offer amendments to no more than six articles of the constitution. In Illinois the maximum number of articles that may be amended at one time is three, and any given article may be subjected to amendment no oftener than once every four years. And in Vermont amendments may be submitted to the voters only once every ten years.

Initiation by Constitutional Initiative. The constitutions of thirteen states now make it possible for the people to amend the constitution through the constitutional initiative.[19] This method of changing the constitution consists of the circulation of petitions to

---

[18] Article XVI, Section 2.

[19] See Chapter 13 for discussion of the various means of direct popular action, including the constitutional initiative.

AMENDMENT BY CONSTITUTIONAL INITIATIVE

State	Signatures Required*	Conditions	Ratification
Arizona	15% votes cast for Governor	—	Majority on amendment
Arkansas	10% votes cast for Governor	5% of legal voters in each of 15 counties	Majority on amendment
California	8% votes cast for Governor	—	Majority on amendment
Colorado	8% votes cast for Secretary of State	—	Majority on amendment
Massachusetts	3% votes cast for Governor	—	Majority on amendment; must be 30% of votes cast[2]
Michigan	10% votes cast for Governor	—	Majority on amendment
Missouri	8% votes cast for Governor[1]	8% in each of two-thirds of congressional districts[1]	Majority on amendment
Nebraska	10% votes cast for Governor	5% of electors in each of two-fifths of counties	Majority on amendment; must be 35% of votes cast
Nevada	10% of registered voters	—	Majority on amendment[3]
North Dakota	20,000 signatures	—	Majority on amendment
Ohio	10% votes cast for Governor	5% in each of one-half of counties	Majority on amendment
Oklahoma	15% of highest vote cast	—	Majority of votes cast
Oregon	10% votes cast for Supreme Court Justice	—	Majority on amendment

* In terms of votes cast at last general election except for Nevada and North Dakota.
[1] Legislature may reduce percentage required. Now set at 5%.
[2] Must be approved by one-fourth of all members of General Court in joint session at two successive sessions before submission to popular vote.
[3] Ratification requires approval at two successive general elections.

collect a prescribed number of signatures. After the signatures have been gathered and verified, the amendment is considered initiated and subject to ratification at the next general election.

Ratification. Not until an amendment has received final approval, that is, ratified in the manner prescribed by the constitution, does it take effect. The instrument of approval in all states except Delaware is the people. Ratification in Delaware is accomplished when two successive legislatures vote favorably on an amendment. Ratification of amendments proposed by constitutional initiative is accomplished by popular vote, with Nevada requiring that such measures win the approval of the electorate at two successive general elections.

Some states are more restrictive than others. In five states an amendment must receive favorable votes from a majority of the total number of voters participating in the election. The states of Illinois and New Hampshire require a majority of two-thirds of those voting on an amendment. Tennessee sets the figure at a majority of the vote cast for governor. South Carolina's constitution requires only a majority of those voting on an amendment, but ratification is not complete unless the legislature concurs at its next session.

Constitutional Amendment—Easy or Difficult? A principal point of controversy with respect to changing constitutions is the question of how difficult it should be to amend a state constitution. In a few states the process is apparently little more than a minor hurdle. The constitutions of California and Louisiana have been amended more than 350 times, that of South Carolina altered on more than 250 occasions, and over 100 amendments have been added to the fundamental documents of Alabama, Florida, New York, Oregon, and Texas. On the other hand, the equally aged constitutions of Illinois, Indiana, Iowa, Kentucky, Tennessee, and Wyoming have been amended with relative infrequency.

There is no fixed formula establishing an ideal amending procedure for all state constitutions. A short, well-written document that contains little more than truly fundamental law obviously would not need to be modified as often as a constitution overburdened with detailed, statute-like provisions. It may well be argued that fundamental law ought to be difficult to change, but at the same time a convincing case can be made for an easier amendatory process if a constitution contains many provisions likely to become outdated. The best solution, of course, is to keep unnecessary detail out of a constitution from the outset, but such reasoning does not meet the real problem.

No single procedure can be said to be best, or even adequate, for all constitutions. It is reasonable, however, to observe that in the interest of discouraging frivolous additions to a constitution, the amending process should not be easy. At the same time, if it is too difficult, as in Tennessee and Kentucky, necessary or highly desirable changes virtually cannot be made. If a balance of these extremes is achieved, the amending provisions of a constitution can be said to be satisfactory.

Revision. When a constitution is badly in need of extensive change and it appears that the usual methods of amendment cannot adequately provide for the changes needed, resort is had to one or another of the revision procedures. Ordinarily, a document that needs alteration to the extent that revision is necessary should be replaced. With few exceptions, therefore, most successful efforts at revision have produced new constitutions rather than reworked versions of constitutions already in force.

Conventions. The constitutional convention is by far the most commonly employed device for constitutional revision. With the exception of the Georgia Constitution of 1945, every state constitution now in effect is the product of such an assembly. While other means are available, the convention remains the generally accepted method for framing new basic documents.

Calling the Convention. Normally, a convention results from cooperative efforts by the state legislature and the people. Even though one-fourth of the state constitutions make no provision for calling a convention, it is generally understood that the power may be exercised by a state legislative body.[20] Prior to the actual calling of a convention a legislature must first submit to the people the question of whether a convention should be held.[21] If a "yes" vote results, the legislature may proceed to call the convention. In the absence of constitutional specifications, the act which formally calls the convention makes the necessary arrangements for the election of delegates, determines the time and place of the assemblage, provides for temporary organization, and appropriates funds to cover the costs of the meeting. The powers of the convention may also be outlined, at least in part. The details of procedure in arranging for a convention vary widely from state to state, and they may also vary in the same state with respect to successive conventions.

In recent years conventions have been prefaced by a considerable amount of research into problems to be dealt with by the delegates.

---

[20] In Arkansas, Connecticut, Louisiana, Massachusetts, Pennsylvania, Rhode Island, and Texas the constitutions are silent as to conventions, but statutes, court decisions, and opinions of attorney generals indicate that the respective legislatures are the proper agencies to call conventions. The constitutions of Indiana, New Jersey, North Dakota, and Vermont are also quiet on the topic of conventions, and the prerogative of the legislature to call them rests upon the effect of custom.

[21] The constitutions of some states require that the question be submitted to the people at designated intervals. The periods prescribed are twenty years in Maryland, Missouri, New York, Ohio, and Oklahoma; sixteen years in Michigan; and ten years in Alaska, Hawaii, Iowa, and New Hampshire.

While again there is wide variance as to organization and procedure among the states, a legislative reference bureau, consulting service, or special commission handles the task. Reports, pamphlets, manuals and the like are produced for the use of delegates once they set about the job of framing a constitution. The value of preliminary research is reflected in the fact that it has become practically an accepted part of the convention process over the past several decades.

Make-up and Organization. State constitutions do not spell out the qualifications to be met by persons desiring to become delegates. In general, they are those of a qualified elector—the same qualifications ordinarily required for candidacy for most public offices. The calibre of conventions is, like that of state legislatures, dependent upon the chance results of elections. It is generally believed, however, that more competent people are attracted to convention membership because of the importance of a convention's work and the fact that conventions usually are of short duration.

In appearance a convention looks very much like a unicameral legislature. As part of organization, officers are chosen, rules are adopted, and committees are appointed. Usually, there is one committee for each article of the existing constitution, with special committees as necessary. The overall pattern of operation is similar to that of a legislative body.

Powers. A constitutional convention is not free to do anything it chooses. In the first place, all constitutional limitations and restrictions must be observed, for until replaced or amended the existing constitution is still the supreme law within a state. The same condition applies in territories or other areas seeking statehood inasmuch as the prevailing organic law remains effective until replaced. Provisions of the legislative act calling the convention are viewed as mandatory in character, although conventions have on occasion successfully ignored legislative directions.

Within the framework of such limitations, a convention controls its own affairs. Once organized and ready for work, it is not subject to limitations by any other organ of government. It proceeds at its task in the manner it chooses and at the rate of speed it desires. However, the product of a convention may be challenged in the courts after the convention adjourns.

Ratification. Beginning with approval by the people of the Massachusetts Constitution of 1780, popular ratification has been a usual step in the adoption of new constitutions. Of the basic documents in effect today only those of Delaware (1897), Louisiana (1921), Mississippi (1890), South Carolina (1895), Vermont (1793), and Virginia (1902) took effect without first being submitted to the people. Altogether the American states have framed over 130 constitutions since 1776. Excluding the original constitutions and the secession documents of the Confederate States, almost ninety per cent of them were popularly ratified.

Throughout most of American history new constitutions have been presented as units to the voters. Accordingly, a new constitution was either accepted or rejected as a whole. The chief disadvantage of this method is that a few controversial provisions may, because of concentrated attacks by opponents, doom the entire document. To reduce the possibilities of complete failure, some new constitutions have been submitted in several parts. Thus the work of the New York Convention of 1938 was presented to the voters in nine sections. One, an omnibus proposal containing forty-nine general, noncontroversial changes, was approved. The other eight dealt with more debatable alterations, three of which were rejected.

The question of how large a majority is required for approval of a new constitution is not settled in all state documents. Half the constitutions are silent, thus leaving the matter for determination by the legislatures or conventions. Fifteen provide specifically that only a majority of those voting on the question of ratification is necessary for adoption. Five states—California, Colorado, Illinois, Montana, and Utah—have constitutional provisions calling for a majority of all votes cast at the election in which ratification is an issue.[22] The states in which extraordinary majorities are required include Minnesota, where a new document must be acceptable to three-fifths of those casting votes, and New Hampshire and Rhode Island, where the majority is fixed at two-thirds. In practically all states a new constitution may be submitted at a special election, a desirable arrangement inasmuch as the proposed document is the only thing at issue and therefore more likely to be accepted or rejected on its merits.

Revision Commissions. From time to time over the past century about one-half of the states have used commissions in the pursuit of

---

[22] Of these states, California, Colorado, and Illinois have constitutional provisions that require special elections for the purpose of ratifying a new basic document. For all practical purposes, therefore, the majority required for approval is a majority of those voting on the question of ratification.

constitutional revision.[23] Unlike conventions, commissions are not recognized by state constitutions, none of which makes provision for the use of a revision commission. Consequently the use that may be made of the commission device depends first upon whether there are conflicts with any provisions of the existing constitution and second, upon the willingness of the state legislature to use it.

Legal Status. Since constitutions do not refer to the revision commission, it is necessarily a creature of the agency which provides for it. While a commission may be appointed by a governor on his own responsibility as in Kentucky in 1949, that function is ordinarily performed by the legislature. As a result, the commission is responsible to the legislature, and the constitutional alterations decided upon by the commission take the form of recommendations to the legislature.

In some states a revision commission may not be practicable due to the effect of certain restrictive constitutional provisions. Since the proposals of a commission are put before the voters by the legislative body in the form of one or more amendments, an unduly restrictive amendatory procedure may severely curtail the extent of revision possible. In fact, true revision may not be possible at all. The Georgia Constitution of 1945, a revised document produced by a commission, was submitted to the voters in the form of a single amendment. The work of a revision commission in Florida was invalidated by a 1958 decision of that state's supreme court on the ground that no one amendment may alter more than one article of the existing constitution. Similar requirements in other states would limit the efficacy of revision commissions.

Make-up and Organization. A revision commission may take any of a variety of forms. Agencies already in existence may function as commissions. The 1947 Oklahoma commission, for example, was in actuality the legislative council acting in a different capacity. The California commission which met in that same year was in reality a joint interim legislative committee. More commonly, however, revision commissions are made up of personnel appointed by the governor upon authorization by the legislature. Members may be drawn from private life as well as from the various branches of government.

---

[23] The revision commission should not be confused with the *convention commission.* The task of the convention commission, discussed above in conjunction with conventions, is to lay the groundwork for a convention to be held later.

The size of a commission is determined by the creating authority, but in practice they have been small groups.

The Commission: Pro and Con. Several convincing arguments may be advanced in support of the commission as a method of constitutional revision. Its small size indicates a saving in costs, and, since small groups operate more expeditiously than large ones, time is also saved. Freer debate is possible since there are fewer members to be heard. Perhaps the strongest argument is the fact that since a commission is not elective, persons with expert qualifications may be induced to accept membership—individuals who might be reluctant to campaign for election as delegates to a convention. Those who favor commissions also contend that pressure groups would be less likely to sway such persons.

Opponents of revision commissions are quick to point out that a constitution, the basic law of the state, should be democratically conceived. And the commission, removed from direct popular control and staffed without particular regard to the desires of the people, is contrary to democratic concepts. Further, it may be contended, the commission is not as free to act as its supporters insist, for being subordinate to the legislature it is conditioned by what it thinks the legislature will accept. It is also easy to "pack" a commission—that is, to appoint members who will suggest changes desired by leaders in the legislative and executive branches. Finally, in answer to the argument that commissions save time and money, opponents reply that such gains are immaterial unless the suggested revision is acceptable and finally adopted. On this point detractors recall that a majority of revision commissions have failed to see their work fully accepted.

Obviously, sound arguments can be posed both in support of and against the revision commission. To condemn all commissions because most have failed is as unrealistic as acclaiming the device because some have produced substantial revisions. The most sensible view judges each individual commission on its merits in the context of the legal structure within which it must operate.

Piecemeal Revision. In some states the constitutionally prescribed method of amending the fundamental law is so easy that frequent and numerous changes are made. Constitutions subjected to such alteration may be said, in effect, to undergo a sort of gradual, continuous revision. One-fourth of the constitutions now in effect are amended on the average of twice at each general election. Georgia and Virginia have averaged three amendments biennially, and the figure is seven in Alabama and South Carolina. The California Constitution is amended an average of eight times at each general election, and the voters of Louisiana approve an average of *twenty-four* alterations every two years!

The undesirability of piecemeal revision is clearly indicated by its haphazard nature. There is no attempt to integrate changes, no pattern according to which a consistent development of constitutional content can be engineered. In the final analysis, extensive piecemeal change can create as much need for further change as it, by chance, remedies.

Revision by the Legislature. Oregon in 1960 and California in 1962 adopted constitutional amendments which provide an alternative method of constitutional revision. Under the terms of each of these provisions, the legislature itself may propose a revision of all or part of the state constitution by means of a two-thirds vote of all members in each house. Revisions proposed in this manner are subject to popular ratification with adoption dependent upon a favorable vote of a majority voting on the issue. In effect, the legislature may choose to perform as a convention or to authorize a convention to recommend a revision. Attempts at implementation have thus far proved unsuccessful, with the work of a revision commission failing to secure the necessary approval at the 1963 Oregon legislative session.

THE MODEL STATE CONSTITUTION

In 1921 the Committee on State Government of the National Municipal League framed the Model State Constitution. That document, intended as a model of what a typical state constitution *ought* to be like, was revised and reissued in 1928, 1933, 1941, 1948, and 1963. It does not, of course, have any legal effect in any state, nor has it been adopted in its entirety by the voters of any state. Rather, its purpose is to serve as a guide to the delegates of constitutional conventions, members of revision commissions, persons and groups sponsoring amendments, and voters who ratify or reject constitutional alterations.

The Model State Constitution is not a radical document. The subjects dealt with are those usually covered by state constitutions.

There is a bill of rights and provisions on suffrage, elections, the legislature, initiative and referendum, the executive, the judiciary, finance, local government, civil service, public schools, intergovernmental relations, general provisions, constitutional revision, and a schedule. Little is included that is not fundamental although questions may be raised on the basis of one's own convictions as to the necessity of some provisions. Still, the provisions included in the model document are generally conceded to comprise an appropriate list of fundamental provisions.

Not all the provisions of the model document have met with general acceptance. Only Nebraska, for example, uses a unicameral legislature as suggested in the Model Constitution. In fact, while some state constitutions contain provisions that are highly similar to corresponding sections of the model document, no state constitution embraces an article that is identical to any found in the Model Constitution. Even so, the Model State Constitution represents the thought of highly competent students of state government and fills well the role of guide to constitution makers across the nation.

SELECTED REFERENCES

Books:

Allen, Tip H., Jr., and Ransone, Coleman B., Jr., *Constitutional Revision in Theory and Practice,* Bureau of Public Administration, University of Alabama, University, 1962.

Dishman, Robert B., *State Constitutions: The Shape of the Document,* National Municipal League, New York, 1960.

Edwards, Richard A., editor, *Index Digest of State Constitutions,* Legislative Drafting Research Fund, Columbia University, New York, 1959.

Graves, W. Brooke, editor, *Major Problems in State Constitutional Revision,* Public Administration Service, Chicago, 1960.

Irvine, Charlotte, and Kresky, Edward M., *How to Study a State Constitution,* National Municipal League, New York, 1962.

Keith, John P., *Methods of Constitutional Revision,* University of Texas Bureau of Municipal Research, Austin, 1949.

McCarthy, Sister M. Barbara, *The Widening Scope of American Constitutions,* Catholic University of America, Washington, D.C., 1928.

National Municipal League, *Model State Constitution,* New York, 1963.

Nevins, Allan, *The American States During and After the Revolution,* Macmillan Co., New York, 1924.

Sturm, Albert L., *Methods of State Constitutional Reform,* University of Michigan Press, Ann Arbor, 1954.

Thorpe, Francis N., *The Federal and State Constitutions*, 7 vols., Government Printing Office, Washington, D.C., 1909.

Wheeler, John P., Jr., editor, *The Constitutional Convention: A Manual on its Planning, Organization and Operation*, National Municipal League, New York, 1961.

——, editor, *Salient Issues of Constitutional Revision*, National Municipal League, New York, 1961.

Articles:

Burdine, J. Alton, "Materials for the Study of State Constitutions," *American Political Science Review*, December 1954.

de Grazia, Alfred, "State Constitutions—Are They Growing Longer?" *State Government*, April 1954.

Dodd, Walter F., "The First State Constitutional Conventions," *American Political Science Review*, November 1908.

Rich, Bennett M., "Convention or Commission?" *National Municipal Review*, March 1948.

——, "Revision by Commission," *National Municipal Review*, April 1951.

Sturm, Albert L., "Making a Constitution," *National Civic Review*, January 1964.

White, Thomas R., "Amendment and Revision of State Constitutions," *University of Pennsylvania Law Review*, June 1952.

CHAPTER 4

State Executives

In his enlightening examination of the development of the office of governor, Leslie Lipson has observed that "in order to render service, democracy must possess powers and structures which equip it for action."[1] Action in the sense of accomplishing the goals and purposes of a governmental unit is the responsibility of the executive branch. The purpose of this chapter is to examine major component parts of this branch of government as found in the states. Attention will be called not only to organizational aspects, but stress will also be placed on the general nature of the executive function. Although each governor has major responsibilities relative to the executive function, he is often in the position of being "first among equals." Consequently, it is important to gain some insight into the authority and responsibility of other executive officers, such as the secretary of state, treasurer, and attorney general.

THE GOVERNOR

Historical Development of the Office. Following the American Revolution, power in the hands of government was considered to be a danger. Serious doubt existed as to the effectiveness of popular control over a government with much authority. Distrust of power in the hands of the executive was especially strong as a result of experience with colonial governors who enjoyed extensive authority as representatives of the King of England or of individual proprietors.[2]

The prevailing tone reflected in the original state constitutions was "confidence in legislatures, mistrust of executives."[3] Since all of these constitutions were the product of legislative action, suprem-

---

[1] Leslie Lipson, *The American Governor: From Figurehead to Leader,* University of Chicago Press, 1939, p. 1.
[2] In Connecticut and Rhode Island, governors were chosen by the state legislatures and possessed few powers.
[3] Lipson, *op. cit.,* p. 12.

acy of the legislative branch was to be expected. Since most of the early state governors were chosen by the legislatures, they possessed little authority.[4] In the effort to guard against the dangers of a strong executive, most power was vested in the legislature, reflecting a failure to realize that the actual risk lay in a concentration of authority in *any* branch of the government.

Although some political leaders by the end of the eighteenth century were aware of certain problems inherent in a governmental system characterized by a weak executive, increases in authority came slowly.[5] According to Lipson, by 1830 there were signs that the governor "will one day develop into an officer existing in his own right, that he will cease to be a mere creature of the legislature."[6] Decreased legislative domination of the executive did not mean, however, that the governor had become chief executive in fact as well as name. Instead, the practice was to diffuse executive responsibility among individual officers, who as a result of the influence of "Jacksonian democracy" were popularly elected and hence were not subject to gubernatorial control.

Writing in the 1880's, James Bryce observed that "the governor remains in solitary glory the official head and representative of the majesty of the State. His powers are . . . more specious than solid . . ."[7] Chief among the reasons why state governors were able to function at all satisfactorily with such diffusion of executive authority was the fact that their responsibilities were few. During the last quarter of the nineteenth century, changes came rapidly. The increased complexity of society resulting in large part from the rapid industrialization of the country made much greater demands upon government. Many new laws enacted by the state legislatures "threw an administrative burden upon an executive branch that was structurally unfitted to bear it."[8] Instead of attempting to develop a cohesive administrative organization, state legislatures chose to create new agencies that were largely independent of the governor.

In the following chapter attention will be called in some detail to

---

[4] Even the popularly elected governors of Massachusetts and New York had little authority.

[5] This realization was clearly reflected in the powers granted to the President in the U.S. Constitution and to the governor in the Illinois Constitution of 1818.

[6] *Op. cit.,* p. 19.

[7] James Bryce, *The American Commonwealth,* Vol. I, The Commonwealth Publishing Co., New York, 1908, p. 533.

[8] Lipson, *op. cit.,* p. 25.

the efforts at reorganization that occurred in the states during the first quarter of the twentieth century. A foremost objective of these movements was "to make the governor chief executive in fact as well as name,"[9] and much effort was expended in this direction during the fifteen or so years following World War I. Although many proposals dear to the hearts of the advocates of thoroughgoing reorganization were not realized, the effectiveness of the executive had been greatly enhanced before World War II. Further efforts at strengthening the executive branch of our state governments followed upon the heels of the report of the first Hoover Commission.

Formal Qualifications for the Office. In every state constitution are found a few minimum qualifications that a person must possess in order to qualify as a gubernatorial candidate. All states require United States citizenship, and over one-third stipulate a minimum number of years of citizenship, ranging from two to twenty.[10] Periods of state residence, varying in length from one to ten years, are required in practically all states. As a rule, a candidate must have reached a specific age. Although the most common requirement is thirty years, a few states accept twenty-one or twenty-five.[11] Even where no provisions are included in the state constitution pertaining to age, custom requires that a candidate for the governorship must be a mature person. Possession of formal qualifications obviously is insufficient to make a person a promising candidate.

Informal Qualifications—"Availability." Much more significant than the formal qualifications are those arising from political necessity. The crucial question is, What qualifications will enhance the vote-getting capacity of the candidate? A party needs a candidate who will make the widest appeal and at the same time offend the smallest number of voters. A good candidate should not be too unlike the mass of voters to whom he must appeal. At the same time he must be sufficiently different for the people to place their trust in him as a leader. Consequently, he must be persuasive; he must

---

[9] J. C. Phillips, *State and Local Government in America*, American Book Co., New York, 1954, p. 184.

[10] In the states with no explicit constitutional requirement as to citizenship, gubernatorial candidates must qualify as voters, who in turn must be citizens.

[11] The only states to impose a minimum age qualification over thirty are Hawaii and Missouri, where it is thirty-five.

possess a superior, practical knowledge of the problems of government; and he must evidence the ability to work with people. Perhaps above all, a good candidate needs to convince the voters that he has a program.[12]

In general, "availability" is measured in terms of such considerations as ability to work with party leaders, affiliation with various organizations, religion, nationality background, financial resources, sex, and experience in public office. A candidate who is acceptable to his party organization in the state or district from which he seeks election usually has a definite advantage over one opposed by the "regulars." Of course, the efforts of "independent" candidates are occasionally crowned with success, an eventuality that may result in part from popular reaction against the policies and practices associated with a particular party at a given time. A good candidate belongs to a number of "desirable" organizations, such as a church, one or more service clubs, professional or trade organizations, and civic action groups. He should also be free from the taint of "undesirable" groups that espouse extremist or radical views or programs.

Although as a people we emphasize the value and importance of religious freedom, candidates to public office are not free, politically speaking, to belong to just any faith. In some areas a Catholic would not be "available," while in others the same would be true of a Protestant; members of the Mormon Church make especially attractive candidates in Utah, but their religion might be a political handicap in other parts of the country. Persons of obvious Irish, Polish, or Scandinavian ancestry, for example, have a definite advantage over persons of other nationalities in certain localities. In general, a candidate needs to have above average financial resources available to him. More often than not, campaigns are expensive. In the absence of personal financial resources, the candidate needs to know where he can go to obtain assistance. This generalization should not be taken to mean that the well-to-do candidate does not need to seek help from persons interested in his candidacy, for the existence of individuals with "a stake" in his success is a definite asset to a person running for public office.[13]

---

[12] See Frank Bane, "The Job of Being a Governor," *State Government*, Summer 1958.

[13] One significant danger is inherent in this consideration, namely, that the voters may feel that the candidate has "sold out" to certain interests. Caution must be exercised with regard to the sources and amount of support accepted by a candidate. Small contributions from a variety of sources are generally to be preferred.

Although it appears that sex is becoming a less critical factor in determining success at the polls, it is still very important. Few women run for the office of mayor or seek membership in state legislatures, and rare indeed is the woman who entertains any hope of becoming governor of her state.[14] The existing political climate clearly indicates that women as well as men prefer male candidates. Numerous studies have been made, especially with relation to gubernatorial candidates, documenting the importance of experience in public office as a qualification desirable for those seeking election to positions in the public service.[15] The candidate with a good record in positions of public trust has "proved" himself and thus has an advantage over the person who has had no such opportunity. Furthermore, the *type* of experience possessed by a candidate will affect his availability. For example, a recent study indicates that prior membership in the state legislature is of particular value to gubernatorial aspirants, particularly in some states, while in others experience as law enforcement officers such as attorney general or judge is very helpful.[16] It seems that "in more than one-half of the states there is a typical office career followed by about a third or more of the governors . . ."[17]

Term of Office. As a consequence of popular distrust of the executive branch mentioned above, early state constitutions generally provided for annual election of governors. Beginning early in the nineteenth century, a lengthening of gubernatorial terms was noticeable. Today the constitutions of all states provide either two- or four-year terms for their governors.

At the same time that some states lengthened the term of office of their governors, restrictions were imposed upon the opportunity of a governor to succeed himself. In approximately half of the states no limitations exist. In the others, a variety of restrictions have been imposed, most often designed to prevent a governor from serving two terms in succession. In a handful of states a governor may serve

---

[14] Only two women have been elected to this office, and they followed their husbands —Miriam A. Ferguson of Texas and Nellie T. Ross of Wyoming.

[15] See the series in the issues of the *National Municipal Review* for November 1927, March 1931, March 1940, and April 1952; also, John K. Gurwell, "The Governors of the States," *State Government*, July 1941; Samuel R. Solomon, "Governors 1950–1960," *National Civic Review*, September 1960.

[16] See Joseph A. Schlesinger, *How They Became Governor*, Michigan State University, East Lansing, Michigan, 1957.

[17] *Ibid.*, p. 19.

LIMITATIONS IN STATE CONSTITUTIONS ON TENURE OF GOVERNORS

State	Regular Term in Years	Maximum Consecutive Terms	State	Regular Term in Years	Maximum Consecutive Terms
Alabama	4	Cannot succeed himself	Nebraska	4	No limit
			Nevada	4	"
Alaska	4	2 consecutive terms	New Hampshire	2	"
			New Jersey	4	2 consecutive terms
Arizona	2	No limit			
Arkansas	2	"	New Mexico	2	"
California	4	"	New York	4	No limit
Colorado	4	"	North Carolina	4	Cannot succeed himself
Connecticut	4	"			
Delaware	4	2 consecutive terms	North Dakota	4	No limit
			Ohio	4	"
Florida	4	Cannot succeed himself	Oklahoma	4	Cannot succeed himself
Georgia	4	"	Oregon	4	2 consecutive terms
Hawaii	4	No limit			
Idaho	4	"	Pennsylvania	4	Cannot succeed himself
Illinois	4	"			
Indiana	4	Cannot succeed himself	Rhode Island	2	No limit
			South Carolina	4	Cannot succeed himself
Iowa	2	No limit			
Kansas	4	"	South Dakota	2	2 consecutive terms
Kentucky	4	Cannot succeed himself	Tennessee	4	Cannot succeed himself
Louisiana	4	"			
Maine	4	No limit	Texas	2	No limit
Maryland	4	2 consecutive terms	Utah	4	"
			Vermont	2	"
Massachusetts	2	No limit	Virginia	4	Cannot succeed himself
Michigan	4	"			
Minnesota	2	"	Washington	4	No limit
Mississippi	4	Cannot succeed himself	West Virginia	4	Cannot succeed himself
Missouri	4	"	Wisconsin	2	No limit
Montana	4	No limit	Wyoming	4	"

Adapted from U.S. Congress, Senate, Committee on the Judiciary, *Hearings . . .* May 4, 1959, Pt. 1, p. 15.

no more than two terms, an arrangement that may prevent a person from ever serving more than two terms or may require an incumbent to retire from office for a specified number of years before seeking re-election.[18]

---

[18] In New Mexico, for example, a governor who has served two terms may not serve again until the expiration of two additional terms (four years). An Oregon governor may not serve more than eight years (two terms) in any twelve.

Although cogent arguments may be advanced in behalf of un-limited succession in terms of the "right" of the people to elect any-one they choose and in behalf of administrative efficiency and leader-ship, the fact remains that on several occasions the people have recently demonstrated their preference for restrictions. On a national scale this attitude was reflected in the adoption of the Twenty-second Amendment to the U.S. Constitution. In three of the six state con-stitutions adopted in recent years—those of Alaska, Missouri, and New Jersey—limitations on gubernatorial succession are found. In Missouri the governor cannot succeed himself. After serving two terms, Alaska and New Jersey governors may not serve again for at least one term (four years).

Compensation. State governors traditionally have been compen-sated inadequately, although significant improvements have ap-peared rather widely in recent years. As late as 1950 the average gubernatorial salary was only slightly in excess of $11,000; today it is about $23,000. Tremendous differences exist, with New York paying its governor $50,000 and a number of states keeping the salary level around $12,000. Of course, these figures do not reflect the total official compensation associated with the office of governor in many states. Governors in forty-one states are provided with a residence or "mansion." Most states also make allowances for expenses, com-monly ranging from $3,000 to $12,000 per year. Too frequently only persons with private means have been able to afford to become governor. Furthermore, the compensation often has been inadequate to attract able and competent men who lacked adequate means to incur expenses associated with attaining the governorship and main-taining a standard of living associated with that office.

Selection and Removal. Viewed superficially, procedures for the selection of governors are not especially complicated. State laws set forth the formal requirements providing that gubernatorial candi-dates shall be nominated by convention or direct primary and elected by vote of the people in a general election.[19] However, complications

---

[19] Governors are elected by a plurality of the popular vote except in Georgia, Maine, and Vermont, where the laws require a majority of the popular vote, and in Mississippi where a majority of both popular and "electoral" votes are required. See J. C. Phillips, *op. cit.,* p. 198.

State	Capital	Term in Years	Annual Salary*
Alabama	Montgomery	4	$25,000 and residence
Alaska	Juneau	4	27,000 and residence
Arizona	Phoenix	2	22,500
Arkansas	Little Rock	2	10,000 and residence
California	Sacramento	4	41,000 and residence
Colorado	Denver	4	20,000 and residence
Connecticut	Hartford	4	15,000 and residence
Delaware	Dover	4	25,000
Florida	Tallahassee	4	25,000 and residence
Georgia	Atlanta	4	12,000 and residence
Hawaii	Honolulu	4	27,500 and residence
Idaho	Boise	4	15,000 and residence
Illinois	Springfield	4	30,000 and residence
Indiana	Indianapolis	4	25,000 and residence
Iowa	Des Moines	2	18,500 and residence
Kansas	Topeka	4	20,000 and residence
Kentucky	Frankfort	4	18,000 and residence
Louisiana	Baton Rouge	4	20,000 and residence
Maine	Augusta	4	20,000 and residence
Maryland	Annapolis	4	15,000 and residence
Massachusetts	Boston	2	35,000
Michigan	Lansing	4	30,000
Minnesota	St. Paul	2	22,500
Mississippi	Jackson	4	25,000 and residence
Missouri	Jefferson City	4	25,000 and residence
Montana	Helena	4	22,000 and residence
Nebraska	Lincoln	4	18,000 and residence
Nevada	Carson City	4	20,000 and residence
New Hampshire	Concord	2	16,587
New Jersey	Trenton	4	35,000 and residence
New Mexico	Santa Fe	2	17,500 and residence
New York	Albany	4	50,000 and residence
North Carolina	Raleigh	4	25,000 and residence
North Dakota	Bismarck	4	10,000 and residence
Ohio	Columbus	4	25,000 and residence
Oklahoma	Oklahoma City	4	25,000 and residence
Oregon	Salem	4	21,500
Pennsylvania	Harrisburg	4	35,000 and residence
Rhode Island	Providence	2	25,000
South Carolina	Columbia	4	20,000 and residence
South Dakota	Pierre	2	15,500 and residence
Tennessee	Nashville	4	18,500 and residence
Texas	Austin	2	25,000 and residence
Utah	Salt Lake City	4	15,000 and residence
Vermont	Montpelier	2	13,750
Virginia	Richmond	4	25,000 and residence
Washington	Olympia	4	32,500 and residence
West Virginia	Charleston	4	25,000 and residence
Wisconsin	Madison	2	25,000 and residence
Wyoming	Cheyenne	4	20,000 and residence

* States provide for expenses, plus increments for longevity and special services in some states.

arise in any effort to describe in detail the entire procedure involved in choosing governors because of "the variety of patterns . . . in the party processes which lie behind the legal pattern and which actually determine who is selected as the gubernatorial candidate of a given party."[20] Every student of government should recognize that the nominating process is a combination of the procedures required by law and the informal system developed by parties over a long period.

Considerable insight into the "character of gubernatorial politics" has been provided by Coleman B. Ransone, Jr., who has noted that the states appear to fall into three major groups.[21] The first group consists of those states where one party "consistently" elected its gubernatorial candidate between 1930 and 1950. According to this classification, the "sure" states for the Democrats are the eleven southern states and Oklahoma, while the Republicans have been able to count on New Hampshire and Vermont.[22] The second group is composed of those states in which the minority party, although weak, has occasionally elected governors and frequently polled a "substantial vote." In this category the Democrats have been dominant in Arizona, Kentucky, Maryland, Missouri, Nevada, New Mexico, Rhode Island, Utah, and West Virginia. The Republicans have been successful most often in California, Iowa, Kansas, Maine, Minnesota, Nebraska, North Dakota, Oregon, Pennsylvania, South Dakota, and Wisconsin. The third category consists of the fourteen states where party competition is keenest, and the two parties characteristically alternate in electing governors.

Professor Ransone is careful to note that there is nothing firm or fixed about these classifications and that the allocation of individual states to them may well be modified with the passage of time, "since it appears that some of the states are even now in the process of change."[23] Also, great care must be exercised in any effort at prognostication on the basis of conditions existing between 1930 and 1950. The basic significance of such an analysis probably lies in the fact that it supports the assertion that formal nominating processes provided by law in the various states have not actually placed control

---

[20] Coleman B. Ransone, Jr., *The Office of Governor in the United States*, University of Alabama Press, 1956, p. 4.

[21] *Ibid.*, pp. 9–10.

[22] The eleven "sure" states for the Democrats have been Alabama, Arkansas, Florida, Georgia, Louisiana, Mississippi, North Carolina, South Carolina, Tennessee, Texas, and Virginia. Democratic governors are now (1965) in office in New Hampshire and Vermont.

[23] *Op. cit.*, p. 11.

in the hands of "the people." Viewed more realistically, the actual decision as to who shall be a party's candidate normally rests with those who work regularly in the realm of politics. In a one-party state, control over the dominant party's choice is tantamount to determination of who shall be governor.

Although seldom used, means of removing governors from office are provided in all state constitutions. The governor of every state, with the exception of Oregon, may be removed upon conviction of impeachment charges. The normal procedure is for the lower house of the state legislature to bring the charges and for the upper house or senate to conduct a trial and determine guilt or innocence.[24] The only penalties usually authorized are removal from office and disqualification from holding office in the state government in the future. If the governor has committed a crime he is liable to criminal action in the courts following his removal. In twelve states, governors may be removed by the recall.[25] Recall procedure involves, first of all, the circulation of a petition setting forth charges against the officer. Such a petition must be signed by a specified percentage of qualified voters and then filed with the secretary of state. If all legal requirements have been met, a recall election is scheduled unless the governor chooses to resign. The only governor to be removed by this procedure was Lynn J. Frazier of North Dakota in 1921.

Succession and Disability. The constitutions of thirty-eight states provide that the lieutenant governor shall step into a vacancy in the office of governor. In the remaining dozen states provision is made for some other state official, most often the president of the senate,[26] to take over the responsibilities of the governorship in case of a vacancy. Vacancies may be "permanent" in the case of death, resignation, or removal; or they may be "temporary" because of illness or short periods of absence from the state. The process of succession stemming from temporary absence may border on the comical at times:

---

[24] Alaska reverses these responsibilities. In Nebraska the supreme court tries impeachment cases. During this century, four governors have been impeached, convicted, and removed from office.

[25] Oregon was the first state to provide for the recall in 1908. Since then it has been adopted in Alaska, Arizona, California, Colorado, Idaho, Kansas, Louisiana, Michigan, Nevada, North Dakota, Washington, and Wisconsin.

[26] Tennessee is unique. There the speaker of the senate, who is the governor's immediate successor, is designated by statute as lieutenant governor. In Alaska, the secretary of state functions as lieutenant governor.

SIX FILL CHAIR OF GOVERNOR
Olympia's Supply Fast Disappearing

Olympia, Wash., June 22 (AP)—Gentlemen, we are running low on governors. The post for which so many vied so ardently last fall has been held, and hastily spurned, by six men in the last five days.

Since Governor Arthur B. Langlie left the state Friday, this is the order in which the scepter was passed along: Governor Langlie to Lt. Gov. Victor A. Meyers to Secretary of State Earl Coe to Treasurer Tom Martin to Auditor Cliff Yelle to Attorney General Smith Troy.

HALF-HOUR REIGN RECORD

Yelle's moment of glory was the briefest of all. Travelling with Martin, his predecessor, to Portland, Yelle stopped off in Vancouver and shouldered the duties of chief executive for half an hour—long enough to telephone Troy, in effect: "I'm leaving. You're governor."

Determined to stay the flight of the plummeting baton, Martin planned to return from his airplane trip to Oregon Wednesday. Governor No. 4 will become Governor No. 7.[27]

On the other hand, the serious aspect of provisions pertaining to succession was dramatically highlighted in 1947 when an airplane crash in Oregon caused the death of the Governor, the Secretary of State, and the President of the Senate. As a consequence, the Speaker of the House became Governor.

Although determination of when the governor is "temporarily absent" from the state within the meaning of a constitutional provision may cause some occasional inconvenience, the major difficulties relate to the matter of disability.[28] In no state is the term defined either by constitutional or statutory provisions. When is a governor sufficiently disabled to warrant the assumption of his duties by someone else? For how long should such disability continue before the governor's duties devolve upon some other officer? Who is to decide these questions of degree and time? The laws of most states provide

---

[27] Portland *Oregonian*, June 21, 1949.

[28] Only the Alabama Constitution provides a definition for the term "temporary absence." It specifically states that the lieutenant governor may assume the powers and duties of the governor after the chief executive has been absent from the state for 20 days (Article V, Section 127). The constitution of Alaska refers to "temporary absence" and further provides that whenever the governor has been absent for six months, the office shall be considered vacant (Article III, Section 12).

neither answers nor machinery designed to provide them. Instead, reliance must be placed upon informal arrangements that are subject to abuse.

The constitutions of four states deal with the matter of deciding disability. In Mississippi the Secretary of State may submit the question of gubernatorial disability to the state supreme court. In Michigan such action may be set in motion by request of the president pro tempore of the senate and the speaker of the house. In both states the court determines disability without assistance from criteria set forth by law. The New Jersey constitution is a bit more specific. It provides for the adoption of a concurrent resolution by two-thirds of the membership of each house of the legislature stating that a vacancy exists in the office of the governor on any of these grounds: (1) failure by governor-elect to qualify for office within six months of his election; (2) continuous absence from the state for six months; (3) continuous inability to discharge the duties of office "by reason of mental or physical disability." Upon a hearing on such a resolution the supreme court may declare the governor's office vacant. The Alabama constitution provides that the question of "unsoundness of mind" of the governor may be presented to the state supreme court for determination. No guidance is provided, however, for determining disability on any other basis.[29]

NATURE OF THE EXECUTIVE FUNCTION

Too often the responsibilities of the office of governor are conceived in unjustifiably narrow terms. Actually, the "executive function" encompasses a wide variety of duties and activities, some formal and others informal. Formal duties include those tasks imposed upon the governor by law, such as "seeing that the laws are faithfully executed," presenting proposals to the legislature, signing or vetoing bills, and granting pardons. Informal activities encompass the many time-consuming, often trivial, functions expected of a governor, such as speeches on many and varied occasions, radio and television appearances, dedication of public works of all types, personal interviews

---

[29] In Oregon a board composed of the Chief Justice of the Supreme Court, the Superintendent of the State Hospital, and the Dean of the Medical School may examine the governor if there is reason to believe he is incapacitated. Upon unanimous finding that the governor is unable to discharge his duties, the next in line becomes governor. In Nebraska similar authority is lodged with a committee consisting of the Chief Justice of the Supreme Court, the Director of the Nebraska Psychiatric Institute, and the Dean of the College of Medicine.

with friends and constituents, as well as attendance at celebrations, festivals, rodeos, and expositions. Although considerable variations stemming from law, custom, and the personality of the individual incumbent exist from state to state, every governor spends long hours each week attempting to perform the many duties required and expected of him.

The formal responsibilities or powers of a governor are commonly divided for purposes of study into three major categories: executive, legislative, and judicial. Although such a combination of powers in the hands of one person is contrary to a strict application of the doctrine of separation of powers, practical considerations have made it necessary in the states as well as the national government.

Execution of the Laws. The basic legal responsibility of the chief executive of any governmental unit is normally reflected in a phrase in the fundamental law to the effect that he shall "see that the laws are faithfully executed." Although the division of responsibilities among various constitutional officers characteristic of our states makes it difficult for him to perform this task, every governor has in his possession certain specific powers designed to assist him. For purposes of analysis it is possible to isolate and describe devices or techniques commonly used by governors in their efforts to *supervise* the administration of state affairs. At the same time it must be recognized that these techniques are not used in a vacuum. Personal and political considerations often determine when they are to be used, if at all, and in what manner they should be applied.

Appointment and Removal. Appointment and removal of principal subordinates constitute a device of major importance in the hands of a chief executive attempting to see that the affairs of a governmental unit are managed as he believes they should be. Often a governor, honestly striving to improve the administration of a particular program, is frustrated because the head of a major department or agency has been chosen in some manner, perhaps by popular vote, that places him beyond gubernatorial control. Where the authority to make appointments is lodged with the governor, senatorial approval usually is required, an arrangement generally considered to be advisable.[30] Very rarely does a governor possess authority in this

---

[30] The requirement found in a few states that gubernatorial appointments must be approved by both houses of the legislature is unnecessarily cumbersome.

regard nearly comparable to that vested in the President of the United States. An examination of the table on page 80 will provide a clearer notion as to the extent of major appointive authority resting with state governors. In many states the governor appoints a great variety of subordinate officers, often members of boards and commissions, as provided by statute. Such appointments, however, may not appreciably increase the supervisory authority of the governor.

Restricted as it is, the typical governor's power of appointment extends to appreciably more officers than does his power of removal. Few state constitutions grant the governor a general power of removal. The most inclusive grants are found in Missouri, New Jersey and Alaska, while in most states the governor may remove officers whom he has appointed only if there is "cause."[31] In a few states removals as well as appointments are subject to senatorial approval. Rarely does a governor become sufficiently desperate to use methods like those employed by Governor Eugene Talmadge of Georgia in 1933. Unable to "remove" certain members of the Highway Board with whom he was in serious disagreement, Governor Talmadge invoked martial law and had the chairman and another member escorted from their offices by members of the National Guard. The governor then appointed two persons to take their places. Efforts by the ousted members to obtain redress through the courts proved unsuccessful.

The Budget. In the following chapter, emphasis will be placed on the importance of control over the budget as a means by which a governor may implement his executive responsibilities. However, brief attention should be directed to the budget at this point. Governmental agencies, like private enterprises, can accomplish very little without money. Personnel must be hired and material purchased. Consequently, the program of an agency will be vitally affected by those persons whose hands are on the purse-strings. In most states today the governor is responsible for preparing an annual or biennial budget for submission to the legislature. Although the legislature usually has complete authority to make any changes it deems best with regard to appropriations made available to individual agencies, recommendations by the governor should and usually do carry great weight. He may be able to persuade the legislature that the pro-

---

[31] For detailed information see The Council of State Governments, *Reorganizing State Government,* Chicago, 1950.

ELECTIVE AND APPOINTIVE STATE ADMINISTRATIVE OFFICIALS

	Governor	Lt. Gov.	Secy. of State	Treasurer	Atty. Gen.	Supt. of P.I.	Comptroller	Auditor	Tax Com'r.	Agriculture	Labor	Utilities
Alabama	E	E	E	E	E	E	—	E	A	E	A	E
Alaska	E	—	E	A	A	A	A	A	A	A	A	A
Arizona	E	—	E	E	E	E	—	E	E	A	A	E
Arkansas	E	E	E	E	E	A	A	E	A	—	A	A
California	E	E	E	E	E	E	E	A	E	A	A	A
Colorado	E	E	E	E	E	A	A	E	A	A	A	A
Connecticut	E	E	E	E	E	A	E	A	A	A	A	A
Delaware	E	E	A	E	E	A	A	E	A	A	A	A
Florida	E	—	E	E	E	E	E	A	E	E	A	E
Georgia	E	E	E	E	E	E	E	A	A	E	E	E
Hawaii	E	E	E[1]	A	A	A	A	A	A	A	A	A
Idaho	E	E	E	E	E	A	E	E	A	A	A	A
Illinois	E	E	E	E	E	E	—	E	A	A	A	A
Indiana	E	E	E	E	E	E	—	E	A	E	A	A
Iowa	E	E	E	E	E	A	A	E	A	E	A	E
Kansas	E	E	E	E	E	E	A	E	A	A	A	A
Kentucky	E	E	E	E	E	E	A	E	A	E	A	A
Louisiana	E	E	E	E	E	E	—	E	A	E	A	E
Maine	E	—	A	A	A	A	A	A	A	A	A	A
Maryland	E	—	A	E	E	A	E	A	A	A	A	A
Massachusetts	E	E	E	E	E	A	—	E	A	A	A	A
Michigan	E	E	A	E	A	E	—	A	A	A	A	A
Minnesota	E	E	E	E	E	A	—	E	A	A	A	E
Mississippi	E	E	E	E	E	E	A	E	A	E	—	E
Missouri	E	E	E	E	E	A	A	E	A	A	A	A
Montana	E	E	E	E	E	E	—	E	A	A	A	E
Nebraska	E	E	E	E	E	A	E	E	A	A	A	E
Nevada	E	E	E	E	E	E	E	A	A	A	A	A
New Hampshire	E	—	A	A	A	A	—	—	A	A	A	A
New Jersey	E	—	A	A	A	A	—	A	A	A	A	A
New Mexico	E	E	E	E	E	E	A	E	A	—	A	A
New York	E	E	A	A	E	A	E	—	A	A	A	A
North Carolina	E	E	E	E	E	E	A	E	A	E	E	A
North Dakota	E	E	E	E	E	E	E	E	E	E[2]	E[2]	E
Ohio	E	E	E	E	E	A	—	E	A	A	A	A
Oklahoma	E	E	E	E	E	A	—	E	A	A[3]	E	E
Oregon	E	—	E[4]	E	E	A	—	—	A	A	E	A
Pennsylvania	E	E	A	E	A	A	E[5]	E	A	A	A	A
Rhode Island	E	E	E	E	E	A	A	—	A	A	A	A
South Carolina	E	E	E	E	E	E	E	A	A	E	A	A

ELECTIVE AND APPOINTIVE STATE ADMINISTRATIVE OFFICIALS (*Continued*)

	Governor	Lt. Gov.	Secy. of State	Treasurer	Atty. Gen.	Supt. of P.I.	Comptroller	Auditor	Tax Com'r.	Agriculture	Labor	Utilities
South Dakota	E	E	E	E	E	E	A	E	A	A	E	E
Tennessee	E	–	A	A	A	A	A	–	A	A	A	E
Texas	E	E	A	E	E	A	E	A	–	E	A	E
Utah	E	–	E	E	E	A	–	E	A	A	A	A
Vermont	E	E	E	E	E	A	E	E	A	A	A	A
Virginia	E	E	A	A	E	A	A	A	A	A	A	A
Washington	E	E	E	E	E	E	E	E	A	A	A	A
West Virginia	E	–	E	E	E	E	–	E	A	E	A	A
Wisconsin	E	E	E	E	E	E	–	A	A	A	A	A
Wyoming	E	–	E	E	A	E	E	E	A	A	A	A

E—Elective
A—Appointive

Adapted from BOOK OF THE STATES 1964–65.
[1] Lieutenant governor acts as secretary of state.
[2] Combined department.
[3] Governor appoints board which chooses a member as President.
[4] Secretary of State serves as auditor.
[5] Treasurer serves as comptroller.

gram of one agency should be cut back while that of another is enlarged because of changing needs of the state or because of fiscal necessity. His conviction that a particular program is of special importance to the state may result in an increased allocation of funds. Although unable to appoint or remove the head of an agency, the governor may vitally affect its program in this way, and his wishes cannot safely be ignored.

Reports. In approximately three-fourths of the states the governor is empowered to require written reports to be submitted to him by officers in various administrative agencies either regularly or irregularly. Although such authority is normally considered to constitute a means by which a governor may implement his responsibility to see that the laws are faithfully executed, it may be largely a matter of form. Usually, no means exists to guarantee that reports will be anything more than routine, perfunctory statements. If the governor is not satisfied with the contents of a report, he cannot order a change. In fact, the practice of sending to the chief executive reports that are too voluminous and too frequent may complicate his problem of supervision.

Formulation of Policy. In recent years it has become fashionable to refer to governors as "chief legislators," an appellation that would have aroused much unfavorable reaction a generation or two ago. Indeed, "the governor's primary concern seems to be determining the policies of the state government during his term of office."[32] In most states the people expect the governor to have "a program" and to use his powers and influence to see that it is realized. The degree to which a governor is expected to seek to influence the legislature to translate his program into law differs from state to state. The great importance of the chief executive in determining "public policy" in the sense of vitally affecting the lawmaking process should be appreciated by all students of state government. "Throughout his term of office, from beginning to end, the governor will give most of his time and attention, inevitably, to the development of . . . policies—and to seeing to it that the legislature enacts the program he bases upon them."[33] A governor's role in policy formulation or determination encompasses far more, however, than relations with the legislature. In this regard special emphasis should be given to relations between the governor and other groups—namely, the public, personnel in the executive branch, and political parties.

Relations with the Legislature. The laws of each state provide for certain specific, formal procedures through which a governor is empowered to affect the deliberations and actions of the legislature. These formal or "constitutional" procedures are usually classified into three major categories: presentation of messages, calling special sessions, and use of the veto.[34] In many of the early state constitutions framed in the eighteenth century provisions were included authorizing governors to recommend programs to legislatures. The general feeling at the time seems to have been that such authority was merely permissive and imposed upon governors no obligation to prepare a program for presentation. In recent times the trend has been to look upon this task as an obligation, a development caused in part by the popular election of many able men as governors.

Today governors customarily present a message to their legislatures at the beginning of each regular session. Such a message is

---

[32] Coleman B. Ransone, Jr., *op. cit.,* p. 157.

[33] Frank Bane, *op. cit.,* p. 185.

[34] Although in nineteen states the governor may adjourn the legislature upon failure by the two houses to agree on a time for adjournment, this power has been of no consequence in affecting executive-legislative relations.

designed to "orient" the legislators with regard to the condition of the state, major problems, and executive proposals designed to meet the needs of the state. These messages may also point with pride to recent accomplishments of the administration, particularly if the administration and a majority of the members of the legislature are of the same party. In most states the general messages are soon followed by a budget message, which is usually much more significant in its effect on governmental policy. Special messages may be sent at intervals and on various topics at the governor's discretion.

Each state constitution empowers the governor to call special or extraordinary sessions of the legislature. This power usually rests exclusively with the governor, but in Connecticut, Massachusetts and New Hampshire special sessions may be called by the members of the legislature. In five states the governor is required to call a special session when requested to do so by a certain proportion of the membership of the legislature.[35] In a majority of states, the legislature in special session is limited to the consideration of items specified by the governor in his call, but in others the range of permissible topics is either unrestricted entirely or limited by the constitution to such matters as impeachment and examination of state accounts. Recently, governors have called special legislative sessions most often to consider financial matters.

The governors of all states except North Carolina are granted the veto power by their respective constitutions. Although this power is viewed by some students of state government as the most significant legislative power possessed by governors, it is most often used only after other methods, formal and informal, have proved to be unavailing. Where the veto power exists, a governor has open to him three courses of action when a bill is sent to him: he may sign it; he may veto it; he may do nothing. If he signs the bill, it becomes law immediately or at some future date specified in the act. If the veto is applied, the governor must return the bill to the house of its origin along with his objections. In all states the legislature may override the veto, a course of action requiring some extraordinary majority in most states—usually two-thirds of the members of each house. The consequences of no gubernatorial action vary among the states. All governors are allowed a specified period of time in which to decide what they wish to do. In all instances absence of guber-

---

[35] Georgia, Louisiana, Nebraska, Virginia, and West Virginia.

natorial action within the designated time results in a bill's becoming law *if* the legislature remains in session. Adjournment of the legislature before expiration of the allotted time may result in the death of the bill because of gubernatorial inaction, in which case it is said that the "pocket veto" has been applied. On the other hand, in some states the bill still becomes law unless it is formally vetoed.

The governors of forty-two states possess the "item veto," empowering them to veto portions of bills and approve the remainder. In all states except Washington this power is generally restricted to appropriation bills. Although the item veto is generally favored as a means of allowing the governor to delete excessive or otherwise undesirable appropriations, "existence of the power may encourage legislators to approve for political reasons items of appropriation which they know the governor will veto, thereby diverting from themselves and to the governor the displeasure of persons who would have stood to benefit from the appropriations concerned."[36] In a few states the governor may reduce items according to his discretion.

In an effort to measure the strength of governors with relation to their respective legislatures, studies have been made of the degree of success experienced by governors in the use of the veto power.[37] It appears that on the whole governors have been quite successful, increasingly so in recent years. The low percentage of vetoes overriden during the last ten or fifteen years (averaging around two per cent) testifies to gubernatorial restraint in the use of the device and to legislative reluctance to override executive disapproval. In the South and in a few other states like California, Illinois, Iowa, and Pennsylvania, governors' vetoes are overriden so infrequently as to be insignificant. Of course, the usefulness of the veto power cannot be measured in this manner with complete accuracy, because such figures cannot reflect possible effects produced on legislation by a *threat* of veto. Legislators are often informed that the passage of a particular bill in a certain form will result in its veto. Although no information is available to measure the effectiveness of this practice, it is an important aspect of the veto power.

In addition to the three courses of action mentioned above as

---

[36] Clyde F. Snider, *American State and Local Government*, Appleton-Century-Crofts, New York, 1965, p. 261.

[37] See Frank W. Prescott, "The Executive Veto in American States," *The Western Political Quarterly*, March 1950; and "The Executive Veto in Southern States," *Journal of Politics*, November 1948.

open to the governors of most states when bills are sent to them, the governors of four states possess an alternative commonly referred to as "executive amendment."[38] The constitutions of these states empower the governor to return a bill to its house of origin accompanied by suggested changes that would make it acceptable to him. If both houses agree to the proposed changes, the bill is returned to the governor; if they cannot agree, the bill may be lost. However, it is possible for the measure to be enacted into law in its original form by an extraordinary majority, in which case it does not need to be returned to the governor. Governors of the four states in question appear to have enjoyed success in their use of the executive amendment.[39] Since governors return vetoed bills to the legislature along with their objections, the veto may be used to serve essentially the same purposes as the executive amendment.

Relations with the Public. Although the proportion varies from state to state, every governor must spend much of his time in activities that may be characterized as "public relations." Public appearances, press conferences, interviews, and correspondence with private citizens play an important role in the lives of governors. Basically, such activities are designed to build public support, and they constitute an important aspect of gubernatorial efforts in regard to the formulation as well as the execution of public policy. Many of the routine activities that occupy a typical governor's day illustrate very well the logical impossibility of dividing the different aspects of the executive function into separate, neat compartments.

According to one study of the routine activities of governors, a typical governor "devotes approximately four and one-half hours a day to conferences and interviews exclusive of press conferences."[40] Most persons conferring with the governor may be placed in one of three categories: administrative personnel, legislators, the public. Usually when a state legislature is in session, the governor meets with a number of legislators each day. Often the chief purpose of these conferences is to enable the governor to explain his viewpoint and wishes concerning matters before the legislature. The governor may solicit the support of a particular legislator for his program, or he may talk "strategy" with legislative leaders. On the other hand, a

---

[38] The four states are Alabama, Massachusetts, New Jersey, and Virginia.

[39] See George W. Spicer, "Gubernatorial Leadership in Virginia," *Public Administration Review,* Autumn 1941, p. 441.

[40] Coleman B. Ransone, Jr., *op. cit.,* p. 125.

legislator may seek clarification of the chief executive's position on a certain matter or attempt to enlist support in behalf of some program or project of special interest to him.

Viewed generally, governors of the smaller or less populous states maintain more of an "open-door" policy toward the public than those of the larger states. Although in accord with democratic traditions, "such a policy is not without severe limitations, not the least of which is the fact that if the governor spends all of his time on interviews with the state's citizens, he has little time left to attend to the state's business."[41] The more time that must be spent with department heads and other administrators, the less remains for other activities. Citizens are often unreasonable in the demands they make. They feel that they have a "right" to an audience with the governor, who in turn has an obligation to acknowledge their social call or to help them with their personal problems. Great care must be exercised lest the belief become widespread that a citizen is likely to receive a "brush-off" in the governor's office. When it is not necessary or feasible to permit an audience with the chief executive, some member of his staff must be prepared to care for the visitor. Failure to make such arrangements will impair efforts to obtain public support for policies and programs advanced by the governor.

An important aspect of public relations concerns gubernatorial efforts to develop public opinion favorable to certain programs and practices. The governor who is convinced of the need to improve educational facilities in his state or to emphasize rigid enforcement of traffic laws will need public support. Particularly if the legislature has indicated opposition to appropriating more funds for the support of education, for example, effective development of public favor for an improved program will be essential. A governor who is able to persuade the people to bring pressure on the legislature in behalf of his proposals possesses a very powerful weapon in dealing with that body. Because this approach to obtaining cooperation is resented by some legislators, it is often used as a last resort. Appeal to public sentiment may be made *in advance* of legislative consideration and thus pave the way for favorable action without creating the impression of attempting to "bludgeon" the legislature.

A favorable climate of public opinion may be created as a by-product of routine activities not specifically designed for that pur-

---

[41] *Ibid.*, p. 123.

pose, such as press conferences, correspondence, speeches, and appearances at functions of all types. The manner in which a governor conducts himself at press conferences may be quite significant. If he is pleasant, forthright, and helpful in providing answers to questions put to him, the chief executive will probably receive a "good press," a consideration of no small significance in view of the importance of the media of mass communication in affecting public opinion. Some governors hold as many as two press conferences a day, while others may hold as few as two a week. Governors generally recognize the importance of speeches and appearances throughout their states and spend a considerable portion of their time meeting demands of this kind. Creation of the impression of "being a Good Joe" and "making sense" extends beyond the subjects of the moment. If a person "makes sense" about one matter, the presumption is at least in his favor that he will do the same about others. Although it is probably desirable to reduce the amount of time that a typical governor must spend on public relations, the importance of this activity to all other responsibilities of his office is very great indeed.

Relations with Personnel in the Executive Branch. Although governors commonly do not possess legal authority adequate to control the activities of many persons generally considered as their subordinates, they must engage in a certain amount of *supervisory* activity over a large number of state functions. Often the difficulties and handicaps involved are very discouraging, and the governor must resort to "coordination by persuasion." Although he may be unable to control them, the governor should keep in close contact with department heads, a necessity met in some states by regular "cabinet" meetings. Such meetings may be attended by all department heads and perhaps certain other important persons designated by the governor. Sometimes, however, they are composed of only selected individuals in whom the governor has special confidence. Such a practice is not conducive to cooperation on the part of those of comparable rank and responsibilities who are excluded. Statutory provisions requiring meetings at stipulated intervals are of very doubtful value—cooperation is indeed difficult, if not impossible, to legislate.

A governor's position in his party affects in many ways his relations with persons in the executive branch. In most circumstances where cooperation is being sought from executive and administrative personnel, it is important for the chief executive to refrain from emphasizing partisanship. A nonpartisan approach is more likely to secure the desired results by stressing the importance of getting the work effectively done for the benefit of all of the people of the state. Such an approach seems particularly important in those states (some two dozen) with strong civil service programs and high-level administrators chosen on the basis of competence in specific fields. In the remaining states emphasis on partisanship is no longer as strong as it once was, even in those often designated as "one-party" states. More and more persons in the public service are adhering to the view that partisanship has little or no place in *carrying out* or *administering* public policy. It is perfectly legitimate for the governor to seek the advice of fellow party members on policy matters that are or are likely to become partisan issues. Indeed, failure to do so will result in the accusation that the governor is trying to run the state's business in a "dictatorial" manner and thus jeopardize his political career.

Relations with Political Parties. Although very difficult to describe or assess, the role of a governor in relation to political parties is highly important. Often a governor is referred to as "leader" or "head" of his party. Such a title may or may not be accurate, depending on local circumstances. In the dozen or so "one-party" states, the governor may represent only the dominant faction within a party, and other party members may repudiate his leadership entirely. Under such circumstances, the governor's efforts must be directed toward building support inside his party with an eye to fending off opposition from within rather than from another party. Even in those states that may be characterized as "normally" Democratic or Republican, governors often represent a dominant intraparty faction. Due to the existence of actually or potentially effective opposition in these states, governors must seek support both inside and outside their parties. Whenever the governor is of one party and the majority in the legislature of another, the need for biparty support is particularly acute. In "two-party" states when the governor and the legislative majority are of the same party, the chief executive becomes the leader of his party in the effective sense.[42]

Even in this last set of circumstances, gubernatorial leadership

---

[42] For an interesting discussion of the significance of party strength in the states as it affects the governor, see *ibid.*, especially Chapters 2, 3, and 4.

may be more apparent than real. An individual seldom becomes governor without incurring extensive political obligations. Sometimes governors are "put into office" by powerful groups or cliques, which then seek to advance their ideas and purposes through the chief executive. Even where no such relation exists, governors may be committed to foster the wishes of those who contributed effectively to their election. Nevertheless, the honor and presige associated with the *office* itself will inevitably gain for the incumbent respectful attention from many persons, and the impact of his program cannot be disregarded by either his party, his faction, or the opposition. On the other hand, the decentralization and lack of internal discipline characteristic of American political parties work powerfully to counteract the influence of any one man.

The Ordinance-Making Power. After the basic outlines of public policy have been translated into statutory provisions, governors may once again make their influence over policy formulation felt through exercise of the "ordinance-making" power. This power to "fill in the details" of legislation by issuing rules and regulations is possessed by most state governors on a limited scale. Unwillingness on the part of state legislatures to expand gubernatorial authority and emphasis by the courts on the principle of separation of powers have combined to restrict the ordinance-making power possessed by the chief executives of our states. Often where delegation of rulemaking has been absolutely necessary, legislatures have entrusted the responsibility to heads of individual agencies such as the director of public health or the superintendent of public instruction. Rules thus issued must be submitted to the governor for approval in some states. By whomever promulgated, such rules and regulations are *law*.

In some instances, exercise of the ordinance-making power of the governor rests upon constitutional provisions rather than upon statutes. As commander-in-chief of state military forces, for example, a governor may issue rules and orders that are not based upon statutory authorization. Similarly, the typical constitutional directive that a governor "take care that the laws be faithfully executed" is sufficient legal basis for the issuance of rules and orders controlling or directing various aspects of administrative reorganization, relocation of government agencies, or creation of special investigatory and study commissions.

Military Powers. In every state the governor is commander-in-chief of the militia or national guard unless it has been "nationalized" to enforce national law and prevent violence.[43] When the President "calls up" a state unit of the National Guard, it ceases to be under state jurisdiction and becomes an integral part of the military forces of the United States. In times of unusual occurrences like riots and natural disasters, a governor may call out the state Guard to maintain law and order and generally to assist in restoring normalcy. In such circumstances the Guard usually functions to assist civil agencies, but the governor may see fit to declare martial law and supplant civil authority with military. On rare occasions a governor has resorted to his military powers to accomplish purposes apparently not contemplated by provisions of either the state constitution or statutes.[44] The United States Supreme Court has indicated that the national Constitution imposes certain restrictions on the free exercise of military power by a state governor.[45]

During World Wars I and II, many state legislatures granted governors extraordinary powers to protect the states and their residents in "emergency" situations. Also, most states have extended to their governors special powers with regard to making necessary arrangements for civil defense. These powers have generally been of a permissive nature, and more often than not the legislatures have failed to appropriate money for their effective implementation. Considered collectively, the military powers of governors are not significant in the conduct of state government except in troubled times. During the depression of the 1930's, for example, governors often called out troops to quell disorder associated with strikes.

Judicial Powers. Governors exercise a variety of powers of a judicial nature, including the granting of pardons, commutations, reprieves, paroles, and authorizing rendition (extradition). With the exceptions of parole and rendition, these actions are usually referred to as "executive clemency." A *pardon* is a release from the legal consequences of a crime. Sometimes conditions are attached to a

---

[43] Although legally responsible, the governor does not normally assume direct command, a task performed by an adjutant-general who reports to the governor.

[44] See especially Robert S. Rankin, *When Civil Law Fails,* Duke University Press, Durham, N.C., 1939. For example, in 1934 Governor Long of Louisiana ordered the militia to seize the voting lists in New Orleans in order to assure the triumph of his political machine in an election.

[45] *Sterling* v. *Constantin,* 287 U.S. 378 (1932).

pardon; if the recipient violates them, the pardon is void. Although legal responsibility for granting pardons is vested solely in the governor in about half of the states, an advisory board empowered to hold hearings and make recommendations to the chief executive is frequently provided. In some dozen states executive pardons may be granted only with the concurrence of some agency like a pardon board. In an equal number of states the pardoning power is vested in a board of which the governor is a member. In Georgia, authority with regard to pardons was removed entirely from the governor's hands in 1943. The power to grant pardons, wherever located, is usually unrestricted except that in most states it may not be applied until after conviction, and in some it may not extend to cases involving treason and impeachment.

A *commutation* is a reduction in sentence. Through the exercise of this power a governor may, for example, change a sentence from death to life imprisonment. The power to commute sentences is less widely vested in governors than other acts of executive clemency. A *reprieve* is a postponement in the execution of a sentence, usually for a period of a few hours or as much as thirty days. Such a delay is normally granted to allow time for an additional appeal to the courts because of the discovery of some new evidence or grounds for appeal not previously ruled upon by the judiciary.

A *parole* is a conditional release of a person who has served part of the term for which he was sentenced to prison. Paroles constitute a regular, integral part of the law enforcement process, and they are often not considered as acts of executive clemency. Where governors do not share the legal responsibility for granting paroles with some sort of board, they usually accept the recommendations of some such agency. Investigation of the records of persons eligible for parole is a difficult and time-consuming task, one in which no governor should be required to participate in any way. *Rendition* or *extradition* involves the return of a fugitive from justice to the state where he has been accused of a crime by order of the governor of the state to which he has fled. Although governors seldom refuse to "deliver up" such a person as provided by the U.S. Constitution, it is their responsibility under federal law to review each such request and decide on the course of action to be taken.[46] A governor may spend

---

[46] In *Kentucky* v. *Dennison*, 24 How. 66 (1861), the U.S. Supreme Court ruled that the obligation to render a fugitive is a moral one that a governor cannot be compelled to perform.

long hours hearing arguments on both sides before he makes his decision, an action that is definitely judicial in nature.

OTHER EXECUTIVE OFFICERS

Responsibility for administration of the affairs of the states is scattered among a number of officers who are commonly independent of the governor as a result of popular election. Such officers are sometimes appointed by the governor or by an independent board or commission. In any event, they bear a large share of the responsibility for carrying on the day-to-day work required by law and expected by the people. No examination of the executive function can afford to overlook them. Included in this group are the lieutenant governor, secretary of state, treasurer, attorney general, superintendent of public instruction and auditor.

Lieutenant Governor. The office of lieutenant governor, which exists in thirty-eight states,[47] is frequently referred to as a "fifth wheel." Indeed, it seems rather difficult to justify the office in view of the relatively unimportant duties regularly assigned to it. The lieutenant governor regularly presides over sessions of the state senate and then "stands by" in case the governor should die, resign, be removed, or be temporarily absent from the state. Occasionally, the lieutenant governor is assigned minor duties like *ex officio* membership on certain boards, but such duties could easily be performed by someone else.

The major argument in behalf of a lieutenant governor is that by electing him the people directly choose the person first in line to succeed the governor. The same goal may be achieved by designating a specific state officer chosen by popular vote, like the secretary of state, as first in line for the position of chief executive. Such an arrangement exists in Alaska, Arizona, Utah, and Wyoming, four of the states having no lieutenant governor. In the other seven states without a lieutenant governor—Florida, Maine, Maryland, New Hampshire, New Jersey, Oregon, and West Virginia—the president of the senate is the governor's successor. Since in these states each senate chooses its own president, that body determines the individual who may have to assume the responsibilities of chief executive.

---

[47] In Tennessee the speaker of the Senate is *ex officio* lieutenant governor. Alaska's secretary of state functions as lieutenant governor.

Everything considered, little seems to be gained by lengthening the ballot and increasing state expenditures in order to have a lieutenant governor in light of the use made of the office in the past. However, it would seem possible to impose certain administrative responsibilities upon the office either by law or by gubernatorial action. One obstacle to this proposal is that the lieutenant governor may represent a party faction unsympathetic toward the governor.

Secretary of State. The office of secretary of state is found in every state, and incumbents are popularly elected in all but twelve.[48] Sometimes called the "wastebasket of state government," the typical secretary of state's office performs a great variety of functions, most of them ministerial and routine in nature. The nature of the functions must not be allowed to obscure their importance, however. A brief examination of some responsibilities of secretaries of state across the nation will reveal their day-to-day value to state government.

The secretary of state is, first of all, keeper of the archives, custodian of public documents like acts of the legislature and proclamations of the governor, which must be filed and maintained in a manner to make them accessible to persons wishing to use them. He is also keeper of the state seal used to authenticate many public documents. He records descriptions of land owned by the state. An important task lodged with the secretary of state involves the supervision of elections to see that legal requirements are met. Many persons, when they go to the polls on election day, fail to realize the great amount of preparation that has been required. State election laws impose upon the secretary of state responsibility to see that nominating as well as initiative, referendum, and recall petitions have been properly filed and the required number of valid signatures obtained. Commissions of election and appointment to various state offices also emanate from his office.

In many states certificates of incorporation as well as automobile and drivers' licenses are issued by the secretary of state's office. Regularly, the collection and publication of a variety of data and statistics on state government in the form of a manual or "Blue Book" is another responsibility of the office. The secretary of state is also

---

[48] The twelve states in which choice is made by appointment are Delaware, Hawaii, Maine, Maryland, Michigan, New Hampshire, New Jersey, New York, Pennsylvania, Tennessee, Texas, and Virginia. In Hawaii the lieutenant governor functions as secretary of state in relation to certain activities.

commonly custodian of certain state buildings, including the capitol. Much of his time may be occupied by membership on various boards and commissions—some important and others insignificant. In a few states the secretary of state has certain audit functions.

Some students of state administration have advocated abolition of the office of secretary of state.[49] There is and never has been any significant support for this proposal. Even the recommendations of "little Hoover Commissions" have not gone so far.[50] The office has long been an accepted part of state government, and its incumbent is usually a politically important individual, one who may have aspirations for the governorship. Because of tradition, administrative importance, and political influence, the office of secretary of state will continue to be a significant agency of state government. On purely logical grounds and in the name of sound administration, there seems to be no good reason why the secretary of state should not be appointed by the governor.

State Treasurer. The treasurer, who is popularly elected in forty-one states, has the important responsibility to act as custodian of state funds and to pay them out on proper authority. Usually he possesses discretion with regard to the selection of banks that will act as depositories of state funds. Treasurers are sometimes required to collect certain taxes, but the responsibility for custodianship extends to practically all state revenue. As in the case of the secretary of state, the importance of this officer in most states cannot be measured solely in terms of the duties he is required by law to perform. A treasurer is usually a well-known figure in his state and has considerable political influence. He is often re-elected for several terms, and as a consequence his opinions, especially with regard to financial matters, are sought and respected. Furthermore, the office may be a steppingstone to the governorship.

Attorney General. The attorney general, a state's chief legal officer, is popularly elected in forty-one states. It is usually the duty of his office to prosecute and defend cases to which the state is a party. He is also supposed to serve as the legal adviser to the

---

[49] See Kirk Porter, *State Administration*, F. S. Crofts and Co., New York, 1938.
[50] The recommendations of these bodies are discussed in some detail in Chapter 5.

governor, various state agencies, and to the legislature. In about one-third of the states, the attorney general provides bill-drafting services for members of the legislature. In many states he also exercises supervisory responsibilities over local prosecuting attorneys. These and similar tasks require a large staff, particularly in the more populous states.

Providing legal advice for officers and agencies of a state is an important duty, although it may sound somewhat casual. In order for laws to be administered, they must be interpreted. It is not practical for each state agency to have its own legal staff to provide needed opinions, nor would such an arrangement be desirable because it would lead to a multiplicity of "official" interpretations. Although a few agencies have their own legal staffs because they must constantly construe the law in order to perform their duties, the great majority of state officers rely on the attorney general to inform them as to what they may and may not do within the framework of the law. In order to facilitate this responsibility, each attorney general regularly issues a series of volumes of "Opinions of the Attorney General" to which personnel in the state government and private citizens may refer in order to determine the meaning of various constitutional and statutory provisions, particularly when specific issues have not been adjudicated by the courts. The importance of these opinions is emphasized by the fact that most of the issues "decided" by them are never reviewed by the courts.

An opinion of the attorney general is seriously weakened when a contrary decision is rendered by any court of record in the state and is voided by such a decision from the state supreme court. Until a specific point has been decided by the courts, any public official who takes action contrary to opinions rendered by his state's chief legal officer is following a perilous course of action. He may find himself subject to civil suit or possibly even criminal prosecution. On the other hand, since these opinions do not actually have the force of law, an administrator may find himself in difficulty when he follows them. If the issue is a serious one, the best course of action is to seek judicial construction of the law.

Another important aspect of the authority of the typical attorney general's office is reflected in the power to conduct investigations. Either upon his own motion or as a result of a request by the governor or some other high state official, the attorney general may investigate the manner in which a state agency is handling its responsibilities with an eye to determining whether the law is being observed. If he finds that it is not, legal action may be instituted against responsible persons. If an investigation does not uncover derelictions that may serve as a basis for prosecution, it may bring to light certain "shady practices" that are contrary to ethical conduct. The consequences for those involved may be serious, administratively and politically if not legally. Also, the attorney general may decide to look into crime conditions, either state-wide or in certain localities. Energetic action on his part with regard to the suppression of crime will greatly hamper the activities of lawless elements, and it will sometimes serve to embarrass other law-enforcement agencies because of the light shed upon their laxity.

Superintendent of Public Instruction. Although public education has been traditionally viewed in this country as primarily a responsibility of local government, the states have played an increasingly important role in supervising and financing this important activity. Today all states have a superintendent of public instruction or comparable official, and in about half of them he is popularly elected. Contrary to the practice with regard to other officials discussed, it is common for the superintendent to be elected without reference to party affiliation. Responsibilities of this officer include apportioning state school support funds, certifying teachers, accrediting schools, developing curriculum requirements for primary and secondary schools, preparing lists of approved textbooks, and supervising programs of special education such as vocational training and education for exceptional children. Also, superintendents of public instruction often render opinions to local school districts interpreting state laws governing the administration of education. Since these laws are voluminous and highly technical, such action greatly reduces the amount of formal litigation required to settle points of law.[51]

Auditor. "Auditors" perform a variety of functions in state governments. Traditionally, their chief function has been to authorize the payment of obligations—the task of preaudit that belongs, more properly, with a comptroller who determines the legality of proposed expenditures and the availability of funds prior

---

[51] For additional information on the responsibilities of states regarding education, see Chapter 26.

to incurring obligations. Approximately two-thirds of the states now provide for comptrollers, and in those states the auditor is concerned with the postaudit.[52] The purpose of the postaudit is to determine the fidelity and legality of expenditures after they have been made. This is a large and important task in every state today, and most experts in fiscal administration agree that it should be performed by someone responsible to the legislature. It is generally conceded to be poor practice to place the responsibility for the postaudit in the hands of a popularly elected official, although auditors are elected in some twenty states.[53]

Other State Officers. A number of other top-level state officers are occasionally elected, including tax commissioners, directors of agriculture, labor commissioners, and public utilities commissioners. However, the more common practice is to have these and similar officers appointed by some authority, most often the governor. The duties usually delegated to these officers are discussed in the following chapters dealing with their respective areas of responsibility.

SELECTED REFERENCES

Books:

Council of State Governments, *Reorganizing State Government,* Chicago, 1950.

——, *The Governors of the States, 1900–1950,* Chicago, 1948.

Lipson, Leslie, *The American Governor: From Figurehead to Leader,* University of Chicago Press, Chicago, 1939.

Phillips, Jewell C., *State and Local Government in America,* American Book Co., New York, 1954.

Ransone, Coleman B., Jr., *The Office of Governor in the South,* Bureau of Public Administration, University of Alabama, 1951.

——, *The Office of Governor in the United States,* University of Alabama, 1956.

Scace, Homer E., *The Organization of the Executive Office of the Governor,* Institute of Public Administration, New York, 1950.

Schlesinger, Joseph A., *How They Became Governor,* Michigan State University Press, East Lansing, 1957.

---

[52] In a few states a limited preaudit is conducted by the auditor, who is also responsible for the postaudit.

[53] For further discussion of the responsibilities of fiscal officers see Chapter 16.

Schlesinger, Joseph A., *How They Became Governor*, Governmental Research Bureau, Michigan State University, 1957.

Articles:

Bane, Frank, "The Job of Being a Governor," *State Government*, Summer 1958.

Ewing, Cortez A. M., "Southern Governors," *Journal of Politics*, May 1948.

Gove, Samuel K., "Why Strong Governors?" *National Civic Review*, March 1964.

Gurwell, John K., "The Governors of the States," *State Government*, July 1941.

Isom, W. R., "The Office of Lt. Governor in the States," *American Political Science Review*, October 1938.

Lipson, Leslie, "The Executive Branch in New State Constitutions," *Public Administration Review*, Winter 1949.

Luke, Sherrill D., "The Need for Strength," *National Civic Review*, March 1964.

Patterson, Robert F., "The Lt. Governor in 1944," *State Government*, June 1944.

Perkins, John A., "American Governors, 1930–1940," *National Municipal Review*, March 1940.

Prescott, Frank W., "The Executive Veto in American States," *Western Political Quarterly*, March 1950.

Solomon, Samuel R., "The Governors as Legislators," *National Municipal Review*, November 1951.

——, "American Governors since 1915," *National Municipal Review*, March 1931.

Spicer, George W., "Gubernatorial Leadership in Virginia," *Public Administration Review*, Autumn 1941.

White, Leonard D., and Sherman, Harvey, "The Governors March On," *State Government*, October 1940.

CHAPTER 5

Executive Direction and Administration

Although the plural quality of the executive branch of state government has been typical throughout most of American history, it has been a source of concern only in relatively recent years. American society was much less complex in the eighteenth and nineteenth centuries than it is today. To a considerable degree, people in earlier days adhered to the belief that the government which governed least was best, and much less was expected of the states then than now. As additional functions and responsibilities have been assumed by governmental units at all levels, the demand has grown for the location of sufficient authority at some point so that direction and coordination may be given to these undertakings. This leadership has been demanded of the executive branch simply because it could not come from any other source. At the same time popular suspicion and distrust of the executive continued to be widespread.

THE EXECUTIVE FUNCTION

When used to designate one of the three major branches of government in the United States—whether on the national, state, or local level—the term "executive" encompasses a great deal. In fact, virtually all functions not obviously a responsibility of the legislature or the courts are normally considered to be the responsibility of the executive branch. In order for these functions to be carried out, the efforts of many people are required; collectively, they constitute the executive branch. Public school teachers, highway engineers, traffic officers, and technicians who administer civil service examinations illustrate the variety of personnel involved. All such persons are carrying out, or administering, policies that have been determined by responsible authorities. In the words of the state constitutions, they are faithfully executing the laws. Their concerted activities are often referred to simply as "administration."

Politics and Administration. It should not be assumed that the executive function involves only responsibility for carrying out policies that have been determined by some outside authority. Efforts have been made by some American scholars to distinguish administration from other elements of governmental activity.[1] Many persons have accepted the idea that all government responsibilities, perhaps with the exception of the judicial, could be neatly divided between administration on the one hand and "politics" on the other. With some modifications, this concept of an essential dichotomy or separation between politics—the formation of public policy—and administration—its execution—has continued to affect the analyses of government and the beliefs of people in general. In this frame of reference, politics is conceived to encompass those activities involved in the expression of the people's will, while administration is concerned with translating that will into action.

In recent years there has been a noticeable trend away from a separation of the responsibilities of policy-making and those of policy-execution. Indeed, many persons take the position that "administration is a branch of politics."[2] Most critical observers of our governmental system today agree that all its processes are necessarily interrelated, and the executive function encompasses both policy-making and policy-execution.

Leadership. In an earlier chapter it was noted that state constitutions place upon the governor responsibility for *seeing* that laws are faithfully executed. In constitutional terms that is his major duty, but at the same time it is important to realize that only part of the governor's job is included in such constitutional provisions. Likewise, to assert that officers subordinate to the governor are responsible for the administration of certain legislative enactments

---

[1] See Woodrow Wilson, "The Study of Administration," *Political Science Quarterly*, June, 1887; Frank Goodnow, *Politics and Administration*, The Macmillan Co., New York, 1900; W. F. Willoughby, *The Government of Modern States*, Appleton-Century-Crofts, Inc., New York, 1920; and John M. Pfiffner, *Public Administration*, The Ronald Press Co., New York, 1935.

[2] See especially J. D. Kingsley, "Political Ends and Administrative Means: The Administrative Principles of Hamilton and Jefferson," *Public Administration Review*, Winter 1945; Paul Appleby, *Policy and Administration*, University of Alabama, Tuscaloosa, 1949. Also, L. D. White, *Introduction to the Study of Public Administration*, The Macmillan Co., New York, 1955; Marshall and Gladys Dimock, *Public Administration* Rinehart and Co., New York, 1964; Herbert Simon, *Administrative Behavior*, The Macmillan Co., New York, 1945; and Dwight Waldo, *The Administrative State*, The Ronald Press Co., New York, 1948.

does not accurately characterize their governmental roles. In addition, a governor and his subordinates must provide *leadership* in the formulation of policies that they will be expected to execute. Instead of fearing the executive as they once did, the American people now look to those who compose this branch of the government, and particularly the chief executive, for initiative in formulating policies. The people *expect* the chief executive to perform this function, and woe to the governor who fails to realize its importance!

What is the nature of the leadership that is expected to emanate from the executive? Political leadership is both personal and institutional. Political leadership involves the representative function. When a popularly elected executive officer uses his influence to translate into public policy the wishes of a number of his constituents, he is exercising political leadership. He also evidences leadership when he seeks to formulate and implement programs designed to promote the public interest in light of his own mature judgment and conscience. These two roles may conflict. In the long run, the elected officer who is unable to develop public support, at least among significant groups, in behalf of his programs must change his position or be overruled. Such leadership may also be exercised by an executive officer who has not been popularly elected. In so doing, of course, his "representative" function is incidental to his other responsibilities. This type of leadership, essentially personal in nature, should be encouraged. Mistakes may be made, but they are the price of progress.

Political leadership is a crucial and difficult task. In order to perform effectively as a political leader in a democratic society, a person "must be skillfully attuned to the popular aspirations and desires of the times."[3] This qualification is very important to the governor of a state. He must have the capacity to "sense" the needs and wishes of the people. Furthermore, he must be able to act with considerable effectiveness in translating these wishes into public policy. For a chief executive to perform his job successfully, he must have the confidence, good wishes, and support of his constituents. Structural arrangements cannot guarantee the effectiveness of political leadership, but they may facilitate it.

As demands upon leadership on the part of top-level state ex-

---

[3] John D. Millett, *Management in the Public Service*, McGraw-Hill Book Co., New York, 1954, p. 39.

ecutives have become increasingly burdensome, more reliance has been placed on subordinate personnel who act in the name of their superiors. As a consequence of the increasing importance of subordinates, the personal element in leadership has decreased in significance. The term often used to describe this process is "institutionalization," and it bears a direct, positive relation to the factors of size and specialization. These factors in turn have a positive correlation with each other. As one increases, the other tends to increase also. Consequently, no one man has the time, energy, or competence to provide adequate leadership in the personal sense. Therefore, leadership must emanate from many persons, some of whom act in concert with the chief executive while others act more or less independently. Adequate organization facilitates the process of giving unity and direction to the efforts of all those exercising leadership.

ORGANIZATION—THE LEGAL FRAMEWORK

In order to achieve any goal or accomplish any purpose, a governmental unit must have organization. As one astute student has observed, organization "is the relating of efforts and capacities of individuals and groups engaged upon a common task in such a way as to secure the desired objective with the least friction and the most satisfaction to those for whom the task is done and those engaged in the enterprise."[4] The task of providing the many services required of state governments has grown tremendously in recent years. As a result, administrative organization in each state has become more complex. Still, the basic legal framework of most states is much the same as it was during the last century. A brief examination of the major organizational patterns is in order.

Basic Types of Organization. Over twenty years ago A. E. Buck identified four types of state administrative organization that are still pertinent: (1) the integrated type in which department heads are subject to appointment and removal by the governor; (2) partially integrated states with a number of top-level elective administrators and certain agencies, especially of the regulatory variety, largely independent of the governor; (3) the fiscal control type where

---

[4] John M. Gaus, *Frontiers in Public Administration*, University of Chicago Press, Chicago, 1936.

reliance is placed on the ability of the governor to control administration of state affairs to a large extent through supervision of budgetary matters; and (4) the commission or plural executive form with emphasis on collective responsibility for the conduct of state administration. Any attempt to allocate each of the fifty states to one or the other of these categories would be extremely difficult because many states might reasonably be placed in two or more.

The Integrated Type. A prime example of integrated state governmental structure is found in New Jersey, where the present organization stems from the constitution adopted in 1947.[5] As an examination of the chart on page 104 reveals, the governor of New Jersey is a chief executive in fact as well as in name. His appointive authority extends directly to the officials who head each of the fourteen departments into which all executive and administrative agencies of the state have been placed. This arrangement is far different from that found in most states, and the constitutional revision that made it possible was accomplished only after years of effort. The constitutional provisions that establish this structural pattern are so unusual as to deserve quotation:

1. All executive and administrative offices, departments, and instrumentalities of the State government, including the office of the Secretary of State and Attorney General, and their respective functions, powers, and duties, shall be allocated by law among and within not more than twenty principal departments, in such manner as to group the same according to major purposes so far as possible. Temporary commissions for special purposes may, however, be established by law and such commissions need not be allocated within a principal department.

2. Each principal department shall be under the supervision of the Governor. The head of each principal department shall be a single executive unless otherwise provided by law. Such single executives shall be nominated and appointed by the Governor, with the advice and consent of the Senate, to serve at the pleasure of the Governor during his term of office and until the appointment and qualification of their successors, except as herein otherwise provided with respect to the Secretary of State and the Attorney General.

3. The Secretary of State and the Attorney General shall be nominated and appointed by the Governor with the advice and con-

---

[5] See C. Wesley Armstrong, Jr., "Administrative Reorganization in New Jersey," *State Government,* December 1948.

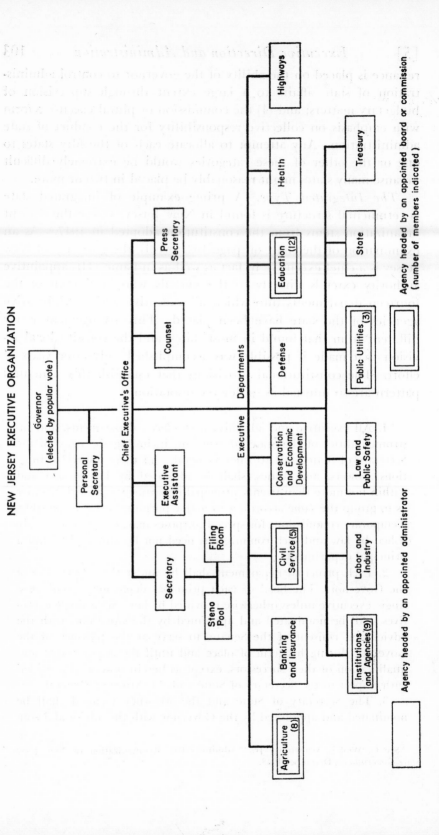

NEW JERSEY EXECUTIVE ORGANIZATION

Governor
(elected by popular vote)

Personal Secretary

Chief Executive's Office

Secretary

Filing Room

Steno Pool

Executive Assistant

Counsel

Press Secretary

Executive

Departments

Agriculture (8)

Banking and Insurance

Civil Service (5)

Conservation and Economic Development

Defense

Education (12)

Health

Highways

Institutions and Agencies (9)

Labor and Industry

Law and Public Safety

Public Utilities (3)

State

Treasury

Agency headed by an appointed administrator

Agency headed by an appointed board or commission (number of members indicated) sent of the Senate to serve during the term of office of the Governor.

4. Whenever a board, commission or other body shall be the head of a principal department, the members thereof shall be nominated and appointed by the Governor with the advice and consent of the Senate, and may be removed in the manner provided by law. Such a board, commission or other body may appoint a principal executive when authorized by law, but the appointment shall be subject to the approval of the Governor. Any principal officer so appointed shall be removable by the Governor, upon notice and an opportunity to be heard.[6]

In this short excerpt from the New Jersey Constitution there are a number of deviations from the usual pattern.[7] The specific requirement that the duties of *all* executive offices and similar agencies shall be allocated among no more than twenty departments by the state legislature is not at all typical. State legislatures usually are free to create as many departments and agencies as they choose, and all such agencies may be legally independent of each other and to a large degree free of control by the governor. In New Jersey they must be "under the supervision of the Governor."[8] In order that the governor may exercise supervision effectively, he is empowered to appoint the head of each of these departments, whether single individuals or plural bodies.

The Partially Integrated Type. Even though organizational details vary appreciably, most states, from the structural viewpoint, belong in the second category identified by Mr. Buck. The chart on pages 106–107 of the executive organization of the state of Oregon is typical of the usual pattern. In obvious contrast to the New Jersey arrangement, the voters of Oregon elect the heads of four major departments. Consequently, it is impossible for the governor to exercise effective control over their activities. The attorney general, the secretary of state, the labor commissioner, and the treasurer owe their primary allegiance to the voters, and it is entirely possible for them to feel that they have a "mandate" to run their respective offices in a manner contrary to the wishes of the governor. In spite of this situation, the Oregon constitution provides that the

---

[6] Constitution of New Jersey, Article V, Section IV.

[7] The New Jersey arrangement is similar to that proposed in the Model State Constitution.

[8] Since New Jersey has no lieutenant governor, the governor is the only state executive officer chosen by popular vote.

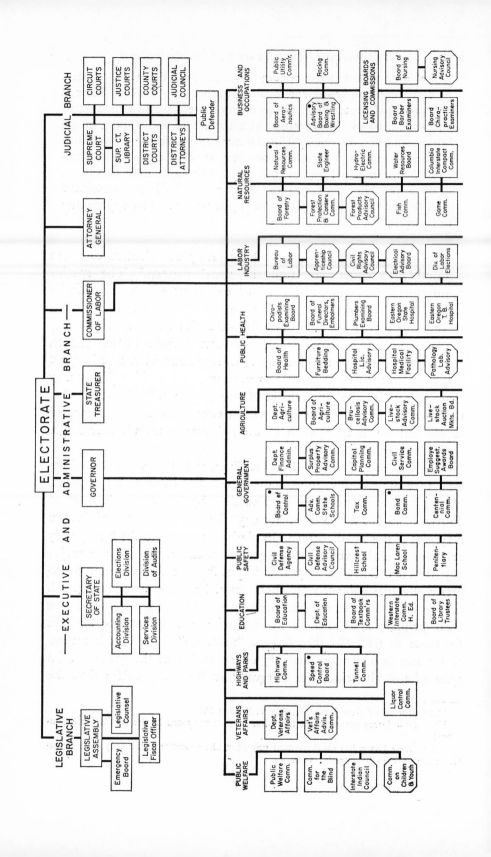

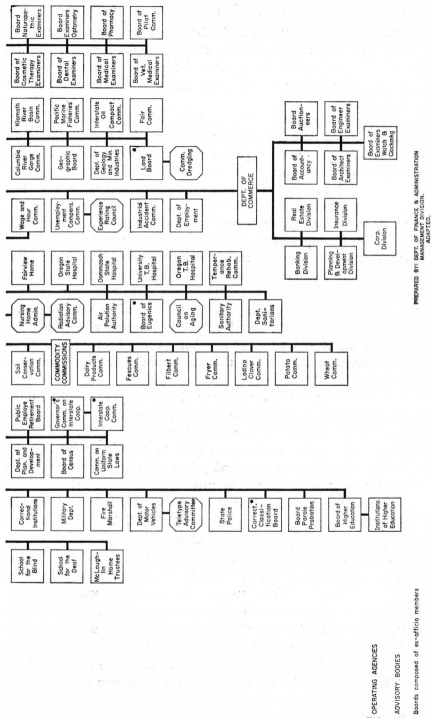

PREPARED BY: DEPT. OF FINANCE & ADMINISTRATION
MANAGEMENT DIVISION.
ADAPTED.

☐ OPERATING AGENCIES

⬡ ADVISORY BODIES

● Boards composed of ex-officio members

governor "shall take care that the laws be faithfully executed."[9] It is true, as noted in the previous chapter, that a governor may influence in various ways the policies of departments headed by elective executives, but he cannot be responsible for their actions in any real sense.

A noteworthy characteristic of executive organization in a partially integrated state is the extent of the appointive authority of the governor. It encompasses a great number of officers, boards, commissions, and agencies, most of which are of a subordinate, unifunctional character. These agencies are in a sense responsible to the governor, but their work often is of such a technical or specialized nature and extends to such a variety of subjects that the governor cannot and should not be expected to supervise or coordinate their activities. Each agency possesses extensive autonomy enabling it to carry out its responsibilities in a highly independent manner. Fortunately, gubernatorial candidates normally do not make campaign commitments with regard to the programs and policies of most such agencies and therefore feel little moral or political necessity to attempt to control them. Appointment of members to such boards and commissions constitutes little more than an unwelcome chore for most governors.

The Fiscal Control Type. The fiscal control type of state administrative organization, unlike those above, is based on considerations not primarily structural in character. Accordingly, a state may belong in this category and at the same time be wholly or partially integrated. It might also conceivably be of the fiscal control type in combination with the plural executive type discussed below.

Who, in the *executive branch* of a state government, has responsibility for determining how much money will be spent during a fiscal period and the manner in which it will be allocated to various agencies and programs? If this responsibility lies primarily in the hands of the governor, the state may be classified as belonging to the fiscal control type. In no state does this task rest entirely with the governor. He possesses it to a greater or lesser degree. Without question, the chief legal responsibility for determining expenditures in any state lies with the legislature. In some instances, the voters may partially determine fiscal policy through the initiative or referendum.

The budget is the most important fiscal device though which

---

[9] Article V, Section 10.

authority of chief executives on all levels of government has been augmented.[10] Not all states place the duty of preparing the budget in the hands of the governor, although most of them have done so. Once a budget has been formulated, it must go to the legislature for approval. An important reason for the consideration normally accorded an executive budget is the realization by individual legislators that it represents a large amount of work over a considerable period of time by people having intimate knowledge and understanding of state affairs the like of which a legislator can seldom possess. Too much emphasis can hardly be placed on the fact, however, that legislators, as representatives of the people, have the primary responsibility to determine what services shall be provided for the people and how much money shall be spent for them. The existence of a plan already worked out by public officials—a budget—is of inestimable value in accomplishing this task.

The Plural Executive Type. It is questionable whether any one of the fifty states today falls logically into this category. Of all the states, Florida probably most nearly evidences the basic characteristic—collective responsibility for the conduct of state administration. The Florida constitution provides that "the Governor shall be assisted by administrative officers as follows: a Secretary of State, Attorney General, Comptroller, Treasurer, Superintendent of Public Instruction, and a Commissioner of Agriculture, who shall be elected at the same time as the Governor and shall hold their offices for the same term . . ."[11] By constitutional and statutory provisions, these same officers, or some of them, serve as *ex officio* members of a number of boards and commissions. Included among these are the Budget Commission, the Board of Education, the Board of Conservation, the Board of Commissioners of State Institutions, the Pardon Board, and the executive board of the Department of Public Safety. As a member of these agencies, the governor has only one vote like the other members with the exception of the Pardon Board, where he must concur in all actions involving pardons, commutations, and the remittance of fines and forfeitures.[12] The six elected officers

---

[10] For a description of the budgetary process and other fiscal controls see Chapter 16.

[11] Article IV, Section 20.

[12] See Wilson K. Doyle, Angus M. Laird, and S. Sherman Weiss, *The Government and Administration of Florida*, Thomas Y. Crowell Co., New York, 1954, pp. 95–96. A somewhat comparable arrangement on a more limited scale exists in other states. For example, Oregon has a Board of Control composed of the Governor, Secretary of State, and Treasurer. This board was created by legislative act in 1913 and has been

mentioned in the above quotation, along with the governor, constitute the "cabinet."

Although the structural arrangement of the executive branch of Florida government would seem to justify its inclusion under the plural executive type, difficulty arises from the fact that in the actual process of administering state affairs there is very little collective responsibility. Instead, responsibility is spread among the elective officials, each of whom feels free to act independently of the others in most matters. Several years ago, a committee created to study the executive arrangement in Florida observed that cooperation "may be obtained only by agreement. The Governor, charged by the Constitution as Florida's chief executive, has no direct authority over the Cabinet or the activities in the several departments headed by those cabinet members. Only through his prestige, personality, and party leadership can the Governor assume the responsibility vested in him by the Constitution. . . ."[13] The committee further noted that to prevent friction, action is sometimes postponed or not taken at all.[14] Such an arrangement is ideally suited to "buck-passing."

REORGANIZATION

Principles of Administrative Organization and Management. In an effort to provide a systematic basis in theory for attempts at structural reorganization, numerous writers have sought over a period of many years to develop "principles" of administrative organization. Advocates of what may be termed the orthodox view have believed that a true *science* of public administration can be developed and applied to problem situations with little concern for the beliefs, attitudes and values of persons closely involved. This viewpoint has prevailed generally, at least until recently, in the literature of public administration in the United States. Such an attitude reflects a conviction that there are certain fundamental principles of general

---

granted full authority over state penal and eleemosynary institutions. Michigan created a State Administrative Board in 1921 (composed of seven elected officials) and gave it supervisory authority over administrative agencies. See George C. S. Benson and Edward H. Litchfield, *The State Administrative Board in Michigan,* University of Michigan Press, Ann Arbor, 1938.

[13] *Florida's State Governmental Structure. Report of the Special Joint Economy and Efficiency Committee of the Florida Legislature of 1943.* Public Administration Clearing Service, University of Florida, Gainesville, 1950, p. 5.

[14] *Loc. cit.*

application that must be observed if efficient administration is to be obtained.[15] What are these principles on which so much emphasis has been placed by advocates of structural reorganization? No one has developed a universally accepted list. However, the following series incorporates some of the more widely accepted ideas as they apply to state governments:

1. There should be a hierarchy arranged so as to fix the lines of responsibility and authority for the administration of the various functions and activities of the executive branch. The lines of authority should run from the governor through the department heads and subordinate officers to individual employees.

2. The principal administrative units immediately under the governor, usually known as departments, should be composed of activities grouped on the basis of function or general purpose. In this way coordination of activities may be facilitated, and overlapping and duplication may be reduced to a minimum.

3. The number of such departments should be sufficiently small to enable the chief executive to exercise an effective "span of control."

4. The governor should possess executive authority commensurate with his responsibilities to the people.

5. There should be staff services adequate to facilitate the exercise of legal authority residing in the hands of responsible officials.[16]

Emphasis should be placed on the fact that these "principles" are in no sense immutable or applicable to all situations without modification. A principle may be defined as a rule of action; it may also be defined as a fundamental belief. According to one authority:

Traditional concepts of administrative organization have been characterized as proverbs and myths. They have been called proverbs in order to emphasize that they are not immutable principles. They have been termed myths because they have some value in rationalizing how people should be treated in organization. . . . But what-

[15] See W. F. Willoughby, *Principles of Public Administration,* Johns Hopkins Press, 1927, for one of the earliest significant efforts to develop this idea. For a later statement see Luther Gulick and L. Urwick (eds.), *Papers on the Science of Administration,* Institute of Public Administration, New York, 1937. Skeptical analyses are found in F. W. Coker, "Dogmas of Administrative Reform," *American Political Science Review,* August, 1922; and Harvey Walker, "Theory and Practice in State Administrative Reorganization," *National Municipal Review,* April, 1930.

[16] This list is an adaptation of the compilation in John M. Pfiffner, *Public Administration,* Ronald Press Co., New York, 1946, p. 65.

ever name one may give them, there are certain principles, dogmas, tribal beliefs, or rules of action concerning administrative structure and behavior which warrant the respectful attention of students of administration.[17]

The important point is that these principles are essentially little more than "guides" or "signposts" to assist students and practitioners in the field of administration.[18] They are helpful, but they are not sacred.

Hierarchy. Essentially, a hierarchy is a system of persons or things based on rank. Thus the chain of command in a military organization is an excellent example of a rigid hierarchical arrangement. To a considerable degree, hierarchy is conceived in terms of legal relations. The structure of the government of New Jersey as depicted in the chart on page 104 illustrates quite well the principle of hierarchy because the governor has control over department heads who in turn control those persons subordinate to them. On the other hand, the arrangement apparent in the chart of the executive branch of Oregon government on pages 106–107 shows disregard for hierarchy because the governor does not have direct control over those department heads elected by the people. The chain of command is broken.

A basic assumption of those who stress the importance of hierarchy is that the definite location of more or less complete legal power is a good thing. Many who do not adhere to this assumption are concerned about the old adage that power corrupts. No known method of selecting chief executives guarantees that men and women of great ability, good faith, or even honesty will always be chosen. Men of superior ability and quality have commonly been elected as governors of the states, but there have been a few notable exceptions. No thoroughly satisfactory answer exists for those who fear serious consequences that would result if a man motivated chiefly by desire for personal power were chosen chief executive in a state where the governor had nearly complete control over all top-level executives responsible for the administration of the affairs of the state.

Functional Grouping. The second principle reflects what has been termed the "dominant dogma of the professional group in

---

[17] John M. Pfiffner and R. V. Presthus, *Public Administration,* Ronald Press Co., New York, 1953, p. 170.

[18] See Dwight Waldo, *The Administrative State,* Ronald Press Co., New York, 1948, especially Chapter 9.

public administration,"[19] commonly known as *integration*. Over the years, there has been a tendency in the states to create new units to administer newly added programs and activities. These units often have been largely autonomous, partly as a result of the efforts of pressure groups. One consequence of this practice has been duplication and overlapping of functions. Efforts aimed at integration are designed to bring together related activities into a single department or agency, and most students of public administration agree that such reorganization should be based primarily on *purpose*. In this way the organizational arrangement of a governmental unit will reflect the major purposes for which that unit exists. To illustrate, all those persons concerned with police and public safety would be located in a Department of Public Safety. Examples of persons included in such a department would be criminal investigators, traffic control personnel, crime laboratory technicians and the staff of a police school, as well as clerks, stenographers, messengers, accountants and others required to run the organization.

Span of Control. According to the third principle, consideration must be given to the number of persons directly supervised by a single official. No one possesses unlimited capacity to supervise others. Studies of administration on all levels of government have noted that executives and administrators often have too many people reporting to them. "The psychological conception of 'the span of attention' places strict limits on the number of separate factors which the human mind can grasp simultaneously."[20] Although efforts have been made to determine precisely the limits to which an individual's span of attention or control may extend, no satisfactory formula has been developed.[21] Failure in this undertaking has resulted largely from the fact that many factors involved are not subject to exact measurement. Individual capacity is one variable; the nature of the work is another; characteristics of reporting individuals constitute a third. Professionally trained persons provide more self-direction than those not so trained. If personalities harmonize and work well together, less supervision is required than under circumstances characterized by discord and bickering. If frequent, complex

---

[19] John M. Pfiffner, *op. cit.*, p. 65.

[20] L. Urwick, "Organization As a Technical Problem," in Gulick and Urwick, *op. cit.*, p. 54.

[21] For one of the more serious efforts at the development of a formula, see V. A. Graicunas, "Relationship in Organization," *ibid.*, pp. 183–187.

decisions have to be made, supervision is usually more difficult than when tasks are of a simple, routine nature. In any event, the number of persons reporting directly to an executive should not be so great that it is impossible to exercise supervision demanded by the responsibilities of his position.

Authority Equal to Responsibility. In the preceding chapter stress was laid upon the constitutional duty of the governor to see that the laws of the state are faithfully executed. Attention was called also to widespread failure to endow the chief executive with sufficient legal power over other executive officers to implement that responsibility in an effective manner. In order to provide a governor with authority commensurate with his responsibility as suggested in principle number four, all the powers discussed in the foregoing chapter must be extended to him plus powers comparable with those of the President of the United States with regard to appointment and removal of subordinates. Chief among the obstacles to the accomplishment of this objective is popular election of subordinate executive officials such as secretaries of state, attorney generals, and treasurers. Election of such officers must be abandoned if this principle is to be observed.

Staff Assistance. In order that the governor may effectively perform the functions imposed upon him, he must have help. Concern for this need is reflected in principle number five. Few persons question the importance to a chief executive of adequate tools for overall management. The first Hoover Commission maintained that "wise exercise of authority is impossible without the aid which staff institutions can provide to assemble facts and recommendations upon which judgment may be made and to supervise and report upon the execution of decisions."[22] Many efforts have been made to describe the role of staff agencies, and still no complete agreement exists as to their proper responsibilities.[23] There may be many varieties of staff agencies, but as one student of state government has pointed out, "The purpose of the staff agency is to help the governor in effectuating control by giving him information and advice and rendering

---

[22] The Hoover Commission, *General Management of the Executive Branch,* Government Printing Office, Washington, D.C., 1949, p. 1.

[23] For good sample treatments of this controversy, see Leonard D. White, *op. cit.;* J. M. Pfiffner and R. V. Presthus, *op. cit.;* M. E. and G. O. Dimock, *op. cit.;* and H. A. Simon, D. W. Smithburg, and V. A. Thompson, *Public Administration,* Alfred A. Knopf, New York, 1950.

service."[24] This statement is pertinent whether the particular unit happens to be a budget bureau, a civil service department, a central purchasing agency, a planning commission or a research agency. Sometimes such agencies are referred to as "auxiliary" or "overhead" units, terms which emphasize the idea that staff agencies are supposed to provide *assistance* of one kind or another to officials responsible for carrying out governmental programs.

Much confusion and misunderstanding exists regarding the proper role of staff agencies. The allegation often has been made that staff units exercise no authority over "line" or operational agencies such as departments of health, public welfare, highways, and safety. At the same time it is asserted that staff units are "closer" to the chief executive than line agencies. Staff people are sometimes said to act as a sort of extension of a chief executive's personality, that is, they are his administrative *alter ego*. This concept is buttressed by the practice of placing staff agencies under immediate supervision of the chief executive, as is illustrated by the Executive Office of the President. A direct consequence of such an arrangement is that staff aides exercise authority over line units. They may do so under the guise of the typical military fiction that action is taken "by authority of" the chief executive. Staff directives may be termed "advice," but they are generally accepted without appeal.

If authority is defined as the ability to elicit obedience or compliance, staff units do indeed control line agencies within certain areas. Only if the line unit makes an issue of the matter of command in a particular case can it be said that authority is not accepted. The claim may be made that if this is so, the authority of the chief executive is accepted, not that of the staff. Recognition must be accorded the fact that an executive is often unaware of and perhaps indifferent to directives issued by staff personnel. Of course, such a situation is in conflict with the principle of hierarchy.[25] The proper role of staff aides is difficult to determine, but their existence and effective performance are essential if governors and other top-level state executives are to perform their jobs effectively.

Use of Boards and Commissions. Some students of public admin-

---

[24] W. B. Graves, *American State Government*, D. C. Heath and Co., New York, 1953, p. 359.

[25] As John D. Millett has observed, "If one insists upon the fiction that no staff aide ever has any identity apart from the personality of the individual administrator, the doctrine of unity of command may continue to have some validity." *Management in the Public Service*, McGraw-Hill Book Co., New York, 1954, p. 164.

istration would add a sixth principle to the list. Boards and commissions, it is frequently contended, are not suitable for "purely
administrative" work and such tasks should not be given to them.
A statement by Leonard D. White goes to the heart of the matter:
"The 'direct performance of work' in a field where major policy and
objectives are generally accepted, where standards are well developed,
and where the public interest is well defined and broadly recognized,
normally calls for agencies managed by a single administrator,
especially those concerned with the vital interests of personal and
community protection."[26] Assuming the validity of White's analysis,
it is difficult to justify a hard and fast rule concerning the "proper"
role of boards and commissions. There is general agreement that
such agencies may perform a valuable service in areas where inquiries
need to be conducted, rules must be made, and disputes resolved
concerning the application of law to controversial areas such as
public transportation, public utilities, banking, and insurance.[27] In
performing such functions boards and commissions are required to
make decisions in much the same manner as a court and to issue rules
and regulations that have the effect of law. Consequently, they are
sometimes termed *quasi*-legislative and *quasi*-judicial agencies. It
seems entirely possible, however, for such duties to be performed
satisfactorily by an agency headed by a single executive.

Considerations like those discussed in the foregoing paragraphs
reveal that many principles of organization and reorganization should
not be accepted without some reservations. Reliance on such principles stems in part from the fact that students of administration are
still rather uncertain as to means for evaluating administrative practices. Much more needs to be done before a true "science" of
administration can be developed.

The Criterion of Efficiency. In the eyes of many persons, the chief
purpose of governmental reorganization is the achievement of a
higher degree of "efficiency," although the precise meaning of the
term is by no means always clear. Actually, few words in the language
of reorganization have such a variety of meanings and implications.
It may mean nothing more than a reduction in expenditures, espe-

---

[26] Leonard D. White, *op. cit.*, p. 189.
[27] For additional information on the use of commissions to regulate business activities, see Chapter 28.

cially when used in conjunction with "economy."[28] Some people are so enamored of the term that they consider efficiency a *goal* of governmental action. This viewpoint is mistaken, for it must be kept in mind that efficiency is not properly viewed as an end in itself; it indicates how well a task is done, not whether it is worth doing.[29]

Probably the most defensible view of efficiency regards the term as descriptive of arrangements and procedures whereby an optimum of "output" is achieved for each unit of "input." Thus an efficient Department of Public Safety would provide the greatest amount of protection possible *for each tax dollar spent,* and an efficient Department of Education would provide the best educational program possible for the amount of money invested. Obviously, the efficiency of these services will improve as knowledge of police science and techniques of education advance. Accordingly, efficiency involves the achievement of the optimum results with the minimum expenditures necessary to achieve those results. Stated another way, a method is efficient if it achieves the best possible results with given costs, or if it achieves a given level of results with the lowest possible costs.

Officials responsible for the conduct of public affairs cannot always be guided by a criterion of efficiency equated in terms of costs. A particular practice or course of action may be inefficient according to such a standard, but it may be advisable because it reflects the desires of the people—and a democratic government must be responsive to the public will. If more elaborate school buildings are desired, it is the responsibility of school officials to provide them even though the input may be disproportionate to the output. If the people want twice as many acres of public parks as information in the hands of recreation specialists indicates will be used effectively, the desired acreage should be provided. It is, of course, legitimate for the "experts" to seek to inform the public and in this way modify popular

---

[28] John A. Perkins has made an excellent comment pertinent to this point: "The late Lent D. Upson, veteran of many reorganization efforts on the state and local levels of government, liked to point out, to the consternation of his tax-conscious friends, that better government seldom meant cheaper government. Good government, like good food, good clothes or any other quality article, is likely to cost more money. Because it is efficient, such government is apt to inspire added services. Well-organized administration often begets professional public servants who are not satisfied with either a low standard or a minimum level of public services." "Reflections on State Reorganizations," *American Political Science Review,* June 1951, p. 509.

[29] For additional insight on this question, see Marshall E. Dimock, *Free Enterprise and the Administrative State,* University of Alabama, Tuscaloosa, 1951, Chapter IV; H. A. Simon, D. W. Smithburg, and V. A. Thompson, *op. cit.,* Chapter 23; and Dwight Waldo, *op. cit.,* Chapter X.

wishes; indeed, such is their responsibility. But once the information has been provided and the arguments heard, popular wishes must prevail.

THE REORGANIZATION MOVEMENT

Early in the current century interest in organization and reorganization was stimulated by developments on all three levels of government in the United States.[30] "Muckrakers" dramatized the terrific waste and inefficiency then characteristic of the governments of many cities.[31] Partially as a result of their efforts and partially because of interest demonstrated by prominent citizens who wanted "more business in government," the municipal research movement got under way with the establishment of the New York Bureau of Municipal Research in 1906. Subsequent to the activities of the People's Power League of Oregon in 1909, efforts were made to advance the cause of reorganization in Minnesota in 1913 and New York in 1915, but little or nothing was accomplished.[32] On the national level, interest in reorganization was stimulated by President Taft's Economy and Efficiency Commission, which made the first detailed study of the national administrative structure in 1910.

In 1917 Illinois became the first state to adopt a fairly comprehensive reorganization plan when it enacted its Civil Administrative Code.[33] Provision was made for the consolidation of a large number of agencies into nine departments, each under the supervision of a director appointed by the governor with the consent of the state senate. A few states followed the lead of Illinois; interest in administrative reorganization continued through the 1920's and was height-

---

[30] In this chapter consideration is given only to structural reorganization. The reorganization movement encompassed other aspects of government, particularly personnel and fiscal management. These topics are considered in the chapters on personnel and fiscal management.

[31] See especially Lincoln Steffens, *The Shame of the Cities,* McClure, Phillips and Co., New York, 1904. Although the term "muckrakers" seems to have been coined by President Theodore Roosevelt as a term of opprobrium applicable to journalists who made frequent charges of corruption against public officials, these writers served a good purpose in bringing public attention to the widespread corruption that did exist.

[32] A. E. Buck, *The Reorganization of State Governments in the United States,* Columbia University Press, New York, 1938. According to Buck, the efforts of the People's Power League marked the beginning of the state reorganization movement.

[33] See J. M. Mathews, "Administrative Reorganization in Illinois," Supplement to the *National Municipal Review,* November 1920. Relative to recent interests in reorganization in Illinois see Samuel K. Gove, "Reorganization in Illinois," *ibid.,* November 1953.

ened by the depression of the 1930's. It was widely believed that structural reorganization would result in saving money for the taxpayer, an especially appealing prospect during the Great Depression. The fact is that it is a very difficult task to demonstrate conclusively how much money is saved as a result of structural reorganization.

Interest in reorganization at all levels of government was stimulated as a result of the work of the Committee on Administrative Management appointed by President Franklin Roosevelt in 1937. This Committee reported its findings and recommendations in 1939, and in the ensuing eight years thirteen states took steps aimed at more or less complete reorganization of their governmental structures.[34] The greatest surge of interest in reorganization in American history followed the work of the Commission on Organization of the Executive Branch of Government (the first Hoover Commission), which reported to Congress in 1949. Widespread consideration of the Hoover Commission proposals so increased public interest in reorganization that many states hastened to make provision for similar surveys.[35] Since 1949 approximately three-fourths of the states have conducted more or less comprehensive surveys of their administrative structure, the work commonly being accomplished by bodies popularly known as "little Hoover Commissions."

In contrast to the success of the Hoover Commission on the national level, organizational arrangements of state governments in the main have not undergone major alterations as a result of recommendations made by their commissions. This situation undoubtedly has been due in part to the fact that major changes in a state generally involve modification of the constitution. Efforts at governmental reorganization always encounter opposition from a variety of sources, largely composed of individuals or groups who have either a vested interest in some aspect of the *status quo*, or fear the unknown consequences of change. Persons in the former category oppose change because they feel the established system is advantageous to them. Members of the latter group oppose change because they prefer to suffer known evils than to risk the unknown. Even the exceptionally bold rearrangement of the executive branch of New Jersey did not provide answers to all administrative problems. In 1954 the New

---

[34] See John C. Bollens, *Administrative Reorganization in the States Since 1939,* University of California, Berkeley, 1947.

[35] See Hubert R. Gallagher, "State Reorganization Surveys," *Public Administration Review,* Autumn 1949.

Jersey Senate created a Commission to Study the Organization and Operation of the Executive Branch of the State Government.

RESULTS OF REORGANIZATION EFFORTS

Although principles for the guidance of reorganization efforts, such as those discussed above, have been known for over a quarter-century, very few states have conformed to them to any appreciable degree. In its outstanding study of reorganization of state governments published in 1950, the Council of State Governments noted that among those states that had undergone partial or "complete" reorganization the great majority still had over twenty major departments and about half of those were under the supervision of boards or commissions.[36] Difficult as it may be to prove that more efficient and economical government has resulted for any appreciable time from efforts at state reorganization, J. C. Phillips has called attention to certain achievements that should be credited at least in part to the reorganization movement.[37] In those states that have reorganized fairly extensively, the ballot has been shortened as a result of a decrease in the number of elected officials, providing greater opportunity for intelligent voting. Associated with reorganization has been an increasing use of desirable administrative techniques such as modern accounting methods, the merit system, and executive budgets.[38] A third achievement was claimed by A. E. Buck some twenty years ago when he asserted that for a few years immediately after reorganization, the costs of administering state government were reduced.[39]

In general, an examination of the results of reorganization on the state level should cause neither great satisfaction nor despair. Opportunities for improvement undoubtedly have been lost, and in some instances much effort has been largely wasted. On the other hand, ambitious and productive reorganization programs have been undertaken in California, Idaho, Illinois, New York, Pennsylvania, Washington, Georgia, Missouri and New Jersey. The last three states recently adopted new constitutions, an action that greatly facilitates

---

[36] Council of State Governments, *Reorganizing State Government,* Chicago, 1950.

[37] J. C. Phillips, *State and Local Government in America,* American Book Co., New York, 1954, p. 221.

[38] For additional information on these subjects, see Chapters 16 and 17.

[39] A. E. Buck, *op. cit.,* pp. 34–36.

administrative reorganization. These states have pointed the way; they are examples of what can be accomplished when citizens are convinced of the need to act.

REORGANIZATION PRACTICE AND POLITICS

Reorganization in practice is a far more delicate matter than reorganization in principle. With reference to the principles of centralization and integration,[40] Clyde Snider observed that they "appear to be basically sound." "But," he adds, "that is not to say that complete reorganization on those principles is the wisest course of action in every state and under all circumstances."[41] His observation is applicable to other principles as well. Experience seems to demonstrate clearly that reorganization for reorganization's sake should not be undertaken. When a particular agency is operating effectively, it probably is best to leave it alone, "even though its organization violates theoretical principles dear to the hearts of 'efficiency experts.' "[42] Such considerations raise the question of how far advocates of reorganization should seek to push their programs. There is no entirely satisfactory answer to this query, and any meaningful answer must emphasize judgment. Compromise usually must play as large a part in a reorganization program as in other proposals involving major changes in public policy. Wisdom may dictate acceptance of "half a loaf," because the alternative may be to achieve little or nothing.

Emphasis on compromise certainly does not mean that all phases of governmental organization and management should not be thoroughly explored. Nor does it mean that those responsible for needed studies and investigations should hesitate to make proposals that they believe will result in more effective government; on the contrary, they have an obligation to do just that. Once studies have been completed and proposals have reached the political arena, advocates of reorganization must take care. At that point they need to develop as much support and as little opposition as possible. In other words, reformers must be cautious lest their goals be "unrealistic in not meeting the demands of practical necessity, and . . . tend to over-

---

[40] Integration is sometimes used to describe the grouping together in a single agency of various related activities.

[41] Clyde F. Snider, *American State and Local Government*, Appleton-Century-Crofts, New York, 1965, p. 293.

[42] *Loc. cit.*

emphasize rational objectives at the expense of value and political considerations."[43]

Plans for administrative reorganization often have come to grief because of failure to give due consideration to three basic factors. First among these is the normal suspicion and conflict characteristic of legislative-executive relations. Legislators often look upon the executive branch as a convenient place to lay responsibility for all kinds of difficulties and failures, and they may evidence hostility toward proposals designed in any way to strengthen the position of the chief executive. This attitude is motivated in part by a concern that a strengthened executive might in some way reduce the importance of the legislature. A second factor is the usual resistance of pressure groups who fear a possible reduction of their influence over activities of agencies with whose programs they are vitally concerned. Interestingly, reorganization proposals are sometimes opposed on the ground that their implementation would result in an increase of "political" control. Thus a proposal to remove a fish and game division from the control of an independent board and integrate it into a department of conservation may cause sportsmen to cry "politics," because the head of the department would be responsible to the governor. A third significant source of opposition lies inside the administrative organization itself. Those officials and employees whose agencies are affected are likely to oppose new proposals. They fear adverse results, real or imagined, to themselves or to their programs, and they may enlist the assistance of their clientele. Opposition on the part of such people is thoroughly understandable. "Their security is threatened by proposed change—not only job security but the psychological security of familiar ways of doing things."[44]

The Task of Salesmanship. The success of reorganization proposals depends in large measure upon the source from which they come. No matter how wise a suggestion may be, it must be "sold." It should be based upon sound reorganization theory; it must not arouse the suspicions and fears of entrenched, key political figures; but above all, it must emanate from or be supported by individuals who are influential in the determination of public policy.

The "little Hoover Commissions," from which a large proportion

[43] Pfiffner and Presthus, *op. cit.*, p. 236.
[44] *Ibid.*, p. 240.

of reorganizational proposals on the state level have come in recent years, are cases in point. These bodies generally have been composed of able, successful citizens; but that alone is not sufficient. On the matter of qualities desirable in members of reorganization commissions, one commentator has observed, "To express it crudely: How many votes can they swing in the legislature, and how effectively can they rally popular support?"[45] In line with this thinking, such commissions ought not to be closely identified with "any limited elements in the political spectrum of the state."[46] If commission personnel are carefully chosen, the task of salesmanship is immeasurably lightened, and the likelihood of success greatly increased.

Building support for a reorganization effort is both important and difficult. Generally, evidence indicates that the greatest degree of success is achieved where reorganization has the active support of the governor.[47] Gubernatorial support alone, however, is not sufficient to guarantee success. Legislative support is vital, and it is wise to have members of the legislature, and perhaps some ex-members, on the reorganization commission. Care must be taken in the choice of these persons, all of whom should have demonstrated an interest in reorganization, although this consideration does *not* mean that they should all be ardent advocates of reorganization. Indeed, wisdom dictates appointment of some individuals who have evidenced skepticism as to the desirability of reorganization. Their doubts facilitate close scrutiny of proposed changes and foreshadow the criticisms that inevitably arise once proposals are made public. One danger inherent in this consideration, however, is that if the opponents of reorganization are members of the legislature who cannot be won over, proposals of the commission may suffer from "built in" opposition when its recommendations go before the legislature.

Another aspect of the problem of building support for governmental reorganization concerns the wisdom of organizing groups of citizens to work in behalf of the commission and its proposals. This course of action was followed with notable success on the national level in regard to the first Hoover Commission; similar efforts with respect to the second Hoover Commission, however, were not so productive. Perhaps some of the difficulties encountered in imple-

---

[45] K. A. Bosworth, "The Politics of Management Improvement in the States," *American Political Science Review,* March 1953, p. 98.

[46] *Ibid.,* p. 90.

[47] *Ibid.,* pp. 88–89.

menting its proposals stem from recommendations made in the area of governmental *policy*. Placing authority to make policy suggestions in the hands of a reorganization commission is of doubtful wisdom.

The use of consulting firms poses a significant problem. According to K. A. Bosworth, "the commissions have apparently learned not to turn the whole job over to one of the national consulting firms."[48] Extensive use of outside agencies creates the possibility that the members of the commission may not participate actively enough in the study to become thoroughly familiar with all its phases, a situation that may prove embarrassing when legislators and private citizens raise critical questions. There is also the danger that outsiders may fail to give adequate attention to all problems, attitudes, and traditions indigenous to a local situation. They may be unaware of, or unimpressed by local values and beliefs that vitally influence popular attitudes. Furthermore, opponents may press the claim that certain recommendations originated with "foreigners" who were ignorant of local conditions. Such assertions may possess sufficient truth to constitute powerful ammunition against reorganization goals.

Responsiveness to Public Opinion. "The administrative state demands results; its god is efficiency. Its efficiency becomes impersonal and knowledge renders it contemptuous of public opinion."[49] This observation is significant; it poses a serious problem that demands consideration by all who are interested in government. Administrators, individually and collectively, exert great influence on public policy, and the vast majority of them are guided by the conviction that their efforts should be exerted in behalf of the public interest. However, administrators often are in a poor position to determine the courses of action best designed to promote the public interest. Their training and experience give them confidence in their own judgment and make them suspicious of persons who do not have knowledge in a particular area of governmental activity. Yet those without such knowledge constitute the mass of citizens who, in the final analysis, must determine what should and should not be done to further the public interest in a democratic society. Many public administrators are unable to act as formal representatives of anyone, particularly if they are not popularly elected. Those who are so

---

[48] *Ibid.*, p. 93.
[49] Francis G. Wilson, *Elements of Modern Politics*, McGraw-Hill Book Co., New York, 1936, p. 393.

elected must be somewhat responsive to public opinion—at least if they plan to run again for public office in the immediate future. This situation may pose serious problems from the standpoint of effective internal control and direction of administration. Accordingly, Professor Wilson is correct in his assertion that "Up to the present time, a solution of the conflict between democracy and the science of public administration has not been found."[50]

Administrators, often referred to collectively as bureaucrats, must be motivated by a desire to be responsive and accountable to the people generally, and the people in turn need to participate more actively in governmental affairs so that accountability may keep pace with increased governmental activity.[51] Although no structural arrangement or reorganization can solve this problem completely, definite location of authority and *legal* responsibility for implementation of the wishes of the people can help.[52] Under our system of government, the primary repositories of legal responsibility are the legislative bodies whose duty it is to translate public will into public policy. Legislatures assign part of this task to the executive branch, which must answer to the people and their representatives for the manner in which administrators perform. It is a fundamental maxim of the American governmental system that ours is a "government of laws and not of men." Among the implications of this statement are the requirements that basic policies shall be determined by legislatures and that administrative officers may not act arbitrarily or capriciously in carrying out these policies.[53]

Structural arrangements are important for the administration of public policy in a manner that is efficient and in accord with the will of the people. If these goals are to be realized, *direction* must be given to administrative activities in order that disagreements and conflicts may be held to a minimum. Under circumstances where each popularly elected official is free to choose his own courses of action, citizens are often at a loss to determine where praise or censure should be placed. The basic direction of administrative

---

[50] *Loc. cit.*

[51] For a good discussion, see M. E. and G. O. Dimock, *op. cit.*

[52] Notice the distinction between responsibility in the sense of the duty of a public officer to perform the tasks imposed upon him by proper authority and responsibility in the sense of accountability to those authorized to impose such tasks. The former may be conceived as legal responsibility and the latter as political.

[53] See Charles S. Hyneman, "Bureaucracy and the Democratic System," 6 *Louisiana Law Review*, 309–349. For a more complete examination of related problems, see his *Bureaucracy in a Democracy*, Harper & Brothers, New York, 1950.

activities must reside in the hands of persons popularly elected, and care must be exercised to locate responsibility in a sufficiently definite manner that the people can know exactly where it rests.

The fact that the people do not hasten to change their governments in accord with the ideas and principles of advocates of reorganization is not surprising. Ideas and institutions change slowly unless great crises give rise to action rather than reason. This fact is disturbing to reformers who wish to see their proposals put into effect without delay. In reference to the reluctance to accept sudden change, there is much truth in the observation that "The fear of insecurity has been the bulwark of conservatism, and it will continue to be."[54] People fear change because of the uncertainty involved.

SELECTED REFERENCES

Books:

Appleby, Paul, *Policy and Administration,* University of Alabama Press, 1949.

Bollens, John C., *Administrative Reorganization in the States Since 1939,* University of California, Berkeley, 1947.

Dimock, Marshall E., Dimock, Gladys O., and Koenig, Louis W., *Public Administration,* Rinehart and Co., New York, 1964.

Doyle, Wilson K., Laird, Angus M., and Weiss, S. Sherman, *The Government and Administration of Florida,* Thomas Y. Crowell Co., New York, 1954.

Goodnow, Frank, *Politics and Administration,* The Macmillan Co., New York, 1900.

Gulick, Luther, and Urwick, L. (eds.), *Papers on the Science of Administration,* Institute of Public Administration, New York, 1937.

Millett, John D., *Management in the Public Service,* McGraw-Hill Book Co., New York, 1954.

Nigro, Felix A., *Modern Public Administration,* Harper and Row, New York, 1965.

Presthus, Robert, *The Organizational Society,* Alfred A. Knopf, New York, 1962.

Public Administration Service, *Proposed Organization of the Executive Branch, State of Alaska,* Chicago, 1958.

Simon, Herbert A., *Administrative Behavior,* The Macmillan Co., New York, 1945.

Simon, Herbert A., Smithburg, D. W., and Thompson, V. A., *Public Administration,* Alfred A. Knopf, New York, 1950.

---

[54] F. G. Wilson, *op. cit.,* p. 241.

Smith, Reed M., *State Government in Transition: Reforms of the Leader Administration 1955–1959,* University of Pennsylvania Press, Philadelphia, 1963.

Waldo, Dwight, *The Administrative State,* The Ronald Press Co., New York, 1948.

White, Leonard D., *Introduction to the Study of Public Administration,* 4th ed., The Macmillan Co., New York, 1955.

Articles:

Armstrong, C. Wesley, "Administrative Reorganization in New Jersey," *State Government,* December 1948.

Bosworth, K. A., "The Politics of Management Improvement in the States," *American Political Science Review,* March 1953.

Brown, David S., "The Staff Man Looks in the Mirror," *Public Administration Review,* June 1963.

Doyle, John C., "Alaska: On Its Way," *State Government,* Winter 1960.

Eley, Lynn W., "Executive Reorganization in Michigan," *State Government,* Winter 1959.

Gallagher, Hubert R., "State Reorganization Surveys," *Public Administration Review,* Autumn 1949.

Gove, Samuel K., "Reorganization in Illinois," *National Municipal Review,* November 1953.

Kendrick, John W., "Exploring Productivity Measurement in Government," *Public Administration Review,* June 1963.

Kingsley, J. D., "Political Ends and Administrative Means: The Administrative Principles of Hamilton and Jefferson," *Public Administration Review,* Winter 1945.

Levy, Sidney J., "The Public Image of Government Agencies," *Public Administration Review,* March 1963.

Musicus, Milton, "Reappraising Reorganization," *Public Administration Review,* June 1964.

Perkins, John A., "Reflections on State Reorganizations," *American Political Science Review,* June 1951.

Walker, Harvey, "Theory and Practice in State Administrative Reorganization," *National Municipal Review,* April 1930.

Wilson, Woodrow, "The Study of Administration," *Political Science Quarterly,* June 1887.

Chapter 6

The State Legislature: Organization and Powers

It is a fundamental principle of the American governmental system that all political authority flows from the people. In many New England towns the people still gather to determine the nature and course of local public policy. In some states the public decides on policy items by initiative and referendum. Throughout the country the people make decisions in regard to the nomination and election of public officials. Except for such examples of direct popular action, however, the authority of the American people is exercised through elected representatives.

THE LEGISLATIVE FUNCTION

The governmental process involves two basic functions—policy determination and policy execution. Government first of all must decide what it is going to do. Secondly, it must adopt means of implementing its decisions. The machinery and procedures of government are intended to accomplish these goals.

Primary responsibility for the determination of public policy rests with legislative bodies. Elected representatives of the people are charged with the duty of deciding the courses of action to be followed by government in serving the interests and regulating the affairs of the public. The executive branch, on the other hand, has the task of carrying out the policy decisions of the legislature.[1] The judiciary functions to settle conflicts that arise in the overall process.

Public policy is a broad, inclusive concept. In its broadest application it encompasses every action of the legislature, for every pursuit

---

[1] It is often difficult to separate policymaking and policy execution. Certainly, instances may be cited in which both the executive and judicial branches make policy. The implementation and interpretation of both statutory and constitutional provisions involve decisions that result in policymaking.

of that body has some influence, great or small, upon decisions that chart the course of government. Ordinarily, however, public policy is understood to embrace only those decisions that result from the legislative powers. Not usually regarded as decisions on public policy, therefore, are such actions as impeachment or removal of officials, appointment of judges and executive officers, and approval of executive appointments.

The relationship between public policy and the public will is often misunderstood. They are not identical or synonymous concepts. The public will is a vague term that refers to the desires of the people—desires that form, in theory at least, the basis of public policy in a democracy. From a practical viewpoint, determination of the nature of the public will is a matter of judgment, of evaluating the interests of contesting individuals and groups. Rarely is there unanimity of the assessment or identification of the public will, even among those intimately concerned with public affairs. Thus legislators often differ as to what courses of action government should follow. At best, therefore, public policy can be regarded merely as a reflection or approximation of the public will.

THE OFFICIAL DESIGNATION

The term *state legislature* is used generally to refer to the legislative bodies in the various states, but it is the official title in only twenty-six of them. Nineteen others designate the legislative body as the *general assembly*. In Massachusetts and New Hampshire the legal name is the *general court;* Oregon, Montana, and North Dakota use the title of *legislative assembly*. The upper house of the legislative branch in each state is known as the *senate*, a term used also to designate the one-house legislature of Nebraska.[2] A variety of titles are used to identify the lower houses although *house of representatives* is most often used. Maryland, Virginia, and West Virginia employ the term *house of delegates*. In California, Massachusetts, New York, and Wisconsin the title of *assembly* has been adopted. In New Jersey alone the lower house is officially referred to as the *general assembly*. No real importance attaches to the particular

---

[2] Article III, the legislative article of the Nebraska Constitution, does not refer directly to the single house of that state as the Senate. Similarly, the members of the legislature are not specifically designated as Senators. The titles derive from a resolution passed at the first meeting of the legislature in which the members officially adopted the name of "Senate."

names used, and the principal disadvantage stemming from the variations is the possibility of confusion in cataloging them.

BICAMERALISM AND UNICAMERALISM

In 1934 the voters of Nebraska approved a constitutional amendment abolishing their bicameral legislature and replacing it with a body composed of a single house. The first session of the new unicameral legislature, held three years later, marked the first time in over one-hundred years that a state legislature had consisted of a single chamber. Georgia, Pennsylvania, and Vermont had unicameral legislatures upon their entry into the Union, but in 1789 Georgia adopted the bicameral plan, and Pennsylvania followed suit a year later.[3] Only in Vermont, where it persisted until 1836, had unicameralism been in effect for an extended period of time.[4]

The predominance of bicameral legislative bodies in the United States can be attributed largely to two basic factors: the influence of English experience and the tendency of new states to follow the example set by earlier states and the federal government. Early colonial legislatures were essentially unicameral, the elected representatives sitting with the governor and council to determine legislative matters. As the popularly chosen representatives gained power, the governor and council assumed the role of a second, or upper, house, leading to the establishment of bicameral bodies in imitation of the English Parliament. After the Declaration of Independence, most states that had not already done so provided for legislative chambers composed of two houses, fixing the pattern that was to be followed by practically all states entering the Union later.

Justification for early resort to the bicameral system was found in

---

[3] Henry Luce states that the unicameral legislature of Georgia "was no more than technically unicameral" because of the existence of a council that had an important part in the making of laws. Only Pennsylvania and Vermont "saw fit to frame a State Constitution intrusting the making of laws to a single body uncontrolled." *Legislative Assemblies*, Houghton Mifflin Co., New York, 1924, p. 24.

From the standpoint of numbers alone, unicameral legislative bodies of all types are more numerous by far than bicameral ones. The legislative, or policymaking, bodies of virtually all local governments in America are composed of one house. So rare, in fact, are bicameral bodies at the local level that only a few small New England municipalities, plus New York City perhaps, may be counted. Unicameral legislatures are found in Guam and the Virgin Islands.

[4] Unicameralism was first adopted in Vermont in 1777 and was in effect for fifty-nine years. For a review of the history of that state's one-house legislature, see Daniel B. Carroll, *The Unicameral Legislature of Vermont*, Vermont Historical Society, Montpelier, 1933.

several considerations. Some feared that a single house might become too powerful and establish itself as the sole authority in government. Since popularly elected bodies were not generally regarded as temperate, it was felt that some kind of check was needed. Further, a unicameral body was not considered to be truly representative of all elements in society. It was also argued that an upper house whose members enjoyed longer terms would give more continuity to legislative policy.

The bicameral nature of early state legislatures reflected a division between the propertied, well-to-do classes and the public in general. Wealthy, landholding elements felt strongly that the lower houses chosen by popular vote were likely to be radical and unmindful of the rights of property. Consequently, members of upper houses were chosen by electors possessing more property than was required of persons permitted to vote only for members of lower houses. For this reason relationships between the houses of the legislatures were not unlike those characteristic of the English House of Commons and House of Lords. With the broadening of the suffrage in later years, however, stress upon property subsided, and the separate houses of today's bicameral legislatures represent highly similar interests.

The Case for Bicameralism. The traditional form of American state legislatures has been defended on various grounds. Essentially the same arguments have been cited by many individuals and groups over a long period of years. The merits usually claimed for bicameral legislatures are as follows:[5]

A bicameral legislature prevents hasty, ill-considered legislation. Thus, if one house approves legislation without giving it due consideration, the other serves to check hasty action and thereby places a major obstacle in the path of unwise policy. However, it is not uncommon for noncontroversial bills to pass both houses with little or no attention paid to them. The "last-minute rush" in both houses almost invariably involves passage of bills with no debate or consideration. Sometimes one house may pass bills in the expectation that the other will consider them more closely, an expectation not always fulfilled. It is, in short, true that a second house *can* act as a check on the first and undoubtedly does so in some instances, but

---

[5] This section and the one that follows are based largely upon Belle Zeller (ed.), *American State Legislatures*, Report of the Committee on American Legislatures, American Political Science Association, Thomas Y. Crowell Co., New York, 1954, pp. 51–58.

experience has shown that the checking function is not always performed.

Two houses are less subject to popular passions and impulses than are unicameral bodies. This point grew out of the fear current in earlier years that a single chamber composed of popularly elected representatives might not respect the rights of property and wealth. However, the gubernatorial veto, the legislative committee system, and constitutional restrictions placed upon legislatures minimize such dangers.

A single legislative house is more likely to usurp the powers of other branches of government. Based upon the assumption of legislative supremacy, this claim loses force in modern governmental situations. Governors are no longer subservient to legislatures, and the independence of courts has long been established.

Bicameral legislatures are less easily controlled by lobbies. It is argued that one house may be corrupted, but to control both houses of a legislature is extremely difficult. This argument loses much of its force, however, when it is recalled that a lobbyist need not control an entire house to achieve his purposes. It is usually sufficient to control a few key members of a legislative committee.

Unicameralism is contrary to traditional American political institutions. Unicameralism has been the exception rather than the rule in American legislative experience at both the national and state levels. At the same time there is precedent in American history for the unicameral system and consequently basis for anticipation of problems and difficulties that might be encountered in establishing and operating a one-house legislature.

Until recent years an argument that could be cited in favor of bicameralism, and still is in many quarters, was the point that bicameral bodies were not limited to population alone as the basis of representation. This argument has lost most of its force, however, since the United States Supreme Court ruled, in 1964, that the Equal Protection of the Laws Clause of the national Constitution requires that both houses of a bicameral state legislature must be apportioned on the basis of population.

The Case for Unicameralism. The arguments usually cited in support of unicameralism are even more numerous than those in favor of the customary system of legislative organization. In summary form they are:

1. Persons with better qualifications are attracted because of the greater prestige and opportunity for public service.

2. A single chamber operates more efficiently.

3. Friction and rivalry between the two houses are eliminated.

4. Responsibility is more easily fixed.

5. Competent leadership is more readily developed.

6. Better legislative-executive relations result because of concentration of leadership in the unicameral system.

7. It is more difficult for lobbies to control a unicameral legislature.

8. The need for conference committees is eliminated.

9. It is easier for the public to know what the legislature is doing.

10. A unicameral legislature is not as expensive to operate as a bicameral one.

There is no mass of data on the operation of unicameral legislatures against which to test the validity of these claims. The Nebraska experience serves as the best available yardstick, and even there the single chamber has met only since 1937. In that state unicameralism has been considered successful although it "has not fulfilled either the most optimistic hopes of its friends or the most pessimistic fears of its opponents."[6]

Support for unicameralism continues to come largely from individuals and groups with a professional interest in the improvement of governmental organization. Political scientists generally favor single-chambered legislatures. The Model State Constitution prepared by the National Municipal League provides for a unicameral body.[7] On the other hand, most persons who serve in, or have formerly served in, state legislatures are opposed to departure from the bicameral system. Perhaps the most important factor to be considered in assessing the desirability of either type of structure is the quality of personnel involved in each, for in the final analysis "no mere institutional device can be substituted for character and intelligence on the part of the body of citizens and of those they elect to public office."[8]

---

[6] Roger V. Shumate, "The Nebraska Unicameral Legislature," *Western Political Quarterly*, September 1952, p. 512. For a defense of bicameralism see Frank E. Horack, Jr., "Bicameral Legislatures Are Effective," *State Government*, April 1941.

[7] Unicameralism has been proposed in each edition of the Model State Constitution.

[8] Roger V. Shumate, *loc. cit.*

Descriptive Features of State Legislatures

Size. The range in size of state legislatures is impressive. While none of them is equal in size to the United States Congress, a few contain several hundred members. In most states apparently little if any attention is paid to the question of the optimum number of members, if indeed such a number can be determined, for getting the work of a legislature done. The question is probably of slight importance inasmuch as the significant consideration is the ability of the legislature to enact sound policy.

The greatest variations in size occur in the lower houses, ranging from thirty-five members in Delaware to 400[9] in New Hampshire. In general, the largest houses are found in the New England states where the numerous towns serve as election districts. The smallest lower houses generally are found in the western states where approximately sixty to seventy members are not uncommon. In other areas of the country the lower houses of state legislatures contain from 100 to 200 members.

Upper houses, known as senates in all states, do not present startlingly wide variations, although only seventeen members sit in the upper houses in Nevada and Delaware, and sixty-seven senators compose that body in Minnesota. Eight senates have fewer than thirty members, and nine number fifty or more. The remaining two-thirds of the states have senate membership falling somewhere between these two figures. No geographical patterns such as those relating to lower houses emerge upon analysis of the figures.

Terms. The length of terms served by members of state legislatures does not vary greatly. In every state they are of either two or four years' duration. Senators serve for four years in thirty-six states and for half that time in the remainder.[10] Only in the New England area, where senate terms are uniformly fixed at two years, can any regional pattern be noted. Members of lower houses usually are elected to two years of service; only four states—Alabama, Louisiana, Maryland, and Mississippi—setting both senate and house terms at

---

[9] This number may vary from 375 to 400 depending upon the number and size of towns eligible to elect representatives.

[10] Current thought appears to favor the four-year term. Senators in the most recent additions to the Union, Alaska and Hawaii, serve for four years. Ohio state senators were elected to two-year terms until 1960 when, by virtue of a 1956 constitutional amendment, their terms were extended.

four years. In Nebraska's unicameral legislature there is, of course, no lower chamber.

No fixed period of time is generally accepted as the optimum length for the term of a state legislator. Certainly, it should be long enough for the incumbent to become sufficiently familiar with the duties and responsibilities of his office to render effective public service. Allowing for individual talent, it is doubtful that a freshman representative or senator can achieve that level of development during a term so brief that he is able to attend only one legislative session. Again, variations in individual capabilities make it highly improbable that a length of term could be determined that would enable all members of a legislature to perform at their fullest potential.

Since most of the state legislative assemblies still meet in regular session only once every two years, the number of sessions attended by a legislator during his term of office is severely limited. In fact, house members in thirty states participate in a single regular session each two-year term; senators in twenty-two states attend only two sessions during their four-year terms; and in eight states members of upper houses experience only one session during a two-year occupancy in office. Taking into account the fact that there is a high rate of turnover among state legislators, it would appear that longer terms, or in some cases more frequent sessions, might contribute to more satisfactory legislative performance.

Compensation. Despite the fact that in recent years a few states have provided substantial salaries for their legislators, no public servant in relation to his responsibilities is more underpaid. As indicated in the table on page 136, states such as New York, California, Illinois, and New Jersey pay realistic salaries of several thousand dollars per year. At the other end of the scale legislators in the states of North Dakota and Rhode Island receive only five dollars per day; those of Wyoming only twelve; and in New Hampshire, regardless of the length of the session, legislative labors are rewarded by the sum of $200 per session. Other states represent gradations between these limits.

In most of the states, legislators also receive expense allowances that range from a few dollars per day to considerable sums. The states also allow "mileage" costs, that is, reimbursement of expenses incurred in travelling to and from the place of meeting; but a limit may be placed upon the number of trips per member.

THE STATE LEGISLATURES

State	Year	Sessions Month[1]	Limit	Senate No.	Senate Term	House No.	House Term	Salary[9]
Alabama	Odd	May	36 da.[3]	35	4	106	4	$10/day
Alaska	Annual	Jan.	—	20	4	40	2	2,500/year
Arizona	Annual	Jan.	—	28	2	80	2	1,800/session
Arkansas	Odd	Jan.	60 da.	35	4	100	2	1,200/year
California	Annual[2]	Jan.–O	120 da.	40	4	80	2	6,000/year
		Feb.–E	30 da.					
Colorado	Annual[2]	Jan.	—	35	4	65	2	3,200/year
Connecticut	Odd	Jan.	5 mo.[4]	36	2	177	2	2,000/session
Delaware	Annual[2]	Jan.–O	90 da.	18	4	35	2	4,500/year
		Feb.–E	30 da.					
Florida	Odd	April	60 da.	43	4	112	2	100/month
Georgia	Annual	Jan.–O	45 da.	54	2	205	2	10/day
		Jan.–E	40 da.					
Hawaii	Annual[2]	Feb.–O	60 da.	25	4	51	2	4,000/biennium
		Feb.–E	30 da.					
Idaho	Odd	Jan.	60 da.[5]	44	2	79	2	10/day
Illinois	Odd	Jan.	6 mo.[6]	58	4	177	2	6,000/year
Indiana	Odd	Jan.	61 da.	50	4	100	2	1,800/year
Iowa	Odd	Jan.	—	59	4	124	2	30/day
Kansas	Annual[2]	Jan.–O	—	40	4	125	2	10/day
		Jan.–E	30 da.					
Kentucky	Even	Jan.	60 da.	38	4	100	2	25/day
Louisiana	Annual[2]	May–O	30 da.	39	4	105	4	50/day
		May–E	60 da.					
Maine	Odd	Jan.	—	34	2	151	2	2,000/biennium
Maryland	Annual[2]	Jan.–O	70 da.	29	4	142	4	1,800/year
		Feb.–E	70 da.					
Massachusetts	Annual	Jan.	—	40	2	240	2	7,500/year
Michigan	Annual	Jan.	—	38	4	110	2	10,000/year
Minnesota	Odd	Jan.	120 da.	67	4	135	2	2,400/year
Mississippi	Even	Jan.	—	52	4	122	4	3,000/session
Missouri	Odd	Jan.	5 mo.[7]	34	4	163	2	4,800/year
Montana	Odd	Jan.	60 da.	56	4	94	2	20/day
Nebraska	Odd	Jan.	—	49	2	—	—	200/month
Nevada	Odd	Jan.	60 da.[5]	17	4	37	2	2,400/session
New Hampshire	Odd	Jan.	—	24	2	400	2	200/session
New Jersey	Annual	Jan.	—	21	4	60	2	7,500/year
New Mexico	Annual[2]	Jan.–O	60 da.	32	4	77	2	20/day
		Jan.–E	30 da.					
New York	Annual	Jan.	—	58	2	150	2	10,000/year
North Carolina	Odd	Feb.	120 da.[5]	53	2	106	2	15/day
North Dakota	Odd	Jan.	60 da.	49	4	109	2	5/day
Ohio	Odd	Jan.	—	33	4	135	2	5,000/year
Oklahoma	Odd	Jan.	75 da.	48	4	99	2	15/day
Oregon	Odd	Jan.	—	30	4	60	2	3,000/year
Pennsylvania	Annual[2]	Jan.	—	50	4	209	2	6,000/year

THE STATE LEGISLATURES (*Continued*)

State	Year	Sessions Month[1]	Limit	Senate No.	Senate Term	House No.	House Term	Salary[9]
Rhode Island	Annual	Jan.	60 da.[5]	46	2	100	2	5/day
South Carolina	Annual	Jan.	—	46	4	124	2	1,800/year
South Dakota	Annual	Jan.–O	45 da.	35	2	75	2	3,000/biennium
		Jan.–E	30 da.					
Tennessee	Odd	Jan.	75 da.[5]	33	2	99	2	10/day
Texas	Odd	Jan.	140 da.	31	4	150	2	4,800/year
Utah	Odd	Jan.	60 da.	25	4	64	2	1,000/biennium
Vermont	Odd	Jan.	—	30	2	246	2	80/week
Virginia	Even	Jan.	60 da.[5]	40	4	100	2	1,080/session
Washington	Odd	Jan.	60 da.	49	4	99	2	3,600/year
West Virginia	Annual[2]	Jan.–O	60 da.	34	4	100	2	1,500/year
		Jan.–E	30 da.					
Wisconsin	Odd	Jan.	—	33	4	100	2	450/month
Wyoming	Odd	Jan.	40 da.	25	4	61	2	12/day

[1] In states having annual sessions, 0 = odd-numbered years; E = even-numbered years.

[2] Session held in even-numbered years (odd-numbered in Louisiana) are limited to consideration of budgetary and fiscal matters.

[3] In actual practice the Alabama legislature meets for eighteen weeks.

[4] Must adjourn by Wednesday after the first Monday in June.

[5] Limit is indirect. Sessions may continue, but salaries stop at end of period indicated.

[6] Laws passed after July 1 do not take effect until the following July 1.

[7] Must adjourn by July 15.

[8] May vary between 375 and 400.

[9] In all states legislators receive travel expenses. Practically all states also provide for other expenses. For example, when not in session Louisiana legislators receive $250 per month, and those in Mississippi and Oklahoma receive $100. Other states allow fixed sums ranging from $5 to $40 per day during sessions.

The inadequacy of compensation in many states is evident upon examination of the costs involved in holding a legislative office. In addition to campaign costs, the legislator must leave his means of livelihood, sometimes for several months, in order to serve. The costs of food and lodging while serving add to his expenses. Again, service upon a legislative council or interim committees is likely to require further expenditures.

Public service is an honor, but in the case of the state legislature it is an honor that many people cannot afford. Consequently, qualified persons who could render distinguished service commonly find it impracticable to seek state legislative offices. Salaries sufficient to prevent personal financial sacrifices have often been suggested, but usually with disappointing results. Although constitutional provisions fixing levels of compensation present obstacles in some states, legislatures usually have authority to raise their own salaries. They do not do so, however, because of concern for hostile public reaction. The problem of adequate compensation for legislators continues to be a chronic sore spot in state government.

Retirement. The idea of retirement benefits for state legislators is new in state government. In 1946 Congress made its members eligible for retirement under the federal civil service retirement system, and since that date about a third of the states have taken similar action.[11] In the states providing for retirement, the legislators participate in existing pension systems or, as in Illinois and California, are covered by a special system adapted to legislative needs. Whatever plan is used, the object is the same as in any retirement system: to lend an aspect of security to employment.

The extent to which availability of retirement benefits affects the quality and character of aspirants to legislative office remains to be seen. Since so few states have adopted them yet, and since existing systems have been in effect for such a short time, no general conclusions can be drawn. But it appears that except in those states where legislative salaries are relatively high, retirement benefits are not particularly attractive.

Sessions. Among the perennial problems concerning state legislatures are the questions of how often regular sessions should be held and how long they should last. In most states legislative bodies convene once each odd-numbered year, but in twenty annual sessions are held.[12] Positive limitations on the length of sessions are found in about half of the states, and in several others legislative salaries stop after a designated period—provisions which have the practical effect of prescribed limits. The range is from comparatively brief periods of thirty-six days in Alabama and forty days in Wyoming to the six-months maximum permitted in Illinois. However, the most commonly prescribed limitation is sixty days.

Ordinarily, a legislature remains in session, with occasional short recesses or daily adjournments, until its work is completed. Some

---

[11] Massachusetts and Nevada have abandoned their retirement plans for legislators. Abuse of the system in Massachusetts resulted in its repeal in 1952, and in Nevada the attorney general ruled in 1953 that legislators were not eligible. Zeller, *op. cit.*, p. 80.

[12] Alaska, Arizona, California, Colorado, Delaware, Georgia, Hawaii, Kansas, Louisiana, Maryland, Massachusetts, Michigan, New Jersey, New Mexico, New York, Pennsylvania, Rhode Island, South Carolina, South Dakota, and West Virginia.

interesting variations have been tried, however. The split session, abandoned by California in 1958, was a practice whereby the legislature convened to organize, introduce bills, and take care of similar procedural matters, then recessed for at least a month.[13] During the interim, the legislators had the opportunity to consult with constituents before returning to the serious business of debate and decision. Never used by more than a few states, the split session is used today only in Georgia where, since its adoption in 1962, its purpose is to afford more thorough consideration of the budget.

The split session is approximated by the "adjourned session" in which a legislature merely recesses during its deliberations to allow time for reflection upon matters under consideration. The main differences between these types of sessions is that the adjourned session is wholly voluntary, and there is no restriction upon the activities of either the first or second portions of the session. Each arrangement is intended to eliminate hurried, careless action, but neither device appears to have been particularly successful.

Special, or extraordinary, sessions may be held in every state. They are, as the name implies, called for the purpose of considering matters that require immediate treatment. In all states the governor is empowered to call special sessions, and the legislators of about one-fourth of the states can call themselves together for such meetings.[14] In recent years special sessions have been called frequently, especially in states where regular sessions are held biennially, to deal with a variety of problems, particularly those occasioned by invalid apportionment of legislative seats.

ELECTION OF STATE LEGISLATORS

In a democratic society the people choose many of their public officials. In conformity with this principle, legislators in every state

---

[13] The split session, which had been used in California since 1911, was tried briefly in New Mexico and West Virginia.

[14] Legislatures in Connecticut, Massachusetts, and New Hampshire may call such sessions as they "judge necessary." Petitions bearing the names of two-thirds of the legislators in Alaska, Arizona, Louisiana, Nebraska, Vermont, Virginia, and West Virginia result in special sessions. A three-fifths majority is required in Georgia. In Florida, twenty per cent of the legislators may, by petition, force the Secretary of State to poll all members of the legislature on the question of a special session, which must be held upon an affirmative response from three-fifths of the members. The governor of New Jersey must call a special session if petitioned by a majority of the members of both houses of the legislature; in New Mexico, a special session may still be called even if the governor ignores a petition from three-fifths of the legislators.

are chosen by popular vote. With some exceptions, the nomination of candidates is also left to the voters in a direct primary.

Every state uses the district system in the selection of members of its legislature. Under such a system the entire territory of the state is subdivided, usually along county boundary lines, into a number of districts. The voters in each district cast ballots for one or more candidates, depending upon the number of positions assigned to the area. Ordinarily, two separate district plans are employed—one for use in the election of members to the lower house, and the other for the selection of senators. Since there are, in every state, fewer senatorial positions than lower house seats, a senatorial district normally encompasses several house districts.

Fixing the boundaries of election districts is a legislative prerogative, a situation that makes gerrymandering possible. Gerrymandering is the process by which the political party with a majority in a legislature prescribes the boundaries of election districts in such a way that as many districts as possible contain a majority of that party's voters. This practice, found in many states, increases the probability that a party can continue its domination of a legislative body even if its total registered voters or adherents falls below that of the opposition. In some instances population shifts across district lines favor one political party over another. If redistricting is prevented, the party so favored is said to benefit from a "silent gerrymander."

The district systems in effect in the states and the dominance of the two major parties militate against independents and minority parties. As a result, candidates who are not backed by one of the two major parties ordinarily have little hope of election. Only in Illinois has any effort been made to improve the chances of election of such aspirants.[15] In that state, since 1870, three representatives have been chosen from each district. Each voter has three votes which he may distribute as he pleases—one vote for each of three candidates, two for one man and one for another, one and one-half for each of two candidates, or all three may be cast for a single individual. Thus a minority group may elect a representative if all or most of his supporters "plunk" all their votes for him. This system does not result in true proportional representation, however, for even though a minority party may manage to elect a member of the lower house, the limited number of representatives makes it possible under the two-

---

[15] See also pp. 308–309.

party system for only one minority group to elect a member. Further, only one senator is elected from each district, a method of selection which, as in other states, makes no concession to minority representation.

Two states, Nebraska and Minnesota, have legislatures chosen on a nonpartisan basis; that is, candidates for legislative offices run without party designation. The idea behind elimination of party labels is to focus the attention of voters upon the issues and the qualifications of candidates. Nonpartisanship, in theory at least, results in a better chance of election for the individual who does not have the blessing of a major party. In actual practice, however, it is difficult if not impossible for a candidate to disassociate himself from past party connections or to avoid affiliation with viewpoints expressed by partisan candidates for other offices. Consequently, nonpartisan election does not fully achieve its theoretical potential.

The State Legislator: Qualifications and Characteristics

The men and women who comprise the membership of state legislative bodies are not a class apart from the rest of society. Rather they are representative of most elements of the social structure, even though they are not an accurate cross section of the public they serve. If any one trait distinguishes them from their fellow citizens it is, upon whatever reason based, their interest in government and their desire to serve in public office.

Qualifications. Constitutionally, the conditions placed upon legislative candidates are not restrictive. Legal qualifications set forth in the state constitutions are based on age, citizenship and residence. In all states a candidate for membership in the lower house must be at least twenty-one years old, and in some states a senatorial aspirant must be several years older. United States citizenship is a universal requirement, as is a prescribed period of state residence. The candidate for legislative office is also required, either by law or by custom to live in the district from which he is elected. By and large, anyone who qualifies as a legal voter is constitutionally eligible to become a candidate.

While it is a fairly simple matter to meet the constitutional requirements for candidacy, the extralegal qualifications may cause more difficulty. Factors which determine the *political availability* of a person vary from state to state and even among areas within a state. They relate to his vote-getting ability and may be determined by religion, occupation, education, race, personality traits, vindictiveness of political enemies, or any number of other matters. Any one factor, or a number of them in combination, may make it unlikely that a candidate can be elected even though he meets all legal qualifications.

Occupational Background. Unlike their counterparts in Washington, D.C., the vast majority of the 7,800 state legislators are not professional politicians. Only a few states pay salaries high enough to enable their legislators to devote most of their efforts to legislative matters. Therefore, when the legislatures are not in session the typical member, like his fellow citizens, is at work earning a living at his chosen profession or trade.

Traditionally, state legislatures have been dominated by lawyers, followed closely by farmers and businessmen. In recent years, however, businessmen have sought legislative offices in increasing numbers and now lead all other occupational fields.[16] It is true, of course, that scores of occupational pursuits are represented in state legislative chambers. In addition to the three largest groups, doctors, teachers, laborers, craftsmen, retired individuals and many others are found. Businessmen, lawyers, and farmers, however, still occupy most of the seats in the typical state legislative assembly.

Turnover. The percentage of new members at each regular session of a state legislature is extremely high. Usually a lower house will have more new faces, proportionally, than a senate, but of the total membership of all state legislatures combined approximately half are serving their first term. Studies have been made to determine the rate of turnover, but no comparative research upon which trustworthy conclusions may be based has been done.[17] Reasons that state legislators in general do not serve for long periods seem to be the discouragement of low salaries, the insecurity of the positions, and political instability. The longer periods of service noted in states

---

[16] Zeller, *op. cit.*, pp. 70–71.

[17] A survey and analysis of tenure and turnover in state legislatures, based on the year 1950, was executed by the Committee on American Legislatures of the American Political Science Association. See Zeller, *op. cit.*, pp. 65–70.

that offer substantial salaries and in which one party is dominant tend to support these points.

Level of Performance. Probably no public servant is more consistently criticized and castigated than the state legislator. Surely some criticism is deserved, for often a young lawyer or businessman seeks the office for the sole purpose of establishing contacts. Or an aspiring politician uses the office as a steppingstone to a higher position. Undoubtedly, some opportunists look upon legislative membership as a means of promoting or protecting selfish interests. At other times poorly qualified persons are elected because the opposition provides such poor competition. Commentators from time to time have lamented the "decay" and incompetence of state legislatures.

Despite admitted shortcomings and obstacles, state legislators do a commendable job. Theirs is a task that requires decisions on matters of tax policy, commerce, industry, agriculture, public health, welfare, criminology, civil rights, conservation, education, law enforcement, public works and a host of other equally vexatious topics. At the same time the handicaps of the short term, niggardly salaries, constant pressure of lobbyists, and threat of executive veto and popular referral limit their freedom of action. Yet, with exceptionally few instances of outright dishonesty and collusion, state legislators generally have lived up to the responsibilities of their office.

Party Control of Legislatures

American state legislatures are organized on the basis of the party affiliations of their members. The political party that succeeds in electing the majority of members of a legislative chamber is in an almost unassailable position to organize and to a certain extent to control the actions of the chamber. Even in Minnesota and Nebraska, where members are elected on a nonpartisan basis, there is partisan activity in the legislatures. Members of the Minnesota body are frankly aligned on a partisan basis, while in Nebraska partisanship is less clearly defined.

Before a legislature begins its session there is little if any doubt as to who will be chosen to fill the Speaker's chair, or who will serve as President of the upper house. Usually, appointees for less important positions also have been informally determined. Party leaders and members, meeting in caucus, reach agreement on such matters before a session convenes, and though party control of members may be lacking with regard to individual bills and even general programs, a legislator does not often desert his party on an organizational vote.

Party control of legislatures generally is not as pronounced in the states as it is in the United States Congress. Whereas the major parties in Washington, D.C., are frequently able to command loyalty to party positions, state parties are less able to do so. In fact, only those states where the two major parties are approximately equal in strength can it be said that parties exert strong controls. The weakest party organizations are found in one-party states, although factions within the dominant party may exercise influence over members.

LEGISLATIVE OFFICERS AND EMPLOYEES

The Speaker. The presiding officer of the lower house of every bicameral state legislature is known as the speaker. He is regularly chosen by the full membership of the house. Except in Minnesota and Nebraska, where representatives are elected on nonpartisan ballots, the vote is cast according to formal party lines. While it is not accurate to refer to him as a virtual dictator, the speaker is normally the most powerful member of the house.

Among the powers of the speaker is the authority to appoint members of standing committees. Seniority, party status, and consultation with party leaders figure prominently in the actual selection of committee members, but since the speaker must ultimately make the decisions in regard to committee membership, he wields great power. Only in Oklahoma must his choices be confirmed by the whole house. The speaker also has full authority to refer bills to committees. In many instances custom or house rule requires that certain types of bills must be sent to designated committees. Where alternative committees may be chosen, however, the speaker is free to determine whether a bill goes to a favorable or to an antagonistic group. The power of recognition is another important instrument of authority available to the presiding officer of the house. Potentially, at least, the speaker can control debate and thereby increase or diminish the effectiveness of various members. Finally, he interprets and applies rules of procedure. Even though his rulings are usually subject to appeal to the whole membership, an astute speaker can, through clever application and manipulation of the rules, profoundly influence the course of legislative action.

The Lieutenant Governor. In thirty-eight states lieutenant governors are elected by the people.[18] Except in two states, Hawaii and Massachusetts, he is constitutionally charged with the duty of presiding over the senate. The powers of a lieutenant governor acting in his legislative capacity vary from one capitol to the next. When presiding, he exercises the power of recognition, applies and interprets the rules, and has authority to refer bills to committees. In only fifteen states, however, does the lieutenant governor appoint the members of committees, and in three of those states his selections are subject to approval by the whole membership. Also, his powers are diminished by the fact that he may cast a vote only if it is needed to break a tie.

The President of the Senate. The senate in each of the fifty states except Tennessee and North Carolina selects from its membership an officer known as the president or president *pro tem.*[19] In states where there is no lieutenant governor or that official is not designated as the presiding officer, the president presides over senate deliberations. Where, as in most states, there is both a lieutenant governor and a president *pro tem,* the latter assumes the chair in the absence of the former.

The authority of senate presidents varies widely across the nation. Where they are second in command, they obviously must share power with the lieutenant governor. The powers of referral, recognition and rules interpretation are exercised by the officer actually presiding at a particular time, but the authority to appoint committees is variously assigned. As noted above, designation of committees is a prerogative of the lieutenant governor in fifteen states. In the remainder this important power is exercised either by the president *pro tem,* the committee on committees, the rules committee, or by the entire senate membership.

---

[18] The office does not exist in Alaska, Arizona, Florida, Maine, Maryland, New Hampshire, New Jersey, Oregon, Utah, West Virginia, and Wyoming. In Tennessee the Speaker of the Senate is designated by statute as the lieutenant governor of the state. In actuality the Speaker of the Tennessee Senate corresponds to the president found in the upper houses of states having no lieutenant governor.

[19] The term *pro tempore,* usually shortened to *pro tem,* means "temporary." Commonly, the lieutenant governor is termed the president of the senate, and the member elected to preside in his absence is called the president *pro tem.* In states where there is no lieutenant governor, the member chosen to preside is entitled president of the senate. In Tennessee and North Carolina the title "speaker" is used.

Other Officers and Employees. Each chamber, whether a senate or lower house, also chooses officers to discharge necessary routine functions. Included are a clerk, chaplain, and sergeant-at-arms, whose responsibilities have little, if any, effect upon the course or content of legislation. In addition, numbers of employees are hired to handle clerical, stenographic, and custodial tasks.

THE COMMITTEE SYSTEM

The array of problems confronting legislatures today are both numerous and difficult. Few, if any, legislators are competent to decide all questions of public policy. Even if competency were not involved, it is doubtful that a legislative body, operating under parliamentary rules in open debate, would have time to consider more than a minor fraction of all bills that are introduced. It is absolutely necessary, therefore, for a legislature to organize in such a way that it at least has an *opportunity* to perform its job. The organizational pattern employed in all states to realize that opportunity is the committee system.

The standing committees, which are organized on a partisan basis, have long been regarded as the "workhorses" of state legislatures. To them all the bills are referred, and measures receive their closest scrutiny in the committee rooms. Bills may be overhauled completely, amended to various degrees, or as is commonly the case, ignored altogether. Whether a bill is considered by the full membership of a legislative chamber usually depends upon the decisions made by the committee to which it was referred.

It is also important to observe that committees are often large and unwieldy and thus subject to control by dominant members. As a consequence, a small number of persons, perhaps a subcommittee or a clique led by the chairman, might for all practical purposes make decisions for the committee. Because of the obviously unfortunate effects of such a development upon the content of public policy, it is important that citizens have an understanding of the organization, procedures, and problems of the committee system.

Number and Size of Committees. Practically all state legislatures are subject to the criticism that they maintain too many standing committees. While no particular number is best for all legislative chambers, it is generally agreed that a small number of committees with well-defined areas of jurisdiction is best adapted to legislative needs. The value of this arrangement is especially notable in light of the fact that most of the bills introduced during a legislative session are referred to a handful of the most important committees.

In most instances the number of standing committees maintained by a house bears little or no relation to the total number of members. The New Hampshire legislature is about fifteen times larger than that of Delaware, yet the latter has more standing committees. The lower houses of Florida and Rhode Island are comparable in size, but the former has three times as many committees. Senates, as a general rule, maintain fewer committees than do lower houses.

The size of a particular committee appears to be determined largely by chance, political desires, or expediency. It is not unusual to find enough committees to provide a chairmanship for each majority party member. Neither is it uncommon for a single legislator to hold membership on a half-dozen or more committees. As a rule little attention seems to be given to the problem of fixing the size of committees at levels that would be most effective from the standpoint of legislative activity.

Use of Joint Committees. With occasional exceptions the gears of legislative machinery turn slowly, and in a great many instances, inefficiently. A prominent factor causing delay is the necessity for independent action by each house of a bicameral legislature. Procedures followed in each house are substantially the same, yet conflicts arise that prevent the effective meshing of house and senate efforts.

Among devices used to save time, effort, money and tempers is the joint standing committee, a permanent working group composed of members of both houses. Such a committee can greatly reduce the total labors necessary in the consideration of a bill. Today over half the states maintain one or more joint committees, but only in New England are they fully utilized. In Connecticut, for example, about thirty joint committees function in the place of conventional standing committees in each house. In Maine and Massachusetts the individual houses have retained a few committees, but the great bulk of work is done in cooperative groups. Vermont has kept the usual standing committees, but ordinarily corresponding house and senate groups meet jointly for the consideration of bills.

Selection of Chairmen. The choice of committee chairmen is usually the prerogative of the presiding officer, although they may be selected by a designated committee or by the whole membership of a house. More important than identification of the appointing authority are the factors that influence the actual choice. Admittedly, logic demands that ability should be a prime requisite. In most cases, however, selection is based largely upon party affiliation, seniority, and personal influence. Frequently, capable individuals who qualify on such bases are chosen, but unfortunately current practices do not guarantee able leadership of committees.

Rules of Procedure. Procedure followed by committees vary widely not only from state to state, but often among committees in the same house. Such variations are justifiable in many instances, for not all standing committees have the same tasks and problems. Differences in jurisdiction and workload of committees make uniformity of procedural requirements impractical and undesirable. Committees that consider large numbers of bills obviously need a more clearly defined system of procedures than do those that rarely function. Nevertheless, an obvious need exists widely for some changes.

Foremost among problem areas are a lack of definitely scheduled meetings, failure to publicize public hearings, poorly kept or incomplete records of committee action, and the practice of keeping in committee bills that should be reported out. When committees indulge in such actions and practices, there is danger that the course and content of public policy will be determined less by the legislative membership and more by a faction exercising committee control. A few states have sought to correct abuses stemming from these practices by a reduction in number and size of committees, the use of joint committees, prohibition of closed sessions, and more workable procedures to force bills out of committees. Nebraska probably has achieved most in this respect, but little has been accomplished in most states.

Research Assistance. The great variety and complexity of matters dealt with in the legislative process make necessary the provision of research and technical assistance. No matter how experienced or competent a legislator may be, he cannot, if limited to his own resources, achieve his maximum potential. Most states have set up legislative reference services; legislative councils operate in more than forty states; and interim committees are now widely used.[20] These aids, however, are intended to serve legislative bodies as a whole without specific reference to individual committees.

Most state legislatures pay scant attention to the need of committees for research and technical staff. In three-fourths of the states committees must depend almost entirely upon permanent agencies in the legislative or executive branches, while a few states permit all or some committees to obtain technical assistance from nongovernmental sources. The remaining one-fourth provide special assistance when needed. In contrast to the unavailability of research and technical aid, adequate clerical and stenographic assistance is generally provided.

PRIVILEGES AND IMMUNITIES OF LEGISLATORS

Special privileges enjoyed by members of state legislatures are very limited, those that are granted applying only to conditions of debate and attendance at legislative sessions. Derived from British and American colonial usage, state constitutions provide typically that

> The Senators and Representatives shall, in all cases, except treason, felony or breach of the peace, be privileged from arrest during their attendance at the session of their respective Houses, and in going to and returning from the same; and for any speech or debate in either House they shall not be questioned in any other place.[21]

Obviously, the phrase "except treason, felony or breach of the peace" is sufficiently inclusive of all possible offenses to reduce immunity from arrest to little more than freedom from detention for trivial matters. On the other hand, immunity from prosecution for utterances in debate is broad. Under it a legislator can, on the floors of the legislature and in committee sessions, say anything he pleases, restrained only by legislative rules of procedure governing his conduct and deportment. While there have been instances of abuse, the

---

[20] These agencies are discussed in the following chapter.

[21] Constitution of Delaware, Article III, Section 13. Note the similarity, typical of most state constitutions, to the corresponding provision found in Article I, Section **6**, of the United States Constitution.

immunity is easily defensible, for without protection from suits for slander, it is doubtful that free and open debate could be maintained.

THE PROBLEM OF APPORTIONMENT

On March 26, 1962, Justice Brennan delivered an opinion of the United States Supreme Court that was to have a profound effect upon every state legislature in the country. As a direct result of that decision the validity of the apportionment of seats in most legislatures has been challenged in both state and federal courts. In the comparatively few states in which law suits have not resulted, reexamination of apportionment criteria has been occasioned. The decision which brought on this turmoil was *Baker* v. *Carr*,[22] in which the Supreme Court ruled that federal courts have jurisdiction to decide whether a state legislature is apportioned in accordance with constitutional provisions.

The Baker Case. The controversy in the Baker case grew out of the failure of the Tennessee legislature to apportion for sixty years. During that period the population of the state increased about forty-five per cent, with most of the gains concentrated in urban areas. The changing character of the population resulted in such inequities under the 1901 apportionments still in effect that in 1960 one-third of the voters elected two-thirds of the legislators. Consequently, a suit was brought by a group of urban voters.

Historically, both state and federal courts have been reluctant to consider questions involving the composition of legislative bodies. The usual judicial response in pre-Baker cases was to follow a self-imposed rule of nonintervention in deference to the political character of reapportionment issues. In other words, the composition of a legislative body was regarded as a political question to be resolved by the legislatures or the voters. The district court in Tennessee which heard the arguments in the Baker case followed this reasoning and dismissed the complaint, although in doing so it expressed doubt as to whether any definite precedent existed in support of a policy of judicial nonintervention.[23]

The decision was appealed to the United States Supreme Court

---

[22] 369 U.S. 186 (1962).
[23] 175 F. Supp. 649; 179 F. Supp. 824 (1960).

which heard arguments and rearguments for a year and a half before announcing its decision. When it did so, it reversed the lower court, holding that courts have jurisdiction to decide questions involving the validity of apportionments and that previous cases had not established a rule of judicial nonintervention.[24] Within a matter of days, suits were instituted in a number of other states, and many others were in preparation.

The Apportionment Background. State constitutions typically provide for reapportionment every ten years on the basis of population or area, or a combination of both. This process is often complicated by provisions fixing minimum or maximum allotments per district. The most serious difficulties in reapportionment arise, however, out of the frequent neglect or refusal of legislatures to fulfill the constitutional obligation to apportion. This difficulty has been relieved in some states by divesting the legislature of responsibility by providing for "automatic" reapportionment by a board, court, or executive officer. Several other states allow the legislature an opportunity to perform the task, with non-legislative personnel taking over in case of failure. In one state, Oregon, the initiative has been used to achieve a valid reapportionment. Until the Baker decision, however, courts declined to assist in effecting reapportionments.

Underlying the widespread controversy over reapportionment is the clash of rural and urban interests. Alloting seats on the basis of population usually results in shifting control of state legislatures from rural to urban majorities, a move strongly resisted by legislators chosen from rural districts. It is ironic to note that prior to 1920, when the federal census revealed a majority of urban dwellers in

---

[24] In its arguments before the Supreme Court, Tennessee relied heavily upon the case of *Colegrove* v. *Green,* 328 U.S. 549 (1946), in which the court had refused, by a 4-3 vote, to consider whether congressional districts in Illinois were validly drawn. In the majority opinion Justice Frankfurter characterized the issue as one which "must be resolved by considerations on the basis of which this Court, from time to time, has refused to intervene in controversies. It has refused to do so because due regard for the effective working of our government revealed this issue to be of a peculiarly political nature and therefore not meet for judicial determination." It is interesting to note that despite the Colegrove ruling, on two occasions prior to the decision in *Baker v. Carr,* federal district courts exercised jurisdiction in apportionment disputes. In fact, *Dyer* v. *Kazuhisa,* 138 F. Supp. 220 (1956), held the Hawaiian territorial legislature invalidly constituted; and in *Magraw* v. *Donovan,* 163 F. Supp. 184 (1958), a federal district court took jurisdiction of an attack on the composition of the Minnesota legislature. Both cases ended inconsequentially, however, because of subsequent reapportionments of the legislatures involved.

the United States, rural primacy in state legislatures was generally consistent with population distribution.

The Population Factor in Apportionment. The Baker decision did not answer the extremely important question of what criteria may be used in reapportionment. The answer to this question was provided in several cases decided the same day in 1964, the principal one of which was *Reynolds* v. *Sims*.[25] In declaring the Alabama apportionment of 1901 invalid, Chief Justice Warren observed that legislators "represent people, not trees or acres," and went on to assert that "as a basic constitutional standard, the Equal Protecttion Clause requires that the seats in both houses of a bicameral state legislature must be apportioned on a population basis." All other factors were rejected as possible bases of apportionment. Thus, the only valid apportionment is one which accords as nearly as possible with population distribution.

Reactions and Implications. The eventual effects of the Baker and Sims cases are both clear and predictable. Reapportionment of state legislatures on the basis of population alone means that the majorities of seats will be controlled by legislators elected from urban areas. In turn, the character of state political systems is bound to undergo fundamental change, with public policy oriented more toward urban needs. Inasmuch as congressional districts are determined by state legislatures, and must also be laid out in accord with population distribution, Congress itself will be profoundly affected. Only in those states having predominantly rural populations and those in which the economic mainstays are primarily agricultural will the effects of the Baker and Sims decisions be minimal.

Reactions to these decisions have been widespread and in some instances intemperate. Opposition has been expressed in many quarters. Unsuccessful attempts have been made in the Congress to deny federal courts jurisdiction in apportionment cases, and many states have requested Congress to propose amendments to the national Constitution which would negate the decisions. Undoubtedly such

---

[25] 377 U.S. 533, (1964). Several months earlier, in *Wesberry v. Sanders,* 376 U.S. 1 (1964), the Court invalidated the statute establishing congressional districts in Georgia. In that decision Justice Black stated that "construed in its historical context, the command of Art. I, § 2, that Representatives be chosen 'by the People in the several States' means that as nearly as is practicable one man's vote in a congressional election is to be worth as much as another's."

efforts will persist, but indications are that the population rule will continue to be the sole criterion in apportionment.

POWERS OF THE LEGISLATURE

In the American federal system governmental power is divided between the nation and the states. Under the United States Constitution the national government has such powers as are *delegated* to it, with the remaining powers *reserved* to the states. As stated in the Tenth Amendment, "The powers not delegated to the United States by the Constitution, nor prohibited by it to the States, are reserved to the States respectively, or to the people." The powers reserved to the states are vested largely in the state legislatures, but they do not exercise their powers free from restraint.

Limitation by National Law. Article VI, Section 2, of the national Constitution provides that the Constitution itself, and all laws and treaties made under it, are the "supreme law of the land." Consequently, no state legislative enactment can be contrary to national law and still be valid. Whenever conflicts occur, the national law prevails.

Many specific limitations upon the exercise of state authority are contained in the Constitution. Article I, Section 10, sets forth a detailed list of prohibitions forbidding the states, among other things, to conclude treaties, join alliances, coin or print money, grant titles of nobility, tax imports or exports, or keep troops in time of peace.[26] In other portions of the document additional limitations are imposed. In effect a delegation of power to the national government is, or can be, a limitation, for it may totally pre-empt an area of authority that would otherwise belong exclusively to the states.

State Constitutional Limitations. The fundamental law of a state, the constitution, is the source of numerous restrictions upon, or denials of, legislative authority. Designed to protect certain rights and powers from legislative encroachment and to prevent abuse of legislative authority, the limitations fall into a number or categories. First, all state constitutions contain Bills of Rights—lists of guarantees

---

[26] The states may maintain troops provided Congress approves. The National Guard serves both as the military organization of the various states and as a component of the armed forces of the United States.

against infringement of individual rights. Second, constitutions in a third of the states contain initiative and referendum clauses that preserve the right of the people directly to enact or repeal legislation. Third, most state legislatures are forbidden to enact special or local legislation of certain designated types. Usually, a state constitution contains a list of prohibitions denying the legislature authority to pass laws that apply to single individuals, groups, or local governments with respect to such matters as granting divorces, changing names, granting franchises, altering the rate of interest, and impaneling juries. The object is to eliminate partisanship and discrimination in individual instances. Fourth, restrictive provisions relating to finance are commonly found in the organic law of a state. Legislatures must levy taxes uniformly, are not permitted to grant tax exemptions except in specified instances, may not borrow money beyond a prescribed limit, cannot appropriate money for the use of religious groups, and may not loan the credit of the state to private corporations. Since every state constitution adheres either by express statement or by implication to the doctrine of separation of powers, legislatures may not, except in designated areas, exercise powers assigned other branches of government.

Extent of Legislative Power. In performing its essential function of policymaking, a wide range of powers is available to a state legislature. It is not possible, however, to develop a comprehensive list of legislative powers. Since any power not delegated to the national government nor prohibited to the states by the national Constitution is a reserved power, it is not feasible to catalog state legislative authority. Stated in general terms, the authority of a state legislature is bounded, in theory at least, only by the negative effect of national law and by the restrictions imposed by the state constitution.

While legislative powers are not detailed in state constitutions, the major areas of authority are set forth or are generally identifiable. The powers to tax, appropriate and borrow money, impose regulations upon commercial ventures within a state, establish courts and fix their jurisdictions, and to define crimes and prescribe punishments are among powers usually mentioned in state constitutions. Not listed is the broad, loosely defined power to legislate in behalf of the public health, safety, welfare, and morals—the well-known "police power."

It is not possible to subject the police power to precise definition. Under it legislatures are empowered to enact legislation imposing quarantines, requiring vaccinations, compelling food inspection, forbidding gambling, prohibiting the manufacture or sale of fireworks, banning ownership of dangerous weapons, fixing automobile speed limits, barring immoral or indecent entertainment, prescribing safety requirements for industrial plants, and a host of other limitations on freedom of action. Often the police power overlaps other areas of legislative authority, or it may be conceived as a part of other powers. For example, a statutory requirement that dangerous machinery be enclosed by wire guards is in the interest of the public safety and therefore an exercise of the police power; at the same time it may be an expression of legislative authority to regulate intrastate commerce. In reality the extent of the police power is so vague that only through the process of examining judicial decisions involving the question of whether it has been exceeded can its limits be approximately determined. Even then judicial interpretations provide only temporary understandings, since future decisions may reinterpret the police power to meet the exigencies of changing conditions.

Nonlegislative Powers. When a legislature exercises authority that is similar to the powers of a court it is said to have *judicial powers.* The most common prerogative of legislatures in this category is impeachment. All state legislatures except that of Oregon are empowered to bring charges against executive and judicial officers and upon conviction to remove them from office.[27] Impeachment itself is merely accusation; thus when a lower house votes to accuse an officer, that individual is impeached. The role of the senate is to sit as jury, hear arguments on the charges, and ultimately to decide the guilt or innocence of the person impeached.[28] Conviction on impeachment charges results in removal from office, and later prosecu-

---

[27] In Oregon public officials accused of improper conduct in office may be removed by action brought in the regular courts. In such proceedings conventional criminal procedure is followed. (Constitution of Oregon, Article VII, Section 6.) The recall may also be used against elective officers in Oregon.

[28] Typically, the lower house of a legislature is vested with the sole power to impeach, and the trial is held before the senate. In Missouri, impeachment cases are tried before the supreme court. The unicameral legislature of Nebraska impeaches, and the trial is conducted before the supreme court. In Alaska the usual roles of the two houses in the impeachment process are reversed; the senate impeaches, and the trial is held before the house of representatives.

tion in the regular courts is not prevented by the outcome of the impeachment trial.

Legislatures also exercise authority of a judicial nature over their members. Since legislators are not subject to impeachment, legislative bodies may subject them to censure, a form of reprimand for improper conduct, or in extreme cases to expulsion. If questions arise as to whether a member was validly elected to his seat, or if two or more persons claim the same legislative seat, the house involved is empowered to decide who shall be seated.

Every state legislature shares in the process of amending the state constitution and the creation of constitutional conventions. These prerogatives are known as *constituent powers* and are of fundamental importance. As indicated in an earlier chapter, the role of the legislature in making changes in state constitutions varies widely across the nation.

Among the broad grants of authority vested in state legislatures are those regarded as *executive* in nature. For example, gubernatorial appointments to high state offices ordinarily are subject to approval by the upper house of a legislature. In some half-dozen states judges of some courts are chosen by the legislature, and in a similar number high-ranking officials such as the secretary of state, attorney general, and treasurer are legislatively selected. Conversely, the legislatures of some states may, by extraordinary majority vote, remove judges from office without resorting to the impeachment process. Frequently, legislatures are empowered to approve or reject actions of a governor in the removal of local officials. In all states interstate compacts to which a state becomes a signatory are subject to approval by the legislature.

Usually not specified in constitutional or statutory provisions, but certainly among the important powers of a legislature, are those that may be designated as *administrative*. It is primarily through these powers that oversight of administration is accomplished. Best known among such devices is the investigation, a process by which a legislative group, most often a standing or interim committee, inquires into some aspect of governmental activity. Conducted ostensibly for the purpose of gaining information upon which to base legislation, an investigation provides a method of supervising the performance of executive officers. Further control is exercised through the device of requiring designated administrative units to submit reports. In conducting hearings preparatory to the consideration of appropriation bills legislatures may probe deeply into administrative affairs. In a few states, legislative bodies require administrative agencies to open their accounts to a complete inspection by a legislatively chosen auditor.

SELECTED REFERENCES

Books:

Baker, Gordon E., *Rural Versus Urban Political Power,* Random House, New York, 1955.

——, *State Constitutions: Reapportionment,* National Municipal League, 1960.

Buck, A. E., *Modernizing Our State Legislatures,* American Academy of Political and Social Science, Philadelphia, 1936.

Council of State Governments, *American Legislatures, Structure and Procedures,* Chicago, 1955.

——, *Our State Legislatures,* revised edition, Chicago, 1948.

Fordham, Jefferson B., *The State Legislative Institution,* University of Pennsylvania Press, Philadelphia, 1959.

Jewell, Malcolm E., *Politics of Reapportionment,* Atherton Press, New York, 1962.

Larsen, James E., *Reapportionment and the Courts,* Bureau of Public Administration, University of Alabama, University, 1962.

Luce, Henry, *Legislative Assemblies,* Houghton-Mifflin Co., Boston, 1924.

Schubert, Glendon, *Reapportionment,* Charles Scribner's Sons, New York, 1965.

Scott, Stanley, *Streamlining State Legislatures,* Bureau of Public Administration, University of California, Berkeley, 1956.

Truman, David B., *The Governmental Process,* Alfred A. Knopf, New York, 1951.

Willoughby, W. F., *Principles of Legislative Organization and Administration,* Brookings Institution, Washington, D.C., 1934.

Articles:

Abram, Morris B., "A New Civil Right," *National Civic Review,* April 1963.

Barrett, Charles, "Reapportionment and the Courts," *State Government,* Summer 1962.

Boyd, William J. D., "Apportionment Facts," *National Civic Review,* November 1964.

"Controversy Over Supreme Court Decisions on Apportionment of State Legislatures," Symposium, *Congressional Digest,* January 1965.

Graves, W. Brooke, "Concepts of Legislative Power in State Constitutions," *Louisiana Law Review,* June 1954.

Horack, Frank E., Jr., "Bicameral Legislatures Are Effective," *State Government,* April 1941.

Larsen, James E., "Awaiting the Other Shoe," *National Civic Review,* April 1963.

McGee, Vernon A., "The Vitality of State Legislatures," *State Government,* January 1958.

Pritchett, C. Herman, "Equal Protection and the Urban Majority," *American Political Science Review,* December 1964.

Shumate, Roger V., "The Nebraska Unicameral Legislature," *Western Political Quarterly,* September 1952.

Tucker, W. P., "Characteristics of State Legislators," *Social Science,* April 1955.

Walker, Harvey, "The Role of the Legislature in Government," *State Government,* Spring 1960.

CHAPTER 7

The State Legislature: Making of Laws

Determination of public policy through the passage of laws is the most important function of a legislative body. There are times, of course, when other functions such as initiating controversial constitutional amendments or bringing and hearing impeachment charges may seem more vital. Such instances are usually accompanied by headlines and a high degree of public interest. However, the deliberations that result in decisions as to what government will or will not do—the formulations of policies and programs—is the very *raison d'être* of the state legislature.

Modern state legislatures must perform tasks of tremendous magnitude. Working within limitations imposed by national law and state constitutions, they determine, to a great extent, the structure of state and local governments. Citizen-government relationships are largely defined through the legislative process. Governmental services and regulation are primarily dependent upon legislative choice. In fact, it is the legislative branch of government which has the greatest responsibility for giving force of law to rules of conduct that both reflect and determine the character of society.

THE LEGISLATIVE PROCESS

In the performance of its basic function, a state legislature follows certain predetermined steps. From the moment a bill is introduced until it clears the legislative halls and is sent to the governor for his consideration, its progress can be noted by reference to those steps. These phases through which all measures must go are termed simply *legislative procedure*—the procedure by means of which laws are enacted.

The *legislative process* entails far more than what takes place within the legislature. Obviously, the governor participates in the legislative process. His veto power, messages to the legislature, recommendations, threats, appeals to the people, or other such expressions certainly have their effect upon the minds and actions of legislators. Viewed broadly, the legislative and gubernatorial phases are only the culmination of the legislative process. The origin and basic development of legislation takes place *before* it is formally introduced in a legislature.

It is not always possible to tell just where the idea for a new law originates. A social worker may feel that existing welfare legislation contains inequities, a businessman may be dissatisfied with prevailing methods of taxing inventories, a teacher may resent restrictions upon his freedom to engage in political affairs, or a housewife may object to the fixing of prices of certain commodities. In each instance someone, or some group, is dissatisfied with existing laws or the lack of them, and desires a change in policy.

A variety of methods is used to bring suggested legislation to the attention of legislators. In many instances individual roles may not be prominent. For example, although solutions may be in controversy, the need for additional revenues, improved highways, better schools, and the like may be generally recognized. But the supporters of proposed laws designed to benefit a single individual, group or industry would have to find ways to gain support for their projects. Circulation of petitions, letters to newspapers, speeches before civic groups, newspaper advertisements, testimony before legislative committees, distribution of handbills, radio and television addresses, and direct mail advertising are a few of the actions that may be resorted to in an effort to enlist public support of proposed legislation. Generally, the chances of actual introduction in the legislature of a proposal and its ultimate passage depend upon the success encountered in lining up support beforehand.[1]

SOURCES OF BILLS

Technically, only a member may introduce a bill in an American state legislature. More than one member may sponsor a bill, or a bill may be authored by a standing committee, but in any event only members of the legislature are *legally* involved. Thus for all legal purposes the members themselves are the sources of legislation. In actual practice, however, the senators and representatives who affix their names to measures placed before their colleagues write relatively

---

[1] In many states availability of the initiative and referendum presents alternative methods of achieving changes in public policy. See Chapter 13.

few of them. Most of the several hundred bills, or several thousand as the case may be, that find their way into legislative halls come from sources outside the legislatures.

Not all bills that reach the hands of legislators are introduced. Some are cast aside as frivolous. Others are of questionable desirability or are obviously unconstitutional. Rejection of still others follows because of conflict with the political convictions of the legislator to whom they are submitted. Nevertheless, large numbers of bills supplied to legislators are introduced. Many are rewritten, rearranged, or edited to some degree, the changes usually being made to adjust them to political realities.

Public Sources. A great many bills introduced in a legislative session come from public officers and agencies. In addition to those written by legislators, a number are provided by standing committees of the legislative houses. Such bills are the result of investigations conducted by those bodies, frequently in conjunction with their consideration of bills already referred to them.

Interim committees, known also as *ad interim* committees—groups of legislators and their assistants who meet between legislative sessions to inquire into a designated topic—may also be a source of new laws. These committees, used virtually since the time state legislatures came into being and particularly during the past thirty years, delve into their subjects in searching detail. Depending upon their findings and conclusions, interim committees then write bills proposing whatever changes they deem necessary in existing laws. At subsequent legislative sessions the bills are introduced, under the guidance of committee chairmen, as committee bills.

Legislative councils, discussed at length below, often prepare bills for introduction at the opening of a legislative session. Since legislative councils are not limited in regard to the subject matter with which they deal, council bills may concern anything the legislature may act on. Bills drawn up by councils frequently enjoy a preferred status, inasmuch as they result from the labors of a permanent research staff and have the support of at least a majority of the legislators who comprise the legislative council.

Special investigating commissions, established by legislatures or governors or the joint action of both, have also been a source of bills. These bodies may or may not include legislators in their membership. When made up wholly or partially by members of the legislature, the derivation of bills is obvious. However, even when legislators are not active members, the utilization by legislators of information turned up by commissions is highly probable.

In the sense that suggestions and proffered information can be regarded as a source of proposed legislation, the governor must also be included. All state executives have what is termed a "legislative program" consisting of a number of proposed changes in, or additions to, existing law. These gubernatorial desires are usually expressed in campaign speeches, inaugural addresses, and messages to the legislature. Budget messages are especially important in this respect. In addition to formal utterances and contacts, governors also participate in behind-the-scenes maneuvers to facilitate realization of their programs. Usually, the more forceful gubernatorial leadership is, the better the chances for passage of the "governor's bills."

Just as the governor may be considered a source of legislation so also, to a limited extent, may the judiciary. Rules of procedure under which courts operate may be determined in part by the courts themselves, but many judicial procedures are governed by statute. Judicial councils, which include judges as members, concern themselves with improvements in judicial organization and procedure. Their sponsorship of legislation on judicial affairs constitutes an important, if not voluminous, source of new laws.

Some of the most prolific authors of proposed legislation are administrative bodies within the executive branch and officers and agencies of local governments. With few exceptions the powers of state departments, agencies, boards, commissions, and the like are determined by statute. The powers and prerogatives of local units are profoundly affected, if in fact not fixed, by state laws. Consequently, changes sought by these entities are drafted in the form of bills and presented to members of the legislature. While there are no reliable, comprehensive figures available for documentation, isolated studies indicate that state and local officials and agencies are responsible for about a third of all bills introduced at a legislative session.

Private Sources. Leading the nonpublic sources of proposed new laws in terms of quantity of suggestions are the large number of pressure groups found in each state. These groups are organized for one main purpose: influencing public policy in order to maintain and increase advantages enjoyed by the interests they represent. A principal method by which they try to achieve favorable changes in existing law is by submission to legislators of bills ready for introduction. Here again, generalization is necessary as to the extent of pressure group activity in this regard, but studies have indicated that upwards of forty per cent of the bills introduced in legislative sessions come from pressure organizations.

Probably never will it be possible to reach full agreement on the question of the extent of pressure group activity, for in many instances private organizations that are not looked upon as pressure organizations temporarily behave like them. Churches, parent-teacher associations, youth groups, civic organizations, private research or consulting services and the like may now and then have an ax to grind. These groups may seek alterations in specific laws, going so far as to draft the bills they want introduced. Thus, depending upon one's concept of the pressure group, these organizations may be included.

A small quantity of bills originates with private individuals. Lawyers, businessmen, farmers or other constituents of a legislator may feel strongly that a certain law ought to be amended or a new law adopted. When this occurs the constituent may merely convey his thoughts to his representative at the state capitol, or, as sometimes happens, prepare a draft of legislation he would like to see enacted.

THE LEGISLATIVE PROGRAM—OR LACK OF IT

Among the worst features of American state legislatures is the lack of a comprehensive legislative program. While legislative councils, discussed below, have brought about some improvement, a typical legislature convenes with little more than a general idea of how it will proceed. The essential pattern of a legislative session, within the context of its organization and rules of procedure, is determined by the vicissitudes of circumstance. Bills that are ready for consideration on the floor are discussed and debated without particular regard to logical subject matter sequence. It is not inaccurate to observe that the effects of pressures, circumstances, and advantages of the moment are more important in determining the course of legislative action than are other factors.

The inadvisability of an unplanned approach is emphasized by the dangers involved. The most obvious peril is that legislation that should be considered may not come to the attention of the legislature at all. This danger is especially present in the many state legislative bodies whose sessions are constitutionally limited to a fixed number of days.[2] In much the same vein, a legislative session that is operated without some preplanning is in danger of acting on bills without the benefit of crucial information. Although this may happen at any time, it is most likely to occur during the latter stages of the session when the members are facing a deadline for adjournment or are eager to return to their regular livelihoods. A third major peril is that without planning, the final days of a session witness a congested backlog of bills, many of which are "must" legislation. As a result, measures which deserve consideration are simply allowed to die, while others are enacted with little or no debate. When such conditions prevail, the incidence of poorly written legislation is likely to be high, and the danger of conflicting bills enacted at the same session is increased. The availability of expert bill drafting services may reduce the number of poorly drafted bills, but amendments and alterations of bills as they proceed to enactment may result in flaws and inconsistencies.

More subtle but no less important is the threat that the absence of preplanning may be fostered or turned to advantage by selfish interests. Lobbies, organizations geared for continuing, year-round activity, are ordinarily careful to capitalize on any turn of events that may produce a result favorable to them. While lobbies and lobbyists are frequently invaluable to legislators in terms of disclosing information necessary to intelligent action, their desire to achieve policy decisions favorable to their interests is paramount. Similarly, administrative agencies, local governments, political party factions, or even individual members of the legislature may be able to exact advantages.

Clearly, the misuse of time and opportunity that permits such shortcomings is not conducive to sound, comprehensive legislation in areas of vital public concern. The problem has not gone unnoticed in state governmental circles, and efforts of a sort have been made to correct it. While no state has come up with a solution regarded as the best that can be obtained, impressive steps have been taken in the form of prelegislative investigation and reports through the use of interim committees and legislative councils.

---

[2] As indicated in the table on page 136, limitations are placed on the length of sessions in almost half of the states and practically the same effect is achieved in several others were legislative salaries stop after a designated length of time.

LEGISLATIVE COUNCILS

Without doubt the most important strides toward achievement of legislative planning have been realized through legislative councils. These bodies are composed of members of the legislature who meet between legislative sessions to consider matters of probable interest to the succeeding session of the legislature.[3] Since 1933, the year the first council was established in Kansas, similar organizations have been created in forty-two states.[4] Various titles are used to identify them, but the most common is simply "Legislative Council."

Legislative councils vary widely in size. The smallest, consisting of only five members, is found in South Carolina; and those of Iowa, Massachusetts, Nevada, and Rhode Island contain only six to eight. At the other extreme are Nebraska, Oklahoma, Pennsylvania, and South Dakota, where every member of the legislature is, by virtue of legislative membership, considered a member of the council. The average size, however, is about fifteen with councils in most states ranging between ten and twenty-seven members. Approximately half of the councils are required to hold quarterly meetings, with the remainder generally free to hold as many or as few as they wish. In no state is there a limit on the number of council meetings.

The legislative council has been characterized as "essentially a super interim committee with an area of action as wide as that of the legislature."[5] It must be remembered, however, that a council is an *advisory* body, possessing no authority to enact legislation or to compel the legislature to act on matters it has considered. In reality it is a permanent joint committee, aided by a permanent research staff, to provide assistance to the legislature on major problems of policy. While no two councils exercise identical powers, all function to pro-

---

[3] In a few instances nonlegislative members are included; the lieutenant governor of Kentucky and the secretary of state of South Carolina are members of the councils in those states. There are three private citizens appointed by the governor to the legislative council in New Hampshire. In Utah the council includes three private citizens, one each of whom is chosen by the governor, president of the senate, and speaker of the house. Care should be taken not to confuse the legislative council with the legislative counsels found in five states.

[4] William J. Siffin, "Footnote to the Legislative Council Movement," *State Government,* July 1955, presents a review of the establishment of the Kansas legislative council, the body which more or less set the pattern for similar agencies later established in other states.

[5] Belle Zeller (ed.), *American State Legislatures,* Report of the Committee on American Legislatures, American Political Science Association, Thomas Y. Crowell Co., New York, 1954, p. 128.

vide factual information on important problems, insure continuing legislative study of major problems between sessions, and issue reports for legislators and the public, usually before a legislative session begins.[6]

Since all states do not have legislative councils, and of those in existence more than half have been in operation for only fifteen years or so, the real worth of councils is difficult to assess. Certainly, they have not solved all the problems occasioned by lack of planned legislative programs. On the other hand, they have facilitated more thorough consideration of major issues, reduced the impact of undesirable lobby pressures through research and reporting, and by means of recommendations and reports expedited the consideration of major policy matters. The fact that legislative councils provide continuing legislative research and contribute appreciably to over-all legislative planning has made them "an indispensable legislative aid for all state legislatures."[7]

INTERIM COMMITTEES

Interim committees resemble legislative councils in many ways, but they are significantly different in two important respects: the interim committee is a temporary legislative agency established to inquire into a specific topic, and it does not have a permanent research staff. Although dating from the earliest days of state legislatures, the interim committee was not widely used until the present century. They were common during the early 1900's, used even more widely in the 1920's, and by 1950 were employed in three-fourths of the states. Since their function is similar to that of a legislative council, interim committees are least common in those states with active councils.[8]

The record of accomplishment of interim committees has not been impressive. Some, of course, have been of great value, contributing much to the intelligent consideration by legislatures of the committees' subjects of inquiry. Because an interim committee can devote its entire effort to a single topic in which its members may have an intense interest, the potential contribution of such a com-

---

[6] Harold W. Sevey, "The Legislative Council Movement," *American Political Science Review*, September 1953.

[7] Zeller, *op. cit.*, p. 139.

[8] For example, in California, New York, and Oregon, where legislative councils have not been established, from fifteen to fifty interim committees have been used.

mittee is considerable. However, time lost in organization, the difficulty of assembling a competent staff for a relatively short period, the fact that the committee itself is temporary, and the lack of integration with other committees are weaknesses difficult to overcome.

LEGISLATIVE SERVICE AGENCIES

In addition to legislative councils and interim committees, various other aids are available to state legislators. Advice, information, and assistance are rendered in different states by reference services, bill drafting agencies, legislative counsels, legal revision and codification bodies, and staff agencies responsible for fiscal management. Without help from such aids, the tasks of individual legislators would be overwhelming.

Legislative Reference Services. The basic purpose of a legislative reference service is, as the name implies, to provide information and other assistance to legislators in the performance of their legislative duties. If a member of a state legislature needs information in the preparation or revision of a bill he is about to introduce, he can turn to the reference service for help. Most such agencies perform a variety of services including bill drafting, law summaries, statutory revision research reports, spot research for legislators, or any other services requested which they are equipped to render.

Legislative research services were among the first aids legislatures created. At the turn of the present century Wisconsin and New York established research agencies and within a decade or so, about a dozen states had followed suit. By 1940, legislative research arms were functioning in half the states. During the past twenty years each of the remaining states has created some type of agency to furnish research assistance to its legislators.

Several state legislative reference agencies function independently of other organizations, but in most instances the reference function is handled by the legislative council, a division of the state library, or a department within the executive branch. In some states the research assistance that ordinarily would be provided by a single reference bureau is rendered by several agencies which serve the legislature.

Bill Drafting. There is a world of difference between the exercise of intelligent discretion in determining what public policy ought to be and the ability to master the technique of expressing policy in the form of legislative bills. The vast majority of state legislators might be described as amateurs, or at best semipros, in drafting legislation. Classic examples of legislative *faux pas* of the past include the Massachusetts law which required all hotel rooms to have plastered walls and floors and an Ohio statute which provided that the state coat of arms was to be engraved on state officials. A prohibition enacted by the Tennessee legislature forbade owners of livestock to run at large, but the most quoted legislative misstep of all is the Kansas measure which required that trains meeting on a single track should each proceed to a siding from which neither should move until the other had passed. Such measures obviously are the result of careless, inept draftsmanship.

Pitfalls to be avoided in the preparation of a bill are numerous. Drafting an adequate bill requires that the author be fully aware of several important points:

1. A bill should be written in clear, precise terms that convey only the meanings intended.
2. The drafter should know how the bill relates to constitutional provisions, existing statutes, and court interpretations touching on matters covered by the bill.
3. The drafter should be aware not only of the effects of the bill upon individuals and groups directly affected, but also those in related fields.
4. Thorough consideration must be given to the question of whether the bill can be effectively administered.

If these cautions are respected, poorly drafted bills can be largely eliminated. Even so, after introduction the actions of committees and amendments on the floor can impair the quality of draftsmanship.

In all states it is now possible for legislators to secure help in bill drafting from at least one governmental officer or agency. The legislative councils, law revisors, legislative reference bureaus, and attorney generals are the usual sources of assistance. In previous years a great deal of reliance was placed upon the attorney generals in the belief that bill drafting could best be performed by individuals with substantial legal training. Today, primary reliance is upon research agencies under direct control of the legislatures, particularly the legislative councils. Reflected in this practice is the view that "effective draftsmanship requires a high degree of research skill and substantive information in addition to technical, legal proficiency."[9]

Legislative Counsels. The office of legislative *counsel*, which should not be confused with the legislative *council*, is found in several states. The word *counsel* refers to a person trained in the law, and a legislative counsel, therefore, is an attorney retained by a legislative body "to counsel members of the legislature concerning the form, substance, and effect of the law."[10] In actual practice, however, the form and duties of the office vary widely where it exists as a separate agency, and in many states the counseling function is performed by other service agencies and the attorney general.

In California the Legislative Counsel Bureau functions as a reference service, bill drafting agency, and legal revision department. The Legislative Counsel in Nevada operates in the manner of a legislative council. The Oregon counsel performs the tasks of legal revision and bill drafting as well as advising legislators on legal matters, and in Georgia the office provides general staff services to the legislative council. In these states the duties are more those of a general service agency than of a legal adviser. Viewing the position as one involving only the functions of a legal consultant, the closest approximations are found in the offices maintained in Massachusetts and New Hampshire.

Legal Revisions. At each regular session of every state legislature at least several hundred new laws are enacted. Some of the laws are completely new; others change specified parts of laws already on the books; still others may complement, conflict with, or compromise already existing law. If some means did not exist to relate the new laws to those already in existence, a state's legal system would soon become seriously entangled.

A legal revisor does not actually enact law. Rather, the function of the revisor is to consolidate overlapping provisions; correct inaccurate, prolix, or redundant expressions; eliminate obscurities and conflicts; and collect the whole into a logical, compact arrangement

---

[9] Herbert L. Wiltsee, "Legislative Service Agencies," *Book of the States, 1964–65*, p. 69.
[10] Zeller, *op. cit.*, p. 141.

without change in effect.[11] Within the last few years several states have authorized revisors to make recommendations as to the substantive content of laws. However, only the legislative body has power to enact laws, and the validity of a compilation, revision, or codification depends upon approval by the state legislature.

If the job of revision is not competently done, a conflicting, confused system of laws may result. Consequently all states provide for compilations, revisions, or codifications of statutory law. Nearly one-fourth of the states, however, do not maintain permanent revision agencies, preferring instead to rely upon periodic revisions by temporary bodies. The remainder of the states, following the example set by Wisconsin in 1909, have established permanent agencies for this important function, either as independent bodies or as a group within an existing department.

Budgetary and Fiscal Analysis. Among the most vexatious problems with which legislators must contend are those of a financial character. Before the functions of state government became so numerous, the budgetary process was handled in legislative stride. Today, however, the multiplicity of regulatory and service programs carried on by state governments has transformed budgetary and fiscal problems into matters that challenge the talents of even the most skilled economists. The trend toward executive budgets has relieved the pressure on the legislator, but it has done little to clarify for him the complexities of modern state financial problems.

During the past twenty years about half the states have created agencies which function as legislative advisers on budgetary and fiscal matters. The first such agency was the Joint Legislative Budget Committee established by the California legislature in 1941. Other states have created similar agencies, particularly during the 1950's. There are strong indications that the trend will continue, and "it is apparent that legislators desire more concrete information as to the dollars and cents effects of bills than has been forthcoming in the past."[12]

LOBBIES AND LOBBYISTS

At each session of every state legislature, decisions are made that alter the content and effect of existing public policy. Since the policy

---

[11] *Ibid.*, p. 153.
[12] Herbert L. Wiltsee, *op. cit.*, p. 72.

decisions made by the legislators are of fundamental importance to various economic, social, or political groups, it is not surprising that those groups should seek to maintain and extend public policy favorable to them. The agents who perform this function are referred to as *lobbyists*.

Lobby and *pressure group* are terms that are often used interchangeably, but it is helpful to recognize that differences between the two may exist. Both are organized groups that seek, by various means, to bring about or maintain what they consider favorable public policy. To be sure, a pressure group may operate as a lobby, but in a manner of speaking the lobby is best characterized as the legislative arm of the pressure group. Thus, railroad companies, labor unions, and veterans' organizations may function as pressure groups and at the same time maintain offices or organizations which operate as lobbies. In any event it is possible to say that all lobbies either represent or are themselves pressure groups, but that not all pressure groups are to be regarded as lobbies.

In a general sense all organizations which actively attempt to influence public policy can be considered pressure groups. However, some organizations such as fraternal lodges, hobbyists' clubs, and civic groups may be only temporarily or casually interested in some aspect of public policy. Ordinarily, issues such as the tax status of club property or the feasibility of public assistance in the purchase of playground equipment for a park represent the pressure activities of these groups. Inasmuch as they do not attempt continuously to influence policy, it is somewhat misleading to regard them either as lobbies or as pressure groups.

In the minds of many, lobbying consists only of the act of contacting a legislator and attempting to convince him of a certain point of view. Such actions are certainly included, but are only one of many tactics employed in lobbying. Direct contacts include not only the "buttonholing" of legislators, but also appearances as witnesses at committee hearings, dissemination of information in the form of pamphlets, tracts and reports directly to legislators, and sponsorship of social functions at which attendance of legislators is sought. More effective are the lobbying activities of an indirect nature. Propaganda designed to win support of the general public, pressures exerted on administrators, maintenance of speakers bureaus, mass letterwriting, advertising and sponsorship of radio and television programs are suggestive of the variety of means used to influence opinion and mold attitudes that are bound to have an effect upon legislators.

It should be noted that lobbying, as such, is not an undesirable practice. In fact, lobbyists frequently perform valuable services in the provision of information, particularly where legislative reference services do not exist or do not function well. There have been, of course, examples of bribery and corruption, and occasional actions of questionable ethical character lend an aura of suspicion to lobbying. Consequently, most state legislatures have made some attempts to regulate the practice.

Lobbyists, like everyone else, are subject to criminal laws. While not directed specifically at lobbyists, the criminal law prohibits such things as bribery and blackmail. In addition to general laws three-fourths of the states have enacted statutes designed particularly to control lobbyists.[13] These lobby control laws generally require lobbyists to register and to file financial reports on pain of possible fine, imprisonment, or both. A fourth of the states with lobby control laws also make provision for disbarment of offenders. The disbarment penalty denies the offender the privilege of registering as a lobbyist for a designated period—usually three years.

Enforcement of lobby laws has not been impressive. Several lobby control acts do not provide for fines, but in most states the penalties range up to $10,000 with the typical maximum set at $1,000. Imprisonment may be fixed at the discretion of the judge to terms up to one year in most instances, although a few states permit sentences of two, three or five years, and Florida judges may impose a twenty-year term for false swearing. However, the possibility of criminal sanctions has not proved effective in the prevention of lobbying abuses. In most states there have been no prosecutions at all, and except for Wisconsin, where enforcement has been most successful, few prosecutions have been attempted.

Various suggestions have been made in the interest of better methods of controlling lobbies and lobbyists, the most promising of which involve wider publicity of pressure activities coupled with closer surveillance. As a burglar prefers darkness, so unethical lobbyists prefer secrecy, or at least a minimum of attention. By requiring

---

[13] About a third of these laws merely prohibit improper lobbying practices. Also, in a few states regulation of lobbyists is accomplished by rules of the legislative houses rather than through statutory provisions.

lobbyists *and* their employers not only to register but also to report itemized accounts of all sums spent in their attempts to influence public policy, the public as well as legislators can be more fully informed. It has been suggested that special agencies be established for the enforcement of lobby regulations, thus securing supervision superior to the part-time efforts of attorney generals, secretaries of state, or legislative officers. Valuable as these proposals are, it is doubtful that greatly improved controls will be achieved until the value of the lobbyist to the legislator has been diminished. By providing adequate staff assistance and research and information facilities, legislators—even those in their first terms—can function more effectively without assistance from lobbyists. It is probable that all lobbying activities can never be fully controlled, especially those that are indirect in character, but suggested improvements offer the promise of curbing most abuses.

LAWMAKING PROCEDURE

Steps involved in the course of a bill through a legislature are much the same from state to state. The unicameral system of Nebraska, of course, represents the greatest departure from the "norm," but even there procedures are much like those of a chamber within a bicameral system. Despite much similarity, there are numerous variations in detail in the passage of bills by state legislatures. These differences can best be noted by an examination of the principal procedural steps.

Rules of Procedure. In each state constitution there are a few provisions that affect the procedures by which bills are passed. The North Carolina document, for example, provides that each bill must be read three times in each house before passage, roll call votes may be demanded by one-fifth of those present and voting, and thirty days' public notice must be given before voting on private bills. The Indiana Constitution requires a full section-by-section reading on final passage of every bill—a requirement that by specific constitutional direction cannot be dispensed with. In Texas the basic law forbids reconsideration of a bill once it has been defeated in either house of the legislature, the prohibition extending to any newly introduced measure containing the substance of a defeated bill.

THE COURSE OF A BILL

THE HOUSE OF REPRESENTATIVES						THE SENATE				EXECUTIVE OFFICIALS	
INTRODUCING MEMBER	CHIEF CLERK	SPEAKER OF HOUSE	HOUSE STANDING COMMITTEES	COMMITTEE ON RULES & ORDER "CALENDAR COMMITTEE"		SECRETARY OF SENATE	PRESIDENT OF SENATE	SENATE STANDING COMMITTEES	RULES AND JOINT RULES COMMITTEE "GENERAL FILE"	GOVERNOR	SECRETARY OF STATE

FOR FILING

READ FIRST TIME BY TITLE — REFERRED TO STANDING COMMITTEE

READING AND RECORD OF COMMITTEE REPORT — CONSIDERED BY APPROPRIATE STANDING COMMITTEE

REFERRED TO — TO BE PLACED ON THE CALENDAR FOR SECOND READING

READ SECOND TIME SECTION BY SECTION — REFERRED TO — TO BE PLACED ON THE CALENDAR FOR THIRD READING

THIRD READING AND FINAL PASSAGE

CERTIFICATION

FOR FILING

READ FIRST AND SECOND TIME — REFERRED — CONSIDERED BY APPROPRIATE STANDING COMMITTEE

READING AND RECORD OF COMMITTEE REPORT — REFERRED TO — TO BE PLACED ON THE CALENDAR FOR THIRD READING

THIRD READING SECTION BY SECTION AND FINAL PASSAGE

CERTIFICATION

ENROLLED — ENROLLING COMMITTEE

SIGNED IN OPEN SESSION

SIGNED IN OPEN SESSION

ORIGINAL SIGNED IF APPROVED

GIVES BILL CHAPTER NUMBER IN SESSION LAWS PERMANENTLY FILED

Source: Bureau of Governmental Research and Services, University of Washington

Note: The above procedure for a non-committee bill introduced in the House is the simplest possible; neither veto nor amendment has occurred. If such a bill is introduced in the Senate, the Secretary of the Senate would perform essentially the same functions as the Chief Clerk of the House indicated above, and the action of the House thereon would occur after passage thereof by the Senate.

Other similar provisions are contained in the basic laws of all other states.

Even though state constitutions contain several stipulations regarding legislative procedure, each house of every state legislature is free to adopt the great bulk of its own rules of procedure. Technically, rules are adopted at the beginning of each regular session, a step which usually amounts to nothing more than adoption of the rules in effect during the previous regular session. Of course, changes in the rules may be made, but practically all alterations in the rules come slowly through interpretations during the course of legislative sessions.

Introduction of Bills. One of the simplest steps in legislative procedure is the introduction of a bill. The process consists of depositing a copy of the bill with the clerk of either house. In three-fourths of the states, bills are printed upon introduction. Procedure in the other states calls for printing at a later stage, ordinarily after standing committee approval or second reading.

The number of measures introduced in all American state legislatures during a biennium—the two year period during which each legislature holds at least one regular session—is approximately 110,000. Of this huge total, about 35,000 to 40,000 are eventually enacted into law. The number of introductions varies widely among the states, statistics indicating about 9,000 bills introduced during a regular session in New York, and nearly 5,000 are introduced in the California legislature. On the other hand, records in states like Wyoming and North Dakota show only 500 or 600 measures placed before their legislatures. In most instances, introductions number from about one to three thousand, of which some thirty-five to forty per cent are ultimately passed, with enactments exceeding fifty per cent in a few states.

Since many legislative sessions are limited in length and there is a tendency to delay consideration of many bills, three-fourths of the state legislatures have limited the period during which measures may be introduced in order to reduce congestion at the end of each session. A unique arrangement is found in Massachusetts, where all bills *must* be introduced a full month before the legislature convenes, with exceptions permitted only by a four-fifths majority or request of the governor! To allow for emergency situations, most state legislatures that have limited the period during which measures may be introduced provide for exceptions by gubernatorial request, an extraordinary majority, or by exempting appropriations and revenue bills. One method of circumventing limitations on introduction is by means of parliamentary technicalities such as amending a bill under discussion in such a way that it embodies provisions that would otherwise have been the subject of separate legislation.

First Reading. All state legislative chambers operate under rules which provide that bills be read to the members before votes are taken. Three readings are usually required, although four are necessary in Montana, and two are sufficient in Delaware, Nebraska, North Dakota, Rhode Island, and South Dakota. Ordinarily, each of the readings must take place on different days, and at least one must be of the entire contents of the bill.

The object of different readings, of course, is to prevent hasty passage of legislation, the extreme forms of which are known as *railroading*. At times, dispatch may be necessary or desirable. Consequently, the rules of most houses permit, usually after an extraordinary majority vote, some readings to be dispensed with or all readings heard on a single day. A reading requirement may often be satisfied merely by reading the title. Indeed, the first reading usually consists of nothing more than a recitation of the title by a clerk. At first glance such a practice may seem ill-advised, but in view of the fact that a newly introduced bill must be referred for committee action a first reading in full would serve only to delay later, important procedural steps.

Referral. In each house of every state legislature provision is made for standing committees to which all bills are referred for consideration. Referral of bills—the assignment of bills to various committees—is usually performed by the speaker of the house or the president of the senate. In only eight lower houses is the referral power not wholly lodged in the speaker,[14] although a third of the upper houses either restrict the president of the senate or place the authority

---

[14] In Kentucky bills are referred by the Committee on Committees. The speaker refers them in Louisiana, but upon motion of the author. Bills introduced in either chamber of the Maine legislature are referred by a joint committee composed of the speaker, president of the senate, two senators, and three representatives. Referral is performed by the clerk in Massachusetts, subject to approval of the speaker. The member who introduces a measure in the Nevada house also refers it, and in both Ohio and Oregon whoever is presiding at the time of introduction of a bill refers it.

in other hands.[15] In the great majority of instances, referral involves no discretion and could be handled adequately by a clerk. Sometimes a bill could reasonably be referred to any of several committees, a decision that properly should be made by a designated officer or committee. The power of referral may determine the fate of a bill, depending upon whether the committee to which it is referred is favorably disposed toward its provisions.

Committee Action. Standing committees of legislative bodies are, for all practical purposes, miniature legislatures. The committee may alter a bill in virtually any way it chooses, ranging from reporting the bill to the floor unchanged with a recommendation that it be passed, to other extremes of changing the content completely or simply failing to consider it at all. Committees in about one-third of the states are required to report all bills back to the floor, but a bill that has received no attention from a committee has little chance of passage. Practice in California, Colorado, and New Hampshire is to report all bills not acted on in committee to the floor on the last day of the session, a procedure that honors the letter but manages to defeat the purpose of reporting requirements. On occasion a committee may refuse to report an important bill for consideration by the whole house. The rules of procedure usually provide that a committee can be forced to *discharge* a bill upon a majority vote of the house. Discharge rules, however, are seldom invoked.

At its executive sessions and public hearings, a standing committee works toward a decision on each bill it thinks worth consideration or has time for. It may go to great lengths in its search for information and opinion, or it may rely upon its own knowledge. Whatever decision the committee makes is likely to be the assessment that determines the fate of each measure referred to it.

Committee Reports. Practically all important bills that committees send to the floor are accompanied by recommendations as to

[15] In Delaware, Oregon, Pennsylvania, South Carolina, and Wisconsin, bills are referred by the presiding officer. The president *pro tem* acts in the senates of Kansas and Tennessee (known as the speaker in the latter state). The power of referral is exercised by the Rules Committee in the upper house of California, the Bills Committee in Illinois, and the Reference Committee in Nebraska. The procedures followed in Kentucky, Massachusetts, Maine, and Nevada are the same as those used in the lower houses of those states as indicated in note 14 above. In Louisiana the president acts on motion of the author, and in Michigan the same officer refers bills subject to approval of the full senate. All measures introduced in the Ohio Senate are sent to committee as directed by the majority leader.

their disposition. Frequently, reports are printed setting forth reasons for the committee's actions, and in many cases both the majority and minority of the committee prepare reports. Decision on the merits of a bill does not take place at this stage. The only decision made is whether to send the bill back to the committee or to place it on a calendar.

The Calendar Stage. After a bill has been reported out by a committee the measure is placed on a *calendar*. A calendar is nothing more than a list of bills, in chronological order, that have been acted upon by standing committees and are ready for debate by the full house. In some chambers there is only one calendar; others have several for bills of different types. In all instances, consideration of bills is required, technically at least, in the order in which they are reported from committees.

Frequently an important bill, or one a majority wants to consider immediately, may be at the bottom or far down on a calendar. Since the rules provide that bills must be taken up in order, special action is necessary before any bill other than the first one on the calendar may be discussed. Inasmuch as rules of procedure are determined by the legislative body itself, the rules can be suspended, and the desired bill then considered. Because suspension ordinarily requires an extraordinary majority vote, an easier process is usually employed. A common procedure is the adoption of a special rule permitting a specific bill to be considered out of order. A simple majority plus favorable action of a rules committee is required before such a rule can be brought into play. The role of the rules committee furnishes a possible obstacle to the process, but since the majority party in the house also has a majority on the committee, special rules are seldom refused.

Floor Action. When a bill is ready for floor action, it receives a second reading. In all states except those with constitutional provisions requiring a third reading in full, it is at this stage that a bill is debated and amendments offered. Usual procedure is for a clerk to read the bill aloud, with the presiding officer inquiring as to the agreement of the house as each section is concluded. At any such interval full, extended debate may occur and amendments may be adopted. Unimportant or noncontroversial bills may be read in a rapid, unintelligible drone, or as has happened in a few instances, several such bills may be read simultaneously!

In some states full reading often occurs in *committee of the whole.* Consisting of the full membership of the house, although fewer members may constitute a quorum, a committee of the whole is not bound by the rules of the house as such and is not presided over by the regular presiding officer of the chamber. Debate and discussion are much freer and more informal. Decisions reached in the committee are "reported" to the house which formalizes them under the regular rules of procedure.

Technically, the decision made by a legislative chamber on second reading is whether to restore a bill to the calendar to await third reading, but technicalities aside, the second reading usually results, for all practical purposes, in a decision by the house. Again, except where a full third reading is constitutionally mandatory, it is common practice that after debate is ended a bill is *engrossed*—printed again to incorporate all changes approved during debate—a perfunctory third reading by title is given, and a formal vote taken.

Voting. The most important single act in the course of a bill through a legislative chamber is the vote of the members to approve or reject it. There are several methods of voting, the most formal of which is the *roll call.* When such a vote is cast, a clerk calls the names of members who verbally announce their decisions. The votes are recorded as announced and become a permanent part of the recorded proceedings. Roll calls commonly are required on the final passage of bills, but when they are not compulsory, other methods may be used either to save time or to escape publicity on what might later prove to be an unpopular vote. The *viva voce,* or voice vote, is the most frequently used method of determining the consensus of a legislative body, but when more accurate assessment is necessary, the *show of hands* or *teller* votes are used. In the former, as the term indicates, members merely raise their hands to be counted. A teller vote requires members to file by a clerk who tallies votes as announced by each legislator.

Much time is spent, even wasted, in the vote-taking process in state legislatures, especially when large numbers of roll calls are involved. During the latter portion of the session when time is at a premium its loss can be costly. Consequently, many states have installed electrical voting devices to speed up the process. Such devices have proved their worth, accurately recording in a few seconds roll calls that formerly took ten to twenty minutes. The first electrical device for recording legislative decisions was installed in the Wisconsin House of Representatives in 1917, and since then they have been placed in use in half of the states. Ordinarily, the devices are found only in the larger lower houses, although the senates of Indiana, Louisiana, Minnesota, North Dakota, Tennessee, and Virginia, as well as Nebraska's unicameral body, are so equipped.

Majorities needed to pass bills vary among states, but they are the same for both houses in a given legislature. In no case is anything more than an ordinary majority required for the passage of bills, but in thirty-two states that majority must be of the total membership. Thus if a legislative body contains 100 members, at least fifty-one members must vote affirmatively before a bill can be passed, regardless of the number of members present. A majority of those *present and voting* is required in fourteen states, but of this group Kentucky and Virginia require that at least two-fifths of the total membership cast ballots. A simple majority of the members present is needed for passage in Florida, Idaho, Montana, and New Mexico. Each of the New Hampshire houses operates under a sort of variable formula. Passage of bills in both houses is normally by a majority of those present and voting, but if less than two-thirds of the House is present the majority is raised to two-thirds; if fewer than sixteen of the twenty-four senators are in attendance, the minimum vote is fixed at ten.

Conference Committees. Valid enactment of a law by a bicameral legislature requires that the bill be passed in identical form by each house. There can be no variation whatever; every comma, semicolon, and apostrophe must appear in identical locations. As frequently occurs, however, especially with important or controversial bills, committee action and amendment on the floor result in differences. The usual formal method for resolving differences is through use of conference committees.

Appointed by the presiding officers of the respective houses, conference committees usually are composed of two or three members from each chamber. A separate committee is appointed for each bill, and the conferees, meeting in secret sessions, normally are limited to discussion of points of difference between the bills in conflict. Some states permit such committees to consider any desirable change, and on occasion, despite limitations in the rules, conference committees substantially rewrite measures. When reported to the legislative chambers, recommendations of the conference may be debated, but only rarely are they amendable. Recommendations normally must be accepted as a whole or rejected altogether. Ordinarily, rejection has the effect of killing a bill, although once in a while a new conference committee is appointed for further efforts to reconcile differences.

Conference committees have been criticized on several grounds. First, since the recommendations of conferences are usually approved, the claim is made that it is unwise to concentrate so much power in the hands of a few legislators. Again, it is said, the small number of legislators invites intensified efforts by lobbyists. Also, since most conference committees perform their work late in the session—often during the last few days or weeks—the legislature has little opportunity to consider alternatives to conference recommendations. Little has been done to correct these shortcomings, but suggestions to restrict the powers of conferees to make recommendations only on points of difference, to require written reasons supporting recommendations, and to restrict appointment of conferees to members thoroughly familiar with the bills in question all offer promise for improvement.

Only in Nebraska, which has a unicameral legislature, has the conference committee been eliminated as a significant step in legislative procedure. Even in those states where wide use is made of joint committees or joint sessions of standing committees, the conference committee has persisted. While cooperative efforts between legislative houses may reduce the number of occasions upon which conference committees are necessary, differences will continue to arise, and some means by which agreement can be achieved will be necessary.

Enrollment. The final step in legislative procedure before a bill is sent to the governor is *enrollment*. After it has been passed in identical form by both houses, a bill is then printed in final form, and the signatures of the presiding officers of the respective houses are affixed. At this point, only the governor stands between the bill and its inclusion as a part of the law of a state.

To the Governor. The governor of every state except North Carolina[16] is constitutionally vested with the veto power. As the chief

---

[16] Bills passed by the North Carolina legislature become law thirty days after final adjournment, unless otherwise expressly directed.

executive of the state a governor has authority, in fact the duty, to examine closely all bills passed by the legislature and to veto, or negate, those which he feels are not expressions of sound public policy. When he does so, he is obliged to return the bill to the legislative house where it was introduced with a message setting forth reasons for his action. Since a veto represents a difference of opinion between two equal, coordinate branches of government, a method of resolving the conflict is necessary. In all instances the disagreement may be resolved by the vote of an extraordinary legislative majority to *override* the veto. Usually a two-thirds majority of each house is required to cancel the effect of an executive veto, a number that is in most cases extremely difficult to muster.

If a governor does not veto a bill, several alternatives are open to him. He may sign the measure, as happens in the vast majority of cases. He may also permit the bill to become law without his signature. Governors have from three to fifteen days, with the limit in most states set at five or ten, to act on bills while the legislature is in session. Should a governor fail to act on a bill, it automatically becomes law at the end of the prescribed period. In about twenty states, bills sent to the governor *after* the legislative session is over, or which are on his desk at the time of adjournment, do not become law if left unsigned. Instead, such bills die, and are said to be subject to the *pocket veto*. Forty-two governors also exercise a power known as the *item veto*.[17] This particular veto is ordinarily limited to appropriations bills although the Oregon executive may also apply it to emergency measures, and the governor of Washington may veto items in any bill containing more than one item or section.

After clearing the governor's desk, a bill does not necessarily take immediate legal effect. Usually there is a fixed date upon which bills passed at a session are legally enforceable. The date may be fixed by the constitution, as in Texas, at ninety days after adjournment. In Florida the lapse of time is sixty days. Indiana laws must be distributed to the counties and proclaimed by the governor, and in Kansas legal force is effective upon publication. Laws enacted in Maryland are considered effective on the first day of June following the legislative session unless otherwise declared. If the constitution is silent on the matter, the effective date is determined by the legislature.

---

[17] The item veto may not be wielded by the governors of Indiana, Iowa, Maine, Nevada, New Hampshire, North Carolina, Rhode Island, and Vermont.

A new law may take effect earlier through a provision known as an *emergency clause*. In the event a legislature desires an earlier effective date for a particular law than is usual, and there is no constitutional restriction on doing so, the law may be written to include a provision declaring the bill an emergency measure. As a result, when the procedural steps of lawmaking are concluded, the law takes immediate effect.

IMPROVEMENT OF STATE LEGISLATURES

Legislative powers, organization, and procedure are human creations, and like their creators have many weaknesses and shortcomings. For purposes of textual examination the various aspects of state legislatures can be separately considered, but in reality, powers, organization and procedure are so thoroughly enmeshed and integrated that true understanding of the legislative process requires that they be considered as a whole. Powers hamstrung by unrealistic constitutional limitations can result in poor organization and cumbersome procedures; poor organization can negate power and complicate procedure; and a confused procedural maze nullifies adequate power and lessens the effectiveness of good organization. Consequently, improvements in legislative procedure necessitate concern with organization and allocation of authority.

Suggestions for improving legislatures have not been lacking. Over a decade ago the Council of State Governments published a list of recommendations that today are still painfully applicable.[18] Although the intervening years have seen improvement here and there, legislatures in all states could be improved through further realization of the Council's suggestions. In summary form, the following improvements were advised:

1. The length of regular sessions should not be restricted. The demands of the legislative task should determine how long, and how often, a legislature should meet.

2. Legislative salaries should not be fixed by constitutional provision and they should be high enough to permit a person to serve without financial sacrifice.

---

[18] Council of State Governments, Committee on Legislative Processes and Procedures, *Our State Legislatures,* revised edition, Chicago, 1948. Zeller, *op. cit.,* contains recommendations much like those of the Council report.

3. Legislative terms of office should be lengthened. Staggered terms would provide more continuity in membership.

4. Skilled and essential full-time legislative employees should be appointed on the basis of merit and competence. Tenure of such employees should not be affected by changes in party control of the legislature.

5. Committees should be reduced in number where practicable and organized with regard to related subject matter, equalization of work, and cooperation between houses. Permanent public records of committee action should be kept.

6. Committees should provide for public hearings on all important bills. Advance notice of the time and place of each hearing should be given.

7. Legislative councils or interim committees, with adequate clerical and research assistance, should be maintained.

8. Legislative reference, research, bill drafting, and statutory revision services should be strengthened.

9. The introduction and printing of bills should be closely regulated to prevent congestion during the latter stages of the session.

10. Legislative rules of procedure should be revised in order to expedite procedure, with due regard for debate and fairness to minority parties.

11. Legislative expenditures should be adequately provided in accordance with a budget.

12. The legislature should not enact special legislation. Judicial or administrative agencies should handle claims against the state. Local affairs should be dealt with through general or optional legislation, or by conferring home rule on local governments.

To be sure, steps have been taken in many states to improve legislatures. During the past twenty years some states have taken impressive strides; others have done nothing. But whatever developments have occurred in any state, one thing is clear: piecemeal or single-shot improvement is not enough. Society changes constantly, the demands of the people fluctuate, and public policy needs continuous adjustment. Similarly, legislative improvement must keep pace.

SELECTED REFERENCES

Books:

Council of State Governments, *Our State Legislatures,* revised ed., Chicago, 1948.

——, *State Regulation of Lobbying,* Chicago, 1951.

Guild, Frederic H., *Legislative Councils After Thirty Years,* Public Affairs Research Bureau, Southern Illinois University, Carbondale, Illinois, 1964.

Luce, Robert, *Legislative Principles,* Houghton-Mifflin Co., Boston, 1930.

——, *Legislative Problems,* Houghton-Mifflin Co., Boston, 1935.

——, *Legislative Procedure,* Houghton-Mifflin Co., Boston, 1922.

Neuberger, Richard L., *Adventures in Politics: We Go to the Legislature,* Oxford University Press, New York, 1954.

Siffin, William J., *The Legislative Council in the American States,* Indiana University Press, Bloomington, 1959.

Walker, Harvey, *Law Making in the United States,* Ronald Press, New York, 1934.

——, *The Legislative Process,* Ronald Press, New York, 1948.

Articles:

Davey, Harold W., "The Legislative Council Movement," *American Political Science Review,* September 1953.

Hamilton, Thomas H., "A Citizen Views the Legislature," *State Government,* Winter 1964.

Jewell, Malcolm E., "Party Voting in American State Legislatures," *American Political Science Review,* September 1955.

Kammerer, Gladys M., "Advisory Committees in the Legislative Process," *Journal of Politics,* May 1953.

Keefe, William J., "Comparative Study of the Role of Political Parties in State Legislatures," *Western Political Quarterly,* September 1956.

Mason, Paul, "Procedures in State Legislatures: The Nature of Rules," *State Government,* Spring 1963.

Neuberger, Richard L., "Aids for the Legislator," *National Municipal Review,* March 1956.

"Symposium on Legislation," *Louisiana Law Review,* June 1956.

Chapter 8

Legal Systems and Legal Procedure

All social relationships, whether public or private, are carried on in the context of law. Today more than ever human behavior is regulated by legal codes of conduct. Virtually every human action is affected either directly or indirectly by legal rules. Family relationships, school attendance, recreation, business activities, governmental affairs—all are conditioned by requirements of law.

The word "law" is a complex and challenging concept. No simple definition can be satisfactorily applied in every context. One of the more informative definitions, however, holds law to be the total of those "rules and principles of conduct which the governing power in a community recognizes as those which it will enforce or sanction, and according to which it will regulate, limit, or protect the conduct of its members."[1] The "community" referred to in this statement can be the nation, a state, or an organized locality. Thus, the rules and principles of conduct may arise at various levels of government.

The character of the legal system of the United States is shaped to a large extent by the influence of federalism. One may speak of the American legal system, for the same general principles of law are applied throughout the country. It is much more accurate, however, to refer to the national legal system and the legal system of each of the fifty states. Despite the great similarity in law from one state to the next, each state is a self-contained legal entity with authority to provide for its own system of laws.

TYPES OF LAW

Within the American legal system there are various types of law. Although each type varies as to content and application, there is much overlapping. Some kinds are superior to others, but all are integral parts of the legal system.

---

[1] *Bouvier's Law Dictionary*, 3rd revision, vol. 2, pp. 1875–76.

Constitutional Law. At the apex of the American legal system is the United States Constitution. Superior to all other law in the country, it is known as the "organic," "basic," or "fundamental" law of the nation. Regardless of source or type, other "laws" are of no legal effect if they are contrary to provisions of the Constitution. Affirming this status, the document itself contains the statement that "This Constitution, and the laws of the United States which shall be made in pursuance thereof; and all treaties made, or which shall be made, under the authority of the United States, shall be the supreme law of the land . . ."[2]

In defining supreme or highest law, the Constitution definitely asserts superiority of national law over that of the states. The Constitution, laws, and treaties of the national government are specifically designated as predominant over state law. To remove all doubt, the Constitution further provides that "judges in every State shall be bound thereby, anything in the Constitution or laws of any State to the contrary notwithstanding."

The status of state constitutions is clearly one of inferiority to national law. At the same time, the organic law of a state remains superior to all other provisions of law within the state. Thus in order to be legally effective, every provision of a state statute must accord not only with federal law, but also with the state constitution.

Common Law. A large part of the law applied in each of the American states, except Louisiana,[3] consists of the common law. It is made up of:

> Those principles, usages, and rules of action applicable to the government and security of persons and of property, which do not rest for their authority upon any express and positive declaration of the will of the legislature.[4]

In less technical language, the common law is a body of unwritten rules or principles of law, developed from generally accepted ideas of right and wrong, which receives judicial acceptance. Common law covers almost all facets of human conduct and is applied in state

---

[2] Article VI, Section 2.

[3] The legal system of Louisiana is based upon French legal concepts which are derived from Roman law. Louisiana law has been deeply affected by the common law, however, particularly in regard to its influence upon judicial decisions.

[4] James Kent, *Commentaries on American Law*, O. Halsted, New York, 1826–30, vol. 1, p. 492.

courts,[5] except when in conflict with written law, which takes precedence over it.

Common law originated in England following the Norman Conquest in the closing years of the eleventh century. At that time there was no adequate body of written law regulating conduct. Consequently, judges of courts throughout the realm decided cases according to local custom tempered with reason. Gradually, through the practice of following earlier decisions whenever possible, an established system of legal principles evolved—a system that was "common" to all parts of the country. During the centuries that followed the common law was expanded and refined. The English settlers of the western hemisphere applied it in the American colonies, and common law was to a large extent adopted by the states upon their entry into the Union.

Common law in effect in the states today is not the same as that applied in modern Britain. In the first place the states have not adopted *all* of the common law, certain portions not applicable to their institutions being omitted. Again, cut-off dates have been designated; that is, only the common law in force in England as of the time of the Declaration of Independence or some other arbitrarily chosen date has been accepted as part of the legal systems of the various states.[6] American experience has wrought changes in the content of the common law—an inevitable development over a course of about two centuries of growth in the United States. During this period, for example, the common law crime has all but disappeared since virtually all crimes under that law have long since become the subject of written, statutory provisions.[7] The common law remains, nevertheless, the broadest, most comprehensive type of

---

[5] Common law is not used in the federal jurisdiction. By virtue of the decision in *Swift* v. *Tyson*, 16 Peters 1 (1842), federal courts were permitted to make independent determinations in the application of common law in certain matters. In *Erie Railroad* v. *Tompkins*, 304 U.S. 64 (1939), however, the earlier decision was reversed. Consequently, when deciding cases involving issues of local common law, federal courts are bound by the interpretations of common law made by the appropriate state courts.

[6] Some states fix the date as July 4, 1776. Most common, however, is the year 1607, the date of the English settlement at Jamestown, Virginia.

[7] Rare instances of conviction of common law crimes in recent times may be noted. In *Hitzel* v. *Maryland*, 197 A. 605 (1938), the Court of Appeals of Maryland upheld the conviction of a Baltimore police officer on misdemeanor charges, saying that "at common law malfeasance in office is a misdemeanor." In the Pennsylvania case of *Commonwealth* v. *Coyle*, 160 Pa. St. 36 (1894), the directors of a poorhouse who had through negligence contributed to the death of a minor child were held criminally liable. The court observed that even though their offense was not condemned by statute, "the common law holds them responsible for it as a misdemeanor in office."

law applied in the states, serving as the basis for deciding the vast majority of controversies not covered by written law.

Equity. As the common law developed, it became somewhat rigid. Relief was available only through various writs issued by the courts.[8] If no writ was suited to the relief requested, then no action could be taken by the courts. In any event no one could seek the assistance of the courts until after an injury had been sustained. Even when it was absolutely certain that a person would be wronged by actions of another, it was necessary to wait until the wrong had been inflicted.

Individuals unable to obtain an adequate remedy at common law appealed to the King. Such appeals became numerous and were referred usually to the chancellor, a member of the King's court. Gradually, a system of rules developed, and by the fourteenth century a special court of *chancery*, or equity, was established. Eventually, a fully developed system of rules and principles were in use, and equity assumed a permanent place in the English legal system.

Technically, equity is not "law." This distinction is based on the fact that equity, at least in theory, exists to supplement the law. It provides remedies where none is available at law, preventing injurious actions before they happen. Yet the *decrees,* or orders, issued by a court of equity are enforced exactly as if they were judgments of a court of law. Obviously, the distinction between law and equity is more a matter of form than of substance.

The Application of Common Law and Equity. The distinction between common law and equity is best understood by illustration. Assume that Smith and Jones are neighbors, and Smith is contemplating building a garage that will extend beyond his property line and damage valuable shrubs belonging to Jones. Jones could wait until the structure is completed, the shrubs destroyed, and then sue Smith for damages under common law. Jones may not be able to replace the shrubs, however, regardless of the amount of damages he might receive. Under such a circumstance he would probably bring action in a court of equity, seeking to prevent Smith from damaging his property.

---

[8] Most simply defined, a *writ* is a court order directed to an individual commanding him to perform or not to perform, a designated act. There are literally dozens of types of writs. The *writ of execution,* for example, is an order commanding a previous judgment to be put in force. Perhaps the best known writ is that of *habeas corpus,* by virtue of which a person illegally held in jail may secure his release.

In some instances there is no adequate remedy at common law for activities already taken. For example, if Smith sells a lot to Jones and the deed does not contain an accurate legal description of the property, Jones may resort to a suit in equity to force Smith to execute another, correct deed. Again, if Smith enters into a valid contract to sell Jones a lot, but then refuses to do so, Jones may sue for damages at common law. If Jones wants the property, a damage suit is not an adequate remedy. Under the rules of equity Jones can obtain the desired relief through a judicial decision compelling Smith to fulfill obligations of the contract. On the other hand, if Jones procured the contract under fraudulent representations, Smith can, by proving the fraudulent actions in a court of equity, be excused from meeting the conditions of the agreement.

Statutory Law. In addition to common law and equity, there exists in each state a large body of legislative enactments called statutes. Statutory law supplements, clarifies, modifies, and to some extent replaces the unwritten law. Its status in the rank of law within a state is second only to the constitution.[9]

While statutory law prevails when it conflicts with common law, it does not as a whole replace the unwritten law. Often, in fact, statutory provisions are derived from principles of common law or equity. Or, when at issue in a judicial proceeding, a statute may be construed or interpreted on the basis of common law principles. Thus even though common law itself may not be applied in a given case its influence is apparent. It should also be noted, however, that statutory law often deals with matters not covered by unwritten law.[10]

In about half of the states statutory law has been collected to varying degrees into *codes*. Strictly speaking a code is "a body of law established by the legislative authority of the state, and designed to regulate completely, so far as a statute may, the subject to which it relates."[11] Since a code "regulates completely," the obvious conclusion is that the common law must be abolished when a code is

---

[9] The term "statutory law" is sometimes used as a synonym for "written law." In this sense statutory law would include legal forms not ordinarily classed as statutes.

[10] The principles of common law or equity that relate to procedure may, for example, be adequate for a suit involving claims arising out of the construction and operation of a power utility operating on atomic energy. The liability of persons associated with the proceedings may likewise be determined by the unwritten law. However, the law relating to the control of the fissionable materials, specifications for construction, institution of safety measures, etc., would be of statutory derivation.

[11] *Bouvier's Law Dictionary*, vol. 1, p. 507.

adopted. In reality, however, codes are based upon common law and are interpreted on the basis of that law. In effect then a code brings together, with some changes, the scattered principles of unwritten law. Moreover, even in code states the collection of laws is limited, for many codes are restricted to selected portions of the law such as criminal procedure, civil procedure, pleadings, or insurance.

CIVIL LAW AND PROCEDURE

Regardless of how wise or comprehensive law may be, human relationships are so varied and intricate that no set of laws can anticipate all conflicts or foresee all human difficulties. Law cannot provide a perfect system of regulation in which all human participants know and accept, in the same way, all legal rules of conduct. It is possible, however, for law to provide rules and conditions in terms of which conflicts can be resolved.

Basically, law can be divided into two primary categories, *civil* and *criminal*. Criminal law consists of a collection of legislative declarations that prohibit certain defined actions on pain of legislatively prescribed penalties. A person who performs a criminal act may be taken into custody and upon a showing that he has in fact committed the crime be subjected to an appropriate penalty. Legally defined, crime is an offense against the governmental unit that prohibits the act and acts as prosecutor. On the other hand, civil law is composed of the great body of regulations relating to human actions not prohibited by criminal law. All aspects of human relationships are affected; when conflicts develop in regard to the meaning, application, or interpretation of law, the government acting through judicial tribunals provides the means by which settlements can be reached.

The distinction between civil and criminal law is simple, yet at times it is difficult for the uninitiated to recognize the difference. It is clear that a person who commits murder has committed a crime, and the criminal law is applicable. It is equally obvious that a person who refuses to pay a valid debt may be sued in court by his creditor, and that civil law governs the matter. But what of the instance in which a drunken driver runs into and damages the automobile of another driver? Applying the principles discussed above it is readily seen that the person driving while intoxicated has performed an act prohibited by the criminal law. For that offense he is liable to the state. At the same time he has inflicted damages upon the property of another person, and for that he is liable under civil law to the individual suffering the loss.

Civil Actions. In the United States a person may begin a *civil suit*[12] whenever he can demonstrate what is known as a *cause of action,* or grounds upon which a suit may be based. A cause of action results from alleged infringement by a person or group of the rights of the person bringing suit. Acts or failures to act that result in causes of action under civil law have been classified under the general headings of *contracts* and *torts.*[13] Included under contracts are those acts relating to the making of agreements and the injuries resulting from their breach. Torts embrace acts other than those relating to contracts that in law are injurious to the rights of individuals.

Criteria of liability under the concepts of contracts and torts cut across virtually all fields of civil law. Whether an act which gives rise to a cause of action occurs in regard to property rights, business activity, domestic relations, matters of taxation or other fields, the criteria of liability are generally applicable. Thus principles of law that relate to failure to fulfill the obigations of a contract would be as applicable to businessmen who renege upon a sales agreement as to homeowners who fail to meet the terms of their mortgages. Similarly, liability for damages under the concept of torts applies regardless of the field in which a tortious action may occur. For example, a trespasser who damages the property of another, a person who fails to confine a vicious dog that bites a pedestrian, or a businessman who slanders a competitor are subject to the same general principles of liability.

There are a few areas in the American system of civil law where the contracts-torts basis of determining causes of action does not appear to be directly applicable. Chief among these is the system of equity, which is fundamentally anticipatory in character. A threatened action is sufficient to warrant a civil suit in equity. The exercise by governmental units of their power of *eminent domain,* the taking

---

[12] In their strictest technical applications the terms "suit" and "trial" can be used interchangeably. In general usage, however, "suit" is used to refer to civil actions and "trial" to proceedings before a criminal court; hence the "civil suit" and the "criminal trial." A court proceeding that is neither a suit nor a trial is usually termed a "hearing."

[13] Under this system of classification *crimes* constitutes a third general heading. Thus acts that are injurious to the public or state are the subject of prosecution by the appropriate governmental unit. That this classification is imperfect is seen in the confusion that may result in attempting to classify an act that is at the same time a breach of contract and a tort, or simultaneously a crime and a tort.

of private property for public uses upon payment of fair compensation, represents another area of departure. Or again, actions seeking *declaratory judgments* are based neither upon an actual nor threatened wrong. In such actions a court is asked merely to settle a question of law; no specific relief is sought, and the court issues no decision that requires any specific action.

Civil Procedure. Civil cases may be divided into two general types, *suits at law* and *suits in equity.* The procedures involved in each are widely at variance even though the same courts, except in four states,[14] hear both types of cases.

Suits at Law. Procedures followed in civil suits at law vary from state to state, and there are variations depending upon the character of the proceeding, but the fundamental steps involved occur in every jurisdiction. A suit for damages, for example, involves procedures not found in an action to recover an item of property. Yet, enough similarity exists to warrant generalization.[15]

The first phase of a suit at law is termed the *pleadings.* Included are various steps involved in bringing a cause of action before a court and securing a response from the person being sued. The *plaintiff,* or person bringing the suit, requests, through his attorney, the clerk of the court having jurisdiction of the case to issue a *writ of summons* to the *defendant,* or person being sued. This writ, usually served by a sheriff, is a notice directing the defendant to appear in court at a specified time to answer charges brought by the plaintiff. The defendant then files, through his attorney, an *appearance* indicating that he will respond.

The next phase is the filing of the *declaration* by the plaintiff. The declaration, also known as a *complaint* or *petition,* sets forth in detail the cause of action. The defendant then files an *answer* to the charges, and the scene is set for argument. A defendant may *demur*— that is, admit the facts recited in the declaration, but contend that under the law they do not constitute a cause of action. Since the demurrer involves questions of law, the judge rules whether or not it is to be sustained or overruled. If the cause of action is held to be sufficient the suit continues; if the demurrer is upheld, the suit may

---

[14] Arkansas, Delaware, Mississippi, and Tennessee maintain separate courts of equity.

[15] Minor civil courts are excluded from this statement. In small claims courts, for example, grievances are typically heard by a judge acting without a jury. The judge hears both sides of a case and makes the decision. Similar procedures are followed in domestic relations and justice of the peace courts.

be dismissed, or as often happens the declaration is amended so that a valid cause of action is stated.

With the declaration and answer agreed upon, the litigants prepare to argue the issues in court. At this stage a settlement out of court may be reached. Pretrial conferences may also be held. Such conferences, now authorized in two-thirds of the states, are meetings of the contesting litigants before the court. Attempts are made to reach a settlement or at least come to an agreement on such things as simplification of issues, clarification of facts, limitation on the number of witnesses to be heard, and any other matter that might shorten the proceeding. Where used the pretrial conference is conceded to be generally successful, but on the whole it is still in its developmental stages.

Normally, suits at law are heard before juries. Some states permit such suits to be heard and decided by the judge alone if both sides agree to dispense with a jury. The great majority of cases, however, are argued before juries composed of twelve members although a smaller number may be used in some states. Jurors are selected from a jury list, with each prospective member being subject to questioning upon his qualifications to serve by the judge and attorneys for the plaintiff and defendant.

After the jury is chosen, the attorney for the plaintiff makes an opening statement before the court. He then calls his witnesses and introduces evidence to support his points. Counsel for the defense follows the same procedure. Counsel for each side questions, or *examines,* the witnesses he presents, and has the right to *cross-examine* the witnesses produced by the opposition. Following oral testimony and argument, counsel for the plaintiff, followed in turn by the defense, makes a concluding statement to the jury. In these *summing-up* addresses the opposing attorneys attempt to point out how and why they have proved their cases and where the opposition has failed.

With the final statements completed, the judge makes his *charge* to the jury. The charge consists of an explanation of the law involved in the suit. The jury then retires to the jury room to consider the facts and reach a *verdict,* or decision. The character of the verdict depends upon the nature of the suit and the issues involved. In a proceeding for damages, for example, the jury determines the extent of liability and may fix the amount of damages. Again, depending upon the issues, a jury may determine the custody of children, ownership of property, infringement of copyrights, or any of various other points. In any event, after the jury reports its verdict, it is discharged.

Although the suit is at an end when the decision of the jury is accepted by the court and an order or judgment announced, the litigation does not necessarily end there. A variety of legal motions may extend the proceeding even after the suit as such is over. Also, appeals frequently can be taken to higher courts, a process that delays final settlement.

Suits in Equity. Proceedings in equity differ from those in suits at law mainly in that juries usually are not used and oral testimony frequently is not taken in court. The first steps in bringing a suit in equity are much like those in other civil cases. The plaintiff, by means of a petition, requests the court to *enjoin,* or prohibit, the defendant from acting in a way that will injure or is injuring him. The answer of the defendant is then filed, the issues determined, and preparations are made for argument.

The suit is usually conducted before a judge, or *chancellor* as he is called in some states, although a jury may be used in some jurisdictions. Where juries are utilized their verdicts are advisory, and the judge may choose not to follow their findings. Oral testimony may be taken, but more often testimony is by *deposition,* that is, heard by an examiner outside the court, reduced to writing, and certified to the judge. Often a *special master* is appointed to inquire into a problem and make a report to the court. After any or all of these procedures have been followed, the judge considers the issues as a whole, arrives at a decision, and announces it in the form of a *decree.*

The most commonly used writ of a court of equity is the *injunction,* a judicial order directed to the defendant prohibiting him from performing a designated act, or from refusing to do so. There are many forms of the injunction, each tailored to meet the demands of a special situation, but perhaps the best known are the *temporary* and *permanent* types. The former may be issued upon complaint of the person seeking relief, but with an opportunity extended to the defendant to "show cause" why it should not be made permanent.

CRIMINAL LAW AND PROCEDURE

A necessary part of the over-all scheme of regulating and controlling human behavior for the good of society as a whole is the prohibition of certain socially undesirable actions. In effect society defines a variety of acts, designates them as "crimes," and forbids anyone to indulge in them. If a person should commit any of the criminal acts, he makes himself liable for the punishment that society prescribes.

The national government may, and does, designate many acts as crimes, but in the great majority of cases it is the state which prosecutes criminals. In a geographical area over which the national government has sole authority, such as the territories, the federal district of Washington, D.C., or military installations, criminal law is a matter of federal concern. Or again, violation of federal laws enacted under the powers delegated to the national government by the United States Constitution involves liability to the national government. For example, a person who evades payment of federal income taxes, transports stolen automobiles in interstate commerce, or burglarizes a post office is subject to prosecution in federal courts. Even so, the great bulk of criminal acts are violations of state laws and are therefore subject to prosecution by state or local authorities.

Crimes. A wide variety of acts are encompassed by the word "crime." It includes not only serious offenses, but also many trivial acts that entail the slightest of punishments. Actions designated as crimes range from murder and treason to such things as jaywalking and overparking. Inclusive as the term is, however, many socially undesirable acts are not crimes. They may be injurious to the rights of some persons, or contrary to generally accepted concepts of fairness, but unless an act is designated by law as a crime, it is not punishable as such.

Criminal acts are classified as falling into one of three categories: *treason, felonies,* or *misdemeanors.* The first of these, treason, consists of attacks upon the existence of a state or the nation. Treason is the only crime defined in the United States Constitution, which affirms that "Treason against the United States shall consist only in levying war against them, or in adhering to their enemies, giving them aid and comfort."[16] Identical or highly similar provisions are found in many state constitutions since treason may, of course, be directed against a single state as well as against the nation.

---

[16] Article III, Section 3, clause 1. This same clause further states that "No person shall be convicted of treason unless on the testimony of two witnesses to the same overt act or on confession in open court." It is interesting to note that the concept of treason followed in the United States is much narrower than that employed in Britain.

There is no precise definition of the term *felony*. It is a general term used to distinguish serious crimes from minor offenses. In many state constitutions or statutes a felony is designated as any offense on conviction of which the offender may be sentenced to death or imprisonment in the state penitentiary.[17] In any event a crime may be termed a felony only if it is clearly identified as such by law. Even though all states have defined as felonies the more serious crimes such as murder, rape, and arson, the list differs from one state to the next.

In contrast to the felony, a *misdemeanor* is generally understood to be a minor offense. It is commonly regarded as including all offenses that are neither felonies nor treason. As such it is a broad term encompassing literally thousands of offenses for which punishment consists of a small fine or a short term in a local jail. In a few jurisdictions a misdemeanor is defined as an offense, other than treason or a felony, for which the offender must be indicted. Where this distinction has been adopted a large number of petty offenses are not considered as either felonies or misdemeanors.

Criminal Procedure. The process by which accused persons are brought before criminal courts and their guilt or innocence determined is often long and complicated. Minor offenses may be dealt with in an almost summary fashion. A municipal, or other local court, usually operates without a jury, making it possible to adjudicate minor offenses in a very short time. Further, in some instances such courts may release an offender who posts a small sum as bail, and if the accused does not appear for trial the bail is forfeited as a "fine." More serious misdemeanors and felonies, however, involve a more drawn-out procedure. In each instance, it must be noted, the state or other governmental unit is the prosecutor, for all crimes are considered legally to have been committed against the government.

Detection or discovery of crimes is the first major step in criminal law enforcement. While a large number of persons are brought to trial on criminal charges, many undoubtedly are never apprehended. Those who are discovered may be taken into custody, or *arrested,* in a number of different ways. It is possible for any citizen to arrest a lawbreaker, but in practically all instances arrests are made by a law enforcement officer. If a crime is in the process of commission, or

---

[17] Federal law similarly states that offenses punishable by death or imprisonment for a term exceeding one year are felonies. 18 *U.S.C.* 1.

there is strong reason to suspect a person in the general area of having committed the crime, he may be arrested on the spot. Otherwise, a culprit is apprehended on authority of a *warrant of arrest* issued by a judge or magistrate. The warrant may be issued at the request of law enforcement officials or upon the *complaint* of a citizen.

After arrest on suspicion of a major crime, if there is not already a formal, legal accusation against the suspect, a *preliminary hearing* is usually held. This hearing is in no sense a trial. Its purpose is to determine whether there is sufficient probability of guilt to warrant holding the arrested person pending action of a grand jury or prosecuting attorney. Regardless of the decision of the magistrate or judge, the offender does not lose his right to *bail,* a right extended by state and federal constitutions, although bail may be denied persons accused of crimes punishable by the death penalty.

The accusation by virtue of which a person is taken into custody to stand trial for a major offense may precede or follow actual arrest and is in the form either of an *indictment* or *information.* An indictment is an accusation made by a grand jury, used in many states to decide whether, on the evidence, a person should be brought to trial. In some states the process of accusation has been simplified by replacing the indictment with the information which is merely a formal accusation drawn by the prosecuting attorney. Some states use both devices, reserving indictment for more serious crimes.

The *plea* of the accused person is heard at the *arraignment.* He appears before the court and listens to the indictment or information, after which he pleads "guilty" or "not guilty." If the plea is "guilty," the judge may immediately pronounce sentence. Often, however, witnesses are heard and evidence examined in order that the court may have a fuller understanding of all circumstances of the offense to insure imposition of a just sentence. If the prisoner refuses to admit guilt, preparations are then begun for holding a trial.

Criminal trial procedures vary in minor respects from state to state, but the fundamental steps involved are basically the same across the nation. First a jury is *impanelled,* or chosen, as in civil cases. Once the jury is agreed upon, arguments of counsel are heard, witnesses presented and examined, and evidence entered in much the same way that civil cases are conducted. After both the prosecution and defense *rest,* or conclude their efforts, the judge makes his charge to the jury, instructing them upon the legal aspects involved. The jury then retires to consider the evidence—to determine the facts—and reach a verdict. If the verdict is in favor of the defendant the decision is *acquittal;* if for the prosecution, a finding of guilty. In the event the jury cannot agree upon a decision it is said to be a *hung jury,* and the trial is void. After reporting its decision to the court, the jury is dismissed.

Sentence is usually imposed upon those found guilty of major crimes at a later date rather than immediately upon the conclusion of the trial. When the judge is required by law to impose a definite, fixed penalty the interval is not significant, but in most cases the judge must determine a penalty somewhere between a minimum and maximum set by law. In such cases the judge needs time to weigh all factors pertinent to an appropriate sentence.

Completion of the trial and sentencing does not necessarily end the process. The state is not permitted to appeal a verdict of acquittal, but a convicted person may, if there are grounds upon which he can do so, appeal to a higher court. Some states have enacted laws requiring review by the highest appellate court in the state of all cases resulting in imposition of the death penalty. Also, if it can be demonstrated that a federal law is involved, review by the United States Supreme Court may be attainable. Commonly, review by the federal court is sought on the grounds that the convicted person was denied due process of law as guaranteed by the Fourteenth Amendment of the United States Constitution.

REVIEW OF JUDICIAL DECISIONS

There are various ways in which a litigant can achieve review of his case by an appellate court, but the two most common methods are by *appeal* and the writ of *certiorari.* In fact, the vast majority of cases that are considered by appellate courts go up the judicial ladder by one or the other of these two methods. And of the two, perhaps as many as ninety to ninety-five per cent are reviewed by virtue of the writ of certiorari.

To most laymen the term appeal means simply the process by which a case is taken to a higher court, but in law it has a much more specific meaning. In the legal sense an appeal is a *right* which may by law be given to a losing litigant to enable him to obtain review. An appeal cannot be taken unless it is made specifically available by law, and since it is a matter of right, the appellate court cannot refuse review. If, for example, a statute provides that a person convicted of a felony may appeal his conviction, the appellate court has no choice but to review the case.

In contrast to the appeal, review by means of certiorari is discretionary with the appellate court. Technically, the writ is addressed to the lower court, instructing it to send up the transcript of proceedings for examination. After looking over the record the appellate court may decide that the litigant's request for review deserves a hearing. If so, review is granted and the court begins its consideration of the case. In respect to certiorari it is important to note that the litigant has no right to review; instead he *requests* it, and his request may or may not be granted.

On rare occasions a court itself may effect review through the process of *certification*. In this procedure an inferior court, if permitted by law to do so, may certify important questions to the state court of last resort. The higher court then renders opinions on them, perhaps in the process directing that the entire case be sent up for decision. Certification, it should be stressed, can be initiated only by a court and never by a party in controversy.

A form of review not used in the federal jurisdiction and gradually being eliminated in the states is the *writ of error*. As the name implies, it permits an appellate court to inquire into allegations that a trial court improperly interpreted and applied the law involved in a proceeding.

In addition to the foregoing methods of review, there are the *extraordinary* writs which may be available at times or in circumstances in which the remedies provided for in written law are considered by an appellate court to be inadequate. For example, if review by certiorari is not made available by statute, an appellate court may, if not forbidden to do so by law, grant an extraordinary writ of certiorari. Under similar circumstances review may be accomplished by means of extraordinary writs of *habeas corpus*, which challenge the sufficiency of the grounds upon which a person is held in custody, or *prohibition*, which request an appellate court to determine whether a trial court has jurisdiction of a cause.

In a few states efforts have been made to regularize the channels of review by abolishing the extraordinary writs and the various forms of statutory writs discussed above. In their place a general *writ of review* has been substituted. These efforts have not been particularly successful, however, because of the tendency of appellate courts to grant or deny review on the basis of criteria long associated with the traditional statutory and extraordinary writs.

SELECTED REFERENCES

Books:

Aumann, Francis B., *The Instrumentalities of Justice,* Ohio State University Press, Columbus, 1956.

Carpenter, William Seal, *Foundations of Modern Jurisprudence,* Appleton-Century-Crofts, New York, 1958.

Fellman, David, *The Defendant's Rights,* Rinehart and Co., New York, 1958.

Hohfield, Wesley N., *Fundamental Legal Conceptions,* Yale University Press, New Haven, Conn., 1964.

Karlen, Delmar, *The Citizen in Court,* Holt, Rinehart and Winston, New York, 1964.

Mayers, Lewis, *The American Legal System,* Harper and Brothers, New York, 1955.

Patterson, Edwin W., *Jurisprudence: Men and Ideas of the Law,* Foundation Press, Brooklyn, 1953.

Phillips, Orie L., and McCoy, Philbrick, *Conduct of Judges and Lawyers,* Parker and Co., Los Angeles, 1952.

Post, C. Gordon, *An Introduction to the Law,* Prentice-Hall, Englewood Cliffs, N.J., 1963.

Rosenblum, Victor G., *Law as a Political Instrument,* Random House, New York, 1955.

Articles:

Davis, Charles H., "The States and the Supreme Court," *American Bar Association Journal,* March 1959.

Hart, Henry M., Jr., "The Relations between State and Federal Law," *Columbia Law Review,* April 1954.

"Judicial Administration and the Common Man," Symposium, *The Annals,* May 1953.

"Lagging Justice," Symposium, *The Annals,* March 1960.

CHAPTER 9

The State Judiciary

Patterns of conduct in human society are controlled, and to some extent determined, through governmentally imposed rules called laws. But laws are intangible; it is only when they are given force that they take on material significance. That force is supplied as a result of a desire on the part of society, or a portion of it, to compel obedience to law. The mechanism through which the law is enforced and applied, or brought to bear on individuals and groups, both public and private, is the system of courts.

Courts and the people who staff them—known as the judiciary—are maintained by governments to perform the basic function of hearing and deciding legal controversies. No matter how much care is exercised in the writing of laws, inexactness and uncertainty seem always to occur to some extent. Consequently, disputes arise as to the meaning of the law, and the disputants, including individuals, groups, and the government itself, must look to the judiciary for the settlement of conflicts.

American judiciaries, both state and national, are derived from the English example. To be sure, there are many differences between American and British court systems today, but the resemblance was strong when the union jack flew in the colonial capitals. Divergence from the English system was fostered by the tendency toward self-rule during the colonial period, and with independence the differences became even more marked. The upper house of colonial legislatures served as appellate courts of last resort in the style of the English until general acceptance of separation of powers as a basic tenet in American government. Alteration of British legal concepts and modifications of judicial procedure were made in the colonial and, later, in the state courts. In short, the typical American judiciary may be considered an offspring of the British model, but the American environment has produced distinct individuality.

THE TASK OF THE JUDICIARY

Regardless of how high or low a court may be in the judicial structure, its basic function is the same as that of all courts—to resolve legal controversies. Again, it makes no difference how simple or how complex a case may be, the same basic process is employed in all courts: the facts must be determined, the law must be ascertained, and the law must be applied to the facts.[1] The function and process are the same; differences among courts and cases are due to such factors as complexity of the law, scope of court jurisdiction, involvement of facts, and status of litigants.

The task of the judiciary is also conditioned by a series of facts that distinguish the courts from the legislative and executive branches of government. According to the principle of separation of powers, all three branches are coordinate and equal. Each branch operates in its own separate sphere, exercising certain checks on the other two. In this scheme of government, however, the judiciary occupies a role limited in a manner unlike the restrictions placed on the legislature or executive.

A distinctive characteristic of courts is their lack of power to initiate judicial action. The judicial power is basically a passive thing that can be brought into play only when it is invoked by a litigant who complains to a court that his legal rights have been violated. Variations occur, for example, when an advisory opinion is sought, or a lower court certifies a question to a higher court. But the principle remains undisturbed—judicial power is at rest until it is set in motion by an individual, group, or government outside the judiciary.

Despite the importance of the judicial function, courts have no power to enforce their decisions. Introductory students are often surprised to learn that courts must depend entirely upon outside assistance for enforcement of their orders and decrees. Basically, the effectiveness of judicial decisions ultimately rests upon the degree of public confidence courts can command. In other words, the strength of the judiciary depends upon its prestige. From a more practical, realistic viewpoint, the effectiveness of judicial decisions is dependent upon the willingness of the executive branch to carry them out. About the closest approach to power to execute its decisions possessed

---

[1] Still one of the best discussions of the judicial function and the judicial process is W. F. Willoughby, *Principles of Judicial Administration,* Brookings Institution, 1929.

by a court occurs when it refuses to take jurisdiction of a cause or complaint based on a statute or rule previously held to be of no legal effect. Such action is not true enforcement of a decision, however; instead it is a new decision based on an older one.

The proper role of the judiciary as it relates to the content of public policy expressed in law traditionally has been that courts interpret and apply, but do not make, policy. In other words, the legislature, and to some extent the executive, perform the function of policymaking and the courts merely clarify and apply that policy in controversies that come before them. If all law were absolutely clear and all issues in every controversy equally unclouded, perhaps such a concept would be completely acceptable. Unfortunately, laws are often indefinite, uncertain, even conflicting, and courts must of necessity determine *what the law is*. In one view the court merely ascertains the meaning of the law as *intended* by the legislature; thus judicial interpretation is not an origination of policy. A more realistic view is that an ambiguous law has no certain meaning and that by interpretation courts give meaning to it, a form of policymaking which produces what is often characterized as "judicial legislation." Whether courts do, or do not, make policy in such instances is an interesting question, but one upon which theorists are not in agreement.[2]

In performing their duties courts follow established *rules of procedure* which cover all phases of judicial action. While it would seem that the courts themselves are best qualified to prescribe rules of procedure, only in the last few decades have they been permitted to share in their determination.[3] Although constitutions occasionally provide for a few general rules, ordinarily most such rules have been, and in many states still are established by the legislature, often on the basis of recommendation by the courts or by state bar associations. Over thirty years ago the results of this practice were characterized as "almost wholly bad,"[4] and attitudes on this point are about the same today. Judicial prescription of rules of procedure is generally

[2] Fred V. Cahill, Jr., *Judicial Legislation,* Ronald Press, New York, 1952, is a well documented treatment of the theoretical aspects of the "legislative function of the judiciary." See also the many sources there cited.

[3] In a few states the constitution vests the supreme court with authority to provide rules of procedure for all state courts. For example, the new Michigan Constitution which took effect in 1964, Article VI, Section 5, states that "The supreme court shall by general rules establish, modify, amend and simplify the practice and procedure in all courts of this state."

[4] Willoughby, *op. cit.,* p. 226.

regarded as preferable to legislative action inasmuch as the courts are more able to devise rules easily adaptable to changing situations. When a legislative body establishes rules, they have the status of statutes and are therefore more rigid; the failure of a court to follow them to the letter may constitute grounds for the invalidation of proceedings.

INDEPENDENCE OF THE JUDICIARY

The vast majority of public offices and institutions in America are operated on the basis of political partisanship. With few exceptions, mostly local, legislative bodies at all levels of government are expected to act, at least to some extent, on the basis of the party affiliations of their members. Public officers in most instances are chosen with a view to their party preferences, and no one is surprised when their actions take on partisan characteristics. In some states even judges are elected on partisan ballots. But whatever the method of choice, a judge and the court he presides over are expected to forego partisanship. The judiciary thus stands apart from the remainder of government in this important respect.

Objectivity in proceedings is another requirement that Americans impose upon the judiciary. Any judge, regardless of whether he sits on the highest court or the lowest, who favors one party to a controversy over another damages the prestige and integrity of his court. Isolated instances of such favoritism may lead to reversal of decisions, and repeated, habitual partiality normally leads to a judge's removal or failure of reelection or reappointment.

The necessity of removing the judicial function from the arena of partisanship was recognized long ago. In fact, the English bench was so regarded before the American governmental system began to take form, and subsequent acceptance of the concept on American soil represents another facet of the Anglo-Saxon heritage. A conviction that the courts should not be, nor should ever become, the tool of any public or private interest is firmly entrenched in the American system. Judges, for example, may not be sued for making allegedly "wrong" decisions. Any person who attempts to interfere with the conduct of proper judicial proceedings may be liable to criminal prosecution. The salaries of individual judges may not be reduced, or raised, during their terms of office. In short, the concept of an independent judiciary is implemented by measures designed to preserve every opportunity for objective, impartial application of the law.[5]

STATE AND FEDERAL COURT SYSTEMS

The system of courts in the United States is compartmentalized in line with the requirements of federalism. Just as it is possible to say that there is a national system of law and a legal system in each of the states, reference may also be made to the national judiciary and the fifty state court systems. The state judiciaries are on an equal plane in relation to the national, or federal, system, and each is a separate, distinct system of courts. However, since federal and state courts operate in the same geographical areas, and in some cases apply the same laws, points of contact and possibilities of conflict are numerous.

Although details are left largely to legislative determination, the basic division of judicial authority is provided by the United States Constitution. Article VI, Section 2, for example, provides that the Constitution, federal statutes, and treaties are the "supreme law of the land" which state as well as federal judges are bound to uphold. In the event state law conflicts with national law, the national law takes precedence. Article III provides that the judicial power of the United States extends to all cases arising under *national law* and to certain designated classes of cases.[6] Inasmuch as the national government, including the national courts, have only such powers as are delegated by the Constitution, all other power, judicial as well as legislative and executive, remains in the states.

It should be stressed that the placement of subjects within the jurisdiction of federal courts does not mean that those subjects must, of necessity, be dealt with *only* by federal courts. In fact, only when Congress, by law, gives the federal courts *exclusive* jurisdiction are the state courts without power to act. Examples of cases which can be heard only by federal courts include prosecutions for violations of federal criminal laws, controversies between states, patent and copyright cases, charges against ambassadors or consuls, and proceedings

---

[5] This is not to say that problems involving "fairness" or "justice" cannot arise. See below, the section entitled "Justice and the Law."

[6] As listed in Article III, Section 2, federal jurisdiction includes cases involving ambassadors, public ministers, and consuls; admiralty and maritime cases, controversies to which the United States is a party; controversies between states; cases between citizens of different states; and certain cases involving land grants.

in bankruptcy. In other proceedings state courts *may* hear cases involving federal law that litigants choose to bring before them.

In diversity of citizenship cases—that is, when a citizen of one state brings a civil action against a citizen of another state—the case may be brought in a state court. If the suit involves more than $10,000, the plaintiff may choose to bring action in a federal court regardless of whether any point of federal law is involved.[7] If the case is started in a state court, the defendant has the privilege of having it removed to a federal district court for trial. Removal privileges also exist in other cases, particularly in instances where violations of state criminal laws are charged against federal officers in the course of performing their official duties.

Frequently a single act may violate both a state and a federal criminal law. For example, a culprit who steals an automobile and takes it across a state boundary may be subject to two separate prosecutions—by the state for auto theft, and by the national government for transporting a stolen car in interstate commerce. In reality there is no conflict of jurisdiction; only a question of which government will prosecute first. National and state laws dealing with narcotics, prostitution, kidnaping, bootlegging, robbery of federally insured banks and the like, multiply the number of such dual offense cases. The order of prosecution is usually determined by informal agreement among law enforcement officials.

Review by the United States Supreme Court of state court decisions is restricted to those cases involving a *federal question*. This requirement means that a case must include an issue of federal law. Review is often sought on the grounds that state action has resulted in a denial of due process of law as guaranteed by the Fourteenth Amendment to the U.S. Constitution. The Supreme Court must then decide whether the federal question is "substantial," or important enough to warrant a review of the case.

It is interesting to note that *comity*, or judicial courtesy, has resulted in the understanding that federal courts will accept and apply the interpretations of state law made by a state supreme court. Thus if a state case is being reviewed by the United States Supreme Court and a question of the meaning of a provision of the state constitution or a state statute must be decided, and if there is no question of conflict with federal law, the meanings imparted by the state court are

---

[7] If less than $10,000 is at stake, the federal courts have no jurisdiction in the absence of an issue of federal law. Until 1958, when the amount was fixed at the current sum, the amount in controversy was set at a minimum of $3,000.

applied. Only if the state courts have not spoken do the federal courts interpret state law in such cases.

Organization and Jurisdiction of State Courts

To the casual observer the typical state court system is a bewildering maze. The array of courts, from the lowest to the highest, and including every tribunal within a state, may number several hundred, and in a few of the more populous states even several thousand. The average citizen is even less familiar with the judiciary in his state than with elective executive officers and members of the legislature.

An erroneous impression held by many individuals is that a state judiciary is divided into two broad classifications, "state" and "local" courts. Since some courts have broad, general jurisdiction and others are associated with localities, the derivation of the notion is understandable. However, in the American federal system all powers not exclusively delegated to the national government are *state* powers. As a result, all power exercised by any local government, or any branch of any local unit, is *state* power. Obviously then, every court in the state system exercises state power and consequently must be regarded formally as a state court.

The pattern of state court organization corresponds directly to the jurisdiction of the various courts. That is, the lower a court is in the judicial hierarchy, the more limited its powers are likely to be. In view of this fact it is possible to group courts into several categories for purposes of examination.

The Justice of the Peace. Centuries ago in medieval England the settlement of local, minor squabbles demanded a mode of judicial administration unhampered by the inconveniences of a highly centralized system. By way of meeting the problem, there was developed the office of justice of the peace, an appointive official with authority to settle petty civil cases and try minor criminal offenses without resort to higher courts. The justice usually was a respected townsman without legal training, but blessed with common sense. The system of local justices became a permanent part of the English system and was transported virtually unchanged to American soil, where it has remained in general use over 300 years.

Today the office of justice of the peace represents the lowest station in the judicial pattern of organization. Formerly an appointive office it has, since the days of Andrew Jackson, usually been filled by election. With few exceptions legal training still is not required, compensation is often in the form of fees collected from litigants,[8] and the term of office is short, usually two years. While the office was at one time found in virtually all localities, it is fast disappearing in urban areas and is now looked upon primarily as a method of *rural* judicial administration.

The jurisdiction of justices of the peace varies among the states, but in all instances it is very limited. He ordinarily has authority to settle civil disputes involving sums of no more than a few hundred dollars. His criminal jurisdiction is restricted to misdemeanor cases. Juries are rarely used in either type of proceeding. Other duties include such things as holding preliminary hearings, issuing various kinds of warrants, and performing marriage ceremonies. Decisions of the justice are commonly appealable to higher courts where the cases may be tried *de novo*—that is, complete, new proceedings may be had.

Decades ago when travel was difficult and communications were slow, justices of the peace served a useful purpose. They could settle petty cases without the expense and loss of time involved in carrying grievances to higher courts. Today, however, the need for the office has diminished, and it is beginning to take leave of the judicial scene. Critics of the system point out that the characteristic lack of required legal training results in the election of many persons totally unfit to administer the law. In fact, illiterates have been chosen on occasion, and the office is commonly filled by small-time politicians more interested in the political opportunities of the office than in its legal responsibilities. The justice also operates without a courtroom, with the result that proceedings may be, and usually are, conducted in any kind of surroundings. No clerical assistance is provided, thus forcing the justice to keep his own records. In the absence of statutory requirements, which is the usual case, this means that no permanent records are kept. Again, the justice is ordinarily left to his own devices, without supervision by any central judicial agency or court.

In view of the weaknesses of the office of justice of the peace as presently constituted, some states have adopted drastic reforms.

---

[8] When income depends entirely upon fees, the more cases a justice handles, the higher his income—an arrangement that invites activities calculated to produce more cases. Probably the best known abuse of this type is the "speed trap." Another lucrative method of increasing cases is the practice of "fee splitting," in which competing justices offer to split their fees with arresting officers who agree to bring cases to them.

Outright abolition of the office has been accomplished in some states, particularly in those which have reorganized their judiciaries in accordance with the principle of unification. In such instances the jurisdiction formerly exercised by justices of the peace has been absorbed by statewide courts of local general jurisdiction. A few states have limited the jurisdiction of justices, a few others have provided for their gradual elimination, and still others have undertaken various reforms calculated to improve the administration of the office. Suggestions for improvement include raising the qualifications to include legal training, furnishing clerical help, providing proper facilities, requiring records and reports, and establishing a supervisory agency. There are, of course, a great many justices of the peace who execute their duties honestly, capably, and fairly, but the worst features of the office coupled with the abuses that prevailed in the past mark it as the weakest link in the judicial chain.

Magistrates' Courts. The urban counterpart of the rural justice of the peace is the magistrate. The courts over which magistrates preside, sometimes termed "police courts," have about the same jurisdiction as the justice of the peace. The most significant contrasts are the urban setting of the magistrate and the resulting differences in character of the cases he handles. Depending upon whether a city maintains special courts for traffic violations, juvenile cases, small claims, and the like, the types of cases heard by a magistrate vary from place to place.

Magistrates' or police courts are subject to the same criticisms that have been directed at justices of the peace. In addition, it may be said that pressures and influences exerted upon magistrates by unethical politicians and other interested persons have been very apparent from time to time. Such conditions have contributed to a general feeling among some students of government that the magistrates' courts are even more in need of reform than the system of justice courts. In fact, one text writer has declared that magistrates "are rarely efficient and rarely honest."[9] This view is undoubtedly much too strong, but it is indicative of the need for improvement of these urban tribunals.

---

[9] W. Brooke Graves, *American State Government*, 4th ed., D. C. Heath Co., New York, 1953, p. 600. On the following page Dr. Graves declares that "In many cases the whole magistrate system is a veritable stench in the nostrils of decent people." He then goes on to cite the 1935 situation in Philadelphia where at one time twenty-seven of twenty-eight magistrates in the city were under indictment for various irregularities.

Municipal Courts. In larger cities across the nation the volume of cases to be tried has warranted the establishment of municipal courts. The jurisdiction of these courts is sufficiently broad to include many cases that might be heard by magistrates or the general trial courts of the state. In general the jurisdiction of a municipal court enables it to hear (1) civil cases involving amounts up to several thousand dollars, (2) misdemeanor cases, and (3) appeals from magistrates' courts if such courts are retained after the establishment of the municipal tribunals. The first municipal court in the United States was established in the city of Chicago in 1906. Today many of the heavily populated cities have followed the Chicago example by creating similar municipal courts.

The judicial climate of the municipal court is much more conducive to proper judicial administration than is the case with magistrates and justices of the peace. Elected to longer terms, the judges, who must be trained in the law, receive adequate salaries and are provided with courtrooms and clerical assistance. Consequently, more capable individuals are attracted to service as municipal judges.

Municipal courts are ostensibly unified, but some are organized on a geographical basis in much the same way as a non-unified state judiciary. Technically, however, there is only one court which has various divisions. Typically, specialized sections exist to hear cases according to whether they involve traffic offenses, domestic relations, small claims, juvenile delinquency, morals offenses, or some other general category. There is a chief judge, either appointed or elected to the position, who has authority to assign or transfer other judges within the court as heavy dockets in some divisions may require, or to take advantage of the special talents of some judges. In municipal courts organized on a geographical basis some specialization of divisions is possible, but to a much less adequate degree.

Other Local Courts. In those cities having municipal courts organized on a functional basis certain divisions hear only cases of a given type. All small claims, for example, would be heard before a single tribunal. Whether a unified municipal court system exists or not, other cities frequently have similar specialized courts. Thus a city or a county, regardless of size, may create special courts for small claims, probation of wills, juvenile delinquency, or disputes between married persons. No pattern of uniformity for the creation of such courts exists from state to state. In fact, unless a constitutional provision or statutory enactment prescribes the method by which localities must set up these bodies, each local government is largely free to create them as it chooses.

At the county level in many states are found courts that stand midway between justices of the peace and the general trial courts. Usually called *county courts,* they are presided over by a salaried, elective judge who in most cases serves for four years. Jurisdiction of the county court varies widely by state, scarcely being a court at all in some while exercising considerable authority in others. Where this court does function as an effective judicial instrument, it has jurisdiction that duplicates the authority of justices of the peace and overlaps to some extent the jurisdiction of general trial courts. In a general sense, a county court may be regarded as the rural counterpart of an urban municipal court.

The General Trial Courts. Every state in the Union is divided into judicial districts, each district usually composed of one or more counties.[10] In each district is a court in which most of the legal action brought under state law is begun. Known by a variety of titles,[11] these general trial courts are presided over by a single judge who is elected in almost three-fourths of the states to terms usually of four or six years. The judge, who must be a member of the bar, presides over scheduled sessions held in courtrooms located in the county courthouses.

Persons accused of major crimes are prosecuted in the general trial courts. The attorney who prosecutes in the name of the state is the locally elected prosecutor known variously as the district attorney, county attorney, or county prosecutor. Trials are heard only after formal accusation, whether by indictment or information, and except in rare instances when such procedure may be waived by the defendant, they are conducted before juries. As a rule, unless trial in some other court is specifically directed, violations of state criminal laws are tried in general trial courts.

There is no limit on the amount in controversy in civil suits heard by general trial courts. Suits at law involving millions of

---

[10] In Louisiana the *parish,* which corresponds to the county in other states, is used as the basic unit in drawing district lines. Connecticut abolished its counties in 1959 and now uses *towns* for judicial purposes, while in Alaska the *borough* is employed.

[11] Depending upon the state they are called County, Circuit, District, and Superior Courts, or Courts of Common Pleas.

dollars in property, claims, or damages are heard as well as minor suits that might have been brought in lower courts. Suits in equity, or chancery, are also heard although four states, Arkansas, Delaware, Mississippi, and Tennessee maintain separate tribunals for such actions.

Practically all the cases heard in general trial courts begin there. In other words, the jurisdiction of the courts is essentially *original*. However, a few cases reach such courts on appeal from lower tribunals. A person dissatisfied with the disposition of his case by a justice of the peace, for example, may ask for review by the general trial court. If statutes make such review possible, a trial *de novo*, or completely new trial, is held regardless of what proceedings may have been held in the lower court.

Decisions made by general trial judges are "final"—that is, all facts are determined as required by law, the law is applied to the facts thus found, and a decision reached. Any further action must be in the form of some type of review by an appellate court higher in the judicial hierarchy.

Intermediate Appellate Courts. In order to reduce the number of cases that must be reviewed by the state supreme court, fourteen states maintain intermediate courts of appeals.[12] These courts are composed of three or more judges, popularly elected in eleven states,[13] who serve during terms ranging from four to twelve years. In some instances there is technically only one intermediate appellate court which is divided into divisions or departments, each of which serves a prescribed geographical district.

The work of intermediate courts of appeals is almost completely a matter of reviewing cases heard originally in lower courts. Only in instances such as settling disputed elections is original jurisdiction exercised. As full-fledged appellate tribunals these courts do not hold trials. In both civil and criminal appeals the usual procedure followed by the judges in considering litigation is to hear oral arguments by attorneys, study the briefs submitted, and examine the

---

[12] The states in which intermediate appellate courts are found are Alabama, California, Florida, Georgia, Illinois, Indiana, Louisiana, Missouri, New Jersey, New York, Ohio, Pennsylvania, Tennessee, and Texas.

[13] In California and Missouri judges are appointed by the governor and at a later date run for election on the basis of their performance in office. New Jersey judges are appointed for seven years with reappointment for life. Appellate judges in New York are appointed by the governor from the number of previously elected trial court judges.

record of the case in the lower court. After consultation, a decision is reached by means of a majority vote. Exceptions exist, of course, but ordinarily an appeals court does not concern itself with the facts of a case, basing most decisions upon whether the law was correctly interpreted and applied. Review may be had of decisions by intermediate appellate courts, but in practice the decisions of such courts represent the final step in the judicial ladder for most cases.

The Supreme Court. Topping the hierarchy of every state court system is an appellate court of last resort usually called the state supreme court.[14] Established by the constitution in every state except New Hampshire, supreme courts are composed of *justices*[15] who range in number from three in Alaska, Delaware, and Nevada to nine in Iowa, Mississippi, Oklahoma, Texas, and Washington, with five or seven the usual size. In about three-fourths of the states justices are elected, with those of the remaining states selected by the governor or the legislature.[16] The terms vary from two years in Vermont to life tenure in Massachusetts and Rhode Island.

One member of a supreme court serves as *chief justice,* presiding over the court and supervising court business, but having no more voting power than the *associate justices.* Chief justices are chosen in a variety of ways, with no particular method predominant. A fifth are popularly elected to the position, and an equal number are appointed by governors. In Rhode Island, South Carolina, and Vermont they are legislatively chosen, and the remainder are so designated by reason of seniority, having the shortest term to serve, rotation of the position, choice by the court, or a combination of these. Tenure as chief justice depends largely on how the position is filled and ranges from the length of a term remaining, which can be very short, up to life in Massachusetts and Rhode Island.

---

[14] The highest court of Connecticut is called the Supreme Court of Errors. The title Supreme Judicial Court is used in Maine and Massachusetts. Virginia and West Virginia use the title Supreme Court of Appeals, and in Kentucky, Maryland and New York the court is called simply the Court of Appeals. Confusion may arise with respect to the court system of New York for in that state the term Supreme Court is used to designate the general trial courts, with the intermediate appellate courts designated as the Supreme Court, Appellate Division.

[15] The use of the term "justice" as contrasted with "judge" implies nothing more than rank and prestige of office. The work done by a justice and a judge is virtually the same, the only differences stemming from the jurisdiction of the courts on which they sit.

[16] In some states the method of choosing the judges of appellate courts is too complex to warrant generalization. See below, the section entitled "Judges."

All state courts of last resort have jurisdiction to review any civil case that may be brought before them. Full jurisdiction to hear criminal appeals is vested in each of the supreme courts except in Oklahoma and Texas where separate three-judge courts of criminal appeals exercise that authority. The original jurisdiction of supreme courts is severely restricted, about two-thirds of them being empowered to issue original writs in special types of cases. A supreme court may also have a few advisory and administrative functions, but the great bulk of its time and effort is devoted to the consideration of cases before it for review.

Supreme court decisions are written and published in an official series of volumes called a *reporter*.[17] Sometimes a decision consists of nothing more than a title, docket number, and a few words on the disposal of the case. Frequently, lengthy opinions are written, each of which is recorded verbatim. A *majority opinion* sets forth reasons for the court's action and contains the decision of the tribunal. If a justice disagrees with all or some of the reasons cited in the majority opinion, but feels that the decision is correct, he may write a *concurring opinion*. Justices who disagree with the decision of the majority often write *dissenting opinions*. All opinions are reported, but the majority opinion settles the issues involved.

For most cases, decision by a state supreme court marks the end of litigation. If a case does not involve some point of federal law, the "federal question" discussed earlier, creating the possibility of review by the United States Supreme Court, the only chance for alteration of a decision is for the court to reverse itself. The court might, for example, grant what is known as a *rehearing*. On the basis of new or further argument at a rehearing the Court may change all or part of a previous decision, but this occurs only on extremely rare occasions.

JUDGES

The men who sit on the bench during sessions of courts—the judges and justices—perform a highly specialized, vital function. It is their job to know the law and to apply it. When presiding they have full charge of their courtrooms. They determine, within the context of the rules of procedure, the course of proceedings. It is

---

[17] In some states all or part of the opinions rendered by intermediate appellate courts are reported in a separate series of volumes.

both their function and their responsibility to maintain a dignified court where the law is fairly and impartially applied.

Qualifications. No greater range in the qualifications required of public officers is found among the states than in those demanded of appellate and general trial court judges. In Connecticut, Massachusetts, and New Hampshire there are no legal qualifications whatever, while in New Jersey judges must be United States citizens, state residents for ten years, at least thirty-one years old, and members of the bar with ten years of legal experience. In general, the imposition of such qualifications is intended to limit judicial selection to citizens of mature years who are experienced in legal matters. In any event, the imposition of legal qualifications, or lack of them, at the general trial court level and above has not been of great concern. The nature of the work of judges at these levels is such that only competent persons could perform it successfully. Even in those states with few or no qualifications the record of such judges has, as a whole, not been open to serious criticism.

Lack of qualifications for judges of minor, local courts—in contrast to the higher offices—produces glaring weaknesses in the judicial system of virtually every state. In fact, the great majority of minor judges have had no legal training at all except the experience gained sitting as judges! The typical citizen would not think of calling in a neighbor to repair his television set, but apparently is willing for him to sit in judgment of frequently important legal controversies. Such a system leads to numerous examples of gross incompetency among justices of the peace, magistrates, and other local judicial officers. As indicated earlier, some larger cities have taken steps to improve their courts, but most minor judicial offices are still administered by untrained amateurs.

Selection of Judges. Several methods are employed in the states for the selection of judges. Most are popularly elected, some are appointed by governors, some are selected by legislatures, and others are originally appointed with continuation in office dependent upon later election. As is the case with most other types of public officials, there are wide variations among the states as well as striking differences in methods used within a single state.

The most widely used method in the choice of judges is popular election. Justices of most of the state supreme courts as well as those who fill the lowest ranking positions of a state judiciary are chosen in this manner. The doctrine of separation of powers and the democratic nature of elections are fundamental propositions which support the elective mode of choice. However, since judgeships are not representative in character and involve a highly specialized function, students of government generally feel that the selection of judges should not be entrusted to the vagaries of public election. Instead, to insure competence on the bench, judges ought to be appointed on the basis of demonstrated ability in the field of law. In reality the over-all performance records of elective general trial court and appellate judges makes it difficult to maintain this position. Still, the qualities of a good judge and a good candidate are not usually found in the same individual. On the basis of this reasoning, appointment is to be preferred over election.

A half dozen states—Delaware, Hawaii, Maine, Massachusetts, New Hampshire, and New Jersey—empower the governor to choose all higher court judges subject to the approval of the senate, or in the New England states, the council. In Connecticut, Rhode Island, South Carolina, Vermont, and Virginia these positions are filled by legislative selection. Six other states—Alaska, California, Iowa, Kansas, Missouri, and Nebraska—utilize plans of judicial selection that involve gubernatorial appointment followed by popular election after a period in office.

The California Plan. The plan of judicial selection instituted by means of a 1934 constitutional amendment in California is an attempt to combine the best features both of appointment and election.[18] In that state incumbent judges of the supreme court and the district courts of appeals may not be opposed for re-election. Instead, a judge declares his candidacy to succeed himself and runs on the basis of his performance in office. If the voters approve his record and vote to retain him, he is re-elected to another term. In the event a judge is not re-elected, or should retire, resign, or be removed from office, the vacancy is filled by gubernatorial appointment subject to approval by a commission composed of the chief justice of the supreme court, the attorney general, and a judge of the court on

---

[18] California Constitution, Article VI, Section 26. It is interesting to note that the plan of judicial selection recommended by the Model State Constitution, Article VI, Section 6.04, is practically the same as that used in New Jersey—appointment by the governor to an initial term of seven years, subject to legislative confirmation, with reappointment for life during good behavior. As an alternative, the Model Constitution, Subsection 6.04(a), suggests an approximation of the California Plan.

which the appointee will serve. After taking office a new appointee serves until the next general election when he must go before the voters on the basis of his record in office. Approval by the voters means that a newly appointed justice of the supreme court or of a district court may complete a twelve-year term. The plan does not apply to the superior courts, the general trial courts found in each county, unless by local option it is adopted by the voters.

Variation of the Plan in Other States. In 1940 the voters of Missouri approved a constitutional amendment, carried over in the Constitution of 1945, for a plan of judicial selection almost identical to that used in California.[19] The principal differences are that the governor must make each appointment from a list of three nominees submitted to him by a commission composed of the chief justice, three attorneys chosen by the organized bar, and three laymen selected by the governor; the plan is made applicable to the two most populous counties; and election to determine retention in office may not come earlier than one year after appointment. Kansans voted in 1958 to adopt a similar plan by adding to the constitution provision for a judicial selection procedure that incorporates the principal features of the Missouri approach.[20] According to the Alaska Constitution, judges of the higher courts are selected by the governor from "two or more persons nominated by the judicial council."[21] Judicial selection in Iowa was altered by a 1962 constitutional amendment which established a plan similar to that used in Missouri. The most recent adoption occurred in Nebraska where the voters, at the general election of November, 1962, approved an amendment which revised the system of choosing judges.

It is only on the basis of experience in California and Missouri that the appointment-election method of judicial selection can be evaluated, for the more recent variations have had too little opportunity to prove themselves. The California and Missouri systems have been in use only twenty to thirty years, a rather brief period in view of the fact that in both states judges affected by the plans of selection serve for twelve years. Nevertheless, there is general agreement that the combination of executive opportunity to choose qualified people with the power of the people to reject candidates at the polls has worked well.

---

[19] Missouri Constitution, Article V, Section 29.
[20] Kansas Constitution, Article III, Section 2.
[21] Article IV, Section 5. Judicial councils are discussed later in the chapter.

Compensation. As a group, state supreme court judges are probably the best paid of state officials. It is true that about thirty states have fixed salaries of their supreme court justices at figures varying from $10,500 to $20,000, but in those states such salaries are among the highest available. Half the states have set the pay of these judges between $20,000 and $25,000, and in the remainder salaries range up to $32,500 in Pennsylvania and $39,000 in New York. Intermediate appellate judges receive somewhat lower compensation, varying from $15,500 in Alabama to New York's high of $36,500. At the general trial court level, variations are more marked, the lowest salary of $6,125 being received by some Massachusetts district judges while in New York a salary of $34,500 is possible. The chief judge of a multijudge court usually is paid an additional amount ranging from $500 to $2,500 depending upon the state.

The salaries of local judges are too varied to permit more than the generalization that in some states their pay is adequate, particularly in California, Illinois, Massachusetts, New Jersey, New York, and Pennsylvania. Generally, however, salaries of local judicial personnel are low. Among the worst features of local judiciaries is the practice still followed in some states of providing no income for justices of the peace other than what they can earn in fees. Obviously such an arrangement is an invitation to abuse and corruption.

Terms. The longest terms of office served by any state public officials as a group are those of judges of courts of last resort. Supreme court justices of Massachusetts and Rhode Island are appointed for life; those in New Jersey may be reappointed for life after serving a seven-year term; and in New Hampshire judges of the high court serve until they reach the age of seventy. In other states terms range from two years in Vermont to twenty-one in Pennsylvania with a six-year term occurring most frequently. Terms of intermediate appellate judges range from a low of four years in Indiana to twelve in California, Louisiana, and Missouri. From the general trial court level on down, variations in tenure are extremely broad. Justices of the peace and magistrates are everywhere limited to terms of two to six years. Judges of lower courts in Massachusetts, New Hampshire, and with some exceptions in Rhode Island, enjoy the same tenure as their brethren on the state supreme court. In general, however, such judges serve for terms of four or six years.

Retirement. All states now have systems enabling judges of general trial and higher courts to retire after service on the bench. About a third of the states permit judges to retire at any age if they have served for long periods or accept reduced pensions, but in most instances the minimum retirement age is sixty, sixty-five, or seventy. Retirement is usually voluntary although a few states have made it compulsory. In over forty states a minimum period of service, from five to thirty years depending upon the state and the options available, must be rendered. The systems of a fourth of the states do not require the judges to make contributions to retirement funds, and in a few others non-contributory options are available. The amounts received by retired judges are determined, as in most retirement systems, in accordance with such factors as age at retirement, length of service, position or rank held, past salary levels, and the amount of contributions made while in office.

Removal of Judges. Occasionally the incompetence, disability, or even dishonesty of a judge leads to demands that he be removed from his position. Death, resignation, retirement, or failure of a judge to win re-election or reappointment may solve the problem, but should such a judge insist upon remaining in office one or more methods for removing him are available in each state. In almost all states judges may be impeached, but since the process is clumsy, time-consuming, and tends to be political in nature, it is rarely used.[22] Another method of removing judges, also infrequently utilized, is termed *legislative address*. Found in about thirty states, this process requires a resolution directing the removal of a judge to be passed by an extraordinary majority of both legislative houses. No trial is involved. The governor simply declares the office vacant following the legislative action. In eight states judges may be removed by the *recall* process.[23] The recall, however, is regarded by many as unsuited to the removal of judges because it places in the hands of the people a means of recrimination for unpopular legal decisions.[24]

---

[22] Impeachment as such does not exist in Oregon.

[23] Arizona, California, Colorado, Kansas, Nevada, North Dakota, Oregon, and Wisconsin. For general discussion of the recall, see Chapter 13, "Direct Popular Action: Initiative, Referendum, and Recall."

[24] At the time Arizona became a state President Taft refused to approve the resolution of admission until such a provision was removed from the proposed state constitution. Arizona complied, but after admission amended its basic document to restore the provision for recall of judges.

To date, argument over use of the recall as applied to judges has been largely academic since it has not been used against judges of higher courts. In a few states judges may be removed from office as a result of action by higher courts or special boards of inquiry. In Alaska and Hawaii, for example, an incapacitated supreme court justice may be retired by the governor upon the recommendation of a three-man board appointed by the governor to investigate the disability of a judge. Lower court judges in Alaska may be ousted by a majority vote of the Supreme Court acting on the recommendations of the judicial council. New Jersey's lower court judges are similarly subject to removal by the state court of last resort.

A unique method of removing judges exists in New York. By virtue of a 1947 constitutional amendment judges may be removed or retired by the action of a *court on the judiciary*. This court is an *ex officio* body composed of the chief judge and senior associate judge of the court of appeals and one justice selected by his colleagues in each of the four intermediate appellate court divisions. Action to remove a judge may be initiated by the chief judge of the court of appeals, the governor, the presiding justice of any intermediate appellate division, the judicial council, or the executive committee of the state bar association. A judge to be tried in the court may still be impeached on the same charges if such proceedings are begun within thirty days after the court on the judiciary convenes and prefers charges. If acquitted of the impeachment charges, no further action may be taken by the court. To date the court has been convened three times, resulting once in reprimands, and on the other two occasions in removal of judges from their posts.

Removing a judge from office is a drastic step, one that is both delicate and dangerous. The question of proper grounds for removal can be highly sensitive. Where a judge proves to be flagrantly dishonest or unethical, there is no doubt that his removal is justifiable. But what of charges of incompetence or a record that is politically unpopular? Who is to assess incompetency? Can removal *ever* be justified on political grounds? In view of these points, difficult methods of removal are to be preferred to those which would be expeditious. Judicial independence requires that judges be secure from hasty, ill-advised demands for ouster, but at the same time the methods of removal currently available tend to protect incompetents as well as skilled judges.

The problem of forcing a patently incompetent or dishonest

judge out of office against his will has not been resolved satisfactorily. Impeachment, legislative address, and recall are all unwieldy processes that are seldom invoked. Too often the only practicable course is to wait until the term of an incompetent judge expires and then hope he is not re-elected. Where appointment is the method of selection, a new judge can, of course, be chosen, but where the judge has resort to the polls he may succeed in gaining another term. It would appear that the best solution lies in a method similar to the one outlined in the Alaska Constitution whereby inquiry into the fitness of a judge may be made by a qualified group, with the final decision to remove lodged in the governor or supreme court. Such a method would be both responsive and responsible.

Other Court Personnel. Nearly everyone is familiar enough with judicial procedure and court organization to be generally aware of the roles of the judge and the jury. The functions of attorneys, both for the prosecution and defense, are also fairly well understood. Not so well known are the lesser officials who form the staff of a court. The principal administrative officer of a court is the clerk. The clerk, who is an elective officer in many states, may have several assistants depending upon the size and nature of the court. The court stenographer is the individual responsible for a verbatim transcript of the proceedings. The sergeant-at-arms maintains order during court sessions. In criminal cases a bailiff has charge of prisoners appearing in court. In equity cases, referees or special masters are often appointed by the judges to inquire into and report to the court on various problems associated with a case. Specialists such as psychiatrists and probation officers may be appointed by the judge. Finally, law-enforcement officials such as sheriffs, municipal police, and their assistants provide protection and assistance in process-serving. The total number of persons who staff a court depends, of course, upon the court. The justice of the peace, for example, functions alone in virtually all cases that come before him, while the staff of a general trial or supreme court may be quite large.

THE JURY SYSTEM

The Bill of Rights of every state constitution contains a guarantee that persons brought to trial on criminal charges are entitled to a trial by jury. The use of juries in civil cases is also preserved although some basic documents provide that the right exists only if a designated sum—usually several hundred dollars—is at stake. As with so many other facets of the American system of government, the jury system is derived from England.

Types of Juries. Two basic types of juries are used today, the *grand jury* and the *petit jury.* The function of a grand jury is to determine whether there is sufficient probability of guilt to bring a person to trial. Obviously it is used only in criminal proceedings. The petit jury, used in both civil and criminal proceedings, is the body which hears and determines the facts at the time a case is tried. There is no direct connection whatever between the two types. In fact, a person who served on a grand jury that ordered an accused individual to be tried would not be permitted to sit as a member of the petit jury used at the trial of the accused.

Grand juries are composed of six to twenty-three persons selected by lot to serve for a prescribed period of time. New juries may be chosen every few weeks or months, but it is common in sparsely settled, peaceful areas for a single, annual jury to suffice. The members of a grand jury deliberate in secret, usually considering only the evidence presented to them by the prosecuting attorney. Decisions of a grand jury are reached by majority vote and are reported by the foreman to the judge in whose court the accused persons will be tried. Grand juries accuse by means of a *true bill of indictment,* or by *presentment* if accusation rests on evidence turned up by initiative of the jury. After its decisions are reported, a grand jury is dismissed.

Experience has shown the grand jury to be cumbersome. It adds to the already excessive delay and expense of enforcing criminal laws. Consequently, some states have virtually replaced the grand jury with a much simpler process by which the prosecuting attorney files a formal accusation known as an *information* with the clerk of the court in which trial is to be held. Indictment by grand jury is still generally used in connection with major offenses, but in the majority of states the information is used for all lesser crimes.

In contrast to the grand jury, the function of the petit or trial jury is to hear and determine all the facts in civil and criminal trials. In a few instances they may have some authority to apply the law, as in capital criminal cases when the failure of a jury to recommend mercy means a mandatory imposition of the death penalty. Juries in some states have power to reduce a charge as when a person tried for *first*-degree murder is convicted of *second*-degree murder. Or, as in Oregon, the constitution itself may vest the jury with authority usually reserved to the judge.[25] In the great majority of instances, however, the jury is restricted to fact-finding.

Under the common law, petit juries consisted of twelve persons who were required to reach unanimous agreement before a verdict could be returned. Today the character of the jury is somewhat altered. Unanimous decisions by twelve-member juries are still required in the trial of major crimes, but for lesser offenses and in civil suits smaller juries reaching decisions by majority vote are common. Misdemeanor cases and civil proceedings involving trifling sums ordinarily are heard before juries only on demand of the parties. Many states permit even major crimes to be tried solely by a judge if the accused, being fully informed of his rights, waives his right to trial by jury.

Selection and Qualifications of Jurors. Juries are always chosen by lot. There are as many different methods of choice as there are states, but there is enough similarity from state to state to permit generalization. At least once a year, and usually oftener, a jury list is prepared by a legally designated local officer or agency—the sheriff, judge, clerk of a court, county governing board, special jury commissioners, or in New England, officers of the towns. The lists are of considerable length and, depending upon the state, may be prepared from voter registration books or tax assessor's rolls. From these lists names are chosen at random whenever jurors are needed. Whenever a judge needs a jury, he informs the designated official who draws slips of paper bearing names or numbered tags from a box. Persons thus selected for jury duty are summoned by the sheriff; some of those called are excused if good reason is given; and the names of the remainder are retained. The list of persons thus determined as eligible for jury service is called the *panel of veniremen*.

In each state the qualifications of jurors are set forth in statutes. Those under twenty-one or over sixty or seventy are excluded. Literacy, residence, education, prior jury service, health, citizenship, eligibility to vote, and ability to speak and understand English are

---

[25] Article I, Section 16: ". . . In all criminal cases whatever, the jury shall have the right to determine the law, and the facts under the direction of the court as to the law, and the right of new trial, as in civil cases."

qualifications found in all or part of the states. Also, certain groups of individuals are by law rendered ineligible for jury service. In many states those engaged in professions, such as physicians, lawyers, teachers, druggists, or in businesses vital to the public interest are excused. Many governmental officials are similarly excluded. In one-fourth of the states women are barred as jurors, and individuals to whom jury duty would entail extreme hardship are not required to serve.

Criticism and Suggestions for Improvement. When the jury system began to form in ancient England, jurors were selected because they were familiar with the persons and issues involved in criminal or civil cases. It was felt that such persons, being better informed, would be able to reach intelligent verdicts. By degrees the character of the jury was altered until by the fifteenth century the theory followed today prevailed: that a juror should be completely uninformed as to the facts and principals in a case, resulting in greater objectivity. The theory is excellent, but when put into practice it does not always work. Too often an uninformed jury at the beginning of a trial is little more than a poorly informed and confused group at the conclusion of proceedings. There is no assurance that a random aggregation of twelve citizens is capable, particularly in a complicated case, of reaching an intelligent, fair verdict. Time and again jurors have been unduly influenced by such factors as a desire to get home early, keeping an appointment on time, the persuasive personality of a litigant, and even the flip of a coin!

Another weakness in the jury system is the fact that jurors are poorly paid. Although jury service is a civic duty and compensation should not be emphasized, no amount of good theory can offset the fact that when it costs money to be a good citizen, many persons will dodge the obligation. Compensation for jury service is generally fixed at only a few dollars a day. At these rates a gainfully employed person would lose daily, in unearned income, about five to twenty times the amount received for jury service. Such sacrifice certainly does not promote willingness to serve.

The calibre of jury personnel is also lowered in that large groups of people who would be highly desirable as jurors are not required to serve. Many professional and business men are exempted. Teachers usually are not required to serve, resulting in the loss across the nation of several hundred thousand prospective jurors of greater than average intelligence. When to this total are added the great numbers of others excepted, the system is literally denied the services of millions whose performances as jurors would be valuable.

Numerous suggestions have been made to improve the jury system, most of which have been implemented to a limited degree. Outright abolition of jury trials, for example, has been accomplished in certain technical fields by empowering expert administrative boards and commissioners to resolve legal controversies. Public utilities commissions, civil service boards, licensing bodies and similar agencies are able to handle many situations which, if litigated in the regular courts, would require juries. Ordinarily, a petit jury consists of twelve persons, but many states now have statutes, and in some cases constitutional provisions, which permit use of a smaller number, particularly in civil proceedings. Over half the states have abandoned the idea that juries must agree unanimously in civil cases, requiring instead an extraordinary majority such as three-fourths or five-sixths. In all states the right to jury trial can be waived in minor cases, and in a third of the states even in trials on felony charges. A promising development within the jury system is the "blue ribbon" jury used in New York. When a judge in that state feels that a case is particularly complex or otherwise requires a jury of superior quality, he may direct that the jury be drawn from a special panel consisting of persons of education and ability, a process that has been approved by the United States Supreme Court.[26]

JUDICIAL REVIEW

One of the most potent weapons in the arsenal of the judiciary is judicial review, the power to declare null and void laws that are contrary to constitutional provisions. Since 1803, when John Marshall, Chief Justice of the United States, handed down the opinion of *Marbury* v. *Madison*,[27] the power has been a mainstay of federal courts. Many persons credit Marshall with origination of the doctrine, and indeed he is responsible for its introduction at the national level, but more than a dozen precedents in decisions of colonial and state courts predated his historic opinion. Colonial cases involving judicial review date from the early eighteenth century, and the

---

[26] *Fay* v. *New York,* 332 U.S. 261 (1947).
[27] 1 Cranch 137.

doctrine was applied or discussed in state court opinions prior to Marshall's enunciation.[28]

No mention is made of the doctrine of judicial review in the United States Constitution, although provision for its use is made in some state constitutions. But whether specifically provided for or not, the courts of all states are empowered to invoke the doctrine in cases brought before them. Frequently, laws that are challenged on constitutional grounds cause almost even splits among justices, leading to the criticism that, in effect, the opinions of one or two justices can spell the difference between validity and unconstitutionality. It is strongly felt in some quarters that before a law is rendered null and void, it should be clearly and unmistakably beyond the pale of legality. Consequently in three states—Nebraska, North Dakota, and Ohio—findings of unconstitutionality must be supported by extraordinary majorities.[29]

The doctrine of judicial review embraces three distinct branches: *national, federal,* and *state.*[30] *National* judicial review refers to the power of all courts, both federal and state, to judge the validity of national laws under the national Constitution. *Marbury* v. *Madison,* the first federal case in which an act of Congress was invalidated, is an example of national judicial review. *Federal* judicial review entails the power and duty of all courts, both federal and state, to give precedence to national laws as required by Article VI of the United States Constitution. Thus if any provision of state law should be in conflict with any federal law, the federal law prevails. Federal judicial review is well illustrated by recent decisions of the United States Supreme Court declaring invalid state laws which unfairly apportion representation in the state legislatures. *State* judicial review relates to the power of state courts to assess the constitutionality of state laws under the respective state constitutions. Among the fifty states there are numerous instances of state laws being set aside on constitutional grounds. In all cases involving judicial review of federal law the United States Supreme Court is the final arbiter on

---

[28] See Edward S. Corwin, *The Establishment of Judicial Review,* Princeton University Press, 1930; and Charles G. Haines, *The American Doctrine of Judicial Supremacy,* rev. ed., University of California Press, 1932.

[29] The Nebraska Constitution, Article V, Section 2, requires a majority of five of the seven supreme court justices; the North Dakota Constitution, Article IV, Section 89, sets the majority at four of five; and the Ohio Constitution, Article IV, Section 2, requires that six of the seven justices concur in findings of unconstitutionality.

[30] This discussion of the branches of judicial review is based on Edward S. Corwin, "Judicial Review," *Encyclopedia of the Social Sciences,* vol. 8, pp. 457–462 (1932).

review. With regard to state judicial review, decisions of state courts are respected by the national judiciary if and when the state rulings arise in actions before federal tribunals.

Considered in terms of the many thousands of statutes, both state and federal, that have been enacted since the beginning of the Union, relatively few have been stricken down by means of judicial review. Almost ninety provisions of federal law and about seven hundred and fifty state laws have been voided by the national supreme court. No count has been made of the number of state statutes voided by state courts. Laws thus invalidated are not expunged from the statute books. They remain in print until repealed or deleted by codifiers or revisors, but after being found contrary to higher law they lose their legal force, and courts will not hear future cases based upon them.

ADVISORY OPINIONS

Ordinarily, courts do no act upon issues unless they arise in a case or controversy. Contrary to usual practice, the supreme courts in eleven states are authorized to render advisory opinions. The constitutions of Colorado, Maine, Massachusetts, Michigan, New Hampshire, and Rhode Island provide that the governor or either house of the legislature may obtain advice. In Florida and South Dakota only the governor enjoys this constitutional privilege. Except in Michigan the court in each of these states is obligated to respond. The governor of Delaware, and in Alabama both the governor and legislature, may request advisory opinions as a result of statutory authorization. In compliance with long-standing custom the supreme court of North Carolina renders opinions when asked to do so by the governor or either house of the legislature.

There are several advantages in the use of advisory opinions. When obtained by the legislature, they may serve to deter the enactment of statutes of questionable constitutionality. The governor of a state also has at hand a useful guide to help him decide whether to sign or veto legislation about which he has constitutional doubts, or whether certain laws already enacted are in fact enforceable. Advisory opinions, as the name indicates, are *advisory* only except in Colorado where they have the legal force of a supreme court decision. Even though a supreme court advisory opinion may serve a utilitarian purpose, it is generally disapproved because the function is properly one which should be performed by an attorney general.

DECLARATORY JUDGMENTS

Beginning with New Jersey in 1915, practically all states have enacted legislation enabling courts to render declaratory judgments. Unlike an ordinary suit at law or in equity, the declaratory judgment does not require a party to allege an actual or impending legal wrong. Instead, all that is required is that there be a controversy between parties as to their respective rights under a legal instrument such as a statute, ordinance, will, deed, or contract. The judgments, which are legally binding upon the parties involved, are available *before* any actual wrong is committed. They serve, therefore, to prevent injury and the needless costs and delay that might be occasioned by a lawsuit.

Declaratory judgments and advisory opinions are often confused since both are designed to forestall subsequent legal difficulties. As indicated earlier, however, the advisory opinion is generally not binding and is available only to governors and legislative bodies. The declaratory judgment, on the other hand, resembles a lawsuit in that *any* party to a controversy can petition for it and the resulting declaration is binding. The usefulness and desirability of the declaratory judgment is readily attested by its nearly universal use among the states and adoption by the federal government in 1934.[31]

CONCILIATION AND ARBITRATION

One of the best ways to prevent crowded court dockets is to provide some means of settling legal arguments before they are taken to court. Conciliation, "the process whereby a third party seeks to secure an agreement between the two parties to a controversy in respect to its settlement," is one method of doing so. Another is arbitration, "the process whereby the parties agree to refer the matter to a third party and abide by his decision."[32] The principal difference between the two procedures is that in arbitration the decision reached is not only binding upon contending parties, but it is also enforceable in a court of law in the same way as a court judgment.

Both conciliation and arbitration are generally regarded as highly

---

[31] The nature and uses of the declaratory judgment are discussed fully and authoritatively by its principal advocate over the years, Edwin M. Borchard, in his *Declaratory Judgments,* 2nd ed., Banks-Baldwin, Cleveland, 1941, and in "The Next Step Beyond Equity—The Declaratory Action," *University of Chicago Law Review,* February 1946.

[32] Willoughby, *op. cit.,* p. 40.

desirable methods of settling legal controversies, but neither has been widely used in the United States. Conciliation, in particular, has failed to win general acceptance as a method of settling disputes. It has been successfully used in a few large cities, beginning with Cleveland in 1913, in conjunction with the operation of municipal courts, but has not been used in other applications to any significant degree. Although it offers a way to avoid the delays and expense of a lawsuit, its dependence upon the willingness of contesting parties to abide by the conditions of settlement and the lack of any coercive restraints to enforce terms of agreement are weaknesses that inhibit widespread adoption. Arbitration is much more common, at least insofar as statutory adoptions are concerned. In practically all states arbitration laws have been enacted, although in most instances they are inadequate and, consequently, infrequently invoked. The most successful application of arbitration has occurred in the settlement of disputes between organized labor and management, but even here the incidence of application is comparatively low.

JUDICIAL COUNCILS

Few of today's state court systems are the result of consciously drafted plans for efficient organization. When New Jersey's Constitution of 1948 was being drafted, the court system was designed to achieve functional and organizational unity. But in most states courts have been added and altered as required, with the result that integration is largely lacking. Consequently, excessive delay and cost, overlapping jurisdictions, and crowded dockets are common. It is to the solution of problems arising out of such shortcomings that the attention of a *judicial council* is focused.

Judicial councils are composed of judges, lawyers, legislators, attorney generals, and laymen. They vary in size from a half-dozen members to more than fifty, but in most instances there are about a dozen members. Councils exist in three-fourths of the states although a dozen or so are largely inactive or defunct. Wisconsin in 1913 and Massachusetts in 1919 created agencies similar to today's judicial councils, but the first modern council was probably that of Ohio in 1923. They usually are created by statute, but in a few states establishment is based upon constitutional provisions.

The functions of a judicial council are primarily investigatory and advisory. They inquire into the organizational and administrative problems of the judiciary and on the basis of their findings recommend desirable changes to the legislature or governor. In a few states the council has power to prepare judicial rules of procedure, but usually this power is exercised by the supreme court, the legislature, or both. Since the judicial council movement is of comparatively recent origin, and since their authority is advisory, the accomplishments of the councils have not been as impressive as their supporters have hoped. The fact, however, that most states now have permanent councils designed to consider judicial problems on a continuing basis bodes well for future improvements.

A Unified State Court

The typical state judiciary is a collection of courts organized on a geographical basis. Compartmentalization into counties or districts or circuits has the effect of denying judges the opportunity to specialize, of allowing backlogs of cases to accumulate on the dockets of some courts, and of increasing the probability of uneven interpretation of law throughout the state. An alternative system which removes the bases for these difficulties is the *unified* court which is organized on a functional basis. In a state having a unified judiciary there is only one court within which there are several divisions. For example, there may be general trial, intermediate appellate, and supreme court sections with divisions in the lower levels for proceedings involving equity, criminal law, juveniles, and others as the creating authority deems appropriate. Also, the chief judge or judicial council is empowered to transfer judges within the court to take advantage of special talents and to reduce heavy dockets.

Within the last twenty years, and primarily during the last decade, Alaska, Illinois, Michigan, New Jersey, and North Carolina have adopted or turned to unified judiciaries. Major reforms in the direction of unification have also been taken in Colorado, Connecticut, Missouri, New Hampshire, and New York. A few others have authorized or undertaken studies on the possibility of future court unification.

Administrative Officers

The principal function of courts is to hear and determine cases, but they also have a great many internal administrative chores. Preparation of payrolls, accounting of funds, budget preparation, purchasing supplies, and many other essential tasks must be performed if the courts are to operate smoothly. Experience at the federal level indicates that centralization of these administrative activities can be highly beneficial. Since 1939 the Administrative Office of the United States Courts, headed by a director, collects judicial statistics, administers all financial matters respecting the courts, and supervises all administrative personnel of the national judiciary. Federal judges have thus been relieved of most administrative tasks and have more time to devote to their judicial responsibilities.

Use of administrative officers by state supreme courts is a phenomenon of recent origin. Today, slightly more than half of the state high tribunals employ these valuable aides, while as recently as fifteen years ago they were found in only five states. In most instances administrators are chosen by the full court, but in some cases are appointed by the chief justice, judicial council, or administrative board. Their titles are varied, including the rather terse Director as well as the more impressive appellations Executive Secretary of the Supreme Court, and Administrative Director of the Courts. In no two states are their duties identical, but in general they perform in much the same manner as their federal counterpart. Now organized in a National Conference of Court Administrators, annual meetings are held at which suggested improvements in judicial administration are discussed and explored.

Nonjudicial Functions of State Courts

In addition to their regular judicial duties, judges of some state courts are assigned various administrative functions. The county judge in some states serves as a member of the county governing body. Justices of the peace in a few instances also double as county commissioners and perform other administrative tasks. The establishment of special districts, granting licenses, appointing receivers in bankruptcy, and probate administration add to the list of administrative duties occasionally assigned to judges. By and large, the performance of administrative tasks by judicial officers is regarded as undesirable. Such jobs properly should be undertaken by officers or agencies of the executive branch, leaving judges free to devote their time to their judicial functions.

The Administrative Tribunal

With the ever-broadening scope of governmental regulatory programs has come a welter of legal controversies. A multiplicity of rules and regulations concerning the operation of utilities, licensing of professional people, marketing produce, regulating the development of natural resources, administering health programs, and other matters have occasioned numerous instances of conflict among individuals and between citizens and their governments. In view of their number and complexity, if all such controversies were carried to the courts, the dockets in many jurisdictions would be swamped.

In order to avoid unnecessary recourse to the courts, certain agencies in all states have been authorized through the exercise of "quasi-judicial" power, to settle disputes. A public utilities commission, for example, may hold a hearing to determine whether an accused person or company has violated rules fixing the rates that may be charged for electricity. At the hearing, procedures resembling those of a court are followed; and the commission, acting as judge, jury, and "prosecutor" reaches a decision on whether a violation has occurred. If so, the commission may impose whatever penalty the law permits. Other agencies act similarly in the revocation or suspension of licenses, violations of franchises, and defiance of quarantines. The hearings are not "cases," since they are not heard by courts, but the results are usually much the same. Ordinarily the decisions of administrative agencies may be reviewed by regular courts, but the review is practically always limited to whether the agency was correct in its interpretation and application of the law, and only on rare occasions is the decision of an agency as to the facts disturbed.

JUSTICE AND THE LAW

"Justice" is a nebulous concept. It means different things to different people with few in real agreement. Perhaps the closest that generalization can come to defining the term is to equate it with *fairness*—but fairness not only in the sense that rights are honored and protected, but also with the proviso that obligations and liabilities are met. Even then difficulties arise, for what of the classic example of the man who burglarizes a home to obtain food for his family? Should he be made to pay the full penalty for burglary? Certainly he committed a crime in terms of the law, but would "justice" be served if he were sentenced to a five-year prison term? Numerous examples could be cited to illustrate the point that justice and what the law provides are not always compatible.

Law enforcement and judicial administration in the United States today are subject to incisive criticism with respect to whether justice is always done. The matter of cost, for example, may put justice beyond the reach of indigent persons. Attorneys' fees and court costs can easily discourage a poor complainant, forcing him to drop a justifiable cause. Costs and delays involved in taking appeals can and do discourage litigants. Uneven imposition of penalties for the same crime from state to state, or even from place to place within the same state, is further evidence that justice is an uncertain thing. It has been said that it is fortunate that "justice is blind," for it would shame her to observe discrimination against members of racial minorities and persons of unorthodox beliefs, or the harsh treatment of alcoholics and vagrants. In addition, a valid cause may be defeated through the ability of unscrupulous lawyers to take advantage of legal technicalities.

While it may be said that far more often than not judicial decisions are fair, sound, and just, there is still room for considerable improvement. So far, meaningful advances have been spotty at best, but at least some corrective measures have been taken. Small claims courts are available in many states for those to whom a petty, uncollected debt is important but would be negated by the costs of a regular suit. Legal aid societies, some provided by government, now exist in at least a hundred municipalities, rendering legal services at minimum fees for those who cannot afford private counsel. Public defender systems to provide indigent persons accused of crimes with capable lawyers now operate in most large cities and on a state-wide basis in a few of the states. Also, lawyers must be provided, if requested, to indigent persons accused of felonies. Considered altogether, the list of improvements is impressive, but a great deal more remains to be accomplished.

SELECTED REFERENCES

Books:

Frank, Jerome, *Courts on Trial: Myth and Reality in American Justice,* Princeton University Press, Princeton, 1949.

Keeney, Barnaby C., *Judgment by Peers,* Harvard University Press, Cambridge, 1949.

Lummus, Henry T., *The Trial Judge,* Foundation Press, Chicago, 1937.

Mayers, Lewis, *The Machinery of Justice,* Prentice-Hall, Englewood Cliffs, N.J., 1963.

Mitchell, Wendell, *Relations between the Federal and State Courts,* Columbia University Press, New York, 1950.

Vanderbilt, Arthur T., *Judges and Jurors: Their Functions, Qualifications, and Selection,* Boston University Press, Boston, 1956.

——, editor, *Minimum Standards of Judicial Administration,* Law Center of New York University, New York, 1949.

Willoughby, W. F., *Principles of Judicial Administration,* Brookings Institution, Washington, D.C., 1929.

Articles:

Broeder, Dale W., "The Functions of the Jury: Facts or Fictions?" *University of Chicago Law Review,* Spring 1954.

Currie, F. A., "Small Claims Courts," *University of Florida Law Review,* Spring 1956.

Gershenson, Harry, "Experience in Missouri with Judicial Selection under the Non-Partisan Plan," *American Bar Association Journal,* March 1960.

Garwood, W. St. John, "Judicial Selection and Tenure—The Model Article Provisions," *Journal of the American Judicature Society,* June 1963.

"Judicial Administration and the Common Man," Symposium, *The Annals,* May 1953.

Keefe, W. J., "Judges and Politics," *University of Pittsburgh Law Review,* March 1959.

McWilliams, J. Wesley, "Court Integration and Unification in the Model Judicial Article," *Journal of the American Judicature Society,* June 1963.

Newton, Isham G., "The Justice of the Peace—An American Judicial Dilemma," *Social Science,* February 1959.

Schaeffer, Wendell G., "Management in the Judiciary," *Public Administration Review,* Spring 1953.

Trumbell, William M., "State Court Systems," *The Annals,* March 1960.

Vanderbilt, Arthur T., "For Better Administration of Justice," *State Government,* February 1957.

——, "The Essentials of a Sound Judicial System," *Northwestern University Law Review,* March–April 1953.

Wood, John W., "State Judicial Selection: Realities v. Legalities," *State Government,* January 1958.

CHAPTER 10

Nature and Functions of the Electorate

The successful operation and continued existence of democratic institutions is dependent upon an informed, politically active citizenry willing and able to control governmental policy and personnel. That control can be effected in a number of ways. The principal mechanism through which the people in a democratic society, acting in a peaceful, orderly manner, exercise and implement their will is the *suffrage*—the process of voting.

Understanding the suffrage necessitates an appreciation of the role of the electorate in a democratic society. After all, the voting process is merely a mechanism operating within the context of a pattern of citizen-society-government relationships. Important as the suffrage is, its real significance derives from the vital role of the people, or that part of them called the electorate, as related to the tasks of government. What is the "electorate"? Who are "the people"? What are their duties, privileges, and responsibilities? What is the role of the individual in the voting process?

In a democratic society the people—the sum total of the citizenry—are the source of all political power. What government is and what government does ultimately are determined by the people. That tremendous power carries with it the responsibility, indeed the duty, to make decisions intelligently. Usually, those decisions are made indirectly through the election of representatives who implement the people's will. Through their representatives the people make decisions as to the basic form and powers of the national government by means of amending the national constitution. At the state level those same decisions are, in part at least, made directly by means of balloting to accept or reject constitutional amendments and revisions. In some states the people participate directly in the making of public policy through the initiative and referendum.

Although the term "people" includes *everyone*—men, women, and children—it is obvious that many of the people are unable or unfit to participate in making basic decisions. Infants, the mentally incapacitated, and certain groups such as aliens, vagrants, persons convicted of felonies, and others are excluded from sharing in legally recognized decision making.[1] In short, certain standards are prescribed, and those who qualify are entitled, but not forced, to take part. That portion of the people is termed the *electorate,* and it is they who, directly or indirectly, make decisions that determine the nature and character of government.

VOTING—RIGHT OR PRIVILEGE?

Confusion exists in the minds of many persons as to whether there is, in fact, a *right* vested in Americans to cast ballots, or whether voting is a privilege extended by government. In partial answer to the question, it is certain that there is no constitutional right to vote. Nowhere in the national Constitution nor in the constitutions of any of the states is anyone guaranteed the right to cast a ballot in the same way that the rights to free speech, press, or religion are protected. Wherever the phrase "right to vote" is used in those documents the context clearly indicates that voting is conditional upon the satisfaction of legal qualifications. At the same time, voting is not a privilege in the sense that the entitlement of a single individual to cast a ballot can be withdrawn by the government whenever it pleases. If voting is to be termed a privilege, then it must be added that it is a privilege made available to all persons on the basis of meeting certain prescribed conditions.

Voting may be compared to a legally regulated activity such as operating an automobile. Before a person may legally drive a car on public roads he must be as physically fit as the law requires him to be, pass a written examination on traffic regulations, and demonstrate his ability behind the wheel. After meeting these standards the individual is entitled to a driver's license. Since laws respecting the operation of motor vehicles apply to all persons alike, a person passing the various tests might be said to have the same "right" to drive as all others who do so. Similarly, qualifications for voting are established by laws, and a person who meets the qualifications has the same "right" to cast a ballot as all others who meet them.

---

[1] Note the use of the word "legally" here, for these usually excluded groups could share in decision-making through such extralegal processes as revolutions, riots, and public demonstrations. They have, in fact, done so in the past.

SUFFRAGE AND THE CONSTITUTION

The United States Constitution does not delegate to the national government power to fix voting requirements. Setting suffrage qualifications is, therefore, among the reserved powers of the states. Since each state is independent of her sister states in suffrage matters, there is no legal connection between the requirements imposed in one state and those established in others. With respect to the federal government, a state need only avoid conflict with the limitations found in the national Constitution and federal statutes.

As written by the framers, the Constitution contained only one provision restricting the power of the states to regulate suffrage. Article I, Section 2 provides that persons eligible to participate in the election of members of the House of Representatives shall be those who "have the qualifications requisite for electors of the most numerous branch of the State legislature." In other words, a person who qualifies to vote for candidates for the lower house of a state legislature, or in Nebraska for members of that state's unicameral legislature, may also vote for representatives in Congress. An identical clause applicable to the election of United States senators was added to the Constitution when, in 1913, the Seventeenth Amendment made senators subject to popular election. These clauses prevent the states from restricting the choice of members of Congress to a privileged portion of the electorate.

Shortly after the Civil War, Congress initiated the Fifteenth Amendment, intended to prevent discrimination against the Negro voter. It should be noted that the Amendment does not guarantee suffrage to the Negro. Instead, it provides that states may not discriminate against *any* person because of his "race, color, or previous condition of servitude." The obvious intent, however, at the time of adoption was to buttress the status of the newly freed Negro.

In 1920 the states were prohibited from withholding the vote from women. The Nineteenth Amendment became part of the Constitution in that year and specifically forbade the states to deny or abridge the franchise "on account of sex." The Amendment is not a specific guarantee of female suffrage. Rather, it is cast in terms of *sex,* a wording that technically includes men as well as women. However, the practical effect was to enfranchise women in those states where they did not enjoy full voting privileges. At the time, women voted on a plane of equality with men in a fourth of the states and could cast ballots in some elections in a few others.

The Twenty-fourth Amendment, added in 1964, provides that "failure to pay any poll tax or other tax" may not be made the reason for denying otherwise qualified persons the right to participate in the nomination and election of federal officials. While this provision broadens the suffrage in regard to the election of national office holders, the states are still free to require payment of poll taxes as a qualification on voting for candidates for state offices.

Another clause of the Constitution that limits the power of the states to control suffrage is the Equal Protection of the Laws Clause of the Fourteenth Amendment. This provision of the Constitution applies to all state law, not just to statutes or state constitutional provisions relating to suffrage. Nevertheless, any action by a state that has the effect of abridging the legal right of a qualified person to vote, even though consistent with other provisions of the United States Constitution, might be challenged as denying equal treatment before the law.

GROWTH OF THE SUFFRAGE

Prevailing democratic ideas in the early years of state government in the United States did not include the concept of universal suffrage. Despite the glowing language of the Declaration of Independence and the tendency of modern writers to eulogize early American figures, opinions concerning the common people held by most founders of the Union reflected suspicion and distrust. Those in a position to influence the nature of the suffrage, generally the aristocratic, educated, landowning, well-to-do element, acted to protect the upper classes. As a result the suffrage was so highly restricted at the time the United States Constitution was written that fewer than five per cent of the total population could vote.[2]

Since fear for the safety of property ownership was a principal motivating factor in restricting the suffrage during those early years, it is natural that property ownership should have been a common voting qualification. After the separation from England, each new state fixed qualifications based either upon owning real estate or the payment of taxes. In either case the emphasis was upon the economic worth of the individual. Such qualifications, in one form or another

---

[2] This small group was composed of free white males over twenty-one who owned prescribed amounts of property or paid specified amounts of taxes.

and with varying degrees of severity, persisted in the states until well after the Union was formed. Property ownership as a general suffrage qualification slowly began to disappear, was found in only a half-dozen states by 1821, and vanished altogether when North Carolina discontinued its property requirement in 1856. Today property qualifications exist only in a few states where voting on local bond issues and assessments is restricted to property tax payers, and in South Carolina property ownership may be substituted as an alternative to a literacy test.

The first few decades of independence saw the states limit the suffrage not only by property restrictions, but by religious qualifications as well. It was a common practice to exclude from the franchise those who did not believe in a supreme being, or in a few instances, did not adhere to the principles of the New Testament. The rationalization was that only the best people were entitled to vote, and the best people obviously were the responsible citizens with a property stake and religious scruples. Pressures based on the absence of a national church and the right of free exercise of religion soon prevailed, however, and religious qualifications were rapidly dropped after the adoption of the national Constitution. By 1810 the imposition of religious tests as a suffrage qualification had disappeared in every state in the Union, and none has been required by any state subsequently admitted.

With the turn of the nineteenth century the suffrage began to broaden. The open frontier, the formation of more unified political parties, improving communications, the beginnings of urbanization, and especially the Jacksonian concept of popular democracy brought on a liberalization of suffrage qualifications. By the time of the Civil War, universal white male suffrage was virtually achieved. The Fifteenth Amendment resulted in legally enfranchising Negro males, and in 1920 women were made eligible. Thus for the past forty years America has boasted a universal suffrage.

PRESENT-DAY VOTING QUALIFICATIONS

Restrictions placed on exercise of the suffrage by the states can be classified into two categories. In the first group are the *universal* qualifications, or those found in all the states. Included in this group are the requirements of (1) United States citizenship, (2) a minimum age, and (3) a minimum period of residence within the state. The second category includes all those qualifications imposed in some, but not all, states. This group includes restrictions based on (1) literacy, (2) registration, (3) payment of poll taxes, and (4) miscellaneous requirements regarding character, oaths, and the like.

In addition to the usual array of voting qualifications each state excludes from the polls certain classes of people. The great majority withhold the franchise, for example, from the insane and feeble-minded. Persons convicted of major crimes may not vote in virtually all states. A fourth of the states do not permit paupers to cast ballots. Persons dishonorably discharged from the armed forces of the United States, those convicted of subversive activities, and those who engage in dueling are disfranchised in one or more states. In most instances it makes little difference whether these groups are excluded, for most of them are unable, mentally or physically, to meet the suffrage qualifications anyway.

United States Citizenship. For almost forty years the states have been unanimous in the requirement that before a person may vote he must be a citizen of the United States. At one time about a fourth of the states permitted aliens who had applied for naturalization to cast ballots. Most of them were western states desirous of attracting residents, while in the east, where large numbers of the foreign born were concentrated, the opposite attitude prevailed. The practice of alien voting was gradually dropped, however, Arkansas being the last state to abandon it in 1926. The theoretical basis of the requirement is that only those persons who are legally part of the people should share in making decisions that affect the people. In imposing the qualification most states make no distinction between native-born and naturalized citizens. Pennsylvania, however, requires a naturalized voter to have been a citizen for a month, and ninety days are stipulated in California, Minnesota, New York, and Utah.

Age. In the legal systems of the American states the age of twenty-one has generally been taken as the age of majority—the time at which a person is entitled to full management of his own affairs. It is quite understandable then that twenty-one became the age at which voting eligibility began. Until 1943, when Georgia lowered its minimum age qualification to eighteen, twenty-one was the minimum voting age in all states. Since then three other states have established lower voting ages. In 1955 Kentucky reduced its age requirement to eighteen. Upon entry into the Union in 1959 Alaska became the only state with a minimum voting age of nineteen, and Hawaii set its minimum age at twenty.

Those who favor reduction of the voting age point out that there is nothing sacred about the age of twenty-one, that it has been merely a convenient legal designation that does not necessarily denote maturity. Also, the young people affected are as informed on political matters as other persons and assume many of the obligations of older citizens. In opposition are the claims of immaturity and lack of experience and responsibility. The slogan "old enough to fight, old enough to vote" is frequently cited in support of lowering the voting age, but this assertion is countered by the point that there is no logical relationship between a person's physical and mental powers— and the millions of young women will never be "old enough to fight"! In the early 1940's almost two-thirds of the states considered measures to reduce the voting age to eighteen, with success only in Georgia. Again in the 1950's attention was centered on the movement when President Eisenhower recommended to Congress that a constitutional amendment be initiated to fix the minimum voting age at eighteen for all states. A number of state legislatures considered changes, but only in Kentucky was the age actually lowered.

No state has seriously considered fixing a maximum age limit. Occasionally, comment is made that with the increasing life expectancy of the American people, the older age group will gain more power. Thus, the reasoning runs, the character of the electorate will change and become more conservative and disposed to maintain the status quo. This consideration, coupled with the complaint that the senile are privileged while the young are not, is cited in support of lowering the age minimum. Any attempt, however, to achieve maximum age limits is simply not feasible.

Residence. Before a person may cast a ballot he must be a resident of the state in which he desires to vote. The period of residence varies considerably, with Mississippi the only state requiring two years before voting eligibility can be established. In thirty-six states the qualifying period is set at one year, while six months is sufficient in the other fourteen. In addition to state residence, every state but Oregon also requires shorter periods of local residence. A typical requirement of this sort calls for sixty days in the county and thirty days in the election district or precinct. Supplemental provisions of law sometimes alter the effect of a general residence requirement. In Pennsylvania, for example, a year's residence is required, but persons born in that state or former residents returning to Pennsylvania may qualify after only six months. The one year local residence requirement in Mississippi is reduced to the extent that ministers of organized churches and their wives acquire voting eligibility in six months. On the other hand, even though Oregon has no local requirement, no one is permitted to register during the thirty days previous to an election—a provision which has the effect of a local residence requirement.

All residence requirements refer to *legal residence,* not necessarily physical presence. Thus a person may spend most of his time working, visiting, traveling, or attending college outside his home state and still retain his voting eligibility. All that is necessary is that an individual's legal *domicile,* or home, be within the state in which he casts his ballot. One problem associated with the legal residence provision for which there seems no satisfactory solution concerns the termination and establishment of residence. When a person leaves a state with no intention of returning he ends his legal residence and his suffrage eligibility in that state. Yet the state to which he moves does not recognize him as a resident for voting purposes for six months to two years, depending upon the state. In the meantime the individual is disfranchised.

The relationship between state and local residence and voting for national officials also poses a problem. It is logical enough to conclude that before receiving a voice in the selection of state and local officers a voter should become a part of his local community. But with respect to national elections, connection with a state and a locality is not necessarily a logical prerequisite. Still, most states make no distinction in regard to the character of the offices to be filled. As indicated in the table on pp. 244-245, slightly more than one-third of the states have made it possible for newly arrived residents to participate in choosing presidential electors either by shortening the residence requirement or by eliminating it altogether. A half-dozen states have enacted statutes which provide for no minimum residence requirements for new residents desiring to cast presidential ballots. In most instances, however, a short period such as forty, sixty, or ninety days is prescribed.

Registration. In order to prevent abuse of the suffrage by persons ineligible to vote, some means must be used to identify those who

STATE SUFFRAGE QUALIFICATIONS

State	Age	U.S. Citizen[1]	Residence				Pres. and V. P. only[1]	Literacy
			State	County	City, Town	Ward, Precinct		
Alabama[2]	21	Yes	1 yr.	6 mo.	—	3 mo.	—	Yes
Alaska	19	Yes	1 yr.	—	—	30 da.	—	Yes
Arizona	21	Yes	1 yr.	30 da.	—	30 da.	60 da.	Yes
Arkansas	21	Yes	1 yr.	6 mo.	—	30 da.	—	—
California	21	90 da.	1 yr.	90 da.	—	54 da.	54 da.	Yes
Colorado	21	Yes	1 yr.	90 da.	6 mo.	15 da.	6 mo.	—
Connecticut	21	Yes	1 yr.	—	—	—	60 da.	Yes
Delaware	21	Yes	1 yr.	3 mo.	—	30 da.	—	Yes
Florida	21	Yes	1 yr.	6 mo.	—	—	—	—
Georgia	18	Yes	1 yr.	6 mo.	—	—	—	Yes
Hawaii	20	Yes	1 yr.	—	—	30 da.	60 da.	Yes
Idaho	21	Yes	6 mo.	30 da.	—	—	60 da.	—
Illinois	21	Yes	1 yr.	90 da.	—	30 da.	60 da.[3]	—
Indiana	21	Yes	6 mo.	60 da.	—	30 da.	—	—
Iowa	21	Yes	6 mo.	60 da.	—	—	—	—
Kansas	21	Yes	6 mo.	—	—	30 da.	45 da.[4]	—
Kentucky	18	Yes	1 yr.	6 mo.	—	60 da.	—	Yes
Louisiana	21	Yes	1 yr.	6 mo.	—	3 mo.	—	Yes
Maine	21	Yes	6 mo.	—	6 mo.	—	No minimum	—
Maryland	21	Yes	1 yr.	6 mo.	—	—	—	Yes
Massachusetts	21	Yes	1 yr.	—	6 mo.	—	32 da.	—
Michigan	21	Yes	6 mo.	—	30 da.	—	—	Yes
Minnesota	21	90 da.	6 mo.	—	—	30 da.	—	—
Mississippi[2]	21	Yes	2 yrs.	—	—	1 yr.[5]	—	Yes
Missouri	21	Yes	1 yr.	60 da.	—	—	—	—
Montana	21	Yes	1 yr.	30 da.	—	—	60 da.	—
Nebraska	21	Yes	6 mo.	40 da.	—	10 da.	No minimum	—
Nevada	21	Yes	6 mo.	30 da.	—	10 da.	—	—

244

State	Age	U.S. Citizen	Residence State	County	City, Town	Ward, Precinct	Pres. and V. P. only[1]	Literacy
New Hampshire	21	Yes	6 mo.	—	6 mo.	—	—	Yes
New Jersey	21	Yes	6 mo.	40 da.	—	—	40 da.	—
New Mexico	21	Yes	1 yr.	90 da.	—	30 da.	90 da.	—
New York	21	90 da.	1 yr.	—	4 mo.	30 da.	90 da.	Yes
North Carolina	21	Yes	1 yr.	90 da.	—	30 da.	No minimum	Yes
North Dakota	21	Yes	1 yr.	40 da.	—	30 da.	—	—
Ohio	21	Yes	6 mo.	2 mo.	—	40 da.	No minimum	—
Oklahoma	21	Yes	6 mo.	—	—	20 da.	No minimum	—
Oregon	21	Yes	6 mo.	—	—	—	No minimum	Yes
Pennsylvania	21	30 da.	1 yr.[6]	—	—	60 da.	—	—
Rhode Island	21	Yes	1 yr.	—	6 mo.	—	—	—
South Carolina	21	Yes	1 yr.[7]	6 mo.	—	3 mo.	—	Yes[8]
South Dakota	21	Yes	1 yr.	90 da.	—	30 da.	—	—
Tennessee	21	Yes	1 yr.	3 mo.	—	—	—	—
Texas[2]	21	Yes	1 yr.	6 mo.	—	—	—	—
Utah	21	90 da.	1 yr.	4 mo.	—	60 da.	—	—
Vermont	21	Yes	1 yr.	—	3 mo.	—	—	—
Virginia[2]	21	Yes	1 yr.	6 mo.	—	30 da.	—	Yes
Washington	21	Yes	1 yr.	90 da.	—	30 da.	—	Yes
West Virginia	21	Yes	1 yr.	60 da.	—	30 da.	—	—
Wisconsin	21	Yes	1 yr.	—	—	10 da.	No minimum	—
Wyoming	21	Yes	1 yr.	60 da.	—	10 da.	—	Yes

[1] New residents who are otherwise qualified, but who have not met residence requirements, may vote for electors for President and Vice President.

[2] These states have poll taxes. Under terms of the Twenty-fourth Amendment, however, they can be enforced only in regard to candidacies for non-federal offices.

[3] Residence in precinct.

[4] Residence in township.

[5] Local residence requirement reduced to six months for ministers and their wives.

[6] Six months for former residents.

[7] Six months for ministers, public school teachers, and their wives.

[8] Property ownership is an alternative to literacy.

State and Local Government

have legally qualified to cast ballots. The method now used in most states is a process by which all persons who can qualify are required to enter their names on official lists—in other words, to register. Registration as a means of preventing voting frauds was begun in Massachusetts in 1800 and was adopted in most states from the end of the Civil War to 1910. Today all states except Alaska and North Dakota require or permit registration, although some registration laws apply only to the larger cities and voting districts. In Texas the legislature is authorized by the constitution to provide for registration in all cities of 10,000 or more, but to date that prerogative has not been exercised. Thus, in three states and in some sections of others, the basic method of checking a voter's qualification is to challenge him at the polls.

Technically, registration is not a qualification on the suffrage. Instead, it is a part of the election process whereby voters who have *already qualified* register their names for future identification at the polls. From the practical viewpoint, compulsory registration has the same effect as an age, citizenship, or residence requirement. If a person is otherwise qualified, but is not registered, he is not permitted to cast a ballot. Hence, registration may well be regarded as a suffrage qualification.

Basically, there are two types of registration systems: the *permanent* and the *periodic*. In a permanent system a voter need not reregister at any time unless he should move from the locale where he is registered or by virtue of some infraction of the law become ineligible to vote. Under a periodic system all voters must at some prescribed time reregister or forfeit their voting privileges. In theory, periodic registration is superior, for by requiring reregistration at stated intervals the lists of voters can be kept accurate and up to date. On the other hand, the process is expensive and voters find it inconvenient. Consequently, practically all states now use permanent systems. In any event, most states with permanent systems approximate some of the advantages of periodic registration by providing that the registration of a person becomes void unless he actually votes in state elections.

Literacy. The only suffrage qualification imposed in the states today that is related to the *quality* of the electorate is the requirement that voters be literate. Connecticut in 1855 and Massachusetts two years later were the first states to require that voters demonstrate their literacy. By 1965, twenty states in all sections of the country had adopted literacy qualifications which, in most cases, required no more than that a person be able to read and write.

The object of literacy requirements is to exclude the uneducated from the franchise and, if fairly administered and enforced, only the illiterate are affected. In New York, where literacy examinations are given by public school personnel, fair testing appears to have been achieved. Unfortunately, however, literacy requirements can be readily perverted and used as effective instruments of discrimination by election officials. This is especially true when a literacy quali-fication is cast in terms of "understanding," as in the case of Article VII, Section 1(d), of the Louisiana Constitution requiring certain reg-istrants to be able to "understand and give a reasonable interpreta-tion of any section" of the national or state constitutions. In a suit brought under the Civil Rights Act of 1960 this provision was held unconstitutional in 1965 by the United States Supreme Court which regarded it as part of a plan of discrimination against Negroes.[3] While the decision technically invalidated only the provision involved in the litigation, by indirection it affected similar provisions in the consti-tutions of Georgia, Mississippi, and South Carolina.

Poll Taxes. The first poll tax imposed as a suffrage qualification was levied by Florida in 1889. In combination with literacy and long residence requirements, the poll tax proved an effective method of dis-criminating against Negroes, and by the beginning of the twentieth century it had been adopted by most southern states. The tax was attacked by liberals as undemocratic, and after repeal was achieved in North Carolina in 1920 it began slowly to lose favor in other states. Today it survives only in the states of Alabama, Mississippi, Texas, and Virginia.

As applied to the nomination and election of federal office holders poll taxes were outlawed in 1964 when the Twenty-fourth Amend-ment was ratified as a part of the United States Constitution. Contrary to the impression held by many people, the Amendment did not for-bid the imposition of poll taxes as such. The states may still require

---

[3] Speaking for a unanimous court, Justice Black observed that "There can be no doubt . . . that Louisiana's interpretation test, as written and as applied, was part of a successful plan to deprive Louisiana Negroes of their right to vote." Further, "This is not a test but a trap, sufficient to stop even the most brilliant man on his way to the voting booth." *Louisiana* v. *United States,* 85 S. Ct. 817, (1965).

that such taxes be paid before a voter may participate in the nomination and election of candidates for state offices. In fact, almost simultaneously with the ratification of the Twenty-fourth Amendment the legislature of Virginia enacted a statute making a poll tax applicable in the selection of non-federal elective officials. However, even though poll taxes may still be imposed, their usefulness as an instrument of discrimination has been substantially reduced by the adoption of the new constitutional restriction.

Other Qualifications. In some states a person is required to take an oath as to the validity of his qualifications, usually at the time of registration. In other instances there are qualifications which are based upon ideas of morality, such as requiring that a voter must be a person of "good character." Rarely, however, are the ingredients of good character legislatively prescribed. Obviously, such qualifications are difficult to enforce fairly and effectively, and they may provide the basis for discrimination. As a matter of fact, in most instances where they are enforced discrimination is the objective, with little attention paid to them otherwise.

THE PROBLEM OF NEGRO SUFFRAGE

Because of the unfortunate antipathies and prejudices between whites and Negroes, particularly in the southeastern United States, a serious problem exists with respect to the voting equality of the Negro minority. The causes of the intense feelings go back over a century to the days when slavery was an accepted American institution. The bitterness of the Civil War and the events that followed nurtured attitudes that still prevail without great modification over a century later.

The Reconstruction Period. During the years following the war, the white southerner was literally divested of any substantial control of his state government. Under the Reconstruction Acts the southern states were organized into military districts commanded by Union army officers. The military commanders had authority to remove civil officers and to control virtually all aspects of civil government. During this period unscrupulous individuals—northerners contemptuously called "carpet baggers" and southerners referred to as "scalawags"—through graft, corruption, and collusion made a mockery of civil government. The newly freed Negro became the goat. Uneducated and propertyless, he found himself a foil being manipulated by those who could exploit him. In short, the Negro was made to appear responsible for many of the excesses of the Reconstruction Period. When President Hayes ordered an end to military occupation of the South in 1877 and the white southerners once again regained control of the governmental reins, it was not surprising that they displayed hatred for the Negro.

The Mississippi Plan. By the 1880's the whites were firmly in control of the political processes in the southern states and set about seeking methods to bar Negroes legally from the polls. In 1890 Mississippi amended its constitution to tighten suffrage qualifications in such a way that most Negroes would not be able to qualify. Included in the plan were (1) a two-dollar poll tax, (2) a two-year residence restriction, and (3) a literacy qualification that required prospective voters to be able to read, write, and understand any part of the state constitution. Obviously, the great bulk of Negroes would be eliminated for they were still largely illiterate, propertyless, and rarely able to afford two dollars for poll taxes. Upheld by the United States Supreme Court[4] as being legal on its face, the Mississippi plan was rapidly adopted by other southern states. While effective in keeping Negroes from the polls, the Mississippi Plan had an unintended effect that rankled many whites: great numbers of poor white voters were also disfranchised.

The Grandfather Clauses. To restore suffrage rights to the large numbers of disfranchised whites, "grandfather clauses" were devised. They provided that persons who were citizens before 1866, or 1867, or a descendant of such a citizen, were excused from literacy qualifications. Since Negroes were not citizens in that year, they were not privileged under the clauses, as were most whites. To avoid conflict with the Fifteenth Amendment, grandfather clauses, though usually in the form of constitutional provisions, were made temporary. By the time a case could be carried to the United States Supreme Court a challenged clause would expire. However, the grandfather clause added to the Oklahoma constitution in 1910 was successfully attacked five years later and found by the highest federal court to be contrary

---

[4] *Williams* v. *Mississippi*, 170 U.S. 213 (1898).

to the provisions of the Fifteenth Amendment forbidding abridgment of the suffrage on the basis of race.[5]

The Democratic White Primary. With the passage of time the effectiveness of Mississippi Plans began to wane, and further refinements of methods of discrimination were sought. The answer to the southerners' search was suggested by a United States Supreme Court decision holding that primary elections were beyond the regulation of Congress.[6] Since the vast majority of southerners were Democrats, whoever won nomination in the Democratic Party primary was virtually certain to be elected. Hence, if the Democratic primary was limited to white voters only, the Negro would, for all practical purposes, be excluded from the polls. After a series of cases in which it was declared finally that states as such could not close the primaries to Negroes, the Democratic Party in Texas, acting on its own volition in convention, adopted a resolution restricting party membership to white persons. In *Grovey* v. *Townsend*, decided in 1935, the United States Supreme Court upheld the action of the convention.[7] Thus the Democratic White Primary, from which Negroes were totally excluded, was sanctioned by the highest court in the land.

For several years after the *Townsend* ruling the outlook for Negro suffrage in the South was bleak. Then, in a 1941 case that did not involve Negroes in any way, the Supreme Court handed down an opinion that seemed to offer grounds for a new attack on the white primary.[8] An election commissioner had been caught falsely counting and certifying ballots in a Louisiana primary and had been convicted under *federal* law. In upholding his conviction the Court ruled that primaries were an integral part of the election process and thus subject to federal control. Soon another Texas case involving the white primary was brought and in 1944, in *Smith* v. *Allwright*, the Supreme Court reversed the *Townsend* decision and struck down the white primary.[9] South Carolina later attempted to retain its white primary by repealing all state laws relating to the subject of primary elections. The idea behind the action was that if the primary did not exist in state law, it would be beyond the reach of the courts. However, a lower court decision which the Supreme Court refused

---

[5] *Guinn* v. *United States,* 238 U.S. 347 (1915).

[6] *Newberry* v. *United States,* 256 U.S. 232 (1921).

[7] 295 U.S. 45.

[8] *United States* v. *Classic,* 313 U.S. 299.

[9] 321 U.S. 649.

to review condemned the action as merely a stratagem to avoid federal law and therefore invalid.[10] Throughout the following decade attempts were made in several southern states to deny the legal right of Negroes to participate in primary elections, but these efforts were also struck down by the Supreme Court.

The Situation Today. The passing of the White Primary did not result in substantially increased Negro participation in elections. Having a legal right to do something and actually exercising that right are two radically different things. Discrimination against Negroes seeking to exercise the suffrage has continued, although considerable progress toward equality has been realized during the last decade.

Improvements were made under federal civil rights legislation enacted in 1957, 1960, and 1964, especially when a pattern of discrimination in suffrage matters was involved. The legislation which seems to offer most promise of achieving equality in the exercise of suffrage rights is the federal Voting Rights Act of 1965. By the terms of this legislation, various state-imposed qualifications can be suspended in any state or county in which less than half of the voting age population was registered for or actually voted in the general election of 1964. Federal examiners may then step in and register persons who comply with such state requirements as age and residency. Undoubtedly the Voting Rights Act of 1965 will result in more extensive enfranchisement of Negroes. Effective as it may be in that regard, however, it is not a final solution, for it does not attack in any significant way the economic and social factors involved in racial prejudice.

Nonvoting

In the United States today about 112,000,000 Americans are potential voters. For various reasons, however, a turnout of sixty to sixty-five per cent of the total possible number of voters is considered good. This level of performance contrasts sharply with voting behavior in many European countries where it is common for upwards of eighty-five or ninety per cent of the eligible voters to cast ballots.

Many factors can be cited to explain why so many Americans stay home on election day. At the head of the list is the plain fact that

---

[10] *Elmore* v. *Rice,* 72 F. Supp. 516 (1947); *Rice* v. *Elmore* 165 F. 2d 382 (1947).

many individuals are simply indifferent to political matters. They take no interest in the affairs of government and, presumably as long as their personal situations are not drastically affected by political activity, they cannot be expected to become interested. Perhaps as many as half of those who fail to vote are included in this group. Swelling the ranks of the nonvoters are the millions of Negroes and members of other minorities who, because of intimidation or discrimination by election officials, are unable to qualify. Other millions are temporarily disfranchised because they have moved from one election jurisdiction to another and are unable to meet residence requirements. Also counted in the millions are those persons who, at the time of elections, are ill or otherwise physically handicapped and either cannot or do not take advantage of absentee voting privileges. Work or study away from home accounts for a large number of nonvoters, and a few do not cast ballots for religious reasons. Still others do not participate for such superficial reasons as inconvenience, distance from the polls, or refusal to take time from other activities.

Frequently, campaigns are conducted by politically interested groups to encourage people to register and vote. The motives behind such activities are praiseworthy, but the result may be a mixed blessing. Everything possible should be done to remind the citizenry that an election is approaching and to encourage people to qualify themselves to cast ballots. At the same time it should be remembered that little is gained when uninformed, ordinarily disinterested people are encouraged to vote simply for the sake of voting. It may reasonably be said that an uninformed vote is as bad, if not worse, than no vote at all. Since nonvoting appears to be most prevalent among those least qualified to cast intelligent votes, efforts by civic-minded individuals and groups to get out the vote would be more meritorious if directed at *informing* the nonvoter on issues and candidates and then prompting him to vote.

COMPULSORY VOTING

Compelling people to vote has been proposed at times on the ground that democracy operates best when there is wide citizen participation. Today compulsory voting exists, or has been used in only a few scattered countries around the world.[11] Its longest, and

[11] Included are Argentina, Australia, Belgium, Bulgaria, Czechoslovakia, Denmark, Greece, Holland, Hungary, Italy, Luxemburg, Paraguay, Rumania, Spain, and Switzerland.

perhaps most successful application has been in Belgium where it was adopted in 1892. The system works in that country on the basis of a small fine for the first offense, the fine increasing with each offense until the fourth when the voter may also be disfranchised for ten years. Compulsory voting has never been looked upon with favor in the United States. It was rejected by the voters of Oregon in 1920 by a margin of two to one. The constitutions of Massachusetts and North Dakota authorize compulsory voting, but the legislatures of those states have not enacted legislation on the subject.[12] What appears to be the only example of a form of compulsory voting in the United States since colonial days occurred in the 1890's in Kansas City, Missouri. The city charter imposed a poll tax but exempted all voters who cast ballots in municipal elections. The charter provision was set aside by the Missouri supreme court which held that a right to vote could not be made a legal obligation.[13]

Whatever fate a compulsory voting law might meet if contested in the courts today, it is certain that the idea is contrary to American tradition. There is little likelihood that a system of compulsion would be seriously considered in any state. It is probably just as well that the idea of compulsory voting has not been well received, for the system has an inherent flaw that makes it of questionable value. It is possible to force most people to the polls, but to do so invites millions of uninformed, unintelligent votes. In such an event the cure for nonvoting would undoubtedly be worse than the ill of abstention! Considering the possible consequences of compulsory voting and the traditions of American democracy, it appears that the best antidote for nonvoting lies in improving the suffrage and electoral systems rather than in herding reluctant voters into the polls.

ABSENTEE VOTING

On election day there are many voters who, for one reason or another, cannot be present to cast ballots in their local precincts. Members of the armed forces, for example, cannot leave their posts and return home to vote. Other voters may be ill, physically disabled, away from home on business, away at school, or, as migrant laborers, forced to go where employment can be found. Since any or all such persons may earnestly desire to cast ballots and are qualified to do

---

[12] Massachusetts Constitution, Article of Amendment 61; North Dakota Constitution, Article II, Section 127.

[13] *Kansas City* v. *Whipple,* 136 Mo. 475 (1896).

so, most states now make it possible for them to participate in elections by means of the absentee ballot.

The use of absentee ballots dates back to the Civil War when they were used, without much success, to enable soldiers and sailors to vote. It was not until 1896, in Vermont, that the first statute extending the privilege of absentee balloting to both civilians and military personnel was enacted. Most of the impetus for absentee voting legislation has come during wartime when large numbers of voters are in the armed forces. During World War II Congress created a War Ballot Commission to facilitate voting by servicemen for candidates for national offices in the 1944 general election. Twenty states recognized the validity of the ballots distributed by the Commission, and the remaining states permitted servicemen to vote on state ballots. Since World War II several states have liberalized their absentee laws, and in a few others provisions have become more stringent.

Casting an absentee ballot is a tedious process. The details vary from state to state, but basic procedures are much the same everywhere. First the voter must apply to the proper official, usually the clerk of the county in which his home precinct is located, for a ballot. The application must be accompanied by a notarized affidavit attesting to the eligibility of the voter and must be received by the appropriate official before a designated date. After the voter receives his ballot he fills it out secretly but *in the presence of* an officer authorized to administer oaths. The ballot is then returned in an official, sealed envelope accompanied by a notarized affidavit declaring that the voter himself marked the ballot in secret. The ballot must be received by a designated deadline if it is to be counted. Since the time during which all these steps must be performed may be less than a month, although usually longer, action by a voter in executing an absentee ballot is convincing evidence of his appreciation of the suffrage.

SUFFRAGE IN THE DISTRICT OF COLUMBIA

When the Twenty-third Amendment became a part of the Constitution in 1961, residents of the District of Columbia acquired the right to participate in the choice of presidential electors for the first time in the history of the Union. Under the Amendment the federal district "shall appoint in such manner as the Congress may direct" presidential electors, "but in no event more than the least populous state." Since presidential electors are chosen by popular vote, qualified residents of the district cast ballots choosing three members of the electoral college.

Although district residents may now vote in presidential elections, they have no voice in the selection of local governmental officials. Beginning in 1802 mayors were appointed by the President, with council members chosen by popular vote. In 1874, Congress revised the system of district government, withdrawing all voting privileges enjoyed by the residents. The only other occasions on which the population of the District of Columbia has participated in the electoral process have been presidential primaries, the first of which was held in 1956.

The fact that district residents were denied suffrage rights prior to adoption of the Twenty-third Amendment can be easily explained. The power to set suffrage qualifications is a reserved power vested in the states—and the District of Columbia is not a state. Congress could restore local elections, but it could not, by legislative act, authorize residents to cast ballots for national officers. Thus it was necessary to amend the Constitution to confer upon residents of the District of Columbia suffrage rights similar to those enjoyed by residents of the states.

SELECTED REFERENCES

Books:

Abraham, Henry J., *Compulsory Voting,* Public Affairs Press, Washington, D.C., 1955.

Aiken, Charles, *The Negro Votes,* Chandler Publishing Company, San Francisco, 1962.

Burdick, Eugene, and Brodbeck, Arthur J., *American Voting Behavior,* The Free Press, Glencoe, 1959.

Campbell, Angus, Converse, P., Miller, W., and Stokes, D., *The American Voter,* Wiley and Sons, New York, 1960.

Campbell, Angus, Gurin, Gerald, and Miller, Warren E., *The Voter Decides,* Row, Peterson and Co., 1954.

McGovney, Dudley O., *The American Suffrage Medley,* University of Chicago Press, Chicago, 1949.

Ogden, Frederic D., *The Poll Tax in the South,* University of Alabama Press, University, 1958.

Porter, Kirk H., *A History of the Suffrage in the United States,* University of Chicago Press, Chicago, 1918.

Price, Hugh D., *The Negro and Southern Politics,* New York University Press, New York, 1957.

Price, Margaret, *The Negro and the Ballot in the South,* Southern Regional Council, Atlanta, 1959.

Articles:

Coulson, Robert E., "Let's Not Get Out the Vote," *Harper's Magazine,* November 1955.

Gerwig, Robert, "The Elective Franchise for Residents of Federal Areas," *George Washington Law Review,* March 1956.

Goldman, Ralph M., "Move—Lose Your Vote," *National Municipal Review,* January 1956.

Ogul, Morris S., "Residence Requirements as Barriers to Voting in Presidential Elections," *Midwest Journal of Political Science,* August 1959.

"The Question of Lowering the Voting Age to 18," Symposium, *Congressional Digest,* March 1954.

"The Question of Poll Taxes and Literacy Tests," Symposium, *Congressional Digest,* May 1962.

Scammon, Richard M., "Why One Third of Us Don't Vote," *New York Times Magazine,* November 17, 1963.

CHAPTER 11

Political Parties and Pressure Groups

Popular participation in public affairs takes a variety of forms. Some methods are direct, some are indirect. Some are violent and illegal, but most are well within the range of legality. Some are not especially politically oriented, while many are designed to affect the content or formulation of public policy. But whatever the nature of the activity, virtually all actions by the people have repercussions within the political framework.

The history of every country records acts of violence that have had political significance. In many nations of the world, revolutions have resulted in the establishment of new forms of government. Riots and demonstrations that follow the implementation of unpopular policies often lead to the modification of governmental programs. Assassinations have led to upheavals in the orderly conduct of government. Shows of violence are the exceptions rather than the rule, however; in the vast majority of cases popular participation in the political process takes more conventional, peaceful forms.

Nearly everyone is interested, either actively or passively, in governmental policies and programs. Most people are, therefore, associated with one or more *interest groups*. These groups are not formally organized, but are merely those portions of the population that are sensitive to changes in the public policy affecting them. For example, a dentist who is a veteran and has invested his savings in oil stocks, but who is not active in a party or in any organization that attempts to influence public policy, may be expected to show concern for governmental decisions on such things as socialized medicine, veterans' benefits, and regulation of the petroleum industry. Radical innovations in any of these fields could convert him from a virtually inactive individual to an active participant in the political process. By the same token, millions of persons with interests in other fields are also potentially active. The latent power of the many interest groups thus serves to fix rather indeterminate limits on the extent to which public policy can be modified at any given time. Legislators and members of the executive branch of the government are always concerned with the attitudes and receptivity of the people and act accordingly. To do otherwise would invite popular dissatisfaction with public policy and probably result in unfavorable reactions at the ballot box.

In contrast with interest group association, but nevertheless building upon the interest group structure, is the *pressure group*. Pressure groups, discussed in more detail later in the chapter, are formally organized groups of people who band together for the specific purpose of attempting to maintain or achieve favorable public policy on a matter of common interest. Just as a person may be aligned with several interest groups, he may also be a supporter of various pressure groups. A principal mark of distinction between interest group association and affiliation with a pressure group organization is that the person who supports a pressure group is, by comparison, much more politically active.

Participation in governmental affairs sometimes takes the form of processes leading to direct legislation. In those states where law permits, the people may themselves make public policy by means of the *initiative* and *referendum*. Through the initiative statutes may be enacted or amendments added to the state constitution. The referendum serves as a medium by which the people may pass upon provisions of state law. Closely related to these procedures is the *recall*, the process by which elected governmental officials may be turned out of office.

The most direct method of participation in political affairs is public service itself. Whether appointed or elected, many citizens serve in a multitude of government positions at the state and local levels. These positions represent the means of livelihood for many individuals, but in the majority of instances the service stems primarily from a desire to take part in the affairs of government. Across the country, for instance, many persons serve on the numerous school boards without compensation except perhaps for expenses incurred in the performance of their duties. The same is frequently true for city councilmen as well as for the members of planning and zoning commissions and bodies such as park, recreation, and library boards.

Large numbers of persons are active in each of the modes of political expression discussed above, but the method by which most

Americans exert themselves politically is affiliation with a political party. By joining a political party an individual shares in the selection of public officials and as a political partisan contributes to the party concept of what public policy ought to be. Party affiliation may take the form of becoming a member of the party organization as such, or it may be merely the expression by an individual of preference for one party over all others. Even those who cannot qualify to cast a ballot, particularly younger people, may align themselves with political parties and become active participants.

It is important to note that a person is not limited to any one of the methods of political expression discussed here. Indeed, an individual may join a party, be active in a number of pressure organizations, hold a public office, and if he happens to live in a state where the processes are used, participate in the initiative, referendum, and recall. The choice is strictly up to the individual. At his option he may elect to detach himself from all modes of political action or he may seize every opportunity to participate.

NATURE OF POLITICAL PARTIES

Definitions. Writing in 1770 the English statesman Edmund Burke defined a political party as "a body of men united, for promoting by their joint endeavours the national interest, upon some particular principle in which they are all agreed." This definition does not accurately describe the major political parties in the United States. In both major American parties—the Democratic and Republican—membership includes persons of widely varying interests. The conservative "Dixiecrats" of the southeastern part of the country are counted as Democrats, but they have little in common with liberal members of the party. Within the Republican Party the "Old Guard" conservatives contrast sharply with the liberal "progressive" wing. Numerous examples of individual party members who cannot agree with their fellows upon "some particular principle" could be cited. Consequently, a more accurate definition must be framed.

Casting a definition in terms of the principles that bring people together in parties invites inaccuracy because of the different ways in which individuals perceive and understand those concepts. More meaningful understanding can be attained by emphasizing the *basic purpose* of political parties and the *methods* they employ. Viewed in terms of these criteria, it is possible to say that a political party is a voluntary association of persons joined together for the purpose of achieving power through the winning of elections and the control of government.[1]

Legal Status. Parties exist as legal entities only if they can qualify according to specifications set forth in state law. These criteria vary widely among the states. In Colorado, for example, a political group is recognized as a party if its candidate for governor received at least ten per cent of the votes cast for that office at the last preceding general election. Nevada parties must attract five per cent of the votes cast for candidates for the state's one seat in the United States House of Representatives. A political party in New Hampshire enjoys legal recognition if its gubernatorial candidate wins three per cent of the votes. In New York a party must poll only 50,000 votes for its candidate for governor—a figure that represents a fraction of one per cent of the votes cast in that state's general elections. Most severe in their qualifications are Alabama, Kentucky, Oregon, and Virginia. In the first three a party must attract twenty per cent of the total vote cast for presidential electors, and in Virginia the figure is twenty-five per cent. Since a party must be in existence before it can offer candidates, some means must be provided for them to get started. Illustrative of this process is the Oregon procedure by which a "minor" party gains legal status by circulating petitions to gather signatures of registered voters equal in number to five per cent of the total votes cast in the last general election for candidates for membership in the lower house of Congress.

Since the legal existence of parties derives from state authority, a question naturally arises as to the legal status of *national* parties. On this point a great deal of confusion may arise in the mind of the student. However, if the state political party is viewed primarily as an organization for the nomination of candidates for public office, the confusion is quickly dispelled. Since the holding of elections is a state function, and parties operate as nominating agents in those elections, it follows that the parties may be subjected to regulation by the state. Since a state may exercise legal authority only over matters within its jurisdiction, it may determine the qualifications for a political party within state boundaries, but it can do no more than recognize the existence of a national organization and, as all states have done, regulate to some extent the ways in which persons

---

[1] For a discussion of definitions, see William Goodman, *The Two-Party System in the United States*, 3rd edition, D. Van Nostrand Co., Inc., Princeton, N. J. 1964, pp. 4–7.

within the state participate in the national organization. Obviously then, there are fifty different state parties in the loose association of groups known as the Republican Party and an equal number in the Democratic Party. There are fewer state parties in the organizations known as *third* parties such as the Prohibitionists, Progressives, and Socialists. Regardless of any show of strength they may be able to make, groups advocating violent overthrow of the government are generally denied legal recognition. As a result, Communist organizations are not political parties.

At the national level, political parties must be regarded as extra-legal entities. Congress does not undertake to establish a legal definition of parties other than to provide that subversive organizations seeking the overthrow of government in the United States may not function as political parties.[2] However, Congress does recognize the fact that political parties exist. Indeed, the organization of Congress itself is based on the party affiliation of the senators and representatives. In many statutes dealing with a wide variety of topics party action and affiliation is recognized. Contributions to parties, for example, are regulated by statute. A civil servant cannot be discharged for reasons of party preference. The membership of certain governmental commissions must be divided as evenly as possible between members of the major parties. Scores of other statutes provide the same type of recognition.

ORIGINS AND DEVELOPMENT

The American political party system dates back to the beginnings of the Union. During the colonial period there were clubs and associations that resembled parties and in many ways acted like them, but not until the work of framing a constitution for the new Union was undertaken did the cleavages appear that were to result in the formation of parties. Those first groups, referred to comtemporaneously as "factions," were the *Federalists,* who supported the Constitution, and the *Anti-Federalists,* who were generally opposed to strengthening the central government.

At the Constitutional Convention of 1787 parties were looked upon with disfavor. So strong was the disposition against them that the Constitution made no mention of parties. By placing the office of the Presidency, the Senate, and the courts out of reach of the

---

[2] 50 U.S. Code 842.

people and by separating the branches of government, it was felt that the "mischiefs of faction" could be avoided. However, despite the attitudes and fears of the framers and men at the head of the government during its first years, political parties were rapidly formed.

The first dozen years under the Constitution were dominated by the Federalists, led by Alexander Hamilton. The opposing Anti-Federalists, later called *Republicans* and then *Democratic-Republicans,* were headed by Thomas Jefferson. These parties set the pattern for today's party system. The Hamiltonian group eventually evolved into the modern Republican Party, and the Democrats trace their lineage directly to the party of Jefferson.

The Jeffersonian Republicans won the first presidential election of the nineteenth century and remained in control for the next twenty years. The Federalists waned and died out completely by 1816. From then until the ascendancy of Andrew Jackson the Jeffersonians were so dominant that their only significant opposition came from dissident elements within their own ranks. During this period strong opposing parties did not exist, with the result that these few years are known, rather euphemistically, as the "Era of Good Feeling." In 1824 the Republican Party split into competing factions with the result that no presidential candidate was able to garner a majority of the electoral votes. The "old" Republicans backed Andrew Jackson while the "new" Republicans, whose views were reminiscent of the defunct Federalists, supported John Quincy Adams. The Adams followers, called the *National Republicans,* won in the House election of the President over the *Democratic Republicans* who had rallied around Jackson.

In 1828 Jackson's followers, organized as the *Democratic Party,* defeated their opponents by an overwhelming majority and continued as the dominant party until the Civil War. The heirs of the Federalists, the National Republicans, soon crumbled and were replaced by the *Whigs* who offered their first presidential candidate in 1836. The Whig Party managed to capture the Presidency twice by nominating military heroes, William Henry Harrison in 1840 and Zachary Taylor in 1848. Both died after short periods in office and, ironically, their successors John Tyler and Millard Fillmore proved to be more sympathetic with the views of the Democrats than with those of their Whig colleagues.

Basically, the Whig Party was a combination of groups who

shared a dislike for the Jacksonians. Included in a tenuous alliance were the commercial, financial, and industrial interests, the prosperous farmers, and large planters. They were unable to agree among themselves on a meaningful, consistent party program, and in the early 1850's when the slavery issue became explosive the party disintegrated.

The present *Republican Party* was formed in 1854 as the Whig organization crumbled. By combining elements of the Whig and antislavery groups, and making a strong bid for the support of the farmer, laborer, and small businessman, the Republicans assumed major party status in the election of 1856. The North-South split in the Democratic Party in 1860 enabled the Republican candidate, Abraham Lincoln, to win the Presidency and usher in a seventy-year period of Republican supremacy. From the beginning of the Civil War until the election of Franklin D. Roosevelt in 1932, Grover Cleveland and Woodrow Wilson, each of whom was elected twice, were the only candidates of the Democratic Party chosen to serve as President. For twenty years, throughout the depression of the 1930's and beyond World War II, the Democrats held the Presidency, relinquishing it in 1952 when Dwight D. Eisenhower defeated Adlai E. Stevenson. Eight years later the Democrats again won the high office when John F. Kennedy narrowly defeated Richard M. Nixon. Lyndon B. Johnson succeeded to the high office upon the assassination of President Kennedy in 1963, and at the general election of 1964 defeated Senator Barry M. Goldwater by a landslide vote.

In many ways there is little difference between the two major parties. Neither advocates profound changes in the basic governmental forms and processes. Differences between parties arise in terms of what they think government ought to be doing at a given time. Consequently, Democrats and Republicans may differ markedly at any moment in respect to some aspects of public policy. On such questions as extending social security coverage, regulating labor-management relations, developing hydroelectric facilities, or financing public housing they may take opposing stands—but often on questions of degree rather than of kind.

Historically, the Democratic Party, the party of Jefferson and Jackson, has been dedicated to the view that the central government should do only what the states or the citizens could not do for themselves. On the other hand, the Republicans, in the tradition of Hamilton, represented the centralist point of view. The evolution of parties has resulted in a virtual switching of positions. Since the turn of the twentieth century when the Democrats absorbed the views of the Populists, they have become increasingly the party of regulation in the public interest with emphasis on the role of the national government. At the same time the Republicans have tended to stress the vitality of the states and the self-sufficiency of the individual. While the change in party outlooks has been developing over the last half-century, the most noticeable alterations in party positions occurred during the period of the New Deal in the 1930's and through the war years that followed.

THE AMERICAN PARTY SYSTEM

Viewed nationally, party activity in the United States has taken the form of a "two-party" system, meaning that two *major* parties are dominant, and to them are attracted the great bulk of voters. Other parties known as *third* parties exist, but usually they are short-lived or do not seriously threaten the supremacy of the major parties.

Many explanations have been offered as to why a two-party system exists in this country when all over the world, except in the English-speaking countries, "multiple" party systems with several parties possessing considerable strength are found. While no authoritative, documented list of reasons may be cited, it appears that the best rationale rests upon a complex of factors.[3] First, the effects of *initial form* must be taken into account. When Americans were confronted with the major political decision of adopting or rejecting the Constitution, only two courses of action were open to them. Political alignments had to be made on that basis, and later when parties began to take form the pattern of alignment tended to persist. Second, *institutional factors* certainly have exerted a profound influence. Most elective offices in the United States are filled by means of the *plurality* system, meaning simply that the candidate who gets the most votes is elected. Since most elective public officials are chosen from single-member districts, only one person can be elected regardless of the number of candidates in a district. The fewer candidates who run for an office, the greater are the mathematical chances of election for each aspirant. Accordingly there is a tendency

---

[3] One of the best, concise discussions of the causes of and reasons for two-partyism in the United States is found in V. O. Key, Jr., *Politics, Parties, and Pressure Groups,* 4th ed., Thomas Y. Crowell Co., New York, 1958, pp. 225–231. Much of the above discussion is based on Professor Key's comments.

for political groups to align themselves into as few parties as possible in order to increase their possibilities of success. Under such a system the minor party is at a distinct disadvantage. The use of electors in choosing the President of the United States is in reality a method of combining the results of fifty single-member districts, the states; and, in view of the plurality rule, this procedure all but eliminates the possibility of a third party's electing a President.

A third factor that tends to strengthen and perpetuate the two-party system is the general approval accorded to it by the American people. Relatively few groups in the United States are so dogmatically attached to a single idea or principle that they cannot merge with other groups in one or the other of the two major parties. This characteristic of American partisans "retards and discourages the growth of population splinters that might form the basis for a multiplicity of deviating parties."[4]

State and Local Patterns. Despite the fact that nationally the two-party system prevails, a variety of systems, or "subsystems," are found at the state and local levels. In some areas the party system is like the national pattern. In others only one party is of any consequence. The party system in a few areas is characterized by third parties that have been able to contend seriously with the Democrats and Republicans. As a matter of fact, third parties have for limited periods become dominant, relegating the traditional major parties to virtual minor party status. In still other areas, formal party designations have been abandoned, resulting in nonpartisan elections, at least in form.

In most states, large cities, and counties there are two principal parties, the Democrats and Republicans, offering candidates for practically all offices. There are areas, however, where deviation from the two-party pattern has persisted. Best known of these exceptional areas is the Democratically dominated southeastern United States, often called the "Solid South." Since Reconstruction days the Republican Party in each of those states has been little more than a hard core of party faithful. In view of the prospects of almost certain Democratic victories, Republican candidacies usually have been limited to only the most important offices. Throughout the South there are only a few areas where Republicans have been able to estab-

---

[4] *Ibid.,* p. 231.

lish themselves as a contending party. Among the combined congressional delegations from the southern states there are only a dozen or so Republicans—all members of the House of Representatives. In New England the pattern of party domination is reversed. Traditionally, the Republican Party has been strong in those states, and particularly in Maine and Vermont Republican supremacy has been characterized as one-party domination.

Nonpartisan Systems. Except for the election without party labels of members of the Nebraska and Minnesota legislatures, many judges, and a few executive officers such as superintendents of public instruction, nonpartisanship is confined to municipalities and special districts. A principal argument in support of nonpartisanship on the local level is that parties are closely identified with national and state issues and when national, state, and local elections are held simultaneously, questions of local importance tend to be obscured. As a result, the local citizenry is not as likely to give as much thought and attention to local matters as they should. Other reasons for the greater incidence of nonpartisanship at the local level derive primarily from the technical or business nature of the functions involved. In choosing the personnel of a governing board for a drainage district, for example, it would be rather difficult to maintain that there is a Republican as opposed to a Democratic method of draining a swamp. The same reasoning applies to other types of governmental programs involving technical problems. Governing a municipality is sometimes said to be similar in many ways to the management of a business, as suggested by the term municipal *corporation.* Operating water systems, power plants, and sewage-disposal facilities, paving streets, maintaining libraries, and providing parks and other such municipal functions are similar to business ventures, and in the judgment of many persons they are hampered more than helped when subjected to partisan control. In short, the theory of nonpartisanship holds that by minimizing the influence of political parties more effective and efficient government can be achieved.

Running a government, no matter how large or how small it may be, always involves making policy—and policymaking is a process that is potentially controversial and contentious. The example of draining a swamp cited above admittedly involves questions of a technical nature that have little or no connection with partisan activity. But what of the question as to whether the swamp *ought* to be drained? Should bonds be issued or new taxes levied to finance the project? These are questions of policy that invite disagreement and partisanship. It is thus almost impossible to conceive of a governmental activity that does not, at one stage or another, take on a partisan character.

Viewed strictly from the standpoint of theory, there is little doubt that a nonpartisan system is highly desirable. In practice, however, the theory often does not hold up. Removing party labels from candidates does not transform them into nonpartisans. A Democrat who is elected to a city council on a nonpartisan ballot remains a Democrat. A Republican similarly chosen to serve on a school board does not drop his party preference after taking office. Although the actions of nonpartisan officials and boards may not be *formally* associated with the programs of political parties, identification is often unmistakable.

Another weakness in the nonpartisan rationale lies in the fact that when political parties as such are dispensed with, other political action groups of a partisan nature assume greater prominence and in a sense replace them. In a given locality, for instance, labor unions, chambers of commerce, farm groups, veterans' organizations, civic improvement clubs, churches, newspapers and the like may campaign for certain policies or endorse some "nonpartisan" candidates in preference to others. When this occurs, as it often does, it is obvious that the theoretical advantages of nonpartisanship are lost. The partisan pattern is merely altered.

It is not to be denied that nonpartisanship can work. When citizens in a community are overwhelmingly like-minded, partisan activity is at a minimum. A lack of controversial issues deadens partisan spirit. Such conditions are not common, however, and when they do prevail they are usually of temporary duration.

Third Parties. In addition to the two major parties in the United States there traditionally has been a varying number of third parties. Some have persisted for long periods of time while others have lasted for only a few years. National prominence and importance have been achieved by some while others have flourished in only a limited number of states. In some instances a third party has been active within only one state or even a single community. Only once in American history has a third party replaced one of the major parties.

That event occurred when the Republican Party of today rose to fill the void created by the disintegration of the Whigs.

Third parties generally have been of two types: those dedicated to the fulfillment of an easily identifiable general principle or goal, and those composed of the devoted followers of an outstanding personality. The Prohibitionists, Socialists, and Populists are examples of groups that are, or have been, "idea" parties. Probably the best example of a "personality" party is the "Bull Moose" Progressive Party which split from the Republicans in 1912 under the leadership of Theodore Roosevelt. Failing to win the presidency in that year, Roosevelt was never again a presidential candidate, and the party disappeared. Other examples include the Progressives led by Robert M. La Follette, Sr., in the 1920's, and the Henry A. Wallace Progressives of 1948.

At the state and local levels particularly, it must not be assumed that a third party is necessarily "minor" in character. A third party may be able to contend on equal terms with the Democrats and Republicans. In fact, a third party may, for a short period at least, become dominant. In 1948 the States' Rights Party, known as the Dixiecrats, was dominant in several southern states. The Liberal Party of New York has been highly influential in that state, and in North Dakota the Nonpartisan League, operating as a faction within the two major parties, has been the controlling factor in the outcome of many elections. Though now merged with the Democrats, the Farmer-Labor Party has been a vital force in Minnesota politics. Sometimes third parties are unable to exert appreciable statewide influence but are important in certain localities. The Socialist Party, for example, has realized successes in Milwaukee, Wisconsin, Bridgeport, Connecticut, and Reading, Pennsylvania, although its influence throughout those states has been negligible. It is important to bear in mind that the national pattern of two-partyism does not, at any one time, necessarily prevail in a particular state or locality.

Third parties never have been able to win a great many public offices or to exercise sustained control over public policy. They have, nevertheless, contributed significantly to the American political system. Their chief effect has been to introduce new ideas which, at the time of inception, were shunned by the major parties as politically risky. Antitrust legislation, income taxes, popular election of United States senators, and female suffrage were matters championed by third parties. After it became obvious that substantial numbers of voters were favorable toward such innovations, those proposals were absorbed into the programs of one or both major parties. Their programs thus taken over, third parties usually declined in importance or disappeared altogether. A significant result of activities by third parties has been to stimulate realignment of groups, factions, and individuals within the major parties. For example, the Republican Party was seriously rent in 1912 when literally millions of voters were wooed away by Theodore Roosevelt. The Progressive and States' Rights movements in 1948 weakened the Democratic Party to a dangerous extent, though not enough to bring about defeat of the party's presidential candidate.

Functions of Political Parties. The principle function of a political party is to choose candidates and secure their election to public office. Parties perform other functions too, but virtually every action of a party can be rationalized in terms of its contribution toward winning votes. This situation should not be surprising, for a party that is unable to attract enough votes to elect at least a reasonable number of its candidates can hardly be regarded as an effective vehicle of political action.

In its drive to win popular following and establish itself in a position of dominance, a political party must discharge certain functions and bear definite responsibilities. First, voters tend generally to hold a party accountable for its candidates who are elected to office. Just as a party profits from outstanding performance by its members in office, its status is likewise damaged by dishonest, incompetent, or even politically unpopular actions on the part of party members in public service. In this respect the party is frequently termed a "bonding agent" to insure satisfactory performance of its electees.

A party also acts as informant to the electorate by presenting a program and taking stands on issues. It is true that each party slants information to favor its own views, but since both major parties and third parties act in their own interests, the voters get a variety of views on issues of interest to political parties. Next, a party serves as "watchdog" or "critic" of governmental affairs. While all parties are active in this capacity, the major party out of power fills the role best. Hoping to capitalize on mistakes made by the party in power, the "out" party stands ready to inform the voters about the mistakes of the opposition. Finally, parties are a means by which cohesion is achieved both within and between the legislative and executive branches at all levels. Party affiliations of officials in various positions in government, especially those that involve the making of policy decisions, provide a basis for cooperation. Legislatures, for example, are organized on the basis of party. An administration controlled by the party possessing a majority in the legislature is more likely to enjoy amicable relations with the lawmakers. Appointments usually are made on the basis of party. Indeed, political parties are the interconnecting tissue in the fabric of government.

PARTY ORGANIZATION

A political party, like any other group, must be well organized to operate effectively. Without organization a party would be little more than a vaguely definable association of individuals sharing similar viewpoints on a number of issues. With effective organization it is a collection of individuals and groups which, potentially, can control the policies and personnel of government.

Since there is no legal connection between state and national party organizations, each American political party is separately organized on the national and state levels. In other words, a major party is made up of fifty different state organizations and a single national organization which is not empowered to exercise full legal controls over the state components. Third parties vary from the pattern in that they do not legally exist in many states and may be treated in a manner different from that applicable to the major parties.

National Organization. At the apex of an American political party is the *national committee*. Each party is free to determine its own organizational structure, and in doing so the major parties have evolved national committees that are similarly selected and composed. The Democratic national committee consists of one man and one woman from each state and territory. In addition, the Republican Party made it possible in 1952 for each state to gain a third national committee member. Included as members of the Republican national committee are the state committee chairman from each state which cast its electoral vote for the party's presidential candidates at the last election, has a majority of Republicans in its congressional delegation, or has a Republican governor. Technically, national committee members are chosen by the national convention, but in actuality they are selected in primary elections, by state conventions, by state central committees, or by the national convention delegation.

PARTY ORGANIZATION IN ILLINOIS

MEMBERS OF EACH POLITICAL PARTY AT THE APRIL PRIMARIES

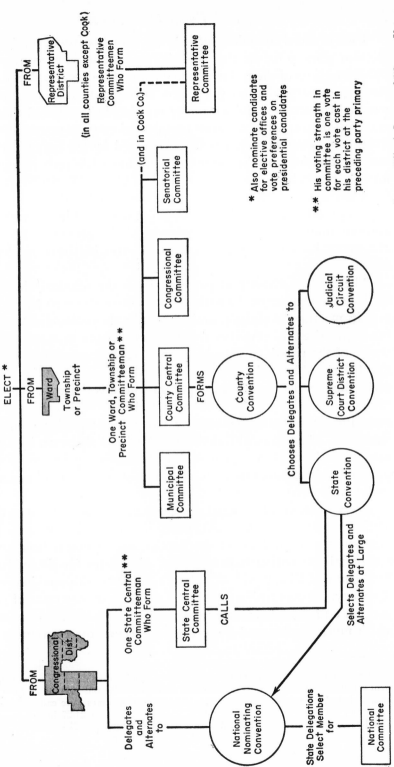

* Also nominate candidates for elective offices and vote preferences on presidential candidates

** His voting strength in committee is one vote for each vote cast in his district at the preceding party primary

Source: Illinois League of Women Voters

Each national committee usually meets in January of presidential election years to fix the time and place of the national convention. Other meetings of the full membership are infrequent, ordinarily including only organizational meetings, an assembly at the time of the national convention, and a strategy meeting held prior to the general election conducted between presidential election years. At other times committee work is actually performed by the national chairman or divisions of the committee dealing with such matters as finance, research, women's affairs, and publicity. Entirely separate from the national committees are the senatorial and congressional campaign committees found in both major parties. These committees are accountable only to the respective legislative groups, but because of common interests they frequently cooperate with the national committee.

The general director of party affairs is the national chairman. He is not a member of the national committee although he presides over its meetings. Officially, he is chosen by the national committee, but in practice the committee usually does no more than approve the choice of the party's presidential nominee. In case of a vacancy in the chairmanship of the party in power, the President of the United States dictates the choice of the person who fills the post. Should a vacancy occur in the defeated party's chairmanship, the national committee, perhaps influenced by party leaders, selects the new chairman. The principal function of a national chairman is to manage the presidential campaign, but after the election he continues to act as organizer, fund-raiser, trouble-shooter, general publicity manager, and outspoken critic of the opposition.

Every four years national conventions are held by American parties. Composed of delegates chosen in accordance with state statutes and the regulations of the parties, the principal function of a national convention is to nominate candidates for the offices of President and Vice President.[5] As the supreme policymaking organ of a party, the convention draws up a *platform* or statement of party position on issues of political interest. Usually a boisterous affair at which much dealing and compromising occurs, the convention has

---

[5] The number of delegates to national conventions is determined by an apportionment formula provided by the convention of each party. At the 1964 Republican convention, held July 13-16 in San Francisco, California, 1,308 votes were cast by an equal number of delegates. The Democratic convention, held August 24-27 in Atlantic City, New Jersey, was attended by 3,052 delegates who cast a total of 2,316 votes.

prevailed as the presidential nominating device of all major and most third parties since 1831.[6]

State and Local Organization. Within each state political party, organization corresponds generally to the boundaries of election districts. That is, a committee exists at the state level, and others are organized in counties, cities, wards, towns, congressional districts, and the like. In no two states are parties organized in identical fashion, but all systems are similar enough to permit generalization.

At the head of a party's state organization is the state *central committee*. Based on state law, central committees present a wide variety of characteristics. Professor V. O. Key comments that

> Variety characterizes their composition, method of selection, duties, and even formal titles. They range in size from a handful to a group that can meet only in a convention hall. Their authority at one extreme amounts to that of a constituent body for the party in a state; at the other it amounts to little more than the ministerial performance of duties minutely prescribed by statute.[7]

Generally, in states where statutory controls are not extensive or excessively detailed, notably in the southeastern area of the country, the discretion of a state central committee is broadest. Even there, however, the one-party nature of state politics with all major candidates in the same party results in pressure for impartiality on the part of the committee.

Chosen by, but ordinarily not a member of, the state central committee is the titular head of the party, the state chairman. He resembles his national counterpart in that promotion of party candidates in general elections and fostering party harmony are his principal functions, but frequently he is not the real leader of his party. Often the governor, a United States Senator, a national committeeman, or some other person or group is much more influential than the state chairman. Moreover, state chairmen commonly have found it

---

[6] One of the most vivid reactions to national conventions in this country was that of the Russian observer, M. Ostrogorski, who declared after watching a convention in action "you cannot help repeating the American saying: 'God takes care of drunkards, of little children, and of the United States.'" M. Ostrogorski, *Democracy and the Organization of Political Parties,* trans. by Frederick Clarke, The Macmillan Co., New York, 1902, vol. II, pp. 278–279.

[7] V. O. Key, *op. cit.,* p. 357.

difficult, if not impossible, to exercise control over local political "bosses."

Between the state central committee and the local units of organization are found various district committees set up on the basis of congressional, state legislative, or state judicial districts. In most states such committees are relatively unimportant. Their only function usually is to assist in the election of the party's candidate in the district, a task often performed by county personnel or the candidate's personal committee. In some instances these committees have authority to nominate candidates in the event of death or withdrawal of the regularly chosen nominees, and they often influence appointment of party followers to governmental jobs.

Precincts are the "building blocks" of local party machinery. These election districts are plotted geographically to contain a certain number of voters, 300 to 500 being common. Party organization within a precinct somtimes consists of a committee, but usually there is a precinct *committeeman* or *captain*. Elected in most instances in the party primary, the precinct captain's function is to win over the voters in his area. The fact that no party, especially in two-party areas, can expect to win consistently without effective precinct personnel attests to the importance of this local office.

At the local level *county committees* are the most significant units of party organization. Members of these committees are selected in various ways. Some are chosen by conventions, a few are picked by candidates, but most are elected in the precincts at party primaries. Election as a precinct committeeman frequently carries with it membership on the county committee. Operating in practical independence from the state committee and with little control over other local committees, the typical county committee performs such functions as managing conventions, carrying on campaigns, and supervising party affairs throughout the county. The county committee ordinarily is an important and vigorous unit in party machinery.

The *county chairman* is ordinarily an important individual in local politics. In many states he is the county's representative on the state central committee. He is influential as a policymaker and frequently supervises campaigns in his county. With his knowledge of local conditions and personalities he can be invaluable to the welfare of his party. Ordinarily, his effectiveness is greatest in rural areas, because urban areas usually are more susceptible to influence by the personnel of ward, precinct, town, village, or other committees.

Party organization in urban areas presents a broad range of patterns. In some states the county organization is all that exists apart from citizens' or candidates' committees. Very often, however, parties in urban areas have a multilevel organizational hierarchy, with large cities tending to have more complex systems. While details of composition, selection, and functions vary, the *ward* is commonly the level next above the precinct, and above the ward is the city-wide organization. Titles differ widely, but usually they are derived from the designation of the election districts involved, such as precinct, ward, city, and town. At each level one person functions as chairman or leader. The duties of all these organizations are similar and are much like those of their counterparts at higher levels.

PARTY MEMBERSHIP

Membership in an American political party is purely voluntary. A prospective member does not have to fill out an application to join, nor does he have to pay dues or work for his party. A party member cannot be expelled; he is required to take an oath of allegiance; he is not compelled to assume party responsibilities; and there is no means of forcing him to support the party's candidates or to accept its whole program. Even when a voter designates a party affiliation at the time of registration, as he is required to do in most states, such designation is not necessarily conclusive. A person who considers himself a Republican may register as a Democrat in order to vote in the latter's primary, or a registered Democrat may change his mind about his party affiliation without changing his registration. Party membership is more a *state of mind* than a legally recognized affiliation.

Party membership often is estimated in terms of the votes cast for a party's candidates and the number of voters registered as party members. Such criteria are merely approximations, however accurate they may at times be. How, for example, is the voter who splits his ticket evenly between two parties to be classified? What is the status of the underage partisan? How are the criteria to be adjusted when registration favors one party, but the opposition elects more candidates? The only logical conclusion is that party membership is, indeed, a vaguely defined thing that is subject to change at any time by individual will.

Undoubtedly, millions of people change their party affiliations during their lives, perhaps several times. As far as individual changes are concerned, the awareness of the general public is not aroused unless the person involved is either well known or occupies a sensitive position. When Theodore Roosevelt bolted the Republican Party and ran for the presidency in 1912 millions followed him. Although Henry Wallace's defection from the Democrats in 1948 was prominently featured in the news, it was not successful in winning a large following. In more recent years Senator Wayne Morse, elected as a Republican from Oregon, announced changes in his party status successively from Republican to Independent to Democrat—and was later re-elected as a Democrat. During the presidential campaign of 1964, Senator Strom Thurmond of South Carolina bolted the Democrats, announcing that he had decided to become a Republican. Such examples support the statement that party membership is a matter of individual will.

PARTY FINANCE

Running for office in the United States is an expensive undertaking. There are times when sizable expenditures are not necessary, as when a candidate is unopposed or when some minor local offices are involved, but ordinarily a candidate and his backers must have a considerable sum of money at their disposal if they expect to win. Election costs have risen steadily over the years. Today there are more voters to be reached, a wider variety of publicity media available to campaigners, and more refined techniques of research and analysis that precede campaigns. A candidate who earnestly desires election can ill afford to neglect any process that may win votes. Consequently, even after discounting the effects of inflation upon the present-day dollar, electioneering costs are much higher today than formerly.

Campaign expenditures vary greatly in proportion to the importance of the office to be filled. The largest sums are spent in behalf of presidential candidates with decreasingly smaller amounts paid out in efforts to secure election to the positions of United States senator, representative to Congress, governor, and lower offices. It must be remembered, however, that at a given time an office may take on importance that it does not normally have. For example, an otherwise comparatively unimportant seat in a state legislature may be the one that determines which party will control a legislative house, or an incumbent running in an unpredictable district may be a key figure in party organization. Greater efforts, financial and otherwise, must be exerted under such circumstances than under other conditions. In any event, money has become an extremely important factor in the conduct of elections, necessitating governmental regulation.

Raising enough money to carry on effective campaigns takes time, organization, and a great deal of energy. Since American parties, except for some third parties, do not collect dues from their members, they must turn to other sources. These sources include (1) individuals and families, (2) persons in office and those seeking office, (3) private organizations such as pressure groups, (4) committees organized to support certain candidates, and (5) party functions such as dinners, dances, and rallies. Despite the variety of sources and the emphasis both major parties place on small contributions from many individuals, the great bulk of funds contributed to parties comes from a relatively small number of donors. This observation is applicable to both the national and state levels and has caused concern over the possibility that parties or candidates may incur "liabilities" or be effectively "controlled" by heavy contributors. As a result, Congress and each state legislature has enacted legislation to regulate party finance and "corrupt practices" in general.

National Regulation. Numerous federal statutes attempt to regulate financial and other affairs of political parties. Since the national government has no authority to control purely state affairs, these laws are limited in application to party activities at the national level and to state activities assisted by or directly involving the national government. Among such regulations is the requirement, in effect since 1910, that parties must file with the clerk of the House of Representatives statements of all contributions and expenditures. Since 1940 the national committee of each party has been limited in the amount it may spend on a presidential candidate's campaign to $3,000,000, and individual contributions have been limited to $5,000. The Corrupt Practices Act of 1925 limited the amounts that candidates for the United States Senate and House of Representatives may spend. Also, corporations and labor unions are prohibited from contributing to campaign funds.

The intent of such laws is good, but evasion has proved to be easy. For instance, even though an individual may give no more than

$5,000 to the national committee of a party, there is no way to prevent his giving similar amounts to private committees supporting his favorite candidates; and, of course, several members of his family may make contributions. Although corporations and unions may not make contributions, the officers of these organizations and members of their families can and do give large sums. Also, political action groups associated with corporations or labor organizations contribute to the campaign chests of various candidates.

Federal corrupt practices legislation prohibits candidates for federal offices from offering governmental jobs, or threatening dismissal of government workers, in order to secure political support. Civil service workers are not permitted to participate actively in political campaigns. Persons or firms entering into contracts with the national government may not contribute to campaign funds. Measures such as these are intended to guard against illegal, unethical practices by government groups. They have been largely effective in preventing illegal actions, but evasions within the letter of the law indicate that unethical conduct has not been eliminated.

State Regulation. Following the lead of New York in 1890, every state has enacted legislation designed to keep political party activities honest. These laws vary greatly in form and coverage, but everywhere certain acts are defined as criminal and therefore prohibited. For example, bribery, which includes giving gifts to influence political activity, is a criminal act. Criminal laws also prohibit embezzlement, libel, slander, extortion and many other acts contrary to public dignity and order. Any candidate or party member who perpetrates any such act would be liable to prosecution.

In some states corrupt practices legislation goes no further than to impose criminal sanctions similar to those mentioned above. By way of contrast other states have fashioned rather comprehensive statutes with detailed provisions pertaining to party finances. Regulating party finance aims generally at four major activities: "(1) publicity of sources of income and expenditures, (2) limitation on sources of income, (3) limitation on expenditures, and (4) prevention of bribery and pernicious political activity."[8] Laws on these matters are difficult to enforce, not so much because of brazen defiance by candidates, but because it is easy to evade them. The evasion tech-

---

[8] Hugh A. Bone, *American Politics and the Party System*, 3rd. edition, McGraw-Hill, Inc., New York, 1955, p. 419.

niques mentioned above in connection with national regulation are practiced at the state level with equal or more success.

Methods of regulation in the states are similar to those adopted by Congress. About thirty states, for instance, limit the amount of money a candidate may spend or that may be spent by others in his behalf. Limitations may be expressed as a flat sum, a percentage of the salary attached to the office sought by a candidate, or in terms of an allowance per vote cast in a preceding election. Over forty states require that statements of contributions and expenditures must be filed. Candidates for state offices usually report to the secretary of state, while county and city clerks receive reports from local candidates. Reports in most states are filed *after* elections although a fourth of the states also require statements *before* the voters go to the polls, and a few insist upon periodical disclosures *during* the campaign. Over thirty states prohibit contributions by corporations, and a half-dozen extend the proscription to labor unions. A few states limit regulation to primaries only, but the great majority regulate party actions in all elections.

PRESSURE GROUPS

Making public policy is a process that necessarily involves compromise of interests. Every cause, movement, and organization has its supporters who would like to see public policy framed in such a way that their interests are favorably treated. But policymakers, chiefly legislators and executive officials, cannot be all things to all individuals and all groups. To satisfy all the requests of one or a few groups would place others at extreme disadvantage. The demands of all groups cannot be met, yet all cannot be ignored. Interests must somehow be compromised so that resulting policy is not determined without regard for the interests of most segments of society.

Viewed in this manner, the formulation of public policy is clearly a process that is susceptible to pressures by interested individuals and groups. Legislators, administrators, and the general public are exposed constantly to the exertions of those seeking changes in policy. In the struggle for favorable treatment groups are formed to promote special interests. The character and purpose of these organizations are revealed in the observation that

> When divisions within a society become so conscious of their desires that they perfect a definite organization, draw up a platform

of objectives, and actively seek to bring about the realization of their aspirations by influencing elected and appointive officials, they have attained the status of a pressure group.[9]

Pressure groups are found everywhere in the United States. They appear in many forms and may be interested in a single phase of policy or in many. Some are tightly organized, while others are loosely knit. Some are affluent, and others are virtually penniless. Whatever their individual composition may be, all pressure groups have one thing in common: the promotion of a particular interest.

Pressure groups, like political parties, serve as means of political expression for millions of people. However, even though political expression is the underlying basis of both parties and pressure groups, there are fundamental differences between them. First, pressure groups do not nominate candidates for office, but they are interested in who is elected and often endorse candidates and give them financial aid. Even so, pressure groups are more interested in what is done by the successful candidate *after* he assumes office. A second major difference lies in the fact that political parties are, indeed must be, concerned with all phases of public affairs, whereas pressure groups are primarily interested in matters that involve the particular interests they seek to promote. Implicit in these distinctions is a third: the broad representation of interests characteristic of a major political party as contrasted with the comparatively narrow interests of the pressure group.

Pressure groups may be classified in several ways. Categories may be based on the level or branch of government to which their attentions are directed. Since many pressure groups exert pressures at all levels and upon numerous governmental agencies and try to popularize their points of view with the general public, they are best classified according to the general subject matter in which they are interested.

Accordingly, the most significant pressure groups are dedicated to promoting the interests of (1) business and industry, (2) labor, (3) agriculture, (4) professions, (5) veterans, (6) religion, (7) consumers, (8) better government, (9) ethnic groups, and (10) government workers. Some groups are not readily classifiable or may fit into more than one of these classifications. This list, as others like it, is not

---

[9] Harold Zink, Howard R. Penniman, and Guy B. Hathorn, *American Government and Politics*, D. Van Nostrand Co., Inc., Princeton, 1958, p. 98.

exhaustive. Nevertheless, it serves to convey an impression of the wide range of interests that stimulate pressure groups and to stress the fact that scarcely a facet of public policy escapes their attention.

The strategy and tactics of pressure groups are such that virtually every avenue of legal—and sometimes illegal—activity is utilized. When engaged in lobbying activities, pressure groups direct their most intensified efforts upon governmental personnel, especially members of legislatures.[10] Pressure groups and lobbies do not, however, cease activity after a legislative session ends. Instead, pressure activities continue, being aimed at governmental officers and employees as well as the general public. Pressuring administrators can be as productive as efforts directed toward legislators, for the meaning and significance of many statutes and rules depend upon interpretations by administrators and the vigor with which they are enforced. Since public acceptance of their ideas is of inestimable value to pressure groups, they constantly strive to achieve that goal. Pressure groups of one type or another work year-round to create public sympathy that may lead to desired alterations in public policy. All communication media are employed to get a point of view across, with the intensity of a group's efforts varying in accord with the resources available to it.

Occasional acts of an illegal or selfish nature have fostered suspicion of pressure organizations as a whole, but regardless of such unfortunate incidents, pressure groups serve a useful purpose. Congress and state legislatures alike use and sometimes depend heavily upon information supplied by these groups. Their representation of functional interests in American society has inspired the observation that pressure groups constitute "the third house of the legislature." It is not to be denied that pressure organizations may stimulate improvement of government. Some pressure groups seek improvement of governmental organization and administration, while others have prodded government into paying more attention to various areas of social concern. Pressure organizations provide channels of political expression for individuals dedicated to the fulfillment of ideas that political parties may or may not endorse. Inasmuch as parties cannot accommodate all persons and all groups, pressure groups play a significant role in politics.

---

[10] See Chapter 7, the section entitled "Lobbies and Lobbyists," where this phase of activity is more fully discussed.

THE LOCAL POLITICAL SCENE

Today more than ever American interests in politics and elections are nationally oriented. Except in the one-party southern states where primary elections are most important, the greatest voter turn-outs occur at general elections in which the President of the United States is chosen. Next in terms of voter interest are the off-year general elections. A distinct third are local elections held separately from the general elections. At some special elections held, for example, to fill a vacant office or to pass on a bond issue, it is not unusual for as few as five or ten per cent of eligible voters to go to the polls! Even when local elections are held simultaneously with general elections, the number of ballots cast for local offices and on local issues is invariably lower than for state and national positions and issues.

There are several reasons for the tendency of modern voters to exhibit slight interest in local politics. The American voter has always been interested in the politics of his nation, but with the advent of rapid communications and constantly expanding functions of the national government his interest has been heightened. Split-second communications keep the interested citizen informed and up-to-date on important and controversial national and international problems. In such areas as taxation, business regulation, labor problems, public welfare, veterans' affairs, selective service, highway construction, transportation, and agriculture the national government has taken the initiative. Thus to many persons local politics seem far less significant.

One of the anomalies of this situation is the fact that in most cases the success of a political party is largely dependent upon how well it is organized locally. It would thus seem that in counties, towns, and cities with well organized parties interest in local political affairs would at least approach that stimulated by national and state issues. Even in such places, however, interest in local affairs tends to lag. There are many localities where interest is high at one time or another and some, usually large, communities where interest is sustained. Controversy, scandal, collusion, reform movements, and active local third parties are examples of stimuli that on occasion jog citizens into awareness of occurrences in their own political back-yard. For a while interest in local politics may soar and even overshadow the affairs of state and nation, but almost inevitably local interest soon subsides.

It is unfortunate that local politics do not command more citizen interest. Efforts have been made to stimulate more interest by holding local elections before or after general elections, but even though direct conflict with national and state issues is thereby avoided, interest still lags. The solution would seem to be somehow to make the citizen aware of the fact that his stake in local government is much more important than he apparently realizes. The condition of his neighborhood, his health, the education of his children, the exercise of many rights and privileges, and even his own personal safety depend largely upon the way local government is conducted. When a citizen neglects his local government, the quality of that government is endangered.

THE POLITICAL BOSS

When political action groups vie with each other, they are struggling to achieve *power*. Political parties, pressure groups, and other organizations represent the normal means by which popular desires are expressed and eventually translated into public policy. In a democracy the privilege of exerting governmental power is the goal of contending political camps, and perhaps the most reassuring indication of a functioning democracy is the earnestness, conviction, and vigor with which contending groups compete. Now and then, however, stagnation of group competition occurs and "a single man seizes so much power in a party organization and exercises this power for such ends that he is known as a political boss."[11]

The term *political boss* is difficult to define. To many persons any individual who exercises extensive political power is a boss. However, an elected official whose power stems from a legal basis and who acts in the public interest within the limitations placed on him is not properly regarded as a boss. Thus the late Fiorello La Guardia of New York City, Governor Thomas E. Dewey of New York, and Governor Earl Warren of California were not bosses even though they exercised great political power. By way of contrast, a political boss seizes power, usually does not hold office, exercises

[11] Harold Zink, *Government of Cities in the United States*, revised edition, The Macmillan Co., New York, 1948, p. 198. One of the best discussions of "old-time" political bosses is Professor Zink's *City Bosses in the United States*, Duke University Press, Durham, 1930.

power that does not stem from legal sources, and acts primarily in his own interests. It is true that strong political leaders may at times resort to actions typical of bosses. In such cases a sort of hybrid boss or Jekyll-Hyde type politician may be said to exist.

In American experience political bosses have been a phenomenon of state and local politics with most of them active in a single large city. Men like William M. Tweed and Richard Croker of New York City, Edwin Vare of Philadelphia, James Curley of Boston, and Frank Hague of Jersey City were municipal bosses. Occasionally, a city boss is able to wield influence on a statewide basis. For a generation E. H. Crump of Memphis, Tennessee, controlled an area that could "swing" state elections. Other areas of the state commonly were split in their support of candidates with the result that Crump, through his control of Memphis, was able to make or break state and national candidates in Tennessee. At times bosses have been able to control the politics of an entire state. The most successful of them, such as Governor Huey Long of Louisiana and Governor Eugene Talmadge of Georgia, differed from their municipal counterparts in that they usually occupied a prominent public office. Such bosses have been highly resourceful men, able to build effective political machines.

Usually, a boss rises through the ranks of his party, serving in precinct, ward, or other local organizations. By establishing himself as a local leader and gaining strength through deals, favors, and compromises, he may eventually emerge as a power to be reckoned with. By trading influence for votes and getting his associates politically indebted to him, he can build up a following. If fortunate enough to continue his growth he may ultimately become *the* power in local politics. His following, including officials who owe their appointments or election to his sponsorship, are the organization or *machine* that supports him. A boss may share his position with a select group of associates or find it necessary to act in concert with other like-minded individuals, a form of alliance referred to as a *ring*.

Boss tactics vary so widely that it is impossible to characterize them in a general statement. What an individual boss does to achieve or retain power depends upon his inclinations and the situation in which he finds himself. In other words, a boss may do anything he feels like if he thinks he can get away with it. A boss may form alliances with the underworld, influence business men through manipulation of licenses, inspections, and assessment of taxes, control election officials, harass his opposition by means of zealous police activity, or engage in many other corrupt actions. If a boss-controlled community is lucky, the worst consequence of bossism may be "honest graft," such as favoritism and use of official information to personal advantage. An intelligent boss knows that his most formidable opposition is an active, informed citizenry. Bosses are careful to see that an appearance of "good" government is made with impressive schools, public improvements, hospitals, and parks. The people are thereby lulled into indifference while the boss continues in his position of power.

Inevitably, the question arises as to why or how a boss is able to exist in a democratic community. Basically, the answer is that the processes which lend vitality to the democratic system break down and stagnate. The citizen simply does not take the time and trouble to inform himself on local affairs or to inquire into matters of local importance. The lack of citizen interest and political participation cripples the effectiveness of democracy. More specific factors can be cited including the absence of discipline in political parties, the long ballot, existence of opportunities for graft, manipulation of patronage, unrepresentative bodies, lack of a vocal minority, the "good works" of bosses, and the fact that modern bosses are usually known to the public as respectable citizens and businessmen. Each of these factors helps to explain bossism, but in the final analysis they all stem from the same basic cause: citizen lethargy and indifference.

INFLUENCE OF PUBLIC OPINION

Holding a public office, regardless of how high or low it happens to be, is usually not easy. Every public official has some connection with public policy: making it, carrying it out, and in some instances both. As a result, the public officer is constantly, at least potentially, under public scrutiny. He is subject to pressures for changes in policy or in the manner in which it is administered. His very job often depends directly or indirectly upon the action of the public at the ballot box. It is not surprising that a public officer is sensitive to the changing attitudes of the public. He is, in short, responsive to public opinion.

The term "public opinion" has been subjected to much analysis by various writers over the years. Interpretations vary, but there seems to be agreement on the point that "public" does not necessarily include everyone. In fact, a public may consist of any group of two or more persons. "Opinion" can be any attitude held by such a group, but the attitude does not constitute real opinion until it is *expressed*. In other words, public opinion consists of expressed group attitudes. Viewed in this way it is clear that public opinion is not necessarily a single, easily recognizable viewpoint held by the entire population. Instead, it consists of many attitudes that conflict as well as those that harmonize. In responding to public opinion, the task of the public officer actually becomes one of trying to decide which public opinions are sufficiently important or influential for him to give them serious consideration.

Because of his connection with public policy and the effect of citizen opinion upon the nature and content of that policy, it is essential that a public officer be as aware as possible of popular sentiments. Every such officer and his supporters have their own ideas as to the tenor of public opinion at a given moment, but that is not enough. Public opinion is so complex and so productive of differing viewpoints that it is dangerous to rely upon personal estimates. Something as seemingly noncontroversial as the street paving program of a small community, for example, can stimulate reactions that might easily bewilder a well-meaning, civic-minded councilman. Motorists may welcome the program; affected property owners may object because of anticipated assessments; real estate promoters may push only for that phase of the program that benefits certain areas; civic clubs may voice concern over total costs; other groups conceivably may object to priorities with relation to street lighting, park development, or library expansion. From such a maze of attitudes and reactions who can say, without risk of error, exactly what "public opinion" is with respect to the paving program?

Despite the difficulties of doing so, efforts to assess public opinion must be made. Every interested individual as well as pressure groups, political parties, civic clubs, professional associations, and other organizations try both to mold opinion and to measure it. In an effort to determine the character of public opinion resort may be had to such procedures as assessing the nature and intensity of pressure group activity, making direct contacts with citizens, and evaluating the results of polls and surveys. These methods involve pitfalls, however, for in practically every case it is not possible to contact every person or group involved, and in any event no method exists to register intensity of feeling or to predict changes in opinion. In the last analysis probably the most reliable index of public opinion, particularly in the view of the public officer, is the election. Such knowledge may come too late, however, to benefit the anxious public official.

SELECTED REFERENCES

Books:

Bone, Hugh A., *American Politics and the Party System,* 3rd ed., McGraw-Hill, New York, 1965.

Committee on Political Parties, American Political Science Association, *Toward a More Responsible Two-Party System,* Rinehart and Co., New York, 1950.

Fenton, John H., *Politics in the Border States,* Hauser Press, New Orleans, 1957.

Goodman, William, *The Two-Party System in the United States,* 3rd edition, D. Van Nostrand Co., Inc., Princeton, N.J., 1964.

Hesseltine, William B., *The Rise and Fall of Third Parties,* Public Affairs Press, New York, 1948.

——, *Third Party Movements in the United States,* D. Van Nostrand Co., Inc., Princeton, N.J., 1962.

Hinderaker, Ivan, *Party Politics,* Holt and Co., New York, 1956.

Kelley, Stanley, Jr., *Political Campaigning,* Brookings Institution, Washington, D.C., 1960.

Key, V. O., Jr., *Politics, Parties, and Pressure Groups,* 4th ed., T. Y. Crowell and Co., New York, 1958.

Leiserson, Avery, *Parties and Politics,* Alfred A. Knopf, New York, 1958.

Ranney, Austin, and Kendall, Willmore, *Democracy and the American Party System,* Harcourt, Brace and Co., New York, 1956.

Salter, J. T., *Boss Rule,* McGraw-Hill, Inc., New York, 1935.

Van Riper, Paul P., *Handbook of Practical Politics,* 2nd ed., Row, Peterson and Co., Evanston, 1960.

Articles:

Butcher, Harry K., "How to Be a Politician," *National Municipal Review,* May 1958.

"Changing American Politics," Symposium, *Current History,* August 1956.

"City Bosses and Political Machines," Symposium, *The Annals,* May 1964.

Clark, Joseph S., "Notes on Political Leadership," *Harper's Magazine,* June 1958.

Leiserson, Avery, "The Place of Parties in the Study of Politics," *American Political Science Review,* December 1957.

Neuberger, Richard L., "Who Should Pay for Political Campaigns?" *New York Times Magazine,* June 3, 1956.

Nevins, Allan, "The Strength of Our Political System," *New York Times Magazine,* July 18, 1948.

"Unofficial Government, Pressure Groups and Lobbies," Symposium, *The Annals,* September 1958.

Chapter 12

Nominations and Elections

In a democratic society the people are the source of political power. Ultimately they are responsible for everything that government is or does. For practical reasons, however, the people cannot, as an assembled unit, make all the decisions required of them. Instead, representative forms and processes must be used. The methods employed in selecting the representatives of the people—nomination and public election—are fundamental procedures in the operation of democratic society.

The processes of nomination and election are separate and distinct, yet intimately related. Most simply defined, nomination is a general term designating a number of methods by means of which individuals are selected as candidates for office. An election is a method whereby the people, by casting ballots, choose from among the nominees those persons who will fill public offices. Except for those public office holders who are selected by means of appointment, all governmental officials, whether legislative, executive, or judicial in character, are subject to some type of nomination and election. These processes operate in much the same manner throughout the United States, but each is found in various forms with wide variations in detail. Differing systems exist in each of the fifty states, and further variations are found in many of the more than 90,000 units of local government.

NATIONAL AND STATE POWERS

Authority to control the processes of nomination and election is lodged chiefly in the states. Since the national government may exercise only those powers delegated to it by the United States Constitution, and since that document does not convey to the central government general power in the matter of selecting public officers, regulation of nominations and elections is largely within the area of reserved state authority. Subject to limitations imposed by the

Constitution, the fifty states provide for methods of nomination and stage the elections in which the great bulk of the more than one-half million public, elective offices in the United States are filled.[1]

Even though state power is paramount regarding nominations and elections, the states are limited by some provisions of federal law. In the first place there are a number of provisions in the national Constitution that affect state authority. Qualifications for the offices of President and Vice President of the United States, United States senator, and representative in Congress are set forth in the Constitution, thereby eliminating any possibility of state-imposed qualifications. The Twelfth and Twentieth Amendments prescribe steps to be followed in the selection of the President and Vice President. Popular election is designated as the method of choosing representatives by Article I, Section 2, and the Seventeenth Amendment applies the same procedure to the choice of United States senators. Section 4 of Article I attests that the states have power to prescribe the "times, places, and manner of holding elections for Senators and Representatives," but goes on to add that "Congress may at any time by law make or alter such regulations."[2]

Pursuant to authority derived from the Constitution, Congress has enacted statutes that profoundly affect the process of selecting public officers. Under an act of 1842, for example, members of the House of Representatives must be chosen from single-member districts, a requirement that goes far in determining the nomenclature of state nomination and election procedures.[3] As indicated in the previous chapter, federal corrupt practices legislation extends to nomination and election processes in the states which involve federal elective offices. To a large extent Congress has, for all practical pur-

---

[1] The only places where the national government may exercise full power over these important processes are the territorial possessions and, subject to the Twenty-third Amendment, the District of Columbia.

[2] This clause also denies Congress authority to regulate "the places of choosing Senators." This provision had real meaning when senators were chosen by state legislatures, but became rather insignificant with the addition of the Seventeenth Amendment which provided for popular election of senators.

[3] In 1872 Congress enacted the requirements that representative districts be "compact and contiguous" and of as nearly equal populations "as practicable," but failed to include these provisions in the Reapportionment Act of 1929. Subsequently, the United States Supreme Court ruled in *Wood* v. *Broom,* 287 U.S. 1 (1932), that the states were no longer bound by these restrictions. However, restoration of the equal populations feature may have been accomplished by judicial decision in *Wesberry* v. *Sanders,* 376 U.S. 1 (1964), in which the Supreme Court held invalid the state statute establishing congressional districts in Georgia. The Court stated that Article I, Section 2, requires that "one man's vote in a congressional election is to be worth as much as another's."

poses, fixed the date upon which most elections are held. In 1872 a national statute fixed the first Tuesday after the first Monday in November of even-numbered years as the day for election of members of the House of Representatives.[4] Following ratification of the Seventeenth Amendment, the same day was designated for election of United States senators. Today some state and local officers are elected at different times, but for the most part the day chosen by Congress has been designated by the states as the day for electing public officials.

The power of the national government to police elections in which national officers are chosen is clearly reflected in decisions of the United States Supreme Court. In the Maryland congressional election of 1878 several persons were arrested for stuffing ballot boxes contrary to state laws. They were brought to trial and convicted in a federal court under a federal statute of 1870 that made it a crime for anyone to interfere with federal supervisors attempting to see that state election laws were fairly administered. This extensive national authority was upheld by the Court.[5] That further supervisory authority may be exercised by the national government was evidenced by the decision in *United States* v. *Classic,* upholding federal conviction of persons found guilty of fraudulent acts in a Louisiana primary election.[6] Thus national power of regulation and supervision includes not only the elections themselves, but also the primaries in which candidates are nominated.

National authority over the processes involved in the choice of elective officials is extensive, but it extends *only* to those in which *federal* officers are chosen. Elections and nomination procedures by which presidential electors and members of Congress are selected can be and are subjected to close national supervision. Federal control of the procedures used to choose *state* and *local* officers is possible if such candidates are nominated or elected on the same ballot with federal officers. In all other instances state and local governments control and supervise nominations and elections.

---

[4] Congress provided, however, that a state might hold elections at other times if its constitution specified a different date. Consequently, congressional elections in Maine were conducted in September until 1960 when, pursuant to a 1957 amendment, the November date became effective. As adopted, the Constitution of Alaska directed that general elections be held in October, but also provided that the date might be altered by the legislature. As the first session of the legislature in 1959 the date was changed to conform to the day established by Congress.

[5] *Ex parte Siebold,* 100 U.S. 371 (1880).

[6] 313 U.S. 299 (1941).

Methods of Nomination

Before a person can be elected to a public office he must be nominated as a candidate. This process can be rather simple with a minimum of red tape, or it can be quite complicated. Today most nominees are selected in primary elections, but other methods also are used. No two states employ precisely the same combination of methods. Some states permit procedures that others forbid, and alternative methods are available in some states. However, even though the details of nomination vary among the states, basic methods are much the same throughout the country.

Self-Announcement. The oldest form of nomination is self-announcement which consists of nothing more than a public declaration of candidacy. A person who aspires to a public office indicates his intentions simply by letting people know that he is a candidate. The announcement may be accomplished by means of a public speech, a published statement, word of mouth, or any other method available to the candidate. Self-announcement was in use in colonial times and is still widely used today.

Use of self-announcement as a method of nomination is largely confined to candidacies for minor local offices. However, public offices of higher station are also subject to this method, with election dependent upon whether the candidate can marshal sufficient write-in votes to outpoll his opposition. An impressive example of these procedures at work occurred in 1954 when Strom Thurmond announced his candidacy for the position of United States senator from South Carolina and, by means of write-in votes, won the office by a substantial margin.

The Caucus. Until the early decades of the nineteenth century, candidates were commonly chosen at meetings—or caucuses—of political leaders. The procedure was simple: acknowledged leaders met and discussed potential candidates, eventually deciding upon whom the group would support for each office to be filled. Since there were no political parties as they are known today and elections were local, the caucus worked satisfactorily as a nominating device. Competing political factions, acting in separate caucuses, produced opposing candidates.

Independence and subsequent union, along with the rise of the party system, occasioned difficulties in use of the caucus. Nominations for state and national offices could not be made practicably in local meetings. To meet this difficulty the *legislative caucus* and the *congressional caucus* were developed. A legislative caucus consisted of all the members of a party or political faction within a state legislature, and its function was to select party nominees for state offices. Presidential and Vice Presidential candidates were nominated by party members in Congress who served collectively as the congressional caucus.

As the political party system became firmly established and demand for more democratic methods of nomination mounted, the nominating caucus fell into disuse. The controls exerted by small groups led to dissatisfaction with "King Caucus." Telling blows were struck by Andrew Jackson and his supporters, and by the 1840's the caucus had been abandoned at the national and state levels. Today only a few local offices, primarily in New England, are subject to the nominating caucus, but all party members may take part in meetings held only after public notice is given.

The Convention. Several decades before the nominating caucus passed from the national and state scenes, the method that was to replace it—the delegate convention—was already in use. Throughout the states in the middle Atlantic area county conventions were in common use by 1804. A state convention was called in New York in 1824, and by 1830 state conventions were used widely in the northeast. The Anti-Masonic Party nominated its candidate for President by convention in 1831 for the next year's election. The major parties followed suit, and within a few years the convention was in general use.

The convention clearly is, in theory at least, a much more democratic device than the caucus. Where a caucus is a "closed corporation," a convention is composed of delegates representing party members throughout the election district involved. At the same time, it is equally clear that conventions can be controlled. Any political process is only as effective and reliable as the people who conduct it. While many, probably most, conventions worked as well as reason could demand throughout the period of their widest use, the last half of the nineteenth century, there were numerous examples of rigged, dishonest conventions.[7] Public reaction to controlled conventions was such that by the early twentieth century the states began to turn to the direct primary.

Today the convention is, or by law may be, used by major parties for the nomination of some or all candidates for state and national offices in about one-fourth of the states.[8] Although the direct primary is now used or is available in some form in all fifty states, the convention has remained the principal method of nominating candidates in a few states such as Connecticut, Indiana, and New York. In some of the southern states the convention exists as an alternative to the primary and is often employed by the "minority" Republican Party.[9] Conventions in Iowa and South Dakota are held *after* the primary election to choose candidates for any office for which no one was able to get a plurality of at least thirty-five per cent of the votes cast.

Several states have nominating systems that include conventions held *before* the primary elections. In Colorado's preprimary convention, which has been in use since 1910, any candidate who receives twenty per cent of the convention vote may run in the primary election. All other candidates must qualify by means of nomination by petition. Convention endorsement in Utah is limited to two candidates, with the second-high contender included on the primary election ballot only if he was able to garner more than twenty per cent of the votes cast in the convention. A similar system is used in New Mexico. In Massachusetts party endorsement is given to convention-certified candidates. Rhode Island uses a system similar to a preprimary convention in that preferred position on the primary ballot is given to candidates, one for each office, who are endorsed by the party central committee.

Nomination by Petition. Aspirants for public office who have no major party affiliation and are thereby unable to secure nominations in conventions or primary elections may in many states formalize

---

[7] Widely cited as an example of the extent to which conventions may be controlled is the Cook County, Illinois (includes Chicago), convention of 1896. That body was composed of 723 delegates of whom 265 were saloon keepers, 148 were public office holders, and 128 were ex-convicts! Only under the oddest of circumstances could such an assemblage nominate a slate of uncompromised candidates.

[8] *Book of the States, 1964–65,* p. 20. The nominating convention is also available for use by minor parties in other states.

[9] In Texas the convention may be used by a party which at the last election received between 10,000 and 200,000 votes.

their candidacies by means of a *nominating petition.* Included in this group are the independents who spurn party membership, candidates in nonpartisan elections, and the members of minor parties which, in some states, are not permitted to select candidates in primary elections. In some states where the nominating petition is not available such candidates may get their names on the ballot by making a deposit of money, the "filing fee," with a designated official. In some instances fees are required of all candidates in primary as well as general elections.

Care must be taken not to confuse the nominating petition which results in placement of a candidate's name upon the general election ballot with filing petitions which authorize candidacies in primary elections. A nominating petition has the effect of making a person a candidate for an office. The primary petition does nothing more than make it possible for a person to present himself in a primary election which, in turn, may result in his nomination.

The Direct Primary. The only method of nomination that is or may be used in each of the fifty states, the direct primary, made its initial appearance at about the time the convention method was achieving general acceptance. In 1842 members of the Democratic Party in Crawford County, Pennsylvania, cast ballots in what is generally considered the first primary election held in the United States. Throughout the next half-century the primary spread slowly but steadily. Party leaders fought hard against it, and in many instances lack of governmental regulation resulted in manipulation and fraud, but gradually the primary took hold. Wisconsin set the pattern for other states by enacting, in 1904, the first state-wide mandatory system of nomination by primary. The convention is still used in some states for some nominations, but nominations for the vast majority of offices today, whether national, state, or local, are made by means of primaries.

As applied to public offices the term "primary election" is a misnomer, for although the process outwardly resembles an actual election, it is simply a method of choosing candidates who, at a later date, will run for office in an election. Except for nonpartisan and open primaries, the primary is a *party* affair in which members select from among themselves the party's candidates.[10] The only sense in

---

[10] This does not, of course, mean that the primary is not related to the electoral process or not subject to governmental control. Indeed each of the fifty states regulates primaries in minute detail, and the United States Supreme Court has declared them to be an "integral part" of the electoral process.

which a primary is truly an election is when it is used as a means of electing people to party offices such as precinct committeeman, national committeeman, and convention delegate.

Running in a primary election is not a privilege free from all legal conditions and available to anyone for the mere asking. A prospective candidate must, first of all, be affiliated with a legally recognized political party.[11] Thus independents and members of so-called minor parties must resort to other nominating methods. State laws may provide that some offices are not subject to primary elections, give parties the choice of whether to nominate in primaries, or limit candidacies by requiring aspirants first to make creditable showings in party conventions. For example, candidates for all major offices in Connecticut, Indiana, and New York are chosen in conventions. Primaries in Connecticut, where they have been available since 1955, are held only on demand of candidates who have won at least twenty per cent of the votes cast in party nominating conventions. State laws also require persons desiring to run in the primaries to post filing fees or present petitions bearing a designated number of signatures.

Even though the legal requirements placed on prospective candidates are designed to discourage frivolous candidacies, they generally are not difficult to meet. How can the fact be explained that large numbers of persons seeking publicity or the satisfaction of seeing their names in print do not clutter primary election ballots? The legal restrictions do deter many who might otherwise present themselves to the voters. However, the most effective deterrents are probably the realization that the likelihood of success without adequate backing is remote and the possibility of being made to look ridiculous too much of a reality. Few people relish the role of fool or laughingstock, although on occasion some seem willing, indeed eager, to play the part.

Open versus *Closed Primaries.* Partisan direct primaries used in the United States can be classified as *open* or *closed.* As the terms

---

[11] Until 1959 candidates in California were permitted to "cross-file," a means by which a person might run in the primary elections of both Republican and Democratic parties. Former Governor Earl Warren won both party nominations in 1946 as did ex-Senator William F. Knowland in 1952. A variation of cross-filing is possible in New York where different parties may, in convention, nominate the same candidate or, for offices subject to the direct primary, the appropriate party committee may permit a nonparty member to cross-file. For a discussion of the cross-filing experience in California, see James C. Findley, "Cross-Filing and the Progressive Movement in California Politics," *Western Political Quarterly,* September 1959.

imply, an open primary, the form in which the direct primary originated, is a nominating election in which *any* qualified voter may take part, while participation in a closed primary is restricted to party members only. Today most states have closed primary elections, the open form being used in only ten states.[12]

The closed primary, which is favored by party leaders and officials, is closed to all voters who are not party members. In most states having such primaries this requirement is met by means of registration or *enrollment*. At the time of registration the voter is listed as a member of the party of his choice. If his party does not or cannot stage a primary election, or if the voter indicates no party affiliation when registering, then his balloting in the primary is restricted to nonpartisan candidacies. A second method of determining party attachment is the so-called *challenge system*. Under this procedure the right of a voter to cast a ballot may be challenged when he attempts to vote. If so, he ordinarily must assert under oath that he is a party member, supported the party's candidates at the last election, and will support them at the next. Enrollment and challenge may be used together, and an oath of party affiliation may be required as a matter of course.

Party membership is not required for participation in an open primary, but with the single exception of Washington, a voter must still confine himself to the primary election of one party. In other words, any qualified voter may cast a primary ballot, but he must make a choice of parties. Party preferences are kept secret either by printing identical but separate ballots for each party and permitting the voter to discard all but one of them, or by listing candidates by party columns on the same ballot with the voter confining himself to a single party column. In Washington's *wide-open* primary, commonly called the "blanket" primary, candidates are listed by office, and the voter may vote regardless of party designations, so long as he casts only one vote for only one candidate for each office.

The fact that the closed form of the direct primary is used in four times as many states as the open type is largely attributable to a practice known as *raiding*. During the early years of the direct primary, the open form was used, making it possible for a party organization to instruct members to vote for the weakest candidate in the opposing party's primary. By securing the nomination of a weak opposition candidate, the raiding party's chances of success at

---

[12] Alaska, Idaho, Michigan, Minnesota, Montana, North Dakota, Utah, Vermont, Washington, and Wisconsin.

the ensuing general election were strengthened. Closing primaries to all but party members made raiding much more difficult.

A comparison of open and clo ed primaries reveals several strong points in favor of each. As already indicated, the closed primary greatly reduces the probability of party raiding. It tends to make candidates more responsible to their parties and to increase the political awareness of the electorate since voters must choose between parties. On the other hand, it can be argued that unlike the closed form, an open primary protects the secrecy of the ballot, makes it possible for *all* qualified persons to vote, and tends to emphasize the quality of individual candidates rather than parties. The arguments in favor of one form indicate weaknesses of the other, and the choice between them is a policy determination to be decided by the people and their representatives in each state.

Run-off Primaries. In the primary elections of most states, whether open or closed, the person who gets the most votes in a particular contest is nominated. If only two candidates are vying for a nomination, one of them is practically certain to get a majority of the votes. However, should three or more persons contend for a nomination and none receive a majority, then the one receiving the highest number of votes would win by a *plurality*.

The plurality rule is followed in the great majority of the states, but in the southeastern United States some primary laws require that nominations must be based upon a majority.[13] In support of these provisions is the fact that in these states nomination in a primary election held by the Democratic Party is a virtual guarantee of success in the subsequent general election. In some southern states over ninety per cent of the electorate is affiliated with the Democratic Party, a situation wherein opposition parties voting full strength in

---

[13] States in which runoff primaries are, or may be, held are Alabama, Arkansas, Florida, Georgia, Idaho, Louisiana, Mississippi, North Carolina, Oklahoma, South Carolina, Texas, Virginia, and Tennessee. In most of these states, candidates for all offices must secure majorities for nomination. A few, however, provide for runoffs only in certain situations. In Idaho, for example, a plurality is sufficient to win a nomination except that candidates for the offices of United States senator, representative in Congress, and governor must win by pluralities of forty per cent or more. If they do not, they are then subject to runoff primaries. North Carolina requires majorities of all candidates, but runoffs are held only if requested by second-high candidates. In Virginia state law repuires majorities in the nomination of candidates for United States senator, governor, lieutenant governor, and attorney general, but permits city or county committees to require majorities for the nomination of local candidates. Even under these circumstances runoffs are held only upon the request of second place candidates in the first primary. The only time a runoff primary may be held in Tennessee is in the unlikely event of a tie.

a general election are unable, except on extremely rare occasions, to defeat a small turnout of Democrats. Consequently, to make sure that a person who fills a public office has been chosen by a majority of the voters, he must secure that majority in the Democratic primary. When necessary, runoff primaries are held about a month after the regular primary to assure that each nominee has obtained a majority vote.

Nonpartisan Primaries. Many local and some state offices are filled by candidates bearing no official party label. Only Nebraska and Minnesota elect state legislators on a nonpartisan basis, while nonpartisan selection generally is confined to judges and certain administrative officers, such as school officials. Nonpartisan primary elections are ordinarily little more than a "sifting and eliminating" process, because in most instances the results are merely to reduce the number of candidates for a particular office to the two highest. Then, at the general election these two candidates contest for the office at stake. Should the highest vote-getter in the primary receive a majority of the total votes cast for all persons seeking an office, he may be declared elected without having to submit himself to the voters in the general election. In such cases the nonpartisan primary becomes the true election.

The Place of the Primary. The direct primary is not without faults, but regardless of its shortcomings it promises to remain the principal method of nomination in the United States. It represents a full swing away from the early days of control by party leaders in caucuses over slates of nominees. Despite the fact that primaries have been and to some extent still can be controlled, their democratic character is favored by American voters.

Attractive as it has proved in comparison with other methods of nomination, the direct primary is open to criticism on a number of logical grounds. First, it is expensive:[14] the process entails mobilization of all, or most, of the election machinery in a state. At the same time, each candidate must finance a campaign for nomination and a second if obliged to enter a runoff primary, as well as a general election effort. Second, the relative ease with which persons may become primary candidates and the tendency to make more and

---

[14] In practically all states the costs of primary elections are paid by government, usually counties and cities. Only one-third of the state governments share the costs of direct primaries. In Arkansas, Georgia, and South Carolina the *party* pays all primary costs. Primaries in Texas are paid for by candidates' filing fees which are determined by party county committees on the basis of anticipated primary expenses.

more offices subject to primary elections have resulted in lengthening ballots that are already too long. A voter often must pore over more than one hundred names, many or most of whom are unknown to him. Third, the plurality rule may result in nomination by a minority of party members. While it is probable that most of the candidates chosen by pluralities would be nominated in any event, some would not. This fact strengthens arguments that candidacies should be limited, majorities required, or that party committees or conventions should be given more control over nominations. Fourth, primaries may be held eight or nine months in advance of the general election although most of them occur in the late spring or summer. Such extended intervals contribute to a loss of voter interest and unnecessarily long campaigns. Next, primaries discourage independent voters. While the independent may participate in an open primary, he must usually align himself temporarily with a political party. Finally, primaries weaken political parties in that intra-party fights are encouraged and candidates must seek favor from the voters rather than approval by the party organization.

Some improvements in the direct primary might be accomplished by legislative action, but some features that have evoked criticism could not be altered without changing the character of the primary. As long as primaries are party elections, for example, little can be done to satisfy the independent voter. Similarly, the direct primary is necessarily more costly than other nominating methods since it involves use of all or most election machinery in a jurisdiction. The complaint that parties do not have adequate control of primary candidates probably cannot be completely satisfied, but party control can be strengthened by permitting parties to endorse one candidate over all others, by limiting the number of candidates, by permitting preprimary conventions, or by a combination of these. As indicated earlier, a few states have such provisions already in effect. The long ballot so often found in primaries can be moderated by reducing the number of offices filled by election. The plurality rule can be re-placed, where it is felt desirable, by a majority requirement, or as in Iowa and South Dakota, supplemented by a post-primary convention. Proper timing of the primary in relation to the general election is probably the easiest improvement to realize, for only a change in dates is necessary.

Presidential Primaries. Although the great majority of nominations are made through direct primaries, the most prominent officers of them all, the President and Vice President of the United States, are subject to nomination by delegate convention. Sentiment has long existed in many quarters for replacing the convention with a national direct primary. President Woodrow Wilson, the only professional political scientist ever to serve in that office, recommended such a primary in his first message to Congress, and public attention frequently has been directed to the issue. However, the only progress of note toward an actual national primary has been in the form of the *presidential primary* and the *presidential preference primary*.

The presidential primary, despite the implications of the title, is *not* a method of nominating presidential candidates. First used in Oregon in 1910 and enjoying its greatest development in the following ten years, the presidential primary is merely a means of choosing, in a party primary, delegates to the national convention of a political party. The popularly elected delegates then participate, in the convention, in the nomination of their party's presidential and vice presidential candidates. All or some delegates are now selected in such primaries in about one-third of the states and Washington, D.C.

In some states where the presidential primary is used the voters not only cast ballots for convention delegates, but also indicate their preferences as to the person they would like to see the convention nominate. This variation has become known as the presidential preference primary. No uniformity exists among the states with respect to the effect of the voters' preferences. The extent to which delegates are bound to support the presidential aspirant receiving the greatest voter support differs from state to state, ranging from no formal requirement at all to compulsory support until released by the candidate.

Whether preference primaries serve a genuinely useful purpose is open to question. Supporters contend that they provide a means of countering abuses and excesses of the convention system and provide a basis for wider popular participation. Perhaps if all states used preference primaries, and if all delegates were directed to honor their results, an approximation of a national direct primary could be achieved. At present two-thirds of the states ignore the process altogether, and those with primaries have made no collective attempt to standardize requirements. One of the glaring weaknesses is that candidates cannot be compelled to enter primaries and are thus able to avoid contests they are not sure of winning. "Favorite son" candidates often divert votes from serious contenders, and little or no attention is given to vice-presidential aspirants. For these and other reasons peculiar to individual states, appreciable expansion of the preference primary to new states in the near future seems improbable.

THE ELECTION PROCESS

After candidates are nominated their battles are only half won. Except in one-party states where nomination by the dominant party virtually assures election, each candidate faces the usually difficult task of winning in the general election. After nomination, whether by means of direct primary, convention, a combination of both, or otherwise, candidates begin to plot their courses of action in preparation for the general election usually held on the first Tuesday after the first Monday in November of even-numbered years.[15]

Campaigns. During the period between nomination and the day upon which the voters go to the polls campaigns are conducted. In one sense, campaigns can be said to have begun during the period when candidates are seeking nomination. Political campaigns vary in nature according to numerous factors, including the personality and status of the candidate, the nature and importance of the office, the character of the times, the size and temper of the electorate, and the disposition of pressure groups. Every campaign is intended to influence voters, but obviously not all campaigns are carried on the same way. A presidential candidate, a person running for a seat in a state senate, and an aspirant for a position on a city council face different problems. Each must tailor his campaign to fit the needs as he and his supporters find them.

There is no reliable way to determine how many votes are won by campaigning. In all but the rarest instances a candidate who does no campaigning is at a disadvantage if his opponent makes any effort at all. *Some* voters can be influenced, and general voter interest can be stimulated. Political observers felt for many years that campaigns actually won few votes because most voters had decided how they were going to cast their ballots by the time candidates took to the campaign trail. Then in 1948, after most observers and commentators had conceded the presidential election to Governor Thomas E. Dewey of New York, incumbent Harry S. Truman was returned to

---

[15] This is the date fixed by Congress for general elections in which presidential electors and members of Congress are chosen. Elections in which only state and/or local officials are chosen can be held at other times.

office. Undoubtedly the arduous, effective campaign conducted by Mr. Truman had won votes. How many, it would be difficult to say. Attitudes toward the value of campaigns have been changed, however, and until more precise assessments can be made, candidates—national, state, and local—will be heartened in their campaign efforts by the Truman experience in 1948.

Holding the Election. Elections are not simple affairs that can be organized overnight and carried off with little effort. Instead, they are highly complex, well-organized activities that demand impressive expenditures of time, energy, and money. Each state has developed extensive legal provisions designed to establish means by which public servants can be honestly and fairly chosen.

As in virtually all areas of governmental activity, each of the fifty states has its own individual election system. Wide variation in detail exists from state to state; local elections within a single state differ; and a state system may be, and frequently is, altered at each legislative session. Nevertheless, the basic procedures involved in the conduct of elections in the states are the same, making it possible to characterize a "typical" mode of election.

Administration. Although there is election machinery at the state level—at least a board to canvass and certify results of designated elections and an official, usually the secretary of state, to see that state laws are observed—most election functions are performed by local personnel. In each local voting district, generally called a *precinct,* an election board mans the polling place and counts the votes. There are usually three or four members, entitled *judges* or *inspectors,* on an election board with clerks to assist them. These officials are chosen by a city or county board of elections, by the governing bodies of counties or cities, by the clerks of these governments, or by popular election. In nearly all states, appointments to precinct election boards are divided equally, or as nearly so as possible, between the major political parties. Consequently, service on such a board has become largely a matter of patronage controlled by local party organizations.

Election laws in each of the states provide in detail for virtually every aspect of elections. Preparing an election is largely a matter of following statutory directions. Laying out precincts, choosing polling places, printing ballots, obtaining booths and ballot boxes, procuring voting machines, choosing precinct officials, and other tasks are carried out as provided by law. Paying the costs of holding an election, as dictated by statute, is generally the obligation of local governments, particularly counties and cities.

Time, Place, and Hours. Except for the elections in which national officers are chosen, fixing election dates is a prerogative of the state legislature. For purposes of convenience, particularly to avoid the costs of a second election, most state officials are elected at the time national offices are filled. However, Kentucky, Mississippi, New Jersey, and Virginia hold their state elections in odd-numbered years. Many local governments avoid coincidence with state and national choices by conducting their elections at other times, commonly in the spring.

In each precinct a poll, or location at which votes are cast, must be designated. To reduce costs, public buildings are utilized where possible. When public buildings are not available, space is rented, often on a patronage basis, in private structures such as churches, business establishments, or private dwellings. The hours during which balloting may take place are determined by state statute, and in virtually all instances it is a continuous twelve-hour period beginning at seven or eight o'clock in the morning.

Casting Ballots. When a voter enters a poll to cast his ballot he must first identify himself. In states where all voters must be registered this step is relatively simple. By requiring each voter to sign his name before receiving a ballot, the signature can be compared with the one appearing on the registration form. In North Dakota, which has no registration system, voter identification depends largely upan successful operation of the challenge system. The problem is not as serious as it might be elsewhere for the state has less than a million population with only about thirty per cent of them residing in a dozen or so cities. The same situation prevails in Alaska which has no general registration system. Texas is today the only populous state without some form of compulsory voter registration, although the Texas Constitution authorizes the legislature to provide for registration in cities of 10,000 or more.

After recognition a voter is ready to mark his ballot. He takes the ballot to a booth where, in private, he checks the names of the candidates he wishes to vote for. Upon leaving the booth and in the presence of the election board, the voter deposits his ballot in a locked ballot box. When mechanical balloting is used, the voter proceeds after identification to a voting machine which is equipped with a curtain to insure voting secrecy. The voter is usually not limited in the amount of time he may take to cast his ballot, and he may request a second ballot should be spoil by mismarking, tearing, or otherwise damaging the first one issued to him. Instructions on the use of a voting machine may also be requested. Where illiterate persons are permitted to vote, they may be accompanied by a literate assistant. The physically handicapped likewise may, on request, be aided in the execution of their ballots.

Tabulation of votes by electronic devices has been used in some states for several years, but Ohio has now made it possible to expedite holding elections by enacting, in 1959, a Punch Card Ballot Law. Under that law ballots may be in the form of cards that can be used in automatic tabulating equipment. In recent general elections card ballots have been used in a few counties in Georgia and Oregon with generally favorable results. Whether the simplicity of the card ballot and the obvious speed with which election results can be determined offset possible voter resistance cannot be assessed until after a longer testing and trial period.

Counting the Votes. The votes are usually counted by a separate board of judges and the process begins soon after the polls are open. Where voting machines are used counting is not done until after the polls close. Counting devices built into the machines keep cumulative totals on all candidates so that it is necessary only to copy the totals. After the figures have been recorded the machines are locked with the counters undisturbed in the event a later recount is ordered. The greatest expenditure of effort occurs where paper ballots are used, for each ballot must be carefully examined and the votes recorded on work sheets. With precinct tallies completed, canvassing boards at city, county, and state levels then assemble totals. The entire process normally lasts many hours and may run into several days. In the 1954 Oregon general election, with machines used in a single county, the effects of the slow count were demonstrated. Returns from other states indicated that party control of the United States Senate hinged on the outcome of the Oregon senatorial race between challenger Richard L. Neuberger and incumbent Guy Cordon. Oregon's tabulating processes eventually showed that Democrat

Neuberger was the winner, but only after the nation waited anxiously for almost three days!

Whether machines or paper ballots are used, measures are taken to reduce temptations to cheat faced by election board members and clerks. It would be strange indeed, for example, to find an election board composed solely of members of a single political party. In some states, courts are empowered to appoint overseers, and in nearly all states *watchers* may be chosen by the political parties offering candidates. These watchdogs are present throughout election day, checking their lists of voters and observing the conduct of the election judges.

THE BALLOT

During the colonial period and early years of statehood, balloting was not regarded as a secret, personal act. Rather, those qualified to cast ballots did so simply by appearing at the polls and publicly telling the elections clerk the names of the candidates they wished to support. Tellers or vote-counters were used when necessary and sometimes, when the situation permitted, a show of hands was adequate. Paper ballots, when used, were furnished by candidates or parties. They were slight improvement over oral voting, for they were usually distinctively colored, bore only the names of one party's candidates, and were already marked when given to the voter!

Although public voting may have been considered by many as a straightforward "manly" form of balloting, it was nevertheless subject to considerable abuse. It was easy to check on a voter who had sold his vote, accepted a bribe, had been intimidated, or was associated with a political machine. Such practices led eventually to adoption of the secret ballot.

The Australian Ballot. As suggested by its title, the Australian ballot derives its name from the country where it was introduced in 1856. It spread from there to several Anglo-Saxon and continental European countries during the next thirty years, at the same time winning advocates in the United States. In 1885, and again two years later, abortive attempts were made to bring about its adoption in Michigan. The Kentucky legislature, in 1888, enacted the first law providing for the Australian ballot but limited its use to municipal elections in Louisville. The first statute requiring statewide employment of the ballot was passed later that year by the Massachusetts General Court. During the following three years—that is, by the end of the general legislative sessions of 1891—over three-fourths of the states had followed suit, and within a decade only a few states had failed to adopt some form of the Australian ballot.[16] For about twenty-five years South Carolina remained the sole holdout, finally capitulating in 1950. Today some form of the Australian ballot is used in all fifty states.

Tersely defined, the Australian ballot is an official ballot which is printed at public expense, contains the names of all duly nominated candidates, is distributed by public officials and is executed in secret at the polls. These features, in combination, made it possible to reduce ballot irregularities impressively. Parties no longer could favor themselves in the provision of printed ballots, and checking on the way an individual voted was rendered extremely difficult if not impossible. The two essential features of the Australian ballot—secrecy and official status—have made it the capstone of integrity in American elections.

There are two basic types of the Australian ballot: the Massachusetts *office-block* and the Indiana *party column*. The original form of the Australian ballot carried no party designation, resembling the nonpartisan ballot of today, and when adopted in Massachusetts candidates were grouped according to the office they sought. Thus a "block" of candidates was listed by office rather than by parties. Since such grouping tends to minimize the influence of party and makes straight-party voting cumbersome, party leaders have been strongly opposed to office-block ballots. Indiana adopted a statewide Australian ballot law a year after Massachusetts had done so, but party leaders achieved an important modification in the Hoosier version. All candidates of the same party were placed in a single column headed by the name of the party—hence the name party column. On such ballots it was possible to vote for all candidates of a party simply by placing a mark by the name of the party, a method termed "straight party" or "straight ticket" voting. Today party column ballots are used in slightly more than half the states.

Voting Machines. Voting machines were first used in an American election in 1892 in the city of Lockport, New York. Since that

---

[16] See Eldon C. Evans, *A History of the Australian Ballot System in the United States,* University of Chicago Press, Chicago, 1917.

time over three-fourths of the states have enacted laws permitting their use by local election boards, and in New York and Rhode Island machine voting is mandatory. Machines are used extensively in about a dozen states and in the large urban areas of many others. Altogether, about half the votes in a nationwide general election are cast on voting machines.

Students of government are virtually unanimous in the opinion that the use of voting machines is a substantial improvement in voting procedures. They eliminate the need for a manual count of votes, reduce the number of persons required to administer elections, speed up voting, make ballot spoilage impossible, and reduce the possibility of cheating. Why, then, are machines not more widely used? The principal difficulty appears to be the initial cost. Machines cost up to several thousand dollars each, and local governments—which bear most election costs—simply cannot manage the initial investment. A second reason is the fact that many voters, especially in rural areas, resist giving up the traditional paper ballot. Finally, machines would be impractical in some instances, particularly in sparsely settled areas where few votes are cast and election costs are low.

Electronic Vote Counting. Within the last few years several states have experimented with electronic processes in the tabulation of votes. Systems tested thus far include the usual paper ballot marked with inks that can be sensed by electronic scanners, ballots in the form of cards that can be processed in automatic tabulators, and cards to which the results of paper and machine balloting have been transferred. Legislation authorizing one or more of these techniques has been enacted in California, Nebraska, Nevada, Ohio, and Oregon, but implementation to date has consisted largely of experimental testing in limited areas.

Consideration of Minor Political Groups. American elections, with their plurality or majority requirements and the single member election district, are a formidable hurdle for minor political groups. In fact, minority parties normally have been unable to elect candidates and almost never in proportion to their voter strength. While no concessions have been made to improve the chances of minor groups in the election of their candidates to national offices, some special balloting methods have been used in regard to various state and local positions.

Since 1870 members of the Illinois House of Representatives have been elected from three-member districts on the basis of *cumulative voting*. Each voter has three votes that he may cast as he chooses; all three for one candidate, two for one candidate and one for another, one and a half for each of two aspirants, or one vote for each of three candidates. Under this system a well organized minor party may succeed in capturing one or more seats in the legislature, if its members "plunk" all their votes within a district on the party candidate.[17]

Another balloting method devised to increase minority chances of success is limited voting. Used in a few states in the selection of some county commissioners and city councilmen, limited voting gives the voter fewer votes than there are offices to be filled. The idea behind limited voting is that since major party voters cannot elect all the members of a board, minority supporters have a better chance to elect the remainder. Like cumulative balloting, limited voting is subject to criticism in that it can be used only when several offices are to be filled and does not result in representation in proportion to voting strength.

Voting systems designed to reflect the voting strength of political groups are known as proportional representation, or more simply as "PR." National and state offices have never been made subject to PR, but a few municipalities have employed it in the selection of councilmen. Probably the best known type is the Hare System.[18] Invented in 1857 by an Englishman, Thomas Hare, and popularized by the political philosopher, John Stuart Mill, the system utilizes what is termed the "single transferable vote." Each voter indicates not only his first choice, but also his second, third, fourth, and so on. When the votes are counted, each candidate receiving enough first place votes according to the Hare formula is declared elected.[19] Second place votes are then added to first choices to select additional winners; then third-, fourth-, and fifth-place votes—and on down the

---

[17] Cumulative voting procedures were not used in the selection of Illinois representatives in 1964. Apportionment of the legislature was judicially invalidated, leading to special legislation providing for at-large election of members of the lower house.

[18] In some western European countries the List System of PR is used. Under this plan a list of candidates is offered by each political party. Votes are cast for the list rather than individuals, and seats are filled, from the top of the list, in proportion to the percentage of votes cast for the list.

[19] A successful candidate must receive votes equal to the "quota," determined by dividing the number of seats plus one into the number of votes cast and adding one to the quotient. Thus, if nine seats are to be filled and 100,000 votes are cast the quota would be $\frac{100,000}{9+1} + 1$ or 10,001.

line as necessary until all positions are filled. In actual use the Hare plan has been subjected to various modifications, but the basic principle of the transferable vote has been preserved in each instance.

Advocates of proportional representation stress that it guarantees representation of minorities, eliminates "wasted" ballots in that each vote helps elect one or more candidates, and helps to minimize the effects of political machines. On the other hand, there is the fear that many parties or factions in a legislative body, a possible result of PR, may introduce an element of instability in government. Whether this development occurs or not, there is no doubt that the Hare System involves a highly complicated vote count—enough so to discourage its adoption or hasten its abondonment. It has virtually disappeared in the United States, although it has been used places as widely separated as West Hartford, Connecticut, and Coos Bay, Oregon. Among the larger cities that have given PR a trial are Cincinnati, Ohio, from 1924 to 1957, and New York City, where between 1937 and 1947 a form of the Hare System was used.

Election Frauds. If elections are not conducted honestly, the spirit and significance of democracy are destroyed. When a few unscrupulous individuals are able to capture public offices by illegal tactics, then the means by which the will of the people is expressed is seriously impaired. It is not surprising, therefore, that both the nation and the states have enacted a great many laws to prevent and punish election frauds.

Before the Australian ballot came into general use and states began to police elections more rigorously, many elections were in fact little more than circuses. Today frauds are not nearly so common as in earlier years, but cheating at the polls has not been eliminated. To list and describe all the ways to cheat in elections would fill several volumes, but a few examples serve to indicate their general nature. Bribery, intimidation, coercion, and violence still occur here and there. Stuffing ballot boxes with stolen or counterfeit ballots is a familiar type of fraud. Casting ballots for voters who have died, moved away, or even for imaginary persons, is still a problem where registration is lacking or poorly administered. The "Tasmanian Dodge" or "endless chain," whereby a bribed voter turns in a marked ballot and collects his money when he returns his own unmarked ballot to be used by the next bribed voter, still occurs, but it has virtually disappeared due to the use of numbered ballot stubs. Most effective are the fraudulent activities of election judges, especially when they act in collusion. Their opportunities to cheat while assisting illiterate voters are obvious. When counting ballots it is possible to mark them, or perhaps spoil them, with a fragment of graphite attached to the finger—a practice known as "short pencilling." Tearing ballots, and thus spoiling them, is an old trick. Substituting tally sheets after the count has altered the results of elections. Transposing figures can work wonders for candidates, as when a vote total of 361 is "inadvertently" recorded as 631.

There are many laws designed to prevent and punish chicanery at the polls. Federal laws apply to primary and general elections in which federal officers are chosen, and the statute books in each state bulge with provisions intended to protect the integrity of the ballot. Although laws providing punishment for dishonest acts are necessary, preventing such actions is more important. Consequently, better results are obtainable through improved registration systems, stricter policing of the balloting process, and improvement of that process to eliminate opportunities for fraud, as by use of voting machines, punch card ballots, electronic vote counters, and similar devices. Laws and voting machines cannot, in and of themselves, produce completely honest elections. If the people who conduct elections are corrupt, there is little reason to believe they will perform honestly. Today little effort is made to insure that election officials are well qualified to do their jobs. In fact, except for literacy, party affiliation and loyalty are the qualifications most commonly required. Unless and until higher qualifications are demanded, instances of fraud will continue, since the honesty of any election depends ultimately upon the honesty of those who administer it.

The Short Ballot. Frequently when a voter examines his ballot preparatory to marking his choices he is confronted with a mass of names and proposals. In some election jurisdictions the voter must grope through the names of more than one hundred candidates plus the text of constitutional amendments and perhaps a number of initiated or referred measures. Casting an intelligent ballot under such circumstances is difficult for a well informed voter and practically impossible for most. Many voters, either in desperation or fear of doing the wrong thing, simply ignore many offices and questions.

The *short ballot,* which ideally contains only the names of

candidates for the most important offices, has been championed
actively during the last half-century as a remedy for the cluttered,
confusing, and excessively long ballot. Advocates of the short ballot
formed the National Short Ballot Organization in 1909, merging
twelve years later with the National Municipal League. The goal of
the short ballot movement can probably best be stated as one of
persuading state and local governments to pattern their ballots as
much as possible after the example of the national government.
Except when vacancies must be filled by election or at-large candidacies occur, voters never find it necessary to consider more than
four national offices—the presidency, vice-presidency, and one seat
each in the United States Senate and House of Representatives.

Progress in achieving the short ballot has been slow. Most states
still have ballots that are much too long, but a few states have shortened their ballots considerably by making all but the most important
state offices subject to appointment or by staggering elections so that
the voters choose officers for only one level of government at a time.
At the state level, short ballots are found in Alaska, Hawaii, New
Hampshire, New Jersey, Tennessee, and Virginia, but it is at the
municipal level that the most encouraging gains in this area have
been made. Most major cities and literally hundreds of smaller ones
have adopted the short ballot.

Contested Elections. After the votes have been counted and
canvassed, the results are certified and proclaimed official. In the
vast majority of instances the election process is then over, and the
winners sit back and wait for their terms of office to begin. Occasionally, however, an apparent loser refuses to accept the result, claiming
it is based upon error, fraud or other impropriety.

If the public office in a contested election is a legislative seat, the
argument is usually settled by the legislative house involved, since
such bodies generally are the sole judges of members' qualifications.
In some states courts are given jurisdiction to hear complaints and
to determine the victor in contested elections. Also, contests may
result in a *recount* of the votes, a process that is easily accomplished
in some states, while in others some proof of fraud or error must be
advanced. Some states require that the costs involved in a recount
must be borne by the person demanding it. Such restrictions create
a risk of putting fraudulent election results beyond correction, but

at the same time they also discourage frivolous, petty demands for recounts.

Except when fraud or other illegal acts are alleged, recounts are rarely demanded unless the results clearly show that slight errors could have changed the outcome. For example, when a winning candidate's margin of victory is less than one per cent of the total votes cast, a request for a recount is reasonable. In the Minnesota gubernatorial election of 1962 the official count showed that Governor Elmer L. Andersen had won re-election by a margin of 142 votes. However, after a recount, his opponent, Karl Rolvaag, was declared the winner by 91 votes out of 1,239,593 cast—a majority by only .000073 per cent!

SELECTED REFERENCES

Books:

Albright, Spencer D., *The American Ballot*, American Council on Public Affairs, Washington, D.C., 1942.

Blair, George S., *Cumulative Voting*, University of Illinois Press, Urbana, 1960.

David, Paul T., *Specifications for a Model State Presidential Primary Law*, Brookings Institution, Washington, D.C., 1956.

Harris, Joseph P., *Election Administration in the United States*, Brookings Institution, Washington, D.C., 1934.

Key, V. O., Jr., *American State Politics*, Alfred A. Knopf, New York, 1956.

Overacker, Louise, *Money in Elections*, Macmillan Co., New York, 1932.

Scammon, Richard M., *America Votes*, 5 vols., Governmental Affairs Institute, Pittsburgh, 1956–1964.

Shannon, Jasper B., *Money and Politics*, Random House, New York, 1959.

Articles:

Adrian, Charles R., "Some General Characteristics of Nonpartisan Elections," *American Political Science Review*, September 1952.

Blair, George S., "Cumulative Voting: Patterns of Party Allegiance and Rational Choice in Illinois State Legislative Contests," *American Political Science Review*, March 1958.

Campbell, Angus, "Voting and Elections: Past and Present," *Journal of Politics*, November 1964.

Cutright, Phillips, "Nonpartisan Electoral Systems in American Cities," *Comparative Studies in Society and History,* January 1963.

Dorr, Harold M., "Nomination by Money Deposit," *National Municipal Review,* June 1954.

Eldersveld, Samuel J., "The Independent Vote," *American Political Science Review,* September 1952.

"Electoral Revision," Symposium, *Congressional Digest,* April 1956.

Hansen, Richard H., "Performance and Potential of Presidential Primary Laws," *Nebraska Law Review,* May 1960.

Harris, Joseph P., "Modernizing Our Election Administration," *State Government,* Winter 1963.

Jones, Harold T., "Electronics in Voting," *National Civic Review,* June 1964.

Kentucky Legislator (anonymous), "How an Election Was Bought and Sold," *Harper's Magazine,* October 1960.

Kerr, Frederick H., "Election Automation," *National Civic Review,* June 1964.

Laughlin, Charles V., "Proportional Representation," *American Bar Association Journal,* November 1963.

Lubell, Samuel, "The New Technology of Election Reporting," *Columbia Journalism Review,* Summer 1964.

CHAPTER 13

Direct Popular Action: Initiative, Referendum, and Recall

Voters in many states are faced not only with large numbers of candidates during elections, they must also decide questions of public policy. Since the end of the nineteenth century nearly half of the states and many cities have provided for direct popular participation in the governmental process through the initiative, referendum, and recall. These devices were conceived as a means of making government more responsive to the people, who may approve or veto acts of legislatures through the referendum and to enact laws by means of the initiative when unresponsive legislatures refuse to act. Through the recall, voters can remove from office public officials against whom there is strong public sentiment.

Although modern advocacy of direct legislation is associated with the Progressive movement and the Populist Party around the turn of the century, popular participation in lawmaking is in no sense a new development in the United States. Some early state constitutions were submitted to popular vote. The New England town meeting exemplified direct democracy. As early as 1825 the voters of Maryland were determining public policy by direct popular vote. In that year the legislature referred to the people the question of establishing free primary schools. Nevertheless, reliance upon legislative bodies to make such decisions was nearly universal during the last century.

Toward the end of the 1800's many persons felt that the orthodox channels of representative government did not provide adequately for expression of popular desires. The conviction was widespread that many legislators had "sold out" to powerful interest groups and were no longer sensitive to the wishes of their constituents. Consequently, reformers urged that the traditional lawmaking processes should be supplemented by devices for direct popular participation. In governmental jurisdictions where the initiative and referendum have been adopted, recognition has been given, in effect, to *two* legislative authorities: the legislature and the people.

The recall, on the other hand, is not directly concerned with the determination of public policy. Instead, it is intended to influence the manner in which public officials, particularly those who have been popularly elected, administer the affairs of government. As a "potential club to wield over recalcitrant officials," the recall seeks to require a minimum of honesty and efficiency. The rationale behind this device for popular control was well stated by W. B. Munro:

> Just when the people have elected a man burning with patriotic zeal, he suffers some sort of intracerebral accident. He is no longer able to interpret *vox populi*. His memory fails him. His formerly clear-cut views upon public questions become confused and incoherent. . . . The ayes and nayes in the legislative journal, when read in the glow of his former zest for public service, appear unintelligible, sometimes villainous. The recall proposes to aid the officeholder in retaining a candidate's state of mind.[1]

Although not as frequently used as the initiative and referendum, the recall on occasion has proved to be a useful weapon in the arsenal of direct democracy—the "shotgun behind the door."

DIRECT LEGISLATION

While under control of the Populists, South Dakota in 1898 became the first state to provide for the initiative and referendum for state legislation. That same year San Francisco and Vallejo, California, adopted these devices. In the next twenty years the direct legislation movement spread very rapidly to nearly all of the twenty states that now provide for the initiative and referendum; two other states use the referendum only.[2] The initiative and referendum have been much more widely used on the local than on the state level. In some cities in almost all states the voters are able to use one or both of these devices.[3]

---

[1] W. B. Munro, *The Initiative, Referendum, and Recall,* D. Appleton and Co., New York, 1912, pp. 299–300.

[2] The initiative and referendum are actually available for use in only nineteen states: Alaska, Arizona, Arkansas, California, Colorado, Maine, Massachusetts, Michigan, Missouri, Montana, Nebraska, Nevada, North Dakota, Ohio, Oklahoma, Oregon, South Dakota, Utah, and Washington. The Idaho legislature has never enacted the necessary enabling legislation to make them operative. The two states that use the referendum only are Maryland and New Mexico.

[3] Exceptions are Delaware, Indiana, and Rhode Island.

The Initiative. The initiative is a "device by which any person or group of persons may draft a proposed ordinance, law or constitutional amendment and by securing in its behalf a designated number of signatures may require that such proposal be submitted to the voters for their acceptance or rejection."[4] This short definition requires explanation. It is possible in thirteen states[5] to amend the state constitution by means of the initiative, a practice commonly referred to as the "constitutional initiative." Procedural details are similar to those required for the enactment of statutes.[6] The major difference is the usual requirement that a larger number of signatures be obtained on a petition for a constitutional amendment than for a statutory provision.

The number of signatures demanded on an initiative petition usually is expressed in terms of a percentage of the votes cast for some state officer elected in a preceding general election. The range is between eight and fifteen per cent. In two states a specific number of signatures is required by law. Occasionally, a state requires that signatures be gathered from various geographical areas of the state. Once the necessary signatures have been obtained and verified, the proposed amendment is ready to be placed on the ballot, usually at the next general election.[7]

In contrast to the "constitutional initiative," the procedure whereby the voters enact or amend statutes is termed the "statutory initiative." In turn, this type of initiative is subdivided into the "direct" and "indirect" forms. In the eleven states[8] that provide for the direct initiative only, a measure must be submitted directly to the voters once the required number of valid signatures has been obtained. In the six states[9] with the indirect initiative, a measure must be referred to the legislature before it is submitted to the voters. In California, Utah, and Washington either procedure may be followed, depending upon the number of signatures obtained. In each of

---

[4] W. B. Munro, "Initiative and Referendum," *Encyclopedia of the Social Sciences*, Vol. VIII, p. 50.

[5] Arizona, Arkansas, California, Colorado, Massachusetts, Michigan, Missouri, Nebraska, Nevada, North Dakota, Ohio, Oklahoma, and Oregon.

[6] For additional information on the procedure required to amend state constitutions, see Chapter 3. For details concerning the differences in signatures required on the two types of petitions, compare data on page 56 with information on pages 320–321. Note that in a few states no differences exist.

[7] Verification refers to the procedure used to determine that a sufficient number of qualified voters have signed a petition.

[8] Alaska, Arizona, Arkansas, Colorado, Idaho, Missouri, Montana, Nebraska, North Dakota, Oklahoma, and Oregon.

[9] Maine, Massachusetts, Michigan, Nevada, Ohio, and South Dakota.

these states a larger percentage is required for the direct initiative. Whenever the indirect procedure is followed, approval by the legislature ends the process, but a measure is submitted to popular vote if the legislature fails to enact it or some acceptable compromise.

When the direct initiative is used, seven general steps are involved in carrying a measure to a successful conclusion: (1) drafting the proposal, (2) preliminary filing, (3) circulation of petitions to obtain signatures, (4) verification of signatures and final filing, (5) education of the public, (6) the election, and (7) promulgation. Submission to the legislature is a substitute for steps five and six in the indirect method. Any individual or group may draft an initiative measure. Adequate legal counsel should be obtained at this point to avoid future complications resulting from poor drafting.

After a draft has been prepared, it must be submitted to some officer designated by law—usually the secretary of state when a state statute or constitutional amendment is involved. The Alaska constitution requires that the names of 100 sponsors accompany the proposal. The officer then specifies the exact form and procedure that must be observed in preparing the petition and obtaining signatures. Next, the proponents must make arrangements for circulation. Abuses sometimes arise because of "petition-hawking," a practice whereby organizations are hired to get persons to sign a petition at a rate of so much per signature. To curtail this commercialization a few states, like Oregon, have enacted laws forbidding persons to receive money for the circulation of petitions.

After signatures have been obtained, they must be verified in order to eliminate names of those who are unqualified. Since "shrinkage" always occurs, it is desirable to have an excess of signers. Some states permit the acquisition of supplementary signatures within a specified time if the original number proves to be inadequate. Once this task has been accomplished, the petition is officially filed so the proposed measure will appear on the ballot. In most states informing the voters concerning arguments for and against initiative proposals is not a governmental responsibility. Instead, interested parties perform this task. A few states like California and Oregon issue to registered voters an official "voters' pamphlet," containing information on candidates and proposed direct legislation. Persons wishing to present arguments in such pamphlets, either for or against proposals, may be afforded an opportunity to do so at moderate cost. In most states a simple majority of those voting on a measure is sufficient for enactment.[10] Following a canvass of the votes, a "proclamation" is issued recognizing as part of the law of the state or locality the measures that received the necessary vote.[11]

The Referendum. The referendum is "an arrangement whereby any measure which has been passed by a city council or state legislature may under certain circumstances be withheld from going into force until the voters have had an opportunity to render their decision upon it."[12] Like the initiative, the referendum is not new. It was known as early as the seventeenth century in Massachusetts, and the constitution of that state was the first to be ratified by popular vote in 1780. For purposes of study and description, three types of referendum are generally recognized: (1) mandatory or compulsory, (2) optional, and (3) protest or "petition." As explained in an earlier chapter, amendments to state constitutions are regularly submitted to popular vote in all states except Delaware. Often bond issues must also be submitted to such a vote. Since it is required by law, this type of referendum is termed *mandatory*.

Under the *optional* referendum a legislative body may refer a measure to the voters for their approval or disapproval. Some confusion of terminology exists with regard to optional referenda, depending upon the *consequences* of the popular vote. Earlier practice was to consider the people's vote as advisory only—hence the term "advisory" referendum often associated with it. The common practice today is to regard the voters' reaction on each issue submitted to them as a final decision. As used here, the term "optional referendum" refers to the latter process.

The third variety of referendum, the *protest* or *petition* type,[13] enables the voters to vote on measures already passed by a legislative body. In order that the people may have an opportunity to vote on such measures, referendum laws provide that statutes shall not take effect for a specified period following passage or for a designated time after the legislature adjourns—usually sixty or ninety days. "Emergency" measures, which become effective immediately, are not subject to the referendum but may be repudiated by popular vote only through the initiative. During the period of suspension any interested group may inaugurate action leading to a popular vote.

---

[10] For details see the table on pages 320–321.

[11] This step is a mere formality and is not required in order that an approved measure become law.

[12] W. B. Munro, *loc. cit.*

[13] Sometimes this type is called the "obligatory" referendum.

INITIATIVE AND REFERENDUM PROVISIONS ON STATEWIDE LEGISLATION

State	Initiative			May be submitted by		Referendum	
	Type: Direct, Indirect, Both	Size of Petition	Vote for Enactment	Petition	Legislature	Size of Petition	Vote for Enactment
Alaska	Direct	10%[1]	Majority	Yes	No	10%[1]	Majority
Arizona	Direct	10% vote for Governor	Majority	Yes	Yes	5% vote for Governor	Majority
Arkansas	Direct	8% vote for Governor[2]	Majority	Yes	—	6% vote for Governor[2]	Majority
California	Both	8% vote for Governor[3]	Majority	Yes	Yes	5% vote for Governor	Majority
Colorado	Direct	8% vote for Secretary of State	Majority	Yes	Yes	5% vote for Secretary of State	Majority
Idaho	Direct	10% vote for Governor	Majority	Yes	Yes	10% vote for Governor	Majority
Maine	Indirect	10% vote for Governor	Majority	Yes	Yes	10% vote for Governor	Majority
Maryland	—	—	—	Yes	—	30% vote for Governor	Majority
Massachusetts	Indirect	3% vote for Governor	Majority[4]	Yes	—	1½–2% vote for Governor[5]	Majority[4]
Michigan	Indirect	8% vote for Governor	Majority	Yes	Yes	5% vote for Governor	Majority
Missouri	Direct	5% vote for Governor[6]	Majority	Yes	Yes	5% vote for Governor	Majority
Montana	Direct	8% vote for Governor[7]	Majority	Yes	Yes	5% vote for Governor[7]	Majority
Nebraska	Direct	7% vote for Governor[8]	Majority[9]	Yes	—	5% vote for Governor[8]	Majority[9]
Nevada	Indirect	10% vote for Supreme Court Justice	Majority	Yes	—	10% vote for Supreme Court Justice	Majority
New Mexico	—	—	—	Yes	—	10–25%[10]	Majority[11]
North Dakota	Direct	10,000	Majority	Yes	—	7,000	Majority
Ohio	Both	3% vote for Governor	Majority	Yes	—	6% vote for Governor	Majority

INITIATIVE AND REFERENDUM PROVISIONS ON STATEWIDE LEGISLATION (*Continued*)

State	Initiative			May be submitted by		Referendum	
	Type: Direct, Indirect, Both	Size of Petition	Vote for Enactment	Petition	Legislature	Size of Petition	Vote for Enactment
Oklahoma	Direct	8%[12]	Majority	Yes	Yes	5%[12]	Majority
Oregon	Direct	8% vote for Supreme Court Justice	Majority	Yes	Yes	5% vote for Supreme Court Justice	Majority
South Dakota	Indirect	5%[13]	Majority	Yes	—	5%[13]	Majority
Utah	Both	5–10%[14]	Majority	Yes	—	10%[14]	Majority
Washington	Both	50,000[15]	Majority[16]	Yes	Yes	30,000[15]	Majority[16]

[1] Applications for initiative and referendum petitions must be signed by not less than 100 qualified voters as sponsors. The 10% requirement is based on "those who voted in the preceding general election and resident in at least two-thirds of the election districts of the State . . ."

[2] Including signatures equal to one-half the percentage in each of fifteen counties.

[3] Only 5% if submission is to the legislature.

[4] Including 30% of total vote cast in election.

[5] 2% if law is to be suspended pending referendum.

[6] Percentage of signatures required in each of two-thirds of the Congressional districts in the state.

[7] Percentage of signatures required in each of two-fifths of counties in the state.

[8] Must include 5% of voters in each of two-fifths of counties in the state.

[9] Including 35% of total vote cast in election.

[10] 25% if law is to be suspended pending referendum. Percentage of signatures required in each of three-fourths of the counties in the state.

[11] Including 40% of total vote cast at election.

[12] Based on number of votes cast for state office receiving highest number of votes in last general election.

[13] 5% of "the qualified electors of the state."

[14] Percentage not set by the constitution. By statutory provision, 5% of votes cast in last election for all candidates for governor required for indirect initiative and 10% of the same number for direct initiative and referendum.

[15] The constitution requires ten per cent and six per cent, respectively, of the legal voters, up to a maximum of 50,000 and 30,000.

[16] Including one-sixth of total votes cast at election.

Steps in the referendum process are very similar to those involved in the initiative. A petition must be prepared; the necessary signatures must be obtained, usually a smaller number than for the initiative;[14] the petition must be filed; the public informed; and an election held. Most often a majority of those voting is sufficient to defeat a measure.

A Constitutional Question. Every schoolboy is aware of the "representative system" of government in the United States. At all levels, national, state, and local, the voters elect a small number of persons to represent the people in the process of translating public will into law. In governmental jurisdictions where the initiative and referendum are available, recognition is given to two legislative powers: the legislature and the people. Shortly after its adoption in Oregon in 1903, direct legislation was challenged in the courts on the ground of unconstitutionality. Specifically, the claim was advanced that the initiative and referendum destroyed the "republican" nature of Oregon's government in violation of the U.S. Constitution.[15] This viewpoint reflected the contention that in a republican government the legislative function must be performed exclusively by a representative assembly.

In a noteworthy opinion, the Oregon Supreme Court observed:

> No particular style of government is designated in the Constitution as republican, nor is its exact form in any way prescribed. A republican form of government is a government administered by representatives chosen or appointed by the people or by their authority. . . . Now the initiative and referendum does not destroy the republican form of government and substitute another in its place. The representative character of the government still remains. The people have simply reserved to themselves a larger share of the legislative process.[16]

Although it presented a cogent statement of the compatibility of the processes of direct legislation with representative government, the opinion did not satisfy opponents of the initiative and referendum. Consequently, the constitutional question was raised again in 1909,

---

[14] For details concerning the number of votes required in each state, see the table on pages 320–321.

[15] Article IV, Section 4 provides, "The United States shall guarantee to every State in this Union a republican form of government . . ."

[16] *Kadderly* v. *Portland*, 44 Ore. 145 (1903).

but the opinion of the Oregon courts did not change.[17] Three years later the United States Supreme Court ruled that the question of whether a state has a republican form of government is a political one, beyond the competence of a court to determine.[18] Instead the issue is a matter to be settled by Congress—and so long as the Senate and House of Representatives seat members-elect from a state, they thereby indicate acceptance of its system of government.

Use of the Initiative and Referendum. Unfortunately, studies on the use of the initiative and referendum are not available for most states. However, especially helpful investigations have been conducted in California, Michigan, and Oregon.[19] Although admittedly not an adequate sample, the information pertaining to three states provides some insight into the operation of these devices of direct democracy. In addition, they make possible some tentative observations concerning the use of the initiative and referendum that are more "scientific" than the general statements often made without adequate investigation of the manner in which these devices actually work.

Even though it is fashionable in some circles to comment critically that the ballot is made excessively long by direct legislation, few serious students of the subject deny that solid accomplishments have been realized through the initiative and referendum. Most proposals voted on by the people have not been of the "ham and eggs" variety. Viewed in general terms, matters voted on by the electorate may be classified into three major groups: (1) modifications in the structure of government, (2) finances, and (3) public policy.[20] Examples of accomplishments by Californians in the first category include an executive budget law, a civil service system, and improved procedures for the selection of judges. Oregonians have provided for county home rule, authorized the reorganization of school districts, removed property qualifications for voters in school district elections, and permitted the subdivision of counties for the election of state legislators.

Voters in Oregon have been especially active with regard to finan-

---

[17] *Oregon* v. *Pacific States Telephone and Telegraph Company,* 53 Ore. 162 (1909).

[18] *Pacific States Telephone and Telegraph Company* v. *Oregon,* 233 U.S. 118 (1912).

[19] W. W. Crouch, *The Initiative and Referendum in California,* The Haynes Foundation, Los Angeles, 1950; J. K. Pollock, *The Initiative and Referendum in Michigan,* University of Michigan Press, Ann Arbor, 1940; J. G. La Palombara, *The Initiative and Referendum in Oregon: 1938–1948,* Oregon State College Press, Corvallis, 1950.

[20] Classification suggested by La Palombara, *op. cit.,* p. 83.

cial matters. Of some 450 measures submitted to them between
1902 and 1964, approximately one-third were directly concerned
with finances of the state and local units of government. A number
of these measures, such as salaries of legislators, the general sales tax,
and the cigarette tax, were submitted to the voters more than once.
Although some persons have hastened to generalize that the people
regularly vote "No" on revenue measures, an analysis of the votes in
Oregon as well as California and Michigan does not support this
assertion. It is true that the people have voted against some major
sources of revenue, but they have acted favorably on others. Thus
the people of Oregon have on several occasions defeated measures
levying direct taxes on consumption and at the same time have authorized numerous levies on real property. It seems more accurate
to conclude that the voters have exercised discrimination.

Through the initiative and referendum voters in the different
states have decided policy questions of just about every type. "Retirement life payments, old age benefits, 'Ham and Eggs,' and 'Thirty
Dollars Every Thursday' pension plans, state liquor regulation, local
option, legislative apportionment, 'hot cargo' labor issues, fair employment practices, and tidelands oil-drilling struggles have all
served to make headlines about the initiative and referendum in
California . . ."[21] Similar issues have been decided in other states.
On the whole, it seems that the people have been rather "conservative" and have voted their opposition to such measures as Townsend
Plans, single taxes, and legalized gambling—to name only a few.

The Case for Direct Legislation. With the exception of Alaska,
where they were a part of the original constitution, no state has
adopted the initiative and referendum for some forty years. Nevertheless, a strong case may be developed in their behalf. Of course,
direct legislation is subject to abuses, and numerous arguments have
been advanced against its use. First the claims of the proponents of
direct legislation will be examined briefly.

Strengthening Popular Sovereignty. It is a fundamental axiom of
the American system of government that political power flows from
the people. Direct legislation was conceived as a means of strengthening the people's control over their government at a time when a feeling was widespread that legislative bodies often were not motivated
by concern for the public welfare. It has never been viewed, except

[21] W. W. Crouch, *op. cit.,* p. 1.

by a few extremists, as a substitute for legislative action; it has been designed to function as a complement. Through it the voters may translate their desires into law regardless of the attitudes of their representatives, who conceivably may *mis*represent the people. Direct legislation strengthens the people's opportunity for accurate political expression.

Control of Special Interests. The influence of special interests, or pressure groups, is a major concern of all persons interested in the legislative process. Advocates of direct legislation argue that it "controls" these groups in the sense that influencing public policy is more difficult when the mass of the voters must be persuaded rather than individual legislators. Hence the effectiveness of pressure organizations may be impaired. In relation to this issue, W. B. Munro asserted that "no individual will ever vote for or willingly assent to a change, unless satisfied that the change will directly benefit him individually, or that the action will bring improved general welfare to the community. . . ."[22]

Hardly anyone denies that the people are susceptible to the propaganda of special interests. Two facts must be noted, however. First, more often than not, there are *competing* interest groups seeking to persuade the voters. If the arguments of one appear more persuasive than those of another, the popular vote may be influenced accordingly, and it is very difficult to argue that it should not be. Second, a basic criticism levied against legislatures when they follow the wishes of pressure groups is that when they do so they are acting contrary to the people's welfare. If the two are in accord, the basis for criticism vanishes.

Influence on the Legislature. It is asserted that direct legislation influences legislative bodies in at least two important ways. First, it serves as a stimulus to action. Where the voters may enact legislation, legislators may be motivated to take action on matters that otherwise would be neglected because of inertia or selfish interests. The people's representatives might also feel, perhaps with some justification, that they could prepare a law which would accomplish desired purposes more effectively than one drawn up by interested citizens.

A second argument frequently advanced is that the initiative and referendum, particularly the latter, function to "check" the legis-

---

[22] W. B. Munro, *The Initiative, Referendum, and Recall,* D. Appleton and Company, New York, 1912, p. 197.

lature by preventing enactment of legislation that does not meet popular approval. Opportunities for overriding the legislature may be somewhat limited, however, by the use of "emergency" clauses. When such a clause is attached to a bill, it becomes effective immediately and is not subject to the usual waiting period of sixty or ninety days. Since legislatures usually exhibit discretion in this matter, the people have the opportunity to vote on the great bulk of significant legislation if they so desire. One careful student has concluded that "this feature of direct legislation appears the most important and effective argument in its favor."[23]

Voter Education. Even though voters may sometimes act on the basis of emotion rather than intelligence and reason, direct legislation stimulates the interest of many persons in public issues. However, the degree to which voters have become more educated and interested in public affairs is difficult, if not impossible, to determine. Still, it cannot be assumed that the many efforts in this direction at election time produce no results. A few states publish an official voters' pamphlet in which arguments are presented for and against measures. Even if a voter does not comprehend all he reads, his knowledge and perhaps his interest will be increased.

Education of the voter is not limited to official efforts. At least three other sources of information are generally significant: (1) groups interested in specific measures, (2) newspapers, and (3) civic organizations of various kinds. Attention already has been directed to the fact that competing interest groups distribute large quantities of information. Although much of the material might more accurately be termed propaganda, the voter is presented with an opportunity to weigh the claims of all sides. In most communities of any size, newspapers run factual and editorial articles on initiative and referendum measures, again presenting the voters with an opportunity to separate the wheat from the chaff. Organizations like the League of Women Voters and businessmen's "city clubs" study proposals carefully and prepare balanced presentations of arguments pro and con. The influence of such groups is not limited to their membership, since they commonly make concerted efforts to disseminate the information that they have prepared.

Effect on Constitutions and Charters. Proponents of direct legislation sometimes maintain that state constitutions and local charters need not be encumbered with so many restrictions on legislative ac-

---

[23] La Palombara, *op. cit.,* p. 118.

tion when the people may directly determine public policy. A cursory comparison of constitutions of those states using direct legislation with the constitutions of other states does not seem to support this generalization. The average of constitutions in the two groups of states is about the same, and restrictions on legislative discretion are numerous in both.

The Case Against Direct Legislation. Numerous criticisms have been directed against the initiative and referendum. Both the theory and practice of direct legislation have been targets of concentrated attack. The fact remains, however, that no state has abandoned these processes, a compelling indication that they have won approval from the people.

Impairment of Representative Government. Attention has been called to court decisions repudiating the idea that, legally speaking, the initiative and referendum destroy the representative nature of government. The existence of devices for direct popular participation in the governmental process means that a *redistribution* of functions has taken place in order to give the people more control. If sovereignty resides with the people, "then it must follow that they enjoy the right to expand or limit the functions of a governmental agency which owes its very existence to the will of the people."[24]

Few persons will deny that the system of representative government found in the states has exhibited some defects. Direct legislation reflects only *one method* of seeking to remedy these defects. The conclusion of one early student of direct legislation with regard to its constituting a threat to representative governments has been justified by experience:

> But whatever the amount of competition with the legislative assembly, from the ever-increasing amount of legislation enacted by the assembly . . . it is clear that there is no danger that the representative legislature will be superseded by the direct action of the people.[25]

Impairment of Legislative Responsibility. Closely related to the foregoing criticism is the claim that direct legislation impairs the

---

[24] *Ibid.,* p. 102.

[25] J. D. Barnett, *The Operation of the Initiative, Referendum, and Recall in Oregon,* The Macmillan Co., New York, 1915, p. 166. A similar view was expressed by C. A. Beard and B. E. Shultz, *Documents on the State-Wide Initiative, Referendum and Recall,* The Macmillan Co., New York, 1912, p. 23.

sense of responsibility of a legislative body. Such a development may stem from two closely related factors. A sense of "timidity" may develop on the part of individual legislators, resulting in the referral of "hot" issues to the voters. In this way the legislator may avoid the necessity of having to take a stand on controversial issues in order to maintain his popularity with his constituents. Early in American experience with direct legislation, J. D. Barnett observed:

> The constitutional provision which permits the legislative assembly to submit statutes to the people of the state for approval or rejection is vicious in that it may tempt the assembly to shift the responsibility for the enactment of legislation, for which it has been chosen, back upon the electors . . .[26]

One writer has aptly noted that this argument "begs the question" because the optional referendum was instituted "for the purpose of allowing the legislature to refer to the people those measures about which it entertained genuine doubts."[27] It could be as logically argued that *failure* by the legislature to use the referendum under such circumstances would reflect a disregard for its responsibilities.

Nevertheless, it is true that the optional referendum *may* be used as a means of abdicating legislative responsibility. If legislators use this device "to refer what they fear to enact," the people are called upon to make decisions that should be made by their representatives. When genuine doubt exists as to the wisdom of a particular course of action with regard to a matter of real public concern, reference to the voters is entirely justifiable.

Lengthening of the Ballot. No one can deny that the initiative and referendum operate to increase the length of ballots. The extent to which this development has been significant differs from state to state and from time to time within a state. Moderate use has been made of these devices in Michigan, where between 1910 and 1939 an average of only three propositions per election appeared on the ballot.[28] On the other hand, the voters of California decided upon 450 measures between 1912 and 1949,[29] while those of Oregon voted on 440 measures between 1904 and 1958. The smallest number of measures submitted at an Oregon general election during this period

[26] J. D. Barnett, *op. cit.*, pp. 169–170.
[27] J. G. La Palombara, *op. cit.*, p. 105.
[28] J. K. Pollock, *op. cit.*
[29] W. W. Crouch, *op. cit.*

was three and the largest was forty-four! The range in California was from four to forty-four.

It is a truism that any virtue may become a vice when carried to an excess. This old saw is applicable to the initiative and referendum. Used discriminatingly, they serve a very useful purpose; employed without discrimination, they impose an intolerable burden upon the voters. However, advocates of the short ballot should not become so ardent as to overlook the value of obtaining an expression of public opinion on certain issues. Occasional abuses do occur, sometimes as a result of repeated referrals of the same question within a short period of time.

Lawmaking by Minorities. Many voters do not go to the polls on election day, and among those who vote on candidates there are many who fail to vote on propositions. As a result, critics of direct legislation argue that it often produces laws enacted by a minority. This claim is undoubtedly true, but its impact is appreciably lessened by recognition of the fact that all lawmaking bodies are subject to the same vice. Thus in many legislative houses a majority constitutes a quorum, and a majority of the quorum is sufficient to pass a law.

Another important observation, however blunt it may seem, is that it is not necessarily desirable that all persons who go to the polls should vote on all measures. There is little if any value in an uninformed, ignorant vote. Furthermore, some voters actually do not care whether a particular measure is accepted or rejected. They are willing to abide by whatever decision is made by those who are interested and informed. Such an attitude may, in fact, be praiseworthy. Of course, there is the risk that selfish minorities may determine public policy. The fact is that within the framework of democratic government no arrangement has been devised to prevent this from happening, regardless of who makes the laws.

Control of Government by Special Interests. Closely related to the foregoing criticism is the claim that direct legislation facilitates control of government by special interests. Some hold the belief that pressure groups are evil and should be curbed, an attitude that ignores the right of people to associate and to seek to influence their government. One writer has observed with much insight that "it can be reasonably assumed that public policy will always be synonymous with the ideas of those groups which have found successful political expression."[30] Special interests are going to influence the

---

[30] J. G. La Palombara, *op. cit.*, p. 109.

formulation of public policy, whether action is taken by legislative bodies or by the people directly.

The ability of pressure groups to get their pet projects on the ballot or to engineer support for them is not nearly so great a threat to public welfare as the opportunity to affect governmental policy secretly. It is true that voters may not always be able to identify the major groups supporting a measure, but the difficulties of hiding such identity when conducting a mass campaign are probably greater than when seeking to influence the votes of a few legislators. Logical analysis does not support the assertion that the people are more susceptible to control by special interests than are their representatives.

Poorly Drafted Legislation. Provisions submitted to the voters through the initiative may be poorly drafted, but so may bills prepared by legislative bodies. Indeed, "there exists no real reason for assuming that the legislature has done a better job of drawing up proposals than have the people."[31] Although this statement was made specifically with reference to the situation in Oregon, there is no reason to believe it is atypical. Indeed, it is reasonable to assume that those groups sponsoring a measure probably exercise care in phraseology so that the desired goals will be obtained should the measure pass. Legal talent is available to such groups so that a creditable job of drafting may be accomplished.

Weakening the Constitution. Basic to American government, national and state, is the idea that constitutions are "fundamental law." Granting the wisdom of the distinction between constitutional and other types of law, it is argued that the initiative is undesirable because it tends to obscure this difference. As early as 1914 one writer advanced the thesis that the initiative "tends to incorporate into the constitution matters that have no proper place there. . . ."[32] Experience in states where the initiative has been most frequently used seems to support this assertion.[33]

High cost. The claim is sometimes made that direct legislation is costly in comparison with the enactment of laws by legislative bodies. Expenses are involved in drafting measures, obtaining signatures on petitions, verifying signatures, educating the public and counting

---

[31] *Ibid.,* p. 111.

[32] A. L. Lowell, *Public Opinion and Popular Government,* Longmans, Green and Company, New York, 1914, p. 218.

[33] See J. G. La Palombara, *op. cit.,* p. 115; and W. W. Crouch, *op. cit.,* p. 42, Table II. According to Crouch's table, 348 of the 450 measures submitted to popular vote between 1912 and 1949 were constitutional amendments.

votes. However, no studies have been made of these costs as compared with those required in order to get a bill through a legislature. Consequently, any conclusions on this point must be based on guesswork.

Evaluation. As indicated by the arguments pro and con, direct legislation has both strengths and weaknesses. It is certainly not a panacea for political ills as some of its early advocates believed it to be. Nor does it constitute the great threat to our basic governmental institutions that many of its opponents have decried. Undoubtedly, the initiative and referendum place a burden upon the voters, but democracy by its nature imposes heavy burdens on them. If government operates more effectively to implement the wishes of the people, the additional burden imposed by direct legislation is hardly a significant argument against it. If as a result of the initiative and referendum many voters take a more active interest in governmental affairs, the effort is worth the price.

Used with moderation, direct legislation can make truly significant contributions to state and local government. Legislatures continue to decide the bulk of public policy questions and to set the tone of government as long as they *choose* to do so. Occasionally, they are overruled by popular vote, sometimes as a result of repeatedly seeking to do things that have already been disapproved by the public. It is also true that the people sometimes make strange and apparently illogical decisions, but such is the price of democracy.

THE RECALL

By means of the recall voters may remove an official from public office prior to the expiration of his term. Although similar to the initiative and referendum in certain respects, the recall is less widely used. It was first adopted in this country by the city of Los Angeles in 1903 and first applied to state officers by amendment of the Oregon constitution in 1908. By 1914 the recall had been adopted by ten other states; since then only Wisconsin and Alaska have provided for the recall of state officials.[34] However, the recall has spread more

---

[34] The recall is applicable to elective state officials in thirteen states: Alaska, Arizona, California, Colorado, Idaho, Kansas, Louisiana, Michigan, Nevada, North Dakota, Oregon, Washington, and Wisconsin. Only in Kansas are appointed as well as elected officers subject to recall. In Alaska, Idaho, Louisiana, Michigan, and Washington, judges are not subject to recall even though they are elected. Some cities also subject

widely on the local level, where it is available in some three-fourths of the states.

The steps in recall proceedings are similar to those involved in direct legislation, but a few important differences should be noted. A major distinction concerns the number of signatures required on a recall petition setting forth the grounds on which the recall of a particular officer is sought. Recall petitions regularly require a much larger number of signatures than either initiative or referendum petitions. The range is from ten to fifty-five per cent of those who voted for some designated officer at the last election; the most common requirement is twenty-five per cent. After the petition has been signed by the required number of voters, it must be filed with the appropriate official, who is responsible for determining the sufficiency and legality of signatures. Once everything is in order, an election must be held within a specified time unless the officer in question resigns.

Although the procedural requirements for the conduct of recall elections differ appreciably from place to place, there are three basic patterns. Under one arrangement, two elections are required. In the first election the people merely vote "Yes" or "No" on the question of removal. If the majority vote affirmatively, a second election is held, usually within thirty days, to choose a successor. An alternative arrangement enables the people to vote simultaneously on removal and for a successor. Thus each person who votes to remove the official also votes for someone to take his place should the election result in his recall. A third variation simply requires the person against whom a recall petition has been filed to run against other candidates whose names have been placed on the ballot. The first practice is to be preferred for several reasons, not the least of which is that the official "runs" against his record rather than against others seeking his position. Since he is normally chosen by a plurality vote, the successor may actually be desired by *fewer* of the voters than the person recalled.

The recall has been used much less frequently than the initiative and referendum. The only instance of its successful use to remove

---

appointed officials to the recall. In addition to the regular recall, Arizona uses the "advisory recall," a device by which candidates seeking election to Congress *may* file a statement indicating willingness or unwillingness to resign if not re-elected at a recall election. Candidates may refuse to file any statement. In any case, a recall vote itself cannot remove a member of Congress from office, since the U.S. Constitution does not recognize the procedure.

officers elected on a statewide basis occurred in North Dakota in 1921, when the governor, attorney general, and secretary of agriculture were recalled.[35] Numerous unsuccessful efforts have been made, however, to remove state officeholders. On the other hand, many local officials have been removed by the recall. Complete figures are unavailable, but attention may be called to a few well-known instances of its use by cities: The mayor of Los Angeles was recalled in 1909 and in 1938, the mayor of Seattle in 1910 and in 1931, and the mayor of Detroit in 1929. The voters of Long Beach, California, recalled their entire city council in 1934, and those of Fort Worth, Texas, removed six of their councilmen in 1938. A recall effort directed against the mayor of San Francisco failed in 1946.[36] Members of the board of the Little Rock (Arkansas) School District were subjected to recall action in 1959.

Evaluation. As in the case of initiative and referendum, experience with the recall has justified neither the fears of its opponents nor the claims of its ardent advocates. It is undoubtedly true that the recall has been used in behalf of the public interest in some instances and to serve selfish, partisan interests in others. The fact remains that limited use has been made of the recall.[37] All the reasons for infrequency of use are not readily apparent. Legal restrictions constitute a part of the explanation. In most jurisdictions, recall proceedings may not be started until an incumbent has been in office for a stipulated period, usually six months. Further, the law commonly provides that recall of an officer may not be undertaken more than once during a single term of office. The large number of signatures required on recall petitions probably contributes to the infrequency of their use. The major explanation for the fact that the recall is seldom used appears to be popular reluctance to resort to it.

It seems reasonable and proper to assess this device of direct democracy in light of its actual use rather than its potential abuses.

---

[35] Governor Frazier, oddly enough, was elected to the United States Senate the following year by the same electorate that had recalled him from the governor's chair!

[36] See Charles M. Kneier, *City Government in the United States*, Harper & Brothers, New York, 1957, pp. 398–403.

[37] According to one study, only seventy-two recall elections were held in the 952 cities in which the device became available during its first quarter-century of use in the United States. See F. F. Bird and F. M. Ryan, *The Recall of Public Officers*, The Macmillan Company, New York, 1930. For a discussion of the use of the recall in California, see W. W. Crouch and D. E. McHenry, *California Government*, University of California Press, Berkeley, 1949.

Along with the initiative and referendum, the recall is sometimes viewed with alarm by those who feel that it reflects an unjustifiable faith in the voters. Nevertheless, there is much wisdom in the observation that "The electorate is neither more nor less judicious and discriminating in the recall of officials than in their election."[38]

SELECTED REFERENCES

Books:

Bird, F. F., and Ryan, F. M., *The Recall of Public Officers,* The Macmillan Co., New York, 1930.

Crouch, Winston W., *The Initiative and Referendum in California,* The Haynes Foundation, Los Angeles, 1950.

La Palombara, Joseph G., *The Initiative and Referendum in Oregon: 1938–1948,* Oregon State College Press, Corvallis, 1950.

Pollock, James K., *The Initiative and Referendum in Michigan,* University of Michigan Press, Ann Arbor, 1940.

Articles:

Crouch, Winston W., "The Initiative and Referendum in Cities," *American Political Science Review,* June 1943.

——, "Direct Legislation Laboratory," *National Municipal Review,* February 1951.

La Palombara, J. G., and Hagen, C. B., "Direct Legislation: An Appraisal and a Suggestion," *American Political Science Review,* June 1951.

Schumacher, Waldo, "Thirty Years of People's Rule in Oregon; An Analysis," *Political Science Quarterly,* June 1932.

---

[38] Charles M. Kneier, *op. cit.,* p. 401.

CHAPTER 14

State and Local Expenditures

Total state and local expenditures now approximate $75 billion. Among the myriad of functions and services provided by the *states* with these funds, four are especially noteworthy. About two-thirds of all state expenditures go for the support of four functions: education, highways, welfare, and health and hospitals. The remainder is spent for protection of persons and property, development of natural resources, correctional institutions, debt retirement and interest payments, recreational facilities, and general government. Major *local* expenditures are for public schools, welfare, public works, and health and hospitals.

TRENDS IN STATE AND LOCAL EXPENDITURES

Every student of government is impressed by the growth of public spending during the twentieth century. Expenditures of state and local governments in 1902 totaled just under $1.1 billion; by 1922 they exceeded $5.6 billion; in 1940 they approximated $11.2 billion; in 1959 the amount was slightly in excess of $58.5 billion, a sum that increased to $75.7 billion in 1963.[1] But these figures are somewhat misleading. Population growth and changes in the gross national product as well as fluctuations in the purchasing power of the dollar must be considered in order to present an accurate picture. In 1902 state and local spending amounted to $12.80 *per capita;* in 1922, $47.41; in 1940, $69.58; in 1959, $331.83; and by 1963 the amount had risen to $379.65. Thus while total expenditures increased about sixty-nine times from 1902 to 1963, per capita amounts were multiplied slightly more than twenty-nine times or well under half as much. A glance at the table on page 336 reveals per capita and total expenditure trends for selected functions. As explained later, the significance of figures on governments spending is further affected by inflationary trends of recent years.

---

[1] See *Governmental Finances in the United States 1902 to 1957.* Bureau of the Census, 1959.

TOTAL AND PER CAPITA EXPENDITURE TRENDS FOR SELECTED STATE AND LOCAL FUNCTIONS, 1902–1963

Function	1902		1922		1932		1940		1948		1953		1957		1963	
	amt.[1]	per cap.	amt.	per cap.	amt.	per cap.	amt.	per cap.	amt.	per cap.	amt.	per cap.	amt.	per cap.	amt.	per cap.
Education	255	3.22	1,705	15.49	2,311	18.51	2,638	19.97	5,379	36.68	9,930	58.82	14,501	85.15	24,012	127.31
Highways	175	2.21	1,294	11.76	1,741	13.95	1,573	11.91	3,036	20.71	4,987	31.25	7,762	45.58	11,136	59.04
Public Welfare	37	.47	119	1.08	444	3.56	1,156	8.75	2,099	14.31	2,914	18.25	3,411	20.03	5,481	29.06
Health & Hospitals (incl. Sanitation)	111	1.59	447	4.07	679	5.45	816	6.18	1,899	12.99	3,198	18.92	4,542	26.67	6,869	36.41
Safety (Police & Fire)	90	1.14	348	3.17	528	4.23	600	4.54	1,050	7.16	1,646	10.25	2,271	13.33	3,468	18.39
Natural Resources	9	.11	61	.55	165	1.32	218	1.65	496	3.38	705	4.41	1,002	5.88	1,588	8.42
General Control	141	1.78	313	2.84	470	3.76	561	4.25	880	6.00	1,263	7.91	1,712	10.05	1,355	7.18

[1] Amounts in millions of dollars.
Source: Bureau of the Census.

Comprehension of governmental expenditures is more complete when viewed in relation to the gross national product, which is the value of the total output of commodities and services produced by the economy of a nation during a specified period of time, one calendar year. Thus the GNP consists of (1) all finished products such as consumer goods, capital facilities, and materiél for the armed forces; and (2) all services rendered by individuals, businesses, and governmental units. In other words, the GNP is the aggregate supply of goods and services resulting from the productive efforts of the nation's economy. Obviously, the value of a nation's GNP fluctuates from year to year. The table on this page indicates how great have been the changes in the GNP of the United States in recent times.

The more wealth a nation has, the more it can afford in the way of services. As wealth increases, larger governmental expenditures can be borne without increased sacrifice. Consequently, the ratio between the value of the GNP and the amount of expenditures by state and local governments is significant. The following figures

STATE AND LOCAL EXPENDITURES AND GROSS NATIONAL PRODUCT
SELECTED CALENDAR YEARS 1929–1963

| | *Millions of Dollars* | | | | *Millions of Dollars* | | |
| | | *State and Local Expenditures*[1] | | | | *State and Local Expenditures*[1] | |
Year	*Gross National Product*	*Actual*	*As % of GNP*	*Year*	*Gross National Product*	*Actual*	*As % of GNP*
1929	$104,436	$ 7,582	7.3	1948	$259,426	$15,581	6.0
1930	91,105	8,256	9.1	1950	284,599	20,089	7.1
1932	58,466	7,419	12.7	1952	346,999	22,812	6.6
1934	64,975	6,346	9.9	1954	363,112	27,171	7.5
1936	82,743	7,381	8.9	1955	397,469	29,663	7.5
1938	85,227	8,138	9.5	1956	419,180	32,458	7.7
1940	100,618	8,378	8.3	1957	442,769	35,552	8.0
1942	159,133	7,891	5.0	1959	482,056	40,745	8.3
1944	211,393	7,487	3.5	1961	518,725	47,225	9.1
1946	210,663	9,990	4.7	1963	583,910	52,800	9.0

[1] Excluding federal grants-in-aid.
Source: Tax Foundation.

reveal that the percentage of the GNP accounted for by state and local spending between 1929 and 1963 ranged from a high of 12.7 in 1932 to a low of 3.5 in 1944. Several other interesting facts are worthy of attention in this regard. For one thing, the ratio of state and local expenditures to GNP was at its highest during the depression of the 1930's. Also, this ratio in recent years has exceeded only slightly the point reached in 1929 and has increased gradually since 1955. Therefore, state and local governments are not spending a great deal more than in 1929 in relation to the nation's wealth.

During the current century appreciable shifts have occurred in the *proportion* of funds expended by the national government on the one hand and state and local governments on the other. In 1902 state and local expenditures accounted for about sixty-eight per cent of total governmental outlay, and in 1923 the percentage stood at sixty-two. By 1940, however, state and local governments spent only about forty-eight per cent of the total, while the federal share had risen to approximately fifty-two per cent; and in 1948 the ratio stood at 32.5 to 67.5 per cent! Since that time a countertrend has developed, and recently state and local spending has amounted to some forty per cent of the total, leaving about sixty per cent for the national government.

Undoubtedly, large increases in public expenditures are to be anticipated in years to come. A study published by the Tax Foundation in 1955 concluded that, assuming a continued high level of business activity and no war, state and local expenditures would probably increase by about two-thirds within ten years.[2] Events have indicated that this prediction was actually too low. Indeed, about half of the projected increase occurred within three years. The best estimates appear unable to account for the many factors operating to push expenditures ever upward.

CAUSES OF GROWTH IN EXPENDITURE AMOUNTS

Increased Demand for Services. Probably the most significant cause of higher governmental costs has been the steady public demand for more and better services. Of the factors producing this demand M. Slade Kendrick has stressed three: a changing social and economic order, a changing theory of the proper role of government, and a changing conception of democracy.[3] Kendrick maintains that the rapid developments characteristic of the American social and economic order have been most important in explaining

---

[2] *Government Finances in 1965*, Tax Foundation, New York, 1955.
[3] M. Slade Kendrick, *Public Finance*, Houghton Mifflin Co., New York, 1951, pp. 46–59.

demands for governmental activity. Automobiles require costly highways, streets, bridges, and policemen. Airports, beacons, radio beams, equipment inspection, and the licensing of pilots have followed in the wake of the airplane. Radio and television have opened new fields of regulation. Early abuses of the public welfare and trust by public utilities as well as banking and insurance companies called forth governmental control. As the proportion of the population employed in industry grew, demands increased for public action to promote healthful working conditions, reduce accidents, and minimize conflicts between workers and employers.

Rapid growth in urban population has spurred governmental activity. Concentrations of people in relatively small areas aggravate many problems, including those of health, welfare, transportation, and the protection of persons and property. The control of communicable diseases, the collection and disposal of waste materials, and the provision of pure water illustrate tasks involved in the protection of public health. Relief for the unemployed, assistance to dependent children, help for the aged, and care for the mentally and physically handicapped become more urgent and the need more apparent in cities than in rural areas.[4] Transporting large numbers of persons safely and quickly to and from work, by private or public means, requires the construction and maintenance of streets, bridges, and similar facilities. Governmental operation of transportation systems is often necessary where private enterprise does not meet local needs. Heavy concentrations of people and property require a large amount of costly protection, resulting in more police and firemen whose work involves the use of expensive equipment.

A second factor contributing to the increased demand for governmental activity has been a changing attitude toward the proper role of government. For many years after the founding of the Union, the consensus was that governmental functions should be held to a minimum in order to avoid encroachments upon individual freedom. Kendrick offers a highly practical explanation for the change in popular attitude: "As more and more public services were offered, each in response to a new problem, the inadequacy of the let-alone theory of government became evident. A view in harmony with

---

[4] Paul J. Strayer has observed that increased governmental activity arises also "out of the changing valuation placed upon health, welfare, and security in a society that can afford for the first time the luxury of systematically making some provision for these areas of concern." *Fiscal Policy and Politics,* Harper & Brothers, New York, 1958, p. 170.

what was being done was needed."[5] Consequently, government came to be viewed as a positive force in promoting the general welfare.

Accompanying the changing idea of what government should do has been a change in the concept of democracy. Early emphasis was almost entirely on equality in political rights, including freedom of speech, press, religion, and assembly, a fair trial, and protection from double jeopardy, self-incrimination, and arbitrary seizure of property. Concern for a degree of economic as well as political equality has become increasingly evident. Demands for unemployment compensation, old-age insurance, minimum wage laws, and price supports reflect this trend. These and similar functions cost large sums of money and necessitate increased governmental expenditures.

Population Growth. Even if the urban-rural ratio in the population had not changed so spectacularly in recent years, the mere growth in number of people would have imposed additional demands on government. When the national Constitution was ratified, slightly less than four million persons lived in the United States. Within 100 years the number multiplied more than fifteen times. About the time of World War I the American population exceeded 100 million, and the 1950 census set the figure at slightly more than 150 million. In the mid-1960's the population is rapidly approaching 200 million. More people have required more services and at the same time called upon government to conserve the nation's resources of water, timber, and minerals—all exploited so freely in the process of rapid growth.

Inflation. During the twentieth century the purchasing power of the dollar has varied greatly; that is, prices have fluctuated widely. Consequently, a billion dollars expended one year might purchase much more or much less in the way of services and improvements than would be the case in another twelve-month period. Put another way, the $21 billion spent in 1948 by state and local governments purchased about the same amount of goods and services as would have been obtained in 1940 by an expenditure of $12 billion because the 1940 dollar had depreciated in eight years to a value equivalent of approximately fifty-seven cents. Because of further deterioration in the value of the dollar, it would have been neces-

---

[5] *Op. cit.,* p. 58.

sary to increase the 1940 amount by more than 100 per cent in 1960 merely to purchase *equivalent* goods and services. If state and local governments had "held the line" and kept expenses at the same level for these twenty years, it would have been necessary to reduce services in 1960 to less than one-half their 1940 level.

MAJOR PROBLEMS[6]

Assuming continued growth of governmental spending and the necessity of providing adequate revenue, certain problems must be faced by those responsible for the financial obligations of governments. In meeting these problems, consideration must be given to (1) achieving effective controls over the purposes for which public money is spent, (2) understanding economic growth, and (3) improving intergovernmental fiscal relations.

Effective Controls. "To gain the financial flexibility necessary to deal with the anticipated growth of demands for state services and local assistance, the disposition of revenues (highway-user taxes generally excepted) should be kept as fluid as possible."[7] Achieving this flexibility is not easy, for legislators and even the people themselves are pressured by groups whose interests are served by earmarked taxes and statutory formulas that result in long-term commitments on expenditures. When pressures to commit funds are successful, collections from specified taxes are channeled *in advance* to designated functions and activities by direction either of statutory or constitutional provisions. A 1954 study revealed that twenty of the thirty-two states then using general sales taxes provided that collections should be used wholly or in part for specific functions.[8] Similar situations existed with regard to taxes on tobacco and alcoholic beverages, and the bulk of income from gasoline taxes is earmarked for highways. The impact of this practice on state finances is reflected in the fact that over fifty per cent of total tax collections for all the states is expended without effective legislative review of needs as balanced against available funds. Not only has the proportion of committed funds grown larger in recent years, but an increasing number of functions has been placed in the "favored" category.

---

[6] This section is adapted from *The Financial Challenge to the States,* Tax Foundation, 1958, pp. 34–38.

[7] *Ibid.,* p. 34.

[8] *Earmarked State Taxes,* Tax Foundation, 1955.

Economic Growth. The importance of continued economic growth as a necessary condition to the support of expanding expenditures has been generally recognized. With varying degrees of success, states have sought to attract new industry and retain existing industries in a variety of ways. Low taxes are sometimes stressed as a means of promoting industrial development. However, there is good indication that "tax differentials are not a primary influence upon industrial development."[9] The manner in which tax money is spent seems to be more significant to business enterprises than total amounts collected. Indeed, "business is entirely willing to pay taxes to provide reasonably for the public service, but it cannot afford to pay out funds which will be dissipated wastefully."[10] Considerations pertaining to such matters as geographical location in relation to markets, transportation facilities, and availability of adequate and relatively cheap power and labor resources are more crucial than tax rates.

Intergovernmental Fiscal Relations. The rapid population growth in urban areas during recent years has produced greatly increased demands for local services, particularly by municipal governments. In an effort to meet these demands local jurisdictions have taxed real property very heavily, in many instances reaching legal limits. Economic, political, and legal considerations have forced local governments to seek additional sources of revenue. Al-

STATE AID FOR LOCAL USES: 1963
Total Aid: $11,885 million

	Millions	Per Cent
Education	$6,993	59
Public Welfare	1,919	16
Highways	1,416	12
Other	1,557	13

though new taxes, such as income and sales levies, have produced appreciable revenue in some jurisdictions, the most significant relief has come in the form of state aid. (The rapid growth in state payments to local governments since 1902 is shown in the table on page 345.) State aid to local governments has tripled since World

---

[9] James W. Martin and William G. Herzel, "The Influence of Taxation upon Industrial Development," *State Government,* July 1957.

[10] *Ibid.,* p. 148.

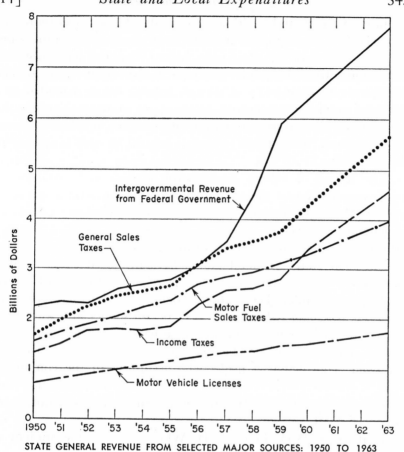

STATE GENERAL REVENUE FROM SELECTED MAJOR SOURCES: 1950 TO 1963

War II, but the bulk of assistance has not gone to cities. Instead, the major recipients have been counties and school districts. Approximately eighty-five per cent of state aid to localities is spent for education, welfare, and highways. (For total amounts in fiscal 1963, see table on page 342.) Since big cities are caught between rising costs and revenue ceilings, it seems inevitable that the states must provide greater assistance to them, "unless they are willing to see the predominant contributors of state taxes turn to the Federal government for aid."[11]

Federal grants to state and local governments have increased rapidly in recent times, and their impact on expenditure patterns has been significant.[12] The most costly state functions are education,

---

[11] *The Financial Challenge to the States,* Tax Foundation, 1958, p. 36.

[12] The importance of federal grants as a source of state and local revenue is considered further in Chapter 15.

highways, welfare, and health and hospitals. These activities receive appreciable federal support in the form of grants-in-aid to the states. In fiscal 1963, and for some years before that, the states obtained more money from the federal government than from any single tax! (See graph on page 343.) Although federal aid is defended as a means of providing "incentive" to the states to increase support for functions considered to be of nationwide concern, it is also criticized on the ground that it tends to impair control by each state over its own finances.

The impact of federal grants-in-aid on state and local governments was studied by the Commission on Intergovernmental Relations.[13] Although an advisory committee of the CIR concluded that in general "the over-all impact of federal grants has had relatively little adverse effect in a majority of the States studied," it was agreed that in some states "Federal grants have produced shifts in State policies. In some instances, services were introduced which would not have been undertaken without federal aid." Furthermore, some functions receiving federal aid "were begun sooner and were done more extensively than would otherwise have been the case." Even though state functions not benefitting from federal assistance have not been "conspicuously neglected," according to the committee, there is considerable evidence to indicate that they have not been "equally well treated."[14] Differences appeared especially noticeable in poorer states.

Writing in 1953, Leonard D. White, a long-time student of American government, voiced the opinion that "if present trends continue for another quarter century, the states may be left hollow shells, operating primarily as the field districts of federal departments and dependent upon the federal treasury for their support."[15] Determination of the accuracy of Professor White's prediction must be left to the future. Nevertheless, some facts do not seem to foretell such an inglorious future for the states. Noting that "the States and their subdivisions bear directly more than two-thirds of the growing

---

[13] The Commission on Intergovernmental Relations was established in 1953 pursuant to an act of Congress directing the Commission to examine the role of the national government in relation to the states and their political subdivisions. The Commission had two dozen members, twelve appointed by the President, six by the President of the Senate, and six by the speaker of the House of Representatives.

[14] *The Impact of Federal Grants-in-Aid on the Structure and Functions of State and Local Government*, June, 1955, p. 12.

[15] Leonard D. White, *The States and the Nation*, Louisiana State University Press, Baton Rouge, 1953, p. 3.

STATE EXPENDITURES FOR SELECTED ITEMS
SELECTED FISCAL YEARS 1902–1963
(millions)

| Year | *Select Direct Expenditures* | | | | *Payments to local governments* |
	Current operation	*Capital outlay*	*Interest[1]*	*Insurance benefits and withdrawals*	
1902	$ 114	$ 2	$ 10		$ 52
1913	218	48	14		91
1922	562	302	45	$ 54	312
1927	762	492	83	71	596
1932	982	786	114	63	801
1936	1,192	634	124	79	1,417
1940	1,570	737	130	601	1,654
1944	2,134	330	101	226	1,842
1948	3,837	1,456	86	1,020	3,283
1950	4,450	2,237	109	2,177	4,217
1952	5,173	2,658	144	1,413	5,044
1954	5,886	3,347	193	2,096	5,679
1956	6,758	4,564	311	1,984	6,538
1957	7,463	5,158	351	2,313	7,310
1958	8,307	5,949	396	3,675	7,943
1959	8,924	7,059	453	4,259	8,540
1960	9,694	6,607	536	3,461	9,283
1961	10,384	6,865	584	4,701	10,114
1962	11,289	7,214	635	4,238	10,891
1963	12,449	8,110	721	4,306	11,885

[1] Does not include sums for repayments of debts.
Sources: Tax Foundation and Bureau of the Census.

fiscal burdens of domestic government," the Commission on Inter-governmental Relations observed that recently "their activities have been increasing faster than the nondefense activities of the National Government." At the same time the Commission stressed the importance of strengthening state and local governments if they are to continue to play their vital role in the affairs of the nation.[16]

PURPOSES OF STATE EXPENDITURES

An appreciation of government spending requires not only an awareness of trends but also an understanding of what the money is spent for. The simplest way of accomplishing this purpose is to examine the financial reports of the states. There are, of course,

[16] The Commission on Intergovernmental Relations, *A Report to the President for Transmittal to the Congress,* June 1955, pp. 36 *ff.*

varied systems of reporting, but expenditures commonly are classified according to *character* and *function*. Character reflects the nature of the expenditure regardless of the function, or functions, involved. Thus all money spent to pay interest on outstanding bonds is of the same character even though the bonds may have been issued to finance roads, hospitals, or school buildings. Function, on the other hand, refers to the nature of the activity such as road construction, public health, or education.

Expenditures According to Character. Major subclassifications under character are (1) current operation, (2) capital outlay, (3) insurance trusts, (4) debt service, and (5) intergovernmental.[17] *Current operation* includes all direct expenditures for the compensation of officers and employees as well as for the purchase of supplies, materials, and services other than capital items. *Capital outlays* are made for the construction of highways, public buildings, public works, and other improvements of a somewhat "permanent" nature. Included also are expenses for the purchase of real property and major items of equipment and for major alterations and additions to existing structures. Differences between expenditures for current operation and capital outlay are sometimes indistinct because items may be arbitrarily classified in one category or the other by different jurisdictions. Thus automobiles and typewriters, for example, are regarded as items of current expense, while road graders and electronic computers may be considered as capital outlays.

Insurance trusts include payments to retired employees, unemployment compensation, workmen's compensation, sickness insurance, and other social insurance programs. Costs of administering such trust activities and state contributions to these funds are *not* included. The major expenses under *debt service* involve the redemption of obligations such as bonds and warrants along with the payment of interest. The bulk of *intergovernmental* expenses stem from fiscal aid to other governments, especially grants and shared taxes.

In fiscal 1963 spending for current operation totaled $12.4 billion, accounting for over one-third of total state expenditures. Capital outlay exceeded $8.0 billion, and trust fund payments amounted to nearly $4.5 billion. During 1963 the states devoted about $2.5 billion to debt redemption and interest payments. State assistance

---

[17] For trends of expenses in these categories see the table on page 345.

to local governments increased to $11.8 billion during the same period. The tremendous growth in state payments to local governments during the current century is indicated in the table on page 345.

DIRECT STATE EXPENDITURES FOR SELECTED FUNCTIONS
SELECTED FISCAL YEARS 1902–1963
(millions)

Year	Total	Education[1]	Highways	Public welfare	Health and Hospitals	Natural resources	General control[2]
1902	136	17	4	10	32	9	23
1913	297	55	26	16	53	14	38
1922	1,085	164	303	38	125	61	69
1927	1,451	218	514	40	170	94	96
1932	2,082	278	843	74	215	119	114
1936	2,445	297	754	422	221	93	130
1940	3,555	375	793	527	300	144	151
1944	3,319	489	540	577	331	164	162
1948	7,897	1,081	1,510	962	663	344	266
1950	10,864	1,358	2,058	1,566	947	468	317
1952	10,790	1,494	2,556	1,410	1,132	539	361
1954	13,008	1,715	3,254	1,548	1,276	563	419
1956	15,148	2,138	4,367	1,603	1,470	670	477
1958	20,137	2,872	5,507	1,855	1,848	874	569
1959	22,585	3,242	6,414	2,007	1,967	976	619
1960	22,313	3,557	6,070	2,221	1,896	842	654
1961	24,578	3,792	6,230	2,311	2,059	906	726
1962	25,494	4,268	6,635	2,509	2,161	973	763
1963	27,698	4,954	7,425	2,712	2,330	1,097	830

[1] Principally higher education.   [2] Includes financial administration.
Sources: Tax Foundation and Bureau of the Census.

Expenditures According to Function. The most important groupings according to function are (1) education, (2) highways, (3) public welfare, (4) health and hospitals, (5) natural resources, (6) public safety, (7) general control, and (8) miscellaneous.[18] State allocations for *education* in fiscal 1963 totaled $11.9 billion, more than was spent for any other function, and a sum representing an increase of eleven per cent over the preceding year. Aid to local governments for public primary and secondary schools reached $7.0 billion. The major portion of the remainder was used to support state colleges and universities.[19] At the same time the states spent $8.8 billion for

[18] This breakdown of expenditures is adapted from the Bureau of the Census.

[19] Funds for the support of agricultural experiment stations and extension services are classified by the Bureau of the Census under natural resources.

highways, also eleven per cent more than in 1962. About $1.4 billion went to local governments to help them finance their road building programs. The bulk of direct state disbursements for highways went for capital outlay, mostly in the form of payments to contractors.

In the field of *public welfare* the states function largely as middlemen. Of the $4.6 billion expended by the states for welfare programs in 1963 transfers to local governments totaled $1.9 billion. During that year the states received over $2.5 billion from the national government for public assistance. Major welfare programs include old-age assistance and aid to dependent children, the blind, and the disabled. State spending for *health and hospitals,* the fourth major function, reached $2.3 billion in 1963. The bulk of these funds was used for hospitals and institutions for the handicapped.

Numerous programs are encompassed within the general category of *natural resources,* for which the states spent $1.09 billion in 1963. With this money the states sought to conserve, develop, and improve the utilization of such resources as soil, water, forests, minerals, and wild life. The programs of agricultural experiment stations and extension services administered by state institutions of higher education are included. It is interesting to note that in 1902 the states spent only nine million dollars on natural resources. In 1963 the states spent $833 million for correction and police functions, including general law enforcement, crime prevention, and prisons.

Expenditures for *general control* in 1963 amounted to $830 million, financing the legislative and judicial branches, the offices of chief executives, and auxiliary and staff services in such fields as finance, personnel, purchasing, record-keeping, and public reporting. Such minor activities as housing and community redevelopment, services for veterans, water transportation facilities, docks, terminals, and airports are usually classified as *miscellaneous.* Indeed, all general expenses for purposes not falling within any standard functional category may be considered as miscellaneous. For these services the states spent over $3.1 billion in 1963.

Purposes of Local Expenditures

Direct general expenditures by all local governments during fiscal 1963 approximated $47.2 billion, including grants of $11.6 billion from state governments. Major functions supported by these expenditures and the approximate amounts involved were as follows: education, $19.1 billion; highways, $3.7 billion; public safety, $3.1

billion; health, hospitals and sanitation, $4.7 billion; public welfare, $2.7 billion; general control, $1.6 billion; housing and community development (including urban renewal), $1.2 billion; parks and recreation, $978 million. (See table on this page for trends in local expenditures for selected functions.)

Of total local expenditures those by municipalities amounted to nearly $18.5 billion in 1963. With two significant exceptions, the bulk of the money allocated to the categories listed above was spent by the 18,000 municipalities in the United States. The two exceptions are education and highways. As noted elsewhere, public schools

AMOUNTS OF LOCAL EXPENDITURES FOR SELECTED
FUNCTIONS 1902–1963
(millions)

Function	1902	1922	1932	1940	1948	1953	1957	1963
Education	$238	$1,541	$2,033	$2,263	$4,298	$7,756	$12,042	$19,058
Highways	171	991	898	780	1,526	2,207	2,877	3,710
Public Welfare	27	81	370	629	1,137	1,380	1,666	2,769
Health and Hospitals (incl. Sanitation)	79	322	464	516	570	2,115	2,890	4,538
Safety (Police and Fire)	90	344	513	566	985	1,517	2,093	3,171
Natural Resources	—	—	46	74	152	173	215	491
General Control[1]	118	244	356	410	614	864	1,181	1,644

[1] Includes financial administration.
Source: Bureau of the Census.

generally are administered by special districts, and the major portion of local road construction is handled by counties. Despite this fact, education took a larger share of municipal expenses than any other single function; highways were second, followed by sanitation and police. More than three-fifths of all municipal expenses were for current operation and about one-fourth for capital outlay.

FINANCING EXPENDITURES

Once decisions have been made concerning the purposes for which public money shall be spent and the amounts to be allocated to individual purposes, then the big problem is, Where is the money coming from? How is the necessary revenue to be raised? Answers to these questions are not easy. Many alternatives are open to legislators who are importuned from all sides by persons who claim their schemes are best. In general, no area of public policy is more loaded with political dynamite than decisions pertaining to taxes and debts. These matters are of vital concern to all citizens. The following chapter examines the means commonly used by states and local governments to raise revenue adequate to meet expenses.

SELECTED REFERENCES

Books:

Advisory Commission on Intergovernmental Relations, *Measures of State and Local Fiscal Capacity and Tax Effort.* A Staff Report. October 1962.

Commission on Intergovernmental Relations, *The Impact of Federal Grant-in-Aid on the Structure and Functions of State and Local Governments,* Washington, D.C., 1955.

Eckstein, Otto, *Trends in Public Expenditures in the Next Decade,* Committee for Economic Development, New York, 1959.

Mosher, Frederick C., and Poland, Orville F., *The Costs of American Governments: Facts, Trends, Myths,* Dodd, Mead & Co., New York, 1964.

Scott, Stanley, and Feder, Edward L., *Factors Associated with Variations in Municipal Expenditure Levels, A Statistical Study of California Cities,* Bureau of Public Administration, University of California Press, Berkeley, 1957.

Strayer, Paul J., *Fiscal Policy and Politics,* Harper and Bros., New York, 1958.

Tax Foundation, *Earmarked State Taxes,* New York, 1955.

——, *The Financial Challenge to the States,* New York, 1958.

United States Bureau of the Census, *Compendium of City Government Finances in 1963,* Washington, D.C., 1964.

——, *Compendium of State Government Finances in 1963,* Washington, D.C., 1964.

——, *Historical Statistics on Governmental Finances and Employment, Census of Governments 1962,* Washington, D.C., 1964.

Articles:

Campbell, Alan K., "Most Dynamic Sector," *National Civic Review,* February 1964.

Kurnow, Ernest, "Determinants of State and Local Expenditures Reexamined," *National Tax Journal,* September 1963.

Spangler, Richard, "The Effect of Population Growth upon State and Local Government Expenditures," *National Tax Journal,* June 1963.

CHAPTER 15

Revenues and Debt

Benjamin Franklin once observed that the only sure things in life were death and taxes. Since the beginning of recorded history people have been concerned with taxes. The Egyptians had a well-developed tax system several thousand years ago. Taxes were a matter of real interest to Biblical writers. "Taxation without representation" was an issue in the American Revolution. Today the revenue of all governments in the United States, federal, state, and local, equals approximately thirty per cent of the total annual income in the United States.

In fiscal 1963 state and local governments raised about $66 billion directly from their own revenue sources, of which $32.7 billion were for the states. When allowance is made for intergovernmental transfers the picture is somewhat different: the national government provided states and localities with some $8.6 billion, and the states paid about $11.6 billion to local governments. Thus in terms of the *final* recipient level of government, public revenues in 1963 were divided roughly in this manner: fifty-eight per cent to the national government, twenty-five per cent to local governments, and sixteen per cent to the states. Although the bulk of these funds came from taxes, significant amounts were derived from such other sources as charges for the performance of specific services, insurance trust revenues, utilities, state owned liquor stores, and interest earnings.

TRENDS IN STATE AND LOCAL REVENUES

Trends in amounts of state and local revenues necessarily have paralleled developments in expenditures—both have grown at a similar pace as revealed by a comparison of the tables on pages 352 and 353, with comparable tables in the previous chapter. The factors basic to the growth of expenditures are equally significant with regard to changes in income. These trends and factors were discussed in Chapter 14. In addition to over-all growth in revenue, two other

STATE REVENUES BY SOURCE
SELECTED FISCAL YEARS
1902–1963
(millions)

| | | From Own Sources | | | | | |
Year	Total	Total	Taxes[1]	Charges and misc.	Liquor stores[2]	Insurance trusts	Intergovern-mental[3]
1902	$ 192	$ 183	$ 156	$ 25	$ 2	$ —	$ 9
1922	1,360	1,234	947	181	—	106	126
1932	2,541	2,274	1,890	266	—	118	267
1940	5,737	5,012	3,313	344	281	1,074	725
1948	11,826	10,086	6,743	774	857	1,711	1,740
1953	17,979	15,218	10,552	1,198	967	2,051	2,761
1958	26,191	21,427	14,919	2,089	1,058	3,361	4,764
1959	29,164	24,448	15,848	2,348	1,085	3,631	6,252
1960	32,838	26,093	18,036	2,583	1,128	4,347	6,745
1963	40,993	32,750	22,117	3,523	1,161	5,950	8,243

[1] Excludes unemployment compensation taxes.
[2] Gross receipts from sale of alcoholic beverages in state monopoly systems.
[3] Principally grants-in-aid from the national government.
Sources: Tax Foundation and Bureau of the Census.

developments have been particularly noticeable during the twentieth century: (1) changes in the relative amounts of income for state and local governments, and (2) changes in revenue sources.

In terms of revenue from their own sources, local governments in 1902 collected nearly five times as much money as the states, and in 1922 the ratio was three to one. By 1940 nearly equal amounts were being collected by states and local governments, an approximate ratio that has been maintained in recent years. State increases have resulted in part from the rapid growth in aid to local governments, which increased some 150 times between 1902 and 1958. During the same period federal grants to the states grew over 500 times! Indeed, in recent years the states have received more money from the national government than from their most productive tax—the general sales tax.[1]

Other major changes have occurred in revenue sources during the last half-century. The proportion of *state* income derived from *taxes* has steadily declined from eighty-one per cent in 1902 to fifty-four per cent in 1963. During the same period taxes decreased as a per cent of *local* revenue from nearly eighty per cent to less than fifty

[1] Intergovernmental payments are discussed in more detail later in the chapter.

LOCAL REVENUES BY SOURCE
SELECTED FISCAL YEARS
1902–1963
(millions)

Year	Total	From own Sources								Intergovernmental
		Total	Taxes				Charges and misc.	Utility and liquor stores	Insurance trust	
			Property	Sales and gross receipts	Income	License and other				
1902	$ 914	$ 858	$ 624	$ —	$ —	$ 80	$ 94	$ 60	$ —	$ 56
1922	4,148	3,827	2,973	20	—	76	476	266	16	321
1932	6,192	5,381	4,159	26	—	89	605	463	39	811
1940	7,724	5,792	4,170	130	19	178	510	717	68	1,932
1948	13,167	9,666	5,850	400	51	298	1,273	1,654	140	3,501
1953	21,007	15,323	9,010	718	103	523	2,331	2,357	280	5,684
1958	31,126	22,906	13,450	1,079	215	676	3,853	3,161	472	8,220
1959	33,791	25,068	14,783	1,150	230	738	4,275	3,410	499	8,723
1960	37,163	27,209	15,798	1,339	254	692	4,831	3,749	549	9,953
1963	46,534	33,846	19,401	1,562	313	867	6,365	4,629	687	12,689

Sources: Tax Foundation and Bureau of the Census.

per cent, and the proportion of income provided by the property tax alone dropped from sixty-eight to forty-two per cent. Major proportional increases in local revenue appeared in insurance trusts and grants from the states.

Principles and Problems of Taxation

Nature of Taxes. Although other sources have become increasingly important in recent decades, the bulk of revenue for most governmental units comes from taxes. In the minds of many, all payments made to governments are taxes, but this idea is not correct. A tax may be defined as "a compulsory contribution, exacted by public authority according to some general rule, the expenditure of which is presumably for the common good without regard to particular benefits to individuals."[2] According to the United States Supreme Court, "A tax is an enforced contribution for the payment of public expenses."[3] These definitions, which are typical of many posed by students of public finance, stress the important characteristics of a tax: its compulsory nature, imposition by public authority on the basis of a general rule, and expenditure for the benefit of the public rather than individuals. Consequently, such payments as charges for specific services, special assessments, and income from governmental enterprises are not taxes.

Principles of Taxation. Since taxes constitute such a large part of state and local revenues, the development of "principles" or "criteria" to guide those who impose the taxes and to inform those who pay them is important. Such principles are even more significant and pertinent as they apply to a *system* of taxation rather than to a single tax. A system of taxation may be defined either as consisting of all the taxes levied *within* a governmental jurisdiction or all those levied *by* a government unit. The first definition is more important to the taxpayer and the second to the tax collector. Thus the system of taxation to which a resident of Gravel Switch is subject consists of all taxes levied by his city, his county, any special districts in which he may live, his state, and the national government. On the other hand, Gravel Switch has its own system of taxation consisting of taxes levied by its authority.

---

[2] Merlin H. Hunter and Harry K. Allen, *Principles of Public Finance,* Harper & Brothers, New York, 1940, p. 169.

[3] *Houck* v. *Little River Drainage District,* 239 U.S. 254, 265 (1915).

Ideally, each governmental unit would construct its own tax system with consideration for all other systems to which its taxpayers are subject. Actually, governments pay too little attention to this problem, although it is not entirely ignored. The trend among states to abandon the property tax in favor of local governments indicates awareness of the problem as does the reluctance of the national government to inaugurate a general sales tax. Because of restrictions imposed upon their taxing authority by state law, local governments normally must raise revenue as best they can with little or no consideration for the taxing practices of other governmental units. In terms of their meaningful application, canons of taxation are most significant as they relate to the taxes levied by each governmental unit.

Ability to Pay. Writing at the time of the American Revolution, Adam Smith, in his *Wealth of Nations,* stated emphatically that "The subjects of every state ought to contribute toward the support of the government, as nearly as possible in proportion to their respective abilities . . ." Although most tax systems evidence concern for ability to pay, none attempts to apply the concept strictly. The fact is that in spite of its popularity no accurate, objective means of measuring this subjective concept has been devised. *Progressive* taxation related to size of income or amount of wealth accords with a major social and political idea of modern times—that those who are "privileged" to have more money at their disposal should be more heavily taxed than those who are "underprivileged" and have less.[4] The proposition is generally accepted that "a scale of progression is likely to result in a greater approximation of justice than if proportionate rates are used."[5] Furthermore, progressive income taxes have been found to be very productive, partially because they obtain "the most feathers with the least squawk"—a consideration that cannot be ignored even though it has not been elevated to a principle of taxation.

Diversity. Diversity in a tax system promotes stability and adequacy of yield. Demands on government revenues are changing constantly, and drastic adjustments are required in terms of emergencies such as wars and depressions. Relatively mild economic fluctuations, to say nothing of depressions or "booms," affect certain

---

[4] A progressive tax is one for which the rate increases as the base increases.

[5] Merlin H. Hunter and Harry K. Allen, *op. cit.,* p. 195. A proportionate tax is one for which the rate remains the same regardless of changes in the base. A gasoline tax of, say, six cents per gallon is a good example of a proportionate tax.

taxes appreciably. Lack of tax diversity caused serious difficulties for many local governments during the depression of the 1930's. Many persons, either by choice or necessity, failed to pay their property taxes, which constituted the chief and practically sole source of local revenue. Governments relying heavily on the income tax may experience unanticipated deficits or surpluses as a result of minor cycles of depression or prosperity. Stability of yield is protected by the presence of other taxes less sensitive to economic fluctuations.

Economy of Administration. Although difficult to measure accurately, economy of administration is an important consideration. Collection costs add nothing to the public treasury. Thus a poll tax, which may consume in the process of collection much of the revenue that it produces, is a poor tax in light of this criterion. Actual costs of administration are often hidden because they are not borne directly by the government imposing the tax. For example, much responsibility for the collection of a general retail sales tax rests with retailers. Expenses incurred by private persons who assist in the collection of retail sales taxes are sometimes not considered officially part of the costs of administration. Because it is so productive, however, the general retail sales tax is widely favored, and little concern is felt for economy of administration.

Simplicity and Convenience. Since a favorable public attitude is important, taxes should be as easy to understand and as convenient to pay as possible. Even though many taxpayers long since have abandoned any effort to understand the complexities of the taxes they pay, changes and additions that confuse them are unwise. Ease of payment is a major consideration with regard to many taxes. Taxes "hidden" in the prices of commodities are especially convenient to pay. In spite of the fact that they may not always be apparent, efforts are made constantly by jurisdictions levying income taxes, for example, to make the process of self-assessment easier and more comprehensible through simplification of forms and required accounting practices. Also, provision is often made for payroll deductions and for time payments. In one sense there may be no such thing as a truly "convenient" tax, but taxpayer irritation may be decreased appreciably by procedures carefully designed and sympathetically administered.

Certainty. The taxes due from each taxpayer should be definite and sure of collection. Uncertainty arises largely from two factors: poorly drawn tax legislation and ineffective administration. Tax laws full of loopholes permitting individuals to escape their tax burden violate this canon of taxation. Inefficient administration that permits some persons to evade their responsibilities while requiring others to assume their burden not only reduces the amount of revenue coming into the treasury, it also promotes public cynicism and disrespect. Much has been done in recent times to improve the administration of many taxes.

Sufficiency. There is no more important test of a tax system than its adequacy to meet the requirements of public expenditures, or at least that portion not met by increased indebtedness. The sufficiency of revenue, including taxes, must be anticipated for each fiscal period. The adequacy of each source of income to meet its share of total expenditures must be estimated by those responsible for the preparation of budgets. If the best educated guesses indicate that an existing revenue system will not provide sufficient income, the chief means of meeting fiscal needs are to raise rates, provide new sources of revenue, go into debt, or reduce expenditures. In any case, if the demands for public services are to be met, money must be available regardless of all other considerations.

No single tax and probably no tax system accords perfectly with all six of the criteria discussed above. Furthermore, the significance of influence and expediency must not be overlooked. Influential groups may be the recipients of special favor in the construction of a tax system. Legislators, hard pressed to provide adequate revenue, may follow the course of least resistance by resorting to expedient tax measures or yielding to the pressures of special interests.

STATE AND LOCAL TAX PROBLEMS

In addition to whatever difficulties may be encountered in devising a tax system in keeping with good principles, legislators and other responsible public officers must face certain problems created by recent social and political developments. Paul J. Strayer has noted a number of difficulties that aggravate the problems of state and local taxation: (1) the increased total tax burden, (2) the growth of population and its increasing mobility, (3) inflation, (4) weaknesses in the property tax, and (5) competition for industry.[6] Despite the growth in national wealth in recent years, state and local governments in many instances are experiencing increasing difficulty in

---

[6] Paul J. Strayer, *Fiscal Policy and Politics*, Harper & Brothers, New York, 1958, Chapter XIII.

their efforts to raise revenue. One reason for this situation is the fact that the national government is first claimant on the taxpayer, relegating states and local governments to secondary roles.

The "baby boom" of recent years has required increased public facilities, especially in the field of education. The larger the population, the more insistent the demands for additional services of all kinds, including welfare, health, police, and fire protection. Not only is the population growing, it is also moving. Some consequences of the outward flow of people to suburban communities are noted in subsequent chapters on local government. As a result of inflation, tax dollars buy less. Nevertheless, taxpayers often view their taxes in terms of a percentage or rate of growth in the number of dollars they must pay. Inflation has produced a special problem for local governments largely dependent upon the property tax. Not only is there popular resistance to increases in the tax rate, but also assessed values usually lag far behind market values in times of inflation. Inequities in assessment and poor administration further emphasize the weakness of the property tax. In an effort to attract new industries and retain the ones they have, state and local governments may engage in unseemly competition by granting special tax favors to certain businesses.

MAJOR STATE TAXES

Growth of State and Local Revenue Systems. The early colonial governments needed small amounts of revenue and relied largely on allowances from the "mother country" supplemented by fees and fines. As tax systems developed, they varied according to the economic characteristics of different regions. Since most people owned land and the distribution of property was fairly equal in New England, states in the northern portion of the country stressed the poll tax and levies on the gross produce of land. These levies developed into real property taxes and later into general property taxes. Because many townspeople were at first largely untouched by such levies, use was made of the "faculty tax," imposed at a fixed rate on various occupations.

In the southern colonies, with their landed gentry, large holdings, and slaves, little reliance was placed on real property taxes. Instead, excise taxes on imports and exports produced most of the revenue. By 1683 the property tax was well established in New York and growing in importance in other states. In colonial days taxes were commonly paid in commodities such as tobacco and corn. Thus at one time in Virginia each planter was required to send a bushel of corn to the public granary to help defray governmental costs, and a tax on land, horses, mares, cows, sheep, and goats was payable in tobacco.

The revenue requirements of local governments in colonial times are illustrated in a description of conditions in Virginia:

> The expenditures of local government were small. For years there were no county buildings. Court was held in the open air beneath a tree by justices who served without payment. There was no public education. A few bridges were needed, but usually passage over a water-course was provided by a ferry maintained by the fees of travelers. The chief expenses of the local government were the building and maintenance of bridges and tobacco warehouses, the minister's or church tithe, and the care of the very poor. The Assembly, however, often relieved local units of the responsibility for building tobacco warehouses. A small expense was bounties for the destruction of wolves, crows, and other pests.[7]

This commentator further notes that "The first evidence of discontent appeared when county buildings began to be erected."[8]

By the time the Revolutionary War was won and the colonial period ended, numerous sources of revenue had been tapped by the states. Poll taxes and levies on property, both real and personal, were widely used. Earnings were taxed, and licenses were imposed on a variety of occupations. The beginnings of luxury taxes were apparent in the form of imposts on coaches. Collection procedures were greatly improved. Early in the nineteenth century the general property tax became the chief source of revenue for both state and local governments. The period from 1796 to the Civil War "witnessed the complete establishment of the American system of state and local taxation. The distinguishing feature of the system may be described in a single sentence. It is the taxation of all property. . . ."[9] Since Professor Ely penned these words in the 1880's, many changes have appeared regarding state and local revenues. Quantities, of course, have been multiplied, sources have become much

---

[7] M. Slade Kendrick, *Public Finance,* Houghton Mifflin Co., Boston, 1951, p. 101.
[8] *Loc. cit.*
[9] Richard T. Ely, *Taxation in American States and Cities,* Thomas Y. Crowell Co., New York, 1888, p. 131.

more varied, and the relative importance of individual taxes has changed.

The tables on pages 352 and 353 reveal some significant revenue trends during the present century in addition to increases in gross amounts. To begin with, sixty years ago the states relied much more heavily on their own sources of revenue than they do today. In 1902 they obtained less than five per cent of their income from other governments, principally grant-in-aid from the national government; in 1963 they received over twenty per cent of their income from this source. When taxes alone are considered, the change has been even more notable. In 1902 the states acquired over eighty per cent of their total revenue from taxes; in 1963 taxes accounted for only about fifty-five per cent of state revenue. In the meantime charges, liquor store revenues, and insurance trusts, as well as intergovernmental revenue, had become important sources of income. Another significant development has been the dramatic decline in importance of the property tax at the state level. At the turn of the century the property tax supplied about forty-five per cent of state revenue; by 1963 his source accounted for less than two per cent of state income. Finally, the major state taxes today, those on general sales, income, and motor fuels were not used at the beginning of the twentieth century.

General Sales Taxes. Sales taxes are used by all levels of government—national, state, and local. Federal sales taxes, commonly called excises, are levied on a variety of commodities, including gasoline, automobiles, alcoholic beverages, tobacco, household appliances, and furs.[10] Levies are also imposed on transportation, entertainment, and telephone service, to mention only a few. Since these taxes are imposed on *selected items,* it is said that the national government does *not* make use of a general sales tax.

More than any other type of governmental unit, the states have come to rely upon sales taxes, both selective and general.[11] A major development in the finances of state governments during the past quarter-century has been a rapid increase in the importance of the general sales tax. In fiscal 1963 these taxes produced about $5.5 billion for the states, or just one-fourth of total state tax yield. Numerous variations exist, but a general sales tax may be defined

---

[10] Customs revenues are sometimes considered as a special form of sales taxation.

[11] Selective sales taxes are discussed later in this chapter.

MAJOR STATE TAXES
SELECTED FISCAL YEARS
1902–1963
(millions)

Year	General sales	Motor fuels	Alcoholic beverages	Tobacco products	Income[1]	Property
1902						$ 82
1922		$ 13			$ 101	348
1932	$ 7	527		$ 19	153	328
1940	499	839	$193	97	361	260
1948	1,478	1,259	425	337	1,084	276
1953	2,433	2,019	465	469	1,779	365
1957	3,373	2,828	569	556	2,547	479
1960	4,302	3,335	650	923	3,389	607
1962	5,111	3,665	740	1,075	4,036	640
1963	5,539	3,851	793	1,124	4,461	688

[1] Both personal and corporate income taxes.
Source: Bureau of the Census.

briefly as a levy at a uniform rate on the sale of property at retail or wholesale. Since it is "general," such a tax applies to all sales not exempted by law.[12] To most people a "sales tax" is a tax on retail sales at a rate of, say, two or three cents on the dollar.

The predecessor of the modern sales tax was the business occupation tax levied on sales, purchases, or receipts. A major difference between these taxes imposed by a number of states during the nineteenth century and the present-day sales tax was the use of fractional rates. Not until the twentieth century did any state realize an appreciable amount of revenue from such taxes; the first to do so was West Virginia subsequent to legislation enacted in 1921, followed by Mississippi in 1930. The urgent need for revenue during the depression of the 1930's accompanied by decreases in income from established tax sources hastened the adoption of sales taxes. Twenty-nine states imposed retail sales taxes between 1932 and 1937; six of these were allowed to expire within a short period.[13] In several other states sales taxes were enacted but defeated by popular vote before they became effective.

---

[12] Robert M. Haig and Carl Shoup, *The Sales Tax in the American States,* Columbia University Press, New York, 1934, pp. 3–4; and John F. Due, *Sales Taxation,* University of Illinois Press, Urbana, 1957, Ch. I.

[13] If Indiana's "gross income tax" is counted, the total would be thirty. Although this tax was not a "true" sales tax, it imposed a levy at a flat rate on the receipts of all businesses, including retailers, as well as personal income. Effective in 1963, Indiana changed to a two per cent general sales tax.

From 1937 to 1947 no state adopted or repealed sales tax legislation. Shortly after World War II, inflation and pressures for increased expenditures increased far more than income. Between 1947 and 1955 sales taxes were provided in ten states and the District of Columbia. Thirty-five states now employ general sales taxes, which "are basically single-stage retail sales taxes, applying to all sales at retail, whether made by retailers or by wholesalers or manufacturers."[14] For details pertaining to these taxes see table on page 363.

Administration. Contrary to opinion held in many quarters, sales taxes are not easily administered if the task is performed effectively. State laws require regular reports from businesses selling goods subject to a sales tax. However, successful administration requires extensive auditing in addition to routine office checks. The audit programs of most states are inadequate, according to John F. Due, who notes that one of the best audit programs is found in California where $5 million dollars were spent in 1955 in the conduct of audits covering about fifteen per cent of the firms that collect the tax. It appears that the cost to the states of administering sales taxes averages around one and one-half per cent of the receipts. In addition, there are compliance expenses for which about half the states compensate retailers at a percentage of their tax liability.[15]

Arguments for a General Sales Tax. Earlier in the chapter attention was called to certain criteria helpful in judging taxes. In light of these criteria proponents of a general sales tax advance the following contentions: (1) When used with other taxes, it diversifies a tax system and consequently promotes stability of income for the governmental unit employing it. (2) Since a general sales tax is highly productive, it can be adjusted to yield *sufficient* revenue to meet expenditure requirements. (3) It is a *simple* tax in the sense that it is easily understood by taxpayers and fairly *convenient* to pay once people become accustomed to it. (4) The amount of tax due is quite *certain,* and opportunities for evasion are minimal. Another argument in favor of a state sales tax is related to the fact that the chief alternative appears to be the income tax, which is so heavily emphasized by the national government. It is asserted that an important tax based on expenditures somewhat offsets the adverse affects on economic incentives produced by a highly progressive in-

---

[14] John F. Due, *op. cit.,* p. 293.
[15] *Ibid.,* pp. 304–306.

STATE SALES TAXES

State	Year of intro-duction	Tax rate	Major exemptions of consumer goods	Major exclusions of producer goods
Alabama	1936	4		Industrial machinery, fuel
Arizona	1933	3		
Arkansas	1935	3		
California	1933	3	Food, medicines	
Colorado	1935	3		Fuel
Connecticut	1947	3½	Food, medicines	Fuel
Florida	1949	3	Food, medicines	
Georgia	1951	3		
Hawaii	1935 [1]	4		
Idaho	1965	3		
Illinois	1933	3½		
Indiana	1963	2		
Iowa	1933	2		Fuel
Kansas	1937	3		Fuel
Kentucky	1960	3		
Louisiana	1936	2		
Maine	1951	4	Food, medicines	
Maryland	1947	3	Food, medicines	Fuel
Michigan	1933	4		Fuel, industrial and farm machinery
Mississippi	1930	3½		Industrial machinery
Missouri	1934	3		
Nevada	1955	2		
New Mexico	1933	3		
New York	1965	2		Coal, farm implements
North Carolina	1935	3	Medicines	Coal, some industrial machinery
North Dakota	1935	3	Medicines	
Ohio	1934	3	Food	All production goods
Oklahoma	1933	2		Industrial machinery
Pennsylvania	1954	5	Food, clothing	Farm and industrial machinery
Rhode Island	1947	4	Food, medicines	Fuel
South Carolina	1951	3		Industrial and farm machinery
South Dakota	1933	3		
Tennessee	1947	3		
Texas	1961	2	Food, medicines	Farm machinery
Utah	1933	3		
Washington	1933	4		
West Virginia	1921	3		Most business goods
Wisconsin	1962	3	Food, medicines, clothing	
Wyoming	1935	2½		Fuel

[1] Hawaii used the sales tax for a quarter-century while a territory.

come tax. It is further maintained that sales taxes used along with income taxes enhance the overall *equity* of the tax structure.

Arguments against a General Sales Tax. The chief contention advanced regularly against sales taxes is that they disregard ability to pay. Such a tax is said to be regressive or, more correctly, *regressive in effect* because it places a relatively heavy burden on those persons in the lower income groups whose expenditures on taxable items constitute a rather large portion of their incomes. This regressiveness can be lessened appreciably by exempting food and perhaps medicine, a practice followed in a number of states. The regressive effect of a sales tax may be somewhat offset by a supplementary progressive income tax with sufficient exemptions to exclude persons in lower income groups, particularly those with families to support.

John Due has summarized considerations pertaining to a general sales tax in this way:

> On the whole, the sales tax must be regarded as a second-best tax —one to be employed only if various circumstances make complete reliance on income and other more suitable taxes undesirable. A carefully designed sales tax is not perhaps as objectionable as it was once regarded; it offers definite advantages over widespread excise tax systems, with their inevitable discrimination among various consumers and business firms and their tendency to distort consumption patterns; and it is definitely superior to high rate "business" taxes with uncertain incidence and possible serious economic effects. But it must be regarded as secondary to income taxation, in terms of usually accepted standards of taxation.[16]

Motor Fuels Taxes. During the past forty years taxes on motor fuels have become one of the most productive sources of state tax receipts.[17] In fiscal 1963 the states realized about $3.8 billion from these taxes. The first state tax on gasoline was levied by Oregon in 1919. It proved so successful that by 1921 fifteen states were taxing gasoline; by 1929 all states had such a tax. In the early years rates varied from one to three cents per gallon. Rates now range from five to eight cents on each gallon, with the most common levy at six cents.

---

[16]John F. Due, *op. cit.*, p. 41.

[17] The bulk of this revenue comes from the gasoline tax, which is so important that all taxes on motor fuels are sometimes loosely referred to as "gasoline taxes." However, òther fuels, particularly diesel oil, are also taxed.

Taxes on motor fuels have been adopted with a minimum of opposition, and they continue to be among the most "popular" of taxes. This situation probably is due in large part to the fact that receipts most often have been earmarked for the construction and maintenance of highways. Since those who use the most gasoline pay the most taxes, there is a close correlation between benefits and payments. Another advantage of gasoline taxes is that they exact contributions from nonresidents in rough proportion to their use of a state's highways. About one-fourth of the state constitutions require use of gasoline tax receipts for highways only. Although the practice of earmarking taxes generally is open to question, it is well established with regard to motor fuels, and any effort to allocate such receipts to cover expenses other than those pertaining to highways inevitably meets stiff opposition.

Motor fuels taxes not only produce large quantities of revenue in good and bad times but are also collected easily, cheaply, and conveniently. Indeed, they are probably the cheapest of all major taxes to collect. States usually collect these taxes from wholesale distributors, who pass them on to retailers, who in turn collect them from consumers.

Some problems are associated with the administration of taxes on motor fuels. When adjacent states impose different rates, there seems to be a temptation to "smuggle" gasoline into the state with the higher rate. By mutual agreements states may require exporters to report out-of-state deliveries and supply this information to the state of import. This arrangement has proved more satisfactory than efforts to patrol points along state borders where entry may be made. Other administrative problems relate to exemptions and refunds. Motor fuel not used on highways is commonly not subject to tax. Thus gasoline used in farm tractors, stationary engines, and airplanes may be exempt. Difficulties arise in determining how much gasoline is used in such engines and how much in motor vehicles when the same taxpayer owns both and purchases motor fuel in bulk. Such problems are especially significant in states with large farm populations.

In recent years, distributing the proceeds of fuels taxes among different political units has become a problem in states where receipts are shared with local governments. Increasingly municipal and county officials have sought and obtained grants from the states to assist in constructing roads and streets. Local officials press the claim that since receipts are collected from persons within local jurisdictions who are operating vehicles on roads and streets built by the localities, the states should help in the construction and maintenance of such thoroughfares. The practice of sharing motor fuels revenues with local governments is widespread, but no uniformity as to the basis of distribution exists.

Income Taxes. In fiscal 1963 state income taxes yielded about $4.4 billion—$2.9 billion from individuals and $1.5 billion from corporations. These taxes are the second most important source of state tax revenue. States used the income tax before the national government experimented with it during the Civil War. Following the panic of 1837 a few states adopted the income tax, but it did not spread significantly until the Civil War period. Early efforts at income taxation were not very successful, due largely to reliance on assessment by local assessors. In 1911 the first modern state income tax was inaugurated by Wisconsin. It was an immediate success as a revenue producer, and in 1917 four states followed Wisconsin's example. There were no further adoptions until 1929 when several states enacted income tax laws, followed by a score more states during the 1930's. Today thirty-nine states levy taxes on personal or corporate income, or both.[18]

A few states tax only income derived from special sources, but usually all income with minor exceptions is taxable. With maximums of about ten per cent, personal income tax rates are progressive, although less so than at the federal level. The picture is different with regard to corporate income rates. Over three-fourths of the states using this type of tax impose flat rates, ranging usually between one and six per cent.

A number of problems are associated with the administration of state income taxes. One concerns the geographical basis of taxable income. Some states tax only the income of residents from whatever sources it may be derived. Other states tax only income earned within their respective boundaries. Still others combine both of these practices. A major argument in behalf of taxing residents on their total income is that full effect is thereby given to graduated rates. A serious disadvantage of taxing residents only is that nonresidents

---

[18] States using neither type of income tax are Florida, Illinois, Indiana, Maine, Michigan, Nebraska, Nevada, Ohio, Texas, Washington, and Wyoming.

who would otherwise be taxed go unscathed. Such people receive the benefits of public services during their working hours, and perhaps at other times also, without bearing their share of the costs.

Certain difficulties surround the collection of income taxes. Traditionally, states have collected income taxes from recipients of income by requiring them to file a report of income by a certain date and to pay at that time all taxes due. In recent years more and more states have resorted to collection at the source. When this procedure is employed, taxes are first collected from payers of income rather than recipients. Thus, taxes on wages are collected from the employer rather than the employee by means of deductions from the employee's paychecks. This action is supplemented by annual reports required of all persons subject to the income tax in order that they may pay additional sums due the state or obtain refunds due them. Collection at the source enhances convenience of payment and minimizes delinquency and avoidance. On the other hand, this practice has the disadvantage of imposing considerable costs upon employers resulting from the maintenance of records and the computation of deductions for each pay period. When these costs are considered, income taxes are not cheap to administer.

OTHER SOURCES OF STATE REVENUE

Now that the three major state taxes have been examined, a look at other sources of state revenue is in order. Although levies on general sales and gross receipts, motor fuels, and income are commonly considered as the "major" state taxes, they account for only about one-third of total state income. Other sources include intergovernmental revenue, license fees, miscellaneous taxes, charges and earnings, and insurance trust revenues. Most important among these in terms of the amount of money received are intergovernmental revenues.

Intergovernmental Revenues. Each year the states now receive some $9 billion from other governmental units. With the exception of some $400–500 million from local governments,[19] all of this amount comes from the national government, mostly in the

---

[19] Funds paid by local governments to the states include payments for local shares in support of state administered programs, reimbursements for services performed by the states directly for local units, application on state debt issued for local benefits, and for repayment of loans made by the states to local governments.

form of grants-in-aid for public welfare, highways, education, employment security, and health and hospitals—in that order. The table on page 352 reveals the rapid growth of intergovernmental revenues as a source of state income since 1902. Since World War II federal grants to the states have more than doubled. The national government possesses much greater financial powers and resources than any state. In recent times Congress has taken the lead to expand governmental support for many important services traditionally considered to be state responsibilities.

The roots of modern federal grants-in-aid to the states extend far back into history. The Land Ordinance enacted by the Confederate Congress in 1785 provided that the national government should give each state a section of land from each township for the maintenance of public schools. Later, grants of land and money were made to promote the development of roads, railroads, and canals. These early grants entailed few conditions and little or no supervision. With the passage of the Morrill Act of 1862 the picture changed. At that time Congress provided for grants of land to the states for the support of colleges emphasizing "such branches of learning as related to agriculture and the mechanic arts." This program was supplemented by the second Morrill Act (1890), providing annual cash grants for instruction in land-grant colleges.

The Morrill Acts were predecessors of modern grants-in-aid inaugurated by the Weeks Act of 1911, authorizing federal-state cooperation in forest conservation. This act was followed three years later by the Smith-Lever Act, providing for agricultural extension work cooperatively administered by the U.S. Department of Agriculture and individual land-grant colleges. These acts first incorporated features now considered characteristic of federal grants-in-aid, particularly requirements for state matching funds and provisions for advance approval of plans by the national government.

More often than not, federal grants have been designed to stimulate state development and improvement of certain activities and services. The impact of such efforts by the national government in recent times has been particularly noticeable with regard to highways, welfare activities, public health, and development of natural resources. Although federal grants often are criticized on a variety of grounds alleging numerous deleterious effects on the states, the fact must be borne in mind that many of these programs were begun at least in part because of urgent requests by state officials for federal assistance.[20] Indeed, it may be argued that the system of grants actually strengthens the states by utilizing them in the process of coping with problems of national scope.[21]

License Fees.[22] License fees constitute an important source of state income. In fiscal 1963 the states realized about $2.8 billion from licenses of all types. Licenses were among the early sources of state revenue. By the middle of the last century license fees were collected from auctioneers, peddlers, and slave traders as well as owners of ferries, toll bridges, circuses, and theaters.

Motor vehicle license fees are collected through the annual sale of plates, or "tabs" to go on old plates, which must be attached to vehicles. The fees vary appreciably from state to state, ranging for passenger cars from a few dollars to as high as $300. Some states impose a flat rate for all automobiles, but others vary the charges according to such factors as horsepower, age or "value" of the vehicle, and weight. Charging variable fees is defended largely on the ground that it gives some consideration to ability to pay in that the owner of a large, powerful, new automobile at least evidences more affluence than the owner of a small, older vehicle.

"Franchise" or "privilege" levies imposed on corporations in the form of licenses provide a significant source of state income. In most states domestic corporations are "taxed" simply for the right to exist and conduct business under state laws. Also, a corporation licensed in one state normally must pay an "entrance fee" in order to do business in another. Licenses on the manufacture, importation, and sale of alcoholic beverages provide income for the states. Fees paid by persons wishing hunting and fishing licenses brought some $127 million into state treasuries during fiscal 1963. Many other activities and privileges are licensed by the states upon payment of small fees, including many professions and matrimony.

Miscellaneous Taxes. As every citizen knows, the states tax many things in their search for revenue. Among the more important selective sales taxes are those on *alcoholic beverages,* from which the states

---

[20] For additional discussion of federal grants to the states, see Chapter 2.

[21] V. O. Key, *The Administration of Federal Grants to States,* Public Administration Service, Chicago, 1937.

[22] Sometimes called "license taxes." However, since levies considered here are made upon those who pay them in return for a special benefit or privilege, a distinction seems warranted.

realized about $793 million in fiscal 1963. These taxes are levied on distilled spirits, wines, and malt beverages. Rates vary not only according to the classification of beverages, but also according to alcoholic content. Even more lucrative are taxes on the sale of *tobacco products,* a levy found in practically all states. More specifically, most of the imposts are on cigarettes, which are taxed at a flat rate per package, ranging up to eleven cents. High levies on alcoholic beverages and tobacco products are defended on the ground that such things are luxuries and therefore "should" be taxed at a high rate.

Once the principal source of state income, the *property tax* has been relegated to a minor role. In fiscal 1963 the states obtained around $688 million from all types of property taxes. The trend in most states has been away from the property tax and toward an emphasis on selective taxes on specific types of property such as utilities and personal property, including automobiles, farm machinery, and livestock. A major reason for the move away from state property taxes has been recognition of the desirability of leaving general property taxation in the hands of local governments.

Nearly three-fifths of the states impose *severance taxes,* from which nearly $470 million were obtained in fiscal 1963. These taxes are imposed upon the privilege of taking or "severing" from the land certain resources, especially coal, oil, and timber. The base for such a tax is generally the quantity or value of the product. Thus the output of coal may be taxed by the ton, and the flow of oil by the barrel. Or a percentage of the value of each of these measures may constitute the tax. Since severance taxes are based on volume of production, they can be adjusted to encourage or discourage production. Consequently, they are sometimes considered as a means of conserving particular resources.

All states except Nevada tax estates or inheritances, and some tax both.[23] An *estate tax* is levied on the property of a deceased person without regard to shares belonging to relatives, friends, and others. An *inheritance tax* is imposed on the share received by each heir, subject to certain exemptions. Both these taxes are characterized by a bewildering complexity, and they defy more than general description. Inheritance and estate taxes were among early levies imposed by some of the states, but they were largely failures as revenue pro-

---

[23] Taxes on estates, inheritances, and gifts are often termed "death and gift" taxes. The U.S. Bureau of the Census uses this classification.

ducers. The New York tax of 1885 appears to have been the first really successful one. During the last half-century most states have patterned their laws on the statutes of North Carolina (1901) and Wisconsin (1903), providing for progressive rates graduated according to the closeness of relationship between heirs and the decedent as well as the amounts of money and property involved.

Following the example of Oregon in 1933, many states have adopted *gift* taxes. These taxes are designed to supplement levies on estates and inheritances in order to prevent evasion of death taxes. Generally, exemptions and exclusions permit transfers of property up to a certain amount, varying with the proximity of kin, over designated periods of time without taxation. Primary responsibility for the payment of gift taxes usually rests with the giver, but his failure to pay may result in a levy against the recipient.

The states derive small quantities of revenue from a variety of minor taxes. Taxes on insurance companies and public utilities are widely used and are commonly imposed on the "gross receipts" of businesses. Levies are frequently imposed on certain types of entertainment, such as parimutuels, horse and dog races, and boxing and wrestling matches. Ten states obtain a little income from poll taxes imposed upon adults at a flat rate.[24] A few states tax document and stock transfers. In 1963 New Hampshire inaugurated a state lottery to help finance education.

Charges and Earnings. Each year the states now realize an annual income of some $4 billion from charges and earnings of various sorts. Most productive of all "business enterprises" conducted by the states are the state-owned liquor stores found in sixteen states. These enterprises have grossed more than a billion dollars annually for several years. Net income, however, has been around one-fifth of that amount. The states also obtain income from fees charged to students in institutions of higher education, tolls imposed for the use of highways and bridges, and charges collected from persons using health and hospital facilities. Earnings on trust funds, excluding insurance trust funds, also produce some income.

Insurance Trusts. Each year the states collect large sums of money for the operation of social insurance programs of one kind or

[24] In 1959 the Idaho legislature imposed a flat $10 levy on each income tax return filed—a sort of selective head tax. Outlawed in *federal* elections by the 24th Amendment to the U. S. Constitution, the poll tax is used as a suffrage qualification in five states.

another. Most important are employee retirement programs and unemployment compensation. Income for the former consisted of contributions required of employers and employees, while income for the latter usually derives from employer contributions. State-operated accident and sickness benefit systems and workmen's compensation schemes are also classified as insurance trusts. In addition, earnings realized on the investment of such funds are counted as trust fund income. Such funds must be held *in trust* by the states until disbursements are authorized to qualified persons in accord with appropriate statutes. In fiscal 1963 insurance trust revenues totaled nearly $6.0 billion.

LOCAL REVENUES

The combined revenues of local governments in fiscal 1963 totaled about $46.5 billion. Of this amount about $33.5 billion came from local revenue sources and some $13 billion from other governments, mostly the states. Of the total income *derived from their own sources,* local governments obtained nearly ninety per cent from property taxes, charges, and utility revenues. About forty-two per cent of *all* local revenues came from property taxes alone. Although recent years have witnessed a struggle by local governments, especially large cities, to tap new sources of income, the major sources remain much as they have been for years and years.

State Restrictions. The snail's pace at which new sources of local income have opened up is partially attributable to restrictions imposed by state laws. Perhaps it is more accurate to say that the states have been reluctant to enlarge the taxing powers of local governments, and they have been particularly unwilling to sanction local use of taxes important at the state level since the practical abandonment of the property tax to local use. Local governments possess, revenue-raising authority only to the extent that the states grant it to them.

In addition to limiting the sources of local revenue, states commonly restrict the amount of taxes that may be levied in a fiscal year. Such restrictions are especially noteworthy with regard to the property tax because of its great importance to local governments. Property tax limitations generally are expressed in terms of one of three factors: (1) a maximum percentage of the assessed value of the property subject to taxation, (2) a percentage increase over the previous year's levy, or (3) a maximum per capita levy. Fortunately, it is usually possible to exceed such limits by vote of the people. Local governments in some states have been further handicapped by the partial exemption of property owned by certain groups of people such as homesteaders and partially disabled veterans.

Major Sources of Local Income

The Property Tax. By far the most important single source of local revenue is the property tax. The ratio of revenue from property taxes to other sources of income varies appreciably for different classes of local governments. Special districts, including school districts, rely very heavily on them—as do most townships. Counties generally are less dependent than special districts and townships on property taxes, and municipalities enjoy a greater variety in their revenue sources than any other type of local government. Even big cities, however, continue to lean heavily on the property tax.

The property tax is no longer as "general" as it once was. Although the laws of a few states indicate that all property, except that which is specifically exempt, is *subject* to taxation, in fact no effort is made to levy taxes against many items of property. For purposes of taxation, property is divided into two major categories, *real* and *personal*. *Real property* consists basically of land and improvements, especially buildings. All other kinds of property are designated as *personal*. Personal property is subdivided into two types: tangible and intangible. *Tangible property,* as the name indicates, may be touched and seen—it has substance as well as value. Included in this category are such things as stocks of goods in stores, livestock, grain, clothes, jewelry, furniture, household appliances, automobiles, and boats. *Intangible property* consists of legal rights to things of value. Mortgages, stock certificates, patents, copyrights, and various kinds of contracts illustrate the nature of intangible property.

Theory of the Property Tax.[25] Property taxes rest on the assumption that the value of a person's property is a valid measure of the amount of tax he is able to pay. Such an assumption may have real validity in an agricultural community where property generally consists of the same items—land, buildings, livestock, and agricultural implements. However, the development of trade and industry com-

---

[25] This section is adapted from Merlin H. Hunter and Harry Allen, *op. cit.,* pp. 308–310.

plicates the picture because incomes are derived from sources other than property ownership.

Furthermore, all forms of real and tangible property do not indicate comparable taxpaying ability. Factories, farms, dwellings, cars, refrigerators, and radios are not equally indicative of taxpaying capacity. The most valid criterion of ability to pay taxes, as far as property is concerned, is productiveness. Some forms of property are not at all productive, while others may be very much so. Although ownership of nonproductive property, such as expensive jewelry or fancy automobiles, may be indicative of ability to pay, taxes other than those on property are better suited to measure this ability.

Administration of the Property Tax. The amount of property tax that a person must pay is determined by multiplying the assessed value of his property by the tax rate. Property tax rates may be expressed in *mills,* or in dollars and cents. A mill is one-tenth of a cent ($.001). Thus the tax on property assessed at $10,000 and taxed at a rate of forty mills would be $400. The same amount of tax would result from a rate of $4.00 per $100 of assessed valuation. Once the value of the property has been set, figuring the tax is a simple matter. The major problem is: How is the value of real property determined?

The *assessment,* or *valuation,* of real property is difficult. First of all, lists must be prepared of all taxable property. With adequate records and tax maps, this undertaking is not too troublesome. The second step, which is much more difficult, is determination of the value of each piece of property. Laws usually require the assessment of property to be based on a "fair," "reasonable," or "actual" value. Many techniques are used to arrive at appropriate valuations. Some are crude and others very involved.

For the bulk of real property, determination of the *assessed value* is usually accomplished in two steps. First, an effort is made to determine "actual" value for which the most common measure is "market" value—that is, the probable price at which the property might be sold on the open market. In times of inflation it is common to reduce market value in order to arrive at a more nearly "true" value. Determination of probable market value is not equally feasible for all property. What, for example, is the market value of the one or two mansions in a small town? Or the value of the Empire State Building in New York City? Other approaches to value-determination must be used in exceptional cases.

The second step in arriving at assessed value involves the use of an "assessment ratio." Once the "fair" or "market" value has been set, it is common practice to multiply that value by an arbitrarily established percentage. Perhaps the market value of a piece of property has been figured at $100,000. Local practice, resulting from administrative practices and political pressures, may have established an assessment ratio for that particular type of property at thirty per cent. Accordingly, the assessed value would be $30,000. Assessment ratios often vary according to classes of property. One ratio may be set for industrial property, another for commercial property, and a third for residential property. Other classifications may, of course, be used.

Adequate administration of the assessment function requires the services of well trained and experienced personnel. The sad fact is that such people are conspicuous by their absence in many jurisdictions. Too often the chief qualification of locally elected assessors is their ability to get votes and prove themselves acceptable to local politicians. No logical defense can be mustered in behalf of the practice of electing assessors. Theirs is in no sense a representative function. Instead their duties, when performed properly, are highly technical. The seriousness of the situation in the offices of many assessors in mitigated somewhat by the presence of appointed employees who, because of their training and experience, possess at least sufficient competence to carry their superior officer along, dead weight though he may be.

In order to reduce some of the glaring inequities and meet the requirements of fairness, assessments are subject to review by an administrative agency, commonly called a board of review and equalization. *Reviews* may be automatic to correct clerical errors and add omitted property to the rolls. They may also result from complaints by individual property owners. Since review may result in raising or lowering assessed value, most property owners do not complain because they know that if any "error" has been made it is probably on the side of underassessment. *Equalization* involves "blanket" increases or decreases within a taxing jurisdiction. The purpose of such action is to guarantee that similar properties will be treated substantially alike. Thus, a board of equalization for a county consisting of four townships may order an increase in the assessment ratio in one township so that its residents will bear their share of county taxes and not benefit from competitive underassessment. Some states provide for review and equalization of county assessment practices by a state agency. Such an agency has proved helpful in many states by guiding, assisting, and training local assessors.

Although the discussion of property tax administration thus far has been concerned specifically with real property, much of what has been said is also pertinent to taxation of personal property. The biggest difference is that the problems of administration are aggravated in relation to personal property. Except when applied to selected items, such as automobiles, boats, airplanes, farm machinery, and livestock, it is practically impossible to administer the personal property tax efficiently. Visiting every home and place of business and setting a value upon the myriad items found there is a hopeless task. Reliance on declarations of ownership and value by individual taxpayers places a premium on dishonesty and has proved unreliable. The costs of effective administration of a general tax on personal property, tangible and intangible, would be prohibitive, and public opposition would be overwhelming. Consequently, taxation of personal property has become increasingly selective and decreasingly important as a source of revenue.

The Case for the Property Tax.[26] In spite of the weaknesses of the property tax, both theoretical and administrative, it continues as the major source of local revenue. What are the reasons for its continued importance? One major reason is the force of tradition. People throughout the country are accustomed to the tax, and they have purchased and sold property in anticipation of its continued use. A second consideration relates to the problems of local administration of major alternative taxes, especially income and sales. These taxes are not as easily administered on the local as on the state level. Third, the property tax has proved that it will produce revenue in large, dependable, and predictable quantities. Fourth, the property tax is easily adjusted to meet the needs of specific areas in that it can be applied accurately to property benefitting from a particular service or group of services, such as schools, water supply, and fire protection. Finally, property appears to many persons to be a justifiable basis for taxation. They reason that the property owner should pay for services rendered to him. Furthermore, if property is fairly well

---

[26] See Harold M. Groves, *Financing Government,* Holt and Co., New York, 1950, pp. 60–61.

assessed, there is normally at least some crude relationship between the value of property owned by an individual and his ability to pay.

Intergovernmental Revenues. In fiscal 1963 over one-fourth of all local governmental revenue came from other governments, mostly in the form of state aid. State assistance to local governments takes two major forms: *grants* and *shared taxes*. Like federal grants-in-aid to the states, state grants to local governments are usually in the form of appropriations, ordinarily from the general fund, to assist local financing of designated functions.[27] Grants are allocated to local governments according to some formula. Thus so many dollars may be provided to local school districts on the basis of the number of children in average daily attendance. Or funds may be allocated to enable poorer districts to maintain school facilities that meet state standards—often called the "equalization allocation." Through grants the states have utilized their superior taxing authority to relieve the burden upon local revenue sources. Local functions benefitting most from state grants are education, highways, and public welfare.

Shared taxes are collected by the state and apportioned among local governments according to fixed percentages of the yield. The income received by local jurisdictions from a shared tax depends on the yield from that tax, not on local needs. Conditions governing the distribution of shared taxes often require that the receipts of each local unit be in direct ratio to the amount of the tax collected there. Thus the revenue from liquor taxes returned to a city depends on the income from the tax collected within that city. Of course, the amounts probably are not the same since the state retains a portion of the tax—at least a sufficient amount to cover costs of administration. Occasionally, taxes are shared on a per capita basis, with local receipts determined by population. Shared taxes most often include those levied on motor fuels, liquor, incomes, and sales.

Utility Revenues. In recent years local governments have realized about ten per cent of their income from *utility revenues*. Government owned and operated "business enterprises" have been numer-

---

[27] States are making increasing use of "general" grants by which funds are made available to local governments without restrictions as to the purposes for which they may be spent.

ous at the local level during much of American history. Local water, electric, gas, and transit utilities and liquor stores gross sizable sums, especially for municipalities. However, *net* income from such sources is generally small because the costs of purchasing, producing, or otherwise providing the facilities largely offset total revenues. Indeed, expenditures related to the operation of utilities sometime exceed revenues, and it becomes necessary to support them partially from the general fund. In a few instances, however, small localities are able to subsidize other functions with income from an important enterprise such as a railroad.

Charges and Special Assessments. Local governments often impose *charges* for the performance of certain services. Prominent among activities financed partially or entirely by charges are sewage disposal, refuse collection, and parking facilities. *Fees* collected for the use of special facilities such as swimming pools, tennis courts, and golf courses also produce small amounts of income. *Fines* usually are not an important source of revenue, but occasionally a small community obtains significant amounts from the operation of a "speed trap."

A *special assessment* is a levy against property made presumably in rough proportion to benefits accruing as the result of a specific service. Special assessments are used most frequently to pay all or part of the costs of paving streets, building sidewalks, installing water and sewer lines, establishing parks and playgrounds, and street lighting. Improvements financed in this way presumably make property more desirable to own and often more valuable as well.

A big problem in the use of special assessments is the determination of the amount of benefit received by each person or parcel of property. The man who has the street in front of his house paved certainly benefits, but he is not the only one who does. His neighbors next door and persons living blocks away who pass his house each day or just on their way to church on Sunday also benefit. So do the delivery truck drivers who frequent his neighborhood. Obviously, assessments cannot be made against all these people. Recognizing that a "general" benefit also stems from paved streets, sidewalks, and similar improvements, cities often pay a portion of their costs from the general fund and assess the remainder against property situated in an arbitrarily determined "benefit district."

Sales Taxes. The first local sales taxes in the United States were enacted by New York City in 1934 and by New Orleans in 1936. Since that time some 1300 municipalities and 150-odd counties have adopted retail or general sales taxes, the bulk of them in California and Illinois. The only major city to try the retail sales tax and voluntarily abandon it is Philadelphia. Many local communities impose selective sales taxes on items such as gasoline, tobacco, and alcohol.

Aside from the fact that in many states local sales taxes are not permitted by law, other considerations have limited their adoption. Probably the most serious objection to the local sales tax is ease of avoidance and consequent shifting of sales to nontax areas. This problem is especially serious for small communities. If a small city adopts a sales tax, many residents will do their shopping, especially for major purchases, in nearby areas without such a tax. Municipal sales taxes also encourage the growth of suburban shopping centers. In an effort to counteract the economic consequences of large-scale buying outside their jurisdictions, some municipalities have resorted to a *use tax*. This type of tax is a levy on the use within the locality of taxable articles purchased outside. However, municipal use taxes are very difficult to administer and are practical only in relation to major purchases such as automobiles.

A more satisfactory approach to the problems of city sales taxes has been adopted in California. In 1956 California counties received authority from the state legislature to levy one per cent sales taxes, provided they arrange for collection by the state agency that collects the state sales tax. Then each city within a county adopting such an arrangement may levy a sales tax up to one per cent and have it credited against the county tax. Thus, if a city sales tax is one per cent all the revenue from the tax comes to the city, but if it is one-half per cent the city receives only one-half of the revenue collected within its boundaries. Sales in unincorporated areas and cities not using the sales tax are still taxed at one per cent, but all the proceeds go to the county. If a county chooses not to levy a sales tax, each city may impose and administer its own.

Income Taxes. Local governments have used income taxes very sparingly in the United States. Although levied by some 650 jurisdictions in five states,[28] local income taxes produced only $313 million in fiscal 1963.

---

[28] Kentucky, Michigan, Missouri, Ohio, and Pennsylvania.

By far the most widespread use of the local income tax is found in Pennsylvania, where Philadelphia pioneered in its use in 1940.[29] Since then many school districts, some 140 cities, and a few townships in that state have adopted income taxes. Outside Pennsylvania its use has been limited to cities, most of which are located in the state of Ohio.[30]

Local income taxes differ from federal and state levies in two major respects: (1) they are imposed at uniform, low rates rather than on a graduated scale,[31] and (2) they generally do not allow exemptions. The most widely used rate is one per cent, although levies of one-half of one per cent are common. These two features, defended chiefly on the ground of administrative simplicity, demonstrate that local income taxes largely disregard ability to pay, since no distinction is made among income levels and family responsibilities. Inequity is further aggravated by the fact that these taxes are imposed only on salaries and wages and do not include other types of income.

In addition to providing additional revenue, local income taxes generally possess two significant features that make them especially attractive: (1) they are relatively easy and economical to administer, and (2) they may exact contributions from nonresidents.[32] As a flat levy on all salaries and wages subject to collection at the source, income taxes are not easily evaded and at the same time are inexpensive to collect. Many people work in cities and live elsewhere. Such persons benefit from city services and should help to support them. A municipal income tax serves this purpose admirably. From both of these standpoints a local income tax appears more desirable than a sales tax.[33]

Other Sources of Income. Local governments, especially cities, obtain income from a variety of sources not yet mentioned. Parking meters produce significant quantities of revenue for cities in spite of the fact that they are justified chiefly on the ground that they regulate the use of public streets. Cities commonly license places of

---

[29] New York City enacted an income tax in 1934, but no collections ever were made.

[30] See Robert A. Sigafoos, *The Municipal Income Tax: Its History and Problems,* Public Administration Service, Chicago, 1955.

[31] The District of Columbia income tax has a mildly progressive rate.

[32] Pennsylvania school districts cannot tax the income of nonresidents.

[33] Of course, nonresidents making purchases in a sales-tax city contribute to the local treasury, but they can and probably will limit the value of such purchases.

amusement such as theaters, cabarets, bowling alleys, pool rooms, dance halls, and restaurants. Fees charged for these licenses may produce sizable amounts of revenue, especially in large cities. A handful of cities in a few states, particularly Washington, California, and Alabama, impose taxes on the price of admission to various types of entertainment, of which the most important are moving pictures and theaters. Cities frequently tax mechanical amusement devices such as pinball machines, juke boxes, and skill-game devices.

Rather high license fees for places of amusement and heavy taxes on admissions and on amusement devices are easily justifiable from the standpoint of equity. Important also is the fact that directly or indirectly they reach nonresidents and transients who benefit from city services. Small communities must, of course, exercise care lest they drive places of amusement outside their boundaries and consequently beyond their regulation in most instances.

Many cities license a variety of businesses and commercial enterprises, including apartment houses, hotels, barber shops, beauty parlors, food stores, laundries, department stores, pawnshops, peddlers, taxicabs, and vending machines. Fees charged for licensing these and similar enterprises produce some revenue but often little more than the costs of administering the licenses. A few cities collect vehicle inspection fees charged for the examination of safety devices on motor vehicles. Local licenses for trailer camps have become increasingly common in recent years. Small amounts of income are realized from rents charged for the use of locally owned property and from interest on investments.

DEBT

When governments are unable or unwilling to finance their activities from current revenues, they may obtain money by borrowing. Debts usually are incurred for three major purposes: (1) to obtain funds in anticipation of revenue, (2) for expenditures arising from emergencies and exceptional circumstances, and (3) construction of public improvements. Yields from taxes often do not come into the treasury in sufficient quantities early in a fiscal year to meet current expenses. As a result, governments must borrow in anticipation of income that will be received a short time later. This type of indebtedness is commonly called "short-term." Occasionally fires, floods, tornadoes, earthquakes, and other disasters require unanticipated expenditures that can be met only by borrowing. Also included in the second category are bonds issued in recent years by the states to finance veterans' bonuses.

By far the most significant purpose for which state and local governments borrow money is financing public improvements. Highways, school buildings, office buildings, city halls, courthouses, hospitals, sewage disposal systems, and airports illustrate the variety of projects often financed by issuing bonds. Best financial practice dictates that the maturity dates on bonds issued for such improvements should be arranged to provide for repayment within the useful life of an improvement. If such a requirement is not observed, taxpayers will not only pay huge amounts in interest, they will also have to begin paying for a new improvement before old obligations are met. Thus if the useful life of a school building is estimated at forty years, the life of the bonds issued for its construction should be somewhat less. Otherwise, it may be necessary to build a new school or thoroughly remodel the old one before the original investment is paid off. Debts for the construction of public improvements are designated "long-term."

Historical Background. The first large state loan was contracted by New York in the 1820's for the construction of the Erie Canal. Several states followed New York's example and financed the construction of waterways; they also established banks and assisted in the financing of railroads. By the time of the financial crisis of 1839 some states were in difficulty, and they occasionally resorted to questionable practices in order to meet their obligations. In spite of their efforts, nine states defaulted. These and similar unfortunate occurrences led to constitutional amendments limiting state borrowing. No such restrictions existed prior to 1840. Although some defaults occurred later, especially in the South following the Civil War, the financial condition of the states improved during the latter part of the nineteenth century.

Problems stemming from borrowing were experienced by the states before local governments were confronted with them. By the middle of the nineteenth century, however, several cities failed to meet their debt payments, including Detroit, Philadelphia, and Chicago. Between 1860 and 1880 municipal indebtedness increased threefold, partly because of widespread corruption and inefficiency. Following the financial crisis of 1873–1874, restrictions were imposed widely on local borrowing.

State and local debt began to grow again in the last years of the nineteenth and early years of the twentieth centuries. In 1902 gross debt for the states stood at $230 million and for local governments at nearly $1.9 billion. Within the next twenty years these sums were multiplied nearly five times and doubled again by 1932. The chief cause of debt expansion at the state level was the construction of more and better highways, while improved public services of practically all types were demanded from local governments. The 1940's witnessed a reduction in state and local debt because construction was severely limited during the war. Pent-up demands for improvements caused state debt to soar from around $3.7 billion in 1948 to $7.8 billion in 1953, to $23.2 billion in 1963. During the same period local debt went from $15 billion to $26 billion to $64.2 billion.

Types of Bonds. Long-term debt is financed by three types of bonds: (1) general obligation, (2) limited obligation, and (3) revenue. General obligation bonds, often called full faith and credit bonds, are guaranteed by the taxing capacity of the issuing government. In other words, a governmental unit pledges to use any and all of its revenue sources to pay off general obligation bonds as they come due.[34] Because of their safety as investments, such bonds normally have relatively low interest rates, assuming that the issuing authority has a satisfactory credit rating. Limited obligation bonds are guaranteed by income from specific taxes or more often by special assessments. Thus bonds issued to pave a street may be backed only by income from special assessments levied against benefited property.

Revenue bonds are issued to finance revenue-producing enterprises, and payment is guaranteed only from such income. This type of bond apparently was first used in the United States by Spokane, Washington, in 1897 to finance a water supply system. Since that time revenue bonds have been used widely by both state and local governments to finance such projects as toll roads and bridges, college and university dormitories, water works, sewer systems, public transportation facilities, housing projects, stadiums, and swimming pools. Since such obligations have no claim upon the general revenues of the issuing government, they are usually considered as less safe investments than general obligation bonds and consequently carry a higher interest rate. If a project financed in this manner fails

---

[34] Rather than pay off bonds when they come due, a government may choose to "re-fund" them, that is, issue more bonds to replace them.

to produce anticipated income, bondholders may suffer a loss. Revenue bonds are especially attractive to governmental units because their use is not restricted by general debt limitations.

Bonds are classified also according to arrangements made for their repayment. If all the bonds in an issue mature on the same date, provisions must be made to have sufficient money available at that time. Common practice is to establish a *sinking fund* into which money is paid at stipulated periods, usually yearly, so that with interest a sufficient amount will be on hand to pay off the bonds when they come due. Bonds amortized in this manner are called sinking-fund or *term* bonds. Interest on them is paid from current revenues.

Frequent mismanagement of sinking funds has caused *serial bonds* to grow in favor to the point where they are more widely used than term bonds. Two chief characteristics distinguish serial from term bonds: (1) staggered maturity dates and (2) payment from current revenues. Thus a twenty-year issue may be set up so that one twentieth of the debt is retired each year from current income. If arrangements are made to repay an equal fraction of the bonded indebtedness each year plus interest, the bonds are called *straight* serials. Since this practice results in larger total payments during the early years of repayment because of large interest charges, the governmental unit may choose to even out the payments. If this practice is followed, payments on the principal are smaller during the early years of the loan and larger in later years when interest payments have been reduced. Bonds paid off in this manner are known as *annuity* serials.

Debt Limitations.[35] Most states and local governments are limited in regard to the amount of debt they may incur. Such restrictions vary appreciably from state to state, with flat-sum limits ranging from $50,000 to $2 million. In a few states limits are expressed in terms of a percentage of assessed valuation. A handful of states prohibit all long-term borrowing. These limits are not absolute, however, for certain exceptions commonly are made to constitutional debt restrictions. Specific authority to exceed debt limits is granted most frequently for two purposes: (1) to protect the state against invasion or domestic violence and (2) to refund existing indebtedness. Also, three procedures are widely used to avoid debt limits:

---

[35] A most helpful source of information on this topic is *Constitutional Debt Control in the States,* The Tax Foundation, 1954.

(1) popular referenda, (2) revenue bonds, and (3) special districts and authorities.

Exceptions to constitutional debt restrictions may be authorized by constitutional amendment, a step that requires a popular vote in all states except Delaware. Thus if a general limit of $50,000 is placed on state debt, the people may vote to amend the constitution to permit bond issues for a special purpose such as veterans' bonuses or highways. A separate maximum amount may be stipulated for such issues, constituting a special debt limit. Furthermore, a state constitution may authorize the incurrence of debts in excess of a general limit simply by a favorable popular vote on each indebtedness. The major difference between these two arrangements is that the latter generally involves a simpler procedure.

In states with strict debt limits a large portion of long-term debt is nonguaranteed, that is, it is payable only from specific sources such as income from revenue-producing activities. In a few states all long-term debt is of this variety. Courts generally have approved borrowing outside debt restrictions by means of revenue bonds on the ground that no state liability is created. Similarly, bonds payable solely from the proceeds of a specific tax, such as the gasoline tax when used for highway construction, are usually not subject to constitutional debt limitations.

Various types of independent authorities have proved highly useful in recent years as a means of avoiding debt limits, particularly for the construction of highways and public buildings and the provision of educational facilities. Debts incurred by such agencies, which are often set up as government corporations, are not considered debts against the state. State universities, for example, often issue bonds for capital improvements unaffected by constitutional restrictions. Sometimes bonds issued by such "independent" agencies are also exempt from limits because they are of the revenue type.

Local governments must operate within debt limits imposed not only by state constitutions but also by statutes and their own charters. Local debt restrictions are imposed to accomplish three major purposes: (1) to limit the amount of borrowing, (2) to prohibit borrowing for certain purposes, and (3) to impose conditions on bonding practices. Most often the amount of indebtedness allowed a unit of local government is expressed in terms of a percentage of the assessed value of property located therein. The percentage may vary according to the manner in which the debt is authorized. A higher percentage often is permitted when a bond issue is sanctioned by popular vote than when it is authorized by legislative action. Indeed, no maximum may be imposed on borrowing approved by popular referendum. Debt limits quite regularly vary according to classifications of local governments, distinguishing, for example, among first-class cities, second-class cities, counties, unincorporated towns, and types of special districts. Although limiting the bonded indebtedness of local governments on the basis of the assessed value of property is not considered satisfactory by most students of public finance and local government, it remains standard practice.

In earlier years local governments borrowed money and then loaned it to railroads, public utilities, and other businesses, some of which proved to be poor investments. As a result of such unfortunate experiences, especially during the last century, states now forbid local loans to private enterprises or to individuals. Requirements pertaining to bonding practices sometimes impose a maximum on the life of bonds as well as on interest rates. Some states require local governments to levy taxes to cover all expenses connected with the use of sinking funds; others stipulate that only serial bonds may be used.

Recognizing the inadequacy of traditional methods of state control over local indebtedness, a few states, particularly Indiana and North Carolina, have moved to substitute state administrative supervision for the older practices. Indiana provides for review of proposed local indebtedness in excess of $5,000 by the State Board of Tax Commissioners upon request by ten or more taxpayers. The decision of the Commission, which has complete discretionary authority, is final. A bond issue may be decreased, otherwise modified, or disallowed. In North Carolina no local bonds may be issued without approval by the Local Government Commission. A decision by the Commission to disallow a bond issue may be overridden, however, by a vote of the people in the local unit involved.

The question of whether *any* restrictions should be imposed on the debt-incurring capacity of state and local governments is academic since past experience, tradition, and the temper of the people support the existence of some limitations. In general, debt limits imposed on state legislatures have worked reasonably well so long as revenue bonds have been exempted and the people have not been too reluctant to vote favorably on special issues. Where local governments are concerned, there seems to be little doubt that supervision by a state agency is superior to the traditional type of limitation. In this way it is possible to promote flexibility and consideration of all factors pertinent to each bond issue. At the same time it must be realized that local officials may oppose any such arrangement on the ground that it places local government in a position of even greater subservience to state supervision.

SELECTED REFERENCES

Books:

Blakey, Roy G., and Gladys C., *Sales Taxes and Other Excises,* Public Administration Service, Chicago, 1945.

Council of State Governments, *State Finances 1942 and 1954,* Chicago, 1956.

Due, John F., *Sales Taxation,* University of Illinois Press, Urbana, 1957.

———, *State Sales Tax Administration,* Public Administration Service, Chicago, 1963.

Groves, Harold M., *Financing Government,* Holt and Co., New York, 1950.

Haig, Robert M., and Shoup, Carl, *The Sales Tax in the American States,* Columbia University Press, New York, 1934.

Hansen, Alvin H., and Perloff, Harvey S., *State and Local Finance in the National Economy,* Norton and Co., New York, 1944.

Hillhouse, A. M., and Magelssen, Muriel, *Where Cities Get Their Money,* Municipal Finance Officers Association, Chicago, 1945.

Hunter, Merlin H., and Allen, Harry K., *Principles of Public Finance,* Harper and Bros., New York, 1940.

Maddox, Russell W., Jr., *Issues in State and Local Government,* D. Van Nostrand Co., Inc., Princeton, N.J., 1965.

Oregon Legislative Interim Tax Study Committee, *Oregon's Taxes,* Portland, 1959.

———, *The Tax Structures of Washington, Oregon, and California,* Portland, 1958.

Penniman, Clara, and Heller, Walter, *State Income Tax Administration,* Public Administration Service, Chicago, 1960.

Sigafoos, Robert A., *The Municipal Income Tax: Its History and Problems,* Public Administration Service, Chicago, 1955.

Tax Foundation, *Constitutional Debt Control in the States,* New York, 1954.

———, *The Tax Burden in Relation to National Income and Product,* New York, 1957.

Utah Foundation, *Property Taxes in the Western States,* Salt Lake City, 1958.

Vieg, John A., et al., *California Local Finance,* Stanford University Press, Palo Alto, 1960.

Articles:

Bird, Frederick L., "How High the Curbs?" *National Civic Review,* February 1963.

Boyle, Gerald J., "Changes in Local Government Revenues," *The Conference Board Business Record,* April 1957.

Chatters, Carl H., "Municipal Financial Needs v. Credit Restraints," *Municipal Finance,* August 1957.

——, "New Money for Cities," *National Civic Review,* June 1961.

Conlon, Charles F., "Some Tax and Revenue Problems of the States," *State Government,* Spring 1960.

Donovan, Clement H., "Special Assessments—Their Place in Municipal Finance," *Municipal Finance,* May 1957.

Freeman, Roger A., "What Ails the Property Tax?" *National Municipal Review,* November 1955.

Funk, Robert L., "A Look at Municipal Revenues," *Public Management,* November 1954.

Heller, Walter W., "Financing State-Local Government in an Age of Expansion," *State Government,* July 1957.

Howards, Irving, "Property Tax Rate Limits in Illinois and their Effect upon Local Government," *National Tax Journal,* September 1963.

Kelly, Daniel M., "Financing State and Municipal Debt," *Municipal Finance,* August 1957.

Mace, Ruth L., "How Cost-Revenue Research Aids Administrators," *Public Management,* October 1964.

Martin, James W., and Herzel, William G., "The Influence of Taxation Upon Industrial Development," *State Government,* July 1957.

Newcomer, Mabel, "The Decline of the General Property Tax," *National Tax Journal,* March 1953.

Scheffer, Walter F., "Problems in Municipal Finance," *Western Political Quarterly,* September 1962.

Senn, John E., "How Taxes Compare in Sixteen Competitive Industry-Seeking States," *Industrial Development,* February 1957.

Simpson, Herbert D., "New Frontiers in City Finance," *National Municipal Review,* May 1947.

"Some Economic Considerations in Municipal Finance,"—Symposium, *Municipal Finance,* May 1964.

Taylor, Milton C., "Local Income Taxes after Twenty-one Years," *National Tax Journal,* June 1962.

Zubrow, Reuben A., "Recent Trends and Developments in Municipal Finance," *Public Management,* November 1963.

CHAPTER 16

Handling Public Money: Fiscal Management

It is important not only to understand how governments obtain money and the purposes for which they spend it, but also to be familiar with the techniques and procedures for handling public money. According to Leonard D. White, "Fiscal management includes those operations designed to make funds available to officials and to ensure their lawful and efficient use."[1] An exhaustive examination of the various aspects of fiscal management is beyond the scope of a single chapter. Emphasis is placed on budgeting, accounting, auditing, and procurement or supply.

This chapter does not undertake a detailed description of financial practices in the states and localities. Such a task would be practically impossible, as the variations are too great. Instead, effort is made to describe the elements in a well developed system of fiscal management. Few governments adhere to any pattern exactly, but a general description provides a guide for understanding existing practices and serves as a sort of criterion by which to judge them. Every governmental unit that receives money engages in financial management, with practices ranging from the extremely crude to the very complicated.

ORGANIZATION FOR FISCAL MANAGEMENT

Excluding the legislature which grants the funds, organization for fiscal management includes (1) agencies in the executive branch that must have money in order to carry out their programs, (2) agencies organized primarily to implement the acquisition of funds and oversee their expenditure, and (3) agencies created to check on the fidelity and legality of disbursements after they have been made. Included in the first category are the great majority of agencies found

---

[1] Leonard D. White, *Introduction to the Study of Public Administration*, The Macmillan Co., New York, 1955, p. 224.

in all multipurpose governments. State departments of all kinds, such as health, education, and highways, are vitally concerned with the management of funds allocated to them. The same is true of agencies at the local level concerned, for example, with the provision of police and fire protection, streets, and schools. The importance of arrangements found in local agencies often is overlooked in an examination of fiscal management. In view of the lack of close central supervision of fiscal procedures characteristic of many governmental units, the practices of spending agencies are especially significant. The trend, however, for some time has been toward increased central control, motivated in part by financial scandals prevalent among governments during the nineteenth century.

Fiscal Officers: *The Chief Executive.* Ideally, the chief executive—governor, mayor, or manager—is in a very real sense the chief fiscal officer. Although his authority in these matters is largely dependent upon constitutional, statutory, or charter provisions and consequently varies from place to place, the chief executive usually plays a major role in the fiscal process. He must assist in the allocation of funds by informing the legislative body and the people of the amount of money required to finance services and meet anticipated needs. Once the legislature has acted, it becomes the chief executive's responsibility to oversee spending insofar as he can, and he must see that appropriate accounts are maintained to provide a record of the use of public money. Of all the fiscal responsibilities borne by the chief executive, those related to securing sufficient revenue are probably most important. They are discussed later in connection with the budget process.

The Treasurer. Although not as important as he once was, a typical treasurer still has a number of important, although somewhat routine, fiscal responsibilities.[2] The great bulk of public funds are either received by the treasurer or deposited with him by receiving agencies. For example, the receipts from a state income tax may be collected by a tax commission and then deposited with the treasurer. The treasurer is at least formally responsible for the custody and investment of public money. He may share these duties, particularly that of investment, with other public officials. In a sense, the custodianship of funds has been shifted to the banks in which they are

---

[2] See Chapter 4 for further discussion of the functions of the treasurer.

deposited. Treasurers also have the task of disbursing money upon proper authorization. In order to perform these and related duties satisfactorily, treasurers must maintain a system of accounts which may be quite complicated. They also prepare reports for the benefit of administrators, budget agencies, and the public.

The Budget Officer. In most states and many municipalities there is an official, commonly known as a budget officer, who aids the chief executive in preparing and executing the budget.[3] Usually responsible directly to the chief executive or an appointed director of finance, a budget officer is in a position to affect profoundly the operations of agencies that come within his purview. Great care must be taken, however, to check the tendency of this staff officer to substitute his judgment for that of line officers regarding the administration of various programs. If he is able to escape the "economizing orientation" that frequently appears to dominate those in his occupation, a budget officer may exert a constructive influence. Once he gets the reputation of being a "nickel-nurser" whose chief aim is to cut expenditures, a budget officer's usefulness is seriously jeopardized.

The Comptroller. As the chief accounting officer, the comptroller's job is to see that records are kept that accurately reflect the current financial status of a governmental unit and its major subdivisions. He not only maintains central accounts but also supervises the accounting systems of operating agencies. In this way uniform accounting procedures may be assured and a basis provided for comparing the financial status and practices of different agencies. Another duty frequently vested in a comptroller is the *preaudit,* by means of which proposed expenditures are compared with available money and authorized purposes. Proposals to spend are checked to determine whether they are legal and proper and whether sufficient money will be available to pay the bills. Individual agencies often perform the preaudit function within their own organizations in accord with procedures outlined by the comptroller.

The Auditor. When properly used, the term "auditor" designates a public official responsible for determining the *fidelity* and *legality* of the manner in which money has been used. This task is accomplished by examining the financial transactions completed dur-

---

[3] At the local level, particularly in small governmental units, budget committees composed of members of the legislative body and laymen assist the chief executive in preparing the budget.

ing a fiscal period, usually a "fiscal year."[4] Occasionally, an official functions in an *ex officio* capacity as auditor. Thus in Oregon the Secretary of State is designated as state auditor by the constitution. Local governments, especially smaller ones, frequently hire private persons to audit their books. Auditors often are elected by popular vote, sometimes chosen by legislative action, and rarely appointed by the chief executive. Legislative selection is generally preferred by students of fiscal management because an auditor should and normally does report to a legislative body, either state or local.

It is important to distinguish between the proper functions of a comptroller and an auditor. Sometimes an auditor is made responsible for checking expenditures prior to disbursement, a task described above as belonging to a comptroller. An explanation of the combination of preaudit and postaudit functions in the hands of an auditor arises from the fact that auditors with authority to check accounts at the end of fiscal periods were commonplace in government before the importance of the comptroller function was recognized. Once the value of the preaudit was accepted, legislatures often assigned the new duty to the auditor rather than create a new officer. Such a combination of duties is considered to be poor fiscal practice because the preaudit, an executive responsibility, is instrumental in providing records on which the postaudit, a legislative responsibility, is based. Self-audit is generally condemned.

The Purchasing Agent. During the last fifty years, state and local governments have made increasing use of centralized purchasing and property control. The older practice is still prevalent, however, whereby each governmental agency purchases all its own equipment and supplies. Centralized purchasing is designed to make a staff officer responsible for the purchase, storage, and distribution of items required by different departments, bureaus, divisions, boards, and commissions. Purchasing is never completely centralized. Specialized items, such as drugs for institutions and experimental equipment used in laboratories, are generally acquired by the agencies that use them. Also, emergency purchases must be made occasionally by line agencies when the central warehouse is unable to provide an item that is needed immediately and unexpectedly.

The Assessor. Administration of the property tax, the principal

---

[4] The fiscal year of most governments coincides with that of the federal government and runs from July 1 to June 30; sometimes it is the same as the calendar year; rarely, some other period is used.

source of tax revenue for local governments, is usually the responsibility of an assessor. Consequently, he is a major fiscal officer at the local level. He has the task of locating, listing, and appraising or evaluating property, both real and personal. The adequate performance of these duties is important both to the taxpayer and to the tax collector. Popularly elected assessors often do not possess the knowledge and training necessary to do an adequate job, causing inequity and injustice in the distribution of the costs of government among taxpayers. Inadequacy on the part of the assessor can often be offset by competent personnel hired to work in his office.

Trends in Fiscal Organization. The "most striking trend in recent years" in organization for fiscal management at both state and local levels has been toward an "integrated" system of finance under the chief executive.[5] Such an arrangement brings together, or integrates, budgetmaking, revenue collection, the preaudit, accounting, central purchasing, and property management. Accordingly, an integrated system of fiscal management requires that the budget officer, treasurer or tax collector, comptroller, and purchasing officer be under the control of the chief executive. At the local level, the assessor should be part of the integrated structure. It is important to note that the auditor is *not* included. He should be independent of the executive and responsible to the legislature.

Procedures for handling financial affairs have been greatly improved in recent years at all levels of government. Fiscal leadership and supervision have been vested increasingly in the chief executive and officers responsible to him, and increased coordination is evident almost everywhere. Opportunities for mishandling public money have been appreciably decreased. Legislative procedures involved in reviewing requests for appropriations and in overseeing the manner in which they are spent have been strengthened, although improvements here have not been as noticeable as in the executive branch. These developments in fiscal management guarantee more efficient use of each tax dollar.

THE BUDGET PROCESS

One of the most important elements of fiscal management is an effective budget process. A budget is "A comprehensive plan, ex-

---

[5] Leonard D. White, *op. cit.,* p. 232. Such an arrangement is provided in the Model State Constitution and the Model City Charter of the National Municipal League.

pressed in financial terms, by which an operating program is effective for a given period of time. It includes estimates of: (a) the services, activities, and projects comprising the program; (b) the resultant expenditure requirements; and (c) the resources usable for their support."[6] In short, a budget is a financial plan for the operation of a governmental unit during a fiscal period, normally one or two years. The term is also used in the sense of a "capital budget," involving a long-term program of capital improvements and operational programs. Discussion in this chapter is limited to a consideration of budgets prepared for specific fiscal periods.

Modern budgeting first developed in this country at the municipal level. All factors contributing to this occurrence are not entirely clear, but three were especially significant. The efforts of "Muckrakers" like Lincoln Steffens and Ray S. Baker at the beginning of the twentieth century aroused public indignation over widespread municipal corruption. Then in 1899 the National Municipal League, an organization active in local government reform, included in its model municipal charter provisions for a budget system. The New York Bureau of Municipal Research, a private organization that proved to be a powerful force in behalf of municipal reform, published in 1907 a study entitled "Making a Municipal Budget." This study contributed to improvements in fiscal management in New York City and later in other cities also.[7] Although it is difficult to set an exact date, "it is appropriate to say that by the mid-1920's most major American cities had undergone a more or less thorough reform in municipal finance practices and had established some sort of a budget system."[8]

Not long after improvements in budgetary practices appeared among municipalities, pressure began to build up for reform at the state level. Public interest was further promoted by the work of the Taft Commission on Economy and Efficiency at the federal level. The first state law providing for an executive budget was enacted in Ohio in 1910, and during the following six years eight states enacted similar legislation. According to Burkhead, the first state to adopt "a thorough system of executive budget-making" was Mary-

---

[6] The International City Managers' Association, *Municipal Finance Administration*, Chicago, 1955, p. 61. This definition was prepared by the Committee on Performance Budgeting and Unit Cost Accounting of the Municipal Finance Officers Association.

[7] For additional details pertaining to early developments in governmental budgeting, see A. E. Buck, *Public Budgeting*, Harper & Brothers, New York, 1929.

[8] Jesse Burkhead, *Government Budgeting*, John Wiley & Sons, New York, 1956, p. 14.

land in 1916; by 1920, budget systems had been established by forty-four states.[9] "As in the case of the cities, the 'friends of budgeting' were of two divergent groups: the reformers, who wanted to make governmental institutions more responsible and responsive, and organized taxpayer groups, who were promoting retrenchment in expenditures and reduction in taxation. Together, these groups were responsible for the rapid spread of the budget system."[10]

Before examining the steps involved in budgeting, it is important to understand the meaning of the term "budget cycle." A budget cycle involves three main steps that constitute a continuous process: budget making, budget adoption, and budget execution. The first step is an executive reponsibility; it ends when the budget is ready for submission to the legislature. The second is the task of the legislature and is complete when appropriation bills are enacted. Responsibility for the third phase, budget execution, is divided between the executive who makes allotments and conducts a preaudit and the auditor who examines the records.

Budget Making and Adoption: *Agency Responsibilities.* The process of building a budget begins when operating agencies prepare their expenditure estimates for the coming fiscal period. General instructions may have been prepared by the central budget office reflecting policies of the chief executive and communicated to the agencies. If these instructions have imposed a ceiling on increases for the next fiscal period, agencies must "hold the line" accordingly. Ceilings may be imposed, for example, in terms of a maximum percentage increase in requests over appropriations available for the preceding fiscal period. If no such limitations exist, each agency is free to make any requests it deems necessary or advisable in light of anticipated or proposed modifications of its program.

Requests for increases usually result from one or both of two factors: (1) increased costs necessary to maintain an established level of service and (2) expanded programs. In times of inflation governmental costs, like those in private industry, continue to rise because of increasing prices of equipment and supplies as well as advances in wage and salary levels. If allowances are not made for such increases, services must be reduced. As already noted, there have been continuous pressures for many years promoting growth in governmental

---

[9] *Ibid.,* p. 23.
[10] *Ibid.,* p. 24.

services. These pressures have come both from inside and from outside government. Highway builders feel we need more and better highways; welfare workers are convinced of the importance of expanded programs; educators are sure they can do a better job with improved facilities and more qualified teachers; and so it goes. Although sometimes accused of "empire building," people dedicated to a function are naturally convinced of its importance. Without such dedication, they will not perform at their maximum level of effectiveness. Outside pressures for expansion come from special groups and from the public in general. Regrettably, some of the same people urge budgetary cuts—and of course, such reductions must always be made in *other* services.

Although responsibility for the preparation of an agency budget rests with the top administrator, as many persons as possible should be given a part in the undertaking. Budget time presents an excellent opportunity for employees to express their ideas concerning possible improvements in the program with which they are working. Large agencies commonly have budget officers to whom the task of budget preparation is delegated, subject to review by the agency head. These officers collect data from operating units, provide assistance in estimating cost increases, and prepare justifications for proposed program expansion. All work must be done in anticipation of the time when representatives from the agency will probably be called before a legislative committee to justify their requests.

The Central Budget Office. Once an agency has completed its budget estimates, they are usually sent to the chief executive or to a central budget office operating as part of his staff. In most states and large municipalities provision has been made for some type of central budget office, which has two major responsibilities, *program review* and *management improvement*. The former consists of an examination of the operations of each agency from a central viewpoint in order to place them in proper perspective in relation to other programs. The central budget office has a major responsibility at this point that is not shared with the operating agencies—namely, the preparation of an estimate of revenues that will be available to meet expenditure requests. A second major task of the budget office relates to the most effective allocation of estimated resources in order to achieve desirable objectives. Involved here is a search for more effective methods of operation.

If it is to be successful, a central budget office must perform its responsibilities in cooperation with line agencies. A major obstacle to effective budgeting develops when line officers feel that the budget officer is attempting to usurp their prerogatives. People working in the field of public health, for example, resent attempts by a budget office to instruct them as to the best way to administer a public health program. The same is true of educators, firefighters, and all other specialists. Consequently, a wise budget officer seeks to assist specialists in "discovering" more efficient methods in the performance of their responsibilities. In the final analysis, a budget office must inform each agency under its jurisdiction as to the proportion of total anticipated income that will be allotted to it.

Within a unit of government not all activities are subject to central budget review. Usually, the expenditures of the legislature and the judiciary are excepted. Expenses involved in debt payments, in welfare and benefit programs, and funds required to match grants from another governmental unit are largely exempt. Also, central control does not apply to revenues from earmarked taxes, but it may limit expenditures from such sources.[11]

It must be kept in mind that a central budget office functions as part of the chief executive's staff and supposedly speaks for him on policy matters.[12] Because of their close relationship to the chief executive, budget officers must resist every temptation to "throw their weight around." At the same time, the chief executive must avoid becoming insulated from the line departments. Opportunities must exist to appeal budget decisions all the way to the top. After all, the budget, when completed, will be presented to the legislature as the chief executive's budget, not the budget officer's.

One of the most important tasks of a central budget office is revenue estimating. A variety of techniques have been used, but the one in general use today is sometimes called "direct valuation," which involves developing a forecast for each revenue source in light of all available information concerning both the nature of the source, such as a general sales tax or income from state-operated liquor stores, and anticipated economic and demographic trends.[13] Some revenue sources are much more stable than others and conse-

---

[11] For a discussion of earmarked taxes, see Chapter 15.

[12] Burkhead states that in all but seven states the governor is responsible for preparing the budget. The exceptions are Arkansas, Florida, Indiana, Montana, North Dakota, South Carolina, and West Virginia. Four states with an executive budget have no central budget office: Arizona, South Dakota, Vermont, and Wyoming.

[13] For additional information on revenue estimating, see Burkhead, *op. cit.*, Chapter 15.

quently subject to more accurate estimates. Grants-in-aid and property taxes are examples of stable sources. Personal and corporate
income taxes, on the other hand, are unstable because they are so
sensitive to economic fluctuations; they are known as "cycle-sensi-
tive" taxes. Revenue estimating is much more difficult for governments that rely heavily on income taxes than for those that depend
on grants and property taxes. In any case, estimates should not be
treated as exact forecasts. Allowance needs to be made for a margin
of error. Consequently, budget officers tend to make "conservative"
estimates.

Legislative Authorization. When the chief executive submits his
budget to the legislature, he normally presents a "budget message" at
the same time. In this message the executive outlines his expenditure and revenue proposals and seeks to justify them. The budget is
then "divided up" and parceled out among various committees and
subcommittees. Program changes and recommendations for new
services are considered by appropriate "subject-matter" committees.
For example, proposals to increase state aid to primary and secondary
schools may be sent to a committee on education and welfare. The
committee will probably divide itself into subcommittees, one of
which will be instructed to report its findings and recommendations
concerning increased aid to schools. Another subcommittee may
consider requests for additional buildings at the state university.
This pattern is repeated many times with relation to different governmental services.

A vital part of budget studies by legislative committees consists
of public hearings at which governmental officials, organized groups,
and all interested persons have an opportunity to present their ideas.
It is at this point that the fact becomes evident that "budgetmaking
is a political process, conducted in a political arena for political advantage."[14] Sometimes hearings are conducted in an honest effort to
obtain information on all aspects of a question and weigh opposing
viewpoints. When such is the case, policymaking functions in the
best democratic tradition. At other times hearings are held as a matter of form, and committee members listen politely with closed
minds—perhaps they have "heard from home," or perhaps in the
absence of pressure they do not wish to be confused by the facts!
The novice in legislative tactics soon learns that the important question often is not, *What* is wanted? Instead, it is, *Who* wants it?

---

[14] Burkhead, *op. cit.,* p. 307.

When a budget is parceled out among committees, those items involving increased expenditures receive special scrutiny by an "appropriations" committee designated among the states by a variety of titles. Such a committee considers *all* requests for expenditures, attempts to decide where increases are most necessary and where decreases are feasible, arrives at recommendations for each agency, and computes a total. The total is likely to be less than that requested in the executive budget. Once the decisions of the appropriations committee are known, then a "revenue" committee, commonly called the ways and means committee, proceeds to develop proposals for raising revenue necessary to finance the recommendations of the appropriations committee. This whole procedure is complicated enough, but the fact that it is substantially duplicated in a second house in a bicameral legislature makes it complex indeed.

Recommendations of both subject-matter and fiscal committees are transmitted to the respective houses of which they are a part. Sometimes joint committees are used, but they are the exception rather than the rule. Recommendations may be accepted quickly without change; they may be debated at length and accepted, or changed appreciably. If the membership of a house feels that additional committee work is desirable, a measure under consideration may be returned to the committee that worked on it, or it may be referred to a different committee. Reference to a different committee is sometimes sought by a minority of members who are unable to gain acceptance of their ideas at the time the measure is considered by the whole house. They may hope that a proposal more to their liking will come from a second committee, or they may seek to stall final action until late in the session in the hope that their chances of success may be better in the end-of-session rush.

The whole process of legislative action on budget requests is intertwined with oversight of administration. Governmental officials appearing before committees often get "cues" as to what is expected of them if they receive certain requests. Throughout the legislative process "understandings" of one kind or another are common. Such techniques of legislative supervision are not likely to be formalized in law, but failure on the part of administrators to honor them are very likely to produce unpleasant repercussions at later legislative sessions. One formal method of supervision relates to the *nature* of appropriations. If the legislature "itemizes" appropriations by specifying in detail the objects of expenditure, it thereby severely restricts administrative discretion by prohibiting transfers of money from one purpose to another. *Lump-sum* appropriations, on the other hand, reflect legislative trust of administrators and a willingness to allow them discretion in using public funds.

Although the foregoing description of legislative authorization of budget requests is couched in terms descriptive of procedures typical of state legislatures, a similar pattern exists at the local level. It is normally somewhat abbreviated and less formal, but the essential steps are similar. Local legislatures ordinarily use committees to consider budget requests. These committees hold hearings and make recommendations which are then acted upon by the legislative body. Legislative efforts to supervise administration are found at the local level as well as at the state level, but their intensity is affected by the form of local government. They are generally less noticeable, for example, in council-manager cities than in weak-mayor communities.

The Performance Budget. Governments at all levels in the United States traditionally have prepared their budgets in terms of objects to be purchased such as equipment and supplies, and salaries to be paid. Classifications in such budgets are in terms of what is to be bought rather than what is to be accomplished. In recent times a few governments have turned to the *performance budget,* which is prepared in terms of services to be performed rather than items to be purchased. Interest in this type of budget was stimulated by the first Hoover Commission, which advised:

> We recommend that the whole budgetary concept of the Federal Government should be refashioned by the adoption of a budget based upon functions, activities, and projects: this we designate a "performance budget." Such an approach would focus attention upon the general character and relative importance of the work to be done, or upon the service to be rendered, rather than upon the things to be acquired, such as personal services, supplies, equipment, and so on. These latter objects are, after all, only a means to an end. The all important thing in budgeting is the work or the service to be accomplished, and what that work or service will cost.[15]

---

[15] Commission on Organization of the Executive Branch of the Government, *Budgeting and Accounting,* Washington, 1949, p. 8.

The performance budget has proved to be especially adaptable to municipal governments, and a number of cities have adopted it, including Los Angeles, Cleveland, Denver, Detroit, and Phoenix.[16] Its use at this level of government has resulted largely from the interest of some local officials and from the nature of certain municipal functions. Changes in the form of government in some cities, especially to the manager type, have been accompanied by experiments with performance budgeting. Also, it is relatively easy to identify the end product of certain municipal activities. Thus the results of garbage collection and street cleaning are more easily reduced to measurable units than education or welfare.

Only a few states have incorporated the performance concept in their budgets. Among these states are California, Connecticut, Illinois, Maryland, Michigan, New York, Oklahoma, and Oregon. A major argument in behalf of the performance budget is that it provides a means by which governmental agencies are able to explain to legislators and citizens their contributions to the community.

Budget Execution. Subsequent to legislative authorization of budgetary requests, the next important phase in the budget cycle is execution or administration. This task belongs to the executive, and a major objective is to preserve legislative intent with regard to expenditures. If they are to assist in the realization of program goals, expenditure controls must be flexible and not allowed to degenerate into a routine application of rules and regulations. Nevertheless, certain basic practices are generally recognized as essential to effective budgetary control, the most important of which are *allotments, preaudit,* and *postaudit.* As noted earlier, the postaudit is not properly considered an executive function, but it is an essential step in fiscal control.

Allotments. One of the most useful devices for controlling expenditures is the allotment by which funds are made available to a spending agency at intervals. Put another way, an *allotment* is a "determination by the budget officer of the amount of obligations which may be incurred under an appropriation or contract authorization during a specified period."[17] Allotments are usually made on a monthly or quarterly basis and provide a means of keeping expendi-

---

[16] See Lynn F. Anderson, "The Role of Performance Budgeting in Municipal Management," *Texas Municipalities,* March 1954.

[17] W. Brooke Graves, *Public Administration in a Democratic Society,* D. C. Heath and Co., New York, 1950, p. 331.

ture programs under constant review to prevent too rapid disbursements early in the fiscal year resulting in later deficits. Like appropriations, they may be itemized or lump-sum. Also, allotments provide a means whereby economies may be effected as a result of changes in work loads or improved management techniques. Allotment systems are now used in a majority of the states and many local governments.

The Preaudit. The preaudit, regarded as a duty of the comptroller, may be defined briefly as a procedure for determining the propriety of a proposed expenditure. In determining propriety, two major considerations are involved: (1) sufficiency of funds to pay an obligation, and (2) legality of a proposed obligation. Obviously, the officer responsible for the preaudit must maintain accounts that reflect the financial status of each agency and subdivision. Sometimes more than one preaudit is required. One may be administered by the spending agency and another by a central fiscal officer. In general, the duplication of effort involved in such procedure is unreasonable and causes excessive delay in financial transactions. Also, government personnel are hampered in performing their duties and merchants are annoyed by the red tape.

The Postaudit. The postaudit, which comes at the close of a fiscal period, is concerned with the honesty and legality of transactions and the accuracy of accounts. It is the duty of the auditor "to verify and check the financial transactions and records with respect to legality, mathematical accuracy, accountability and the application of accepted accounting principles."[18] The officer or private person responsible for conducting this audit normally has the duty of reporting his findings to a legislative body. State laws may require the accounts of local governments to be audited at specified intervals. Such audits are occasionally performed by a state official but more frequently by someone designated by the local legislature. Postaudits are absolutely essential as a guarantee that public funds are handled in an honest and legal manner.

ACCOUNTING AND REPORTING

Although sometimes viewed as part of the budget process, accounting and reporting seem to be sufficiently distinct to warrant separate treatment. Accounting is the heart of fiscal management

---

[18] International City Managers' Association, *op. cit.*, p. 29.

since it provides information for the conduct of all operations. Morey and Hackett have identified four main purposes behind the maintenance of governmental accounts: (1) To provide information about past operations and present conditions. (2) To serve as a basis for guiding future operations. (3) To establish controls over the acts of public bodies and officers in the use of public funds. (4) To publicize the financial operations and conditions of governments for the benefit of interested citizens.[19] The value and importance of accurate and complete accounts to administrators, rank and file employees, legislators, and citizens are apparent.

Cash and Accrual Accounting. Two principal bases for the maintenance of accounts are known as *cash* and *accrual*. When accounts are kept on a strictly cash basis, revenues are recorded only when collected and expenditures are recorded only when paid. When the accrual system is followed, revenues are recorded when earned or billed, and expenditures are recorded at the time liabilities are incurred. Combinations of these two systems are found frequently because of advantages and disadvantages inherent in each. With regard to revenues, a difficulty associated with accrual accounting is that all earned revenue will not be collected because some taxes always prove uncollectible, particularly during the fiscal period in which they are due. A separate account must be created reflecting an allowance for uncollectible taxes based on past experience, and collections subsequent to the fiscal period must be considered as an offset against this allowance.

A chief weakness of a cash accounting system is that it is impossible to prepare an accurate balance sheet from the accounts because only cash is shown as a current asset, and there are no entries to reflect liabilities. Thus, cash assets may total $100,000 on a certain date, which might be considered quite adequate. However, contracts may have been let to purchase $50,000 in equipment and supplies, all of which may be delivered and billed within the next thirty days. Under a cash accounting system, there is no way to indicate the $50,000 in liabilities except by means of memoranda that are not part of the accounts. Accrual accounting, on the other hand, requires that the $50,000 be deducted from the $100,000, the deductions actually occurring when each purchase order is approved. In this

---

[19] Lloyd Morey and Robert Hackett, *Fundamentals of Governmental Accounting,* John Wiley & Sons, New York, 1942, pp. 10–11.

way the true financial picture would be presented, namely, that actual liquid assets are only $50,000.

Financial Reports. All governmental units issue financial reports of one type or another and for a variety of purposes. Some are comprehensive and are designed for the use of executive and fiscal officers, while others are mere leaflets intended to show the citizen what he receives for his tax dollar. As James C. Charlesworth has so aptly noted, "In between are the forbidding and functionless books put out by state auditors and controllers, containing hundreds of pages of columns of figures in fine print, unrelieved by textual interpretation, and altogether unintelligible to the layman. These volumes are more useful as paperweights or doorstops than as sources of information about the state of the government."[20]

Even though many large and cumbersome reports are required by law, opportunities exist for the development of useful reports. The format of a report should be related to the purpose it is supposed to serve. A report useful to an auditor is generally of little value to an administrator and completely useless to most citizens. Considerable improvement has become apparent in the contents and format of governmental reports in recent years. On the whole, the greatest strides have been made by cities, many of which regularly issue reports that are short and readable, containing well written text supplemented by charts, graphs, and pictures to attract and hold the attention of those who are only mildly interested.

PROCUREMENT

Procurement is concerned with the acquisition of equipment and supplies needed by governments in the performance of their functions. Under traditional procedure, which is still used in some places, "goods were bought in the open market at prevailing prices (or higher) not only by individual departments and agencies, but by each separate bureau, division, or section."[21] Gradually, laws were changed to provide for "competitive bidding," requiring that each supplier desiring to do so must be given an opportunity to enter a bid indicating the price at which he will deliver specified goods. At a designated time and place bids are opened, and the contract is awarded to the "lowest responsible bidder." Laws usually provide

[20] James C. Charlesworth, *Governmental Administration*, Harper & Brothers, New York, 1951, p. 373.

[21] W. Brooke Graves, *op. cit.*, p. 347.

that items costing less than a stipulated amount need not be subjected to bids. Still, a great waste of motion, duplicated efforts, and opportunities for favoritism exist.

Recent years have witnessed the rapid spread of *centralized purchasing,* involving the maintenance of a central office within a governmental unit to procure items needed by most, if not all, of the subdivisions within that unit. Most states and large cities as well as many smaller units of local government have inaugurated centralized purchasing. Although viewed by some persons as a mixed blessing, central purchasing has demonstrated a number of advantages if handled wisely: (1) Lower prices result from quantity-purchasing and increased competition among suppliers. (2) Additional savings may be realized as a result of expedited payments, a reduction in the number of purchase orders and vouchers, and simplification of accounting controls. (3) Lists of qualified vendors are maintained in the hope of preventing acquisition of shoddy materials. (4) Through the development of standard specifications for items bought in large quantities, the variety of articles used is reduced, and bulk buying is facilitated. (5) Standard specifications facilitate bidding because competing vendors are aware of the quality of merchandise required. (6) By keeping a record of the service provided by each vendor, those whose records are poor may be eliminated from the list of qualified suppliers. (7) Centralized inspections help to prevent the acquisition of inferior goods.[22]

Those who question the desirability of centralized purchasing advance a number of considerations in opposition: (1) Each agency is better able to determine the nature and quality of goods most suitable to its needs. (2) Delays result from the steps required in order to acquire an item through central purchasing. (3) The development of adequate specifications is so complicated and time-consuming as to offset advantages accruing from their use. (4) Losses may result in the long run from too great emphasis on cost and too little on quality. (5) Friction and distrust often characterize relations between central purchasing and line agencies. (6) Establishment of a central agency for purchasing is no guarantee against inefficiency or dishonesty in the acquisition of equipment and supplies. (7) As a result of "bargain buying," goods may be stocked in such large quantities

---

[22] This list of advantages is adapted from International City Managers' Association, *op. cit.,* p. 367.

that excessive sums of money are tied up in large inventories, and some items become outmoded before they are used.

Considerable care and wisdom are required in the installation and administration of a successful central purchasing program. The ever-present question is, How much centralization should there be? Complete centralization of all purchases is neither desirable nor achievable. Too great a degree of centralization is wasteful. Witness the case of an operating unit in a state that requires desk blotters to be obtained from central stores located in the state capitol. An operating unit, located fifty miles away, requests a half-dozen blotters obtainable locally for ten cents each. The blotters arrive packed in a cardboard cylinder on which there is forty cents in postage! If central purchasing is to be justified in such circumstances, all other costs of acquiring each blotter and getting it to its destination must average less than three and one-half cents—a very unlikely situation. Once a balance has been established on the basis of a determination of those things best purchased centrally and those best obtained locally, a degree of central purchasing seems highly desirable.

ASSESSMENT AND COLLECTION OF TAXES

In the context of fiscal management, "assessment" has two meanings that should be distinguished. In one sense, assessment refers to the process of determining the value of something, particularly income and property, for the purpose of taxation.[23] It also means the procedure of fixing the amount of a tax. Assessment is accomplished in one of three ways: (1) by self-assessment, (2) automatically, or (3) by governmental action. The personal income tax, as used by the national and state governments, is administered basically through a process of self-assessment. Each person is responsible for determining the value (amount) of his income and the exact tax he is obligated to pay.[24] Of course, his action is subject to review by a governmental agency. Many taxes are assessed automatically. Probably the best known examples are retail sales and excise taxes. When a person knows that he must pay two cents on each dollar that he spends for

---

[23] For additional discussion of assessment with regard to property tax, see Chapter 15.

[24] The fact that some jurisdictions provide for "collection at the source" whereby deductions are made from pay checks does not mean that each person is relieved of responsibility for determining the amount of his tax. At some date, each recipient of taxable income must still file a return indicating the amount of tax he is obligated to pay.

clothes, the tax is automatic. The same is true of gasoline taxes, which are included in the price of each gallon. Hidden taxes incorporated in the prices of items, such as food and clothing, without being identified as such are generally termed excise taxes, and they, too, are assessed automatically. Among those taxes to which governmental assessment is applicable, the most important is the property tax. Responsibility for determining the value of property and for fixing the amount of the tax rests with governmental agencies.[25] Because of the importance of governmental action, the significance of the property tax as a source of local revenue, and the problems related to its administration, assessment of the property tax demands special consideration.

The Personal Property Tax. As described in an earlier chapter, property is generally classified as real or personal. Real property consists of land and improvements, while all other property is considered personal. Although decreasing in importance, local jurisdictions and some states continue to receive revenue from the personal property tax. Taxes on personal property are selective, that is, they apply to some kinds of property and not to others. Tangible personal property, including such things as automobiles, furniture, appliances, farm machinery, and livestock, is more easily subjected to taxation than intangible property which consists of stocks, bonds, mortgages, patents, copyrights, and similar evidences of wealth. The latter are much more easily concealed than the former. Since taxes on intangibles are very difficult to administer and tend to penalize the honest taxpayers, they are used much less widely than they once were.

In earlier days the assessment of personal property was based almost entirely upon declarations submitted by taxpayers. Some supplementary information was provided by assessors on the basis of their general but rather haphazard knowledge of property within their respective jurisdictions. In recognition of the inadequacy of such procedure, assessors have resorted to personal visits to view taxable tangible property and record information concerning its quantity, quality, and valuation. Each taxpayer is usually visited only once every two, three, or more years since time and staff do not permit annual visitations in most places. Assessment of the assets of

---

[25] The fact that in the administration of the property tax partial reliance may be placed on statements submitted by taxpayers does not relieve the assessor of legal responsibility for the assessment of this tax.

business firms other than real property must be based largely on accounting records, which may be subject to more or less thorough and regular checks.

The Real Property Tax. Much as in the case of the personal property tax, the assessment of real property requires discovery, listing, and valuation. The problems are different, however. Land and buildings are much more easily discovered and listed than most varieties of personal property. Nevertheless, as a result of poor administration considerable amounts of real property have regularly escaped taxation because they have not been placed on the assessment rolls. The cure for this situation lies in a system requiring that land be surveyed and property lines be recorded on scale maps which must be kept current on the basis of alterations in property lines and changes in ownership. In addition to land maps (commonly called lot and block maps in cities), information must be recorded concerning improvements on each parcel of land. An actual viewing of each piece of property by someone from the assessor's office is the only satisfactory method of accomplishing this purpose. Assistance may be obtained from aerial maps.

Maintaining current records pertaining to improvements is much more difficult than with regard to the parcels of land themselves. Each year buildings are constructed, and old ones modified, torn down or moved. Unless building permits are required, chief reliance must be placed on personal observation to keep abreast of such changes. Even where building permits are required and serve as the major source of information for the assessor, personal viewing cannot be abandoned since changes may be made by property owners who neglect to obtain permits.

The most serious difficulties in the administration of the property tax are associated with valuation. Some of the major reasons for these difficulties are: (1) No two parcels of property are identical because they cannot have identical locations, and the location of property is a major factor in determining its value. (2) Sales of real property often occur too infrequently to provide adequate data on value. (3) Since land is irreplacable, there are no reproduction costs that may be used in the valuation process. (4) Since land and buildings generally exist over long periods of time, estimates pertaining to income and depreciation are difficult to make. (5) Too often assessors and their employees, insufficiently trained in the techniques of assessing property, must rely on the routine application of rate-scale formulas.[26]

Nevertheless, local assessors are required by law to arrive at a taxable value for most property within their jurisdiction.[27] Even under the best circumstances this is a difficult task. When approached unsystematically, property valuation is characterized by inadequacy, inequity, and even chicanery. In an effort to provide assistance to assessors, the National Association of Assessing Officers has developed the concept of "constructive market value" as a guide in determining real property values for purposes of taxation. Constructive market value has been defined as "an approximation of market value arrived at through the application of reasonable rules and procedures of appraisal, such as corner influence and depth rules, building classification and cost schedules, and physical depreciation schedules."[28] An examination of the import of this definition is beyond the scope of this chapter, but one important fact should be noted. Reference is made to an "approximation of market value" through the use of "reasonable rules and procedures." Thus valuation is recognized as an *estimate* based on reason reinforced by standard methods of procedure. Since an estimate smaller than true value is generally preferred to one that is larger, underassessment is the rule. From the viewpoint of a popularly elected assessor, overassessment must be avoided at all costs.

Review and Equalization. Due process of law requires that each taxpayer have the right to a hearing before taxes on his property become final. The standard practice is to establish an administrative agency, commonly an *ex officio* board, to *review* individual assessments against real or personal property, and raise or lower them or uphold the assessor's valuation. The number of appeals to such bodies is kept to a minimum partially by the usual practice of underassessment. Where the distribution of state property taxes among counties or of county taxes among smaller units of government is involved, arrangements must be made for adjustments by the central units to facilitate equitable distribution of such taxes. The procedure whereby these adjustments are made is called *equalization,* and it is intended to minimize inequalities in the administration of the property tax. Equalization is not concerned with adjusting in-

---

[26] This list is adapted from International City Managers' Association, *op. cit.*, p. 229.

[27] Some types of property, such as that belonging to utilities and railroads, are assessed by a state agency.

[28] Quoted in International City Managers' Association, *op. cit.*, pp. 230–231.

equalities in the assessment of individual properties. Instead, it is intended to make adjustments in the level of assessments within jurisdictions like townships, villages, and cities. Thus if the assessor in one township is valuing property appreciably higher than the assessor in another township, the county board of equalization may make them more comparable.

Recent years have witnessed increased state activity with regard to the equalization of property assessments. In many states a "tax commission" is empowered to review and equalize assessments among counties and to assess public utility properties directly. Generally, these commissions use persuasion and education in their efforts to improve the quality of local assessments. They may advise local assessors and conduct schools for them. If such procedures prove inadequate, the state agency may order reassessments by local officials in accord with state rules and regulations, or it may direct local boards of review to correct inequities.

Common Defects. Many of the difficulties associated with the property tax stem from defects in administration. First and probably most important, local assessors are often inadequate in relation to the demands of the job. Popular election, which is the rule, emphasizes the need for gaining favor in the eyes of voters rather than fearless application of the best assessment techniques. Short terms of office further stress the importance of keeping popular favor. In most states no formal qualifications are required of assessors. As a consequence, valuation may be based largely on guesswork; some property escapes taxation; and there is little incentive to install modern procedures. Of course, it sometimes happens that a well qualified assessor is elected, and his office is a model of effectiveness and efficiency.

Defects in property tax administration also stem from the fact that assessors often are provided insufficient funds to perform their duties. Even if they are familiar with modern practices and wish to install them, assessors may be prevented from inaugurating changes by lack of money. Assessors are sometimes paid on a per diem basis, reflecting legislative intent to keep costs to an absolute minimum. Furthermore, assessors may be severely limited in the number and quality of personnel they may hire. "One of the chief causes of poor assessment is the entirely unwarranted belief that almost anyone can do the work."[29]

---

[29] *Ibid.*, p. 219.

Tax Collection. The collection of taxes for any governmental jurisdiction is usually scattered among a number of officers and agencies. Treasurers collect some taxes; separate boards or commissions collect others; and sheriffs may collect still others. The variations are legion, but there has been a trend in recent years toward improvement. It was not uncommon at one time for a taxpayer to have to pay part of his property tax to a county collector; part to a township collector, part to a city collector, and part to a school district collector. Today the collection of the local property tax is usually centralized in a county official who is responsible for allocating to the other jurisdictions their appropriate shares. Practically all states have established a central agency, often a commission, to collect a variety of state taxes. The collection of earmarked revenues frequently rests with the agencies authorized to spend them.

Where assessment of a tax is a governmental responsibility, economy and efficiency would seem to dictate combining assessment and collection in the same agency. Such an arrangement is seldom found, however—a fact that may be partially explained by the different skills and abilities required of those persons responsible for these functions. A major consideration in the collection of a tax is that the procedure should be economical, as Adam Smith observed nearly two centuries ago. Today it is generally conceded that "no tax is a good one that eats itself up in costs of collection."[30] Whatever official is responsible for collecting a tax should also possess the authority and responsibility to follow up cases of delinquency and collect delinquent taxes whenever possible. In order to insure the safe custody of public funds, all persons involved in their collection should be bonded.

Department of Revenue. A few states, including Missouri, Georgia, and Alaska, recently have organized departments of revenue. A number of other states have given serious consideration to the creation of such an agency. Advocates of a state department of revenue argue that the enforcement of major tax laws as well as the collection, custody, and management of state moneys should be brought together under a single authority in the name of efficient and economical management. Opposition comes largely from agencies with vested interests in the administration of certain aspects of a state's finances and from those who have a special interest in the use of specific state funds. Thus a liquor commission with authority over

---

[30] W. Brooke Graves, *op. cit.,* p. 299.

collecting and spending alcoholic beverage taxes may oppose a department of finance, and sportsmen may fight against taking control over the income from hunting and fishing licenses from the fish and game commission. These and other pressures have succeeded in defeating most proposals to create a state department of revenue.

Long-Range Financial Planning

The allocation of financial resources of governmental units is often haphazard. Fiscal plans are limited to each budgetary period of one or two years. No serious effort is made to foresee either operating or capital needs. Competition rather than cooperation among agencies within a government is common practice. Funds are apportioned to meet one "emergency" and then another—most of which might well have been anticipated. Pressure inside and outside government may cause unwise expenditures because no orderly system of priorities has been established.

A long-range comprehensive plan helps to prevent such unfortunate developments. Although an exact time span is difficult to specify and must vary with conditions, a period of fifteen to twenty-five years probably should be encompassed in such a plan. Estimates must be developed in four major areas or phases: (1) services, (2) capital improvements, (3) priorities, and (4) finances. Projections must be made with regard to foreseeable needs for public services such as education, transportation, health, sanitation, and police protection. Preparation of estimates for these and the many other functions of state and local governments is difficult, and the task becomes truly formidable when other aspects of planning are included.

Plans for capital improvements consist of a list of projects and facilities needed to implement the service program. In order for education to be provided, school buildings must be constructed. If people are to be transported, streets and highways must be built. Sanitary conditions in urbanized areas necessitate the construction of sewers and sewage disposal plants. So it goes. Since planned capital improvements reduce the need to rely on long-term bonding, the costs are consequently lowered. Bond issues are an expensive method of financing because of interest charges.

The third phase of long-range planning concerns the establishment of a hierarchy of needs. Since some will be more crucial than others at different times, a system of priorities is very helpful in preparing the budget for each fiscal period. Without a plan, less pressing needs are likely to be pushed ahead of more urgent ones. Of course, a plan provides no guarantee that such a thing will not occur, but it diminishes the likelihood. Finally, ways of financing expanded services and capital improvements must be developed. Certain assumptions must be made concerning economic conditions during the plan period, and unfolding events will necessitate modifications. Flexibility must characterize all aspects of a good long-range plan, and a number of alternative approaches should be prepared. A plan that is too rigid is as bad as no plan at all.

SELECTED REFERENCES

Books:

Buck, A. E., *Public Budgeting,* Harper and Bros., New York, 1929.

——, *The Budget in Governments of Today,* The Macmillan Co., New York, 1934.

Burkhead, Jesse, *Government Budgeting,* John Wiley and Sons, New York, 1956.

International City Managers' Association, *Municipal Finance Administration,* Chicago, 1955.

Maddox, Russell W., Jr., *Issues in State and Local Government,* D. Van Nostrand Co., Inc., Princeton, N.J., 1965.

Wildavsky Aaron, *The Politics of the Budgetary Process,* Little, Brown and Co., Boston, 1964.

Articles:

Cookingham, L. P., "Budget Review and Adoption—Opportunity or Ordeal?" *Public Management,* August 1960.

Hamann, A. P., "Long-Term Capital Budgeting—A Case Study in Effective Procedure," *Public Management,* July 1960.

Harrell, C. A., and Koch, Vernon E., "Basic and Supplemental Budgets," *Public Management,* June 1960.

McDonald, A. M., "Appraising Residential Property," *The Appraisal Journal,* April 1953.

"Municipal Accounting and Financial Reporting," Symposium, *Municipal Finance,* November 1958.

"Performance Budgeting: Has the Theory Worked?" Symposium, *Public Administration Review,* Spring 1960.

Reynolds, John W., and Hollander, Walter G., "Program Budgeting in Wisconsin," *State Government,* Autumn 1964.

Reed, Homer D., "Preparing Budget Estimates," *Public Management,* April 1960.

Schick, Allen, "Control Patterns in State Budget Execution," *Public Administration Review,* June 1964.

Snyder, Ralph W., "Reappraising Program Budgeting," *Public Management,* May 1960.

CHAPTER 17

Staffing State and Local Governments: Personnel Management

"The history of public administration is littered with the wreckage of well planned organization structures which failed because of inefficient or inadequately trained personnel." In earlier chapters, stress was placed on the importance to good government of sound structural arrangements and adequate financial resources. Important as they are, these factors alone cannot produce effective government. Qualified, industrious, loyal people are essential. The magnitude of personnel management problems experienced by state and local governments is reflected in part by the fact that they now employ over six million persons, necessitating payroll costs in excess of two billion dollars per month.

Around the close of the eighteenth century, government employment was considered a privilege. This viewpoint, coupled with the relatively simple governmental activities characteristic of the times, produced a group of public servants who performed their duties satisfactorily. During the first quarter of the nineteenth century, the "spoils system" infested state and local governments generally throughout the nation. In the eyes of the spoilsmen positions in the public service were viewed as booty for the party in power. Accordingly, a change in party resulted in a wholesale turnover of public employees because "to the victor belong the spoils."

Under the spoils system, now as then, persons are appointed to positions on the basis of party and personal considerations. Elected officials reward fellow partisans and personal friends by providing them with jobs at the taxpayers' expense. Little if any attention is paid to such matters as ability and competence. Many people in the early days of the nineteenth century probably thought the spoils system a less serious threat to democratic institutions than a "bureaucracy" resulting from the retention of employees for long periods of time. Any effort to justify the practice today on such grounds is doomed to failure. Nevertheless, the spoils system is still widespread in state and local governments.

In 1877 public-spirited citizens, under the leadership of Dorman B. Eaton, organized the New York Civil Service Reform Association, the first of many such groups. This organization contributed materially to the enactment in 1883 of the federal civil service act (Pendleton Act) and of the first New York state civil service law. Massachusetts followed suit in 1884. No other state passed similar legislation during the next twenty-one years, although by 1963 slightly more than half the states had provided for "general" civil service coverage.[1] Some fifteen other states have voluntarily enacted civil service laws that apply to employees of selected departments. Because of federal requirements, every state provides that employees handling funds granted under the Social Security Act and other grant-in-aid programs must be chosen according to civil service procedure, including competitive entrance examinations.

At the local level the quality of personnel management varies greatly. Most cities with populations in excess of 100,000 now operate under civil service laws, as do numerous smaller communities. In counties and other units of rural local government the picture is discouraging because of the continued widespread existence of the spoils system. It is estimated, for example, that only about seven per cent of the nation's counties have civil service laws or are included under state statutes designed to provide general coverage. Like some states, many cities apply civil service regulations only to members of certain departments, particularly police and fire.

A word of caution is in order. Too often the assumption is made that the existence of civil service guarantees good personnel management. Facts do not warrant this conclusion. The intent of civil service laws may be thwarted in a number of ways. Legislatures may fail to appropriate sufficient money to implement them effectively; responsible officials may be hostile; the people may be indifferent; or provisions of the law may be unworkable. These and other factors may sabotage the administration of civil service rules and regulations. On the other hand, it is possible to have efficient personnel manage-

---

[1] These states are Alabama, Alaska, California, Colorado, Connecticut, Georgia, Hawaii, Illinois, Kansas, Kentucky, Louisiana, Maine, Maryland, Massachusetts, Michigan, Minnesota, Nevada, New Hampshire, New Jersey, New York, Ohio, Oklahoma, Oregon, Rhode Island, Vermont, Washington, and Wisconsin. The effectiveness of these laws in a few instances has been impaired by inadequate appropriations. Developments in recent years indicate that other states will provide increasingly complete civil service coverage for their employees.

ment in public jurisdictions and individual agencies without civil service, particularly in smaller governmental units and agencies staffed with professional personnel.

TERMINOLOGY

Frequently, in discussions of personnel management in the public service, numerous terms appear that are sometimes misunderstood. Some of these will be defined and discussed later in the chapter, but attention should be directed to certain concepts at this point. Students often are confused concerning the differences between "civil service," "merit system," and "career service." Although it may be impossible to distinguish them completely, some differences can be noted. As used in this text, *civil service* refers to a system of personnel management *formalized* by a government through laws, rules, and regulations. The term is also used to refer to the employees subject to such a system. Originally, civil service laws were enacted primarily to keep the rascals and incompetents out of public office. Employees were to be chosen on the basis of competence or "merit" rather than political affiliation or personal friendship. As a result, the terms "civil service" and "merit system" often have been used interchangeably.

An arrangement for managing personnel in which various actions, such as hiring, promoting, and firing, relate closely to the individual employee's fitness and performance qualifies as a *merit system,* whether in public or private employment. Thus any governmental unit that operates on the basis of tradition and practices emphasizing individual fitness for the job may be said to possess a merit system. Civil service never exists in private employment. The real difference between the two lies in the fact that civil service must rest on laws, rules, and regulations that spell out in considerable detail permissible personnel practices, while a merit system may be informal. Confusion is further compounded by the fact that laws and regulations specifically provide for the establishment of a "merit system." Whenever this happens, civil service exists, regardless of the name applied to it, particularly if persons are admitted to the service on the basis of competitive examinations. Consequently, civil service may be equated with a formalized merit system.

The third term to be examined, "career service," is not so difficult to distinguish. "By a *career* is meant a life work. It is an honorable occupation which one formally takes up in youth with the expectation of advancement, and pursues until retirement. A *career service* in government is thus a public service which is so organized and conducted as to encourage careers."[2] Accordingly, in a career service competent young people are recruited with the expectation that they will have long tenure in an agency or governmental unit. Advancement is along recognized promotional ladders, and very few persons fill intermediate or higher positions unless they have "worked their way up." It is probably correct to state that at the present time no governmental unit as a whole operates on the career principle. Young people do not accept employment in a state or city, for example, with any clear idea of the path of advancement open to them as employees of that *unit* of government. Instead, at best they must think in terms of promotion with a particular agency, such as a department of health or welfare. Even then, their future may be quite uncertain because of the absence of clearly established career ladders.

Employees of a governmental unit are often divided into three categories: "classified," "unclassified," and "exempt." Generally, those positions over which the central personnel agency is granted jurisdiction are in the *classified service*.[3] Their selection, advancement, removal, etc. are governed by rules and regulations issued by the central agency. The *unclassified service* normally encompasses such personnel as private secretaries, deputies to executive officers, lawyers, doctors, and staffs of educational institutions. In the *exempt service* are usually found popularly elected officials, members of boards and commissions, department heads, judicial officers, and employees of the legislature. The allocation of personnel to the unclassified and exempt services is normally a matter of legislative discretion. In general, however, the exempt service is limited to persons in the categories indicated here.

SOURCES OF PERSONNEL POLICIES

Although not always strictly observed, the formal sources of personnel policies are state constitutions and local charters, state statutes and local ordinances, and the rules and regulations issued by the central personnel agency. State constitutions and local charters often contain brief statements concerning the creation, nature, and powers

---

[2] Commission of Inquiry on Public Service Personnel, *Better Government Personnel*, McGraw-Hill Book Co., New York, 1935, p. 25.

[3] In the federal government the term "competitive service" has been substituted for "classified service."

of central agencies for the administration of civil service or merit systems. More detailed provisions are reserved to statutes and ordinances that outline the basic purposes and policies to be observed in personnel management, including such items as requirement of competitive examinations, prohibitions against political assessments, and procedure for the dismissal of employees. Additional details are normally set forth in rules and regulations prepared by the board or commission.

ATTRACTING GOOD PEOPLE

Public Attitudes. Norman J. Powell has observed, "It is commonly agreed that Americans in general stereotype the people who work for government as pallid refugees from the brutal realities of industry, commerce, and agriculture."[4] Although this statement may represent a somewhat extreme viewpoint, it nevertheless reflects an attitude sufficiently widespread to produce serious consequences for the public service. The simple fact is that the public service does not generally enjoy high prestige in the United States, although there are great variations in attitude toward different governmental agencies. Studies indicate that the "prestige value" of the public service has increased during the last quarter-century or so.[5] It is true, of course, that discriminating persons do not view the public service as a homogeneous mass and consequently have higher esteem for some groups of public employees than for others.

In a democracy the public service is what the people make it. At least two considerations support this conclusion. In the first place, a democracy draws its public servants from the people, and they constitute a reasonably good cross section of the population. Hence, their basic ideals, aspirations, and beliefs are much the same. In the second place, the conditions under which public employees work, as well as their responsibilities, are determined at least in broad outline by the people through their representatives. Too often the canard is voiced that public employees "do not work as hard" as those in private employment, although no substantial evidence ever has been advanced to support such an assertion. Wherever peculiar circumstances lend support to that viewpoint, the explanation probably lies

---

[4] Norman J. Powell, *Personnel Administration in Government*, Prentice-Hall, New York, 1956, p. 9.

[5] Compare information presented by L. D. White in his *The Prestige Value of Public Employment*, University of Chicago Press, 1929, with that developed in opinion surveys by the National Opinion Research Center and reported in *Public Opinion Quarterly*, 1947–48, pp. 658–61 and *ibid.*, 1949, p. 553.

in lack of incentives. Who determines what incentives shall exist? The answer must be, the people. Since talented individuals tend to prefer to work under high-prestige conditions, the importance of public attitudes toward the public service is apparent.

Competition. Especially in periods of prosperity, governments must compete among themselves and with private employment in order to attract competent employees. Although this necessity is recognized in theory, it is often overlooked in practice. As a group, governments are *not* model employers. Consequently, it is important for each jurisdiction to follow two courses of action to obtain able employees. They must stress their strong points and strengthen their weak ones. They cannot expect their advantages to balance their disadvantages. Thus, a superior retirement program will not effectively counterbalance an inferior pay plan. It is important that the whole program of personnel management be attractive in order to be generally competitive. Furthermore, it is imperative that those persons responsible for shaping such programs *not* accept the fatalistic idea that governments are unable to compete effectively with private employment. Such a philosophy contributes to the creation of a second-rate service.

Recruitment. Recruitment encompasses those processes and practices designed to discover and attract talent into the public service. It is complete once an applicant has filled out an application blank. Although it will not always result in obtaining the most highly qualified personnel, the crucial importance of a good recruitment program is widely recognized. In the words of one acute observer, "The ultimate possibilities of solving problems of government lie in the nature of the men and women who compose the institution."[6] A poor recruitment program is likely to attract applicants who are, as a group, mediocre at best.

Although it is true that "For the 'selling' campaign to be successful, there must be something worthwhile to sell,"[7] the importance of techniques of salesmanship cannot be disregarded. The best recruitment practices will not produce miracles, but they play a vital role in attracting qualified people. Increasing recognition has been given recently to the validity of this assertion. For many years public jurisdictions generally followed a pattern of "passive" recruitment,

---

[6] Herman Finer, *The Theory and Practice of Modern Government*, rev. ed., Henry Holt and Co., New York, 1949, p. 609.

[7] Norman J. Powell, *op. cit.*, p. 209.

characterized first by the preparation of uninteresting, unattractive announcements of job openings. The next step was limited distribution of these announcements for display on bulletin boards and for the files of employment agencies. Sometimes announcements appeared in the classified advertisements of larger newspapers. Little additional effort was exerted.

During periods of depression when many more people are seeking jobs than there are openings available, such a course of action may be successful. In times characterized by a tight labor market, much more needs to be done. Over twenty years ago, even during the depression of the 1930's, the Commission of Inquiry on Public Service Personnel emphasized the great importance of good recruitment practices.[8] Since then the value of a "positive" approach has been increasingly recognized. A good recruitment program must be designed to discover and develop sources of potential employees and to sell the public service to them. Such sources include high schools, trade schools, colleges, professional schools, unions, civic organizations, employment agencies, and friends and relatives of employees. Pinpoint recruiting is much more effective than shotgun publicity.

Once sources have been identified and cultivated, methods of attracting applicants must be developed. The possibilities are legion and are limited chiefly by the ingenuity of those responsible for recruitment and the money available to implement their ideas. Included are attractive advertisements in newspapers, over the radio, and on television. Only the first of these media is widely used, probably because of the greater cost involved in using the other two. Most jurisdictions have been unwilling to appropriate sufficient funds to underwrite costly recruitment efforts. It is also important to prepare attractive announcements and brochures and to distribute them according to a well conceived plan. Notices should be timely and should include all pertinent information to enable a prospective recruit to decide whether he is qualified to compete. Recruitment teams are very useful in surveying known sources of applicants and in arousing interest in the service.

One technique possessing great potential as a recruitment device often is not classified as such. Some public jurisdictions have developed programs through which young persons still in college are brought into the service for short periods, usually during the summer. This practice is one of the soundest recruitment devices for

---

[8] *Op. cit.*, pp. 37–41.

certain types of jobs, particularly those requiring college or other specialized training. Its scope is restricted by available money and by the willingness of responsible officials to appreciate its value. At the same time it has an advantage possessed by no other practice in that it enables the recruit to get a "taste" of the service under relatively favorable circumstances.

Effective recruitment is affected adversely by lengthy delays commonly characteristic of the interim between contact and employment. These delays are sometimes so long that they cause the whole process to partake of the nature of an endurance contest. Such delays and uncertainties are less often associated with private employment. A "successful" candidate for public employment often must have patience, time to spare, and a lack of attractive alternatives. These factors may result in the loss of the most highly qualified candidates. A significant advantage enjoyed by recruiting teams from private industry compared with those from public agencies is their ability to make job commitments at the time of contact. Although it is generally not feasible for public agencies to emulate this practice, every effort should be made to shorten the time between arousing the interest of a good applicant and offering him a job.

When a central personnel agency such as a civil service commission exists, primary responsibility for recruitment usually rests, at least formally, with that agency. When a strong, effective recruitment program has been developed by the personnel agency, it is generally preferable to centralize responsibility. In this way the services of recruitment specialists may be most effectively utilized. However, the needs of line agencies under some circumstances may be better served by conducting their own recruitment programs. As the size of a government increases, difficulties associated with centralized recruitment increase for various reasons, including the number of recruits needed and the variety of skills and specialties required. The latter consideration constitutes a strong argument in favor of decentralized recruitment. Specialists are most likely to be familiar with sources from which persons with similar training and qualifications may be obtained. Thus people in welfare work should be most familiar with the "market" from which to obtain fellow workers.

Putting the Right Man in the Job

Position Classification. Included among the most important elements in any well developed program of personnel management is a system of position classification. Although it is not important that students of state and local government be familiar with the details of this highly specialized function, a general understanding of its nature is helpful. "Position classification is the name given to the orderly arrangement and definition of categories of employment on the basis of the kind and level of work performed."[9] Major groups or *classes* of positions are identified, such as clerks, stenographers, carpenters, automotive repairmen, and statisticians. Individual positions are assigned or "allocated" to the appropriate classes on the basis of the duties and level of responsibilities involved. Each class, then, includes all positions sufficiently alike to be designated by the same descriptive title, such as clerk-typist, stenographer, or budget analyst. These classes are further refined on the basis of rank, as reflected in the titles "Clerk-Typist I," "Clerk-Typist II," and "Clerk-Typist III." Incumbents of each class are expected to possess substantially the same qualifications and to receive the same scale of pay.[10]

The value of position classification is evidenced by the example described by Norman J. Powell:

> . . . a survey of jobs in Philadelphia disclosed that 105 persons were doing work that could be described under the standard title "Telephone Operator." Here are some of the titles under which the telephone operators had worked prior to the survey: Ladderman, Laborer, General Duty Nurse, Ward Maid, Attendant, Stenographer, Housemaid. Differences in pay rates ranged up to a top rate that was more than 200 per cent greater than the bottom pay. For the category of work "clerk," there were 85 titles in use covering 269 employees paid at 33 different salary rates.[11]

This situation is typical of the chaos usually existing in any sizable jurisdiction operating without the benefits of position classification. Obviously "equal pay for equal work" can be no more than a slogan in such circumstances.

Although position classification does not eliminate inequities, it does diminish them appreciably. Individual inequities may be explained largely on two grounds: (1) inaccuracy in original classification of a position, and (2) inadequacy of procedures for reclassifica-

---

[9] Norman J. Powell, *op. cit.*, p. 321.
[10] For details pertaining to position classification, see *Position Classification in the Public Service*, Civil Service Assembly, Chicago, 1941.
[11] *Op. cit.*, p. 323.

tion. Errors are inevitable, especially in view of the necessity of frequently exercising *judgment* throughout the entire process. More important as a source of difficulty, however, is the absence of adequate reclassification procedures. Positions change as duties are added or taken away, and changes may warrant moving a position from one class to another. Even in the absence of a significant change in duties, "upgrading" a position may be required in order to retain experienced, efficient employees. Although personnel technicians commonly decry such action, it may be wise in terms of the effective performance of work in an agency.

In order to keep a classification plan up to date, periodic surveys are needed. If provision is made for such surveys, changes in jobs can be noted and appropriate reassignments made throughout the service, instead of being confined to agencies where officials make the loudest complaints. Only rarely do central personnel agencies have sufficient staff to perform this important task. Since they are less pressing than the demands of day-to-day tasks, surveys are often postponed indefinitely.

Examination. Once applications have been accepted for a particular opening, they must be "sifted" to check the completeness of data and to determine whether applicants possess the legal qualifications necessary for eligibility. Those who pass this first screening are then admitted to an examination. In jurisdictions without civil service, selection is usually made on some more "informal" basis. A great variety of examinations have been used in an effort to determine the fitness of applicants, and they may be classified in many ways for purposes of description and study.

Examinations sometimes are classified as *assembled* and *unassembled*. Actually, examination procedures are frequently a combination of both. When applicants are required to meet in groups for purposes of testing, the examination is designated as assembled. When an unassembled examination is used, applicants' qualifications are determined on the basis of training and experience. For certain types of positions, particularly those requiring professional training or administrative experience, the unassembled procedure is generally preferred. For others a combination may be desirable. For positions that do not require professional training or much varied experience, reliance may be placed entirely on the assembled examination.

The varieties of assembled examinations are legion, but in general they may be divided into three major types: (1) written tests, (2) oral interviews, and (3) performance tests. Although written tests are subdivided into "objective" and "subjective" types, these terms are misleading. Multiple-choice, true-false, and short-answer questions are classified as *objective* because the answers do not have to be evaluated—they are definitely either "right" or "wrong." Such tests, however, are subjective in their construction, that is, in the choice of questions. Essay questions, on the other hand, are *subjective* both as to selection and grading. Written tests are relatively inexpensive and easy to administer, and they provide a better basis for making choices among applicants than judgment founded on thoroughly unreliable information.

A highly specialized variety of the written examination is the *personality* test, which has been used much more widely in industry than in government. The value of this type of test is questionable because its ability to test what it is supposed to test has not been demonstrated.[12] Whenever evaluation of the personal traits of candidates is considered essential, the formal *oral interview* is standard practice. The oral examination can do little more than formalize *impressions* of individuals. It is most useful as a means of observing how people react to certain stimuli under conditions of stress. A significant weakness of the oral test stems from the tendency of raters to generalize on the basis of such reactions. Thus it may be assumed that a candidate who becomes disturbed under questioning will evidence "instability" on the job. Not only may this be a false assumption, but a further difficulty arises from the fact that "stability" in this sense may not be an important qualification for the particular position. Interviews may partake of the nature of "fishing expeditions" in which interviewers make random efforts to discover unrelated bits of information about applicants.

The performance test, sometimes called a "practical" test, is especially useful in measuring physical abilities and skills. Such tests usually reproduce work situations, such as those encountered by stenographers, carpenters, and cooks. Designed to discover how effectively an individual will perform under specific conditions, the performance test indicates nothing about an applicant's potential. A major disadvantage of this type of test is that it is time-consuming and often expensive to administer.

Veterans' Preference. Since World War I, public jurisdictions

---

[12] For a perceptive discussion of personality tests, see William Whyte, *The Organization Man,* Simon and Schuster, New York, 1956, Chapter 15.

generally have followed the practice of giving priority to persons who have served honorably in the nation's armed forces.[13] A variety of methods have been used to implement this policy, but the most widespread has been to add a number of points to the veteran's examination score—usually five or ten. Disabled veterans are given more "bonus" points than those who are not handicapped. Preferred practice dictates that extra points shall be added only to passing scores, although they are sometimes added to all test results. Veterans, particularly those who are disabled, may be accorded preference ahead of all other applicants, after they have passed entrance examinations.

Controversy has centered around the use of veterans' preference. Viewpoints on the issue often are founded on emotions rather than impartial analysis. The nature of the problem has been well stated by O. G. Stahl: "In essence there are two basic philosophies underlying veteran preference in public employment: (1) the idea of preference as a continuing reward for service to the country and (2) the concept of preference as a readjustment aid to help veterans adjust to civilian life."[14] In terms of their consequences for public employment, these views are quite different. If the reward idea is accepted, the veteran is accorded a permanent privilege insofar as public employment is concerned. This practice is subject to criticism from many standpoints, not the least of which is the fact that it is diametrically opposed to the idea that civil service employment should be on the basis of merit as evidenced by fitness to fill a position and by potential for future growth. Acceptance of the readjustment concept implies the granting of such privilege only on a temporary basis, and its implications are consequently not so serious from the standpoint of efficient personnel management.[15]

Certification and Appointment. Following examinations, the names of those who have "passed" are placed on lists along with the scores received. Appointments are made from these lists of *eligibles.* When a vacancy exists, a *requisition* is forwarded to the agency

---

[13] The practice of granting preference to veterans has long been used in this country. However, it did not become widely established by law until the period following World War I.

[14] O. G. Stahl, *Public Personnel Administration,* Harper & Brothers, New York, 1956, p. 130.

[15] The Personnel Task Force of the second Hoover Commission suggested a five-year limitation on veterans' preference. *Task Force Report on Personnel and Civil Service,* Washington, D.C., 1949, pp. 114–115. This recommendation was not included in the Commission report.

responsible for maintaining the lists, and the names of a number of eligibles are *certified* to the appointing authority. The number of eligibles that may be certified at any one time is usually limited by law, with the most common restriction being the "rule of three." According to this rule, only the names of the three persons receiving the highest scores on the examination for a particular type of job are certified. In some jurisdictions only the top person on the list may be certified, a practice that places great faith in the accuracy of the examining process; in others a larger number may be certified. Usually the appointing authority may reject the first list "for cause" and request another group of eligibles. "For cause" implies that he must give some reasonable explanation of his rejection. Although this procedure may be abused, some flexibility is desirable to diminish the likelihood of appointing persons who will be "misfits" because of working conditions peculiar to a particular position.

Sometimes when a vacancy occurs no current eligibility list exists for that position. It is impossible to maintain lists of eligibles for all possible openings at any one time, perhaps with the exception of classifications in which there are a large number of positions characterized by a relatively high turnover, such as clerks and typists. Consequently, provision is normally made for *provisional* or temporary appointments until examinations are held and applicants qualify. Unless constant vigilance is exercised, temporary appointments may become permanent, even in the absence of satisfactory performance. Of course, such temporary appointees should be given the opportunity to take the appropriate examinations and qualify as permanent appointees.

The Man on the Job

Orientation. It is common practice for a new appointee to undergo a *probationary* period of six or twelve months during which he is "on trial" to determine his suitability for the job. At any time during this period his services may be terminated. Good personnel management requires that the new employee be observed carefully and *oriented* to his position. Public jurisdictions are often negligent with regard to these matters—even more so than private employers. The attitude of a new employee toward his job and his fellow workers may be determined largely by the manner in which he is introduced to them. Haphazard orientation is not conducive to enthusiasm, and time consumed in an adequate program of orientation is well invested. The probationary period may well be considered essential to adequate selection procedure. Responsibility for its success rests with those who directly supervise new employees.

Evaluation of Performance. Adequate determination of the effectiveness of each employee relative to the demands of his job is very difficult. Few aspects of personnel management have caused more dissatisfaction. A huge variety of methods and devices have been used to measure job effectiveness, but no generally satisfactory scheme has been devised.[16] Distrust and skepticism relative to "merit ratings" is widespread, and the obvious fallibility of many systems provides some justification for such an attitude. The failure of many rating procedures to produce the desired results has motivated the proposal that they be abandoned. Such a simple solution to the problem is not feasible because *everyone who manages people performs the act of rating.* The act may be formalized or completely informal and irregular. Evaluations may be based on conscientious efforts to assess the quality of an individual's work and his value to the service, or they may be founded entirely on personal prejudice. The alternative to formalized systems of rating is dependence on judgment unguided by formal criteria.

Merit ratings should not serve as the *sole* basis for personnel actions, including promotions, transfers, salary changes, layoffs, and discharges. Even though they may not provide a "scientific" basis for such actions, ratings may be administered in such a manner that those concerned will *feel* that emphasis is placed on fairness and impartiality. Beyond question, evaluation devices may help to identify factors pertinent to an employee's effectiveness and focus attention on his strengths and weaknesses. Such information may be used in setting up training programs and indicating to each individual how he may obtain the greatest benefit from them. In any event, it is imperative that the results of ratings *not* be filed away and seldom, if ever, consulted. If they are, employee evaluation becomes a routine task, performed as quickly as possible with a minimum of effort and reflection.

Promotions and Transfers. A major deterrent to effective personnel management is a feeling among many employees that there is "no place to go." The incentive of advancement resulting from superior qualifications and performance is significant for efficiency. Although many difficulties are inevitably encountered in its estab-

---

[13] Such devices are commonly called "service ratings," "efficiency ratings," "merit ratings," or "performance reports."

lishment and application, a *definite promotion policy* is vastly superior to the practice of considering promotions individually as the opportunities arise. Such a policy is often opposed because it limits the opportunity for arbitrary discretion on the part of administrators.

When promotions in a small jurisdiction or a small agency are limited to personnel already employed, opportunities may be unnecessarily limited. Under such a policy an employee is forced to forego opportunities for higher positions in other agencies or governmental units. Although some value may be attached to familiarity with administrative procedures and the personnel of an agency, the advantages of familiarity are often overemphasized. "It is the general growth, the ability to meet situations that arise, the training in the general duties of the line of work, and the breadth of vision that count . . . ; the preliminary knowledge of the special details of administrative procedure, personnel, subject matter, layout and records is of minor importance in comparison."[17] On the other hand, the hostile reaction sometimes felt by the "old hands" toward a newcomer placed over them cannot be disregarded. As a rule, it is best to give first consideration to qualified persons already part of a working unit. When no such persons are available, the machinery should be geared for the transfer of a qualified person from another unit.

The use of *promotional examinations* is common in large jurisdictions operating under civil service. Although these examinations may test with reasonable accuracy the knowledge necessary to perform duties associated with a particular position, they have not yet succeeded in measuring capacity for administrative responsibility and personality traits that may be important. Promotional exams should, and usually do, include not only formal, written portions, but also an evaluation of an employee's record and experience. In combination such procedures are not entirely satisfactory, but they may be administered with better results than can be obtained by informal selection.

Although *seniority* is seldom relied upon exclusively, it should be given serious consideration along with other factors when a promotion is contemplated. Emphasis on seniority is favored generally by employees, and their viewpoint is not without foundation. Reliance on seniority reduces discord and favoritism in that it is

---

[17] International City Managers' Association, *Municipal Personnel Administration*, Chicago, 1950, p. 174.

most subject to accurate, impartial measurement. Too great emphasis on this factor, however, may produce complacency and result in the advancement of mediocrity. The basic difficulty in the use of seniority as the ground for advancement is that it can reflect only quantity, not quality, of service. Used in combination with a reasonably good rating system, seniority should be given weight in a promotional program. Where the number of persons eligible to fill a vacancy is quite large, formal examinations may also be desirable.

Transfers not involving change in rank are generally used ineffectively in public jurisdictions. Nevertheless, they may be useful in meeting a variety of personnel problems such as getting employees out of "blind alley" jobs, counteracting major fluctuations in work loads, alleviating personal frictions, relieving monotony, and implementing training programs. Although the management of a large administrative unit may be able to develop a good internal program of transfers, such action should be taken in cooperation with the central personnel agency.

Compensation. In spite of the difficulties that inevitably arise in determining salaries and wages, it is imperative that some *plan* be developed and administered as fairly as possible. If this goal is to be accomplished effectively, cooperation among the legislature, the executive branch, the central personnel agency when one exists, and the employees themselves is essential. In any case a wage plan must be so constructed as to attract and maintain a working force of able, efficient people.

A governmental unit's pay plan must be competitive in relation to those of other jurisdictions, both public and private. Certain disparities have existed traditionally between private and public compensation plans, especially with regard to high-level positions. Salaries and wages for employees performing routine activities in the public service have been much more competitive with private employment. Serious disparities often develop regarding professional, technical, and management personnel—crucial areas from the standpoint of program effectiveness. Low salaries accorded to top-level personnel like department heads tend to "freeze" the compensation of subordinates. Thus a public health department may experience difficulty obtaining doctors because of the low salary provided for the director of public health.

Not only should a pay plan be competitive, it should also be internally consistent. In some ways, this is the more crucial require-

FULL-TIME PUBLIC EMPLOYEES, BY LEVEL OF GOVERNMENT AND ANNUAL RATE OF PAY
OCTOBER, 1962

Level of Government	Total	Annual Rate of Pay							Median annual rate
		Less than $1,800	$1,800 to $2,999	$3,000 to $4,199	$4,200 to $5,399	$5,400 to $6,599	$6,600 to $7,799	$7,800 or more	
Number (1,000)									
Total	8,084	267	647	1,517	2,307	1,626	820	897	$5,246
Federal (civilian)	2,415	82	43	279	809	616	262	324	5,390
State and local	5,669	185	604	1,283	1,498	1,010	558	573	4,841
State	1,404	26	204	410	316	176	105	170	4,413
Teachers	121	—	2	2	9	20	24	64	7,971
Other	1,284	26	202	408	307	156	81	105	4,224
Local	4,264	159	401	826	1,184	836	454	403	4,964
Teachers	1,666	2	20	178	522	434	267	244	5,680
Other	2,598	157	381	648	662	402	187	159	4,391
Percent									
Total	100.0	3.3	8.0	18.8	28.5	20.1	10.1	11.1	—
Federal (civilian)	100.0	3.4	1.8	11.6	33.5	25.5	10.8	13.4	—
State and local	100.0	3.3	10.7	21.8	26.4	17.8	9.8	10.1	—
State	100.0	1.9	14.5	29.2	22.5	12.5	7.5	12.1	—
Teachers	100.0	—	1.7	1.7	7.4	16.5	19.8	52.9	—
Other	100.0	2.0	15.7	31.8	23.9	12.1	6.3	8.2	—
Local	100.0	3.7	9.4	19.4	27.8	19.6	10.6	9.5	—
Teachers	100.0	0.1	1.2	10.7	31.3	26.1	16.0	14.6	—
Other	100.0	6.0	14.7	24.9	25.5	15.5	7.2	6.1	—

Source: Bureau of the Census.

ment insofar as the majority of employees are concerned. An employee may not be aware of the pay received by his counterpart in some other jurisdiction, but very probably he will be aware of the compensation of fellow employees. Pay inequities are regrettable, but the implication of unfairness on the part of management that stems from them is even more serious for morale. Small, regular pay increases granted to competent employees until they reach the top of their grade are advisable. In addition, provision must be made for special increases given in recognition of exceptional merit.

Other Incentives. The level of compensation is recognized as a major incentive to good work, but other important ones should not be overlooked. Employees are much concerned about such matters as hours of work, vacations, leaves, suggestion programs, grievance procedures, and retirement provisions. In most jurisdictions with civil service, hours of work, vacations, and leaves have been largely standardized. Reasonably liberal policies in these areas help to offset inadequacies in pay. Vacation periods ranging from two to four weeks per year depending on length of service are common. Government policies with regard to vacations are often more liberal than those in private employment.

Properly handled, *suggestion systems* constitute a valuable aspect of personnel management. They encourage employees to take a greater interest in their work, especially when arrangements are provided to give awards and other types of recognition to persons who initiate good ideas. Even when individual suggestions are not adopted, the opportunity to "let off steam" is valuable. Adequate provisions often are not made for the formal handling of employee grievances. Statements to the effect that employees should feel free at all times to go to their superiors with their problems are not realistic. Such procedure is obviously inadequate when an employee believes that his superiors are largely responsible for his troubles, regardless of the truth of his conviction.

"Until the 1930's the separation of employees from the public service by reason of age, disability, or death was handled in a haphazard, often in an unjust and unintelligent manner."[18] Consequently, "payroll pensioners" were retained on the job or allowed to become public charges, and employees injured in the line of duty became objects of charity. Passage of the federal Social Security Act in 1935 provided great impetus toward improvement in public re-

---

[18] O. G. Stahl, *op. cit.*, p. 480.

tirement practices in order that they might be somewhat competitive with private employment.[19] Most states now have retirement programs covering all full-time personnel, many of them participating in the national Old Age and Survivors Insurance system. All states have retirement programs covering selected groups of employees. A somewhat comparable situation exists on the local level, but small jurisdictions operate under a severe handicap because of an insufficient number of employees to establish a sound retirement program. Statewide systems in which small communities may participate are highly desirable.

When both the employer and the employee make formal contributions toward the employee's retirement, the system is said to be *contributory*. Most public retirement programs today are of this type. When such responsibility rests solely on the employer, the system is termed *noncontributory*. These systems may operate under the *cash-disbursement* plan, in which money is appropriated by the government during each fiscal period to cover the benefit payments anticipated during that time. The longer the plan is in existence, the larger the appropriations must be. Others are administered by means of an *actuarial reserve*, or "pay-as-you-go" plan, in which contributions are made regularly to a fund that is built up for each employee during his years of employment. Money in this reserve is then invested, and the contributions and earnings are figured to anticipate and provide for future retirement payments as well as withdrawals resulting from changes in employment and death. In the more adequate systems, retirement payments average about fifty per cent of an employee's income over a specified period of time, such as the last five or ten years of employment. Membership in retirement systems usually is compulsory for all eligible employees.

Employee Conduct. The position of a government worker differs from that of other persons because in a sense he is a repository of public faith and trust. Accordingly, the public employee's attitudes and behavior are more subject to popular reproach than is the conduct of the ordinary citizen, and the seriousness of his ethical and moral deviations is magnified. General distrust and suspicion of

---

[19] Retirement systems existed much earlier in some states and municipalities. Massachusetts adopted the first general state retirement law in 1911, followed by Connecticut, Maine, New York, New Jersey, and Pennsylvania during the succeeding dozen years. The first municipal pension fund was established for New York City policemen in 1857. All of the early systems applied only to selected groups of employees.

government may result, at least temporarily, from one or a few instances of unwise conduct in the public service.

Every government has the unquestioned right to specify in detail the conduct expected of its employees *on the job*. Attempts to regulate conduct *off the job* are different. Illegal conduct cannot be condoned. Efforts to require private conduct on the part of public employees that is significantly different from that expected of people in general tends to place public servants in a category apart, an undesirable situation in a democratic society. Potential recruits to the public service may hesitate to place themselves in such a position.

A major problem of public employees, particularly those under civil service, is the extent to which they may participate, if at all, in political activity. *Political neutrality* on the part of civil servants in the performance of their duties is generally considered desirable. At the same time, participation in public affairs by interested and informed citizens strengthens democratic institutions. Logic dictates that some of those most able to participate intelligently are among public servants. The basic query is, To what extent are public employees to be limited politically? No easy answer to this question, whether positive or negative, can withstand critical analysis.[20]

Through the Hatch Acts and other requirements, the national government has made strenuous efforts to "neutralize" federal civil servants.[21] Most state and local governments have not found it necessary or wise to go so far, although civil service laws generally provide some restrictions on the political activities of employees. "Most laws, however, do not expressly prohibit political activities of their public employees, though many expressly prohibit 'enforced' or compulsory political activities."[22] Discretion should be the rule. Some limitations on political activity are desirable, but too great severity makes public employment unattractive to many persons who are vitally interested in public affairs. "The end to be achieved is prohibiting solely offensive partisan political activity clearly inimical to the public interest."[23]

Training. Although training programs for public employees are

---

[20] See Leon D. Epstein, "Political Sterilization of Civil Servants: The United States and Great Britain," *Public Administration Review,* Autumn 1950; and Wallace S. Sayre, "Political Neutrality," in *Public Management in the New Democracy,* Fritz M. Marx, ed., Harper & Brothers, New York, 1940.

[21] Provisions of the Hatch Acts extend to state and local personnel paid from federal funds.

[22] H. Eliot Kaplan, *The Law of Civil Service,* Matthew Bender & Co., New York, 1958, p. 343.

[23] *Ibid.,* p. 350.

frequently neglected, "no program of personnel administration can be considered complete or balanced unless it gives as much attention to the development of its employees as it does to their selection or to their separation from the service."[24] Conceived broadly, training occurs regularly as a result of increased familiarity and facility with the duties of a position. In the usual sense, training is apart from routine work. The basic steps in a formal training program are: (1) identification of needs, (2) development of programs and choice of techniques of execution, (3) implementation of program, and (4) checking on reactions and results.

In spite of its importance, formal training has been traditionally neglected in public jurisdictions, much more so than in large private concerns. Reliance has been placed on the costly practice of learning by doing. Today many varieties of programs and techniques are included under the term *in-service training*. Formal courses, institutes, demonstrations, apprenticeships, and internships are included, to name only a few. Especially valuable are programs designed to improve opportunities for promotion. Development and implementation of such undertakings in large jurisdictions require the services of specially trained persons, for whose salaries legislatures often are unwilling to appropriate money. A successful training program requires cooperation from all concerned, not only the efforts of training specialists.

Once a program has been organized, employees must be motivated to avail themselves of training opportunities. In general, they should *not* be required to participate. If top management is sold on training, little difficulty is likely to be experienced in this regard. Failure on the part of an employee to participate may be officially noted as indicating a lack of interest and initiative, factors relative to such personnel actions as merit increases and promotions.

Morale. Although morale is an elusive concept, it may be defined as an attitude that causes individuals and groups to evidence confidence and zeal in accomplishing a goal or program. O. G. Stahl has stressed the importance of "developing among the employees of an organization a *sense of 'belonging'* and a *sense of unity of purpose* which combine to maintain what all of us can understand but rarely see, namely, *high morale*."[25] The morale of an organization reflects the quality of management.

The more progressive segments of private industry have long

---

[24] International City Managers' Association, *op. cit.,* p. 136.
[25] *Op. cit.,* p. 245.

recognized the importance of creating and maintaining high morale, and much time and money have been spent on efforts to promote it. Little comparable effort has been exerted in government. Numerous studies have been made to identify specifically the factors on which the morale of a group normally depends. Among the more important are (1) confidence and understanding that individual members have in regard to the purposes and objectives of the group, (2) confidence in leadership, (3) confidence members of a group feel in each other, (4) efficiency of the group, and (5) the mental, emotional, and physical health of members. All of these combine to create a "will to work."

Since morale is largely a matter of attitudes, a program of morale-building must be founded on knowledge of actual feelings and beliefs. Public jurisdictions have failed almost universally to exert a serious effort to measure morale. The common practice has been to rely upon impressions when more accurate methods have been available, particularly in recent years. *Attitude surveys* provide much more definite information about the status of morale in an organization than is obtainable through guesses. Known by a variety of names, these surveys are available from a number of organizations devoted to research in personnel management. Such surveys, widely used in private industry, are "a means of analyzing not the employees but the effectiveness of management and supervision, the training programs, the communications, the plans and policies of a company."[26]

REMOVING THE "WRONG" PEOPLE

Necessity for Occasional Removals. In all organizations, regardless of the care with which employees are selected, it is sometimes necessary to remove incumbents from their positions. Contrary to a popular misconception, civil service employees are frequently discharged at all levels of government. Uninformed persons may assert that it is impossible to dismiss someone who has "tenure" under civil service, but the fact is that "Few jurisdictions do not have adequate provisions for forced separation when the work situation demands it."[27] Stress should be placed on the feasibility of removals *when the work situation demands them.*

It is true that unregulated, unrestricted "firing" of employees under civil service is generally not permitted. Civil service laws are

---

[26] American Management Association, *Management Review*, June 1955, p. 388.
[27] O. G. Stahl, *op. cit.*, p. 454.

designed to guarantee that persons shall be recruited, examined, appointed, paid, and promoted with careful regard for job responsibilities. It is only logical that the same principle apply to dismissals. Consequently, laws and regulations stipulate that certain procedural requirements be observed in discharging employees, both for their benefit and for the benefit of the service.

Open vs. Closed Back Door. Most jurisdictions set forth at some length the procedural requirements that must be followed in removals, including formal, written notice stating the grounds for discharge, and an opportunity for a hearing. Civil service laws normally require review of dismissals allegedly made on racial, political, or religious grounds, and they empower central personnel agencies to reinstate any employee whom they find was removed on such grounds. When employees are dismissed "for cause" as required by law and no questions pertaining to race, politics, or religion are raised, authority to make the final decision may be vested either with the employing agency or with the central personnel agency. If final responsibility rests with the employing agency, the *open back door* is said to exist; if it rests with the central agency, the arrangement is referred to as the *closed back door*.

Even with the open back door it is possible for a central personnel agency to review cases of removal "for cause." Where this procedure is provided, the function of the agency is to consider the sufficiency of the stipulated grounds for discharge and to make recommendations as to the best course of action. Responsibility for the final decision rests, nevertheless, with the employing agency. The open back door is generally preferred by operating officials, and good administrative practice dictates that the final decision as to removals should rest with them. Quite naturally, employees tend to prefer the closed back door because it provides them with additional protection against possible arbitrary action. Despite opinions often voiced to the contrary, the fact is that "in general, appeals systems have resulted more often in the upholding than in the undermining of the authority of removing officers."[28]

Transfers. Circumstances indicating a need to move an employee from a particular position may not justify dismissal. Instead, a change of surroundings may be in order, and a *transfer* may serve the purpose admirably. In this way an employee may move to an-

---

[28] *Ibid.*, p. 459.

other position in his same class situated in another organizational unit. Unfortunately, transfers without change in rank are generally not used effectively in public jurisdictions. This fact is explained in part by the reluctance of a supervisor to accept someone who is transferred from another position because of the implication of lack of success in the former job. Such prejudice may be decreased by a program of regular, planned transfers among agencies for the benefit of employees, who may in this way increase their potential for advancement. Personnel in small agencies are especially handicapped by a lack of opportunity to transfer and in this way avail themselves of promotional opportunities elsewhere.

EMPLOYEE ORGANIZATION

Importance of Organization. Free men tend to combine in order to further their interests and objectives. Public employees are no different in this regard, in spite of a widespread feeling that they should be. A major function of personnel management is to establish a cooperative relationship with employee organizations and attempt to arrive at solutions to any clashes and disagreements that occur. The rapid increase in the number and size of organizations among public employees in recent years reflects a general feeling that their common interests and needs can best be met through organized effort.

Although the detailed objectives of public employee organizations differ from time to time and place to place, certain major categories may be identified: (1) establishing and strengthening the merit and career concepts, (2) emphasis on seniority and tenure, (3) improvements in wages and hours, (4) more adequate retirement programs, (5) improved machinery for handling grievances, and (6) a variety of minor "fringe benefits." All of these are entirely legitimate objectives, and their realization results in making the public service more attractive.[29]

One of the major concerns of many public employee organizations has been more widespread recognition of the importance of merit and career practices. Many such organizations have lobbied before legislative bodies for improvements in personnel practices. (It must be admitted, however, that their programs have been motivated sometimes by selfish interests contrary to best personnel practices.) Also, employee groups have functioned to bring atten-

---

[29] For an excellent examination of the role of employee organizations in the public service, see O. G. Stahl, *op. cit.*, Chapter 12.

tion to legitimate grievances of public employees. Complaints supported by organizations representing large numbers of employees and presented by competent people are more likely to receive favorable consideration by legislators and the public in general than the "gripes" of individuals.

Right to Strike. Strikes by federal employees are forbidden by law. Similar legislation is found in some states and localities, but a policy of silence has been observed in most jurisdictions. This situation is probably explained by the fact that "A study of judicial decisions relating to the right of public employees to strike . . . leads to the conclusion that there is no inherent right to strike against the government, and it would appear that a statute prohibiting such strikes is unnecessary."[30] Furthermore, the constitutions of many public employee organizations explicitly disavow the use of the strike.

In spite of legal restrictions and unsympathetic public opinion, a number of strikes by public employees have occurred.[31] Their relatively small number attests to the truth of the assertion that "The public employee strike is nearly always a measure of desperation; if conditions are sufficiently bad, it will be resorted to, whether or not its use is legally recognized."[32] Arguments advanced against permitting public employees to strike usually stress the sovereign nature of government and the urgency of its functions. Emphasis on sovereignty in this context harks back to the outmoded concept that "the king can do no wrong." The alleged life-or-death character of all governmental activities is refuted by L. D. White:

> The inconvenience caused by a public service strike . . . is not necessarily so great as that which would be involved in a stoppage in some privately managed undertakings. A strike on the nation's railroads . . . would bring instant disaster to the whole country . . . a strike of milk handlers would be as grave as a strike of almost any group of municipal employees. The relative inconvenience of a strike of street maintenance men, or of public welfare case workers, or of seamen on a government-owned barge line is clearly less.[33]

[30] H. Eliot Kaplan, *op. cit.,* p. 325.
[31] See David Ziskind, *One Thousand Strikes of Government Employees,* Columbia University Press, New York, 1940.
[32] O. G. Stahl, *op. cit.,* p. 308.
[33] L. D. White, "Strikes in the Public Service," *Public Personnel Review,* January 1949.

A realistic distinction between those workers who may strike and those who may not must rest on the nature of their work rather than on the nature of their employer. Whether in private industry or the public service, the potential dangers and discomforts associated with strikes can be forestalled by good personnel management. Equitable working conditions, a spirit of teamwork between employees and management, recognition of the right of collective representation by employees of their needs, and adequate grievance procedures are far more effective in building an efficient organization than restrictive measures designed to curtail employee activities.

ORGANIZATION FOR CENTRAL PERSONNEL MANAGEMENT

Bipartisan Commission. Where general civil service laws exist, responsibility for personnel management is divided between a central agency and operating or "line" agencies. Impetus for this arrangement stemmed originally from the desire to remove personnel administration from "politics." The belief was that this goal could be best accomplished by creating an independent commission that could withstand attacks from spoilsmen. Consequently, the *bipartisan commission* or *board* is the traditional and still dominant organizational pattern for central personnel management. Commission members in most instances are appointed by the chief executive with senatorial approval for long terms, staggered to promote continuity of policy and to curtail control by the appointing authority.

Conceived to implement the negative goal of "keeping the rascals out of public office," bipartisan commissions undoubtedly have contributed much to the improvement of public personnel management. They have several weaknesses, however, that tend to make them ill-suited to implement the modern emphasis on positive objectives that necessitate strong leadership. In this regard, attention is usually directed to the emphasis on political allegiance in choosing members, and the inevitable lack of expert knowledge of personnel matters on the part of commissioners, often resulting in indecision and lack of decisive action. With effort these difficulties can be largely overcome, but a serious, often neglected problem remains, namely, inadequacy of time available to the commissioners. Standard practice has been that commissioners are chosen from among persons who have achieved prominence in some field such as law, education, or mass communication. They are busy people who may experience difficulty in allocating sufficient time to a sideline—even an important one like serving on a civil service commission which may meet only twice a month. Consequently, the knowledge and leadership needed to meet personnel problems are not forthcoming.

Obviously, such multimembered bodies cannot administer directly the details of personnel management. In order to meet this need, commissions follow the practice of appointing someone, often called a director, to administer their policies and all pertinent laws. The director may be required by law to be a "career person" in the sense that he must have demonstrated competence in the field of personnel management or he may be chosen for other abilities that he possesses. In any event, the duties of such a position require impartiality and nonpartisanship as well as technical competence if civil service is to function most effectively.

Single Director. Under the single director arrangement, central administration of personnel matters is lodged entirely in one man appointed by and responsible to the chief executive. Although found in a few localities and in Illinois and Maryland, this organizational pattern has not been widely adopted. The main arguments in its favor are that it centralizes personnel management under the chief executive and facilitates quickness of action when necessary. It is argued that by placing responsibility with the chief executive, leadership is facilitated. Thus, if the governor favors a program to improve the compensation of civil servants, the position of *his* personnel director is greatly strengthened with the public, the legislature, and especially with members of the governor's party.

Single Director with Commission. The Model State Civil Service Law advances a proposal designed to combine the advantages of both of the structural patterns described above and at the same time to overcome their weaknesses.[34] Provision is made in the Model Law for a civil service commission composed of three members appointed by the governor for staggered terms of six years. Commissioners may be removed by the governor "for cause" following an opportunity for public hearing. A director of personnel, appointed to an indefinite term by the governor upon recommendation of the commission, may be removed by the commission "for cause" following opportunity for a hearing.

---

[34] The Model Law has been issued in several editions by the National Civil Service League and the National Municipal League and has been influential in shaping civil service laws in several states.

In the Model Law provision is made for only partial separation of administrative responsibilities from those usually designated as *quasi-legislative* and *quasi-judicial*. The director is the chief administrative officer under the chief executive, and he is required to see that the laws, rules, and regulations governing civil service are faithfully executed. He has responsibility for formulating the rules and regulations as well as administering them. Such rules and regulations must be submitted to the commission for approval, becoming effective within thirty days unless disapproved. Thus the quasi-legislative task of rulemaking is shared between the director and the commission.

The quasi-judicial role of the commission stems from its authority to hear appeals by employees who have been dismissed, demoted, or suspended for more than thirty days. If the commission finds that the action was based on racial, political, or religious grounds, the employee must be reinstated. In all other cases, the findings and recommendations of the commission must be considered by the appointing authority, with whom the final decision rests. If the appointing authority dismisses an employee whose removal is disapproved by the commission, it may order his name placed on an appropriate reemployment list.

It is impossible to say that any one form of organization for personnel management is universally preferable. The most desirable type depends upon the major functions that the central agency is supposed to perform. Also, the total environment in which the system must operate requires consideration. Local attitudes, beliefs, practices, and customs vitally affect the way in which any system operates. If emphasis is on negative "police" functions, the bipartisan board or commission may serve satisfactorily, assuming appointment by the board of someone competent to administer the activities required by law. Whenever the need is for a "positive" program designed to attack and solve operational problems, a single director appointed by the chief executive and assisted by a commission created to hear appeals and to participate in rulemaking presents an attractive alternative. Under such an arrangement, it is especially important for chief executives to pledge unqualified determination to maintain an effective public service through support of the merit idea. This consideration further emphasizes the importance of competent, well-informed chief executives.

SELECTED REFERENCES

Books:

Civil Service Assembly, *Position Classification in the Public Service,* Chicago, 1941.

Godine, Morton R., *The Labor Problem in the Public Service,* Harvard University Press, Cambridge, 1951.

Goode, Cecil E., *Personnel Research Frontiers,* Public Personnel Association, Chicago, 1958.

Hoslett, Schuyler D., editor, *Human Factors in Management,* Harper and Bros., New York, 1951.

International City Managers' Association, *Municipal Personnel Administration,* Chicago, 1950.

Kaplan, H. Elliot, *The Law of Civil Service,* Matthew Bender and Co., New York, 1958.

Maddox, Russell W., Jr., *Issues in State and Local Government,* D. Van Nostrand Co., Inc., Princeton, N.J., 1965.

Powell, Norman J., *Personnel Administration in Government,* Prentice-Hall, Inc., Englewood Cliffs, New Jersey, 1956.

Stahl, O. Glenn, *Public Personnel Administration,* Harper and Bros., New York, 1962.

Strauss, George, and Sayles, Leonard R., *Personnel: The Human Problems of Management,* Prentice-Hall, Inc., Englewood Cliffs, New Jersey, 1960.

Ziskind, David, *One Thousand Strikes of Government Employees,* Columbia University Press, New York, 1940.

Articles:

Aronson, Albert H., "Promise and Performance," *Public Personnel Review,* January 1957.

Clapp, Gordon R., "What Price Ability in the Public Service?" *Personnel Administration,* May 1948.

Epstein, Leon D., "Political Sterilization of Civil Servants: The United States and Great Britain," *Public Administration Review,* Autumn 1950.

Nigro, Felix A., "The Modern Concept of Personnel Administration," *Public Personnel Review,* July 1957.

Pfiffner, John M., "The Personnel Function in Government," *Public Personnel Review,* October 1956.

Stahl, O. Glenn, "Outdated Political Activity Rules Unfair to Employees," *Public Management,* January 1965.

White, Leonard D., "Strikes in the Public Service," *Public Personnel Review,* January 1949.

CHAPTER 18

The Nature and Legal Position of Local Governments

While the spotlight of citizen interest focuses on national and international affairs and shines less intensely on the activities of state governments, the functions of local governments may be obscured in the shadows. Many factors combine to produce this situation, not the least of which is a difference in the dramatic quality of the tasks involved. "No incumbent mayor or city councilman will ever sign a treaty of peace ending all war; no city engineer will ever build a hydrogen bomb; no police chief will ever command a victorious United Nations Army; but these local officials . . . will determine whether the several communities in which we live will remain relatively civilized and decent."[1] People tend to take their local governments for granted and to forget that they provide such essential services as public education, welfare and health programs, utilities, streets and roads, fire and police protection, airports, and waste disposal. Without these local activities, the nature of American society would be drastically altered. Hardly anyone would maintain that the change would be an improvement.

Interest in local affairs occasionally becomes very strong. As a result of outbursts of civic virtue and the strenuous efforts of small groups of practical reformers, tremendous improvements have highlighted the history of local government during the twentieth century. Lincoln Steffens wrote of widespread municipal corruption in 1902 and 1903, and he concluded that the greatest need was an awakening of the people's conscience.[2] Stirred by the disclosures of Steffens and other "muckrakers" and spurred on by the efforts of groups dedicated

---

[1] S. K. Bailey, H. D. Samuel, and S. Baldwin, *Government in America*, Holt-Rinehart-Winston, New York, 1957, p. 455.

[2] Written as a series of articles in *McClure's Magazine,* Steffens' observations were published in the well known volume entitled *The Shame of the Cities*, McClure, Phillips and Co., New York, 1904.

to civic reform, the people demanded and obtained improvements in municipal government. Graft, corruption, and bribery still exist, but they are no longer regarded as inevitable accompaniments of local government.

What Is a "Unit of Local Government?" According to the U.S. Bureau of the Census, a unit of local government must exhibit three qualifications. First, it must exist as an *organized entity*, possessing organization and some minimum powers such as the right to enter contracts and own property. Second, it must have *governmental character* as an agency of the public, to whom it must be accountable. Its officers must be elected or appointed by elected officials. Third, it must possess *substantial autonomy*, particularly as reflected in the right to prepare a budget and raise the revenue necessary to meet it.[3] In his study of governmental units, Professor Anderson has identified seven characteristics: (1) territory, (2) population, (3) organization, (4) separate legal identity, (5) a degree of legal independence, (6) authority to exercise governmental powers, and (7) the power to raise revenue.[4] Viewed in the light of *all* these requirements, administrative areas such as judicial districts, election districts, police precincts, and city wards do not qualify as "governmental units."

NUMBER AND VARIETY OF LOCAL UNITS

The serious study of local government is greatly complicated by the multiplicity of units. In January, 1962, the Bureau of the Census counted 91,236 units of local government in the United States. This figure included 3,043 counties, 17,997 municipalities, 17,144 towns and townships, 34,678 school districts, and 18,323 other special districts.[5] Between 1952 and 1962 the number of local units declined about twenty-two per cent; since 1942 there has been a significant decrease of more than forty per cent. These decreases are attributable entirely to a steady reduction in the number of school districts

---

[3] United States Department of Commerce, Bureau of the Census, *U.S. Census of Governments: 1957,* Vol. I, No. 3, Local Government Structure, Washington, D.C., 1957, p. 3.

[4] William Anderson, *The Units of Local Government in the United States,* Public Administration Service, No. 83, Chicago, 1949, pp. 8–10.

[5] Bureau of the Census, *Census of Governments: 1962,* Vol. I, *Governmental Organization,* Washington, D. C., 1963, p. 1. Counted by the Bureau of the Census as townships are fifty-six organized "plantations" in Maine.

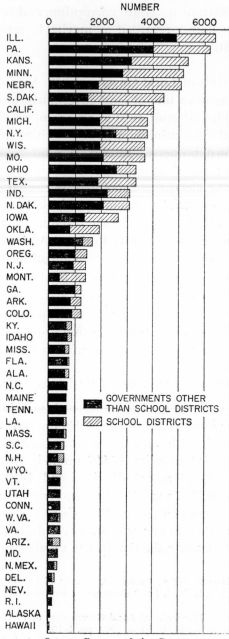

NUMBER OF LOCAL GOVERNMENTS, BY STATES: 1962

through consolidation. Understanding the nature of these local governments requires a brief examination of each type.[6]

Counties. Most people in the United States live within the boundaries of a county. No organized counties exist in Alaska, Connecticut, Rhode Island, and the District of Columbia. Also, the inhabitants of some two dozen of the larger cities in Virginia are not subject to county government. Although counties are primarily units of rural government, they regularly provide services to urban dwellers. In legal terminology, counties often are designated as "quasi-municipal corporations," reflecting their nature as administrative subdivisions of a state, created to administer functions of statewide concern, such as law enforcement, justice, and welfare. Since counties also provide services primarily of interest to their residents, such as libraries, recreational facilities, and record maintenance, they partake of the nature of a municipality.

Although counties are found almost everywhere in the United States, they are not uniformly important. New England counties perform very limited functions because of the primacy of the town. In about one third of the states, located in the northern portion of the country, counties share their responsibilities with townships. In the South and the West the county has no peer as a unit of rural local government.

Municipalities. No precise, universally accepted definition of "municipality" or "municipal corporation" exists. The Bureau of the Census takes the position that a municipality is an incorporated political subdivision of a state within which a government has been established to provide services for a concentration of population within a defined area. Several implications in this definition need to be spelled out. Like counties, municipalities are political subdivisions of the states in which they are situated. Unlike counties, however, municipalities are organized (incorporated) primarily to provide in specific areas services desired by *concentrations of population*. But municipalities are *not* organized *solely* for this purpose. They also act as agents of the state in providing certain services to their inhabitants, such as law enforcement and health protection. An important consideration with regard to municipal corporations not clearly indicated in the Bureau's definition is that municipalities

---

[6] For detailed information on each type, see the appropriate subsequent chapter.

normally are created at the behest of their residents rather than by the desire of the state legislature.

Cities. Depending on local custom and statutory provisions, municipalities may be known as "cities," "towns," "villages," or "boroughs." The meaning of these terms varies among the states. Larger municipalities everywhere are designated as cities, but the laws of some states provide that all municipal corporations organized in a certain manner shall be known as cities regardless of size. Thus New York is a city, and so is Granite, Oregon, with a 1960 population of two persons. Although laws regularly stipulate that a minimum number of persons must live in a given area before a municipality may be organized, later shifts in population may reduce it to little more than a "ghost town."

Towns. Much confusion is associated with the use of "town." The term sometimes is used to refer to a unit of rural government more properly called a "township." Unincorporated settlements with no governmental organization of their own may be called "towns." The basic units of rural local government in the New England states are "towns."[7] In popular usage in some states, any small municipality may be referred to loosely as a "town." In order to qualify formally as a type of municipality, however, a town must be *incorporated,* that is, certain steps taken as required by law to bring it into legal existence for the purpose of providing services to its inhabitants.

Villages. The smallest of municipalities are commonly known as villages. Indeed, the concentration of population in a village may be so small that it is in reality a unit of rural government. On the other hand, quite populous places may continue to be designated as villages because the official action required for change to some other designation is not taken. Suburban communities, located near large cities, may be organized as villages. Generally, the governmental organization of a village is rather simple, and its powers are less extensive than those of larger municipalities.

Boroughs. In Connecticut, New Jersey, and Pennsylvania, certain small municipalities are designated by law as boroughs. They differ in no essential respects from incorporated towns and villages in other states. Boroughs were established in New Jersey and Pennsylvania during the colonial period and were modeled after the English borough; lawmakers in these states have chosen to continue the use

---

[7] Classified as townships by the Bureau of the Census.

of the term. The first borough was organized in Connecticut in 1800, and about a dozen boroughs now exist there. These units of government are not to be confused with the Alaskan borough, which is a substitute for the county.

Towns and Townships. In almost half of the states there are governmental subdivisions known as towns or townships.[8] Although the Bureau of the Census classifies all of these governments as townships, some distinctions can be made. New England towns generally are not municipal corporations and have been created directly by state statutory provisions. Except for cities, towns are the chief units of local government in the New England states. Their importance stems from the fact that they administer functions performed elsewhere by counties and by small incorporated towns and villages. Consequently, a New England town may function as a unit of rural or urban government and sometimes as both.

In a band of states running westward from New York and New Jersey, townships are significant units of rural government.[9] Although townships occasionally are active in highly urbanized places, particularly in New York, New Jersey, and Pennsylvania, they normally provide a number of services such as roads, poor relief, and property assessment in rural areas. Commonly, such activities are shared with counties. Townships often serve also as election districts. Recent years have witnessed a trend for townships to lose responsibilities to the counties in which they are located.

Special Districts. As the name indicates, a special district is organized for the provision of a *special* function.[10] Hence, a special district is usually a unifunctional unit, providing only one service to the people residing within its boundaries. Occasionally, two or three related functions are provided, such as water and fire protection. Although most special districts are small in area, some are quite large and may include several counties. Great variety in organizational

---

[8] These "civil" townships must be distinguished from *congressional townships*, which are areas for land surveying and are not governments.

[9] These units are called "towns" in New York, but they are functionally like townships in other states and unlike New England towns. The township states are Illinois, Indiana, Kansas, Michigan, Minnesota, Missouri, Nebraska, New Jersey, New York, North Dakota, Ohio, Pennsylvania, South Dakota, Washington, and Wisconsin. Not all the territory of each of these states is divided into townships.

[10] As a result of this characteristic, special districts are sometimes described as *ad hoc* districts, indicating that they are created "for this purpose."

patterns characterize these governmental units, which as a group provide many services, including education, water, sanitation, flood control, street lighting, recreational facilities, and fire protection. All told, special districts account for nearly two-thirds of local governments in the United States.[11]

Complexity of Picture. Because of sheer numbers, local governments present a complicated and confusing picture. Other considerations such as difference in powers, variations in structure, and relations with the parent state and other local units contribute to the difficulties involved in any attempt to describe their nature and their role in relation to the people who live under them. The picture is further complicated by the fact that the typical citizen lives under at least five or six "layers" of government: national, state, county, municipal, town or township, and at least one special district. This number may rise easily to ten or more when several special districts are superimposed. Often the multiplicity of governmental units under which he lives is not appreciated by the average citizen because they do not make comparable impacts upon his consciousness.

The city dweller is constantly aware of the existence of his city because of its ever-present physical manifestations, such as streets, policemen, parks, and water supply. He may at the same time almost forget that he is a county resident because county services are not so important to his day-to-day existence—at least until he receives his tax bill. The urbanite, and perhaps the rural resident, may overlook the activities of a sanitary, park, library, flood control, or utility district in which he lives, thinking that such services are provided by the city or the county. The reality of the typical multiplicity of layers is further obscured by the fact that the citizen commonly receives a consolidated property tax bill from the county, a bill which includes levies imposed by several governmental units. Counties regularly act as collection agencies for governments within their jurisdiction, particularly with regard to the property tax.

The usual pattern of local government across the country is complex, and it is greatly complicated by numerous exceptional situations. A few illustrations are worthy of note. Cities are normally located within counties, both legally and geographically, but the

---

[11] Although counted separately by the Bureau of the Census, school districts are included in this number since they are special districts. Their nature and responsibilities are considered in Chapter 26.

counties of Bronx, Kings, New York, Queens, and Richmond are subdivisions of New York City and are not considered as separate governments. Over thirty "independent" Virginia cities are legally outside counties and constitute "islands" of government surrounded by county areas. Similar situations exist with regard to Baltimore and St. Louis. Although still in existence, Iowa townships are so lacking in functions that they are no longer considered as governmental units. California, Montana, and North Carolina have no township governments, but counties are divided into townships that serve merely as election districts. Michigan cities are outside townships, but villages remain in them. In New England, cities are usually outside towns, while villages are within the jurisdiction of town government.

It is very difficult to acquire complete, detailed knowledge of even a major portion of all local units. It is feasible, however, to obtain sufficient information and insight to understand their general nature, appreciate their importance, and become familiar with their problems. Armed with such knowledge, a citizen is equipped to participate intelligently in the public affairs of his community.

LEGAL STATUS OF LOCAL GOVERNMENTS

Each of the fifty states is a *unitary* government. Consequently, each possesses complete authority and control over local governments within its boundaries. As "creatures of the state," local units are created by and derive their powers from state law, either constitutional or statutory. The accuracy of this observation is more readily apparent in relation to quasi-municipalities than in relation to "true" municipal corporations. The former, particularly counties and townships, function largely as administrative subdivisions of their states.[12] The latter are organized at the behest of local residents and have as their chief responsibility the provision of services to their residents, but they are still created under the authority of state law.[13] The states follow a variety of procedures in the creation of municipal corporations.

---

[12] County home rule, provided in a dozen states, does not significantly modify this basic relationship. In these states, counties are granted by state law more freedom in certain areas, especially with regard to governmental structure. See Chapter 20.

[13] For a classic statement of this rule by the U.S. Supreme Court, see *Barnes* v. *District of Columbia,* 91 U.S. 540 (1875). See also Eugene McQuillin, *The Law of Municipal Corporations,* 3rd ed., Callaghan and Co., Chicago, 1949, sec. 4.03.

CHARTERS

Special Charters. Immediately following independence from England, the first state legislatures assumed responsibility for organizing local governments. Each municipality was organized and granted powers by a separate, special legislative act called a charter. This practice was standard procedure for about three-quarters of a century, and it still exists in about ten states.[14] Although special charters provide flexibility to whatever degree the legislature is willing to sanction, they subject municipalities to regular, continuing, and detailed legislative supervision. Occasionally, legislatures have taken advantage of the opportunity to dictate by controlling local services and such projects as the construction of public buildings.[15] Under this system, state legislatures spend much time in each session considering local matters.

Inadequate, ill-considered, sometimes punitive laws caused a reaction against special laws of all kinds, and most states have included provisions in their constitutions designed to prohibit or severely curb their enactment. Constitutions sometimes prohibit special legislation whenever a general law can be made applicable. A more satisfactory type of restriction, and the one most widely employed, itemizes subjects upon which special laws are specifically forbidden, usually including affairs of local governments. Instead, other methods of organizing and controlling municipal corporations were devised.

General Charters. Reflecting a strong reaction against special local acts, some states went to the opposite extreme and provided that all municipalities should be organized under the same laws. Providing the same form of government and the same powers for all cities prevented discrimination and created uniformity—in fact, too much uniformity. It is not feasible to govern all communities alike. Differences in size produce differences in needs and problems. Governments of large, complex cities require more varied authority than

---

[14] The use of special legislation to provide municipal charters is still common in the New England states, Delaware, Florida, Georgia, and Tennessee. Florida municipalities are also established under general law.

[15] The Louisiana legislature enacted punitive laws directed against New Orleans in 1935 and 1948. See L. L. Moak and H. R. Moak, "The Rape of New Orleans," *National Municipal Review*, September 1949. In 1870, the Pennsylvania legislature decided that Philadelphia should have a new city hall regardless of local opposition and created a commission with power to levy taxes to pay for the edifice.

the governments of small, relatively simple ones. Local preferences vary, and the people in one place may prefer a form of government quite different from that of their neighbors in a nearby community. The needs of some cities may change rapidly while those of others may remain rather static.

Classified Charters. In an effort to give recognition to different local needs, states have adopted plans whereby municipalities, especially cities, are classified into groups on the basis of population. All localities within each class are treated alike, each operating under a charter enacted by the legislature and applicable to all local units within a certain class. For example, the cities of a state might be classified into six groups according to population as follows: I—over 500,000; II—100,000 to 500,000; III—50,000 to 100,000; IV—25,000 to 50,000; V—10,000 to 25,000; VI—under 10,000. All cities within the same group or class would be governed by the same statutory provisions, with those in Class I enjoying greatest authority and those in Class VI the least. Of course, some powers would be common to all, such as regulating traffic, paving streets, and building city halls.

Designed to minimize discrimination and at the same time to provide flexibility, classification systems have proved generally superior to special acts or general charters. Special treatment for individual cities, especially the largest ones in a state, is possible under a classification system. In terms of the six hypothetical classifications set forth in the preceding paragraph, one charter would be applicable only to city A and another applicable only to city B if they were the only cities in groups I and II, respectively. It is possible for a legislature to construct a classification scheme specifically in order to give special attention to certain cities. It is fairly common practice to have the largest city in a state occupying a class by itself, and occasionally a class covers such a small population range—such as 45,000 to 50,000—that only one city is affected.

A basic weakness exists in all schemes for classifying municipalities, even those that are administered in the fairest manner possible. Every such arrangement must be based on the assumption that communities of approximately the same size have similar needs. They may, or they may not. Differing social and economic conditions, rate of growth, and age are illustrative of many factors that impose different demands upon local governments. An allied problem stems from the fact that a city may be required to change its form of government when it moves from one population class to another. Under some circumstances a change may be desirable, but under others it may only serve to disturb well balanced working arrangements.

Optional Charters. A noteworthy modification of traditional classification practices is provided by use of the optional charter. This device, which has been used in a number of states,[16] makes available to all cities, or those within each population group, alternative forms of government that are spelled out in detail by statutory provisions. For example, residents of Class III cities may be able to choose among three types, while the inhabitants of Class I cities may have only two options. The number and variety of choices may be the same for all cities, or they may differ for some or all classes. Sub-options may also be allowed, providing minor variations within a major type. In this way a rather wide range of choices may be available from which the people of each community may choose, but no modifications may be made in any plan. Each option must be accepted or rejected in its entirety.

Home Rule Charters. A significant and controversial modification of traditional practices for the provision of local charters is home rule, of which there are two major types: constitutional and statutory. "Constitutional home rule is a form of state-local relationship in which local governmental units are granted, by state constitutional provision, authority to exercise certain local powers free from control by the state legislature."[17] Under statutory home rule, a comparable relationship is established by legislative act. Since a legislature may take away whatever authority it gives, statutory home rule is very different from constitutional—so different that "home rule" is often ascribed only to those states where it is based on constitutional provisions.

In spite of variations in detail, constitutional home rule is always intended to increase the freedom and authority of those units of government to which it applies.[18] This freedom relates to two areas

---

[16] Illinois, Iowa, Massachusetts, Montana, New Hampshire, and New Jersey are examples.

[17] Clyde F. Snider, *American State and Local Government,* Appleton-Century-Crofts, Inc., New York, 1965, p. 72.

[18] The fact that a state has home rule does not mean that *all* local governments of any given type enjoy its advantage. In about half of the home rule states specific minimum population requirements exist for cities, commonly ranging from 2,000 to 10,000, and only communities of stipulated size enjoy home rule privileges.

of responsibility, structural and functional. Uniformly, the residents of home rule communities are empowered to prepare and adopt charters and provide the form of government they feel is best. Home rule is also supposed to provide local control over matters primarily of local concern as distinguished from those in which the state has paramount interest. Although this statement of the functional significance of home rule may be helpful as a guide, it is pregnant with difficulties.[19] Specifically, what matters are of local concern and what matters are of state concern? Who is to make the decisions?

Any effort to allocate all municipal functions on the basis of primacy of local or state interest is doomed to failure. Local interest may be considered paramount in such matters as terms and qualifications of local officials, procedure for the enactment of ordinances, recreational facilities, standards for street cleaning and lighting, municipal utility services, and zoning ordinances. State interest may be conceded as paramount, on the other hand, with regard to municipal debt limits and major taxes, jurisdiction of local courts, procedure for annexation of territory, and regulation of private utilities. Both levels of government usually exercise considerable authority in relation to education, welfare, sanitation, the police power, and certain types of physical planning. Such an arbitrary and incomplete division of responsibilities does not describe the situation in any particular state, but it provides concrete illustrations of the complexity of the problem.

Who makes the decisions concerning the allocation of responsibilities in a home rule state? The people themselves and state agencies do so, with their determination taking the form of specific constitutional provisions, statutes, court decisions, or acquiescence in the assumption of functions by local governments. If a favorable climate of opinion exists toward local self-government in the courts and the legislature of a state, chances for the effective implementation of home rule are excellent. On the other hand, if unfavorable or hostile attitudes exist, no conceivable constitutional provision will provide effective self-government for localities. Since attitudes and traditions differ from state to state, similar constitutional provisions produce dissimilar results.

Rarely have all communities within any state received their

---

[19] The proper division of responsibilities under county home rule does not pose as great difficulties since counties function primarily to administer state services at the local level.

MUNICIPAL HOME RULE

I. CONSTITUTIONAL HOME RULE STATES

State	Date	Constitutional Basis	Application
Alaska	1959	Art. X, Sec. 9	First class cities and boroughs
Arizona	1912	Art. XIII, Secs. 2–3	Cities of 3,500 or more
California	1879	Art. XI, Secs. 6 et seq.	Cities and city-counties of more than 3,500
Colorado	1902	Art. XX, Secs. 1–6	Cities and towns of 2,000 or more
Hawaii	1959	Art. VII, Sec. 2	All political subdivisions
Kansas	1960	Art. XII, Sec. 5	All cities
Louisiana	1952	Art. XIV, Sec. 40	Any municipality
Maryland[1]	1954	Art. XI-E	Cities and towns
Michigan	1908	Art. VII, Sec. 22	Each city and village
Minnesota	1898	Art. IV, Sec. 36	Any city or village
Missouri	1875	Art. VI, Secs. 19–20	Any city over 10,000
Nebraska	1912	Art. XI, Secs. 2–5	Any city over 5,000
Nevada	1924	Art. VIII, Sec. 8	Any city or town
New Mexico	1949	Art. X, Sec 4(a)	City-counties over 50,000
New York	1923	Art. IX, Secs. 12–13	Cities, towns, and villages
Ohio	1912	Art. XVIII, Secs. 2–3, and 7–9	Any municipality
Oklahoma	1908	Art. XVIII, Secs. 2–7	Any city of 2,000 or more
Oregon	1906	Art. XI, Secs. 2–2a	Every city and town
Pennsylvania	1922	Art. XV, Sec. 1	Cities, towns, and boroughs over 10,000
Rhode Island	1951	Amend. XXVIII	Every city and town
South Dakota	1962	Art. X, Secs. 4–5	Any municipality
Tennessee	1953	Art. XI, Sec. 9	Any municipality
Texas	1912	Art. XI, Sec. 5	Cities over 5,000
Utah	1932	Art. XI, Sec. 5	Any incorporated city or town
Washington	1889	Art. XI, Secs. 10–12	Any city of 10,000 or more
West Virginia	1936	Art. VI, Sec. 39a	Each municipal corporation over 2,000
Wisconsin	1924	Art. XI, Sec. 3	Cities and villages

II. LEGISLATIVE HOME RULE STATES

State	Date	Statutory Basis	Application
Connecticut	1951	Gen. Stats. of Conn. (1949) Sec. 619 as amended 1953	Any city, town, or borough
Florida	1915	F. S. A., ch. 166.01	Every city and town
Georgia	1947	Ga. Code Ann. (1936–37) 69-1001-3 as amended 1951	Any municipal corporation
North Carolina	1917	Gen. Stats. of N. C. (1952) Sec. 160-353	Any municipality
South Carolina	1899	Code of Laws of S. C. (1952) Sec. 47-3	Any city or town

[1] Art. XI-A, providing home rule for Baltimore only, was adopted in 1915.

charters in the same manner. In a state with general classification statutes, cities may continue to operate under charters granted earlier by special act of the legislature. Thus in Nevada, a "classification" state, Las Vegas and Reno continue to use special charters. In an optional charter state, a municipality may function under a charter granted by special act or provided under a general classificaiton law. Municipalities entitled to acquire home rule charters may choose to retain charters granted by special law, by classification statute, or by optional charter procedure. Such home-rule communities, however, may amend their old charters by local action without replacing them. Regardless of the manner in which it is acquired, every charter must be in harmony with the state constitution and general laws.

STATE ADMINISTRATIVE CONTROL AND SUPERVISION[20]

A major aspect of the recent history of local government in the United States has been the continuing struggle, particularly on the part of municipalities, to reduce legislative domination and interference with regard to local affairs. At the same time, it has been generally recognized that each state, having an interest in many local activities, may exercise reasonable control and supervision. When such control takes the form of statutory provisions, such as a specific debt limit, enforcement must normally be sought through the courts. Not only does a restriction of this type possess the disadvantage of rigidity, its enforcement is cumbersome. As the number and variety of governmental activities have increased rapidly during the past generation or so, the need for frequency and flexibility of supervision has grown. Activities and policies of a local government may affect not only its own residents but also people outside its jurisdiction. For example, a substandard health program may threaten the welfare of residents, visitors, and persons who live nearby.

Since increased supervision of any type runs contrary to increased demands for local self-government, it is often opposed by local residents and officials. Nevertheless, the necessities of modern living have dictated increased control in certain areas, control sufficiently adequate and flexible to meet the needs of each individual community. Seven methods or procedures are especially noteworthy: (1) advice and information, (2) reports, (3) grants-in-aid, (4) inspection, (5) review and approval, (6) state appointment and removal of

---

[20] For additional information see Arthur W. Bromage, *Introduction to Municipal Government and Administration,* Appleton-Century-Crofts, New York, 1957, Chapter 9.

local officers, and (7) instructions to local agencies. Viewed legally, the first three of these techniques are noncoercive in that no enforcement procedures are associated with them, and the localities may accept them or ignore them. The last four are normally accompanied by some means to compel acquiescence.[21]

LEGAL LIABILITY

As noted earlier, local governments function in a dual capacity as state agencies and as means of providing services to local residents. Although blurred, this distinction is important in determining whether a person may successfully sue a locality for damages. Unlike the national government and the states, local governments may be subject to suit without consenting to be sued. Such suits arise from acts involving *torts*[22] and *contracts*. The law of tort liability is very confusing, and its principles can be sketched here only in the broadest outlines. Where valid contracts are involved, the rule is that local governments are responsible for observing their provisions and are subject to legal action for any breach of contractual obligations. Regardless of the nature of the function, the local unit is liable to civil suit for breach of contract.

Tort Liability. Actions in tort against local governments most often stem from injury sustained by someone because of the manner in which a local function has been performed. Thus a suit for damages may be instituted by someone who falls into a manhole because the cover has been removed and no warnings or barricades have been put up. A person injured on the icy steps of the city hall may seek redress. A bystander wounded by the police in pursuit of a criminal probably cannot recover damages from the city, but may be able to sue the policeman. Although it is impossible adequately to blanket these and comparable circumstances with a general rule, the following judicial statement serves as a guide in most jurisdictions:

> Those acts which are done by a municipal corporation in the exercise of powers for the benefit of the people generally, as an arm of the state, enforcing general laws made in pursuance of the general policy of the state are "governmental" acts, from the negligent manner of doing which no liability follows; while those acts which are

---

[21] Detailed examination of these and other aspects of administrative relations between states and their local governments is found in Chapter 23.

[22] Briefly defined, a tort is a private wrong not arising from a contract. See Chapter 8.

done in the exercise of the powers of the municipal corporation for its own benefit, or for the benefit of its citizens alone, or the citizens of the municipal corporation and its immediate locality, are corporate or ministerial actions which are governed by the same rules that govern private corporations.[23]

The courts of most states accept the proposition that the powers of true municipalities may be viewed as "governmental" or "corporate."[24] The common law rule is that damages may be recovered by persons harmed or injured as a result of the performance of functions considered as corporate, but in the performance of governmental activities municipalities are free from suit.[25] This distinction is founded on the dual role of municipal corporations as agents of the state and as organs for the satisfaction of local needs. Functions considered governmental in most states include fire and police protection, public health, hospitals, poor relief, education, traffic regulation, and the management of jails and similar institutions. Activities generally classified as corporate include municipally owned and operated utilities, transportation facilities, and other enterprises operated for profit. Considerable difference of opinion exists with regard to functions such as construction and maintenance of airports, quarries, cemeteries, sidewalks, bridges, sewers, parks, and recreational facilities in general.

Although the logic of the distinction between governmental and corporate activities is somewhat obscure, its existence must be recognized. Further application of this distinction is found in the fact that quasi-municipal corporations are generally held not to be liable in tort in connection with any of their functions. In 1961 the California supreme court ruled that a patient in a hospital maintained by a hospital district could recover damages for injuries allegedly caused by the hospital staff, even though the district was a state agency. The court expressed the opinion that the "rule of government immunity from tort liability must be discarded as mistaken and unjust."[26] Both types of municipal corporations may be made subject to suit by state statute, an action that has been taken in some

---

[23] *City of Mobile* v. *Lartigue,* 223 Ala. App. 479, 127 So. 257, 259 (1930).

[24] Governmental functions sometimes are called "political" or "public," and corporate activities are referred to as "proprietary" or "private."

[25] The importance of the common law rule arises from the fact that in most states this matter is not covered by statutory provisions. For an expression of judicial refusal to follow this rule, see *Kaufman* v. *Tallahassee,* 84 Fla. 634, 94 So. 697 (1922).

[26] *Muskopf* v. *Corning Hospital,* 359 P. 2d 457.

states like New York. Reluctance to extend the liability of local governments has stemmed in part from the fear that excessively large and frequent awards might be made by juries whose sympathies lie with the plaintiffs rather than with the taxpayers.[27] In an effort to forestall fiscal difficulties associated with possible damage awards, some municipalities have resorted to liability insurance.

Employee Liability. An example of a tort mentioned earlier concerned the wounding of an innocent spectator by police in pursuit of a criminal, and reference was made to the fact that the offending policeman might be sued. Performance of a governmental function would not protect the local officer although it would probably prevent a suit against the city. "The municipal official or employee is liable as an individual for his torts."[28] Negligence or culpability must normally be proved, however, to justify an award of damages against the employee. Superior officers may be considered a party to the negligence if it can be proved that they were aware of former actions by an employee indicating that he might abuse or wrongfully use his authority.[29] From the standpoint of an injured person, employee liability is not a satisfactory alternative to governmental liability because employees may be "suit proof" due to lack of financial resources. The infrequency of awards against local employees probably reflects in part a realization that the constant threat of such action would not foster effective performance of duties. On the other hand, the possibility of civil action for damages is conducive to the exercise of care by employees.

SELECTED REFERENCES

Books:

Fordham, Jefferson B., *Local Government Law,* Foundation Press, Brooklyn, 1949.

Kneier, Charles M., *City Government in the United States,* 3rd ed., Harper and Bros., New York, 1957.

McQuillin, Eugene, *The Law of Municipal Corporations,* Callaghan and Co., Chicago, 1949.

Rhyne, Charles S., *Municipal Law,* National Institute of Municipal Law Officers, Washington, D.C., 1957.

---

[27] The correctness of this assumption is open to question. See George A. Warp, "Tort Liability Problems of Small Municipalities," 9 *Law and Contemporary Problems* 363 (1942).

[28] Charles M. Kneier, *op. cit.,* p. 184.

[29] *Fernelius v. Pierce,* 22 Cal. 2d 226, 138 P. 2d 12 (1943).

Articles:

Beckman, Norman, and Brazer, Marjorie C., "Governments Galore," *National Civic Review,* March 1963.

Brachtenbach, Robert F., "Home Rule in Washington—At the Whim of the Legislature," *Washington Law Review,* August 1954.

Breckenridge, A. C., "The Mockery of Classification," *National Municipal Review,* November 1947.

Bromage, Arthur W., "Home Rule—N M L Model," *National Municipal Review,* March 1955.

——, "Home Rule as of Now," *National Civic Review,* July 1964.

Faulkner, Bayard H., "New Road to Home Rule," *National Municipal Review,* April 1955.

Fordham, Jefferson B., "Home Rule—A M A Model," *National Municipal Review,* March 1955.

Kerstetter, John R., "Municipal Home Rule," *The Municipal Yearbook, 1956,* International City Managers' Association, Chicago.

——, "Status of Municipal Home Rule," *Public Management,* April 1956.

Richland, W. Bernard, "Courts Nullify Home Rule," *National Municipal Review,* December 1955.

Willoughby, Alfred, "The New Model City Charter," *Public Management,* March 1964.

CHAPTER 19

Municipal Government

Today almost three-fourths of the population of the United States is urban. Since the greatest numbers of people are found in those municipalities known legally and popularly as cities, this chapter emphasizes the structure and functions of cities. Viewed by some as "abnormal" and as centers of corruption,[1] cities very largely set the tone of society. "The city is an economic, social and political organism. It is a product of need, man's need when he lives in close proximity to his fellow man. . . . The city *is* civilization."[2]

The size of urban populations and the rapidity of their growth during the past century have imposed tremendous demands on urban governments. In 1790 only about five per cent of the people were urbanites, and the largest city, Philadelphia, boasted 42,000 souls. By 1850 urban dwellers composed barely fifteen per cent of the country's population. The next sixty years witnessed such rapid urban growth that by 1910 about half of America's population was urban, and recent trends indicate that the urban-rural ratio will soon be three to one. Although the causes of this phenomenon are numerous and complex, a few major ones have been identified.[3]

Factors Contributing to Urban Growth. Important factors contributing to urban growth include improvements in agricultural practices, advances in techniques of production, growth of commerce and trade, changes in methods of transportation, advances in medical science, and new engineering techniques. Before men can gather in large numbers to engage in manufacture and trade they must be freed from the soil. When the great bulk of the working force of a

---

[1] See Elmer T. Peterson (ed.), *Cities Are Abnormal*, University of Oklahoma Press, Norman, 1946; Robert S. Allen, *Our Fair City*, Vanguard Press, New York, 1947.

[2] Benjamin Baker, *Urban Government*, D. Van Nostrand Co., Inc., Princeton, 1957, p. 20.

[3] A good discussion of these causes and their consequences is found in Benjamin Baker, *op. cit.*, Chapters 1 and 2.

nation must spend most of its time in the production of food, impressive urban growth is impossible. By increasing the productivity of agricultural practices, the ratio of farmers to nonfarmers can be appreciably diminished. The erstwhile farmer can then seek his fortune in other endeavors; he can heed the lure of the city.

Urban growth has depended also upon advances in technology. The use of steam to provide power to run machinery made possible the growth of the factory system, which in turn demanded increasing numbers of workers concentrated in proximity to the factories. Then "the baker, the butcher, and the candlestick maker," along with many others, set up business in order to meet the needs of the factory workers. As means of transportation improved, markets widened, demands for manufactured goods increased, and more workers were needed. Railroad centers grew in importance along with ports. According to one theory, cities develop wherever the flow of raw materials and manufactured goods is interrupted.[4] The proximity of important natural resources, such as iron, coal, and water, has made some places especially attractive as centers of industry and trade.

When births lag behind the death rate and the difference is not compensated by emigration, population growth is checked. Dangers from diseases of all kinds are greatly increased whenever people congregate in large numbers. Plagues that ravaged ancient and medieval cities posed a constant threat to the lives of urban dwellers and at more or less frequent intervals reduced their numbers appreciably. Advances in medical knowledge and improvements in methods of sanitation have made cities more attractive and accelerated their growth. The modern city is also dependent upon the application of engineering techniques to build skyscrapers, to construct water distribution systems, to dispose of sewage, and to provide other amenities of community living.

Consequences of Urban Growth. The concentration of large numbers of persons into relatively small areas has produced many problems and increased the severity of others. Provision of new services and improved performance of traditional ones are inevitable consequences of urban growth. Urban living would soon become unsafe without more police protection than can be usually provided by county sheriffs and state police. This situation stems not from

---

[4] See Charles H. Cooley, "The Theory of Transportation," in *Sociological Theory and Social Research,* Holt and Co., New York, 1930.

characteristics of the urbanite, but from the increased opportunities for crime in the city. There are simply more houses to be burglarized, more people to be robbed and swindled, and more traffic to be regulated. The suppression of crime, along with the provision of a great variety of services, means that there must be many more policemen per capita in the city than in the country.

The proximity of residential, commercial, and industrial property in urban areas requires fire protection facilities totally different from those found in rural areas. Large sections of cities, if not entire communities, would be devastated by conflagrations if trained personnel and specialized equipment were not available at all times to fight fires at their inception. The terrible consequences of inadequate fire-fighting equipment and techniques have been experienced by some American cities in rather recent times—Chicago and San Francisco, for example. Although not as spectacular as fighting fires, combatting disease is also an important local function. Since major reliance is placed on private physicians, urban residents are not as dependent upon government in this area as in many others. Certain local functions performed to promote public health are generally classified as public works, including water supply systems and sewage disposal facilities.

Some of the most troublesome municipal responsibilities relate to the transportation of people and goods. Urban residents move about a great deal, traveling to and from work as well as for purposes of shopping and recreation. Many cities, especially the larger ones, provide public transit systems. All cities build and maintain streets on which people travel. Also, they regulate the flow of traffic by means of signs, lights and policemen.

The functions already mentioned by no means encompass the range and variety of tasks demanded of municipalities today, but they indicate the vital role played by these units of government in the lives of most of the people.[5] Their importance is further stressed by the costs of providing services. In fiscal 1959, municipal expenditures amounted to approximately $14.5 billion, an increase of some five per cent over the previous year.

State Restrictions. In the legal sense, each unit of local government is a creature of the state in which it is located. All states impose restrictions, explicit and implied, on the powers of local governments,

---

[5] The powers of municipalities are further discussed later in this chapter.

including municipalities. The traditional pattern of these limitations is revealed in the oft-quoted "Dillon's rule":

> It is a general and undisputed proposition of law that a munici-pal corporation possesses and can exercise the following powers, and no others: First, those granted in express words; second, those neces-sarily or fairly implied in or incident to the powers expressly granted; third, those essential to the accomplishment of the declared objects and purpose of the corporation—not simply convenient but indispen-sable. Any fair, reasonable, substantial doubt concerning the exist-ence of power is resolved by the courts against the corporation, and the power is denied. Of every municipal corporation the charter or statute by which it is created is its organic act. Neither the corpora-tion nor its officers can do any act, or make any contract, or incur any liability, not authorized thereby, or by some legislative act applicable thereto. All acts beyond the scope of the powers granted are void.[6]

The implications of "Dillon's rule" have been somewhat modified in those states that have extended home rule powers to municipalities, particularly where such powers have been granted by constitutional provision. Furthermore, the scope of home rule authority is deter-mined in the final analysis by state courts.[7] Local governments have no inherent rights or powers.[8]

Although local affairs are no longer run from the state capitol as they were fifty years ago, much time in practically every state legis-lative session is occupied in considering questions pertaining to local governments. However, there is a material difference between then and now. During the nineteenth century, legislative concern with local matters characteristically took forms that would now be con-

---

[6] John F. Dillon, *Commentaries on the Law of Municipal Corporations*, 5th ed., Little, Brown & Co., Boston, 1911, I, Sec. 237. Some question as to the correctness of the assertion that cities are merely creatures of the state is implied in *City of Tacoma* v. *The Taxpayers of Tacoma*, 357 U.S. 320, 78 S. Ct. 1209 (1958).

[7] For an explanation of the nature of home rule, see Chapter 18.

[8] The idea that municipalities possess an "inherent right" to local self-government, not stemming from state constitutions or statutes, was first given judicial expression by the Supreme Court of Michigan in *People ex rel. Le Roy* v. *Hurlbut*, 24 Mich. 44 (1871). Courts in other states have toyed with this viewpoint, especially in Indiana, Iowa, Kentucky, Montana, Nebraska, and Texas. However, the doctrine has been repudiated in Indiana and Nebraska, seriously questioned in Texas, and only hesi-tatingly advanced in Iowa. In Kentucky and Montana a distinction between govern-mental and corporate functions has been made, and inherent rights associated only with the latter. On the other hand, the decisions of state courts are filled with posi-tive denials of such rights. See Eugene McQuillin, *The Law of Municipal Corpora-tions*, 3rd ed., Callaghan and Co., Chicago, 1949, Sec. 4.03.

demned as "meddling." Legislatures sometimes went so far as to change the powers of cities according to the political party in power! If the majority in the legislature and the majority in the city government were of the same party, additional powers might be granted. A change in political complexion on either level could result in a reduction of local authority. Making appointments to specific local offices, changing municipal boundaries, authorizing the construction of local public works, and granting utility franchises illustrate legislative interference in local affairs characteristic of earlier years.

Although similar legislative actions occasionally occur today, they are not nearly so common. Instead, legislative concern with local affairs usually relates to problems involved in *extending* local authority. Cities request permission, for example, to levy a new kind of tax, to issue bonds for the construction of off-street parking facilities, to regulate subdivisions immediately outside their boundaries, or to license house trailers. Although city fathers continue to chafe under state restrictions, the trend in recent years unquestionably has been toward increased powers for local governments.

Urban Underrepresentation. In spite of increasing state recognition of local needs, many local officials as well as students of local government feel that developments have been inadequate to meet rapidly changing conditions. The lag is attributable at least in part to the fact that urban areas are seriously underrepresented in most state legislatures. Nationwide, almost three-fourths of the population is urban, but only about one-fourth of all state legislators are elected by urban voters. To put the matter another way, three-fourths of the representatives in the state legislatures are chosen by less than one-third of the people.[9] Rural majorities naturally experience difficulty in understanding and sympathizing with urban problems and needs. Also, inequities inevitably result from conflicts of interest, for example, with regard to the distribution of state funds for local projects.[10]

Several factors have contributed to the curtailment of urban representation in state legislatures. A major cause is found in constitutional provisions requiring equal representation for certain governmental units such as counties and towns without regard to population.

---

[9] See G. E. Baker, *Rural Versus Urban Power,* Doubleday and Co., New York, 1955.
[10] See G. E. Baker, "Cities Resent Stepchild Lot," *National Municipal Review,* September 1953.

Variations of this requirement establish a minimum or maximum representation for each such unit. If a state constitution requires, as is often the case, that each county shall have at least one senator and at the same time sets a limit on the total number of senators, significant inequities inevitably appear in the representation of people. On the other hand, prohibition against more than one senator from a county or representative from a town may produce equally obvious inequalities, as witnessed by the California constitutional provision that limits Los Angeles county to a single senator.

Another cause of inadequate urban representation has been the frequent failure of state legislatures to honor constitutional directives to reapportion on the basis of population following each decennial census. Legislators from rural areas have demonstrated an understandable reluctance to vote themselves out of office and reduce the representation permitted to their constituents. The broader implications of this failure were noted by the Commission on Intergovernmental Relations:

> Reapportionment should not be thought of solely in terms of a conflict of interests between urban and rural areas. In the long run, the interests of all in an equitable system of representation that will strengthen State governments is far more important than any temporary advantage to an area enjoying overrepresentation.[11]

The Commission observed that "The problem of reapportionment is important in the area of study of this Commission because legislative neglect of urban communities has led more and more people to look to Washington for more and more of the services and controls they desire."[12] Thus the bypassing of state legislatures to obtain assistance desired by urban areas may be partially attributed to inequities in representation. Improvements have resulted from judicial action following the decision in *Baker* v. *Carr*.[13]

MAJOR FORMS OF GOVERNMENT

One consequence of the existence of some 18,000 municipalities is a multitude of variations in the details of governmental machinery.

---

[11] Commission on Intergovernmental Relations, *A Report to the President*, June 1955, p. 39.

[12] *Loc. cit.*

[13] 369 U.S. 186. For further analysis of legislative reapportionment, see Chapter 6.

Fortunately, most of these governments display the basic character·
istics of one of three major types of municipal government: mayor·
council, commission, and council-manager. In view of this fact, it is
possible to describe city government in general and consider certain
of its strengths and weaknesses by analyzing these types. Although
some well known commentators, including Alexander Pope and
Lincoln Steffens, have minimized the importance of structure in
determining the effectiveness of government, most students of government agree that good organization *and* good people produce
better government than either alone. Alfred Willoughby truthfully
observed that "it is almost too obvious a fact that a good workman
does better with good machinery."[14]

MAYOR-COUNCIL GOVERNMENT

Quite logically, eighteenth-century local government in the
United States was patterned after that of England. Urban government resembled that of the English borough, with authority vested in
a "common council" composed of the mayor, recorder, aldermen,
and councilmen. In those days, the burden of responsibilities on
urban governments was very light. Few ordinances were enacted,
and limited administrative activities were carried out by the council
as a body, often acting through committees. The mayor, recorder,
and aldermen, as justices of the peace, formed a local court of limited
jurisdiction.

As urban problems grew, the need for leadership became increas·
ingly apparent, and the position of mayor assumed greater importance. Mayors came to be popularly elected rather than appointed by
governors or chosen by local councils as in the past. Popular election
did not result in a sudden and appreciable increase in the mayor's
formal authority. Nevertheless, it separated the "chief executive"
from the legislative branch. This application of the principle of
separation of powers endured, becoming a basic characteristic of
mayor-council government. The people of the United States repeatedly have affirmed their confidence in this principle and have em-
bodied it in the governments of the nation and the states. Popular
acceptance of the desirability of separation of powers undoubtedly
accounts in part for the fact that mayor-council government is the
oldest and still the most widespread form of city government.

---

[14] Alfred Willoughby, "Good Men and Good Machinery," *National Municipal Review*, March 1944, p. 116.

The Mayor: *Selection.* City charters regularly impose minimum qualifications on the office of mayor, a number of them being implied in the requirement that candidates be qualified voters in the community. Occasionally, other age and residence requirements are imposed. In order to be elected mayor, a person must possess numerous qualifications not reflected in law. Like a gubernatorial candidate, he must be "available." Those qualifications that produce "availability" differ in detail from community to community. In general, however, they must result in acceptance by those groups in a community that play a dominant role in influencing public opinion with regard to political issues and more especially with regard to candidates for public office, including party organizations, business leaders, and nonpartisan political groups.

Although mayors in a few small cities are still chosen by the council, the usual method of selection today is popular election. In those cities with partisan election, some formal procedure for the nomination of candidates is necessary so that the elements within each party may unite in support of its slate of candidates. The caucus, the convention, and the direct primary have been widely used for this purpose at different times. Of the three methods, the direct primary is used in most communities today. In order to get his name on the primary ballot, a candidate may file a declaration of candidacy and pay a token fee or he may obtain a stipulated number of signatures of qualified voters on a petition.[15] In some states a choice of methods is open to candidates, while in others no option is available.

In recent years, increasing use has been made of nonpartisan elections for city officials. The major difference between partisan and nonpartisan election is simply that the names of candidates are placed on the ballots of primary and general elections without party designation. Placement of names on the nonpartisan primary ballot may be accomplished by the same means used with regard to the partisan primary. Usually, among contestants for an office the two persons obtaining the highest number of votes in the primary run against each other in the final election. Sometimes, a candidate receiving a majority of the votes cast for the office that he is seeking is declared elected, and there is no further contest. Nonpartisan elec-

---

[15] In a few cities, candidates may get their names on the *election* ballot by petition, thus avoiding the primary. Seldom used, this method is criticized because it may easily result in the election of a "plurality" candidate, that is, one who has received more votes than any of his opponents but less than all others combined.

tion does *not* mean that the voters are unaware of the political affiliation of candidates. With a minimum of inquiry a person may discover the party allegiance of most candidates and then vote his party preference just as in partisan elections.

Popular election of mayors is sometimes criticized by those who prefer an appointed chief executive on the ground that election is not the most reliable means of picking someone endowed with administrative ability. This contention is unquestionably correct. An obvious rejoinder is that a major *should not* be chosen solely, or perhaps even mainly, because of his administrative capacity. The most important role of a typical mayor is that of political leader—not necessarily a partisan leader, however. Some really great mayors of large cities, like Fiorello La Guardia of New York, Brand Whitlock of Toledo, and Charles Taft of Cincinnati, were first of all molders of public opinion and leaders of diverse groups interested in good government. Had they not succeeded at this task, their administrative abilities alone would never have raised them to the heights they achieved. Particularly in big cities like New York and Los Angeles recognition has been given to the need for placing administrative responsibilities in the hands of someone other than the mayor who can then perform tasks of community leadership.[16]

Powers. The mayor-council form of government is commonly divided into sub-types known as "weak-mayor" and "strong-mayor" according to the degree of authority granted to the mayor. Throughout history until the present century in this country, local governments almost uniformly had "weak" executives, and many still do. In general, weak executive arrangements possess four significant characteristics: (1) a strong legislative body, most often called a "council" in cities, possessing not only law-making authority but also power to appoint and perhaps to remove a number of administrative officers; (2) popular election of several administrators; (3) very limited appointive and legislative power in the hands of the chief executive, often including absence of the veto; and (4) short terms of office, commonly two years.[17]

---

[16] By providing an administrative assistant to the mayor, the performance of many routine tasks may be delegated. San Francisco provided for a general manager of this type in 1932, and since then several large cities have adopted the idea, including Boston, Chicago, Louisville, Newark, New York City, New Orleans, and Philadelphia. A number of smaller cities also have created such an office.

[17] See J. C. Phillips, *State and Local Government in America*, American Book Co., New York, 1954, pp. 408–409.

A major feature of the reform movement in city government during the twentieth century has been a trend to strengthen the chief executive or chief administrative officer. The absence of an officer with formal responsibility for over-all supervision of municipal affairs facilitated the rise of local bosses who filled the power vacuum. Rather than go to city officials who could only express sympathy and perhaps make promises, people turned to unofficial but actual leaders who could get things done. Although strengthening the power of mayors did not ring the death knell for bosses, it contributed to their downfall. Leadership and control came to rest where they belonged, in the hands of an official elected by the people.

No fine line can be drawn to divide municipalities neatly into two groups on the basis of the strength of the chief executive because strength is a matter of *degree*. Some mayors are very weak and others are very strong, but the great bulk are in between these extremes. In general, strong mayors exercise relatively extensive authority to appoint and remove administrative officials, with consent of the council in some cases, and they regularly possess the power to veto ordinances passed by the council. They frequently serve longer terms in office, often four years. Few administrators are elected by the people or chosen by the council in a strong-mayor city. Under such circumstances, local residents may logically hold the chief executive and legislative body responsible for the manner in which local needs are met.

In addition to the powers directly concerned with day-to-day supervision of city affairs, mayors have a variety of other duties. Responsibility for the preparation of a budget and its submission to the council commonly rests with the mayor in a mayor-council city. He may propose other measures for consideration by the council, and he may even preside over meetings of that body. As head of the city, the mayor is expected to deliver frequent addresses to civic organizations, women's clubs, political assemblies, and meetings of all types. Many persons impose upon his time daily with complaints and proposals, and the mayor cannot afford to adopt a "closed-door" policy if he has political ambitions. Regardless of his effectiveness as an administrator, a mayor must be a good mixer.

Removal. Four methods of removing mayors have been adopted in the United States: (1) action of the council, (2) recall, (3) judicial action, and (4) action of the state governor. Parallel to the practice at the state level, the most common method available for removing

local chief executives is impeachment. Since almost all city councils are unicameral, the same body brings charges, decides guilt or
innocence, and votes on removal. An extraordinary majority is
usually required to accomplish removal. Since its inclusion in the
charter of Los Angeles in 1903, more than 1,000 cities have provided
for the recall by which officials may be voted out of office.[18] Easily
subject to abuses, the recall has been used with restraint. Common
practice provides that local officials shall be removed from office upon
conviction of a felony, and courts are occasionally empowered to
remove persons for malfeasance or misfeasance in office. In a few
states, including Florida, Michigan, New York, and North Dakota,
the governor may remove mayors.[19] For political and other reasons,
this authority has seldom been used.

The Council. The legislative bodies of most municipalities, particularly cities, are known simply as "councils." Almost all local
councils today are unicameral.[20] Following the American Revolution,
cities began to use the bicameral council, and by the middle of the
nineteenth century it was in general use. During the last quarter of
the past century, the unicameral council grew in favor, and the shift
to this arrangement developed very rapidly during the first three or
four decades of the current century. The single house of most city
councils today is considerably smaller than either house of the old
bicameral councils. Very few cities have more than a score members
on their councils, and many have less than half that number.[21]

Selection. Two major trends in the selection of councilmen are
especially worthy of note: (1) election at-large and (2) nonpartisan
selection.[22] Although not so widespread as in other types of city
government, at-large election of council members is receiving increasing favor among mayor-council cities. Traditionally, cities have

---

[18] For a discussion of the recall, see Chapter 13.

[19] The governor of Florida must receive the approval of the state senate in order to
remove a mayor. In Louisiana the legislature may remove mayors.

[20] The bicameral council, which has been abandoned by several communities in
recent years, is now found in Everett, Mass., and Waterville, Me. The governing
body of New York City consists of a "Council" and a "Board of Estimate," but the
latter is concerned only with fiscal matters.

[21] The range among cities over 500,000 is from fifty councilmen in Chicago to seven
in New Orleans—a wider range than is found among smaller cities.

[22] A noteworthy innovation is the selection of councilmen in a few cities by proportional representation—commonly called "PR." For excellent discussions of this
device see Charles M. Kneier, *City Government in the United States,* Harper & Brothers,
New York, 1957, pp. 226–236; and Arthur W. Bromage, *Introduction to Municipal Government and Administration,* Appleton-Century-Crofts, New York, 1957, pp. 227–233.

been divided into *wards,* and one or more councilmen have been elected from each ward. Advocates of the ward system argue that it guarantees that the interests of sections and even neighborhoods will be represented and considered in the deliberations of the council. Critics maintain that the promotion of sectional interests should be discouraged by requiring all councilmen to seek election at the hands of all the voters in a city. "The chief weakness of the ward plan is that the members of the council often work for the interest of their own wards rather than those of the city as a whole. It brings into the municipal field the 'pork barrel' system of legislation."[23] This criticism is especially relevant to large cities. In the spirit of compromise, some communities elect part of their councilmen at-large and the remainder from wards.

It is estimated that about half of the mayor-council cities continue to elect their councilmen on a partisan basis. In these cities nominations usually are made through the partisan direct primary. More and more cities recently have turned to nonpartisan nomination and election of council members. Proponents of nonpartisan selection argue that "there is no Democratic way to pave a street or Republican method of laying a sewer." Also, they maintain that partisan issues and cleavages should not be extended to questions relating to municipal services such as improvements in police and fire protection and more adequate recreational facilities, as well as many other matters that should be settled on more objective grounds. Those who favor retention of partisan selection claim that questions such as changes in taxation and the provision of new municipal services may properly become issues between parties. Furthermore, it is asserted that formal separation from local issues will weaken political parties at the "grass roots" and thereby impair their effectiveness at all levels of government, although no proof has been advanced in support of this assertion.

Organization. Due to the small size of most city councils, their organization is relatively simple. Provision is always made for a presiding officer, who may be the mayor, an independently elected "president," or someone chosen by the council from among its membership. Commonly, the city clerk or recorder serves as clerk to the council. Municipal councils often perform much of their work through committees, and many decisions pertaining to council action on major as well as minor issues are made by them. Committee

---

[23] Charles M. Kneier, *op. cit.,* p. 225.

reports and recommendations are nearly always seriously considered and usually accepted by the council with only minor modifications. Although subject to abuse, the use of committees may be very helpful. Most councilmen do not possess the time or inclination to become well versed with regard to all municipal functions. Instead, they develop interest in certain areas, such as public works, police, or finance. The needs of a community are better served by enabling each councilman to devote his special competence to particular local problems. To prevent "government by committee," the council must restrain its committees from meddling into the responsibilities of administrative departments and agencies.

Powers. Within the limitations imposed upon it by state and federal law, each local council determines public policy within its jurisdiction. All powers possessed by a city and not conferred by law upon some other officer or agency belong to the council. Although governments of limited powers, municipalities provide many services and impose numerous regulations that are of vital concern to local residents. Fire and police protection, recreational facilities, water, refuse collection and disposal, and street construction and maintenance are illustrative of the variety of services provided. Regulations are imposed, for example, in relation to health, traffic, use of property, and the conduct of many kinds of business. The very existence of these activities and their quality depend largely upon decisions made by local councils. Also, of course, determination of the amount of money to be spent for municipal functions is a responsibility of the council.

In addition to their ordinance-making authority, local councils have numerous other responsibilities. Investigations must be conducted. They may be concerned with uncovering information pertaining to proposed projects or changes in policy, or their purpose may be to determine the efficiency with which municipal affairs are being administered. Long-range plans must be considered, especially with regard to public works such as streets, water supply, and sewage disposal. Contracts and franchises must be reviewed. Petitions from individual citizens and organized groups within the community must be given attention. Careful consideration needs to be given, at least occasionally, to appointments to municipal offices. Although this list of responsibilities is by no means exhaustive, it provides some insight into the variety of tasks imposed upon municipal councils.

Removal. Although members of municipal councils are seldom removed from office prior to the expiration of their terms, such action is occasionally desirable. Three methods of removal are common: (1) recall, (2) expulsion by the council, and (3) conviction of crime. Where permitted, removal by recall requires the circulation of a petition setting forth the charges and the acquisition of a certain number of signatures of legal voters on the petition, followed by a vote on removal. Usually, a special election is called for this purpose. Some city charters empower councils to expel members. A person convicted of a serious crime during his term of office must normally relinquish his position on a local council.

COMMISSION GOVERNMENT

The stepchild among the major varieties of city government is the commission form, which grew in favor during the first quarter of the twentieth century but has been on the decline ever since. This type of government received widespread attention as a result of its adoption in Galveston, Texas, following a tidal wave that killed thousands of persons and destroyed millions of dollars worth of property.[24] The mayor-council government of Galveston proved unable to cope with the serious situation produced by the disaster. A committee of civic leaders drew up a new charter and requested the Texas legislature to adopt it as the basic law for Galveston.[25] The legislature complied, and commission government was established in 1901. Three of the five commissioners were originally appointed by the governor, an arrangement held unconstitutional, and the charter was amended to provide for popular election of all commissioners.[26]

During the next dozen years, between four and five hundred communities adopted commission government. Although accurate figures are not available, the high point in the number of adoptions of this form of government appears to have occurred around 1920. Since then the trend has been downward. In 1963 only about 250 of the cities of over 5,000 population were reported as operating with

---

[24] The commission form of government was used by a few cities during the nineteenth century, including Sacramento, California (1863), New Orleans, Louisiana (1870), Memphis, Tennessee (1878) and Mobile, Alabama (1879). Washington, D.C., has operated under a type of commission government for three-quarters of a century.

[25] This was a "special act" charter.

[26] *Ex parte Lewis,* 45 Tex. Crim. 1, 73 S.W. 811 (1903).

commissions. Very few cities have adopted the plan in recent years, while many have abandoned it. On April 19, 1960, the people of Galveston voted commission government out in favor of the council-manager plan. "So the commission plan, in the light of abundant experience, dwindles out."[27]

The Nature of Commission Government. Most notable among the features of commission government is the concentration of major legislative, executive, and administrative responsibilities in a single body, the commission. Consequently, there is a fusion rather than a separation of powers. Although details vary from community to community, three major features are characteristic: (1) a small, popularly elected commission, sometimes known as the "council," (2) a mayor who is usually a member of the commission and is often chosen by that body to serve as "chief executive," and (3) members of the commission serving individually as top-level administrators in charge of major departments. This arrangement is structurally simple, but it has proved complex in operation.

The Commission. Membership on the commission or council rarely exceeds seven; three or five members are most common. Collectively, the commissioners serve in a legislative capacity and perform duties comparable with those belonging to councilmen in the mayor-council system. In other words, the commission decides issues of public policy and enacts the ordinances necessary to implement its decisions. More often than not, commissioners are selected on a nonpartisan basis from the entire city rather than from wards.

Executive Officers. In commission cities various methods are employed to designate the chief executive, a position normally carrying little more authority than belongs to individual commissioners. The mayor usually does not possess the veto power. He may be specifically chosen by popular vote as mayor, or the commissioner who receives the largest number of popular votes may automatically assume that position. In many cities the commissioners choose one of their own number to serve as mayor. He functions as head of a major city department, usually the one including fire and police services. Due to his position as "first among equals" and as titular head of the city government, the mayor enjoys more influence, if little more formal authority, than other commissioners.

---

[27] "Wane of the Commission Plan," *National Municipal Review*, November 1954, p. 517. Another major defection occurred in November 1960 when the people of Jersey City voted to change to the mayor-council form.

Since commissioners serve individually as administrators of major departments, there is no organizational distinction in commission government between policymaking and policy-execution. A commissioner may be elected to head a particular department, but more often the commissioners allocate the departments among themselves. In a few communities, the mayor is empowered to designate the department for which each commissioner will be responsible. Because the number of major departments is limited by the number of commissioners, each department is responsible for a variety of duties, many of which may be functionally unrelated. Titles of departments vary from place to place, but these may be considered typical: Public Safety, Public Works, Finance, Welfare, and Parks and Recreation. Practically all municipal activities are divided among these five departments. Depending on the size of the city and the predilections of the commissioners, professional personnel are hired to supervise each of the subdepartments. Thus a police chief, a fire chief, an engineer, and a recreation specialist may be placed in immediate charge of functions for which they are specially trained.

Assessment of Commission Government. Although generalizations concerning the effectiveness or desirability of a particular type of government are fraught with danger, a brief review of the claims of proponents and opponents of commission government is in order. The major advantages of this type of government are alleged to be: (1) simplicity, (2) small size of commission, (3) concentration of authority and responsibility, and (4) close relation between policymaking and administration. Structural simplicity is unquestionably characteristic of commission government, which substitutes a single small body for separate executive, legislature, and independent administrative officers. On the other hand, the variety of functions lodged in a single agency may create difficulty for the average citizen when he attempts to pinpoint responsibility for the manner in which a particular task has been performed or for failure to meet certain needs of the community.

The chief advantage associated with a small commission is a short ballot. However, the short ballot is in no sense peculiar to commission government, since small councils and few elected administrative officers may be provided in any type of municipal government. It is sometimes maintained that the small number of commissioners combined with the importance of the responsibilities attaching to each position attracts superior personnel. This claim appears to be entirely in the realm of conjecture.

That official authority and responsibility are concentrated in a few hands in commission government is undeniable. That such concentration produces good government is debatable. Since responsibility for the administration of local affairs is placed in the hands of a *group,* opportunities for "buck-passing" are always present. Whenever anything goes wrong in a department, the commissioner in charge may attempt to avoid unpleasant consequences by asserting that his actions are controlled by the majority of the commission of which he is only *one* member. He may imply or perhaps even state that he is required to follow a particular course of action in spite of his better judgment.

Location of responsibility for making policy and administering it in the same hands is favored by some persons and criticized by others. Proponents of this arrangement maintain that the combination of responsibilities reduces legislative-executive friction and minimizes opportunities for mutual misunderstanding of the problems faced by each branch of government. However, one astute student of local government has observed, "To entrust these divergent processes to the same body is to invite confusion. . . . Making policy calls for a different type of ability from the conducting of administration. The amateur may be desirable in the former but never in the latter role. . . . In principle, the commission idea errs in its merger of legislative and executive operations."[28]

Critics of commission government usually emphasize the following points: (1) absence of a chief administrator, (2) inexpert administration, (3) joining of politics and administration in the same hands, (4) rigid departmental organization, and (5) inadequate provision for political leadership. Effective administration of municipal affairs requires coordination. "Everybody wants coordination, at least on paper, but nobody wants to be coordinated in practice. Every agency wants to go its own way and have other agencies build around their own program. Unless there is strong leadership at the top, leadership with ability to induce different departments or units to work as a team, then in all probability these units will be proceeding simultaneously in all directions."[29] Structurally, no provision is made in commission government for such leadership.

---

[28] Arthur W. Bromage, *op. cit.,* p. 285.
[29] W. Brooke Graves, *Public Administration in A Democratic Society,* D. C. Heath and Co., New York, 1950, pp. 66–67.

It has been said often that "experts should be on tap and not on top." Expert administration of governmental services is very much needed today. Political leaders seldom have the time or inclination to acquire knowledge and techniques necessary for effective administration of fire and police departments, public works programs, and other important municipal activities. Commission government, particularly in smaller communities where it is most common, seeks to combine political finesse and technical *expertise* in the same persons. Such a combination is rarely found. Since commissioners must be elected, their primary emphasis must be on politics.

Combining policymaking and policy-execution in the same hands contributes to "horse-trading" among commissioners, according to critics. Each commissioner is primarily concerned with his own administrative responsibilities. In order to win commission approval of his own proposals, each member is inclined to treat the requests of other commissioners with sympathy rather than critical analysis. Consequently, commission government has been likened to "a spending machine without a brake." Although somewhat inaccurate, this observation reflects certain difficulties inherent in any system that places responsibility in the same hands for determining how much shall be spent and for supervising actual expenditures.

Since the number of major departments cannot exceed the number of commissioners, all governmental activities must necessarily be allocated to a predetermined number of departments. If commission government is to retain its characteristic advantage of a small council, the number of departments must be strictly limited regardless of the size of a city. Combinations of unrelated, or at best remotely related, functions are inevitably found in most if not all departments. Detailed supervision by one person of such varied activities is difficult at best.

Another major criticism of commission government is that from the viewpoint of *structure* it makes inadequate provision for political leadership. However, the same criticism can be leveled against all forms of municipal government with the exception of the strong-mayor type. Furthermore, it is possible for mayors in commission communities to *assume* positions of leadership. A popular mayor with a strong personality and a determination to "get things done" may accomplish more under commission government than a mayor without these qualities in a strong-mayor city.

COUNCIL-MANAGER GOVERNMENT

The third major variety of municipal government, the council-manager form, was inaugurated in Staunton, Virginia, in 1908.[30] As in the case of commission government, a natural disaster brought manager government to prominence. The Miami River flooded portions of Dayton, Ohio, in 1913, drowning many and destroying large amounts of property. The government of Dayton was so ineffective in meeting the resultant problems that the city was placed under martial law, and a group of business men took responsibility for overhauling local services. A proposal to "put business in government" by adopting council-manager government was approved in late 1913, and a new charter became effective on January 1, 1914. Municipalities using this type of government have increased steadily and now number more than 1800.[31]

The Council. Responsibilities of the council in council-manager government are, with one major addition, much the same as in mayor-council government. That addition is the task of choosing a manager. The manner in which this responsibility is handled largely determines the success or failure of this type of government. In council-manager cities authority to run city affairs is definitely located in the council. The council not only determines policy, but it also selects the top-level administrator empowered to implement that policy. Furthermore, the council normally has authority to terminate the manager's services at any time.[32]

Although many variations exist, council-manager cities typically have a small council of five to nine members who are elected at-large on a nonpartisan basis. Terms of office are commonly two or four years and occasionally six. Councilmen often serve without compensation except for payment of expenses, and where pay is provided it is usually nominal. Monetary remuneration is not a major concern of public-spirited citizens who spend hours each week investigating,

---

[30] Sometimes called "city-manager government," but the designation used here is preferred. The first city to adopt council-manager government by charter amendment was Sumter, S.C., in 1912.

[31] Only Hawaii, Indiana, and Louisiana have no council-manager cities.

[32] Occasionally, managers are hired for fixed terms, a practice that is opposed by the International City Managers' Association and most students of local government. Some charters provide that the manager shall be removed only for "cause," but any council wishing to remove a manager can develop reasons for the action.

considering, and hearing citizen viewpoints on the many problems of local government.

The Mayor. Mayors in council-manager cities may be popularly elected or chosen by the council from among its membership. Since administrative responsibilities are separated from the office, the mayor is concerned with policymaking and ceremony. Ideally, a mayor provides the political leadership in which a manager may not dare indulge. Usually the only popularly elected executive officer, the mayor occupies a position of potentially significant influence. His knowledge of public sentiment and his efforts in "selling" projects and programs may provide invaluable assistance to the council and to the manager. Although he has little or no responsibility for the administration of city functions, the mayor's role need in no sense be insignificant.

The Manager: *Selection and Tenure.* Beyond prescribing "executive and administrative ability," most local charters say nothing about the qualifications of a manager. Consequently, councils are legally free to choose anyone who appears best suited to meet community needs. Such intangible qualities as honesty, tact, energy, foresight, resourcefulness, and a sense of humor must always be considered. Experience in the public service in some professional capacity, preferably on the local level, is usually demanded. Although a council may consider local talent for promotion to the position of manager, someone from outside normally is brought in to fill the position, particularly where it is a full-time job. This practice is favored because citizens who have been active in local affairs will have friends and enemies along with definite notions concerning the manner in which certain matters should be handled.

The opportunity to move from community to community promotes professionalization of city-manager work. It is estimated that the average tenure of managers today is about seven years. Although managers occasionally are dismissed by council action, the great majority of separations are voluntary.[33] Especially since World War II the demand for qualified managers has exceeded the supply, and when a larger city needs a manager it looks to smaller communities. The higher salaries and greater challenges offered by the large city

---

[33] Very rarely, managers are subject to removal by recall.

are attractive to many administrators who have begun their careers in small cities and towns.

Duties. Although the duties of a manager necessarily vary from city to city, he should have full responsibility, subject to council approval, for the administration of city affairs. In order to accomplish this task, he must have control of most, if not all, departments implemented by authority to appoint and remove their heads. His must be the basic responsibility for preparing an annual budget and submitting it to the council. He must review and coordinate agency plans in all fields of municipal activity. The manager must submit proposals to the council on any and all matters that he feels should be brought to their attention, and he must prepare information and recommendations on questions submitted to him by the council. Reports to the council at stipulated intervals on the financial condition of the city must come from the manager's office. The manager should prepare an agenda prior to each council session so that members may anticipate matters that will be brought before them. Finally, a major portion of the manager's time needs to be allocated to the implementation of a "public relations" program designed to keep interested persons and the public in general informed about the operations of city government. Each of these tasks might well be the subject of a short essay. Together, they vitally affect all phases of local government.

Arguments in Favor. The major arguments in behalf of council-manager government may be summarized briefly. Although legal responsibility for the conduct of local affairs definitely rests with the council, adequate provision is made for separation of legislative and administrative functions. Managers normally are chosen on the basis of training, ability, and experience rather than political considerations. Because of the conditions surrounding his selection and tenure, the manager is less subject to political pressure than a popularly elected official. Council membership involves relatively fewer demands on incumbents than in other forms of local government, thus encouraging larger numbers of civic-minded persons to seek membership. Reduction in the number of elected officials shortens the ballot. Managers possess authority commensurate with responsibility for overseeing local activities. Opportunities for "buck-passing" are reduced to a minimum. Finally, communities using this form of government generally praise it as providing increased efficiency.

Arguments Against. Opponents of council-manager government stress a number of considerations. Too much authority is placed in the hands of an appointive official, and manager government is consequently less democratic than those types in which the chief administrative officer is popularly elected. Since the supply of qualified managers is limited, municipalities, particularly small ones, experience serious difficulty in their efforts to secure and retain capable, experienced managers. Separation of responsibilities between the council and the manager may be clear in theory, but in practice it is difficult to maintain. Councils tend to interfere in matters of administration, and managers become involved in major policy decisions. Inadequate provision is made for effective political leadership. Salary costs required to attract and keep competent managers are excessive. Several communities have tried the plan and abandoned it.

Council-manager government is in no sense a cure-all for the problems besetting local government. Its success requires sympathetic understanding and cooperation on the part of many persons and groups. The voters must accept the idea that the manager's qualifications as a professional administrator are more important to efficient local government than are his political views. They must be willing to exert their control over local affairs through their influence over the council, which in turn controls the manager.

Basic to council-manager government is a division of responsibilities between the council and the manager, a division that is not easily realized in practice. Although final authority to make decisions on major questions of policy is lodged with the council, many persons other than councilmen participate in the process, including the manager and subordinate administrative personnel, the mayor, and various groups in the community.[34] From these and other sources councils receive information, suggestions, and recommendations, all of which influence their deliberations. But once a decision has been made the manager must see that it is carried out in the most effective and expeditious manner possible. Selection and supervision of necessary personnel is the manager's responsibility, and many local charters specifically prohibit councilmen from seeking to influence him in regard to such matters. If the council as a body concludes that the affairs of a community are not being adequately

---

[34] For additional insight into the role of the manager in formulating policy, see C. A. Harrell and D. G. Weiford, "The City Manager and the Policy Process," *Public Administration Review,* Spring 1959.

administered, it has the legal and moral duty to obtain a new manager.

Some of the most vexatious problems in council-manager communities pertain to political leadership. There appears to be no reason why a popularly elected mayor *cannot* fill this important need. However, experience shows that mayors often do not assume this responsibility. Where they are chosen by the council, the inability or reluctance on the part of mayors to assume leadership is understandable. Studies indicate, however, that even elected mayors may be willing to allow leadership to emanate from other sources such as the manager, prominent administrators in various city departments, and leaders of pressure groups in the community.[35] "Throughout the history of the council-manager movement, some city managers have ventured into overt community leadership in the settlement of public problems. Through the same period, some students and proponents of the plan have feared that the role of active policy leadership would bring discredit to the form of government."[36] The problems inherent in the assumption of leadership by the manager are reflected in the assertion by a former mayor of Philadelphia to the effect that "top leadership in American politics is never hired; it is always elected . . ."[37]

The manager's position as top administrative official is jeopardized when a subordinate is able to assume a position of community leadership with regard to a particular area of responsibility. Thus a city engineer with a quarter-century of service may exert more influence over the street-paving or sewer-construction programs than the newly appointed manager. Or a police chief with long tenure may similarly determine the quality of law enforcement. Such officials may be beyond the effective control of the manager because of their standing in the community even though legally subject to removal by him. Although pressure groups have a legitimate function to perform in the presentation of their wishes, their activities become particularly deplorable when they seek to control the manner in which functions and programs are administered. It is important that some official selected by the voters be able, ready, and willing to use his influence to champion programs considered beneficial to the

---

[35] See the symposium entitled "Leadership and Decision-Making in Manager Cities," *Public Administration Review*, Summer 1958.

[36] Karl A. Bosworth, "The Manager Is a Politician," *ibid.*, p. 219.

[37] Quoted in Dorothee Straus Pealy, "The Need for Elected Leadership," *ibid.*, p. 214.

entire community and to counteract the influence of special groups. In order for council-manager government to function most effectively, this task must be performed by the mayor. His failure to assume these duties does not, however, reflect an inherent weakness in the manager system.

Hybrid Forms. Diagrams on pages 486–487 of the major varieties of municipal government depict each type in its "pure" or "ideal" form. Governments in many communities do not fit any of these patterns. Thus the prominence of an appointed chief administrator is the central characteristic of council-manager government, but a similar arrangement is found in some mayor-council cities. The "chief administrative officers" in these cities are appointed by the mayor and function to assist him in various capacities.[38] This arrangement originated in San Francisco in 1932 and has been used in a number of large cities, including Boston, Los Angeles, Louisville, Newark, New York, New Orleans, and Philadelphia. Advocates of the plan stress its combination of a strong, elected chief executive with a professional administrator.

The government of Jacksonville, Florida, clearly illustrates difficulties involved in the classification of city governments according to major types. The government of that city is designated as the "Mayor-Commissioner-Council" form. A "mayor-commissioner," who is the chief executive of the city, is popularly elected like the council, which is the city's legislative body. The city commission, an administrative body much like a governor's cabinet, is composed of elected administrators responsible for the operation of the various city departments. The council passes the ordinances and makes appropriations, subject to the mayor-commissioner's veto. In terms of the threefold classification of city governments, Jacksonville's system would have to be considered as belonging to the mayor-council type.

Innumerable minor variations appear from community to community. In some manager cities certain department heads are not subject to appointment and removal by the manager. They may be selected by the mayor, by popular vote, or even occasionally by departmental personnel. The last arrangement is most common among volunteer fire departments. In a few manager communities the legislative bodies are called commissions rather than councils. The

---

[38] For an examination of the situation in California, see John C. Bollens, *Appointed Executive Government*, Haynes Foundation, Los Angeles, 1952.

WEAK-MAYOR AND COUNCIL GOVERNMENT

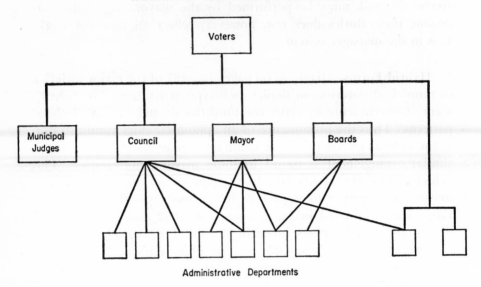

Administrative Departments

STRONG-MAYOR AND COUNCIL GOVERNMENT

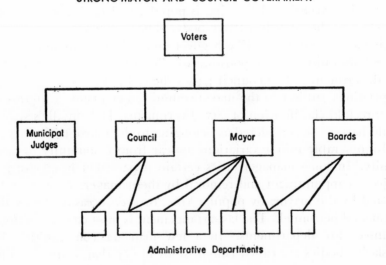

Administrative Departments

COMMISSION GOVERNMENT

Voters

Boards

Commissioners

Commissioners Make up the Council

Municipal Judges

Administrative Departments

COUNCIL-MANAGER GOVERNMENT

Voters

Municipal Judges

Council

Mayor*

City Officers

Manager

Administrative Departments

* Chosen by council in some cities

voters in "true" commission cities occasionally elect important administrative officials in addition to members of the commission. Consequently, in these municipalities some functions are assigned to departments or agencies not under the immediate supervision of a commissioner. Such illustrations could be multiplied many times. The governmental structures found in many municipalities do not fit any pattern exactly. This fact is not too significant, however, since these patterns still serve as guides for the deliberations of those responsible for determining the form of government in each community.

MAJOR MUNICIPAL FUNCTIONS

Public Safety. Some of the most important activities of municipal governments are related to the promotion of public safety. Police and fire protection, traffic engineering, street lighting, building inspection, and civil defense are important illustrations. Beginning with the night watch in colonial times, cities have had important responsibilities for the protection of persons and property. From New York City with about 24,000 policemen to hundreds of small communities with one or two members in their police forces, municipalities spend major portions of their budgets for the apprehension of criminals, recovery of stolen property, suppression of vice, crime prevention, and traffic control, to name some of the more common activities. Despite the large number of crimes regularly reported, much credit is due police forces for the appreciable advances made in the control of crime during the last half-century.

"American cities have the finest fire equipment in the world, but they also have the greatest annual fire losses."[39] To compensate for their negligence, Americans annually spend millions of dollars to man and equip local fire departments. Although not so dramatic as fire-fighting, fire-prevention activities are assuming increasing importance. Particularly in larger communities, it is important that firemen be mentally alert, physically agile, and professionally trained. Training schools for firemen have proved their worth in reducing fire losses and property damage.

Although sometimes considered as part of planning rather than public safety, traffic engineering is vitally important to the safety of citizens, especially in congested areas. Laying out thoroughfares,

---

[39] Charles R. Adrian, *Governing Urban America,* McGraw-Hill Book Co., New York, 1955, p. 364.

widening streets, designating one-way arterials, locating lights, and setting speed limits indicate the close relationship between traffic engineering and safety. Adequate street lighting is important to traffic control, but it also bears a close relation to crime detection and suppression. Dangers to persons and property lurking in poorly lighted areas have stimulated many local councils to provide more modern facilities. Review of plans for the construction of buildings, industrial and commercial as well as residential, and inspection of wiring, plumbing, fire escapes, elevators, heating systems, structural strength, and many related matters contribute significantly to public safety. Under federal civil defense legislation since 1950, local governments have primary responsibility for civil defense. In spite of the appalling lack of concern among citizens, many cities have undertaken sizable projects designed to decrease the devastation of possible nuclear attack.

Health and Welfare. As noted earlier, advances in medical science have contributed to the growth of urbanism. Because of the necessity of controlling communicable diseases in heavily populated areas, cities have long assumed responsibilities relating to the protection of health. In earlier times, pesthouses and quarantines were established to isolate those seriously ill. With the growth of medical knowledge, the importance of sanitation was recognized. Cities began to construct sewage disposal systems and dispose of garbage and other wastes. Responsibility for the provision of an adequate supply of pure water has long been a major municipal function. Cities occasionally have vaccinated and innoculated large numbers of their residents against certain communicable diseases. Municipal hospitals have been established in many communities. Smoke abatement constitutes a recent addition to municipal efforts in the field of public health.

Until recent times cities played a major role in the provision of welfare services. Municipal almshouses and poor farms cared for indigent aged, invalids, orphans, and other persons mentally and physically disabled. During the last quarter-century or so, responsibility for the provision of welfare has been assumed by the national and state governments, with counties generally serving as the primary agencies for local administration. Since the depression of the 1930's the concept of welfare has expanded to encompass those persons temporarily out of work and in need of assistance to "tide them over" until they resume gainful employment. Some cities recently have cooperated with the national and state governments in support of programs for slum clearance and public housing.

Utilities and Transportation. Many municipalities provide services that may be classified broadly as utilities, including electricity, water, gas, airports, auditoriums, port facilities, public markets, and slaughterhouses. Also sometimes considered as utilities are transportation facilities. Municipal streetcar and bus systems have been a familiar part of the local scene for many years. Most public transit systems today are either operating at a deficit or on a very narrow margin of profit because of greatly increased use of private automobiles. Fewer public transit passengers cause higher rates, which in turn mean fewer passengers. No one has yet proposed an adequate solution to this dilemma. An allied problem for cities has been the provision of adequate parking facilities for automobiles. Municipal parking lots and garages are becoming increasingly common.

Planning and Zoning. Most American cities have grown largely without plan, but fortunately increasing attention is now being given to the future. Although other types of planning are not ignored, attention is given primarily to physical planning. Planners with an eye for the future are concerned about such matters as street patterns, parking facilities, water and sewer systems, mass transportation, parks, airports, schools, public buildings, and sites for industrial, commercial, and residential developments. This list by no means exhausts the areas of concern to planners, but it indicates the difficulty of their task, which is further complicated by the necessity of relating projected population growth and financial resources to physical needs.

Planning and zoning go hand in hand. The best laid plans for the orderly development of a community will certainly go awry unless legal restrictions are imposed on indiscriminate uses of property. Zoning is intended to implement the orderly development of a community by regulating the use of land and buildings within precisely defined districts. Restrictions are imposed upon the size of buildings as well as the uses to which they may be put, the proximity of structures to each other, and the density of population. Zoned cities are usually divided into industrial, commercial, and residential areas with subcategories within each. Thus residential areas may be subdivided into one-family districts, two-family districts, and multiple-family districts, controlling the number of families that may reside within each residential building. Except in areas developed after the adoption of a zoning ordinance, some nonconforming uses normally exist in each zone. For example, a few multiple-family dwellings may be located in a section zoned for single-family residences, or vice versa. Through "spot-zoning" small segments of land are set aside for special uses different from those authorized for the zone in which they are situated. In this way, for example, neighborhood commercial areas may be permitted to encroach upon residential zones.

Judicial Functions. All states have granted to municipal courts limited authority for the administration of justice in both civil and criminal cases arising within their territory. The number and variety of these courts often bear a close relation to the size of the city. The charters of large cities may establish a variety of courts, including special courts dealing with domestic relations, juveniles, small claims, and traffic offenses. In many small cities the jurisdiction of municipal courts is limited largely to violations of local ordinances, particularly those pertaining to traffic, punishable by small fines and short jail terms. These courts must not be confused with state courts that happen to be physically situated within the environs of individual municipalities. The jurisdiction of state courts, in terms of types of cases and geography, is much broader than that granted to municipal courts.[40] The importance of city courts must not be measured solely in terms of their jurisdiction, however. The fact that many citizens have their only contact with the judiciary in these courts gives them an importance that is often overlooked.

SELECTED REFERENCES

Books:

Adrian, Charles R., *Governing Urban America,* McGraw-Hill Book Co., New York, 1961.

Allen, Robert S., *Our Fair City,* Vanguard Press, New York, 1947.

Baker, Benjamin, *Urban Government,* Van Nostrand Co., Princeton, 1957.

Banfield, Edward C., and Wilson, James Q., *City Politics,* Harvard University Press, Cambridge, Mass., 1963.

---

[40] Technically, municipal courts are also state courts in that their authority is granted to them by state law.

Bromage, Arthur W., *Introduction to Municipal Government and Administration,* Appleton-Century-Crofts, New York, 1957.

——, *Councilmen at Work,* George Wahr Co., Ann Arbor, 1954.

Dahl, Robert A., *Who Governs? Democracy and Power in an American City,* Yale University Press, New Haven, Conn., 1961.

Kneier, Charles M., *City Government in the United States,* 3rd ed., Harper and Bros., New York, 1957.

MacDonald, Austin F., *American City Government and Administration,* 6th ed., T. Y. Crowell Co., New York, 1956.

Maddox, Russell W., Jr., *Extraterritorial Powers of Municipalities in the United States,* Oregon State College Press, Corvallis, 1955.

National Municipal League, *Manager Plan Abandonments,* New York, 1959.

——, *The Story of the Council-Manager Plan,* New York, 1959.

Articles:

Baker, G. E., "Cities Resent Stepchild Lot," *National Municipal Review,* September 1953.

Bebout, John E., "Management for Large Cities," *Public Administration Review,* Summer 1955.

Bollens, John, "The Most Important Problems Confronting Cities Today," *Western City,* February 1964.

Gruen, Victor, "Who Is to Save Our Cities?" *Harvard Business Review,* May-June 1963.

Harrell, C. A., and Weiford, D. G., "The City Manager and the Policy Process," *Public Administration Review,* Spring 1959.

Jones, Russell D., "The Changing Role of the City Manager," *Public Management,* June 1962.

"Leadership and Decision-Making in Manager Cities," Symposium, *Public Administration Review,* Summer 1958.

Miller, Roy L., "Getting a Good Council," *National Civic Review,* March 1959.

Nelson, Otto L., Jr., "Will Our Cities Survive?" *National Civic Review,* April 1959.

Pfiffner, John M., "The Job of the City Manager," *Public Management,* June 1961.

Schnore, Leo F., and Alford, Robert R., "Forms of Government and Socioeconomic Characteristics of Suburbs," *Administrative Science Quarterly,* June 1963.

Stene, Edwin O., "University Training for City Management," *Public Management,* January 1952.

Wagner, Robert F., "Help for Our Cities," *National Civic Review,* January 1960.

CHAPTER 20

The County

The American county is a direct descendant of the English shire established in the ninth century. At that time "the affairs of each shire were managed by a semiannual court, composed of the representatives of each township and the individual landowners . . ."[1] The chief function of the court was the administration of justice. Officials of the shire were the earl, the shire-reeve or sheriff, and the bishop. Shortly after the Norman conquest earls and bishops disappeared as administrators of shire business; shires came to be called counties, and the sheriff became the dominant officer in county affairs as the representative of the King.

When the English forefathers settled this country, they naturally established governmental forms with which they were familiar. In Virginia the English system of local government was followed closely, and as early as 1634 that state was divided into eight shires or counties. Counties were established in Massachusetts in 1643, Maryland in 1650, Connecticut in 1663, and Rhode Island in 1703. Similar developments took place in other states about the same time.

Following the Revolution, state constitutions made frequent reference to counties, and considerable authority for self-government was granted. Increases in local authority were apparent especially in regard to more pronounced local influence over the choice of county officials formerly appointed by the governor or other state officials. By the end of the first quarter of the nineteenth century the basic characteristics of county governmental structure as they exist today were taking form. Throughout the last century increased local control by virtue of more widespread popular election of county officers characterized developments at that level of government.

---

[1] John A. Fairlie, *Local Government in Counties, Towns and Villages,* The Century Co., New York, 1906, p. 5. Information for this section on historical background is drawn largely from Dr. Fairlie's volume.

PRESENT STATUS OF THE COUNTY

The county is the most nearly universal unit of local government in the United States. In name at least, almost the entire area of the country is included in the 3,041 organized counties.[2] Organized county governments are found in every state except Alaska, Connecticut, and Rhode Island. The five counties of Rhode Island serve merely as judicial districts. Scattered across the country are a few areas situated in so-called "geographic" counties that lack governmental organization. Included in this category are four "unorganized" counties in South Dakota, five counties in New York City, five that have merged with their central cities and lost separate existence for all practical purposes, and the city-counties of Denver and San Francisco.[3] There are also thirty-four cities, the District of Columbia, and Yellowstone National Park that lack county government. The number of counties per state ranges from three in Delaware to 254 in Texas, and in size they vary from 20,131 square miles in San Bernardino County, California, to twenty-five square miles in Arlington County, Virginia. According to the 1960 census, the population of counties varied from 6.5 million in Los Angeles County, California, to less than 1,000 in a few sparsely populated areas in the western states.

Understanding county government in the United States today requires knowledge of several basic considerations. First, counties are legally geographical subdivisions of a state for the administration of certain governmental activities of statewide concern, such as construction and maintenance of highways and other roads, conduct of elections, and the application of justice. Accordingly, the area and governmental organization of counties are determined by state constitutional or statutory law.[4] Second, counties are primarily units

---

[2] Included in this number are the parishes of Louisiana that are legally and politically comparable with counties. The county of Kalawao, Hawaii, is not included since it does not have responsibilities for local administration. Counties were abolished in Connecticut, effective in 1960, and a new county was created in Wisconsin in 1961. As of January 1963, Norfolk and Princess Anne counties, Virginia, became respectively the cities of Chesapeake and Virginia Beach.

[3] The mergers include the parishes of East Baton Rouge (counted by the Bureau of the Census as the city of Baton Rouge) and Orleans (New Orleans), counties of Nantucket and Suffolk, Massachusetts (counted as the township of Nantucket and city of Boston, respectively), and county of Philadelphia (counted as the city of Philadelphia). The New York City five counties are Bronx, Kings, New York, Queens, and Richmond.

[4] Even in those few states with county home rule, county charters are adopted pursuant to provisions of state statutes.

for rural government in most places. Although not so universally true as earlier in history, the fact remains that county functions considered as a whole are more vital to people living outside city boundaries than to urban dwellers. At the same time, rapid population growth in suburban areas around many cities has imposed upon counties the responsibility of providing suburbanites with certain municipal services. A third fact worthy of note is that county boundaries in most instances were determined many years before the advent of modern means of transportation. In earlier years it was important to have the county seat near all parts of a county so that residents having business at the courthouse could make the trip in a day or so.

The importance of the county varies considerably in different parts of the country. In New England the town overshadows the county to the point that responsibilities allocated to county governments are meager. In fifteen states outside New England, certain functions are divided between counties and townships.[5] Township governments sometimes cover the entire state; but in Illinois, Missouri, Nebraska, and Washington, organization of township government is optional within each county. Consequently, townships are found in some parts of these states and not in others, creating a confusing and varied pattern of local government. In the remaining states (not counting Alaska), particularly in the South and the Far West, the county is the dominant unit of rural local government. Although counties have been called the "dark continent of American politics," they play a vital role in our system of government. Indeed, recent years have seen a notable increase in the responsibilities and functions assigned to counties. This generalization appears justified in spite of the fact that control over certain functions has been transferred in some instances from counties to states, especially highways and phases of relief programs.[6]

Counties have been regarded primarily as political subdivisions of the states in which they are located. Legal sanction was given to this viewpoint by the supreme court of Ohio a century ago:

---

[5] Illinois, Indiana, Kansas, Michigan, Minnesota, Missouri, Nebraska, New Jersey, New York, North Dakota, Ohio, Pennsylvania, South Dakota, Washington, and Wisconsin.

[6] Responsibility for construction and maintenance of highways has been transferred from county authorities to the state in Delaware, North Carolina, Virginia, and West Virginia.

Counties are local subdivisions of a state, created by the sovereign power of the state, of its own sovereign will, without the particular solicitation, consent, or concurrent action of the people who inhabit them . . .

A municipal corporation proper is created mainly for the interest, advantage, and convenience of the locality and its people; a county organization is created almost exclusively with a view to the policy of the state at large, for purposes of political organization and civil administration . . .[7]

This viewpoint has been repeated by courts in other states and is accepted as a settled point of law. In the foregoing quotation reference is made to the idea that a county should be distinguished from "a municipal corporation proper" created for the convenience of those who live within its boundaries. Cities, villages, and incorporated towns are examples of municipal corporations. Recognizing that counties partake of certain characteristics commonly assigned to such corporations, courts have classified counties as "quasi-municipal corporations," along with townships, New England towns, and special districts.[8] Lest too much emphasis be placed on this distinction, the following admonition by Professor Snider should be kept in mind:

Although the distinction between quasi and true municipal corporations is important for legal purposes, it is not always clear in actual application. Corporations of both types may serve at the same time as state administrative areas and as organs of local self-government. The difference is merely one of degree—the quasi-municipal corporation being *primarily* an administrative subdivision of the state and the true municipal corporation *primarily* an instrumentality of local government. Moreover, the attributes noted . . . as characteristic of quasi-municipal corporations apply more fully to some units ordinarily placed in that category (notably counties) than to others. And, with the tendency to increase the powers of counties and other quasi-municipal corporations in local matters, the distinction is gradually becoming of less practical significance.[9]

---

[7] *Commissioners of Hamilton County* v. *Mighels,* 7 Ohio St. 109 (1857).

[8] "Quasi" means "semi" or "almost." Accordingly, it is used to distinguish governmental bodies that are almost municipal corporations from those that are of the "true" variety, such as cities, villages, and incorporated towns.

[9] Clyde F. Snyder, *American State and Local Government,* Appleton-Century-Crofts, New York, 1965, p. 353.

Counties are always established under state authority, either constitutional or statutory. They are created by constitutional provisions in a few states, but this practice is exceptional. In most states counties are established directly by legislative act; in a few states they are brought into existence by local action under the authority of legislative acts.[10] Furthermore, the powers of counties are determined by the same authority. Earlier in history, mandatory responsibilities whose performance was *required* by state law accounted for most county activities. In recent years emphasis has been shifted increasingly to optional activities that are *permitted* by state law but are of particular interest to local inhabitants. This trend has been especially significant in highly urbanized counties where densely populated areas have developed outside city boundaries. Illustrative of newer, optional functions are provision of utility services, collection and disposal of waste materials, and maintenance of recreational facilities.

County Home Rule. Traditionally, direct control by state legislatures has extended to matters of county organization. State constitutions and statutes usually specify what officers shall be responsible for county government, the manner in which they shall be chosen, and their terms of office as well as their duties. In a few states the people have in recent years extended to individual counties increased freedom with regard to organization. In some instances this goal has been accomplished by means of optional-charter provisions authorizing counties to choose among alternative patterns of organization set forth more or less in detail by statutory provisions. For example, New York counties may choose among four options, North Dakota counties among three, and Virginia counties between two or three depending upon population. In Montana and North Carolina, counties are offered a single alternative to their traditional pattern of organization, namely, the county-manager arrangement. The basic purposes of such optional-charter laws are to enable counties to adopt a type of organization better suited to the new demands placed upon counties and at the same time to keep control over the structure of county government in the hands of the state legislature.

Eleven states extend even greater freedom of action to counties than that granted by optional-charter laws. In the constitutions of

---

[10] Examples of the creation of counties have been rare in recent years. A new county was created in New Mexico in 1949 and in Wisconsin in 1961

California, Hawaii, Maryland, Michigan, Minnesota, Missouri, New York, Ohio, Oregon, Texas, and Washington, *county home rule* is provided for.[11] As in the case of cities, a major purpose of home rule for counties is to permit the people to determine by popular vote the form of government they want. Basic to this privilege is the authority to frame and adopt their own charters.

An important difference exists between the usual grant of home rule to cities on the one hand and to counties on the other. State constitutional provisions authorizing home rule for cities usually confer considerable authority over local matters as distinguished from those of general state concern. But county home-rule provisions have *not* appreciably increased the substantive authority of counties; that is, they have not empowered counties to enter previously forbidden fields of activity to any significant degree. Instead, home rule has served almost entirely to enable individual counties to arrange their governmental structure to meet their particular needs. Complete freedom does not always exist even in this regard, for in some instances counties are required to provide for certain specified officers. For example, California counties must provide for a clerk, sheriff, treasurer, recorder, district attorney, auditor, assessor, tax collector, license collector, public administrator, coroner, surveyor, and superintendent of schools. Since home rule is in effect there, the method of choosing these officers is left to local determination.

Although some reformers and students of local government view home rule as a significant means of improving county government, experience with it has proved somewhat disappointing. In the eleven states that provide for county home rule, over 500 counties are entitled to frame and adopt charters designed to meet local needs and wishes, but about twenty have done so. Ten are found in California, three in Maryland, three in Oregon, one in Missouri, and three in

---

[11] The years in which these provisions were adopted are: California, 1911; Maryland, 1915; Ohio and Texas, 1933; Missouri, 1945; Washington, 1948; Minnesota, New York, and Oregon, 1958; Michigan, 1964. Constitutional amendments adopted in 1956 authorize adoption of charters by Dade County, Florida, and Jefferson Parish, Louisiana. Since these authorizations are in the nature of special grants for a single county in each state, they do not justify inclusion of Florida and Louisiana in a list of home rule states. With regard to county home rule in Texas, John Keith has observed, "The ambiguity and contradictions found in the language of the amendments as well as the lack of a proper enabling statute render it inoperative." John P. Keith, *City and County Home Rule in Texas*, Institute of Public Affairs, University of Texas, Austin, 1951, p. 146. Alaskan boroughs may also adopt home-rule charters.

New York.[12] In Minnesota, Ohio, Texas, and Washington no county has taken advantage of home rule.[13] Charters have been drafted in several counties, but they have failed to obtain the popular vote required for adoption. The most distinctive feature of home-rule charters adopted by counties is that in some dozen of them provision has been made for a chief executive officer, either appointed by the county governing body or popularly elected.

In fairness to advocates of county home rule, it should be noted that the small number of counties availing themselves of the opportunity to adopt their own charters and rearrange their governmental structures does not prove the idea defective. In those counties where it has been tried, people appear to be generally well satisfied with the arrangements created under home-rule authority. The fact remains, however, that experience thus far indicates that the presence of provisions in a state constitution making home rule available to counties will not result in any appreciable improvement in county government on a statewide basis. Indeed, in about one-third of the states where it is found no improvement in *any* county has resulted. The greatest use of county home rule has occurred in California, where approximately seventeen per cent of the counties have adopted charters. The small number of home-rule charters in states where they are available may be due in part to public apathy and indifference. Yet, many of the same people who have been indifferent to county home rule have taken advantage of municipal home rule.

---

[12] The ten California counties with home-rule charters are Los Angeles (1912), San Bernardino (1912), Butte (1916), Tehama (1916), Alameda (1926), Fresno (1933), Sacramento (1933), San Diego (1933), San Mateo (1933), and Santa Clara (1950). The city-county of San Francisco also operates under a home-rule charter, but it is usually considered as a city. The counties of Kern, Mendocino, Merced, Napa, Plumas, San Luis Obispo, Santa Barbara, Siskiyou, and Stanislaus have attempted unsuccessfully to acquire home-rule charters. Charters must be submitted to the California legislature after they have been ratified by the people, but none has been denied approval.

County home rule was adopted in Maryland in 1915, but Montgomery County in 1948 was first to adopt a charter, followed by Baltimore County (1956) and Anne Arundel (1964). In Missouri, home rule is extended only to counties with over 85,000 inhabitants. Among the few eligible counties, only St. Louis County has succeeded in adopting a charter. Proposals have been defeated in Buchanan and Jackson counties.

[13] In seven of the first eight Ohio counties attempting to secure home-rule charters, the effort was defeated by popular vote. The charter adopted in Cuyahoga County was ruled unconstitutional by the Ohio supreme court. See Earl L. Shoup, "Judicial Abrogation of County Home Rule in Ohio," *American Political Science Review*, June 1936. In Texas only El Paso County has attempted to secure a home-rule charter, and it failed to obtain the necessary popular vote. The charter drafted for King County, Washington, was defeated at the polls in 1952. This failure marked the only significant attempt to obtain a county home-rule charter in Washington.

ORGANIZATION OF COUNTY GOVERNMENT

County governmental organization is characterized by diversity, not only from state to state but even within states. Since detailed examination of the many existing variations is impossible here, a general treatment interspersed with illustrations must suffice. One writer has aptly observed that if any "principle" could be distinguished in American county government, it would be the principle of confusion.[14] The chart on page 501 reveals some of the reasons for this assertion.

Governing Bodies. In most counties the governing body is composed of several members, ranging from three to fifty.[15] Most commonly, this body is designated as the board of commissioners or board of supervisors, often referred to simply as the "county board." Titles vary among the states, including county court, commissioners court, fiscal court, police jury, board of freeholders, and commissioners of roads and revenue.[16] In spite of the variety, the United States Bureau of the Census has distinguished four major types of county governing bodies:[17]

1. board of commissioners or supervisors,
2. board composed of township supervisors,
3. board composed of one judge and commissioners,
4. board composed of one judge and justices of the peace.

Approximately two-thirds of county governing bodies belong in the first category. Members of boards in this group are elected specifically to perform the duties belonging to these bodies collec-

---

[14] Roger H. Wells, *American Local Government*, McGraw-Hill Book Co., New York, 1939, p. 80.

[15] Occasionally, particularly in Arizona, Georgia, and South Carolina, a single individual performs the duties usually assigned to a multimembered body. In a few instances, especially in Vermont, these duties are performed by bodies with only two members. By far the largest number of county governing agencies are composed of three or five members. At the other extreme are a few counties where the number of members on governing bodies ranges as high as eighty or more. The largest boards are usually found among the "township supervisors" type because each township is represented regardless of size, and additional membership is accorded to populous areas.

[16] For a detailed statement of the various titles of county governing bodies, see *County Boards and Commissions*, U.S. Bureau of the Census, 1947.

[17] The governing bodies of a few counties cannot be properly included in any of these four categories. Five minor types are distinguished in order to accommodate approximately six per cent of all counties. For a detailed breakdown of the various types with the number of counties belonging to each, see *ibid.*, p. 2.

ORGANIZATION OF TYPICAL COUNTY GOVERNMENT

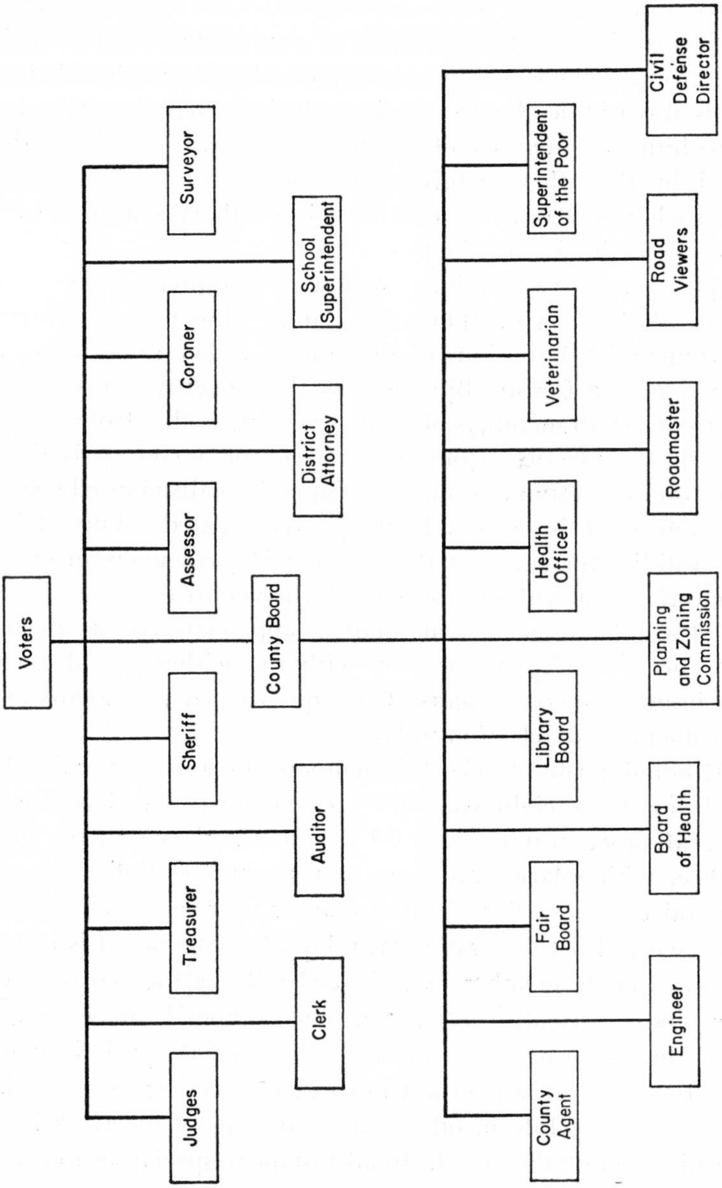

tively, and they normally hold no other public office. Members of boards of the second type are chosen from townships composing each county and regularly have responsibilities as township officers in addition to those that they possess as county officials. Boards in the third group differ from those in the first largely in that their chairman is also a judicial officer who has duties other than those belonging to him as a member of the county governing body, duties not shared by the other members. In the fourth category are those boards where not only the chairman is a judicial officer, since other members are justices of the peace.

With very few exceptions, members of county governing bodies are popularly elected. They are usually chosen from districts or governmental subdivisions of the county rather than at-large. According to the Census Bureau, less than twenty per cent of the counties elect all members of their governing bodies from the county as a whole. Election from subdivisions of a county is defended chiefly on the ground that membership will be distributed geographically and local interests adequately represented. This claim has some validity for counties that are not homogeneous in character, but election from subdivisions entails the very real danger that members of a governing body may fail to appreciate county needs as a whole because of preoccupation with the wishes and demands of their immediate constituents. Consequently, most students of local government favor election at-large.

Although terms of office for members of county governing bodies vary from one to eight years, the great majority are elected for four years. Members usually are paid an annual salary or a per diem allowance, with salaries ranging from about 100 dollars to several thousand per year. Per diem allowances vary in most instances between five and ten dollars for each day when the board is in session, and occasionally members are allowed mileage for necessary travel. County boards usually meet at least once a month, but meetings may be held less often in rural counties and more frequently in populous ones. In some states a certain number of meetings per year is prescribed by law, while in others the frequency of meetings is left to determination by the board. In all instances, special sessions may be called as needed.

The powers of county governing bodies are determined by state constitutional and statutory provisions. According to one commentator, all powers conferred by law upon a county, and not specifically delegated to some other county officers, are normally exercised by the county board.[18] County boards commonly exercise legislative, administrative, and judicial powers, an arrangement contrary to the principle of separation of powers characteristic of American government generally. The most important legislative powers pertain to finances.[19] A county board levies taxes, makes appropriations, and incurs debts for the county, subject to restrictions imposed by provisions of the state constitution and statutes. County boards also possess a variety of minor legislative powers, particularly in the regulatory field. Counties license and regulate businesses situated outside the boundaries of incorporated municipalities, such as liquor dispensaries, dance halls, circuses, and sporting events. They may also enact health and zoning ordinances as permitted by state law.

County boards are regarded principally as administrative agencies. Subject to varying amounts of state control and supervision, they exercise a wide variety of administrative functions. Probably the most important single function of a "typical" county board is supervision of the road and highway program. The significance of this activity is reflected in the time and money commonly allocated to it. Indeed, this responsibility is often exaggerated to the point where others are neglected. Another important duty concerns the control of county property. Administration of the courthouse, jail, poor house, county hospital, and various recreational facilities may rest with the county board. The board oversees the purchase and sale of property, construction and repair of buildings, and the general maintenance and upkeep of all county property. The county board may be responsible for the administration of elections and the supervision of poor relief, subject to control by state law. In addition, the board appoints certain officers, assistants, and deputies of many kinds, as well as a number of employees. It may also fix the salaries of county officers and employees, often subject to limitations imposed by state laws.

The judicial powers of most county boards today are insignificant. In some states these bodies have the legal status of judicial tribunals in spite of the fact that they perform few if any judicial functions. In other states county boards cannot be vested with judicial authority. Despite such restrictions, individual members of

---

[18] Clyde F. Snider, *op. cit.*, p. 363.

[19] On rare occasions authority over the financial affairs of the county may be vested in some agency other than the county board. See below, "Collateral Agencies."

county boards may have judicial responsibilities when acting as county judges or justices of the peace.

Collateral Agencies. A practice has long existed in county government of establishing a variety of inferior boards and commissions, usually unifunctional, to administer or supervise such functions as welfare, health, property assessment, libraries, elections, and hospitals. One student of county government, writing in 1950, noted that "there are 72 different functions for which one or more special function boards or commissions have been authorized by general law alone," not taking into account those created by special act.[20] Further complicating the picture is the fact that there may be more than one special agency responsible for different aspects of a single function. The existence of boards and commissions engaged in such activities as planning, airports, recreation, and personnel reflects recent developments in county government, usually involving the addition of new functions. Such new functions are significant with regard to the nature of county government today because they are primarily of *local* interest. Because of the increasing importance of such activities, counties can no longer be correctly viewed almost exclusively as subdivisions for the administration of state programs.

On rare occasions authority over county financial affairs may be lodged in an agency other than the county board. According to the Bureau of the Census, approximately 270 counties possess some type of collateral fiscal agency. An unusual arrangement is found in three New England states. In New Hampshire, the power to tax, make appropriations, and borrow money for counties rests in the hands of the members of the state legislature from the respective counties. The Maine legislature levies county taxes, and in Massachusetts the legislature authorizes county appropriations. In South Carolina, county levies and appropriations are made nominally by the state legislature as a whole, but actually the determination is made by the members of the legislature from each county. Four counties in Tennessee, three each in Florida and Georgia, and Wayne County in Michigan have collateral fiscal agencies. Although arguments may be advanced in behalf of such an arrangement, it undoubtedly serves

---

[20] Paul W. Wager, *County Government Across the Nation,* University of North Carolina Press, Chapel Hill, 1950, p. 13. It is not uncommon for the county board to serve *ex officio* as some of these special boards and commissions. Thus in Oregon the county court serves as the equalization board, the welfare commission, the board of health, and the dog control board.

to complicate the organizational pattern and the allocation of responsibilities in a county government.

Officers and Employees: *The Sheriff.* The most time-honored and universal county officer is the sheriff, who is generally elected by popular vote. His term of office is usually two or four years. Although the law in some states provides that a sheriff may not succeed himself, such a provision does not prevent his wife from being elected to the office and his serving as her chief deputy! Traditionally, the sheriff has served as conservator of the peace in his county. Although legally the chief law enforcement officer in his county, the modern sheriff has devoted less and less time to this responsibility, a trend due largely to two factors. First, increased urbanization has placed more and more policing responsibilities in the hands of municipal police. For several reasons sheriffs are willing to leave crime control in incorporated areas to city policemen and town constables even though their legal authority to enforce state laws and county ordinances extends into all units of government in their respective counties. Second, many law enforcement activities formerly in the hands of sheriffs have been transferred to state police who are generally more adequately trained and better equipped to perform them. Nevertheless, the county sheriff and his deputies still constitute an important agency for law enforcement in counties generally. In some urban areas, such as Los Angeles County for example, the sheriff's office is staffed with men well trained and organized to investigate crimes and to apprehend persons who break the law.

In addition to being conservator of the peace, the sheriff is an officer of the courts of record in his county. He or one of his deputies is required to attend court sessions and perform a variety of duties as directed, including the service of warrants, summonses, and subpoenas. The sheriff also conducts foreclosures and confiscates abandoned and illegal property. In addition, he is responsible for persons being held in jail pending indictment or trial, for taking convicted persons to institutions to which they are committed by court action, and frequently for the custody of persons who have been sentenced to the county jail. Sheriffs in some states are required to perform functions not directly related to law enforcement, such as collecting taxes and issuing licenses.

Frequently, county jails are administered by the sheriff on the basis of fees. Especially serious and reprehensible is the practice of allowing the sheriff or jailer a stipulated sum per day for each prisoner. Not only does this arrangement serve as an incentive to keep the jail filled, it also constitutes an ever-present temptation to provide substandard meals and inadequate care of all kinds for prisoners. Knowledge of the evils of this system is widespread, but it is often impossible to arouse sufficient interest on the part of citizens to make changes.[21] In recent years the fee system as a means of financing county jails has been abolished in many jurisdictions, and provision is made in some counties for a separate jailer.

The Prosecuting Attorney. Another county officer intimately associated with law enforcement is the prosecuting attorney, who is known by such titles as state's attorney, district attorney, or solicitor. This official, who may serve more than one county, is essentially a state officer, although he is popularly elected on a local basis in some three-fourths of the states. When a crime is committed, it is his job to investigate, collect evidence, institute formal proceedings against suspected persons, and represent the state at the trial. Although he may have a staff for purposes of investigation, it is important that the prosecuting attorney work in close cooperation with sheriffs and other local police officers. He may also be responsible for giving legal advice to county officers and conducting civil cases to which the county is a party, a task performed in some counties by an attorney retained by the county governing body.

From the standpoint of effective law enforcement, it is difficult to overestimate the importance of the prosecuting attorney. Without his cooperation effective law enforcement is impossible. To begin with, grand juries which in a majority of the states are responsible for indicting persons suspected of serious crime, usually consider only evidence presented to them by the prosecuting attorney. As an alternative to grand jury indictment, the prosecuting attorney in many states may bring criminal charges directly by a process known as "information." Whether a grand jury is used or not, the prosecutor largely determines who shall and who shall not be prosecuted for crime.

After a person has been charged with crime, the prosecuting attorney is responsible for conducting the prosecution. Once again

---

[21] For interesting insights pertaining to county jails, see Louis N. Robinson, *Jails: Care and Treatment of Misdemeanant Prisoners in the United States,* Winston Press, Philadelphia, 1944; and Mryl E. Alexander, *Jail Administration,* Charles C. Thomas, Springfield, Ill., 1957.

the role of this officer is critical. Legally responsible for prosecuting the guilty, a prosecutor also is obligated to seek justice, and this task involves acquitting the innocent. When a prosecuting attorney believes he has insufficient evidence to prove a person guilty of crime, he may seek dismissal of the case. Such action may be entirely justifiable in order to save the time, effort, and expense involved in a trial that can lead only to acquittal. On the other hand, the prosecutor may act for personal or political reasons. In spite of the great importance of the office, it "is often held either by a young lawyer fresh from school, who seeks by this means to widen his acquaintance and at the same time gain some experience, or less frequently, by an older attorney whose career in private practice has not been outstanding."[22]

The Coroner. Only slightly less ancient than the office of sheriff is that of the coroner, who is most often popularly elected.[23] His principal function is to hold inquests to determine the cause of deaths occurring under violent or suspicious circumstances. A few states require coroners to be physicians, but they are often undertakers whose official fees are determined by the number of corpses they bury. Usually there is only one coroner per county, but in a few localities there may be two or more.[24] In some counties, especially more highly urbanized ones, the coroner has been supplanted by a medical examiner who is required to be a physician. Even this arrangement is not entirely satisfactory, however, since the duties of the office involve legal as well as medical questions and decisions. Rare is the person who possesses training desirable for handling both types of problems. As a consequence, it is often necessary that the medical examiner and prosecuting attorney maintain a close working relationship. Although subject to much criticism and the object of proposals for its abolition, the office of coroner performs a significant function in counties across the nation.

The Clerk. The office of county clerk is found in about half of the states, and the incumbent is usually chosen by popular vote. The duties of county clerks may be divided into three major categories: (a) preparation and custodianship of records, (b) issuance of warrants against the county, and (c) administration of elections. The

---

[22] Clyde F. Snider, *op. cit.,* p. 471.

[23] Several states have recently abolished elective coroners.

[24] In Michigan provision is made for two coroners per county, and three may be found in New Jersey counties. In all states, coroners frequently name deputies to assist them.

clerk serves as secretary of the county board and "clerk of court" for many local courts of record. His office is commonly the repository for all books, records, and papers of the county and often of special districts located in the county. Deeds, mortgages, leases,[25] plats, marriage certificates, divorce records, birth certificates, adoption papers, and similar documents may be filed with the county clerk. He may also issue passports and naturalization papers in accord with procedures specified by federal law.

When issuing warrants against the county treasury, the county clerk is sometimes called the "auditor," if there is no separate officer with that title. Prior to the issuance of a warrant, a claim must be allowed by the county board. Once it has been prepared by the clerk, the warrant is countersigned and paid by the county treasurer. In practice, actual determination of whether a claim will be allowed against a county often lies with the clerk. This situation stems from the fact that he has available the records to determine the validity of a claim, and his recommendation is likely to be accepted by the board.

The county clerk performs many essential functions with regard to the administration of elections. He usually registers voters where there is no separate registrar to perform this important task. He prepares ballots, receives nominating as well as local initiative and referendum petitions, establishes election precincts, canvasses the vote, and issues certificates of election to local officers. In addition, the county clerk is often responsible for issuing licenses, such as those required for marriage, hunting, fishing, and operation of certain types of businesses.

The Treasurer. Most counties have a treasurer, who may be popularly elected or appointed by the county board. The duties of this office fall into three major categories: (a) receipt of county revenues, (b) custodianship of county funds, and (c) disbursement of money as directed by proper authority. Although certain revenues are received by other officers in many counties, some authorities believe that the collection of all county income should be centralized in the treasurer.[26] Such an arrangement simplifies administration of

---

[25] In about half of the states provision is made for a recorder or register of deeds, and documents relating to property transactions are entrusted to his care.

[26] Alternative arrangements have been adopted in a few states whereby the treasurer's office has been merged with some other office or abolished, and banks have been designated to serve as depositories and disbursing agents. See Melvin C. Hughes, *County Government in Georgia,* University of Georgia Press, Athens, 1944.

financial affairs and facilitates the preparation of adequate reports. Furthermore, it may be advisable for the treasurer to collect income due governmental subdivisions within a county, particularly special districts.

When revenues are received by other county officers such as the sheriff or the clerk, they are usually turned over to the treasurer.[27] Earlier in history, county treasurers often retained for their own use any interest paid on county bank deposits, a practice generally recognized as intolerable today. Treasurers usually are required to provide an indemnity bond as a guarantee against any possible loss or misuse of public funds. The third major responsibility of the treasurer is to disburse funds as directed, usually on order of the county board.

The Assessor. Administration of the property tax involves determination of the value of property, a task commonly placed in the hands of the assessor of a county, township, or city. Most often the county assessor evaluates all taxable property within his jurisdiction, and his assessments are accepted by other governmental units for purposes of taxation. In those states where townships function, assessment of property may be lodged with the township assessor. The importance of the assessor is indicated by the fact that the revenue of local governments is largely derived from the property tax. Many serious problems result from the election of persons not qualified adequately to perform the assessment function.[28] In an effort to overcome evils associated with such a practice, some states have enacted laws providing that only individuals certified by a state agency as qualified appraisers may actually set the value of real property. Such a requirement means that elected assessors frequently must hire persons qualified to do the work for which they are responsible.

The Superintendent of Schools. Found in over three-fourths of the states, the county superintendent of schools may be elected or appointed. His duties and responsibilities vary greatly from state to state. In the fifteen states that use the county-unit plan[29] for providing primary and secondary education, the responsibilities of this

---

[27] Fees received by county officers for the performance of certain particular functions constitute an exception.

[28] See Chapter 15 for additional discussion of property valuation.

[29] The county-unit system provides for financing and administering most of the schools, if not all, by county authorities. City schools are sometimes not under direct county supervision and have their own school boards and superintendents.

officer are especially important because most schools are managed on a county-wide basis. In the other states the duties of the county superintendent are less numerous, and he serves primarily as an agent of the state department of education in seeing that state requirements are met. This generalization does not mean that in the states without the county-unit arrangement the responsibilities assigned to the county superintendent are unimportant. His duties often include assisting in the development of improved curricula and methods of teaching, encouraging parental interest in the schools, observing physical conditions in school plants, advising school district authorities, making reports to state agencies, and keeping records on all teachers in the county.

Miscellaneous Officers. The foregoing list of county officers is by no means complete. Many others are found in counties across the United States. For purposes of illustration, mention may be made of the *surveyor,* who is usually popularly elected and compensated by fees. His chief task is to conduct land surveys and determine boundary lines, a job that can be done equally well by private surveyors. Many counties have an *engineer,* often on a part-time basis, who is in charge of the location, design, and construction of roads and bridges. In addition, there may be a county *roadmaster* who supervises the actual construction and maintenance of county roads, as well as *road viewers* charged with the task of establishing the most feasible route for a proposed road. Some counties, located in about one-third of the states, have an *auditor,* who is normally responsible for preparing budgets and maintaining accounts. Another important function of the auditor is the preaudit of claims against the county to determine their validity and the existence of funds available for payment. It appears that seldom, if ever, does this officer perform a postaudit to determine the fidelity with which public funds have been handled. Many other county officers exist, but their number and variety are too great to permit mention here.

Employees. Although an adequate distinction between officers and employees is difficult to make, the general consensus seems to be that an officer is an individual who holds an office or position created specifically by law and who is responsible for the preformance of certain duties set forth by law. An employee, on the other hand, is a person hired by an officer or agency to perform tasks specified by his superiors. According to the Bureau of the Census, there are between

800,000 and 900,000 county officers and employees in the United States.

A chief defect of county government today is reflected in the fact that the spoils system is almost universal. In other words, the great majority of county employees are appointed on the basis of party and personal allegiance. Although it is *not impossible* to have efficient government without a merit system, it is difficult and unlikely. Although no authoritative list exists, probably about ten per cent of the counties in the United States have established civil service procedures for the selection and appointment of employees on the basis of demonstrated merit.[30] The situation has improved slightly in recent years, but the bulk of these counties still are situated in New York and Ohio, the only states requiring counties to operate under a merit system. With the exception of these states, the largest percentage of counties with a merit system is found in California, where in 1955 some forty per cent were reported as having made some arrangement for selecting employees on the basis of merit.[31] In most other states only a few of the more populous counties have taken similar action. Since sabotage of established merit systems has occurred in some instances, the picture is discouraging for advocates of civil service reform.

Even in counties that make no provision for a general merit program, certain employees are under a merit system. Those engaged in administering welfare programs are commonly selected on the basis of merit. This situation is *not* due to a widespread voluntary decision by county authorities to place welfare workers in a different category from other county employees. Instead, it is attributable to a federal requirement that personnel administering welfare funds received from the national government must be employed under some sort of merit plan. Consequently, counties have been forced to make provision for a merit system for such people in order to receive federal monetary assistance.

Employees in the great majority of counties work under conditions largely untouched by modern methods of personnel administration. Rarely have such techniques as job classification, well-developed pay plans, organized training programs, and adequate retirement systems become an integral part of county administration. Advances

---

[30] This number does not include school employees.

[31] Harry W. Graham, "County Personnel Administration—Wide Variety in California Systems," *The Tax Digest*, March, 1955.

usually have occurred piecemeal as the result of necessity, such as improvement in pay scales and provision for retirement benefits. Subsequent to changes in the federal Social Security Act in 1950 and 1954, many state and local governments have taken advantage of the opportunity to include their employees under social security. Greater improvements have occurred with regard to the development of retirement programs than in most other areas of personnel administration in American counties.

STRUCTURAL REORGANIZATION

Consolidation. Many proposals have been made for the modernization of county government. In addition to home rule, discussed earlier, a proposal that has received some support is county consolidation. Many counties are too small and possess inadequate financial resources to be effective. Numerous studies have been made with consolidation in mind, and serious proposals have been advanced in several states, but almost nothing has been accomplished.[32] During the present century only two consolidations involving organized counties have occurred.[33] Many factors have contributed to the rarity of county consolidations, but the basic reason is probably reflected in this highly perceptive statement: "Consolidation often seems to be a logical solution, but political decisions are often illogical. The people of one county may be willing to merge with another, providing the *other* county gives up its county seat, courthouse, and officeholders."[34] County officials, politicians, and many citizens look with disfavor upon the idea of losing their identity as residents of *their own* county.

Another type of consolidation that has experienced more success is city-county consolidation, involving the merger of city and county

---

[32] For illustrations of such proposals, see S. R. Heckart and G. S. Klemmedson, *County Consolidation in Colorado,* Colorado Agricultural College, Fort Collins, 1933; V. G. Sorrell and J. R. Stuart, *County Consolidation in New Mexico,* University of New Mexico, Albuquerque, 1934; and Nevada Legislative Counsel Bureau, *County Consolidation and Reorganization in Nevada,* 1948.

[33] In 1919 James County was consolidated with Hamilton County, Tennessee; and in 1932 Campbell and Milton Counties were merged with Fulton County, Georgia. In addition, two unorganized counties in South Dakota have been eliminated. In 1943 the legislature of South Dakota consolidated the unorganized county of Washington with that of Shannon. In 1951 the unorganized county of Armstrong was annexed to the organized county of Dewey by act of the legislature. On December 17, 1957, the voters in Alabama approved a constitutional amendment authorizing the legislature to abolish Macon County and divide it among neighboring counties.

[34] Marguerite J. Fisher and Donald G. Bishop, *Municipal and Other Local Governments,* Prentice-Hall, New York, 1950, p. 627.

governments. The best known instances are found in Baltimore, Denver, Honolulu, St. Louis, and San Francisco.[35] Partial mergers have been undertaken in Baton Rouge, Boston, New Orleans, New York City, and Philadelphia.[36] A special situation exists in Virginia, where cities with 10,000 or more people are legally separated from the counties in which they are situated and perform both city and county services for their residents.[37] No pattern has emerged from the actions taken in different localities; each consolidation has been unique in certain of its aspects. "The greatest merit of the city-county consolidation approach lies in providing a unified, coordinated program of service, development and control over an area larger than that previously served exclusively by one general local government."[38] Accordingly, this device is generally viewed not so

---

[35] Denver, Honolulu, and San Francisco are known as city-counties, while Baltimore and St. Louis are designated simply as cities. Technically, these cities were separated from the counties of which they were once a part. The only one of these separations to become effective during the present century was that of Denver in 1902. (Litigation delayed progress for another ten years.) The boundaries of the city-county of Honolulu include the island of Oahu and all nearby islands not assigned to another county. In 1962 a consolidation of the governments of the city of Nashville and Davidson County, Tennessee, was approved by the voters, creating the Metropolitan Government of Nashville and Davidson County. A different type of merger was accomplished in Virginia in 1963 when Norfolk and Princess Anne counties became the cities of Chesapeake and Virginia Beach.

[36] The first of these consolidations, involving New Orleans and the Parish of Orleans, was accomplished by special act of the Louisiana legislature in 1813. The second, involving Boston and Suffolk County, resulted from a special act of the Massachusetts legislature passed in 1821. The third consolidation act was enacted by the Pennsylvania legislature in 1854, extending the boundaries of the City of Philadelphia so as to be coterminous with those of the County of Philadelphia. The degree of consolidation provided by the act of 1854 was lessened by the constitution of 1874. More thorough consolidation was authorized by a constitutional amendment adopted in 1951. For details of the history of the Philadelphia consolidation, see Bureau of Municipal Research of Philadelphia, "Taking Stock of Consolidation," *Citizens' Business,* December 21, 1953, and Bureau of Municipal Research of Philadelphia and Pennsylvania Economy League, Eastern Division, "Supreme Court Delays Completing City-County Unity," *Citizens' Business,* January 24, 1955. Three consolidations have occurred involving New York City. In 1730 the boundaries of the City of New York and the County of New York were made identical by charter provision. In 1894 the boundaries of the City of Brooklyn and the County of Kings were made coterminous by legislative act. In 1896 the legislature authorized consolidation of the governments in the area of the three counties of New York, Kings, Richmond, and part of Queens. A legislative charter for the consolidated unit became effective on January 1, 1898. In 1949 an amendment was added to the New Mexico constitution permitting city-county mergers in counties with a population of 50,000 or more. Recent proposals for the unification of the City of Durham with Durham County, N.C., and the City of Chattanooga with Hamilton County, Tenn., were defeated by popular vote.

[37] See R. B. Pinchbeck, "City-County Separation in Virginia," *National Municipal Review,* July 1940.

[38] The Council of State Governments, *The States and the Metropolitan Problem,* 1956, p. 74.

much as a means of improving county government as of meeting the problems of metropolitan areas.

A Chief Executive. One outstanding weakness of county government in general is the absence of a chief executive. There are far too many independent "executives" and department heads whose activities are subject to no effective supervision and coordination. Recognition of the evils of this arrangement has been widespread, and efforts at improvement have taken three major forms: (a) adoption of the county-manager plan; (b) provision of an appointed chief executive with less authority than is usually granted to a manager; and (c) an elected chief executive. Since the first two of these arrangements are similar in form, they are sometimes not distinguished.

County-manager government is organized in essentially the same manner as the city-manager form.[39] (See the chart on page 515 for a graphic presentation of county-manager government in its "pure" form.) Its basic feature is appointment by the county board of a manager who serves as the county's principal administrative officer. Duties of the manager include enforcement of the official policies of the board, appointment and removal of administrative officers, preparation of budgets, and provision of advice and recommendations to the board. Under this arrangement, *legal* responsibility for the conduct of county affairs rests with the county board, which vests *administrative* responsibility in the hands of a person chosen supposedly without regard to political considerations. "Thus, the manager plan leaves policy determination in the hands of the popularly elected board but emphasizes the professional element in administration and places responsibility for administrative supervision upon a single official—the county manager."[40]

Over two dozen counties operate under the manager form of government.[41] Unsuccessful efforts have been made in other counties to adopt manager government, which is opposed on a variety of grounds, many of them rather specious. The allegation is often made that manager government is "undemocratic." The popularity of this

---

[39] For a discussion of the council-manager type of city government, see Chapter 19.
[40] Clyde F. Snider, *op. cit.,* p. 174.
[41] The manager counties are Sacramento, San Mateo, and Santa Clara in California; Dade in Florida; Fulton, Glynn, and Wayne in Georgia; Ann Arundel and Montgomery in Maryland; Washoe in Nevada; Petroleum in Montana; Monroe in New York; Anson, Catawba, Davidson, Durham, Forsyth, Gaston, Guilford, Hertford, Mecklenburg, Rockingham, and Wake in North Carolina; McNinn in Tennessee; Albemarle, Arlington, Fairfax, and Henrico in Virginia.

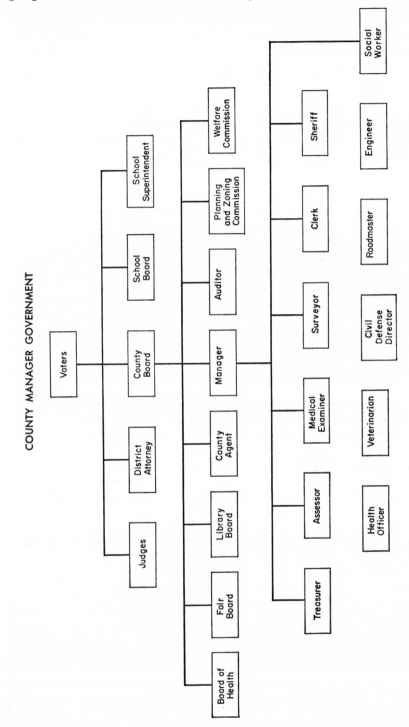

COUNTY MANAGER GOVERNMENT

claim stems from the belief that in order for a government to be democratic, the people must elect those officers responsible for the execution of public policy as well as those responsible for its formulation. Nowhere is this attitude better illustrated than in county government. Persons advancing this argument against the manager system often choose to disregard the fact that basic responsibility continues to rest in the hands of popularly elected officials. The fact must be admitted, however, that appointed officials sometimes actually make decisions that appear to be made by representative bodies.

Managers are sometimes opposed on the ground that there is too little county business to justify hiring them. Even in rural counties where this claim may have some merit, arrangements may be made for hiring part-time managers as is done in some cities. Another possible means of meeting this problem is to put the manager directly in charge of certain county functions, thus eliminating some positions. Others maintain that the adoption of the manager plan would interfere with the work of state officials who have responsibility for supervising county functions, such as health, welfare and highways. Certainly, appointment by a manager of agency heads to administer such activities would make them no less amenable to state supervision than choice by popular election.[42]

More common than managers are *chief administrative officers* who have less power than is normally granted to managers, especially with regard to making appointments and preparing budgets.[43] Chief

---

[42] County-manager government appears to have met with notable success in most instances, including the most rural county where it has been adopted, Petroleum County, Montana. For glowing accounts of the accomplishments of manager government in Petroleum County, based on facts and figures, see R. R. Renne, "Too Small to Be Efficient?" *National Municipal Review*, February 1947; "Petroleum County Thrives with Manager," *ibid.*, May 1954; and R. R. Renne, "Montana Pace Setter," *ibid.*, March 1958. See also H. G. Halcrow, *County Manager Government in Montana: Presenting a Case Study of Petroleum County*, Montana State College Agricultural Experiment Station, 1949.

In 1953 reports from Monroe County, New York, indicated that manager government had been instrumental in reducing county debt by over eighty per cent in sixteen years and in holding administrative costs to a relatively small increase. See W. E. Weller and C. M. Smith, "Sixteen Years of Progress," *National Municipal Review*, September 1953. For a critical viewpoint, see Kirk H. Porter, "A Wet Blanket on the County Manager Plan," *ibid.*, January 1929; and "County Government and State Centralization," *ibid.*, August 1932.

Although factual details have been inadequately reported, available information indicates that manager government has contributed appreciably to the efficiency and economy of operations in those counties that have tried it.

[43] These officers sometimes are designated as managers, but they are not recognized as such by the International City Managers' Association, the professional organization of local managers.

administrative officers commonly are limited to making recommendations on appointments to the county board, which retains final appointing authority over officers not elected. In respect to budgets
they are generally responsible merely for collecting annual departmental estimates and submitting them, perhaps accompanied by
suggestions, to the board. The chief administrative officer constitutes
a sort of compromise between the no-executive arrangement traditional in our counties and the strong manager system.

No complete tabulation exists of the total number of counties in
the United States possessing some sort of chief executive. However,
attention may be called to a few well-known examples. Among the
first counties to provide for a chief administrative officer was Los
Angeles in 1944.[44] The plan appears to have enjoyed considerable
success there, and at least thirty other counties in California have
adopted something similar.[45] The list of counties in other states
adopting a comparable arrangement includes Hamilton County, Tennessee, Clark County, Nevada, Charleston County, South Carolina,
and Cuyahoga, Hamilton, Lake, and Summit Counties, Ohio. Although organizational details differ, results appear to have been
praiseworthy in every instance.[46]

The third alternative followed in some counties that have reorganized their administrative structure is the elected president or
supervisor, an arrangement very similar to the mayor-council form of
city government.[47] Again, variations in titles and organizational details abound. Efforts directed along this line began during the last
century. Among the first counties to provide for an elected president
was Cook County, Illinois, where the president is popularly elected as
a member of the county board. In addition to being chairman of the
board, the president possesses powers of appointment and veto. A
majority of the chief county officers are still popularly elected.

Popularly elected chief executives called county supervisors are
found in Essex and Hudson counties, New Jersey, where they have

---

[44] The official title is now "county administrative officer." A variety of modifications
of the generic title exists. Particularly in California, the designation often is shortened
to "CAO."

[45] See John C. Bollens, *Appointed Executive Local Government*, Haynes Foundation,
Los Angeles, 1952.

[46] See William F. Larsen, "Tradition Bows to Efficiency," *National Municipal Re-
view*, November 1950; "Cuyahoga County Gets Administrative Officer," *ibid.*, April 1952;
"Three Counties Appoint Administrative Officers," *Public Management*, March 1952.
For a more complete list, see *Recent Council-Manager Developments and Directory of
Council-Manager Cities*, International City Managers' Association, 1961.

[47] For a discussion of the mayor-council form of city government, see Chapter 19.

been authorized for first-class counties since 1900. Although supposedly responsible for supervising the activities of county officials and employees, these supervisors are without effective authority because they lack control over appointments and budgets. Consequently, their effectiveness as executive officers is quite limited. In Nassau and Westchester counties, New York, elected county executives possess greater control over county affairs since they are empowered to appoint and remove a number of important county officers as well as to prepare budgets. A similar pattern is found in St. Louis County, Missouri, where the elected supervisor exercises more administrative control than in most counties with this form of government. Elected county executives have been recently established in Baltimore County, in Jefferson Parish, Louisiana, and in Milwaukee County, Wisconsin.

In an effort to overcome some of the evils resulting from the lack of a county executive officer, a few counties, especially in Wisconsin, have strengthened the position of the county clerk. The degree to which the clerk's powers are broadened depends largely upon the wishes of the county board. If the members choose to rely upon him in a variety of matters, they may in effect make him *primus inter pares,* first among equals. Since such an arrangement involves no reorganization of governmental structure, it does not qualify as constituting a significant change in the traditional pattern of county government.

County government still is regarded by many as the "dark continent of American politics." Important among the reasons for this opinion are the usual organizational complexity and the lack of coordination that stem from a multiplicity of independent elective officials responsible only to the voters. Although more or less serious attempts have been made in most states during the present century to improve county government, significant progress has been made in very few instances. No other major type of governmental unit in the country, perhaps with the exception of the township, has been so little affected by efforts at reform.

COUNTY FUNCTIONS

Of the many functions performed by the county some are required by state law, while others are optional; some are traditional, while others are new. Considered generally, those required by state law are the traditional functions, while optional activities are the newer ones. In the former category belong such duties as law enforcement, administration of justice, public welfare, construction and maintenance of roads and highways, assistance to agriculture, and responsibility for phases of public education, a particularly important function in certain parts of the country.

Law Enforcement. From the time of their beginning in England, counties have had responsibilities with regard to preserving public peace and order. While the prevention of crime and the apprehension of criminals now rests in large part with municipal and state police, the sheriff and his deputies usually constitute the only local police force with county-wide jurisdiction. With the exception of highly urbanized counties and a few others, the unfortunate fact is that the sheriff's office is poorly prepared to cope with modern crime. "We have in reality retained a medieval functionary with almost unchanged status and powers to cope with a criminal class which has completely mechanized itself and taken full advantage of every improvement in transportation and communication."[48] In spite of this fact, many law-enforcement activities outside municipal boundaries rest with county officers. Two important officers, other than the sheriff, concerned with law enforcement are the prosecuting attorney and the coroner, whose duties have been briefly described above.

Administration of Justice. One of the most important county functions involves provision of courts and other agencies for the administration of state civil and criminal laws. Although local courts are viewed legally as components of the state judicial system, responsibility for their organization, staffing, and financial support often rests with counties. The interrelations existing in this area are stressed by the fact that local judicial officers often serve as members of county governing bodies. Throughout most of the rural United States, a person who commits a minor infraction of the law or who wishes to institute a minor civil suit must go into a justice of the peace court. The justice of the peace is a traditional county officer in England and in the United States.[49] At a time when "the law was not yet developed into that morass of refinements inseparable from a varied and complex economic order, and plain men were compe-

---

[48] Lane W. Lancaster, *Government in Rural America*, D. Van Nostrand Co., Inc., Princeton, 1937, pp. 191–192.

[49] Justices of the peace often are chosen for subdivisions of a county, such as the township or special district.

tent to manage tribunals devoted to settling the controversies of their neighbors," much could be said in behalf of this office.[50]

Persons committing more serious infractions of the law or wishing to institute a major civil action commonly begin proceedings in a "court of general jurisdiction." Known most often as circuit, district, or superior courts, the geographical jurisdiction of these courts is often coterminous with county boundaries. More often, however, special judicial districts are provided by state law. These districts frequently comprise two or more counties, each of which is required to supply funds for the support of the court; and the court must hold sessions in each county at prescribed intervals. Although popularly elected in over three-fourths of the states, judges of such courts generally must be qualified both as to training and experience.

Provision is sometimes made for a trial court intermediate between the justice of the peace and the general trial court. The county commonly constitutes the geographical jurisdiction of such a court, which may hear criminal cases more serious than those taken into a justice of the peace court and less serious than those that must go into a general trial court. Some states permit only counties with a specified minimum population to establish such a court. A fourth type of court found in some counties is the probate court, whose chief duties involve supervision and disposition of the estates of deceased persons. In those counties without probate courts, the administration of estates is generally performed by courts of general or limited jurisdiction as described above.

One phase of the administration of justice that is poorly handled throughout most of the United States is the defense of persons accused of crime who are financially unable to hire capable legal talent. According to one estimate, as high as eighty per cent of accused persons do not possess sufficient funds to secure adequate counsel.[51] In more serious cases involving such individuals, it is the duty of the court to see that defense counsel is provided. The traditional method of meeting this requirement is through the device of assigned counsel, whereby the court designates a lawyer to represent the defendant. This practice is generally unsatisfactory either because the better lawyers do not draw the assignments, or if they do, the accompanying fees are insufficient to arouse their best efforts. In an attempt to

---

[50] Lane W. Lancaster, *op. cit.*, p. 201.

[51] See J. E. Lumbard, Jr., "For Equal Justice—A Public 'Defender,' " *New York Times Magazine*, Nov. 2, 1947, pp. 17, 68.

make "equality before the law" a fact as well as a slogan, a few counties and cities have made provision for the office of public defender, who is required by law to defend the accused just as the prosecuting attorney is required to prosecute him.[52] Of course, persons able to do so must still provide their own counsel.

Public Welfare. The care of dependent poor is a traditional function of American counties. Although the *portion* of the public welfare burden borne by local governments has decreased appreciably in the last quarter-century, counties still play a vital role in the administration of welfare services; they are the major agencies through which so-called "outdoor" assistance is usually provided.[53] Outdoor assistance, sometimes called home relief, consists of grants of food, clothes, fuel, medical supplies, utilities, shelter, or in some cases the provision of funds for the purchase, by the recipient, of such necessities. Counties also share in the administration of assistance to the aged, the blind, and dependent children, although most of the money for these programs comes from the federal and state governments. Recent years have witnessed greatly increased state supervision of county welfare activities, a development stemming in large part from provisions of federal law requiring effective administration of federal welfare funds in all political subdivisions of a state.

Roads and Highways. Provision of ways for public travel is another traditional function of counties and other units of local government. Indeed, it was not until World War I that all states participated in the construction of highways.[54] Today, in all but four states, responsibility for this important activity is divided between the state

---

[52] First provided in Los Angeles County in 1914, the office of public defender in 1957 was found in nineteen California counties and municipalities, according to the National Legal Aid Association. At the same time this organization noted that Connecticut had several municipal public defenders. Also, public defenders existed in twenty-seven counties in Illinois and Dade County, Florida. A sprinkling of cities were reported to have such officers, including Boston and Cambridge, Massachusetts; St. Paul, Minnesota; St. Louis, Missouri; Omaha, Nebraska; Columbus, Ohio; Oklahoma City and Tulsa, Oklahoma; Providence, Rhode Island; and Memphis, Tennessee. Privately supported voluntary defense organizations existed in New York City, Cincinnati, Philadelphia, Pittsburgh, and Rochester, New York.

[53] "Indoor" assistance, typefied by the county almshouse or poorhouse, has been of decreasing importance in recent years. Many persons earlier committed to such institutions are now cared for in state institutions, while others are kept out of institutions by improved programs for outdoor relief.

[54] See U.S. Bureau of Public Roads, *Highways in the United States* (1951) and *The Local Rural Road Problem* (1950).

and local units.[55] Rural public ways are commonly classified as primary or secondary highways and farm-to-market roads. Highways of the first class are generally designed to facilitate cross-state or interstate traffic. Secondary highways, referred to in many localities as county highways, are designed to link small towns and to feed traffic into first-class highways. As their name indicates, farm-to-market roads are designed chiefly to carry traffic to and from farms and in turn to feed traffic into highways of the first two classes.

Everywhere, states have assumed most of the responsibility for construction or supervision of the construction of primary highways.[56] Generally, chief responsibility for secondary highways rests with counties, which in recent years have been increasingly responsible for farm-to-market roads that were formerly constructed and maintained by towns or townships.[57] Although they carry less than one-fourth of the total traffic, secondary highways and farm-to-market roads comprise some seventy-five per cent of the total road mileage in the United States. Despite the fact that construction and maintenance of roads in these categories are vested in counties and other units of local government, more than half of the necessary money is provided by the states, largely in the form of allocations from gasoline taxes. Counties continue to spend a very large portion of their revenues for roads and highways, a fact reflecting the importance of the rural vote in electing members of county boards.

Assistance to Agriculture. Agricultural extension work is found in most counties in the United States. Often called "cooperative extension," this program is financed by the national government, the states, and counties.[58] The basic purposes are to provide farmers and other rural dwellers with practical information on agriculture and home economics and instill in them a desire to use that information to increase productivity and improve their standard of living.[59]

---

[55] The four exceptions are Delaware, North Carolina, Virginia, and West Virginia. Three counties in Virginia have retained control over local roads.

[56] This situation has resulted in large part from federal grants-in-aid given to the states with the understanding that certain standards must be met in highway construction. For further information on state activities with regard to highways, see Chapter 27.

[57] Such transfer has been mandatory under state law in some instances and optional in others.

[58] The basis for federal participation is found in the Smith-Lever Act of 1914.

[59] The efforts of extension workers are not limited to these undertakings. Particularly in recent years, they have branched out into social and recreational activities as well as adult education programs designed to promote interest in community, national, and international affairs. See Wallace E. Ogg, "The Cooperative Extension Service in Today's World," *State Government*, September 1952.

Actual administration of the program rests with county extension offices working in close cooperation with state agricultural colleges. Each extension office is under the supervision of a "county agent," who usually has a home-demonstration agent and sometimes a 4-H Club agent working with him. These agents most often are appointed by the county board, subject to the approval of other governmental units sharing the cost of the program. At present the national government bears over forty per cent of the costs of extension work, the states something over thirty per cent, and the counties slightly under twenty-five per cent, with a small amount coming from farmers' organizations. At least two-thirds of the total available funds are spent by county extension offices.[60] Although activities of extension agents do not represent the only efforts of counties to assist the farmer, they include many of the more important ones.

Education. In fifteen states[61] the county is the dominant governmental unit in the administration of public education on the primary and secondary levels. Under this arrangement, the schools in a county are financed and administered on a county-wide basis, although city schools may be separately controlled. Major arguments in behalf of the county-unit system are that it promotes uniformity of educational opportunities throughout a relatively large area and that by pooling the resources of this area the likelihood of better educational facilities is enhanced. On the other hand, counties were not created with the specific intention that they serve as units for administering public education. Furthermore, there eixsts in many places a strong desire on the part of the people to keep control over schools "close to home," and local school districts accord with this wish. In counties not under the county-unit arrangement, county school officials may still serve an important function, particularly in enforcing the rules and regulations of state departments of education.

Newer County Functions. Contrary to the frequently repeated views of some skeptics, counties in recent years have demonstrated their capacity to assume a variety of new functions. Included among these newer responsibilities are health protection, parks and recreational facilities, libraries, and zoning. This list is in no sense com-

---

[60] See United States Department of Agriculture, *Report of Cooperative Extension Work in Agriculture and Home Economics: 1952.*

[61] Alabama, Florida, Georgia, Kentucky, Louisiana, Maryland, Mississippi, Nevada, New Mexico, North Carolina, South Carolina, Tennessee, Utah, Virginia, and West Virginia. Nevada became a county-unit state as the result of legislation enacted in 1955.

plete, but it serves well the purpose of illustration. Assumption of these activities has been largely a matter of necessity, resulting from the rapid growth of heavily populated areas outside municipal boundaries.

Although much emphasis has been placed on "healthful" country living, deaths from certain diseases, such as malaria and typhoid fever, are higher today in rural areas than in cities. Many problems complicate the development of adequate health programs in counties across the nation. A large portion of the rural counties are financially unable to create and maintain adequate health departments.[62] Efforts along this line were given impetus by the Social Security Act of 1935, which made federal funds available to assist in establishing and maintaining local health services. On occasion counties have cooperated to provide joint health programs. Nevertheless, the United States Health Service reported in 1952 that only about half of the counties had full-time health officers.[63] County health organizations have accomplished much in the areas of disease-control, sanitation, and health education. Also, many counties have performed an important service by establishing hospitals.

Many counties own and operate parks and other recreational facilities such as playgrounds, swimming pools, golf courses, and camping and picnic grounds. These facilities serve not only county residents, but city dwellers as well. Failure on the part of many cities to plan for adequate recreational facilities within their confines has increased the need for county action. County libraries for the benefit of both city and rural dwellers have been established in many localities. In some instances counties have entered into contracts with city libraries or other county libraries to provide service to their rural residents, or they may have joined with a city to establish a joint city-county library. In recent years, increasing use has been made of regional libraries established cooperatively by two or more counties, especially poorer, less populous ones.[64]

Zoning has been a generally accepted practice in cities for many years, involving the creation of districts in which only specified land uses and building arrangements are permitted. The authority under

---

[62] According to the Commission on Intergovernmental Relations, only 476 counties were able to support public health programs. *Report to the President,* 1955.

[63] U.S. Public Health Service, *Report of Local Public Health Resources: 1950* (1952).

[64] See M. H. Satterfield, "Intergovernmental Cooperation in the Tennessee Valley," *Journal of Politics,* February 1947; Helen A. Ridgway, "Library Legislation and Planning," *The Book of the States: 1950–1951.*

which counties are able to zone derives from state enabling legislation. Under such permissive statutes, a county may, by means of a zoning ordinance, impose reasonable restrictions upon the use of real property. Wisconsin, in 1929, was the first state to provide for full-fledged rural zoning. Approximately three-fourths of the states have passed laws granting zoning powers to counties or townships. In those states suburban lands, areas with relatively dense population, are subject to zoning; but in only about a dozen of them can counties zone rural lands.[65]

Rural zoning is intended basically to conserve natural resources and prevent wasteful scattering of rural population on unproductive land. Ordinances designed to accomplish these purposes commonly provide for three types of districts: recreational, forest, and agricultural. Lands in recreational and forest districts may be put only to certain specified uses, including playgrounds, parks, hunting and fishing, cottages, and growth of forest products. Agricultural land, on the other hand, may be put to any lawful use. Through zoning, privately owned land may be reserved for particular uses as specified by law. Zoning serves in part as an alternative to public ownership. Linked with a program of submarginal land purchase, such as the land utilization program of the Soil Conservation Service, zoning can effectively change a wasteful and unproductive pattern of land use into one that will bring material benefits to a county.

Although financial and legal limitations generally stand in the way of the assumption of new activities by counties, a major reason for their failure adequately to meet many needs has been public indifference and even hostility. A number of studies in different states have concluded that the county is the logical unit of government to provide many services and controls necessary for the "good life" in rural and suburban areas. Counties may even assist cities in providing typically municipal services to urban residents, as has been done to a considerable extent in Los Angeles County. Too often, however, counties are dominated by an attitude as antiquated as their administrative structure. Rural residents particularly may be slow to see advantages accruing from increased governmental activity. Suburbanites often move into the "country" to get away from the city, and they oppose extension of urban controls and services. Many of them prefer to drink unsafe water, travel on poorly

---

[65] See Erling D. Solberg, *Rural Zoning in the United States,* U.S. Department of Agriculture, 1952.

paved and inadequately lighted streets, and live with insufficient police and fire protection.

REVENUES, EXPENDITURES, AND DEBTS[66]

In financing their functions, counties today rely chiefly on two sources of revenue: property taxes and state aid. Proportions differ so greatly from state to state and county to county that it is difficult to generalize, but it appears safe to say that, nationwide, counties obtain slightly less than half of their revenues from property taxes, a little over one-third from state aid, and the remainder from a variety of sources. It is important to keep in mind that counties possess only those taxing powers permitted them by state constitutional and statutory provisions. Rather than increase the taxing powers of counties, states have gradually increased the amount of state-collected revenue that is turned over to the counties.

Counties spend the great bulk of their income for the traditional functions of highways and welfare. Education runs a poor third, with health and hospitals coming fourth. All told, county expenditures represent approximately one-third of the total amount spent by local governments across the nation. Relatively, county debts are not large. Their debt-incurring capacity is generally limited by state law, and county residents appear reluctant to authorize deficits by popular vote.

PROSPECTS FOR THE COUNTY

Counties and municipalities are the dominant units of local government, and there is a trend to grant counties many powers formerly exercised almost exclusively by cities. One reason for the increasing importance of the county is that "the National Government has found the county more convenient than the municipality as a base for a number of grant-in-aid programs."[67] Especially important are the fields of welfare, agriculture, and health. Another reason for recent growth in the importance of the county lies in the rapid development of suburban areas over which no other unit of local government has general authority. Where the county is unable or unwilling to act, the needs of such areas often become acute. In order that the county may prove equal to the responsibilities thrust upon

---

[66] For a discussion of state and local revenues, expenditures, and debts, see Chapters 14 and 15.

[67] Commission on Intergovernmental Relations, *op. cit.*, p. 53.

it, some changes are badly needed, since the organizational structure and powers of most counties were designed to meet the needs of the rural society of a century or more ago.

Solutions to many problems facing local governments today can be achieved only if they are as dynamic as the society they serve. Many people view with alarm the centralizing trend so widely evident in recent years, and at the same time they resist efforts to strengthen local units of government that provide the only alternative means of providing needed services. No panacea, no sure cure exists; but the problems can be met if citizens shake off their lethargy and overcome their reluctance to use established governmental institutions effectively to meet the needs of the time.

SELECTED REFERENCES

Books:

Booth, David A., *Metropolitics: The Nashville Consolidation,* Institute for Community Development and Services, Michigan State University, 1963.

Lancaster, Lane W., *Government in Rural America,* 2nd ed., Van Nostrand Co., Princeton, 1952.

Phillips, Jewell C., *State and Local Government in America,* American Book Co., New York, 1954.

Shamburger, Harold J., *County Government and Administration in West Virginia,* Bureau for Governmental Research, West Virginia University, Morgantown, 1952.

Snider, Clyde F., *Local Government in Rural America,* Appleton-Century-Crofts, New York, 1957.

Spicer, George W., *Fifteen Years of County Manager Government in Virginia,* University of Virginia Extension, Charlottesville, 1951.

United States Bureau of the Census, *County Boards and Commissions,* U.S. Government Printing Office, Washington, D.C., 1947.

Wager, Paul W., *County Government Across the Nation,* University of North Carolina Press, Chapel Hill, 1950.

Articles:

Bollens, John C., "Administrative Integration in California Counties," *Public Administration Review,* Winter 1951.

Collier, James M., "Elected County Chief Executives in New Jersey," *The County Officer,* February 1955.

Grossman, Howard J., "Counties Come to Life," *National Civic Review,* September 1964.

Larsen, William F., "Tradition Bows to Efficiency," *National Municipal Review,* November 1950.

MacDougall, William R., "Meaning of County Home Rule Analyzed," *National Civic Review,* April 1964.

Porter, Kirk H., "A Wet Blanket on the County Manager Plan," *National Municipal Review,* January 1929.

Renne, R. R., "Montana Pace Setter," *National Municipal Review,* March 1958.

——, "Too Small to Be Efficient?" *National Municipal Review,* February 1947.

Snider, Clyde F., "American County Government: A Mid-Century Review," *American Political Science Review,* March 1952.

Spicer, George W., "Manager Counties Evaluated," *National Municipal Review,* July 1953.

Wager, Paul W., "The Case for County Manager Plan," *Public Management,* March 1930.

Weller, W. E., and Smith, C. M. "Sixteen Years of Progress," *National Municipal Review,* September 1953.

CHAPTER 21

Other Local Governments

Three types of local governments that often escape understanding are the New England town, the township, and the special district. The variety of usages of the word "town" has produced much confusion. At least three distinct types of governmental units are known as towns. Generally outside New England, New York, and Wisconsin, a town is a small urban place that may or may not be incorporated. In a few states, particularly New York and Wisconsin, units of government known elsewhere as townships are officially designated as towns. In the six New England states, *towns* are the *principal units of local government* except in the more populous urban areas that have been incorporated as cities or in some instances as villages.

In the strict sense, *townships* are subdivisions of counties created to provide certain services to the inhabitants of relatively small areas without regard to population concentration. Townships usually provide services largely if not exclusively to rural residents, but they sometimes perform functions for the benefit of persons living in urban areas that are not incorporated as municipalities.[1] *Special districts,* occasionally called ad hoc districts, are found throughout the United States. Typically, a special district provides only one service, such as schools, water, or fire protection. It is not uncommon, however, for two or three closely related functions to be performed by a single district. Such districts are organized most often by local residents under the authority of state enabling legislation.

NEW ENGLAND TOWNS

Most of the area of New England is divided into towns, each usually encompassing between twenty and forty square miles. These towns frequently include both rural and urban territory—much like

---

[1] The civil township discussed in this chapter must not be confused with the congressional or survey township, which is not a governmental unit. The latter was created by Congress under the Articles of Confederation in 1785 as a means for surveying land in the Northwest Territory.

counties in other states. As will be noted later, New England towns perform a variety of important governmental functions. Their unique character stems not so much from their structure or their powers as from the manner in which they conduct local business.[2]

Organization of Town Government: *The Town Meeting.* "The New England town affords the outstanding example in the United States today of a governmental unit which operates as a direct democracy instead of employing a representative body for purposes of policy determination."[3] Annual town meetings are held regularly on a date specified by law. Every voter is eligible to attend and participate in his own town meeting. Many voters, particularly in large, urban towns do not attend the meetings, and decisions are made by a small minority of residents. In an effort to meet the problems inherent in this situation, some larger towns, especially in Connecticut and Massachusetts, have established the representative town meeting. This arrangement requires the popular election of a number of voters from "districts" or "precincts" within each town to serve as "town meeting members." Although voting at the town meeting is restricted to such elected members, all voters are still eligible to attend and voice their opinions.

Important decisions are made at town meetings. Ordinances or "bylaws" are enacted; appropriations are voted for the following year; taxes are levied; borrowing is authorized as necessary; and town officers are elected. Less important matters are also considered, such as the construction and repair of roads, the purchase of individual items of property and equipment, street lighting, improvement of library facilities, and employee salaries. The necessity of having to make decisions on such a variety of matters undoubtedly causes some citizens to absent themselves from town meetings. The increasing complexity of government has caused the town meeting to lose much of its "pristine vitality."[4]

The Selectmen. One of the important tasks of a town meeting is the choice of selectmen,[5] in whose hands rests the executive authority

---

[2] For information concerning the details of the government of a particular town, see Town Government Study Committee, *Wilton—A Study of Its Town Government,* (1956).

[3] Clyde F. Snider, *Local Government in Rural America,* Appleton-Century-Crofts, New York, 1957, p. 195. (The material on New England town government relies heavily on Professor Snider's discussion.)

[4] *Ibid.,* p. 198.

[5] Selectmen may be chosen at separate town elections.

of the town. The board of selectmen, most commonly consisting of three members, is responsible for the conduct of town business between town meetings. Consequently, the board performs a variety of routine functions, such as issuing licenses, awarding contracts, conducting elections, and supervising the maintenance of town property, the repair of streets, and the construction of sewers—to list a few. One selectman frequently assumes a position of leadership on the board and may function much like a "mayor" in spite of the fact that all authority is formally vested in the board as a body. Selectmen also make the rules and regulations necessary to govern a town between town meetings.

Other Town Officers. Among other important town officers is the town *clerk*, whose responsibilities are comparable to those of the county clerk outside New England.[6] Although his duties are primarily concerned with record-keeping, the town clerk is typically the chief source of help and information concerning town affairs, a situation resulting in part from the long tenure characteristic of the office. As a rule the clerk receives most of his compensation from fees. The town *treasurer* is the recipient and custodian of town funds, from which he makes payments upon proper authorization. The same person often serves both as clerk and treasurer. Judicial functions of the town are generally performed by the justice of the peace.[7]

Evaluation of property for purposes of taxation is the duty of town *assessors* or *appraisers,* of whom there are commonly one to three per town. The town law enforcement officers are the popularly elected *constable* and *attorney.* The duties of these officers have decreased in importance in recent years, as law-enforcement activities have been assumed increasingly by state, city, and county officials. Popularly elected *auditors* check the books of small towns, while larger ones usually hire professional help. Responsibility for the condition of rural town roads rests with the *road commissioner,* who most often has learned his trade by experience rather than training. Minor officers found in some but not all towns are *overseers of the poor; fence viewers* who settle disputes between farmers concerning the proper location of fences; *sextons* who look after cemeteries; and *water commissioners* with responsibility to maintain

---

[6] For an examination of the duties of the county clerk, see Chapter 20.

[7] Although justices of the peace are technically state officers, they are generally elected by the voters of each town and are identified with town government.

an adequate supply of pure water. Some towns recently have provided for civil service commissions and planning boards.

Among the more recent and important additions to town government is the *town manager* whose duties are similar to those of the city manager.[8] Subject to the requirements of state law, typical procedure is for the town meeting to instruct the selectmen to hire a manager who is answerable to the selectmen. The manager typically is responsible for seeing that state laws and local ordinances are enforced. It is common practice for a manager to assume the duties of some of the other officers, often including the treasurer, the road commissioner, the water commissioner, and overseer of the poor. In addition, the manager usually acts as purchasing agent for his town. One student has observed that in a small town the manager *"is* town government."[9] In order to obtain the benefits of manager government, some small New England towns have hired managers jointly with other units of local government. These joint efforts may involve two or more towns or in some instances towns and villages.

Functions of Town Governments. The foregoing discussion of the organization of town government reveals the major functions of New England towns. Functioning in a capacity somewhat similar to that of counties elsewhere, New England towns perform many duties that vary according to the needs and demands of local residents.[10] In general, towns are concerned with roads, education, libraries, parks, sanitation, water supply, health, recreation facilities, and police and fire protection, as well as the assessment and collection of taxes. Towns, particularly the more urbanized ones, may provide many municipal services. Consequently, the distinction between an urban New England town and a city may be more of form than of substance.

TOWNSHIPS

Townships exist as functioning governmental units in fifteen states outside New England.[11] As noted earlier, these governmental

---

[8] For a discussion of the duties of city managers, see Chapter 19.

[9] Lawrence Pelletier, "New England Pioneers Again," *National Municipal Review,* February 1949, p. 83.

[10] See John P. Wheeler, "Towns in Transition," *National Civic Review,* February 1959.

[11] The fifteen states are Illinois, Indiana, Kansas, Michigan, Minnesota, Missouri, Nebraska, New Jersey, New York, North Dakota, Ohio, Pennsylvania, South Dakota,

units are officially designated "towns" in New York and Wisconsin.[12] Townships are numerous in some states and scarce in others. The Bureau of the Census reports, for example, the existence of 1,433 townships in eighty-five of the 102 Illinois counties and only sixty-six townships in two counties in the state of Washington.[13] Only in the state of Indiana does township government encompass the entire area of the state. In a few states, establishment of township government is optional with each county. Some states include municipalities within the jurisdiction of townships, while others exclude them.

Organization of Township Government: *Township Meetings.* In half of the township states, township meetings are authorized by statute.[14] Like their New England prototype, these gatherings are in theory composed of all qualified voters of each township. Attendance is generally very poor, however, and "township government has largely become government by default."[15] Often no one attends except officeholders. Those who do attend have important matters to consider. They levy taxes, provide appropriations, authorize bond issues, enact ordinances and bylaws, and elect township officers. They may also perform a variety of less important duties such as authorizing acquisition of property for various public uses, entering into contracts for the provision of goods and services, and receiving reports from various officials. Recent years have witnessed a gradual decrease in the powers of township meetings.

Township Boards. Every township has a board known variously as the board of trustees, board of supervisors, board of auditors, or just simply the township board. Members of such boards, usually three or five, may be elected directly to membership or they may acquire membership as a result of some other office which they hold. Persons in the latter category are said to be *ex officio* members.

Washington, and Wisconsin. Vestigial townships exist in Iowa, but they evidence so little governmental activity that they are not considered as governmental units by the Bureau of the Census. *U.S. Census of Governments: 1962*, Vol. I, *Governmental Organization*.

[12] In a few states, Minnesota and Pennsylvania for example, the terms, "town" and "township" are interchangeable in popular usage with reference to township governments.

[13] *U.S. Census of Governments: op. cit.*

[14] Illinois, Michigan, Minnesota, Nebraska, North Dakota, South Dakota, Washington, and Wisconsin.

[15] Robert S. Babcock, *State and Local Government and Politics*, Random House, Inc., New York, 1957, p. 104.

Township clerks, treasurers, and justices of the peace often serve in an *ex officio* capacity. About half of the township boards are composed of both *ex officio* and elective members; the entire membership of the others are directly elected. Terms of office are usually two or four years. Regular meetings are held monthly in some states and only two or three times a year in others.

Where township meetings exist, duties of township boards are largely administrative, including preparation of budgets for presentation to the meetings. In the absence of a township meeting, the board may be both chief legislative and administrative authority, an arrangement somewhat similar to the commission form of city government.[16] The similarity is especially striking where individual board members are responsible for supervising certain town functions such as road construction and maintenance or the assessment of property. Townships occasionally are divided into sections, with each board member responsible for administering affairs in one of the sections.

Other Township Officers. A noticeable parallel exists between officers of townships and those of New England towns. Great variety is evident among the approximately 15,000 townships as to the number of officers, their duties, and the methods of their selection. Provision is made regularly for a *clerk,* a *treasurer,* an *assessor,* a *constable, justices of the peace,* and *road commissioners,* whose duties are much like those of their counterparts in New England towns. Among the less important township officers are *fence viewers, overseers of the poor, poundkeepers,* and *weed commissioners.* The last two officers, respectively, are concerned with impounding stray dogs and livestock and with eradicating noxious weeds.

In about half the township states provision is made for a chief administrative officer in each township. Such an officer is known by a variety of titles in different states, including *supervisor, trustee,* and *chairman.* He is usually a member of the township board and in a few states is also a member of the county board. Some comparison may be drawn between this officer and a mayor in the commission type of city government, since he typically combines the roles of legislator and administrator. First and foremost a politician by necessity, the supervisor is seldom a professional administrator. Nevertheless, this arrangement is preferable to the headless administrative structure characteristic of many townships.

---

[16] For an explanation of commission government, see Chapter 19.

Functions of Township Governments. Township activities differ from state to state and even within individual states. Urban townships may provide such a variety of functions that they resemble municipal governments. The great bulk of townships, however, are units for rural government, and their most important activities generally relate to roads, welfare, education, and law enforcement. Undoubtedly, the most important of these is the construction and maintenance of roads. Although townships are too small to function economically and efficiently in this area, the desire of local residents to keep control of roads "close to home" has deterred shifting the task to counties. Nevertheless, such a shift has occurred in a few states. Townships occasionally serve as administrative units for the distribution of welfare funds under supervision by state agencies. In a few states the township rather than the school district serves as the basic agency for providing public education. Township police officers are normally active only in the enforcement of township traffic ordinances. Other services provided by some townships include fire protection, public health programs, recreational facilities, cemeteries, licensing and regulating certain businesses, planning, and zoning, as well as the construction of public works like sanitary sewers, disposal plants, and waterworks.

Future of Township Governments. Nearly thirty years ago Professor Lane W. Lancaster observed, "There is not a function now performed by the township which could not be better performed by other units."[17] But the township continues to play a significant role in rural government in nearly one-third of the states. In spite of the passing of pioneer days for which townships were well suited, many persons prefer to adhere to time-honored arrangements. Attitudes favorable to retention of the townships are not found among students of local government, but they are not the ones who count. So long as the rank and file of people in township states maintain an attitude of toleration or even admiration toward its institutions and practices, the township will survive.

It is true, as Professor Snider has noted, that logic and recent events point toward the eventual demise of the township, but the process is certain to be slow.[18] Modern means of communication and

---

[17] Lane W. Lancaster, *Government in Rural America,* D. Van Nostrand Co., Inc., Princeton, 1937, p. 77.

[18] *Op. cit.,* pp. 229–233. See also, James W. Drury, "Townships Lose Grounds," *National Municipal Review,* January 1955.

transportation have rendered small township areas somewhat anachronistic. Township ogranization for the provision of services such as roads and welfare overlaps and duplicates comparable arrangements in other governments, especially counties. Recognition of this duplication is reflected in major transfers of some township functions to counties. This shift has been most noticeable in relation to roads and welfare, but it has also occurred with regard to education, property assessment, and law enforcement. Such a transfer has been so complete in Iowa and Oklahoma that townships in those states are no longer significant governmental units. Another factor that has weakened the townships has been the incorporation of portions of their area either by annexation to existing cities or by creation of new municipalities, particularly villages. Incorporation is especially detrimental to townships where state law provides that incorporated areas shall be severed from township jurisdiction.

Despite the advantages that would seem to accrue from the abandonment of townships, a basic reason for their continued existence has been well stated by Professor Lancaster:

> Formal abolition of the township is beset with a number of difficulties. In many states it would require a constitutional amendment. Still more to the point is the fact that the number of township officers is so large as to constitute a powerful vested interest . . . in spite of a supposed American aversion to what is called bureaucracy, most rural and village people apparently seem to enjoy their turn in office, and the township form of government gives such opportunities to a very large share of the population. These offices are petty and part-time but politically they are probably far more significant than the choicer 'plums' at the state house. . . . Defenders of small governmental units often rationalize this itch for crumbs of power by saying that in this way the small unit trains people in the responsibilities of government.[19]

In conclusion, it may be said that townships find favor in the eyes of many of their residents and for many years to come will remain a part of the rural government scene.

SPECIAL DISTRICTS

Early in the century the county was dubbed "the dark continent of American politics." It is appropriate, says John C. Bollens, to

---

[19] Lane W. Lancaster, *op. cit.,* p. 78.

describe the special district as the "new dark continent of American politics."[20] The number and variety of special districts make any effort at general description difficult. In 1962 the Bureau of the Census counted 53,001 special districts in the United States, including 34,678 school districts, which were enumerated separately. This count noted a decrease of 11,850 special districts since 1957. The Bureau found special districts in every state and in the District of Columbia and noted the absence of a consistent pattern relative to their organization and financing. Their importance is attested by the fact that special districts comprise nearly sixty per cent of all governmental units and are responsible for approximately one-fourth of the expenditures made by all state and local governments. The great bulk of this money is spent by school districts.

Reasons for the Growth of Special Districts. In the most thorough study of special districts available today, Professor Bollens has identified five major reasons for the growth of special districts: (1) unsuitability of other units of local government, (2) desire for independence, (3) advocacy by existing governments, (4) expediency and finances, and (5) unadorned self-interest.[21] When the need for a particular service such as fire protection or soil conservation becomes evident to the people residing in a given area, no existing, general-purpose local government may be able, ready, and willing to take steps necessary to meet the need. Area is a major problem because the boundaries of established governments such as counties and cities often are not coterminous with the area of need. Thus when suburbanites desire fire protection they are unable to obtain it from an existing government. Since they are outside the city, it has no duty to serve them, and counties and townships generally do not provide such services. The easy and quick solution is to create a fire district by vote of the residents, levy a tax on the property in it, and then establish a fire department or contract with a nearby city to provide protection.[22]

Unsuitability of established governments stems from factors

---

[20] John C. Bollens, *Special District Governments in the United States,* University of California Press, Berkeley, 1957, p. 1.

[21] *Ibid.,* pp. 6–15.

[22] Although not yet causing an increase in the number of special districts, the unsuitability of other governments has been cited as an argument for *multipurpose* special districts as a possible solution to problems of metropolitan areas. See *Metropolitan Government in California,* Assembly Interim Committee Reports, Vol. 13, No. 23, March 1959.

other than area. Expansion of services may be restricted by financial and functional limitations imposed by constitutional or statutory provisions. Thus the residents of a city may wish to expand the recreational facilities of their community. At the same time the city may have reached or come close to a legally imposed tax or debt ceiling, and no other means of raising revenue may be available. A possible solution may be the creation of a park district to levy the necessary tax and provide the desired facilities. Variations of this hypothetical situation are almost unlimited in practice. Another problem arises from the lack of authority of general governmental units to provide needed services. Counties and townships, for example, may not possess authority under state law to provide fire protection and a supply of water to suburban dwellers, who then seek to solve their problems by creating special districts.

Even when financial and functional restrictions do not prohibit action, established local governments sometimes promote the creation of special districts because of their administrative inability to assume the burden of expanded services. Elected officials, often concerned primarily with keeping the tax rate down, may be reluctant to expand activities. Furthermore, the quality of administration may be so poor that an extension of services may be impractical and undesirable. Such an extension might lead to a complete breakdown of established practices and would be unlikely to provide the level of service desired by those seeking a solution to their problems.

The second major reason for the growth of special districts has been a desire for independence. Persons strongly interested in the success of a particular activity or program commonly seek to give it some sort of independent status. An excellent example of this tendency as it relates to the topic at hand is the school district. In the great majority of states public education is provided partially, if not entirely, by school districts. A major consideration leading to the establishment of these districts has been the conviction on the part of educators, legislators, and the public in general that such an important function should not be entrusted to a general-purpose governmental unit. This attitude is often expressed in terms of keeping education "out of politics." The implication is that where "politics" dominate, professionalism and efficiency must suffer. A related concern is the feeling that a relatively small, single-purpose unit is more responsive to the wishes of the people than a larger one. Although the accuracy of this idea is debatable, it has unquestionably contributed to the proliferation of various types of special districts.

Advocacy for special districts has also come from existing governments. Jealousy among local governments may generate support for the creation of a new government rather than the augmentation of one already in existence. Thus township authorities may promote special districts to provide services to new suburban areas instead of supporting annexation to a city, especially if incorporated areas are not within township jurisdiction. On the other hand, efforts to organize special districts may stem from a conviction in the minds of local officials that only in this way can needed services be provided. A city may recognize the importance of extending fire protection to surrounding areas, and a special district may appear to be the only feasible method of meeting the need. Also, support for special districts may arise from national and state laws designed to enhance the provision of particular functions, usually by means of financial support. The large number of soil conservation districts attests to the impact of national legislations.

Expediency and financial condition constitute important fac-

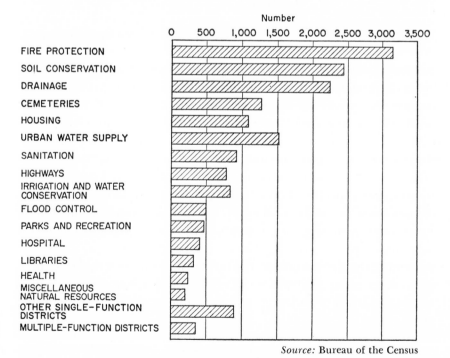

Source: Bureau of the Census

NUMBER OF SPECIAL DISTRICTS, BY FUNCTION: 1962

tors in explanation of the growth in number of special districts. The simple fact that it is often more expeditious to provide a governmental service by creating a new district rather than setting up the required machinery within an established unit explains the existence of many special districts. Another consideration is that an area with limited population and financial resources may need and be able to afford only a few functions that it cannot obtain from a general-purpose government. Under such circumstances, the obvious solution is to create a low-cost government capable of providing the limited functions required, that is, a special district.

Although not related to the reasons examined in the foregoing discussion, self-interest on the part of small groups may be decisive in creating special districts. Concerns interested in selling supplies and equipment may also induce some persons to favor the establishment of a new government. Another, probably somewhat more important selfish consideration, has been noted by Emmett Asseff, who expresses the opinion that "the special district has a psychological attraction, for there a specific tax is applied to a specific function and area" in which the taxpayer is especially interested.[23]

Formation and Organization of Special Districts. Details pertaining to the organization of special districts are spelled out in the statutes of each state.[24] Quite naturally, great variations exist, and generalization is difficult. Individual districts occasionally are formed by special legislative act, but in most instances they are organized by local residents according to the provisions of general statutes. Four major steps are usually required to set up a special district. First, a petition must be circulated among those to be affected, stipulating the type of district to be created and defining its area, and a specified number of signatures of residents or property owners must be secured. Second, the petition must be filed with some governmental agency, commonly the county board. The board may simply pass on the legality of the petition, or it may possibly determine the desirability of the district and grant or deny the petition. Most often, a third step in the form of a local referendum is required. If the popular vote is favorable, the fourth step by the

---

[23] Emmett Asseff, *Special Districts in Louisiana,* Bureau of Government Research, Louisiana State University, Baton Rouge, 1951, p. 3.

[24] Rarely, special districts are organized directly under the authority of constitutional provisions.

appropriate government authority, usually the county court, is in
order, establishing the new district.

The variety of organizational patterns found in special districts
defies general description. Nevertheless, it is important to get an
idea of the manner in which they are organized. The governing body
of a district is generally a board composed of three, five, or seven
members. These persons, variously known as commissioners, directors, trustees, and supervisors, may be appointed or elected. Only
rarely is a single officer made responsible for the affairs of a district.
Among school districts common practice dictates that policymaking
shall be in the hands of a popularly elected board, which in turn
hires a professional administrator, or superintendent, to oversee the
affairs of the district. Terms of office for board members are usually
two, four, or six years.

An outstanding characteristic of many special districts is their
informality in organization and procedure. This is not surprising in
view of the fact that about one-third of all nonschool districts have
no paid personnel, and only about one per cent have a payroll of 100
or more persons. School districts employ over nine-tenths of all
special district employees. District boards normally possess practically unlimited discretion in hiring and firing employees. Teachers
may enjoy "tenure," but this status does not constitute very effective
protection against removal by the board. Civil service is practically
unknown. In the smaller districts, officers often perform their duties
and maintain records in a desultory and haphazard manner.

Finances. Property taxes, special assessments, service charges, and
grants from the states and federal government constitute most of the
income received by special districts. The relative importance of these
sources varies appreciably with the type of district. School districts
obtain almost all of their income from local property taxes and state
grants. On the other hand, water, sanitary, and similar districts
acquire most of their revenue from special assessments against benefited property and service charges collected from those using district
facilities. It is estimated that about one-third of the nonschool districts have no authority to levy taxes.[25] Some special districts, especially soil conservation districts, must rely for their revenue entirely
on contributions from other governmental units and residents within
their boundaries. Most special districts possess authority to issue

[25] Bollens, *op. cit.*, p. 42.

bonds, usually subject to approval by the voters. Strict limits are generally imposed by state law upon the taxing and bonding capacity of districts.

Taxpayers often fail to appreciate the impact imposed upon their pocketbooks by special districts within which they live. It is not uncommon for a person, particularly someone living outside a municipality, to be taxed by four or five special districts. For example, many people live at the same time in a school district, a water district, a fire district, and a sanitary district. All of these districts may levy property taxes, and commonly all of the levies are incorporated in the tax bill prepared by the county. The share of taxes paid to the county treasurer and actually remaining with the county may be very small. In this way the county serves as a collection agency for special districts within its boundaries.

Quasi-Special Districts. Scattered across the country are many subordinate agencies that do not possess sufficient administrative and fiscal autonomy to be classified as separate governmental units. Often known as "districts" or "authorities," these agencies are generally dependent for their creation and continued existence upon some government such as a state, county, or municipality. Thus, California has created fish and game districts, game refuge districts, and highway districts, all of which function as adjuncts of the state government and engage in no independent action. Florida counties have established sanitary, water, and zoning districts, as well as airport, bridge, and port authorities. Each of these agencies is created by the county in which it is located, and they function under the direct and immediate supervision of the respective boards of county commissioners. New York municipalities similarly use garbage and refuse districts, water districts, and parking authorities. Municipal park, sewer, and zoning districts exist in South Dakota. Such examples could be multiplied many times.[26]

Like true special districts, quasi-districts may be organized so that their boundaries are coterminous with the area in which a particular service is needed or desired. Thus zoning districts may be desirable in only a few, scattered sections of a county. Possessing authority to establish such districts, the county board can take steps to provide the necessary machinery for the enactment and adminis-

---

[26] Occasionally, authorities are established by the cooperative efforts of two or more governments. Probably the best known example is the Port of New York Authority.

tration of zoning rules and regulations in selected areas. The county board probably would serve *ex officio* as the governing body of each zoning district, an arrangement typical of the practice in most quasi-districts. A significant consideration in favor of quasi-districts is that they do not require the establishment of separate governmental units. Consequently, the people do not have to elect additional officers and be burdened further with the multiplication of governments.[27]

Special Districts—a Summary. Professor Bollens has observed quite aptly that the characteristics of special districts "are a mixed blessing."[28] So long as general purpose governments are unable or unwilling to meet the different needs of the various areas within their jurisdiction, special districts will continue to flourish. In order to curtail the growth of nonschool districts, to say nothing of reducing their number, at least two major steps must be taken. First, general purpose governments such as counties and municipalities must be granted adequate authority to meet the varying needs that develop within their jurisdictions. This step requires action on the state level through either constitutional amendment or statutory change, or probably a combination of both. Second, the officers of general-purpose governments must become increasingly sensitive to the importance of action to meet area needs before they become acute. A keener interest on the part of the average citizen in the problems of neighborhoods other than his own would also be helpful.

Considered as a group, special districts are a costly means of providing governmental services. They often duplicate activities in which general-purpose governments are already engaged. Thus sanitary districts may lay sewers in areas that could be more economically serviced by nearby cities; hospital districts may build hospitals when more adequate care might be afforded through the expansion of county facilities; and fire districts may establish small fire departments incapable of providing protection equivalent to that available from a large municipal department. Small fire districts also illustrate certain "hidden" costs often associated with obtaining services

---

[27] Authorities have been established with unusual frequency in Pennsylvania. See Tina V. Weintraub and James D. Patterson, *The "Authority" in Pennsylvania: Pro and Con,* Bureau of Municipal Research of Philadelphia, 1949.

[28] *Op. cit.,* p. 251.

from special districts. Fire insurance rates are regularly much higher in such districts than in neighboring municipalities.

Other factors contribute to the costliness of special districts. Few districts other than those in the field of education are sufficiently large to benefit from bulk purchasing. As a result, unit costs are often higher than for larger governments. Personnel costs may also be relatively high. Lacking formal machinery for hiring, supervising, training, and dismissing employees, most nonschool districts handle personnel matters somewhat haphazardly. The quality of personnel suffers, and the most effective use of employees is not made. Usually, there is no one in a special district who is responsible for long-range planning designed to anticipate future needs and develop means of meeting them. The resulting uncoordinated and sometimes ill-conceived programs do not provide the taxpayer with the most service feasible for his tax dollars.

Regardless of the criticisms that may be levied against special districts, the fact remains that they have served a useful purpose, and it appears that they will continue to do so for a long time to come. Any call for their elimination is visionary. Future history may record that special districts constituted an important phase in the development of local governmental institutions. In any case, an understanding of their nature and their role in the scheme of things is important to every citizen who takes seriously his public responsibilities.

SELECTED REFERENCES

Books:

Asseff, Emmett, *Special Districts in Louisiana,* Bureau of Government Research, Louisiana State University, Baton Rouge, 1951.

Babcock, Robert S., *State and Local Government and Politics,* Random House, New York, 1957.

Bird, Frederick L., *Local Special Districts and Authorities in Rhode Island,* Bureau of Government Research, University of Rhode Island, 1962.

Bollens, John C., *Special District Governments in the United States,* University of California Press, Berkeley, 1957.

Dowling, Edward T., *Administrative Organization in Massachusetts Town,* Bureau of Government Research, University of Massachusetts, 1960.

Lancaster, Lane W., *Government in Rural America,* 2nd ed., Van Nostrand Co., Princeton, 1952.

Nuquist, Andrew E., *Town Government in Vermont,* Government Research Center, University of Vermont, 1964.

Snider, Clyde F., *Local Government in Rural America,* Appleton-Century-Crofts, New York, 1957.

United States Bureau of the Census, *Census of Governments: 1962,* Vol. I, *Governmental Organization,* Washington, D.C., 1963.

Articles:

Alexander, John W., and Berger, Monroe, "Is the Town Meeting Finished?" *American Mercury,* August 1949.

Drury, James W., "Townships Lose Ground," *National Municipal Review,* January 1955.

Kalijarvi, Thorsten V., "Town Meeting vs. Town Management," *National Municipal Review,* August 1940.

Pelletier, Laurence, "New England Pioneers Again," *National Municipal Review,* February 1949.

Scott, Stanley, and Bollens, John C., "Special Districts in California Local Government," *Western Political Quarterly,* June 1950.

Wheeler, John P., "Towns in Transition," *National Civic Review,* February 1959.

CHAPTER 22

Metropolitan Areas

WHAT IS A "METROPOLITAN AREA"?

One consequence of the rapid increase in urbanism has been the growth of the *metropolitan area,* sometimes called the metropolis. Although large "urban aggregations" have been the subject of much study and concern in recent years, metropolitan areas are not easily defined. They are large social, economic, and cultural communities characterized by a complex governmental pattern. A metropolis may be a "concept that is foggy in spots and fuzzy around the edges,"[1] but it definitely implies the presence of a large, heavily populated urban area that transcends the borders of numerous governmental units, including cities, towns, special districts, and often even states.

Recognizing the need for precise, even though arbitrary, terminology, the United States Bureau of the Census in 1949 established criteria for a *standard metropolitan area.* Except in New England, such an area consisted of a county or group of counties containing at least one city of 50,000 population or over. Counties without cities of this size but contiguous to a county possessing such a city were included within a standard metropolitan area if they were "socially and economically integrated with the central city" and not essentially agricultural.[2] In New England the town was substituted for the county as the basic governmental unit for determining the geographical boundaries of standard metropolitan areas.

About three-fifths of the country's population lived in the 174 standard metropolitan areas in the United States in 1957, which contained about fifteen per cent of the nation's local governmental units. In June, 1959, the official designation for metropolitan areas

---

[1] Mabel Walker, "Fiscal Aspects of Metropolitan Regional Development," *University of Pennsylvania Law Review,* February 1957, p. 489.

[2] U.S. Bureau of the Census, *U.S. Census of Governments: 1957,* Vol. I, No. 2, *Local Government in Standard Metropolitan Areas,* pp. 2–3. The detailed criteria for determining the nonagricultural quality of counties and their integration with the central city are set forth here.

was changed from "standard metropolitan area" to "standard metropolitan statistical area." As a result of changes in designation, eight new areas were added to the list, raising the total to 188 within the continental United States, plus three in Puerto Rico and Honolulu, Hawaii. The most notable changes resulted from the splitting of two bistate areas, New York–Northeastern New Jersey and Chicago, into five single state areas.[3] Minor changes included the addition of counties to a few areas and the subtraction of counties from others. A count in 1963 revealed the existence of 215 standard metropolitan statistical areas in the continental United States, plus one in Hawaii and three in Puerto Rico. The population of these areas approximated 117 million, nearly two-thirds of the national total. Recognizing the special importance of more inclusive metropolitan statistics for the New York–Northeastern New Jersey and Chicago–Northwestern Indiana areas, the Bureau of the Census coined the term "standard consolidated areas" to apply to these population complexes.

Most of the nation's increase in population since 1950 has occurred in these areas, chiefly in the suburbs around the central cities. Care must be taken in discussing the characteristics of metropolitan populations, however. One complication arises from the fact that not all residents of metropolitan areas are classified as urban. The Bureau of the Census considers only places of 2,500 or more population and closely contiguous areas as urban. Since the county is the basic unit for determining the boundaries of standard metropolitan statistical areas, some rural population is included within them. Consequently a few states—Delaware, Maryland, New Jersey, and Pennsylvania—have more metropolitan than urban residents!

Useful though it is, the standard metropolitan statistical area is not an entirely satisfactory concept as a basis for studying metropolitanism. From the practical standpoint, the important task is to identify the problems resulting from the rapid growth of large urban areas and to develop means of meeting them. The difficulties associated with water supply, police protection, waste disposal, and transportation, to name only a few, are not restricted to cities with 50,000 or more residents. Indeed, the problems of urban growth in

---

[3] Specifically, the New York-Northeastern New Jersey S.M.A. was divided into four standard metropolitan statistical areas, and the old Chicago S.M.A. was divided into two. The Wheeling, West Virginia-Steubenville, Ohio S.M.A. was also divided into two parts. Three new areas were designated: Ann Arbor, Michigan; Fitchburg-Leominster, Massachusetts; and Lynchburg, Virginia.

and around a community with 35,000 people, for example, may be more complex than in one of 50,000 or more. When action by numerous and independent local governmental jurisdictions is required to meet the needs of an urban area, that area has metropolitan characteristics.

Recognition of the Metropolis. Serious study of the growth, characteristics, and problems of the metropolis is largely a product of the last quarter-century. An early study published in 1933 under the direction of the President's Research Committee on Social Trends combined three approaches to the metropolitan community which may be identified as the governmental, the sociological, and the economic.[4] Comprehensive understanding of the metropolis requires the best efforts of the political scientist, the sociologist, and the economist. Some studies of metropolitan problems have been oriented largely, if not exclusively, toward only one of these disciplines. Fortunately, others have sought to combine them. By its very nature, a textbook on state and local government must stress the governmental aspects of metropolitanism, but it is important that the student be aware that they by no means constitute the whole picture.

Much information necessary to a thorough comprehension of metropolitan problems has been provided by detailed studies of individual communities, including Cleveland, Dayton, Houston, Kansas City, Los Angeles, Miami, Nashville, Philadelphia, and St. Louis. The fact that the millions of dollars to conduct these studies were obtained testifies to a widespread recognition of their importance and value. In recent years bills have been introduced in Congress to establish a national Department of Urban Affairs with a secretary who would serve in the President's cabinet. Also, a Council on Metropolitan Areas in the Executive Office of the President has been suggested.[5] Only a few years ago such proposals would have been considered ludicrous.

CONSEQUENCES OF METROPOLITAN GROWTH

Governmental Inadequacy. Luther Gulick has offered an incisive analysis of causes for the "breakdown" of local government in

---

[4] R. D. McKenzie, *The Metropolitan Community*, McGraw-Hill Book Co., New York, 1933.

[5] Robert H. Connery and Richard H. Leach, "U.S. Council on Metro," *National Civic Review*, June 1959.

metropolitan areas. He suggests four major reasons: (1) a governmental vacuum, (2) fractionalization of assigned duties, (3) political
and economic imbalance, and (4) lack of political leadership accompanied by inadequate recognition of the nature of the overall problem.[6] A governmental vacuum exists, according to Gulick, because
in each metropolitan region there usually is no governmental body
with authority to cope with the major problems of the area, whether
they be water supply, air pollution, or transportation. "Nowhere
has anybody been given the job of looking at the total geographic
region of any metropolitan complex . . . to decide what can and
should be done."[7] Governments functioning in metropolitan areas
are inadequate in terms of geographical jurisdiction, functional authority, or both. Thus central cities are always geographically inadequate since their powers are essentially limited to their boundaries; in the circumstance where a county encompasses the critical
area it probably lacks power to exercise general control of such necessary functions as public transportation and police protection.

Fractionalization of duties results from the independent operation of numerous governments within an area that has in many ways
become a unit. For example, cities situated miles apart may construct their separate sewage disposal facilities and draw up their own
plans for orderly growth. Once grown together, each disposal facility may not only be inadequate but may actually contaminate the
source of water for the other city. Their street and land-use plans
may not fit together at all. Such circumstances result from explosive
growth that is difficult if not impossible to foresee. Fractionalization
may result also from failure to appreciate the nature of a problem
currently at hand. Civil defense is a prime example. Certain important civil defense functions have been assigned by law to existing
local governments within metropolitan areas that are totally inadequate geographically to handle the massive tasks that would inevitably result from attack. Fractionalization likewise produces difficulties in such matters as air pollution, health, fire protection, crime
control, traffic flow, and taxation.

A third reason for governmental inadequacy in metropolitan
areas is political and economic imbalance. Assuming that the presence of some sort of "balance" of forces and interests is important to
an effective governmental unit, the tendency for some communities

---

[6] Luther Gulick, *Metro: Changing Problems and Lines of Attack*, Governmental
Affairs Institute, New York, 1957.
[7] *Ibid.*, p. 10.

to become predominantly upper or lower class in terms of economic status is disturbing. The outward flow of people and commercial establishments to suburbs not only deprives central cities of an important portion of their tax base, but it also removes persons from whom community leadership is normally expected. On the other hand, suburban communities may be rich in leadership but poor in taxable resources. "Democracy needs balanced constituencies, balanced leadership groups, balanced economic interests, balanced taxable resources, and powers of government which are balanced and appropriate to these other elements."[8] Obviously, not every minor constituency can be balanced in this sense, but Gulick's point is that in an area of the size and complexity characteristic of a metropolis such balance is important to effective governmental action.

The inadequacy or even total absence of area-wide political leadership in metropolitan regions is largely due to the fact that no elected public officials have the entire area as their constituency. Candidates for office in a city do not have to dwell on matters of concern to residents of surrounding areas and nearby cities. "No one gets elected in jurisdiction A by appealing courageously to the people of B, C, or D."[9] Few community problems, regardless of their nature, are effectively handled unless impetus is provided by persons who can rally public support for their cause.

Duplication and Overlapping. Taxpayers everywhere, aware of the high cost of governments, deplore unnecessary duplication and waste. Yet few appreciate the costliness of many independent agencies, side by side, providing parallel services. If anyone were to suggest the establishment of two or three police or fire departments, planning commissions, or departments of public works within a municipality, he would not be taken seriously for obvious reasons. Nevertheless, comparable situations exist in metropolitan areas. The residents of each municipality support such agencies and many others like those of their neighbors in other cities. Simultaneously the same people support county, district, town, and township agencies with responsibilities related to police, fire, planning, public works and many other services. Too often various governmental officials proceed with duties within their own limited jurisdictions without any apparent awareness or concern for the efforts of their

---

[8] *Ibid.*, p. 15.
[9] *Ibid.*, p. 16.

neighboring counterparts, who may even be housed in the same building!

Unevenness of Services. Within a metropolitan region many levels of service exist in regard to individual governmental functions. Residents of one section may receive excellent fire and police protection while those living in other sections may be served in a fair, poor, or totally inadequate manner. Disposal of wastes may not be a problem in some places while in others the inadequacy of this service may pose a real threat to health. Some streets may be adequately lighted, and others may have no lights at all. This list of examples could be greatly lengthened, but it illustrates the unevenness of services characteristic of metropolitan areas.

Disparity and inadequacy of services are especially noticeable in so-called "fringe areas." These suburban zones, located outside municipal boundaries, are generally unable to turn to any unit of local government possessing responsibility for meeting their needs. Water supply, sewage disposal, fire and police protection, drainage, street lighting, and zoning are often inadequate in fringe areas. The picture is further complicated by the fact that the quality of services differs greatly among various fringe zones, a situation explained largely by the relative adequacy of special district arrangements. Fringe areas are an especially fertile breeding ground for special districts.[10]

Fiscal Inequity. Since metropolitan areas are major centers of income and wealth, fiscal problems stem largely from inadequate machinery for the effective use of financial resources. The problem has been summarized in this way:

> The policy of providing city-wide services on the basis of need rather than the fiscal resources of each block, precinct or ward is not extended in the great majority of instances to metropolitan areas. Instead, the individual governmental unit relies upon a small amount of territory for its local financial resources. Thus some units are wealthy but have relatively few needs; others are extremely poor and have extensive needs. Such disparity between needs and resources

---

[10] For a discussion of special districts see Chapter 21. See also Charles Press, *When One Third of a City Moves to the Suburbs—A Report on the Grand Rapids Metropolitan Area,* Institute for Community Development and Services, Michigan State University, East Lansing, 1959.

is particularly apparent in the central cities, which must furnish services to many nonresidents but cannot tap the financial resources of the localities in which these people reside. The broad variations between needs and resources make for gross inequalities in financial burdens.[11]

Problems faced by some satellite communities are equally as great if not more severe than those of central cities. "Bedroom" communities housing low- and middle-income groups are illustrative. Property valuation in such places is rather low, but at the same time the need for services is high. At the other extreme are "wealthy tax colonies," where only the well-to-do reside.[12] Neither of these types of communities benefits from the tax base supplied by large commercial and industrial enterprises.

Another major cause of fiscal difficulties in metropolitan areas arises from the many revenue and debt limitations imposed upon local governments by state laws. Local governments are generally able to levy only those taxes specifically authorized by state law, and most state legislatures have been jealous of revenue sources (excepting the property tax) and unwilling to relinquish them to subordinate governments. The problem is further compounded by the fact that some localities are too small for effective and economical administration of revenue sources. Taxes may be avoided through changing residence by a few blocks or going to a nearby community to shop. The unsatisfactory record of some cities during the depression of the 1930's in meeting their financial obligations to bondholders resulted in the imposition of strict debt limits. Legislatures dominated by representatives from less congested areas are often unsympathetic with the needs of metropolitan regions.

SUGGESTED SOLUTIONS TO METROPOLITAN PROBLEMS

Responsibility of State Legislatures. In an earlier chapter attention was directed to the fact that local governments are creatures of the states in which they are situated. Before effective local action to meet the needs of metropolitan areas is possible, important changes in state constitutions and statutes are necessary. Old restrictions, procedural as well as substantive, require modification. Laws per-

---

[11] The Council of State Governments, *The States and the Metropolitan Problem,* Chicago, 1956, p. 20 (John C. Bollens, Director of Study).

[12] See Lyle C. Fitch, "Metropolitan Financial Problems," *The Annals,* November 1957.

taining to the incorporation of cities or annexation of territory to them may require modernization. New sources of local revenue await legislative authorization. Restrictions on municipal forms of governments need to be repealed. Counties require more varied powers. These examples serve to stress the crucial role of the state legislatures.

In spite of the obvious need, legislative reluctance to alleviate metropolitan problems has been apparent. Although a number of reasons may be advanced to explain this dereliction, rural domination of most state legislatures has been a major factor. Through constitutional provisions specifying minimum or maximum representation for designated governmental units, especially counties, heavily populated areas have suffered increasingly from underrepresentation. Legislatures have held urban representation to a minimum by repeated failures to reapportion their membership at intervals as required by their constitutions.[13] During these periods of inaction the percentage of urban population has increased rapidly. In 1953 sixty-four per cent of the population was urban and thirty-six per cent was rural, but seventy-five per cent of the state legislators were elected by the rural thirty-six per cent of the people![14] As noted earlier, "urban" and "metropolitan" are not synonymous in describing population characteristics, but these figures indicate the extent of underrepresentation suffered by large urban areas across the country.

Encouraging signs have appeared in recent years. National recognition has been given to the vital role of the states in meeting metropolitan problems. According to the Commission on Intergovernmental Relations, "It is clearly the responsibility of the states to assume leadership in seeking solutions for the problems of metropolitan government."[15] A number of states, including California, Connecticut, Illinois, Minnesota, North Carolina, Ohio, Oregon, Utah, and Wisconsin, have undertaken studies of municipal and metropolitan needs and ways of meeting them. Such investigations constitute an essential first step in any intelligent program of action.

---

[13] See Chapter 6 for a discussion of representation and reapportionment problems in state legislatures.

[14] Congress of Industrial Organizations, *Government by Minority*, 1953. Quoted in Charles M. Kneier, *City Government in the United States,* 3rd ed., Harper & Brothers, New York, 1957, p. 105.

[15] Commission on Intergovernmental Relations, *A Report to the President for Transmittal to the Congress,* June 1955, p. 52.

In 1956 the Conference on Metropolitan Area Problems was established. Financed by private funds, this organization is dedicated to a continuing nationwide study of needs and developments in metropolitan regions.

Annexation. Viewed historically, the standard method of providing increased service to expanding urban areas has been to add these areas to a central city through *annexation,* which is the process of adding territory to an established government. When created, most cities were much smaller than they now are; their growth has resulted from the annexation of surrounding, contiguous territory— usually in a piecemeal, haphazard manner. From their date of incorporation to 1900, Chicago grew from 10.5 to 190 square miles, Boston from 4.5 to 38.5, and Pittsburgh from .5 to 28.[16] Most annexed areas are unincorporated, but occasionally small incorporated communities have been added to larger ones. The great bulk of nineteenth-century annexations were accomplished by legislative act, a fact that helps to explain their frequent use.

Although there has been some increase since World War II, the twentieth century has witnessed a sharp decline in the use of annexation. "The simultaneous decline of annexation and the rise and growth of metropolitan areas were not simply coincidental."[17] Although it is difficult to isolate factors accounting for the decline, these have been significant: (1) ability of fringe-area dwellers to obtain desired services without annexation; (2) hostility of suburbanites toward the central city and their consequent determination to take advantage of increasingly stringent procedural requirements governing annexation; (3) incorporation of satellite communities; and (4) reluctance on the part of central cities to assume the expense required to increase services and facilities in newly annexed areas to a level comparable with that existing in the remainder of the community.[18]

Particularly through the use of special districts and in some instances by means of increased county activity, fringe-area residents have satisfied their desire for municipal-type services such as pure

---

[16] The Council of State Governments, *The States and the Metropolitan Problem,* Chicago, 1956, p. 26.

[17] *Ibid.,* p. 27.

[18] Ralph T. Jans, *The Urban Fringe Problem: Solutions under Michigan Law,* Bureau of Government, Institute of Public Administration, University of Michigan, Ann Arbor, 1957, p. 21.

water, fire protection, and waste disposal. A consequent reduction in the urgency of annexation has occurred. Alternative methods for obtaining services without annexation have been authorized by state legislatures whose members viewed such methods as easy "solutions" to vexatious problems. Hostility toward core cities is widespread among suburbanites. Because of fear of increased taxes, dislike for city regulations, or concern over loss of local identity, people living near a city on which they are dependent may not wish to become part of it. Of all the factors contributing to the decrease in municipal annexations, suburban antipathy toward the central city is among the most important.

When individual annexations were accomplished by state legislative act, local opposition was not crucial. Today, however, the situation is quite different. Typically, annexation proposals must be subject to a popular vote in the area to be annexed. Action on the part of the annexing city may be accomplished by council action or by popular vote. Where approval by city voters is required, a favorable majority usually must be obtained separately within the city and in the area to be annexed. Favorable council action or popular vote within a city is often negated by an unfavorable vote outside. In this way "local control over local matters" has hindered the orderly development of many communities. In a few states, particularly Missouri, Ohio, New Mexico, Texas, and Virginia, annexations may be accomplished without popular vote.

A technique that appears promising as a means of reducing suburban opposition to annexation is the *tax differential*. This device enables a municipality to enter into an agreement to the effect that upon annexation and for a period thereafter residents of a newly added area will be taxed at a rate different from that applied generally throughout the city. The theory behind such an arrangement is that for some time following annexation an area cannot receive full advantage of all municipal services and consequently should enjoy a lower tax rate. In view of its importance as a source of municipal revenue and its susceptibility to adjustment, the property tax would probably be scaled down in some manner to achieve the desired result. Thus an adjustment period of five years might be agreed upon, and for the first year in the newly annexed area the millage rate might be ten mills less than in the rest of the city; for the second year it might be eight mills less, for the third year six mills less, and so on until a uniform millage would be achieved. Although numerous difficulties would attend any effort to establish a plan of municipal tax differentials, they do not appear insuperable.[19]

Although a promise of lower taxes for a period of time may serve as an inducement to encourage suburbanites to accept annexation, the fairness of this practice from the standpoint of city residents is questionable. Granting reduced tax rates to newly annexed areas disregards the fact that the costs of improvements and services in such places are generally greater in proportion to assessed valuation than in other parts of the city. Occasionally, cities have accepted this premise and assessed higher taxes for a short time in new additions or required payment of some sort of entrance fee. Intended to discourage annexations, such a policy is feasible only when suburban zones desire to join a city that is not especially interested in extending its boundaries.

The record clearly indicates that annexation has proved inadequate as a means of meeting the problems of rapidly growing urban areas. Urbanization regularly outruns annexations. Since urban growth does not respect legal boundaries, county lines and state boundaries are crossed. State laws may not allow municipalities to expand across county lines, and annexations across state boundaries are not permissible because such action would involve surrender of territory by one state to another. Furthermore, the incorporation of small satellite communities around a large city seriously impedes annexations. Procedure for annexation of incorporated territory is nearly always cumbersome. A favorable vote is usually difficult to achieve within a community marked for absorption, and arrangements concerning the disposition of the assets and liabilities of the disincorporated municipality are complicated.

Extraterritorial Jurisdiction.[20] One approach to the metropolitan problem is to empower municipalities to extend their authority beyond their boundaries for certain purposes. Specific territory is a

---

[19] See Orval Etter, "Municipal Tax Differentials," *Oregon Law Review,* December 1957; and Kenneth C. Tollenaar, "Taxation Differentials," *National Civic Review,* March 1959.

[20] "Extramural" is often used in place of "extraterritorial." Extramural means literally "beyond the wall." In the Roman language and practice this term was applied to powers exercised beyond the territory of a municipality. The boundaries of major Roman cities were marked by walls, and the area around such cities for a certain distance beyond the walls was under municipal jurisdiction. For additional information on the historical aspects of municipal extraterritoriality, see Russell W. Maddox, *Extraterritorial Powers of Municipalities in the United States,* Oregon State College Press, Corvallis, 1955, pp. 6–8.

necessary attribute of a municipality, and municipal powers are intended chiefly for use within municipal boundaries. Cities regularly extend their authority beyond their geographical limits for many purposes which may be considered in terms of two broad classifications: (1) implementation of services and acquisition of facilities for the benefit of city residents and (2) provision of services to fringe areas which are usually unincorporated. Municipalities frequently must go outside their boundaries to obtain water, locate parks and sewage disposal works, build bridges, and operate airports. At the same time they supply water to nonresident consumers, provide fire protection for nearby property, extend transportation facilities to surrounding areas, and regulate the subdivision of property within a specified distance beyond their limits.

Municipalities can exercise only those extraterritorial powers that are permitted them by their respective state legislatures.[21] Some states have been more generous than others, and within a single state jurisdictions over various functions have been treated differently. "Accuracy requires recognition that most municipalities possess a *number* of 'jurisdictions.' A municipality may extend its powers over one territory in order to acquire water and over another in order to inspect dairies that supply milk for its residents; it may acquire property for sewage disposal facilities within one area and for parks in another; it may be able to collect taxes only from its residents and at the same time provide a variety of services to nonresidents."[22]

Extraterritorial jurisdiction for cities has proved unsatisfactory as a means of meeting metropolitan needs for a number of reasons. Although cities are permitted to extend services beyond their limits, they exercise very little regulatory authority and almost no taxing power over nonresidents. Under such circumstances, no city can administer a plan to control the development of an area because its authority and resources are not commensurate with the need. A basic obstacle to the expansion of extraterritorial regulatory power is that it is "government without the consent of the governed" since nonresidents have no direct voice in city government. Another complication arises from a conflict of jurisdictions. Competition among cities and with other local governments for spheres of control and

---

[21] Such powers may be expressed or implied. For example, the power of eminent domain may be implied in a specific grant of power to provide an adequate water supply or construct sewage disposal facilities.

[22] Russell W. Maddox, *op. cit.,* pp. 88–89.

influence may produce rivalry and disharmony rather than cooperation.[23]

Intergovernmental Cooperation. Related to municipal extraterritorial jurisdiction are numerous arrangements for the promotion
of cooperation among local governments on problems of common
concern. This approach involves minimum disturbance to established patterns and relationships and consequently does not encounter the hostility directed toward some other suggested means of
solving metropolitan difficulties. "The most feasible solution politically is generally some type of intergovernmental arrangement which
leaves the structure of government untouched, but provides a means
of meeting a particular problem at a particular time through voluntary cooperation."[24] Such arrangements take a number of forms
which for purposes of discussion may be divided into two major categories: (1) Counties may provide services for governments within
their borders. (2) Two or more governmental units may undertake
joint efforts. A third category, extension of services by a central city,
has been considered above under extraterritorial jurisdiction.

County Services. Strengthening counties and extending the scope
of their services constitute a potentially significant means of alleviating metropolitan problems for several reasons. First, the territories of counties more nearly approximate the limits of metropolitan
regions than do the boundaries of other local governments. Second,
recent years have witnessed numerous increases in authority vested in
counties by state law. Third, using county governments is probably
more feasible than attempting to create other general-purpose governments.[25] In nearly all instances, however, reorganization of
county government is essential prior to any appreciable increases in
authority and responsibility. Leadership and support at the state
level are necessary if such changes are to be realized.

A few states have enacted general laws empowering counties to
perform any municipal function for local governments within their
jurisdiction. Most states have expanded the authority of counties
activity by activity, usually to a very limited extent. Functions per-

---

[23] See Robert T. Daland, *Municipal Fringe Area Problems in Alabama,* Bureau of
Public Administration, University of Alabama, 1953.

[24] Betty Tableman, *Government Organization in Metropolitan Areas,* Bureau of
Government, Institute of Public Administration, University of Michigan, Ann Arbor,
1951, p. 24. Chapter III provides an excellent discussion of the cooperative approach.

[25] See the Council of State Governments, *op. cit.,* pp. 114–15.

formed by counties in lieu of action by other local governments include property assessment and tax collection, public health and welfare, library service, sewage disposal, and fire protection. In approximately one-fourth of the states county assessors evaluate property, and all local governments must use their assessments for purposes of taxation. In other states municipalities have agreed to accept county valuations; in still others assessments are duplicated by county and municipal assessors. Less frequently, counties function as collection agencies for certain municipal taxes.

County responsibility for public health and welfare is common. City-county health units are widespread throughout the country, including some metropolitan areas. Many counties provide health services to municipal residents on the basis of contractual agreements whereby the city reimburses the county according to a formula. Cities sometimes contribute to the support of county welfare departments which then administer all welfare activities. Very few county libraries serve all governmental units within their boundaries, but contractual arrangements are frequently made between counties and a number of their cities. Sewage disposal is rarely handled on a county-wide basis, but precedents exist, running as far back as 1901, when Jefferson County, Alabama, took over this task. Although county police and fire departments seldom protect incorporated areas, it would seem that cooperative arrangements might easily be worked out to provide more adequate services, especially to small communities. In no other place have county services to local governments developed to an extent comparable to the practice in Los Angeles County. In addition to a variety of functions performed for the many small cities within its boundaries, Los Angeles County provides all municipal services for the city of Lakewood.[26]

Joint Undertakings. As noted earlier, communities within a county may turn over to the county responsibility for administering activities such as health and welfare programs and property assessment. Joint undertakings, on the other hand, involve arrangements among governments whereby ownership and control of facilities as well as program supervision remain at least partially in the hands of all participants. Cooperation between cities and counties as well as among cities is especially significant. Services provided in this man-

[26] For a discussion of this very interesting arrangement, see S. B. Sweeney and G. S. Blair, *Metropolitan Analysis,* University of Pennsylvania Press, Philadelphia, 1958, pp. 113–16.

ner include purchase of equipment and supplies and the construction and maintenance of recreational facilities, hospitals, airports, sewage-disposal systems, bridges, and a variety of public buildings. Police radio facilities, fire protection, and aspects of personnel management are provided cooperatively in rare instances.

A major problem facing most governments pertains to ways of procuring materials and equipment at minimum costs while maintaining adequate standards of quality. According to one estimate, cooperative purchasing among local governmental units can save from three to ten per cent of costs.[27] Lack of uniformity in the laws governing purchasing procedure for individual governments is a major obstacle to joint efforts. Another difficulty stems from the usual desire on the part of local officials in each government to enjoy independence of action in spending "their" money. Nevertheless, progress has been made in numerous localities, including Cincinnati, Los Angeles, Milwaukee, and Broward County, Florida.

Recreational programs are often financed and administered jointly by cities, school districts, and counties.[28] City-county hospitals and public health units exist in many communities, including Louisville, Kentucky; El Paso and Fort Worth, Texas; and Chattanooga, Tennessee. City-county cooperation in the construction and maintenance of airports is a common arrangement facilitated by Congressional legislation making federal money available. New Jersey cities have resorted frequently to joint development of sewage disposal systems. An early joint undertaking between two cities involved the construction of a bridge. In 1870, New York and Brooklyn, then separate municipalities, cooperated in the construction of the Brooklyn Bridge. Joint efforts of this nature are not common. Courthouses, office buildings, and jails in a number of communities are the products of city-county cooperation.

Although joint efforts represent progress in meeting some problems, they have proved to be too slow an approach to the great problems of metropolitan areas. Legal restrictions and financial limitations accompanied by a mutual lack of determination on the part of local officials to work cooperatively have seriously hampered progress. The multiplicity of governmental units characteristic of metropoli-

---

[27] See Robert K. Lowry, "Advantages of Intergovernmental Purchasing," *Public Management*, March 1959, pp. 61–63.

[28] See, for example, Earl B. Smith, "High School Recreation Program Is Jointly Planned in Merced," *Western City*, February 1959.

tan regions constitutes an additional obstacle. Major progress toward a solution of the problems of these regions must be sought along other lines.[29]

Federation. Metropolitan federation, sometimes called the borough plan, appears to be potentially the most promising approach to metropolitan area problems. In a federated metropolis, authority to administer certain matters of regional concern would be transferred to a "central" government. Local governments would continue to exist and maintain control over local functions. Representation on the governing body of the metropolitan authority would be guaranteed to each government within its jurisdiction. The resemblance between such an arrangement and the federal system on the national level is apparent.

Federation as a means of meeting urban problems is not a new idea, as it was first seriously considered for the Boston area in 1896. The proposal never came to a vote, however, because the legislature failed to take the necessary action. Similar reluctance was again evidenced by the Massachusetts legislature in 1931. Efforts to establish federated arrangements were defeated by a vote of the local residents in Alameda County (Oakland) in 1922 and in Allegheny County (Pittsburgh) in 1929. In 1930, a proposed constitutional amendment authorizing the drafting of a federation charter for St. Louis was defeated by a state-wide vote.

Interest in metropolitan federation was heightened appreciably in 1954 when the Municipality of Metropolitan Toronto (Canada) began to function. This new unit of government had been created the previous year by act of the Ontario provincial legislature. Included within its boundaries were the City of Toronto and twelve suburban municipalities, all of which continued to function. The law creating the metropolitan municipality specified that it should assume responsibility for the following functions: water supply, sewage disposal, arterial highways, metropolitan parks, housing and redevelopment, certain health and welfare services, and over-all planning. It was also empowered to appoint the governing body of

---

[29] In spite of the apparent lack of promise of cooperative arrangements, the Northeastern Illinois Metropolitan Area Local Governmental Services Commission reported in 1959 that "we have attempted to encourage a system of voluntary cooperation among the traditional units of local government" as the most feasible approach to the problems of the Chicago Metropolitan Area. See *Metropolitan Area Problems,* Conference on Metropolitan Area Problems, May–June 1959, pp. 1–2.

the Toronto Transit Commission, provide a courthouse and jail, assist in financing education, review and issue bonds for member municipalities, and set a uniform assessment rate for all taxable property within its jurisdiction. Municipalities within Metropolitan Toronto continued to administer law enforcement, fire protection, most public health services, public relief, libraries and building regulations—to name only the more important functions. By authority of a 1956 amendment to the original law, the metropolitan authority was authorized to provide area-wide police protection.

Hailed as "a bold new development in metropolitan government," the accomplishments of the Municipality of Metropolitan Toronto have been too numerous to review here.[30] Suffice it to say that on balance the achievements of the new government have been favorably received by its residents. Nevertheless, the experiment has been criticized on several counts. It is asserted that some functions retained by the individual municipalities should be in the hands of the federation and that its geographical jurisdiction is inadequate to meet the needs of a rapidly growing urban area. Some critics claim that representation on the metropolitan governing body is inequitable and that the administrative structure is top-heavy. However, these criticisms relate to matters of detail and do not reflect basic weaknesses in the concept of a metropolitan federation.

In 1955, a plan of federation for Dade County (Miami), Florida, was approved by a board created to study the problems of the area. A constitutional amendment authorizing federation was submitted to the state legislature, which altered it to make the board of county commissioners the metropolitan governing body. This amendment was approved by popular vote in 1956 along with a home rule charter for Dade County. Since the federation boundaries are limited to Dade County which is designated as the metropolitan government, there is some question as to whether this arrangement is a "true" federation.[31] Dade County is not geographically coterminous with the heavily urbanized area around Miami, even though it does encompass the bulk of it. Nevertheless, the experiment in southern

---

[30] See Eric Hardy, "Progress in Toronto," *National Municipal Review*, October 1958, and John G. Grumm, *Metropolitan Area Government*, University of Kansas, Lawrence, 1959.

[31] For a detailed analysis of the Dade County arrangement, see Edward Sofen, *The Miami Metropolitan Experiment*, Indiana University, Bloomington, 1963. See also, Richard Carpenter, "Is Dade County Plan Applicable to the California Experience?" *Western City*, November 1958.

Florida is generally conceded to be the first instance of federation at the local level in the United States.

Miami "Metro," as it is generally known, experienced difficulties getting under way, not the least of which stemmed from opposition on the part of municipalities in Dade County. Shortly after the federation was organized an "autonomy" amendment to the county charter was supported by the Dade County League of Municipalities. This amendment was designed to prohibit the Dade County government from taking any action infringing upon the right of municipalities "to exercise all powers whether granted by their several charters, or by special act, or by general law." The effect would have nullified its usefulness as a metropolitan authority. The voters of Dade County defeated the amendment by a large margin in 1958. One factor that may have contributed significantly to the support of Metro was the first annual report of progress issued by County Manager O. W. Campbell. His report cited a number of accomplishments, including halving the number of county departments, installation of modern budget and accounting systems, reduction in the county tax rate by 6.5 per cent, extension of civil service accompanied by pay increases, reorganization of welfare and hospital programs, inauguration of long-range planning, inauguration of a plan to meet the recreation needs of the county, acceleration of the county's highway program, and uniform subdivision regulations. Such a list of accomplishments in so short a time was undoubtedly quite impressive in the eyes of many voters who supported Metro.

Success in Dade County and Toronto heightened interest in federation as a means of attacking metropolitan problems. In 1958, the voters of Davidson County (Nashville), Tennessee, and of King County (Seattle), Washington, defeated proposals for metropolitan government. In the same year, the Quebec Provincial Legislature created the Montreal Metropolitan Corporation, which was described as "a limited and skeleton form of Metropolitan Government." Too little authority was granted to the Corporation, however, to classify it as a federation although it represented a halting step in that direction. In 1959, the voters of Knox County (Knoxville), Tennessee, defeated a charter creating The Knoxville-Knox County Metropolitan Government providing a federated approach to some of the major problems of that area. During the same year metropolitan plans were also defeated in Cleveland and St. Louis.

In 1960, the Metropolitan Corporation of Greater Winnipeg was created by the Manitoba provincial legislature.[32]

Although it is premature to evaluate federation as a means of handling metropolitan problems, preliminary conclusions seem justified. Certainly federation is no cure-all, and attempts to establish such an arrangement in a community will encounter numerous difficulties. Three major centers of controversy must be resolved. One concerns the distribution of powers between the metropolitan government and the local units situated within it. Local governments generally fight reduction of their powers. A second major source of controversy is the composition of the governing body of the metropolitan unit. Involved here are such questions as the number of members, whether they shall be elected at-large or by units of government, and how they shall be apportioned among the units.[33] A third category of problems relates to the nature of the state laws, including constitutional amendments, that may be required to establish federations. Shall a new unit of government be created? What shall be its boundaries? Shall a county be empowered to function as a metropolitan government? How much home rule authority shall be extended to the new government? If home rule already exists for cities, what effect will the change have upon them? These sample questions indicate the nature of the problems involved. In spite of such difficulties, the flexibility inherent in federation and the fact that it does not entail the abolition of established governments constitute important advantages in its favor.[34]

City-County Consolidation or Separation. City-county consolidation consists of a partial or complete merger of the area and government of a county with the area and government of a city. City-county separation consists of detaching a city from its county so that the city performs most if not all county functions within its territory. Although this arrangement is common practice in some countries, it has found little use in the United States except in Virginia where every city upon reaching a population of 10,000 is

---

[32] See "Greater Winnipeg Agency Created," *National Civic Review,* September 1960.

[33] See Arthur W. Bromage, "Political Representation in Metropolitan Areas," *American Political Science Review,* June 1958.

[34] Nevertheless, unfavorable popular reaction to major changes, either structural or functional, in metropolitan areas in the last few years casts doubt upon the future of metropolitan federation in the United States. See Henry Schmandt, "The Area Council —Approach to Metropolitan Government," *Public Management,* February 1960.

separated completely from its county. An obvious difficulty associated with this practice, particularly in heavily urbanized regions, is the reduction in taxable resources suffered by the county.

An early instance of city-county consolidation in the United States occurred in New Orleans in 1813, when the state legislature authorized the city to perform within its boundaries certain functions assigned to parishes (counties). Although there have since been a number of readjustments of jurisdiction, both in terms of area and functions, New Orleans remains an example of city-county consolidation. A similar arrangement became effective in Boston in 1822. The boundaries of the City of Philadelphia were made coterminous with those of the County of Philadelphia in 1854, and twenty-eight local governments in the county became part of the City of Philadelphia. Again consolidation was partial because a number of county officers were continued in existence. The extent of this consolidation was diminished by the constitution of 1874. Consolidation in Pennsylvania was given additional impetus by a constitutional amendment adopted in 1951.

Probably the best known example of city-county consolidation is found in New York City. In fact, a number of consolidations have taken place, the first occurring in 1730, the second in 1894, and the third in 1898 when the boundaries of New York City were extended to encompass four counties (five when the Bronx was divided from the County of New York in 1912). Most county functions were turned over to the city government. A unique feature of the New York plan is the arrangement whereby local areas, called boroughs, are permitted administrative powers and representation on the legislature of the consolidated government, the city council. Representation actually is granted to the boroughs on the Board of Estimate, which is the "upper chamber" of the council.

Few consolidations have occurred during the present century. The city and county of Honolulu were consolidated in 1907. Today the entire island of Oahu is organized as one unit of local government, namely, the City and County of Honolulu.[35] Consolidation was accomplished in Baton Rouge, Louisiana, in 1949. At that time, East Baton Rouge Parish was divided into an urban area, two industrial areas, and a rural area. The boundaries of Baton Rouge

---

[35] For an interesting discussion of the situation in Honolulu, see Charlton F. Chute, "The Honolulu Metropolitan Area: A Challenge to Traditional Thinking," *Public Administration Review*, Winter 1958.

were defined to encompass only the urban area. Partial consolidation was accomplished in 1951 between Atlanta and Fulton County, Georgia.[36] The most recent city-county consolidation followed a favorable popular vote in Nashville and Davidson County, Tennessee, in 1962. The same proposal was defeated in 1958.[37]

Less frequently advocated as an approach to the solution of metropolitan problems, city-county separation has been effected in more communities than city-county consolidation. With the exception of those found in Virginia, most city-county separations were achieved during the nineteenth century. The separation of Baltimore and San Francisco from their counties was accomplished during the 1850's, followed by the separation of St. Louis in 1876. Denver was officially separated from its county in 1902 by terms of a constitutional amendment, although litigation postponed its effective operation for about ten years. Virginia is the only state where systematic use has been made of city-county separation. The practice in that state is to provide separation for municipalities of 10,000 or more. Where complete separation has been achieved, a city is in no way subject to county jurisdiction or taxation.

Numerous difficulties are associated with city-county consolidation and separation. Both have usually required the absorption of small municipalities and fringe areas by a large central city. The characteristic determination of such communities to retain their identity leads their residents to vote against any constitutional amendment or local referendum measure authorizing or implementing consolidation or separation. Furthermore, if consolidation or separation is accomplished with a view toward anticipation of future growth and problems, some rural land must be included within the city-county. Residents of such areas also regularly oppose consolidation. Territorial circumscription has posed another problem. Consolidations have been based on the area of individual counties and consequently have provided no assistance in the solution of intercounty problems. Experience has demonstrated that it is very difficult, if not impossible, to enlarge the original boundaries of the consolidated area. The same problem exists in regard to city-county separations. The boundaries of St. Louis and San Francisco are the

---

[36] An unsuccessful effort was made in the 1950's to establish a consolidated city-county of Albuquerque, New Mexico. In 1949, an amendment was added to the New Mexico constitution permitting city-county mergers in counties with a population of at least 50,000.

[37] See David A. Booth, *Metropolitics: The Nashville Consolidation*, 1963.

same as when they were separated from their counties, and only very limited additions have been made to Denver. Of the three examples of separation mentioned above, only Baltimore has increased appreciably in territory, but each annexation required a special act of the state legislature. Since annexation is a judicial process in Virginia, separated cities have been able to add appreciably to their territory.

The City-State. The most radical proposal for dealing with metropolitan problems involves the creation of city-states. Proponents of this idea advocate the separation of large urban areas from their states and the admission of such areas as new states in the Union with powers and privileges equal to all other states. A major argument in behalf of such a step is that it would free these areas from control by legislatures dominated by rural interests. Each city-state would be free to work out its own salvation under the Constitution of the United States. A little reflection reveals the thoroughly fanciful nature of such a proposal. The U.S. Constitution forbids the creation of a new state within an existing state or by joining parts of two or more states without the consent of the state legislatures concerned as well as of Congress. No state legislature is likely to agree to such a proposal!

Special Districts. Since special districts were discussed in an earlier chapter, they will be considered only briefly here. However, a few comments are in order concerning the use of special districts as means of handling certain metropolitan problems. Of the 18,442 local governments in the 212 standard metropolitan areas reported in 1962 by the Bureau of the Census, 11,415 were special districts, including school districts. It appears that a special district was first used on what might be called a "metropolitan basis" in 1790 when a special district was established in the Philadelphia area to administer prisons. Special districts were created in the New York area to administer the police function in 1857, fire departments in 1865, and public health in 1866. The growth of special districts in metropolitan areas and elsewhere has been especially rapid during the last quarter-century or so.

According to Professor Bollens, metropolitan special districts have been used most frequently to provide port facilities, sewage disposal, water supply, and parks. They also operate bridges, tunnels, housing projects, airports, libraries, and transit facilities; furnish public health services, power, ice, gas, and coke; and develop regional plans.[38] Some of these districts are truly big government. It is interesting to note that the oldest active independent metropolitan district in the United States, the Metropolitan Sanitary District of Greater Chicago, covers about 500 square miles and includes about fifty per cent of the area of Cook County and ninety-five per cent of its population and assessed valuation. The Metropolitan Water District of Southern California contains approximately 2,700 square miles and serves over six million people living in five counties.

Although the cumulative effect of increasing use of special districts is to complicate governmental structure, this disadvantage does not outweigh their several advantages, including these: (1) their creation does not disturb the existence of other governmental units; (2) they may cross county and even state lines; (3) they may circumvent tax and debt limits imposed by state law; and (4) they are easily organized.[39] The fact is that of all the approaches to metropolitan problems, particularly as they pertain to the provision of services, the special district has been most widely used. However, the special district has not been used as a comprehensive solution to metropolitan problems.[40]

Evaluation of Solutions. Victor Jones, a widely known and highly respected student of metropolitan regions, has developed a number of propositions as guides for the evaluation of various approaches to metropolitan problems. His propositions provide such an excellent basis for critical insight that they are quoted here in full.

(1) Metropolitan communities are growing so large and becoming so complicated that the effort to find solutions to their problems should be shared by federal, state, and local governments.

(2) Whenever possible, a metropolitan government responsible to

---

[38] John C. Bollens, *Special District Governments in the United States,* University of California Press, Berkeley, 1957, p. 68.

[39] See Victor Jones, "The Organization of a Metropolitan Region," *University of Pennsylvania Law Review,* February 1957, p. 545.

[40] The use of multipurpose special districts organized to encompass entire metropolitan areas was suggested in a report to the Assembly Interim Committee on Conservation, Planning and Public Works of the California legislature in 1959. See *Metropolitan Government in California,* Assembly Interim Committee Reports 1957–1959, Vol. 13, No. 23.

the inhabitants of the area is preferable to direct federal or state administration.

(3) It would be undesirable to attempt to govern the modern metropolis with its large area, huge population and many divergent interests as if it were a small, compact, homogenous city.

(4) A metropolitan government should be devised that will provide effective services, guidance and controls where desired over the whole of the metropolitan area, that will equalize the burden of supporting such governmental functions, and that will facilitate effective citizen control of governmental policies which affect them at their places of work and recreation, as well as their places of residence.

(5) There should be an area-wide government with sufficient authority to make policy decisions about, and to administer, those matters that the community considers to be of metropolitan interest and concern.

(6) All or part of a governmental function might be assigned to a limited metropolitan government (a) when coordination of a function over the whole area is essential to effective service or control in any part of the area; (b) when it is desired to apply the ability-to-pay theory of taxation to the area as a whole, instead of allowing each part to support its own activities at whatever level its own economic base will permit; (c) when services can be supplied more efficiently through large-scale operations and when the advantages of large-scale operations are desired; and (d) when it is necessary in order to assure citizens a voice in decisions that affect them in other parts of the metropolitan area, as well as the part in which they reside.

(7) There should be a network of submetropolitan governments, perhaps existing counties and municipalities, to legislate and administer those matters that the metropolitan community does not consider to require uniform treatments throughout the metropolitan area.

(8) The metropolitan government should be a *general* government with responsibility for enough functions so that it can weigh the claims of one function against those of other functions. Only a general government can, in planning and administering the government of a metropolis, take account of the delicate and intricate relations among governmental and private services and controls.[41]

No solution thus far suggested accords completely with all these criteria, but federation seems more promising than any other approach. Metropolitan areas provide a sort of frontier in society today. New problems, new dangers, and new threats to established

[41] Victor Jones, *op. cit.*, pp. 551–52.

ways of doing things are appearing all the time.[42] Only through ingenuity, resourcefulness, and informed effort on the part of leaders and citizens can large communities prosper.

SELECTED REFERENCES

Books:

Advisory Commission on Intergovernmental Relations, *Alternative Approaches to Governmental Reorganization in Metropolitan Areas,* Washington, D.C., 1962.

——, *Factors Affecting Voter Reactions to Governmental Reorganization in Metropolitan Areas,* Washington, D.C., 1962.

Bollens, John C. (ed.), *Exploring the Metropolitan Community,* University of California Press, Berkeley, 1961.

Booth, David A., *Metropolitics: the Nashville Consolidation,* Institute for Community Development and Services, Michigan State University, 1963.

Bromage, Arthur W., *Political Representation in Metropolitan Agencies,* Institute of Public Administration, University of Michigan, 1962.

Council of State Governments, *The States and the Metropolitan Problem,* Chicago, 1956.

Greene, Lee S., et al., *The Problem of Government in Metropolitan Areas,* Arnold Foundation, Southern Methodist University, Dallas, 1958.

Gottman, Jean, *Megalopolis: The Urbanized Northeastern Seaboard of the United States,* The Twentieth Century Fund, N.Y., 1961.

Greer, Scott, *Governing the Metropolis,* John Wiley & Sons, New York, 1962.

——, *Metropolitics: A Study of Political Culture,* John Wiley & Sons, New York, 1963.

Gulick, Luther, *Metro: Changing Problems and Lines of Attack,* Governmental Affairs Institute, New York, 1957.

Hoover, Edgar, and Vernon, Raymond, *Anatomy of a Metropolis,* Harvard University Press, Cambridge, 1960.

Lyon, Leverett S., editor, *Governmental Problems in the Chicago Metropolitan Area,* University of Chicago Press, Chicago, 1957.

Maddox, Russell W., *Extraterritorial Powers of Municipalities in the United States,* Oregon State College Press, Corvallis, 1955.

——, *Issues in State and Local Government,* D. Van Nostrand Co., Inc., Princeton, N.J., 1965.

---

[42] For a minority viewpoint, see Robert C. Wood, "Metropolitan Government, 1975: An Extrapolation of Trends." *American Political Science Review,* March 1958. "In short," says Mr. Wood, "there may not be the metropolitan crisis which so many of us have expected for so long, either now or in the future."

Robson, William A., *Great Cities of the World: Their Government, Politics, and Planning,* 2nd ed., Macmillan Co., New York, 1957.

Sweeney, S. B., and Blair, G. S., *Metropolitan Analysis,* University of Pennsylvania Press, Philadelphia, 1958.

Tableman, Betty, *Governmental Organization in Metropolitan Areas,* Bureau of Government, Institute of Public Administration, University of Michigan, Ann Arbor, 1951.

Wood, Robert C., *Suburbia: Its People and Their Politics,* Houghton Mifflin Co., Boston, 1959.

——, *1400 Governments,* Harvard University Press, Cambridge, 1960.

Articles:

Beckman, Norman, "Alternative Approaches for Metropolitan Reorganization," *Public Management,* June 1964.

Bible, Alan, "Uncle Sam's Metro Job," *National Civic Review,* December 1960.

Bollens, John C., "Urban Fringe Areas—A Persistent Problem," *Public Management,* October 1960.

Campbell, Alan K., and Sacks, Seymour, "Administering the Spread City," *Public Administration Review,* September 1964.

Chute, Charlton F., "The Honolulu Metropolitan Area: A Challenge to Traditional Thinking," *Public Administration Review,* Winter 1958.

Connery, Robert H., and Leach, Richard H., "U.S. Council on Metro," *National Civic Review,* June 1959.

Gulick, Luther, "Goals for Metropolis," *National Civic Review,* December 1960.

Hardy, Eric, "Progress in Toronto," *National Municipal Review,* October 1958.

Jones, Victor, "The Organization of a Metropolitan Region," *University of Pennsylvania Law Review,* February 1957.

Maddox, Russell W., "Cities Step over Line," *National Municipal Review,* February 1955.

Parker, John K., "Cooperation in Metropolitan Areas through Councils of Governments," *Public Management,* October 1963.

Schmandt, Henry, "The Area Council—An Approach to Metropolitan Government," *Public Management,* February 1960.

Studenski, Paul, "Metropolitan Areas 1960," *National Civic Review,* October and November 1960.

Walker, Mabel, "Fiscal Aspects of Metropolitan Regional Development," *University of Pennsylvania Law Review,* February 1957.

Wood, Robert C., "Metropolitan Government, 1975: An Extrapolation of Trends," *American Political Science Review,* March 1958.

CHAPTER 23

Local Governments: Their Role in Intergovernmental Affairs

"Intergovernmental relations, not always recognized as such, have been with us from the beginning of our history."[1] Popular awareness of their importance has increased perceptibly in recent years. Solutions to many problems in such fields as finance, civil rights, law enforcement, and urban renewal are sought through cooperation among different levels of government. In this chapter three major categories of intergovernmental relations will be examined: (1) state-local, (2) federal-local, and (3) interlocal.

STATE-LOCAL RELATIONS

Previous chapters stressed the basic legal relationships between local governments and states. Consequently, in the area of state-local relations attention is centered here on those aspects that may be termed "administrative," involving the direction of local affairs by a state agency. The importance of day-to-day contacts between local governments and state administrative agencies varies greatly according to the activity. State-local administrative relations have become especially significant in the fields of education, welfare, highways, and finances. These relationships have developed largely during the present century and have resulted in greatly increased state supervision of local actions. In earlier days state supervision of the activities of local governments, such as it was, took the form of laws that local officials were expected to observe, with judicial action directed against those accused of flagrant violations. Such a system, productive of rather spasmodic control, was reasonably adequate when governmental services were relatively simple and their administration uncomplicated. As government became "big gov-

---

[1] W. Brooke Graves, "Maze of Governments I," *National Civic Review*, May 1960, p. 230.

ernment," demands grew for more effective and uniform administration of major services. It is noteworthy that the three functions over which state supervision has increased most notably are also those on which the greatest amounts of state and local money are spent.

Education. Public education at the secondary and primary levels traditionally has been a local concern. Well into the nineteenth century local authorities, sometimes even groups of private citizens, regularly built schools, hired teachers, and determined the curriculum according to the needs, wishes, and resources of each local community. As a result, within each state tremendous variations in quality characterized the education received by youngsters in different localities. In an effort to reduce inequities, state agencies were created and authorized to set minimum building standards, determine qualifications for teachers, establish minimum requirements concerning curriculum, and assist in the selection of textbooks. By 1900 each state had a school superintendent or commissioner who gave advice and assistance to local authorities, but effective central supervision had not yet developed in most states. Economic disparities among communities continued to result in less adequate education for some children than for others. State aid appeared to be the only solution, and with state money came additional controls.

Welfare. State supervision of local activities in the field of public welfare is even more recent than in education. Although some signs of state centralization were evident prior to the depression of the 1930's, welfare was considered a local problem, consisting largely of help for the indigent. State supervision was chiefly concerned with the administration of institutions such as almshouses, orphanages, and charity hospitals. The Great Depression witnessed an expansion of the concept of welfare to include such programs as old-age assistance, aid to dependent children and widows, help for the blind and disabled, and unemployment compensation for the able-bodied jobless. The Social Security Act of 1935 required that an agency be created in each state to administer and supervise local administration of those programs supported partially by federal funds. More recently, other programs, particularly those providing assistance for the needy aged, have further stimulated state supervision of local efforts.

Highways. Throughout most of the nineteenth century, road construction and maintenance was a local task. Cities and towns built streets within their boundaries, and counties and townships undertook to connect these centers of population. As late as 1910 only seven states had made provision for state aid in the construction of highways, but by 1917 all states had done so.[2] Since that time the typical arrangement has been for the state to construct and maintain major or primary highways and for counties, with some assistance from the state, to assume responsibility for other roads outside city limits. In some states counties and townships share this responsibility. Only four states have assumed complete responsibility for highway and road construction and maintenance: Delaware, North Carolina, Virginia, and West Virginia. Again state centralization has been hastened by federal action. When the federal government inaugurated its grant-in-aid program for highways in 1916, one of the requirements was that each state have a highway department to work with the national government and supervise the expenditure of federal money.

Finances.[3] State supervision of local finances relates especially to the assessment of property, budgeting, maintenance and audit of accounts, and indebtedness. In an effort to mitigate inequities in the valuation of property for taxation, practically all states have provided for some control over local assessors. Supervision ranges from giving advice, interpreting laws, and requiring reports to setting standards, equalizing assessments, and instituting removal proceedings against unusually incompetent and uncooperative assessors. Often state agencies choose not to exert their legal authority but rely instead on seeking cooperation.

Although most states require local governments to prepare budgets and to observe certain procedural requirements in the process, very few have sought to control local fiscal policies by means of extensive review. Budgets reflect public policy in terms of dollars and cents, and strict state supervision of local budgets in regard to contents would undermine local self-government. In most states the accounts of some or all local governments are subject to some type of supervision or audit by state authority. Many states prescribe accounting forms and classifications of accounts for local use, but the local units may be free to decide whether or not to use them. Only about one-fourth of the states require the use of uniform local accounting systems and uniform reports that must be filed with a state agency. State requirements concerning an audit of local accounts

---

[2] W. Brooke Graves, *American State Government*, D. C. Heath and Co., New York, 1953, p. 828.

[3] See William Anderson, *Intergovernmental Fiscal Relations*, University of Minnesota Press, Minneapolis, 1956.

are much more common. Most states require annual or biennial postaudits of the accounts of some or all local governments to discover any irregularities or violations of statutory requirements. Such audits may be the responsibility of a state agency, or private firms may be engaged to conduct them and file reports with the state. It is not uncommon for local officials to request state audits more frequently than required by law in order that their records may be kept in the best possible condition.

Miscellaneous. State supervision of local governments is by no means limited to the major areas discussed above. Some states recently have evidenced increased interest in certain local activities. In 1959 municipal incorporations, annexations, and consolidations were made subject to review by a state official in Wisconsin and by a state commission in Minnesota. In the same year the New York legislature created the Office of Local Government to provide a number of services to local governments, including assistance in the coordination of state activities relating to local governments and in the promotion of cooperative efforts among local governments to solve common problems. The states generally demonstrate their concern for the problems of local governments in many ways, although often not in the manner preferred by local officials.

Techniques of Supervision and Control. The devices used by states to supervise local activities may be allocated to seven categories: (1) advice and information, (2) reports, (3) financial assistance, (4) standards and inspection, (5) review and approval, (6) appointment and removal of local officials, and (7) directives to local agencies. *Advice* and *information* may be more properly considered as a means of influencing local governments than supervising them in the usual sense. Their importance must not be underestimated, however, because administrators favor a cooperative approach to the solution of problems whenever possible. Many improvements have been accomplished in local practices through advice and information in such fields, for example, as police administration, public health, and financial practices. More often than not, the superior resources of state agencies, especially technically trained personnel, enable them to render helpful advice that might otherwise be unavailable to local governments. Wisdom generally dictates its voluntary acceptance.

Particularly in regard to fiscal affairs, public health, and education, requirements that localities file certain types of *reports* with a state agency at regular intervals have become very common. Information obtained in this way may serve many valuable purposes. It may reveal relative deficiencies among local units in providing services and provide a basis for study and action leading to improvements. A community may discover that its expenditures for a function are disproportionate to achievements and consequently inaugurate administrative reforms. A need for tightening state requirements and increasing supervision may also be indicated. Information of great value may be made available to state legislators considering problems of local government. If adequate publicity is given to such reports, the information may serve as incentive to local officials to perform more adequately or to local residents to demand improvements.

State *financial assistance* in the form of aid and reimbursements to local governments now exceeds $12 billion a year. A major portion of these expenditures consists of grants-in-aid, which have become increasingly important in recent years as a means of controlling local activities. These conditional contributions to local governments are usually designed to encourage specific local programs and to guarantee that they meet minimum state standards. Grants-in-aid are most widely used in relation to education, health, and welfare. Great variations exist as to the degree of discretion permitted state agencies administering such subsidies. The amount of administrative control depends basically upon the manner in which a state legislature chooses to word the relevant statutes. Since the receipt of grant-in-aid funds is voluntary from the legal standpoint, very stringent conditions may be attached to their acceptance, and consequently they possess great potential as a means of control.

In order to increase the effectiveness of reports and grants-in-aid as supervisory devices, states have developed *standards* and resorted to *inspection* to oversee their application, especially in the fields of finance, health, welfare, and education. As noted earlier, states impose requirements concerning such matters as assessment of property and audit of local accounts. Waterworks and sewage disposal plants are often subject to state inspection to determine that they are constructed and operated according to minimum standards. Local administration of welfare programs is closely scrutinized by states to guarantee uniformity of eligibility requirements and payments. Since public welfare is financed largely by state and federal funds, such scrutiny is logical and reasonable. Each year the states pay a larger share of the costs of public education. Use of state funds to support substandard programs and facilities is contrary to the laudable goal that all children in a state should receive an education that at least meets minimum standards as conceived by educators.

Review and *approval* are often used to forestall action not in harmony with state requirements. Properly handled, they may save much time, effort, and money otherwise expended on inadequate, improperly administered programs. In a few states, such as Indiana and North Carolina, municipal debts are subject to close control by a state agency. Municipal utilities are sometimes under state supervision regarding rates, methods of accounting, and extension of services. Local assessment of property for purposes of taxation has long been subject to review by state boards of equalization or state tax commissions. Some states require that plans for the construction of municipal water and sewage systems be submitted to a state agency for approval. Numerous other local activities are subject to review and approval by a central agency in one or more states.

Although the laws of a number of states vest in the governor or some state agency authority to *remove* certain local officials, few recent examples of its exercise are recorded. State *appointment* of local officials is authorized less frequently but exercised more often, particularly in regard to health officers. Local opposition to central appointment or removal of local officials is generally strong, with the state authority viewed as unjustifiable interference in local affairs. The record indicates that there is little danger that such authority will be abused, for reliance has usually been placed on more effective and acceptable means of supervision.

Directives to local agencies may take the form of general regulations applicable to certain types of actions or of specific instructions applicable to individual cases. The former are commonly called *ordinances,* while the latter are known as *orders.* Ordinances are most widely used in relation to education, finance, and public health. The major arguments in behalf of vesting a state agency with such power are that the state legislature is relieved of the burden of enacting detailed statutes and that more adequate regulations are produced since they are prepared by specialized agencies.

State Assumption of Functions. When supervision proves inadequate, states may assume responsibility for the administration of local functions. Such a development has occurred most frequently in regard to highways and education. Complete control over the construction and maintenance of local roads and highways has been vested in the state government in Delaware, North Carolina, Virginia, and West Virginia. Except for Virginia, responsibility for public education in these states has been largely assumed by the central governments, although in Delaware school districts continue to possess considerable discretion concerning curricula. Centralization of control over certain aspects of education, such as certification of teachers, is generally accepted without question. As an expedient to meet unusual circumstances, substitute administration is sometimes considered as a technique of supervision over local affairs.

Merits of State Administrative Supervision. Assuming the value of state supervision of some local functions, the major advantage of *administrative* action is, broadly, that it is superior to any other approach thus far devised. The alternative of detailed legislative specifications enforceable through judicial action is cumbersome, expensive, time-consuming, and unnecessarily restrictive.[4] Administrative supervision, on the other hand, can and should be flexible, expert, and continuous. It is possible to consider each situation on its own merits rather than attempting to cover an entire problem area with a "blanket" provision. Thus, rather than provide by law that the debt limit for cities may not exceed five per cent of the assessed valuation of property located therein, responsibility for determining the debt limit for each city individually might be placed in the hands of a state agency. Each case would be handled on its own merits by a trained staff familiar with those factors pertinent to determining the economic strength of a community. Continuous oversight of such matters as minimum standards for school buildings and curriculum requirements is much preferable to spasmodic efforts by parents to exert pressure on local school authorities who neglect or disregard them.

Arguments in behalf of state administrative supervision of local affairs are founded on certain assumptions that may not always be valid. State agencies are not necessarily more effective than local ones. This fact is particularly evident in those states where the merit principle is not closely observed in the selection and management of personnel. The qualifications of administrative personnel in a large

---

[4] See the Council of State Governments, *State-Local Relations*, Chicago, 1946, pp. 141–81, for a good discussion of the way in which legal restrictions impede local governments.

school district may be superior to those of employees in a state department of education. Over a period of time, large central agencies tend to handle matters as "routine." Unless great care is exercised, potential flexibility is not realized in practice. Individual requests for review and assistance may become so bogged down that the effectiveness of local governments may be lessened rather than increased.

Administrative Cooperation. Too much stress often is placed on formal control and too little on informal cooperation. State and local officials work together through personal contacts and by correspondence to seek solutions to problems and to discover improved methods for providing public services. Professional meetings of educators, public health personnel, engineers, tax assessors, librarians, purchasing agents, and personnel engaged in many other types of work provide opportunities to exchange ideas, thus paving the way for future contacts and cooperation. Annual meetings of state leagues of municipalities to which state officials are invited as program participants or interested observers strengthen mutual understanding and open channels of communication. Advice and assistance are generally more effective when voluntarily sought and given than when they are required by law. Voluntary arrangements have not wholly dispelled the need for administrative supervision, but they have supplemented formal controls and diminished their rate of growth.

A State Department of Local Government. In spite of the increased number and complexity of relationships between each state and its local governments, no state has established an agency or department to coordinate all such activities. Only a few states have taken even halting steps in that direction. New Jersey, New York, North Carolina, and Pennsylvania have central agencies with titles such as Local Government Commission and Department of Municipal Affairs. These general titles are misleading, however, because in each instance the primary emphasis is on supervision of local finances. In Indiana, state supervision over municipal indebtedness is lodged in the State Board of Tax Commissioners.

Some students of local government have advocated the creation in each state of a department of local government with general responsibility for the bulk of state activities involving direct relations with local governments. Such a department would serve as a clearinghouse for information about and inquiries from all units of local government in the state. It would also function as a coordinating agency between various state agencies and individual local governments as well as among local units. Local requests for all types of assistance would be directed to this department which would either handle them itself or direct them to the appropriate place. The department would oversee the application of state laws pertaining to local government and report to the legislature and chief executive concerning problems and deficiencies requiring legislative adjustment.

Although the case for a department of local government has been presented on many occasions, the idea has received little support. The fact is that both local and state officials are concerned about the manner in which such an agency would actually work. Local officials fear that it would function to bring local activities under stricter state control, perhaps by persons unfamiliar and unsympathetic with local needs. They look upon such an agency as just another device for "centralization," a term charged with much emotion if little specific content. State officials associated with agencies working closely with local governments are generally convinced that assistance and supervision are more adequately provided by specialized rather than general-purpose agencies. Concern is also felt at the state level that a department of local government may function as a special pleader for local causes. Sufficient data are not available to provide an adequate basis for assessing these viewpoints, but their mere existence deters experimentation.

FEDERAL-LOCAL RELATIONS

Prior to the depression of the 1930's, contacts between the federal government and local governments were few and rather insignificant. The generally accepted view was that any such relations should be channeled through state governments. Federal activities directly affecting localities were considered as either actual or potential infringements of "states' rights." Indeed, it seems that very little consideration was given to the matter until recent times. A pioneer effort to call attention to developments in this area was made by Professor William Anderson in 1924.[5] He noted that federal

---

[5] W. M. Anderson, "The Federal Government and the Cities," *National Municipal Review*, May 1924.

court decisions involving municipal ordinances often constituted "federal restraints" upon municipalities, and he recalled that during World War I military officers in some instances "practically superseded" local authorities in suppressing vice in the vicinity of military establishments. The United States delegation at the International Congress of Cities in London in 1932 reported that no direct administrative relationships existed in the United States between the national and local governments. Nevertheless, there were numerous federal services of interest and value to localities.

Because of the importance of chronology in federal-local relations, they are most profitably examined within the framework of three major periods: pre-Depression, Depression, and World War II and its aftermath. Although the rapid increase in federal-local relations since 1930 has resulted largely from "abnormal" conditions, it seems safe to venture that they will continue to grow.

Pre-Depression Relations. By the early twentieth century, more or less regular contacts had been established between local governments and national agencies. Most of these contacts were related to services provided to localities by departments of the national government, especially Commerce, Treasury, Interior, War, Agriculture, and Justice. As late as 1930 the services rendered by the Department of Commerce to local governments, particularly municipalities, were "greater in number and more varied in scope than those of any other department."[6] At that time six units of the Department were providing such services, the most important of which were the Bureau of the Census, the Bureau of Standards, and the Bureau of Mines.

The Census Bureau collected and published data on population, educational facilities, occupations, wages and hours, manufactures, and births and deaths. Also of local interest was information on waterworks, sewers, fire and police departments, parks, and schools. In addition, some information was collected on receipts and expenditures, taxes, debts, etc., of localities over 30,000 population. The Bureau of Standards assisted local governments in regulating weights and measures by establishing standards and assisting in the development of methods. The Bureau also engaged in engineering research on such problems as electrolysis of water and gas pipes as well as

---

[6] Paul V. Betters, *Federal Services to Municipal Governments,* Municipal Administration Service, Chicago, 1931, p. 5.

sewers caused by street railways, standards of electric light and power service, and properties of structural materials. Tests were conducted on water meters, incandescent lamps, fire hose, brick, tile, and many other items. Safety codes were developed, including those on electrical installations, buildings, and traffic. The Bureau of Mines conducted research and experiments on matters of local interest such as explosion hazards of gases in sewers, fire-fighting techniques, hazards of handling and storing gasoline, and ventilation of tunnels.

The chief subdivision of the Treasury Department so far as the localities were concerned was the Health Service, which collected and disseminated information on sanitation legislation and control. It also conducted studies on diseases that posed threats to public health, stream pollution, and rat extermination. In natural disasters the Coast Guard offered assistance to local governments.

The Bureau of Education of the Department of the Interior provided three general types of services to local units: information, surveys, and consultation. Large quantities of information were disseminated to school authorities. Data on the ways in which school problems had been solved in other places, accompanied by suggestions pertinent to the needs of an individual community, were available upon request. If local authorities desired the Bureau to make a survey of their schools, they merely had to request such help and assume the expenses.

The direct services of the War Department to local governments were quite limited. They related almost entirely to the control that department exercised over river and harbor improvements. Frequently, in the development of such improvements cities were required to contribute money and land, and they generally had to assume claims for damage resulting from the improvements and make necessary alterations in streets. During the pre-Depression period as well as today, the chief activities of the Department of Agriculture involving federal-local contacts were related to agricultural extension and experiment station work. Financed and administered jointly by the national government, the states, and local governments, particularly counties, these programs have provided important services to farmers. In addition, the Food and Drug Administration sought the cooperation of local authorities in the fight against the sale of impure and adulterated products. The Forest Service assisted any locality whose source of water was situated in a national forest.

Through its Division of Identification and Information the

Department of Justice rendered assistance to local law enforcement agencies in the apprehension of criminals. The files maintained by this organization have grown increasingly important to local law enforcement officers. During the period under consideration the Bureau of Prohibition sought the assistance of local governments in its efforts to enforce prohibition, but with a minimum of success.

Depression Relations. As the Great Depression fastened its stranglehold on the economy in the 1930's, local governments often found themselves in awkward and difficult circumstances. Relief rolls skyrocketed and with them went demands on local treasuries, demands far beyond their resources in many instances. Simultaneously, local revenues were depleted. Assistance had to come from a higher level of government with greater financial resources. Logically, it would seem that the states would have been the source of help, but they proved either unable or unwilling to assume the burden. Only the federal government remained.

In July, 1932, Congress passed the Emergency Relief and Reconstruction Act, which "for the first time in the history of our country established definite and intimate contacts between American cities and the federal government."[7] This act enabled the Reconstruction Finance Corporation to give aid to governments as it had to businesses. Three hundred million dollars were made available to states and cities for relief and $1.5 billion for public works projects. When securing loans for self-liquidating projects, a city dealt directly with the RFC, which purchased the securities of the applicant. This practice proved unsatisfactory, and it was terminated in 1933 by the National Industrial Recovery Act.

Title II of the NIRA authorized expenditure of $3.3 billion by the newly created Public Works Administration. The federal government made grants up to thirty per cent of the cost of works projects and loans of seventy per cent on the securities of the borrowing agency. PWA subjected proposed projects to close examination, requiring communities in some instances to amend their laws to conform with federal standards. Governments accepting PWA grants had to agree to federal requirements concerning wages, hours, and other conditions of employment. Arrangements were made for federal inspection of the work and review of all financial transactions.

---

[7] Paul V. Betters, "The Federal Government and the Cities," *The Municipal Year book,* 1934, p. 33.

These and other regulations caused one observer to express the opinion that it was only after PWA allotments had been made that local governments came to a full realization of "the extent of federal influence over affairs formerly considered of purely local concern."[8]

In 1933 Congress passed the Home Owners Loan Corporation Act. The chief significance of this act for local governments lay in the provision for payment of delinquent taxes with HOLC funds, an arrangement that proved to be of very real assistance to local finances. By 1937 HOLC funds had been used to pay approximately $230 million in delinquent taxes.[9] In order to implement the work relief program outlined in the Emergency Relief Act of 1935, the President created the Works Project Administration by executive order. States and their political subdivisions were able to apply for federal money for such projects as the construction, repair, or improvement of public buildings or public works; improvement of parks, sewers, and streets; tree-cutting and pruning; and statistical or clerical projects in libraries and city and county clerks' offices.

The foregoing examples of federal-local cooperation during the Great Depression are by no means exhaustive. Additional examples include the Civil Works Administration, which financed many projects "sponsored" by local governments, including road repairs and improvements of school buildings and grounds, as well as other public buildings, parks, and playgrounds. Almost from the time of its creation in 1933, the Tennessee Valley Authority worked closely with counties and cities.[10] Numerous contacts have been established between localities and the Rural Electrification Administration since its organization in 1935. Federal-local cooperation was very important in implementing the intent of the Housing Division of the Public Works Administration and the United States Housing Authority to provide low-cost housing. Projects constructed under these acts were locally conceived, planned, constructed, and operated.

War and Its Aftermath. As the war in Europe got under way, the national government increased the tempo of defense activities. Dur-

---

[8] J. K. Williams, *Grants-in-Aid under the Public Works Administration*, Columbia University Press, New York, 1939, p. 170.

[9] See Carl H. Chatters, "Cities Look At Their Federal-State Relationships," *Minnesota Municipalities*, November 1937.

[10] See Tennessee Valley Authority, *County Government and Administration in the Tennessee Valley States*, U.S. Government Printing Office, 1940.

ing the period of preparation for war and the war itself, federal-local relations were strengthened and expanded in many areas. Some programs of long standing assumed increased significance. Airport construction is an illustration. As of 1940, "More than 85 per cent of all airport and landing field construction in the past five years has been done through WPA projects, and more than half of all airport construction since the beginning of aviation in this country has been done under WPA projects in the last five years."[11] Thus a program administered for several years as a depression recovery measure became significant for national defense. In the same year the Civil Aeronautics Administration was granted $40 million for the construction and improvement of a maximum of 250 publicly owned and operated airports. Generally, the interested localities provided the land and pledged to maintain the facilities. Construction of airports became primarily a military concern during the war, but with the return of peace the earlier program was continued. The Federal Airport Act of 1946 authorized $500 million for airport construction over a period of seven years. Funds were to be matched by local units sponsoring the projects.

In 1940 the Division of State and Local Cooperation was established within the Advisory Commission of the Council of National Defense. This agency, which was intended as a two-way channel for information and service, was short-lived. In the following year it was superseded by the Office of Civilian Defense. In addition to pointing the way for local organization of air-raid wardens, fire-watchers, and similar emergency groups, the OCD performed specific services for cities, including distribution of fire-fighting equipment. The Committee for Congested Production Areas was organized in 1943 to coordinate federal, state, and local activities in areas congested by defense programs. Analyses were made of such local problems as housing, hospitals, water supply, refuse disposal, and transportation facilities. Close cooperation among federal, state, and local authorities was required by these efforts.

Two months after war was declared the President created the Federal Public Housing Authority, which assumed the duties of the United States Housing Authority concerned with making housing available to persons engaged in defense activities. The FPHA was specifically empowered to use local public housing agencies in the

---

[11] H. O. Hunter, "The Relation of WPA City Programs to National Defense," *The Annual Proceedings of the U.S. Conference of Mayors,* 1940, p. 33.

construction and operation of necessary projects. At the request of this agency many local authorities assumed a large part of the construction and management of federal war housing projects. As the war came to an end, another phase of the housing problem faced the nation. Many returning veterans with families were unable to find acceptable places to live. Veterans taking advantage of the G. I. Bill filled college and university towns to overflowing. Once again part of the solution lay in federal-local cooperation.

By 1946 more than 700 mayors' emergency housing committees had been organized. Federal "locality expediters" were sent into many communities to assist these committees. FPHA funds were used to transfer temporary housing from areas where the need was not great to those where the demand for veterans' housing was acute. Local communities usually provided the land for the housing and made available the necessary utilities. Arrangements were made whereby local governments gained title to the housing on the condition that they would remit to the federal government income over and above operating costs. Some localities took advantage of an offer by the FPHA whereby surplus army and navy structures were given to them if they agreed to move and install them at their own expense.

During World War II local governments had frequent and close contacts with such agencies as the Office of Production Management, the War Production Board, the War Labor Board, the Office of Price Administration, and the War Manpower Commission. A section within the OPM was known as the State and Local Governments Requirements Branch, and it applied a priority-rating scheme to purchases by governmental units. Localities were required to obtain authorization and allocations of materials from the WPB to construct buildings, public works, streets, etc., as well as for the purchase of fire equipment. Local operation of rationing boards under OPA supervision was common practice.

Following World War II some established programs involving federal-local relations were continued, and others were inaugurated. In order to accelerate airport development, the Federal Airport Act of 1946 authorized grants to state and local governments over a long period of years. The Federal Public Highway Act of 1944 for the first time specifically provided aid to cities for road construction. In the War Mobilization and Reconversion Act of 1944 Congress appropriated $65 million for state and local planning, and by 1947 most of this money had been disbursed to assist in planning public works.[12] Since 1949 the national government has assisted many municipalities with urban renewal programs to clear slum areas for redevelopment. Cities may obtain federal grants to offset as much as two-thirds or three-fourths of any deficit incurred in such projects. Control of the program has been placed in the Urban Renewal Administration located in the Housing and Home Finance Agency. Federal law has decreed that the task of developing a program of civil defense shall be a responsibility of national, state, and local governments. Provision has been made for federal advice and assistance, but state and local governments have the primary responsibility.[13]

Many more examples of federal-local relationships might be noted, but the foregoing indicate clearly that since 1930 there has been a strong and steady tendency for these relations to increase rapidly.[14] Although they have by no means been unopposed, the forces in favor of the trend seem to have won the day. A major reason for this development was well stated by Paul Betters over twenty years ago: "Yet the fact remains that in the main the cities have had a more sympathetic and understanding audience in Washington than they have had in their own states."[15] City officials continue to seek more federal help. At the annual meeting of the American Municipal Association in 1958 resolutions were adopted requesting Congress, among other things, to provide more money for civil defense, create a department of urban affairs, provide additional urban renewal funds, and increase the annual authorization for federal matching grants to help in the construction of sewage plants.

INTERLOCAL RELATIONS

Relationships among local governments, particularly counties, municipalities, and special districts, are numerous and significant. However, it is very difficult to describe them satisfactorily for at least two principal reasons. First, a large portion of interlocal relations are informal, resulting from personal contacts and arrangements that

---

[12] See J. K. Williams, "Federal Aid Due to Continue," *National Municipal Review,* February 1948.

[13] Responsibility for coordinating civil defence efforts rests at the national level with the Office of Emergency Planning in the Executive Office of the President.

[14] See Commission on Intergovernmental Relations, *An Advisory Report on Local Government,* 1955, Chapter 3.

[15] P. V. Betters, "The Federal Government and the Cities: A Problem in Adjustment," *Annals of the American Academy of Political and Social Science,* September 1938.

are not recorded in a manner that makes possible ready and meaningful analysis. Second, in the absence of agencies in the various states to collect data state by state even in regard to formal agreements, a survey of the 90,000 units of local government in the country is not practical. Consequently, a description of interlocal relationships must be in general terms.

Cooperative interlocal arrangements have been instrumental in seeking solutions to problems that plague the nation's metropolitan areas.[16] Another significant development in recent years has been the notable increase in city-county cooperation. In the name of economy and efficiency more and more cities and counties are entering into formal agreements to perform a variety of functions, including public health, care of prisoners, election administration, planning, collection of taxes, property assessment, libraries, police and fire services, refuse disposal, water supply, airports, streets, building inspection, personnel services, recreational facilities, and civil defense.[17] Such arrangements are more common in some states than in others because of the presence or absence of state laws authorizing a variety of agreements. They are especially common in California since the legislature in 1891 extended permission to each county to perform any administrative function for any of its cities upon city request. In fact, in 1960, the League of California Cities classified sixteen municipalities as "contract cities."

Cooperation among counties is less significant than between cities and counties. Nevertheless, intercounty arrangements are found pertaining to planning, sewers, air pollution control, welfare, and the construction and maintenance of institutions such as tuberculosis sanitariums and hospitals for the mentally disturbed. Airports, libraries, and bridges are also occasionally provided by intercounty cooperation. Counties also enter into cooperative arrangements with special districts, most often to assist them in the collection of taxes, assessment of property, legal advice, and selection and management of personnel. On the other hand, counties may obtain services from special districts, such as sanitation, flood control, water supply, and pest abatement.

The earliest examples of interlocal cooperation on record in the

---

[16] See Chapter 22.

[17] See Bernard F. Hillenbrand, "Urban Counties in 1958," *Public Management*, May 1959; James A. Norton, "Benefits of Intergovernmental Cooperation," *ibid.*, September 1959; and Peter Barry, "Cooperation Pays Off," *National Civic Review*, April 1960.

United States were in the form of mutual defense arrangements among New England towns in colonial times. Since those days and particularly in recent years, many activities have been facilitated by agreements among municipalities of all sizes. Small municipalities as well as New England towns sometimes pool their resources to hire personnel such as managers and engineers in order to obtain qualified persons. In some instances supplies, materials, and equipment are purchased jointly by neighboring communities. Public works such as bridges, airports, and sewage disposal facilities are constructed on a cooperative basis. Mutual aid agreements among municipal fire departments are common, and informal cooperation is often helpful in the apprehension of criminals. A few states have gone so far as to empower local governments to enter into contracts for the performance of any function common to the contracting units. The Minnesota law, enacted in 1943, is a good example. It authorizes two or more local governments, including cities, counties, villages, towns, boroughs, and school districts, to agree by action of their governing bodies jointly to exercise any power common to the contracting parties. Other states conferring broad authority for interlocal cooperation include California, Connecticut, Georgia, Louisiana, Missouri, Nevada, Ohio, Pennsylvania, and Wisconsin.[18]

Another important aspect of interlocal relations concerns agreements between special districts and other local governments, especially cities. Special districts frequently enter into agreements with cities for fire protection, water supply, sewage disposal, and other services. The usual procedure requires that a formal contract be approved by the governing bodies of the special district and of the city, specifying conditions of service. Cities occasionally obtain services from special districts.

One final aspect of interlocal relations remains. Much cooperation among localities stems not from formal agreements among governments but from contacts among local officials. Almost all states have municipal leagues whose membership consists of cities and villages and occasionally other local units. These leagues hold an-

---

[18] A 1958 survey indicated that in Pennsylvania alone a total of 617 agreements involving 1,794 "municipalities" in the performance of governmental services were in force. This enumeration included cities, boroughs, townships, counties, and school districts. J. Martin Kelly, Jr., "617 Agreements Link 1,794 Municipal Units in Cooperative Action." *Internal Affairs,* Commonwealth of Pennsylvania, Harrisburg, July 1958. See also, George Goodwin, *Intermunicipal Relations in Massachusetts,* Bureau of Government Research, University of Massachusetts, 1956.

nual meetings at which city officials get together to study and discuss their mutual problems and discover better ways of meeting them. Frequently, officials of city A will discover that city B has developed a superior technique for performing some activity. Conferences and correspondence may ensue, resulting in a change of practice for city A. Furthermore, friendships formed at such meetings may facilitate future cooperation. State municipal leagues are federated in the American Municipal Association, which serves as a national clearing-house of information.

Statewide organizations are also common among other local officials, including county commissioners, county clerks, sheriffs, coroners, assessors, prosecuting attorneys, and justices of the peace. County officials are organized on a national basis in the National Association of County Officials. National professional associations also provide important means of contact and collaboration among local officers. Especially noteworthy are the International City Managers' Association and its regional organizations, the Municipal Finance Officers Association, the International Association of Chiefs of Police, and the National Institute of Municipal Law Officers.

In the words of one observer of local government, ". . . there is a great deal more cooperation and integration existing on the local level than is sometimes imagined. Compared to the amount which might ultimately be achieved, it may appear rather small. But, if what we now have were to be suddenly cancelled out, the resultant increased cost and confusion would be instantly felt and the change-over regarded with considerable regret."[19]

SELECTED REFERENCES

Books:

Advisory Commission on Intergovernmental Relations, *Intergovernmental Responsibilities for Water Supply and Sewage Disposal in Metropolitan Areas,* Washington, D.C., 1962.

———, *State Constitutional and Statutory Restrictions on Local Taxing Powers,* Washington, D.C., 1962.

Anderson, William, *Intergovernmental Fiscal Relations,* University of Minnesota Press, Minneapolis, 1956.

Council of State Governments, *State-Local Relations,* Chicago, 1946.

---

[19] From a speech by Roger Arnebergh, quoted in Bernard F. Hillenbrand, *op. cit.,* p. 106.

Graves, W. Brooke, *American Intergovernmental Relations,* Charles Scribner's Sons, New York, 1964.

Hein, Clarence J., *State Administrative Supervision of Local Government Functions in Kansas,* Governmental Research Center, University of Kansas, Lawrence, 1955.

Howards, Irving, *Selected Aspects of State Supervision over Local Government in Illinois,* Public Affairs Research Bureau, Southern Illinois University, Carbondale, 1964.

McMillan, T. E., Jr., *State Supervision of Municipal Finance,* Institute of Public Affairs, University of Texas, Austin, 1953.

Articles:

Barry, Peter, "Cooperation Pays Off," *National Civic Review,* April 1960.

Bromage, Arthur W., "Federal-State-Local Relations," *American Political Science Review,* February 1943.

Graves, W. Brooke, "Maze of Governments," Series of three articles in the *National Civic Review,* May, June, and July 1960.

Grumm, John G., "Do We Need a State Agency for Local Affairs?" *Public Management,* June 1961.

Moran, Carlos, "Era of Cooperation for Cities," *National Municipal Review,* November 1945.

Norton, James A., "Benefits of Intergovernmental Cooperation," *Public Management,* September 1959.

Reinhold, Frances, "Federal-Municipal Relations—the Road thus Far," *National Municipal Review,* August 1936.

Short, Raymond, "Municipalities and the Federal Government," *The Annals,* January 1940.

Weidner, Edward W., "State Supervision of Local Government in Minnesota," *Public Administration Review,* Summer 1944.

CHAPTER 24

Public Safety

Governments perform many functions in the interest of the well-being of society. Arguments have been raised over the question of whether some functions ought to be performed by government, but rarely if ever are objections heard to governmental attention to public safety. In fact, virtually all comment on the topic mirrors a desire for more and better protection.

Defining "public safety" is difficult because of the wide range of activities that may be viewed as protective in nature and the large number of officials and agencies involved. In a sense, public safety includes every action undertaken by any unit of government to secure not only the personal safety of every individual but also to preserve his rights and privileges within the legal system. From this point of view virtually all governmental personnel and every program is related, either directly or indirectly, to some aspect of public safety. A more restricted and generally applied interpretation of the term embraces only those functions and activities devoted exclusively or primarily to the prevention and punishment of acts prohibited by law because they are harmful to persons, property, or the government.

Enforcement of criminal law is undoubtedly the best known aspect of public safety. Combatting crime and criminals involves vast amounts of time, money, and effort. However, public safety encompasses other vital activities. Protecting the nation from invasion and rebellion; emergency action in the event of natural disasters such as earthquake, hurricane, or flood; investigating and policing certain occupations and professions in the interest of adequate standards of service and performance; fire protection; and accident prevention are significant areas of action. Thus, even when regarded in a limited fashion, the scope of public safety is broad.

THE NATIONAL ROLE

As with all other federal activities, the scope and nature of providing for public safety at the national level are qualified by the constitutional division of powers. In contrast to the power of the states to enact general laws on the basis of the reserved powers, the national government must base its actions upon powers delegated to it by the Constitution. National efforts in the interest of public safety are scattered among many agencies whose power to act derives from authority of the national government to regulate interstate commerce, levy taxes, coin money, establish post offices, maintain an army and navy, or from other delegated powers.

Defending the country in time of war is obviously a paramount federal function. The military powers of the national government are so extensive, in fact, that state military authority has been virtually pre-empted.[1] In the event of natural disasters such as floods, fires, hurricanes, earthquakes, or storms, the national government may assist state and local governments. Under present law the President may direct a federal agency to give help in the form of loans, surplus federal equipment, clearing of debris, providing temporary shelter and housing, and distributing, through the National Red Cross, food, clothing, and medicines. Various administrative agencies prescribe rules and regulations designed to promote public safety. For example, the Federal Aviation Agency looks after safety in air travel; the Interstate Commerce Commission enforces rules designed to make surface transportation safer; the Security and Exchange Commission attempts to alert the public to chicanery in the investment field; and the Food and Drug Administration tries to keep adulterated food, drugs, and cosmetics out of interstate commerce. The entire country is organized into districts in which U.S. District Attorneys and Marshals, working under the Attorney General, are the principal law enforcement officers.

Probably the best known national law enforcement agency is the Federal Bureau of Investigation, located in the Department of Justice. Not only has the FBI distinguished itself in the apprehension of criminals, it has also performed valuable services through collection and publication of crime statistics and operation of the FBI National Academy which offers courses of instruction in modern law enforcement techniques to selected state and local officers. In the Treasury Department is the Secret Service, the famous "T-Men," who uncover counterfeiters, protect the President and his family, and assist in the enforcement of the nation's tax laws. The Coast Guard, another

---

[1] See below, the section entitled "National Guard," for discussion of state military authority.

Treasury arm, helps enforce maritime laws, especially those relating to smuggling. Postal Inspectors have as their primary function detection and apprehension of persons using the mails illegally. A variety of other national agencies and officers perform similar duties in the enforcement of such diverse national laws as those controlling immigration, customs, illicit traffic in liquor and narcotics, unfair trade practices, and conservation of fish and wildlife.

Although the national and state governments are separate entities in matters of law enforcement, there is much cooperation between the two levels. Officers and agencies of both governmental levels work together regularly in handling criminal cases. The FBI, for example, maintains a huge fingerprint file and modern laboratories for scientific detection used in assisting state and local police; federal narcotics agents work closely with enforcement officers of cities and states. The fact that such cooperative arrangements are not formalized by written agreements but exist on an informal basis attests not only to the importance of the function of public safety but also to the vigorous character of cooperative federalism.

STATE AGENCIES

The governor of each state is constitutionally charged with the responsibility of seeing that all laws, civil and criminal, are executed.[2] He must, therefore, be regarded as the principal official in implementing public safety measures. Obviously no one man, regardless of how learned and competent, could personally supervise and guide all state programs. There are simply too many things that have to be done. The function of public safety alone, involving widely varying agencies and programs, would prove too much for a single director. Consequently, state efforts to provide for public safety are not performed by a single, central agency but represent instead the activities of numerous officers and agencies.

Attorney General. The chief legal officer of a state is the attorney general, an elective official in forty-one states.[3] His main functions consist of representing the state as such, or state agencies, in suits to

---

[2] Typically, state constitutions echo the phrase of the U.S. Constitution, Article II, Section 2, which states that the President shall "take care that the laws be faithfully executed." Even when such clauses do not appear, as in the Ohio and South Dakota constitutions, the duty of the governor is clear and unmistakable.

[3] For more information on the attorney general, see Chapter 4.

which they are parties, advising the governor and other executive officers on legal matters, and in many states supervising local prosecuting attorneys. In actual practice the attorney general personally does not have time to tend every duty of the office. Depending upon the size of a state and the volume of legal business to be handled, he is aided by a number of assistant attorney generals.

The attorney general does not play a prominent part in criminal law enforcement. Conducting local prosecutions is a responsibility of the attorney general only in Delaware and Rhode Island—the two smallest states. Although he usually has authority to function at the local level, an attorney general rarely does so because prosecutions are conducted by district or county prosecuting attorneys. Only in cases of extreme importance does an attorney general undertake prosecution locally, since possible conflicts with local prosecutors are dangerous both professionally and politically.

State Police and Highway Patrols. Today each of the fifty states maintains a police organization to assist in the enforcement of its criminal laws. These units may be classed as state police, with broad powers of law enforcement; or as highway patrols, with functions generally limited to the enforcement of traffic laws. Of the organizations found in the states today, half can be regarded as true police forces.[4] Variations in size are pronounced across the nation. In some of the more populous states the police forces consist of several thousand officers and employees, and in many other states the personnel rolls list up to a thousand, and the remainder range downward to a few dozen patrolmen.

The first modern police system was established by Pennsylvania in 1905, although other states had established state agencies with limited law enforcement functions in earlier years. Forerunners of today's state organizations date back to 1835 when Texas, then an independent republic, created the Texas Rangers for patrol duty along the Mexican border and to Massachusetts' system of state constables organized in 1865. At the turn of the present century Arizona, Connecticut, and New Mexico also established police agencies, but each was severely limited in its jurisdiction.

At the head of a state police force is usually a director or superintendent chosen by the governor. In some states, Connecticut,

---

[4] State-by-state classification and further commentary may be found in Frank D. Day, "State Police and Highway Patrols," *Book of the States, 1964–65*, pp. 461–466.

Michigan, and West Virginia, for example, control is vested in an administrative board. Selection of personnel for police work is based on merit examination in only about a dozen states. Elsewhere, hiring and firing are left to the discretion of police administrators. Recruits are given training in all states, but the quality of the preparation varies considerably. Extensive instruction in police methods is given in states with well-developed systems, while in others very little is done.

State police jurisdiction extends to all parts of a state including the area within incorporated municipalities. However, in order to avoid conflicts with municipal forces, state police generally confine themselves to rural areas. When it is necessary to enter a city on police business it is common practice for state patrolmen to contact the municipal police department. Experience has shown that tactless "invasions" of municipalities by state police cost dearly in terms of state-local police cooperation.

Military Force. Throughout the history of the Union, state military forces have been made up of the *militia* composed of all able-bodied male inhabitants between specified minimum and maximum ages. Inasmuch as a state may not maintain troops or warships in time of peace without congressional consent,[5] national law has, since 1792, set the pattern for state military organization. Under present law the membership of a state militia is still composed of all eligible, able-bodied male citizens, but the only *active* members are those in the *organized* portion of the militia—the National Guard.

The pattern of command and organizational structure of the National Guard dates from the National Defense Act of 1916.[6] A National Guard unit is ostensibly commanded by the governor who is empowered to commission officers. Actual command in day-to-day administration is exercised by an adjutant general, and all gubernatorial appointments must be nationally approved. That the National Guard is, for all practical purposes, a unit of the national

---

[5] United States Constitution, Article I, Section 10, Clause 3.

[6] The power of Congress to legislate in matters relating to the militia is quite broad. In the U.S. Constitution, Article I, Section 8, Clause 15, Congress is delegated the authority "To provide for calling forth the militia to execute the laws of the Union, suppress insurrection, and repel invasions;" and in Section 16 "To provide for organizing, arming, and disciplining the militia, and for governing such part of them as may be employed in the service of the United States, reserving to the States respectively the appointment of the officers, and the authority of training the militia, according to the discipline prescribed by Congress."

armed forces is forcefully indicated by the extent of national control. Size of the National Guard, types of units to be maintained, qualifications of officers, periods of enlistment, and salaries are nationally determined. Equipment is provided by the national government to all Guard units, which may be summoned into national service by the President.

Basically, the function of the National Guard is to help provide for military security, but it also serves, in a stand-by capacity, as an agency of law enforcement. At the direction of the governor, National Guard troops may be called upon when violence erupts or is threatened during strikes, racial conflicts, or other civil disorders.[7] The most frequent use of the Guard, however, occurs during emergencies occasioned by natural disasters.

Administrative Agencies. Although they are not designed as criminal law enforcement bodies, administrative agencies render valuable service in the field of public safety. Agencies of all descriptions implement legislation that involves virtually every aspect of social intercourse. Through their regulations these agencies strive to maintain or establish standards of performance and integrity in their respective areas of concern. Public health personnel, for example, work constantly to check disease. Bank examiners keep banking practices under perpetual surveillance. Licensing and examining officials have the duty of preventing incompetents, quacks, and charlatans from masquerading as physicians, lawyers, engineers, and the like. Agricultural inspectors, utilities commissioners, insurance inspectors, and other such officers perform duties in the public interest.

Disciplinary techniques available to administrative officers and agencies vary widely. Revocation or suspension of a license, refusal to certify a product as salable or edible, or imposition of a quarantine may be all that is necessary to secure compliance with statutes or regulations. In some cases fines and damages can be assessed. Failing of success by these means, more drastic steps usually can be taken. For example, an agency may obtain a judicial order directing compliance with an administrative decision. Refusal by an offender to

---

[7] On a few occasions governors have abused their power. The most fantastic example is probably that of Oklahoma Governor Walton who, in 1923, used the Guard to prevent the state legislature from convening. He was later impeached, convicted, and removed from office. When Huey Long resigned as governor of Louisiana in 1930 to assume his seat in the United States Senate, he used the National Guard to prevent the lieutenant governor from taking over the gubernatorial chair.

obey then becomes contempt of court, an offense punishable by the court issuing the order. Another method of enforcement often available is the bringing of criminal charges by an administrative agency. When this occurs the state becomes the prosecutor as in other criminal cases. Finally, an agency may, if it has no authority to institute criminal proceedings and no other remedy is available, enlist the aid of the state attorney general or a local prosecuting attorney.

Local Agencies

At the local level public safety figures prominently in the functions of many officers and agencies. Public health offices, licensing boards, building inspectors, planning bodies, fire departments, zoning commissions, and maintenance crews are among agencies performing meaningful functions in the area of public safety. Some agencies are purely local, some work closely with state counterparts, and some are branches of state departments. Probably the most important of them all, and certainly the best known, are the local agencies of criminal law enforcement: the sheriff, the prosecutor, and the municipal police.[8]

The Sheriff. Local law enforcement in rural areas is primarily the responsibility of the sheriff, an elected official. The duties of a sheriff vary considerably from state to state, but in all instances he has jurisdiction to enforce state laws throughout his county, including the areas within cities. Since he does not enforce municipal ordinances, and because the chance of conflict with municipal police forces is constantly present, the sheriff and his deputies nearly always confine their activities to rural areas. There the sheriff shares jurisdiction with the state police with whom probability of conflict is slight since relatively few state police attempt to enforce all laws.

The quality of law enforcement achieved by sheriffs varies tremendously both among the states and within a single state. In some places, such as Los Angeles County, the sheriff's office is a highly effective, vigorous organization. At the other extreme the sheriff of a small, sparsely populated county may be little more than a process server and keeper of the county jail. In such instances law enforcement in rural areas leaves much to be desired.

---

[8] For a general discussion of the duties and functions of the county sheriff, see Chapter 20. Similar treatment of the public prosecutor appears in the same chapter.

The Public Prosecutor. Bringing criminals to justice involves more than detection and arrest; they must be prosecuted before a court. This task forms the basic function of the public prosecutor who is known by such titles as district attorney, county attorney, county prosecutor, state's attorney, and solicitor. Usually, his jurisdiction covers a single county although several counties may be combined into a district under his authority. In the more populous areas of the nation the prosecutor's office includes a staff large enough to handle the preparation of cases as well as to conduct investigations and to gather evidence.

The importance of the prosecutor is indicated by the fact that the effectiveness of local law enforcement depends largely upon the success of his efforts. It is the prosecutor's duty to seek or to bring formal accusations against persons suspected of crime, and he may decide whether to prosecute or to continue a prosecution already in progress. Obviously, an inept prosecutor can nullify good police work, and a corrupt one can easily sabotage the best efforts at law enforcement.

Municipal Police Departments. Most incorporated places in the United States, whether called cities, towns, or villages, maintain agencies whose primary function is law enforcement.[9] These municipal police departments, ranging in size from over 25,000 in New York City to the many small communities that hire only a few officers, are with few exceptions locally chosen, financed, and administered. State operation of local police departments was in vogue a century ago, but lack of anticipated improvements resulted in re-establishment of local control. Today only a few large cities, including Baltimore, Boston, St. Louis, and Kansas City, Missouri, are situated in metropolitan police districts administered by the state.

Municipal police departments staffed by professional career policemen originated in New York City in 1844. The idea quickly spread to other large cities and in due time to municipalities throughout the country. Municipal police enforce both local and state criminal laws, ranging from prohibitions against jaywalking and overparking to the most serious offenses against state law, including

---

[9] Unincorporated places, many small rural communities, and some municipalities located adjacent to large cities do not support police departments. In the first two instances reliance upon the county sheriff is considered adequate. Small incorporated municipalities in metropolitan areas may depend upon a combination of the sheriff and police services rendered by larger cities on a "contract" basis.

murder, rape, arson, and robbery. Police departments sometimes are assigned a variety of other duties such as elevator inspection, dog pound management, licensing bicycles, censorship of motion pictures and night club shows, and operation of emergency ambulance services. In the opinion of one student of local government, all too often the police department has been made "a sort of municipal wastebasket."[10]

Police department organization varies, of course, but the larger cities follow much the same basic pattern. Administrative boards were once in common use and are still found in a few cities, but they have been largely abandoned in favor of a single administrator usually called the police commissioner. Immediately below the commissioner is the chief of police, ordinarily a career man with several years of service. The pattern of intradepartmental organization depends upon the number and nature of tasks assigned a given department. In smaller cities the office of commissioner usually does not exist, and small town departments frequently consists of a mere handful of patrolmen.

Today the merit principle is widely accepted as the best way to recruit personnel for a police force, and promotion is frequently dependent upon passing a qualifying examination. Dismissal is in most cases controlled by the chief although appeals may be taken to a commissioner or civil service board, a procedure criticized by some students of police administration as detrimental to discipline. Special training schools for recruits are conducted in some cities, supplemented by on-the-job instruction. Small cities are at a disadvantage in this regard due to lack of funds and facilities for training.

The record of American municipal police departments has suffered because of many examples of corruption. Even today the newspapers carry occasional reports of collusion between police and organized crime. However, the gross transgressions of many nineteenth century police departments should not be cited as evidence of corruption today. Granted that policemen are human and must face numerous temptations to which some will succumb, widespread corruption is not apparent. Rather, the level of police efficiency is a much more serious matter in view of inadequate salaries, equipment, and training.

---

[10] Austin F. MacDonald, *American City Government and Administration*, 6th ed., Thomas Y. Crowell Co., New York, 1956, p. 465.

Treatment of Criminals

Punishment. Upon conviction for violation of the criminal law, a person is subject to punishment. The exact nature of the punishment depends upon a variety of factors. The crime itself, of course, is the principal determinant. Felonies involve more severe penalties than do misdemeanors, and violations of state law usually occasion more serious consequences than infractions of local ordinances. Punishment depends also upon the person convicted, for in most instances sentences imposed vary according to whether an adult or child, male or female, and sane or mentally deficient person is involved. Severity and type of punishment may also be affected by the underlying rationale of the penal system of a state. If vengeance is the object, punishment is likely to be severe with little thought for rehabilitation of the criminal—a situation that contrasts markedly with policies followed when deterrence of crime and reformation of criminals are the basic motives.

One of the challenging problems faced by society is whether capital punishment—infliction of the death penalty—should be continued. Death may be imposed as punishment in not quite forty states upon conviction of premeditated murder and a few other serious felonies.[11] In recent years the question of the propriety and efficacy of capital punishment was brought into national and international focus by the case of Caryl Chessman, a condemned California convict whose conviction was delayed about twelve years during which numerous appeals were heard. By the time his sentence of death was carried out in 1960, California Governor Edmund Brown had called the state legislature into special session to consider whether to retain the death penalty. Among the strongest arguments in opposition to capital punishment are the claims that it does not deter crime; it involves a profound question of morality; and it eliminates all possibility of correcting any error of conviction that may be discovered later. In rebuttal those who favor death as the ultimate penalty answer that it applies only to the most serious crimes, that a person who commits those crimes does so in full aware-

---

[11] Life imprisonment is the most severe penalty that may be imposed in approximately one-fourth of the states. In the remainder (and in the federal jurisdiction) capital punishment may be imposed. The methods used to carry out death sentences include electrocution, lethal gas, hanging, and in Utah either hanging or shooting. The list of crimes for which the death sentence may be imposed is varied, but not a long one. Included in some or all states are murder, treason, rape, arson, kidnaping, robbery, burglary, and trainwrecking.

ness of the possible consequences, and that society has both the right and the obligation to defend itself against criminality with whatever measures it deems appropriate. Compromise of the two views is hardly possible, and the people in each state, either directly or through their representatives, must decide which view will prevail.

Pardons, Commutations, and Reprieves. In all states the governor has some power to intercede in the punishment of criminals.[12] Except in Georgia, all governors may either *pardon* criminals or share in the process by which a criminal is absolved from legal consequences for his crime. Governors may also exercise the power of *commutation* whereby the severity of a sentence is reduced. A third means by which governors may alter the course of punishment is the *reprieve,* a postponement of the execution of a sentence.

Probation and Parole. In some cases the sentence imposed upon a convicted criminal involves a mandatory prison term that may not, under any circumstances, be shortened. When this occurs there is no alternative but for the prisoner to serve out the full sentence. On the other hand, if there is no statutory direction that the full term be served, it is possible for courts or penal officials to permit conditional freedom to convicted persons who evidence potentiality for full rehabilitation. Under such circumstances the convicted person may be placed on probation or parole.

Probation involves the imposition of conditions to which a convicted person must conform while remaining free from custody. It is possible that probation is the only consequence a convicted person may suffer, especially in cases involving juveniles and first offenders, but commonly probation is used in conjunction with a suspended sentence of confinement. In other words, failure to live up to the conditions of probation usually means the violator must serve the remaining portion of the suspended term. *Parole* is conditional release of a prisoner after he has served a portion of the confinement to which he was originally sentenced. A growing trend in recent years has been toward the indeterminate sentence under which a convicted criminal may be sentenced to prison for, say, two to ten years. He must serve two years and may be held in confinement for as many as ten, but he may be released on parole at any time after two years should he show promise of rehabilitation.

---

[12] These powers of the governor are discussed at greater length in Chapter 4.

The success of probation and parole hinges largely upon care in judging the fitness of persons for such privileges and on skillful supervision of them after release. Thoroughly trained social workers are necessary to the operation of a good probation and parole system. Without such people, who are not attracted in sufficient numbers by typically low salaries and heavy case loads, chances of satisfactory results are minimized. Even so, probation and parole programs have produced good results in many states.

Prisons and Jails. Local jails maintained and operated by cities and counties serve as the places of detention for persons accused of crimes and those sentenced to short terms. Inmates of jails include persons awaiting trial who, for one reason or another, are unable to gain their freedom on bail and those convicted of a variety of misdemeanors such as speeding, reckless driving, simple assault, and public drunkenness. Those accused of more serious crimes usually remain in local confinement only until conviction, and then they are transported to some unit of the state prison system.

Students of penology are virtually unanimous in their condemnation of local jails. Except where new buildings have been constructed in recent years, jails are likely to be old, dirty, poorly ventilated, without facilities for preparation of food, and too small to permit separation of youthful or first offenders from hardened criminals. Usually little or no provision is made to occupy the time of inmates who consequently sit in idleness. In most cases operation of local jails is handled by people who are more interested in keeping costs down than in the welfare of the prisoners. Less subject to harsh criticism, but still not considered truly modern penal institutions, are county workhouses and houses of correction where persons serving short terms are engaged in productive occupations. However, such facilities represent only a tiny fraction of the thousands of local jails in the United States.

Facilities for confinement of criminals are much more adequate at the state than at the local level. Several types of penal institutions are found in each state. Altogether, about 200,000 prisoners are detained in some 300 state correctional facilities.[13] Most widely known are the state penitentiaries such as Sing Sing and San Quentin. Separate institutions for women and for maximum security prisoners

---

[13] See *Book of the States, 1964–65,* pp. 447–460.

may be provided, although segregated divisions of the penitentiary may be utilized for such purposes. Also, the criminally insane are imprisoned in separate facilities. Reformatories are operated for women, youthful offenders, and those who indicate probability of early rehabilitation. Industrial schools for juveniles have become numerous since their inception about a century ago.

When compared with their status a generation or two ago, state penal systems have undergone substantial improvement. There are still many physical facilities that have long since become outmoded, but with enough money such shortcomings can be corrected. The area of greatest improvement—and one in which greater improvement still is needed—has been in understanding what a correctional system ought to accomplish and in implementing that understanding. The first major steps have been taken, for penologists and the general public alike no longer feel that the sole purpose of imprisonment is vengeance. Instead, it should be reformation and rehabilitation. The death sentence, lengthy terms, and solitary confinement belie this awareness. At the same time wider use of the indeterminate sentence, probation and parole, special treatment for juveniles, and concern for the health, education, and welfare of prisoners indicate a trend toward a more enlightened view.

CIVIL DEFENSE

Throughout most of the last hundred years Americans have regarded war and international hostilities as fearful events that occurred in far-off places. The United States was seemingly insulated from the locales of conflict by two wide, protective oceans. However, with the development of the long range bomber, nuclear weapons, and guided missiles the possibility of attack on American shores became all too menacing, and the protection of geographical isolation vanished. These developments, coupled with the concept of total war in which any resource, civilian or military, is a target, indicated the need to organize for emergency on the home front as on the battlefield.

During World War II the national Office of Civilian Defense, an independent executive agency, directed a locally oriented program that emphasized aircraft spotting, auxiliary police and fire services, first-aid centers, air-raid shelters, and a warning service. In 1950, after the OCD was abolished, a new agency, the Federal Civil Defense

Administration, was created to head a program in which each state established a civil defense organization. Eight years later the FCDA was merged with the Office of Defense Mobilization to form the Office of Civil Defense Mobilization. Further reorganization occurred in 1961 when the civil defense functions were vested in the Office of Emergency Planning in the Executive Office of the President, and the Office of Civil Defense in the Defense Department. OED advises the President regarding total nonmilitary defense planning and OCD has the responsibility for developing an overall plan of civil defense. Since the Cuban crisis in 1962 substantial progress in planning has been made, but significant implementation is still to be realized.

Civil defense programs are based on the concepts of self-help and mutual aid. That is, each locality is responsible for assessing its own strength and resources with regard to how it may best protect itself and assist other stricken communities. State organizations serve primarily as sources of over-all leadership and coordination. The problems that would stem from an actual attack stress the need for an effective civil defense program. Nuclear bombing of a metropolitan center, for example, would leave thousands dead and thousands more wounded. Tremendous efforts would be required to provide adequate food, water, medical supplies, communications, police and fire protection, and transportation facilities. The horrors of a general attack on numerous targets are obvious. Only by effective preparation for such emergencies can the danger of total disaster be averted.

What progress toward the goal of preparedness has a decade of civil defense planning been able to realize? The terrifying prospect of nuclear attack would appear to be sufficient to shock states and cities into action. Yet, in terms of what ought to be done, very little has been accomplished. Each state has set up a civil defense organization, and some cities have decided upon plans of action in case of attack. Most cities, however, have not gone beyond the discussion stage. Underscoring the inadequacy of present civil defense programs is the fact that millions of adult Americans have not the slightest notion of what civil defense is.

Correcting the dangerous attitude of complacency that seems to have throttled any real progress in civil defense would necessitate drastic overhaul of the program. The present approach is based on the assumption that material progress must come at the state and local levels within the framework of general leadership and encouragement by the national government. Since little has been accomplished and local governments have given few signs of increased future activity, substantial progress probably cannot be expected until more financial aid from the nation and the states is extended and stronger central leadership and supervision is asserted.

FIRE PROTECTION

An aspect of public safety that is of fundamental importance to every individual is protection from personal injury and property losses by fire. The magnitude of the problem is indicated by the fact that each year in the United States about one billion dollars' worth of property is consumed by fire, and thousands of lives are lost. Consequently, national, state, and local governments administer fire prevention and protection programs.

National efforts in fire protection are not as extensive as those of state and local governments. National properties, national forests, and shipping facilities are the principal objects of federal efforts. Probably the most valuable federal services consist of research on matters relating to fire prevention and control. Many federal agencies such as the Office of Education, Bureau of Mines, Bureau of Standards, and the Forest Service render valuable assistance to state and local governments by disseminating information on fire prevention and control techniques.

State contributions in the field are varied, but they rarely involve fire fighting as such. The criminal laws of every state make arson—the deliberate and malicious setting of fires—a crime punishable as a felony. State-wide building codes, civil defense legislation, and fire hazard laws on handling of combustibles and explosives represent other areas of state concern in fire protection. About forty states have created the office of fire marshal, an officer who investigates causes of serious fires, conducts fire prevention educational campaigns, and enforces all state fire laws that are not specifically assigned to other state officials.

Local governments perform the basic function of protecting lives and property from damage and destruction by fire. Virtually every community provides some organized effort to control fires. In small towns and cities fire-fighting forces are usually composed of volunteers, often supplemented by a few full-time, paid firemen. Several small governmental units may be included in a fire control district; a town or county fire department may be maintained; or a large city may, by formal agreement, provide protection to smaller, neighboring communities. Fire departments of large cities employ professional, full-time firemen involving, in cities like New York and Chicago, thousands of personnel. The larger the community, the more varied are the types of property to be protected, and consequently the more specialized must be the training and equipment.

When compared to European countries the record of American fire losses is high. Even after allowances are made for the greater amount of property involved and its higher value in dollars, the American record does not measure up to European efforts. The difference is emphasized further by the fact that fire-fighting equipment used in the United States is superior and more abundant than in any other country. The difference seems best explained by general attitudes toward fire prevention, with Americans typically exhibiting indifference unless exhorted by such campaigns as "fire prevention week" or sobered by experience with a destructive blaze.

SELECTED REFERENCES

Books:

Camp, Irving, *Our State Police,* Dodd, Mead and Company, New York, 1955.

Federal Bureau of Investigation, *Uniform Crime Reports,* Washington, D.C., published semi-annually.

Johnson, Elmer H., *Crime Correction, and Society,* Dorsey Press, Homewood, Ill., 1964.

Smith, Bruce, *Police Systems in the United States,* revised edition, Harper and Row, Publishers, New York, 1960.

Wilson, O. W., *Police Administration,* 2nd edition, McGraw-Hill, New York, 1962.

Articles:

Bennett, James V., "Probation and Parole Among the States," *State Government,* June 1957.

"Crime and Correction," Symposium, *Law and Contemporary Problems,* Autumn 1958.

Finsley, Fred, "Parole and Probation," *State Government,* Summer 1963.

Hall, Jerome, "Police and Law in a Democratic Society," *Indiana Law Journal,* Winter 1953.

"Law Enforcement," Symposium, *County Officer,* May 1960.

Moses, Robert, "The Civil Defense Fiasco," *Harper's Magazine,* November 1957.

"New Goals in Police Management," Symposium, *The Annals,* January 1954.

Peterson, Val, "Civil Defense and Law," *Nebraska Law Review,* March 1956.

"Prisons in Transformation," Symposium, *The Annals,* May 1954.

Rich, Bennett M., and Burch, Philip H., Jr., "The Changing Role of the National Guard" *American Political Science Review,* September 1956.

CHAPTER 25

Health, Welfare, and Housing

Social problems very often are, or may become, governmental problems. This statement is dramatically borne out by the course of development of government in the United States. During the colonial period and early statehood, American governments were essentially "negative" in character. That is, they did very little by way of providing services to the people or regulating private affairs. Over the years, however, government became increasingly "positive," doing more and more for its citizens and paying more attention to their problems.

Among the areas in which government has undertaken an increasingly important role are public health and public welfare. In former years these matters were generally regarded primarily as responsibilities of the individual, his family, and his church. As the population grew, industrialization and urbanization became national characteristics, and self-sufficiency of the individual was largely replaced by a condition of social interdependence. Accordingly, the ability of each individual to solve many of his own problems was diminished. Solutions to such problems as disease control in densely populated areas, general unemployment of workers trained in narrow specialties, and the prevalence of slums and depressed areas demanded something more than individual efforts. Slowly but surely, government assumed responsibility for seeking solutions to those problems.

PUBLIC HEALTH

Governmental concern for matters of general health reflects a very real connection between public well-being and the obligation of government to provide for the general welfare. Epidemics, poor sanitation, lack of hospitals and laboratory facilities, and the like are not only serious problems themselves—they also create other problems. There is no doubt that health problems can result, for example, in economic loss and dependency. Viewed in this light, governmental action in the health field is both reasonable and justifiable.

Although organized governmental efforts in public health can be traced to the final years of the eighteenth century,[1] they did not become significant until after the Civil War. There had been local activities before that time, but from mid-century on the states became increasingly active. Federal concern dates back to the first decade of union but did not assume prominence until the last generation.

The tardiness of meaningful governmental effort in regard to public health was not due to arbitrary refusal to act. Public officials were mindful of the ravages of disease. Scourges such as smallpox, yellow fever, and tuberculosis elicited governmentally imposed quarantines and such sanitary measures as were thought necessary. The major difficulty was lack of medical knowledge. It was not until Louis Pasteur's discoveries in 1866 on the causes of disease that truly effective strides could be taken. After that date public health programs based on preventing ills rather than curing them began to develop.

THE NATIONAL ROLE

The United States Constitution does not give the national government express authority to engage in public health activities. Consequently the power to protect the public health is a reserved power lodged in the states. Even so, the national government has managed, through its implied powers and by means of grants-in-aid, to carry on extensive health activities itself and at the same time promote broadened programs in the states.

Of all federal agencies engaged in health work, the most important is the Public Health Service, located in the Department of Health, Education, and Welfare. Dating from 1798, when it was first created as a hospital for American seamen, the Public Health Service has expanded until now it administers most national health programs. It operates hospitals and outpatient clinics, administers grant-in-aid programs, trains researchers, cooperates with private research agencies, assists states in drawing up health legislation, and maintains the National Institutes of Health. The contributions of the Public

---

[1] Wilson G. Smillie, *Public Health Administration in the United States*, 2nd ed., The Macmillan Co., New York, 1940, p. 369, reports local boards of health in Massachusetts in 1797. Interestingly, it was in 1798 that the national government, by act of Congress, created the Marine Hospital Service for the care of American seamen.

Health Service have been characterized by one eminent health authority as having "raised the level of work performed in every county, city and state health department with which it has had even indirect contact."[2]

It would be difficult to say exactly how many national agencies are involved in public health activities. Some are directly involved, but others created to perform tasks considered outside the health field certainly *affect* public health work. Thus the Food and Drug Administration, medical agencies of the armed forces, and the Veterans' Administration's medical department may be classed as health agencies. At the same time it would be unrealistic to assert that the Federal Trade Commission, National Bureau of Standards, and research agencies of the Department of Agriculture do not also contribute to improvement of national health.

STATE HEALTH AGENCIES

As noted earlier, general health programs at the state level did not take form until after the Civil War. In 1855 Louisiana created a state board of health in the wake of a yellow fever epidemic, but within a few years it became inactive. The first board of health to become a permanent part of state organization was created in Massachusetts in 1869. California established a health organization the following year, and in the next ten years more than two dozen states followed suit. By 1909 every state had set up a department to administer health laws of statewide application.

Practically all states maintain boards of health composed of members appointed by the governor. Serving four to six year overlapping terms, they are responsible for all policy decisions in the administration of programs under their jurisdiction. Serving under the board is an executive officer, known as the state health officer, health commissioner, director of public health, or some similar title. He is chosen by the governor in over forty states and serves an indefinite term. The state health officer supervises day-to-day administration and enforcement of state health laws.

The functions of state health organizations vary from one state to the next. Such factors as geographical location, size and character

[2] Harry S. Mustard, *Government in Public Health,* Harvard University Press, Cambridge, 1945, p. 59. A concise presentation of grant-in-aid programs in the field of public health is found in Commission on Intergovernmental Relations, *A Description of Twenty-five Federal Grant-in-aid Programs,* Washington, D.C., 1955, pp. 80–110.

of population, climate, and occupational pursuits of the inhabitants result in differing health problems in different states. However, there is enough similarity in the various programs to warrant general classification of health activities. These functions, which include the principal areas of concern in public health, are discussed later in the chapter.

LOCAL ORGANIZATION

Most routine health services rendered to the general public are performed by personnel of local health organizations. Yet, it is at the local level that the most glaring inadequacies are found. Despite the existence of a large number of local health agencies administering comprehensive programs, it is nevertheless true that many Americans reside in areas where health services and facilities are demonstrably inadequate or totally lacking.[3]

Despite the fact that local health organizations appeared over 165 years ago, it was not until the present century that full-time, permanently staffed local organizations came into existence. In fact, prior to World War I most local organizations consisted of private physicians serving part-time. In view of these facts it is surprising that during the past forty years local health services have developed as rapidly as they have.

Local health units exist in many forms. When considered in detail, administrative variations seem endless. Nevertheless, basic patterns of organization similar to those at the state level can be delineated, with both boards and single administrators being used. Local organization is often based on the county, or as an alternative, the township or town. Sometimes two or more counties band together, sharing costs of health services. Cities commonly operate health units, with the more competently staffed and better equipped ones found in the larger cities around the nation. Another general type of health organization is the health district that combines several counties and is administered under direct supervision of the state health department. A pronounced trend in public health organization in recent years has been in the direction of the district plan. This development has been occasioned largely by the difficulties experienced by local governments in meeting the necessary

---

[3] Haven Emerson and Martha Luginbuhl, *Local Health Units for the Nation,* Commonwealth Fund, New York, 1945.

costs of securing competent personnel and modern, up-to-date equipment.

The functions of public health at the local level are no different, in principle, from those of the states. In most instances, however, local governments confine their activities principally to disease control, particularly to checking the spread of communicable ills. The main reason for such restricted activity is the expense of a general health program.

State supervision and control over local activities is definite in some states and virtually nonexistent in others. Responsibility for supervision is lodged in many state health departments, but lack of personnel, funds, and adequate enforcement authority leave the local units relatively free. In other states county health officers are chosen by the state health officer or are subject to his approval if locally chosen. Supervision often is tied in with administration of state grants to local health units, making it possible to stimulate or channel local efforts by manipulation of the purse strings.

PUBLIC HEALTH FUNCTIONS

Areas of concentrated health activity vary widely among the states as well as at the local level. Nevertheless, it is simple to list the major categories into which most public health efforts can be classified. Generally considered, the most important areas are: collection and publication of vital statistics, disease control, sanitation, and sanitary engineering. These functions comprise the heart of a state public health program. In addition, states commonly undertake such activities as provision of diagnostic laboratory services, health education, industrial hygiene, maternity and child hygiene, dental health, public nursing, and public school nursing.

Vital Statistics. Health statistics are indispensable to an effective public health program. Consisting of data on births, deaths, causes of death, incidence of disease, and the like, these statistics are measurements of the effectiveness of health programs and indications of areas in which future efforts should be concentrated. The value of such information can be illustrated in countless ways. Tabulations on mental illness and hospital space available forewarn shortages in that area. "Keeping books" on communicable diseases may foretell possible epidemics; records of infant mortality may point the way to necessary changes in nursing and maternity and infant care.

Disease Control. The first public health departments, state and local, were organized primarily to fight the spread of communicable diseases. Epidemics of smallpox, typhoid, and yellow fever were combatted largely through the imposition of strictly enforced quarantines. Today these diseases and others such as diphtheria, pneumonia, polio, syphilis, and gonorrhea are countered with a vastly superior arsenal of medical weapons. New medicines, improved techniques, better hospitals, rapid reporting, and emphasis upon prevention have brought these diseases more nearly under control. Today more money is spent to control contagious diseases than ever before, but the expenditure is a smaller percentage of the total health outlay than in earlier years.

A great deal of effort is concentrated on diseases that, while not communicable, disable or claim the lives of many Americans. Cancer, heart ailments, and mental diseases head the list of ills that are subjected to intensive research by government health specialists. National and state organizations are especially active in this field.

Sanitation and Sanitary Engineering. Promotion of sanitation has long been a major function of public health organizations, particularly since the causes of disease have been more fully understood. All levels and units of government have enacted laws, ordinances, and regulations designed to eliminate unsanitary conditions that endanger public health. Many such laws are administered by health officials, of course, but enforcement authority, especially at the local level, is often lodged in other officers. Illustrative of the broad range of sanitation laws are those designed to protect the purity of water and milk supplies, assure cleanliness of food handlers, prevent pollution of rivers and other bodies of water, provide safe means of garbage disposal, eradicate rodents and insect pests, eliminate unsanitary conditions in public recreation facilities, require safe methods of sewage disposal, and prevent or correct air pollution.

The term sanitary engineering refers to the profession of developing methods and programs to eliminate and prevent the dangers to health that lack of sanitation involves. In recent years, for example, air pollution in industrial centers has proved a thorny problem. Improved methods of treating raw sewage, safer and more economical ways of providing supplies of potable water, and more effective application of plumbing skills are constant challenges. Solution to such problems is a task for sanitary engineers.

Other Functions. A standard function of state departments of health is to provide diagnostic laboratory services for local health units as well as private physicians and hospitals. Assistance is rendered to expectant mothers and infants through maternity and child hygiene programs that include operation of clinics, prenatal instruction, training midwives, care of premature babies, and nursing assistance. Industrial hygiene programs promote more healthful working conditions to prevent occupational diseases. Public health nursing, particularly in low-income areas, is a usual health activity. Public school nurses often are provided by school districts, but some are supplied by health departments. Both health units and school districts provide for dental inspections and treatment. Every state department of health, and most local ones as well, conduct health education programs in the valid belief that a public well informed on health matters is better able to protect the public health.

HOSPITALS

In the United States there are more than 7,000 hospitals with a total capacity of approximately 1.7 million beds. Eight of every ten hospitals are general institutions, while the remainder are designed for the treatment of selected illnesses. Of the total number of hospitals in America, about thirty-five percent are governmentally owned and operated.

Publicly owned hospitals are of various types, depending upon the level of government involved and the use to which the hospitals are put. Hospitals are operated by the national government, the states, counties, cities, city-county combinations, and special districts. National facilities include many operated for research purposes, veterans' hospitals, military hospitals, and those maintained in federally administered territories. University hospitals and medical centers conduct research and treatment at the state level. States also operate facilities for the treatment of tuberculosis, mental illnesses, and venereal diseases. Hospitals operated by local governments are usually of the general type, although special treatment centers may also be maintained.

PUBLIC WELFARE

Society has always been plagued by poverty and its consequences. In good times and bad there are those who, because of such factors as sickness, physical handicaps, old age, mental condition, and economic disruptions, are unable to make their way unaided. Provision of assistance to these people today is regarded as a proper function of government. Indeed, assuring minimum conditions of subsistence is looked upon as a *duty* of government.

Broadly viewed, most governmental programs designed to combat social problems can be classed as welfare activities. Thus legislation to promote health, housing, and education are included in the concept. More narrowly conceived, however, public welfare may be said to consist of those activities designed to render immediate, and perhaps continuing, assistance to individuals who, for reasons usually beyond their control, are financially or physically unable to provide themselves with the minimum needs for subsistence. What is and what is not included in public welfare is often subject to debate. The inclusion of social insurance programs, for example, is admittedly arbitrary. In the final analysis, the concept of public welfare defies precise definition, and only through arbitary, majority acceptance can its meaning be even temporarily fixed.

Regardless of how the term public welfare may be defined, certain methods of rendering assistance may be identified. The term "relief" is used to identify direct assistance to the needy. Relief may be *general,* or applicable to all persons needing help, and it may be *categorical,* or limited to specified groups such as widows, the blind, or the tubercular. Relief may be classified as *indoor* or *institutional.* Indoor assistance is given within institutions such as hospitals and schools. *Outdoor* relief, on the other hand, refers to noninstitutional help whereby the recipient is given food, clothing, housing, and other necessities. A form of assistance, widely used during the depression of the 1930's, that does not fit well into either the indoor or outdoor classifications is *work* relief, consisting of jobs created by the government for the sole purpose of providing employment for idle workers. These forms of assistance are, or have been, used at all levels of government, national, state, and local.

THE MODERN APPROACH TO WELFARE

The concept of public welfare held by Americans today is the culmination of a development reaching back to the Elizabethan poor laws of sixteenth- and seventeenth-century England. According to Elizabethan theory, responsibility for welfare activities rested with the individual, his family, and local governments. The influence of this line of thought upon American practices is indicated by the fact that down to the present century the national government had very little to do with public welfare, and the states were not organized to administer general welfare programs.

For the first three decades of the twentieth century the largely local situs of welfare functions was not disturbed. During the 1930's, however, the catastrophic Great Depression wrought fundamental changes in outlook. With at least a fourth of the labor force idle, long bread lines, and little promise of improvement, local governments were unable to meet demands for welfare assistance. In turn some states virtually exhausted their resources trying to cope with the situation. Out of sheer necessity the national government entered the welfare picture, at first modestly and later on a grand scale. Many federal welfare programs of the thirties were temporary, but out of that era a whole new system of national-state cooperation evolved— a system still in effect today.

During the critical 1930's the national government first extended loans to state and local governments for relief purposes. Outright grants were made in 1933, and the earlier loans were written off. Throughout the rest of the decade numerous agencies and programs designed to lighten individual hardships were inaugurated. Most important was the Social Security Act of 1935, which today forms the heart of the federal-state system of public welfare. This basic law established an old-age insurance program and set up grants-in-aid under which the national government and the states administer programs of old-age assistance, unemployment compensation,[4] and aid to dependent children, the blind, and the disabled.

WELFARE ORGANIZATION

Prior to the passage of the Social Security Act, state welfare organization was for the most part a jumble of agencies, boards, and commissions. Since there was no concerted pressure for centralized administration, common practice was to establish a separate board for each welfare function. Although some states, following the lead of Illinois in 1917, had unified most welfare activities in a single administrative authority by the time of the Depression, most unification occurred after 1935 in view of the requirement of the Social

---

[4] Even though provision of unemployment compensation may be regarded as a welfare function, it is considered in this volume in conjunction with labor problems. See pp. 693–694 for a discussion of unemployment compensation programs.

Security Act that participating states provide administrative agencies acceptable to the national government. However, since the Act pertained only to certain forms of public assistance, many states still have not placed *all* welfare activities under one department.[5]

Historically, the county has been important as a local welfare unit, maintaining poor farms, almshouses, orphanages, and dispensing direct relief. Large cities and New England towns also provide such services. Since the advent of the Social Security Act local welfare agencies, particularly those in the counties, have taken on new significance. Commonly, they function as field extensions of the state welfare agency in administering federally aided programs. As such they are subject to close supervision by the state agency. In addition, local agencies also perform other welfare functions that may be assigned to them by the states.

THE PROBLEM OF THE AGED

The economic structure of the United States is of such nature that as a person approaches retirement age, demand for his services diminishes. Unless he is self-employed or has some special professional or technical skill, his sixty-fifth birthday may signal a virtual end to his earning capacity. Despite the fact that a worker of such advanced age may be able to perform on a par with younger workers, his productive years generally are regarded as over, and he usually must face his remaining years without assurance of sustained employment.

Before the present system of social insurance and public assistance was inaugurated, aged workers frequently experienced hardship during their years of retirement. Without savings accumulated over the years, insurance annuities, support contributed by friends or relatives, or some other help, many aged persons were without the necessities of life. Many were forced to seek public assistance. The Great Depression dramatized the needs of the aged whose problems are made even more evident by longer life expectancy. The Social Security Act was designed to ameliorate these difficulties by establishing broad programs of public assistance and social insurance.

---

[5] Nor is it wise always to do so. For example, the education or training of mentally retarded public charges should probably be controlled by state education officers. By the same token, rehabilitation of criminals is ordinarily a function of correctional personnel, and medical treatment of indigent persons is assigned to health officials.

Old-Age, Survivors and Disability Insurance

In the strictest sense, OASDI is not a public welfare undertaking. The benefits received under this program are based upon contributions paid in the form of taxes by each participant and his employers. The program, in which the states do not participate, is in fact a system of compulsory retirement and disability insurance administered by the Social Security Administration in the Department of Health, Education, and Welfare.

Now covering the vast majority of employed persons in the country,[6] the program is financed by a tax levied equally upon employees and employers.[7] The payments are made to the national government which credits the social security accounts of employees. Benefits are payable at age sixty-five, or at reduced rates, as early as sixty-two. The benefits are payable irrespective of age in the event of disablement. Surviving dependents, such as a widow and children under eighteen, are entitled to the benefits a deceased worker would have received.

OASDI was begun too late to be of much help to workers nearing retirement when the Social Security Act was passed. Also, the coverage of the act was not extended to millions of others until later amendments were added. Help was provided to these individuals in the form of federally aided state public assistance programs.

Old Age Assistance

Public assistance in the form of pensions for the needy aged was undertaken on a statewide basis about forty years ago. In 1923 Montana established such a program, and by 1935 thirty states had done so. Both coverage and benefits, however, were generally inadequate. It was not until the states took advantage of the public assistance provisions of the Social Security Act that adequate systems were approximated.

There are various conditions to which states must agree before being eligible for old age assistance funds from the national govern-

---

[6] The major groups of workers not included are those covered by the national civil service retirement program, employees of state and local governments which have not elected OASDI coverage, and persons with incomes too low to qualify for benefits.

[7] The amount of tax paid by each employee is determined by two factors, the tax rate and the earning base. In 1965 the rate was fixed at 3.625%, and the base against which it was levied was the first $4,800 earned. However, revisions enacted in 1965, effective in 1966, raised the earnings base to $6,600 and the rate to 4.2%, and provided for graduated rate increases scheduled to reach 5.65% by 1987.

ment. Assistance must be extended to persons over age sixty-five on the basis of need. The program must be statewide and administered by a single agency staffed with personnel selected on a merit basis, and fair hearings must be given to applicants denied assistance. Most important, the federal funds granted the states must be supplemented by state money according to a federally determined ratio. Every state has accepted these conditions.

The magnitude of the problem is indicated by the fact that over 2.2 million aged persons now receive public welfare assistance payments. Moreover, the changing character of the population suggests that the probable number of recipients in the future is likely to be much higher. Life expectancy has increased impressively during the past few decades, and the percentage of persons surviving beyond age sixty-five has risen dramatically. There are now about 18 million Americans in this age group as compared to approximately half that number only twenty-five years ago. During that same period the total population increased by slightly less than one-third.

In the United States today one of every eight persons over the age of sixty-five receives old-age assistance payments. Although this proportion is lower than in many recent years, one may still wonder why there are so many in view of the existence of OASDI. Several reasons may be cited. First, OASDI was not begun in time to benefit many already aged persons and others approaching retirement. Second, coverage was not extended to certain large groups of workers, notably farm workers, domestic employees, and the self-employed, until a few years ago. Finally, the modest OASDI benefits may be inadequate because of the high costs of living. In time the OASDI program promises to eliminate old-age assistance; indeed, today in only a few states are there more persons receiving assistance than OASDI benefits.

MEDICAL ASSISTANCE FOR THE AGED

Among the many problems besetting the needy aged is that of securing adequate medical care. With financial resources at low ebb elderly persons in need of medical care have often found it difficult to receive needed treatment. To reduce the severity of this problem Congress, in the closing days of its 1960 session, enacted the Kerr-Mills Act which established a cooperative federal-state system of medical care for the indigent aged.

Under the system two programs are in operation. The first is in reality an extension of the old age assistance program with the federal government paying fifty to eighty per cent of the costs, depending upon the level of per capita income within a state. The second is designed to help elderly persons who are not on assistance rolls. State funds are matched as in the assistance programs, but no limit is placed on the total amount of federal payments.

Further action was taken by Congress in 1965 when it enacted the controversial "medicare" legislation, scheduled to take effect July 1, 1966. The act established a program of medical care for the aged as a part of the OASDI system. First proposed by the late President Kennedy and later by President Johnson, the so-called medicare program is a compulsory system administered directly by the national government through the Department of Health, Education, and Welfare. As in the case of retirement benefits, it is financed through taxes paid in equal amounts by both employees and their employers. The combination of the programs under the Kerr-Mills Act and the medical benefits available under the new legislation make it posssible, at least in theory, for virtually all persons over the age of sixty-five to receive adequate medical care.

POVERTY PROGRAMS

Even in prosperous times when most segments of society enjoy substantial material benefits, there are those who, for a variety of reasons, exist in conditions of poverty. In recent years, efforts in Congress have been directed toward the passage of measures designed to eliminate or at least reduce the severity of these "pockets of poverty." Legislation intended to achieve this goal was enacted in 1964 in the form of the Economic Opportunity Act.[8]

Administered by an Office of Economic Opportunity headed by a single director, a variety of programs to be undertaken in cooperation with state and local governments are authorized by the new legislation. Included are a Job Corps, consisting of work and training camps for youths in the 16 to 21 age group; financial assistance for state and local training programs, higher educational institutions, and both urban and rural development programs; transfer of funds to

---

[8] The Economic Opportunity Act of 1964, popularly known at the time of its passage as the "poverty bill," was the first enacted of several measures proposed by President Lyndon B. Johnson in his "war on poverty."

other national welfare agencies; and creation of volunteers in service to America—a sort of domestic Peace Corps.

DEPENDENT CHILDREN

Federal law states that a dependent child is "a needy child under the age of eighteen, who has been deprived of parental support." Included are those whose parents are living but who, for one reason or another, do not support or care for their offspring. Prior to the Social Security Act, dependent children commonly were cared for in institutions such as orphanages. Today the trend is to preserve or construct the home situation by extending aid to mothers, near relatives, or foster parents who care for these children. The emphasis is apparent in that the aid, while primarily for the support of children, is known as aid to families of dependent children.

These programs, administered by state welfare departments, are financed by state appropriations and federal grant-in-aid funds. Payments may be made not only for the support of dependent children, but also for the support of those who care for them. Recent amendments to federal child welfare laws provided that, until 1967 at least, aid may also be extended for the care of the needy offspring of unemployed parents. Today, almost a million families receive aid for the support of nearly three million children.

THE BLIND AND DISABLED

Another category of persons aided under the provisions of the Social Security Act are the needy blind, including those having some sight but not enought to be able to hold a job. The terms under which states are granted federal funds are the same as those for old age assistance except for the age requirement. About 100,000 persons are aided through the various state programs.

In 1950 the Social Security Act was amended to extend federal aid to state programs for support of permanently and totally disabled persons over eighteen years of age. In this program the states exercise a wider degree of discretion than in many other federal-state cooperative ventures. Criteria of disability are left to state determination and, while there are variations, most states regard a person as totally disabled if, because of disease or disability, he is permanently unable to provide for himself through gainful employment.

Public Housing

Until recent years government took little direct action in regard to housing problems. Regulation through building codes, sanitation laws, and zoning ordinances, all of which still are used, were the usual modes of governmental action through the first quarter of the twentieth century. With the coming of the Great Depression, housing problems assumed a new importance, and governmental participation in the housing field took on a different character. The pressing need for new housing, particularly of the low-rental type, was so great that the national government entered the field.

To some people, governmental efforts to promote or provide housing are somehow "improper." Such actions are in reality profitable investments when measured against costs occasioned by substandard slum areas. When adequate housing is not available, slums and depressed areas inevitably develop, and such areas are costly in terms of police and fire protection, health services, and welfare assistance. Normally, taxes on slum property and other taxes collected from slum dwellers are but a fraction of the cost of the public services they require.[9] Further, since the great need is for low-rent housing that low-income families can afford, some sort of subsidy is required. Private capital cannot sustain such housing. The logical solution is government help.

Governmental activity in housing represents a departure from the usual pattern of intergovernmental programs. Usually, federally aided ventures involve grants-in-aid to the state with administration centered in a single state agency. Housing problems, however, are basically local in nature. Thus public housing programs are primarily federal-local undertakings. With the exception of a few states such as Connecticut, New Jersey, New York, and Massachusetts, which conduct public housing programs of considerable proportions, the primary role of the states has been to enact legislation authorizing their local governments to participate in federally assisted housing programs.

There are two general facets to housing ventures supported by the federal government: construction of low-rent housing projects and slum clearance programs. Before the national government agrees

---

[9] For concise treatment of this and other aspects of public housing, see Benjamin Baker, *Urban Government,* D. Van Nostrand Co., Inc., Princeton, 1957, pp. 540–549; and Arthur Bromage, *Municipal Government and Administration,* 2nd. ed., Appleton-Century-Crofts, New York, 1957, pp. 151–155.

to give financial aid, a locality must have what is called a "workable program." In summary, a workable program is one that involves an over-all plan of development with due regard for minimum housing standards, building and zoning regulations, effective administration, citizen participation, slum clearance, provisions for financing improvements, and relocation of displaced families. Such requirements discourage piecemeal or half-hearted efforts by participating communities.

The method by which low-rent public housing projects are provided is one that calls for local initiative and action with federal approval and assistance. A city must first create a "housing authority" to administer a contemplated project. After reaching agreement with the city for provision of services in return for about ten per cent of the rentals in lieu of taxes, the authority then negotiates contracts with the national Public Housing Administration.[10] These contracts call for federal assistance over periods up to forty years to pay the difference between construction and operation costs and the collections from rentals. Local housing authorities today operate public housing units occupied by approximately 2.0 million low-income families, the elderly, veterans, and families displaced by slum-clearance projects.

In the Housing Act of 1949 Congress provided a means by which cities are able to clear slum areas without incurring large financial deficits. By agreement with the Urban Renewal Administration, local renewal authorities acquire the land to be cleared, remove the slum dwellings, and sell or lease the property to private developers. The local agency is then reimbursed to the extent of two-thirds of any loss represented by the difference between the cost of acquiring and clearing the land and the income from sales and leases. Grants and loans are also available for planning such redevelopment projects. Since 1949 completions have not been numerous, but throughout the fifty states approximately 1,500 projects have received federal approval.

SELECTED REFERENCES

Books:

Abrams, Charles, *Forbidden Neighbors: A Study of Prejudice in Housing*, Harper and Row, Publishers, New York, 1955.

---

[10] The Public Housing Administration, in operation since 1947, is the successor of the Federal Public Housing Authority created in 1942, which in turn replaced the original United States Housing Authority set up in 1937.

Banfield, E. C., and Grodzins, Morton, *Government and Housing,* McGraw-Hill, New York, 1958.

Hanlon, J. J., *Principles of Public Health Organization,* 2nd ed., C. V. Mosby, St. Louis, 1955.

Hiscock, Ira V., *Community Health Organization,* 4th ed., Commonwealth Fund, New York, 1950.

Leyendecker, Hilary M., *Problems and Policy in Public Assistance,* Harper and Brothers, New York, 1955.

Smillie, W. G., *Public Health Administration in the United States,* 3rd ed., Macmillan Co., New York, 1947.

Vasey, Wayne, *Government and Social Welfare,* Holt and Company, New York, 1958.

Woodbury, Coleman, editor, *Urban Redevelopment: Problems and Practices,* University of Chicago Press, Chicago, 1953.

Articles:

Brown, J. Douglas, "The American Philosophy of Social Insurance," *Social Service Review,* March 1956.

Cohen, Wilbur J., "Needed Changes in Social Welfare Programs and Objectives," *Social Service Review,* March 1959.

"The Controversy Over the Administration's New Medicare Plan for the Aged," *Congressional Digest,* January 1962.

"The Controversy Over the 'Equal Employment Opportunity' Provisions of the Civil Rights Bill," *Congressional Digest,* March 1964.

Dunn, Loula, "Public Assistance Administration," *State Government,* July 1957.

"Health and Urban Development," Symposium, *American Journal of Public Health,* May 1964.

"The Local Health Officer," Symposium, *American Journal of Public Health,* February 1964.

Perkins, Ellen J., "State and Local Financing of Public Assistance, 1935–1955," *Social Security Bulletin,* July 1956.

Phalan, J. Laurence, "The Private Business of Public Housing," *Harvard Business Review,* September–October 1955.

"Programs and Problems in Child Welfare," Symposium, *The Annals,* September 1964.

CHAPTER 26

Education

Democracy as it is known in the United States requires participation in the governmental process by a large portion of citizens. Since political activity for its own sake is of doubtful value, the quality of that participation is a matter of prime importance. Political activity of a kind that strengthens rather than weakens democratic institutions "presupposes that each individual be mentally, socially, and emotionally competent to the fullest possibility of his inborn capacities."[1] A desire on the part of each individual to realize his potential is also assumed. At a time when approximately nine out of ten young people between six and seventeen years of age are enrolled in public schools, a major share of the responsibility for such an accomplishment rests with the primary and secondary schools, as well as colleges and universities, that are publicly supported and administered. Of course, other institutions, such as the family and the church, have an important share in this great undertaking.

According to Henry Steele Commager, schools have made self-government work; they have created a national unity, swiftly made Americans of immigrants, and taught the equality of man.[2] In the early years of American history the fortunate few who were the beneficiaries of formal education received their training in private schools. Far into the nineteenth century public schools were commonly considered as schools for the underprivileged. Although provisions pertaining to education were included in six of the original state constitutions, the idea behind them was that government should supplement private facilities, and these provisions were later revised to indicate clearly that public responsibility was limited to the pro-

---

[1] Arthur B. Moehlman, *School Administration,* Houghton Mifflin Co., New York, 1951, p. 11.

[2] H. S. Commager, "Our Schools Have Kept Us Free," *Life,* October 16, 1950, pp. 46–47.

vision of some type of minimum training for those unable to pay the price of a private education.[3] As late as 1800 only a "small minority of the children of the country attended school and only for short periods and at sporadic intervals."[4]

A great expansion of educational opportunity occurred during the nineteenth century, and basic features of modern public education emerged. Legal responsibility was recognized as belonging to the states, but "both geographical necessity and the political mores fixed the actual control of the educational program in the local units."[5] During this period the typical school was an individual enterprise unconcerned with the programs of other schools and largely unencumbered by state controls. By 1900, fifty per cent of the population between five and seventeen years of age attended school an average of about seventy-two days per year. However, only twelve per cent of those of high-school age were in school. An even more rapid increase occurred during the first half of the twentieth century, so that by 1950 eighty-two per cent of the young people between five and seventeen were in school, average school attendance was 150 days a year, and seventy per cent of those of high-school age were enrolled.[6] Now some eighty-five per cent of school-age young people are enrolled.

Much credit for advancement of public education belongs to such leaders as Horace Mann, Henry Barnard, Caleb Mills, and Calvin Stowe, who helped to convince Americans that public schools were worthy of generous support. Many able laymen and members of state legislatures rallied to the cause of education. Standards were developed by which the quality of school buildings and the qualifications of teachers and school administrators were greatly improved. Professional educators, in turn, made their influence felt throughout the land in behalf of better schools. As a nation, America sought to achieve a system of schools to realize Goethe's observation that if children fulfilled their promise the world would be peopled with geniuses.[7]

---

[3] See H. G. Good, *A History of American Education,* The Macmillan Co., New York, 1956, pp. 88–89, and 134.

[4] Walter D. Cocking and Charles H. Gilmore, *Organization and Administration of Public Education,* U.S. Government Printing Office, Washington, D.C., 1938, p. 4.

[5] *Ibid.,* pp. 9–10.

[6] Walter D. Cocking, "The Role of the States in Education Since 1900," *State Government,* June 1950.

[7] See Lee M. Thurston and William H. Roe, *State School Administration,* Harper & Brothers, New York, 1957, p. 3.

PRIMARY AND SECONDARY EDUCATION

Local Responsibility. Throughout the history of America public education has been primarily a local responsibility. Costs have been met in large part by some unit of local government with authority to construct buildings, provide equipment, hire teachers and administrators, and control curriculum content. Increasingly, local authorities have been required to accept numerous controls imposed by state law, a development that has accompanied increased state financial support of primary and secondary schools. There is no doubt as to the legal right of each state to regulate all aspects of public education within its domain, but the wisdom of greatly augmented control is questioned by many who feel that the more effective approach is to strengthen local systems.[8]

The Special District. Five types of local governments are concerned with providing education: (1) special districts, (2) counties, (3) municipalities, (4) New England towns, and (5) townships. The district system appears to have originated in Massachusetts, where by the middle of the eighteenth century "a multitude of petty local boards and 'directors' ruled supreme in their infinitesimal districts. Each district was a law unto itself; of uniformity and system there was none."[9] The district pattern spread to other states and was carried into frontier regions where pioneer conditions provided fertile ground for its growth. Scattered neighborhood settlements had to provide their own educational facilities if there were to be any, and the school district, locally organized, controlled, and financed, served the purpose.

In better than half of the states responsibility for public schools rests largely with school districts that are independent governmental units. In 1962 the Bureau of the Census counted 34,678 school districts, not all of them independent, comprising over one-third of all governmental units. These districts were characterized by striking disparities. Approximately six per cent of the districts had over 3,000 students, while half of them had less than fifty. Variations in size were very noticeable. Some districts, particularly in the western

---

[8] See The New York State Regent's Inquiry, *Education for American Life*, McGraw-Hill Book Co., New York, 1938, especially Chapter IV; and Council of State Governments, *The Forty-Eight State School Systems*, Chicago, 1949.

[9] William C. Webster, *Recent Centralizing Tendencies in State Educational Administration*, Columbia University Press, New York, 1897, p. 24.

part of the country, encompassed several thousand square miles, while elsewhere districts of less than twenty-five square miles were common. A study published in 1958 noted the financial disparity between two small school districts in the suburbs of Des Moines, Iowa. One of the districts had an assessed taxable valuation per pupil of $216,271, while the other had $1,668 per pupil. In the wealthy district, property was taxed at a rate of slightly over two mills; in the poor district the rate was 154 mills.[10] Although this instance was extreme, similar inequities are still not uncommon.

Every school district has a school board, known variously as the board of education, the board of directors, or the board of trustees. Board members are popularly elected in most instances, but occasionally they are appointed. Important responsibilities are vested in school boards, including constructing and maintaining physical facilities, hiring teachers, arranging the curriculum, purchasing supplies, providing transportation for pupils, and approving claims against the district. Particularly in larger districts, school boards commonly appoint superintendents to whom responsibility for many of these and other functions is delegated, subject to board approval. Board members in small, rural districts are still burdened with many routine chores.

Inadequacies so painfully evident in many small districts over the years have promoted their consolidation into larger units. In 1942 there were over 108,000 independent school districts in the United States. As noted, that number has been reduced to approximately 34,000. The consolidation movement has resulted largely from action at the state level. Some states have enacted legislation designed to compel consolidation, while others have sought to reach the same goal by providing incentives for "voluntary" consolidation. Often the incentives have taken the form of cash subsidies made available to districts of a certain size (measured in terms of area, valuation, or some other criteria) and withheld from others. Because of increased financial resources, consolidated districts are able to provide better school plants and improved curricula and to attract more highly qualified teachers. Nevertheless, much room for improvement still remains.

The County-Unit. The plantation system in the South early favored the county as the chief unit of local government. When educa-

---

[10] American Association of School Administrators, *School District Organization*, Washington, D.C., 1958, p. 84.

tion was recognized as a public function in the South, the county became the principal unit for its administration. Today more than half of the states employ the county-unit to administer some or all schools. Three states, Florida, Nevada, and West Virginia, use the county-unit exclusively, but its principal use is still in the South.[11] The county-unit plan calls for the administration and financial support of all or most primary and/or secondary schools on a *county-wide* basis. Frequently, high schools are under county-wide administration while elementary schools are controlled by districts within the county. Occasionally, schools located in large municipalities are operated independently of county-unit administration.

Relationships between public schools and the county governing body under a county-unit arrangement differ significantly from state to state. Officials administering schools normally enjoy considerable independence. The fact is reflected in the term "county-unit school district," commonly used to designate the agency responsible for providing public education under the supervision of the "county board of education." These districts are quasi-corporations recognized by state law as enjoying an existence independent from the county. The degree of independence, particularly in regard to finances, varies from state to state. Typically, a county governing body exercises very little control over the county board of education.

The county-unit plan of school administration has gained in favor among educators in recent years, although it by no means guarantees the elimination of small, independent schools. In 1957, a number of county units in Florida, Georgia, and Kentucky had less than 1,000 pupils. "However, these examples are exceptional, for the majority of county school districts have more than the minimum number of pupils necessary for providing a modern educational program at reasonable per-pupil cost. Their adequacy in size is the basic advantage of the county as a unit of school administration."[12]

The Municipality. Urban school districts are commonplace in most parts of the country. Much like county units, these districts normally are quasi-corporations whose boundaries are usually coterminous with those of the city or village with which they are identified. In earlier times, cities frequently encompassed numerous school

---

[11] The great bulk of county-unit systems are found in Alabama, Florida, Georgia, Kentucky, Louisiana, Maryland, Mississippi, Nevada, North Carolina, South Carolina, Tennessee, Utah, Virginia, and West Virginia.

[12] American Association of School Administrators, *op. cit.*, p. 98.

districts, much as most counties do at the present time. In most cities today all schools are administered by a single district. Indeed, many districts include urbanized territory outside city boundaries along with the city itself. Under such circumstances, the administration of the district and the government of the city are usually completely separate.

Although most urban school districts are organized independently of municipal government, some function as municipal departments. Sometimes control over city schools is divided between the district and the municipality. A 1950 study by the National Education Association of 1,892 city school systems revealed that in fifty-four per cent of them the school budget was not subject to review by a municipal authority, and in eighteen per cent the budget was subject to only nominal review. In the remaining twenty-eight per cent varying degrees of municipal control existed. In more than sixty per cent of these districts the school boards were empowered to set the school tax rate without municipal interference. Review and control were found most often in the larger city school systems.[13]

The Town and the Township. School systems operating as adjuncts of town or township governments are much less common than county-wide schools. Only in the six states of New England and in New Jersey is the town the principal governmental unit for school administration. In all the New England states except New Hampshire town school districts are fiscally dependent upon town government, while township districts are as a rule fiscally independent of the township. In New England and New Jersey large municipalities frequently possess independent school districts. Like counties, towns and townships are more adequate administrative and financial units for the provision of public education than many small districts that are unassociated with a general purpose government. Of course, use of the town or township as the basic administrative area does not guarantee the elimination of small and inadequate schools, a fact reflected in the elimination of township schools in several states.

State Responsibility. During the first century of American independence, state activity in regard to public education was minimal and did not assume significant proportions until the end of the nineteenth century. According to a New York law of 1812, the state

---

[13] *Ibid.,* p. 102.

superintendent of common schools was authorized to prepare plans for improving public schools, to report the manner in which school money was used, and to provide information concerning schools to the legislature. By 1850, many states had provided for state superintendents who often were *ex officio*. Their chief duties were to administer certain state funds and oversee the manner in which they were spent by local school authorities.

By the end of the nineteenth century, state supervision had been extended in some states to such matters as textbooks, courses of study, selection of teachers, educational methods, and construction standards for buildings. Throughout the twentieth century there has existed a definite trend toward centralization in education. This trend has been evidenced by a greatly increased number of statutory provisions and by an appreciable growth in professional leadership emanating from state agencies. Local school administrators voluntarily seek the assistance of specialized personnel in state agencies. In Delaware and Hawaii the administration of education is sufficiently centralized for these states to be classified as state-unit systems.

State Board of Education. Most states have a board of education which exercises some control over elementary and secondary schools. Board members are selected in a variety of ways, but the great majority are either *ex officio* or appointed by the governor. The use of *ex officio* members, such as treasurers or attorney generals, is in part a carryover from earlier days when supervision of public school lands and custodianship of state aid money were the chief responsibilities of the board. Gubernatorial appointment subject to legislative approval is generally considered by students of education as the preferable method of selecting board members today.[14] A number of states provide for popular election, and other methods of selection are employed in a few states. The number of members on state boards of education ranges between three and twenty-one.

Ideally, a major task of a state board of education is to help "unify the educational forces within the state."[15] The board should be the dominant statewide agency concerned with public education, particularly at the primary and secondary levels. Unfortunately, facts appear to justify this assessment: "In the majority of states, state boards of education have been slow in developing into important,

---

[14] The manner of selection in a particular state may logically be related to the functions of the board.

[15] Thurston and Roe, *op. cit.*, p. 108.

responsible educational agencies despite the fact that most educators today would favor having them serve in this way."[16] If this situation is to be remedied, state legislatures must grant more authority and discretion to their state boards of education, reduce the number and power of competing authorities, and place in the hands of the board the authority to choose a chief state administrative officer, usually known as the superintendent of public instruction.

The Superintendent of Public Instruction. The chief state administrative officer immediately concerned with the supervision of public education generally has the title of superintendent of public instruction, but other designations are used, including commissioner of education, director of education, and state superintendent of schools. The impact of this officer and his staff, commonly called the department of education, on the operation of schools stems not so much from formal controls as from assistance extended to local units. Although conditions surrounding the early development of the superintendent were not auspicious, "it is obvious that no position has greater potential for the unification and leadership of education in each of the states than that of the chief state school officer."[17]

The great majority of state superintendents of public instruction are either popularly elected or chosen by the state board of education, while a handful are gubernatorial appointees. All of those popularly elected or appointed by a governor serve definite terms in office, while some chosen by a board serve definite terms and others at the pleasure of the board. In nearly half of the states the superintendent is a member of the board, and in about an equal number he serves as secretary to the board. As a consequence, he may function both as a policymaker and as an administrator. Such a combination of responsibilities, especially in view of the fact that they often result from popular election, decrease the probability that the superintendent will be a skilled professional administrator and educator. People of the desired calibre often are deterred from seeking office because of the risks involved in popular election. Problems associated with popular election may be ameliorated somewhat by nonpartisan selection. "It is an error to suppose that an educational official will gain strength from periodic contact with the people at election time. Getting elected is so pleasing an experience as to

---

[16] J. T. Wahlquist, W. E. Arnold, R. F. Campbell, T. L. Reller, and L. B. Sands, *The Administration of Public Education,* The Ronald Press Co., New York, 1952, p. 80.

[17] Thurston and Roe, *op. cit.,* p. 113.

sharpen the average appetite for more political conquests of the same sort and to cause an official to steer his course accordingly."[18]

The Department of Education. A strong state department of education, under the leadership of an able professional superintendent, engages in a variety of functions of great importance to public education. Such departments originally performed routine tasks like compiling statistics, making reports, publishing state laws pertaining to education, and apportioning state aid money to local schools. In 1900, personnel in departments of education numbered 177, an average of about four per state. In 1955, staff members numbered approximately 1,500, an average of about thirty-one per state. The value of a department is measured, of course, not so much in terms of the number of personnel as by their quality and the nature of their responsibilities.

Major activities of state departments of education include planning, research, appraisal of present conditions and future needs, presentation of needs to legislatures and the people, provision of leadership to the teaching profession, and administration of regulations. Only a state agency can gather and interpret pertinent data pertaining to all aspects of public education in a state so as to provide a comprehensive picture of current conditions and relate resources to anticipated needs.[19] It is important for school authorities in each state to know, for example, the number of classrooms in existence and their capacity as well as their structural condition; they also need to know the number of teachers on hand, the number potentially available, and the qualifications they possess; school administrators must also have up-to-date information on population trends. These examples merely serve to indicate the variety and importance of plans and supporting data made available to local educators by central agencies.

Plans for the future are of little value unless they can be effectively presented and interpreted to those persons able to implement them. If they are to be effective in promoting the kind of education they feel is desirable, state departments of education must constantly explain their programs to legislators and to the public in general and enlist their support. Implementation of plans rests, in the final analysis, upon those persons who are "on the firing line." In the

---

[18] *Ibid.,* p. 115.

[19] Theoretically, such information might be provided by a national agency, but this arrangement is not practical at the present time.

field of education these people are the teachers, and it is imperative that a central agency inspire them to improve their teaching methods, advance their educational qualifications, enhance their pride in their profession, enrich the curricula where possible, and in every way seek to perform their mission more effectively. The regulatory responsibilities of state departments of education, although important, are more likely to be of a routine nature than those mentioned above. Included in this category are such functions as certification of teachers, inspection of sanitary facilities and fire escapes, review of curricula to ascertain that state requirements are met, and apportionment of state subsidies, especially when conditions are attached.

The importance and complexity of larger state departments of education are evident in this summary of their activities:

> There is no one pattern of organization, but the larger state departments are likely to have divisions or departments to give aid and supervision to the general fields of elementary education, secondary education, teacher education, certification, and guidance services, as well as instructional services in such special fields as art, music, physical and health education, education for the handicapped, and the vocational fields (agriculture, home economics, trade and industrial education, commercial and distributive education). There are also likely to be special departments concerned with textbooks, libraries, audio-visual materials, evaluation and research, school buildings, transportation, school lunches, budgets, accounts, finance, attendance, accrediting of schools and colleges, school law, pension systems, rehabilitation and education, and the like.[20]

State Financial Assistance. A major development in recent times has been the rapid increase in the relative importance of state money used to assist in paying the costs of primary and secondary education. Traditionally, most of the costs of public education have been defrayed by local governments. Little change occurred in the traditional pattern until the depression of the 1930's when revenues, coming largely from property taxes, decreased sharply. Rather than allow education to be crippled almost irreparably, public opinion favored state aid. A sharp upturn in state assistance occurred around 1930 and has not abated. Within fifteen years about one-third of the states were paying at least half of the cost of public elementary

---

[20] R. Freeman Butts and Lawrence A. Cremin, *A History of Education in American Culture,* Holt and Co., New York, 1953, pp. 577–78.

and secondary education, whereas only Delaware had done so at the onset of the depression.[21]

Factors causing the growth in state aid are numerous and complex. One underlying cause was the change in the nature of the economy from an agricultural to an industrial one. As industrialization spreads, disparities in taxpaying capacity of localities become increasingly evident. The more highly industrialized a state is, the more severe the discrepancies. Thus the taxpaying capacity of the area around Detroit is much greater than that of the upper peninsula in Michigan. The same is true of the areas around Philadelphia and Pittsburgh as contrasted with many sections of Pennsylvania. Although local differences exist in states like Iowa, Mississippi, and Nebraska, they are not so great. If revenue is to be collected from areas of concentrated wealth and spent in proportionately larger sums in less wealthy communities, responsibility for the undertaking logically rests with the states.

Intertwined with the collection of money in one locality and spending it in another is the problem of equalization of educational opportunities. Only a few parochially minded persons now claim that because a child is born in a "backwoods" community he should be deprived of educational opportunities at least broadly comparable with those of his fellow state citizen who enters the world in a more prosperous locale. Absolute equalization may be neither practical nor desirable, but steps in that direction have constituted a major reason for the increase in state aid. Related to equalization has been increasing acceptance of the idea that each state should assume responsibility for acquiring or encouraging *minimum* standards for *all* schools within its jurisdiction. For example, a state may stipulate that no local school may receive certain state aid unless it remains open at least nine months in each year; or a state may withhold state assistance if a school is permitted to become excessively crowded, or if the ratio between pupils and teachers exceeds a stipulated maximum.

Motivation for state aid has stemmed from many other considerations, including a desire to establish new services such as guidance, to enrich existing programs, to equalize the tax burden, to improve organizational arrangements, or to encourage research and experimentation in educational practices such as special curricula for ex-

---

[21] Thurston and Roe, *op. cit.*, pp. 140–42.

ceptional children. As an alternative a state could, of course, assume direct responsibility for the provision of all public education, but there has been and continues to be a strong demand for retaining basic responsibility at the local level.[22]

Although the trend is definitely toward increased state (and federal) support for schools and the end is not in sight, there is some question as to the wisdom of this trend aside from the perennial concern over centralization. On the basis of research prepared by the U.S. Office of Education, the following observation has been made:

> Thus the public school systems which depend most heavily on property taxes and receive the smallest share of their income from state sources generally have the highest expenditure per pupil in average daily attendance and the least need for additional funds; conversely, the public school systems which depend most heavily on state support and receive the smallest share of their income from property taxes generally have the lowest expenditure per pupil in average daily attendance and need the greatest increase in school funds to bring their education to a desirable level.[23]

Although this finding by no means proves that appreciable state aid is not desirable, it at least raises a question as to the relationship between state aid and the adequacy of local schools. Furthermore, information uncovered in the same investigation revealed that "liberal property tax exemptions, property tax limitations and under-assessments are most common in high-state-support-low-local-tax-burden states. . . . State aid has often served more to lighten the burden of local taxation and to relieve local officials of an onerous duty than to support the schools."[24] There is much wisdom in the observation that "The taxes that somebody else levies and you spend are, of course, the most desirable kind."

It has been said, "He who pays the piper calls the tune." This homely observation points to the heart of a major question in public education today. How should control be devided among local, state,

---

[22] Complete centralization of the administration of schools is found only in Hawaii, but it has been approached in Delaware, where a minimum school program is financed by state funds. Special districts, created by the Board of Education, supplement state funds. Administration of schools in Wilmington is tied in with city government.

[23] Roger A. Freeman, "State Aid and the Support of Our Public Schools," *State Government,* October 1953, p. 239.

[24] *Loc. cit.*

and federal authorities? When schools were financed locally, they were also controlled locally. Increased state financial support has been accompanied by increased state regulation, a situation now generally accepted as a matter of course. The big debate now revolves around increased federal assistance and accompanying federal controls. In 1935–1936, state support of schools accounted for less than thirty per cent of total costs; twenty years later state support amounted to more than forty per cent of costs. During this same period federal support increased from one-half to approximately two and one-half per cent—not a large amount but reflecting a five-fold growth.[25] A case may be made for increased central control over education in the name of effectiveness and efficiency, but most Americans experience a feeling of uneasiness at the prospect of supervision over education moving further and further from the local community.

NATIONAL RESPONSIBILITY

"Today . . . because technological development has largely nullified state and local boundaries, because functional groups, powerful in the formulation of policy, are significantly national in character, because wealth is concentrated and economic control is centralized, and because problems have arisen that have made it necessary for the federal government to . . . become a center of activity and power, education appears to be on the threshold of an appreciable increase in federal control."[26] National support for education is no recent occurrence. The federal government began making land grants for educational purposes even before the national Constitution was adopted. Millions of acres were granted to the states without imposing federal controls on education policies. Although not related to primary and secondary education, federal controls emerged with the Morrill Act of 1862, and they were strengthened by later acts of Congress, particularly the Smith-Lever Act of 1914. Federal controls over public education at the primary and secondary levels, specifically in regard to vocational training, were inaugurated by the Smith-Hughes Act in 1917.

For the past quarter-century or more, bills have been introduced at every session of Congress to provide federal aid for schools in gen-

---

[25] See Thurston and Roe, *op. cit.*, pp. 152–153.

[26] Dawson Hales, *Federal Control of Public Education*, Teachers College, Columbia University, New York, 1954, p. 54.

eral, not merely for special aspects of education. Interest in such proposals has been noticeably sharpened in recent years, partially as a result of presidential leadership. In his State of the Union message in 1954, President Eisenhower urged Congress to make federal funds available to the states for school construction, saying "the Federal Government should stand ready to assist States which demonstrably cannot provide sufficient school buildings." In 1956, the House of Representatives debated a school construction bill to which an amendment was adopted providing that no federal funds should be allotted to any state failing to comply with the desegregation decision of the Supreme Court.[27] Costing the support of members of the House from the South, this amendment contributed significantly to the defeat of the bill. A similar bill was defeated a year later.

Launching of the Russian Sputnik in 1957 spurred nationwide interest, if only briefly, in education. Partially as a result of this event, Congress in 1958 enacted the National Defense Education Act. This act was designed to advance the cause of education at both the higher and lower levels. Federal loans were made available to college students on liberal terms, and money was appropriated to help public schools strengthen their offerings in science, mathematics, and modern foreign languages and to improve their guidance, testing, and counseling programs. In line with President Kennedy's broad program, Congress in 1964 more than doubled funds for use by the United States Office of Education to strengthen public education.

Proposals to inaugurate a large federal program to provide aid to general education as contrasted with specialized training have stirred great controversy. Many arguments pro and con have been advanced by educators, legislators, pressure groups, and many others. The major claims in behalf of federal assistance may be summarized under eight points.[28] (1) Because states differ so greatly in wealth, income, taxpaying ability, and other pertinent factors, federal aid is needed to equalize educational opportunities. (2) Judged on the basis of the proportion of tax revenues spent on education, poorer states generally exert greater efforts to provide their facilities than do richer states. This unfair situation can be remedied only by federal action. (3) Since citizens of the respective states are also

---

[27] The problem of segregation is discussed later in this chapter.

[28] See Robert L. Morlan, *Intergovernmental Relations in Education,* University of Minnesota Press, Minneapolis, 1950, p. 94.

citizens of the United States, the national government has a responsibility to see that they are provided with adequate educational opportunities. Mobility of the population stresses the national significance of the consequences of poor education. (4) Wealth should be taxed where found and services provided where needed. (5) Numerous precedents already exist to testify to the value and wisdom of federal aid. Vocational training and agricultural extension programs are generally cited as examples. (6) Functions of the national government are expanding in other areas, and its responsibilities in education should keep pace. This argument is among the weakest. (7) Increasing national taxes leave other governmental units with inadequate revenue sources. (8) Federal aid will not necessarily involve federal control.

Opponents of increased federal aid to education present a number of arguments in support of their position in addition to denying the validity and significance of the claims of the proponents. (1) Responsibility for education is reserved to the states, and this reservation should not be impaired. (2) Control of education by state and local authorities guarantees that it will be better suited to local needs than if supervised from Washington. (3) National dictation of educational practices opens the door to national regimentation of the nation's youth. (4) Federal aid will tend to weaken and destroy local initiative. (5) Increased national expenditures for education will further unbalance the national budget. (6) The states are able to do an adequate job without federal help. (7) Local school authorities might be less careful in the expenditure of money obtained from the federal government than from local taxes. (8) There exists no widespread popular demand for federal action, which has been urged upon Congress primarily by representatives of pressure groups like the National Education Association and the AFL-CIO.

Typical of the viewpoint of those who look with favor upon federal assistance is the statement of Robert Morlan that:

> Many of these arguments seem to ignore obvious situations and past experience, and insist that because perfection is impossible, improvement should not be attempted. Wealthy states have often argued that proposals for federal aid mean taking money unfairly from rich states to give to poor states, and they overlook the fact that it is not the states who pay, but the citizens, who are also citizens of the United States. It is a matter of taxpayers of the United

States providing education for children in the United States, not of one *state* giving money to another. . . .

The real bogey to the average person in this question is, however, the time-honored fear of federal control. Most people also tend to repeat as a sort of ritual the words "federal aid without federal control." Just what is meant by this varies from person to person and is rarely very coherent. . . .

One will find a few educators who are willing to say that they feel that some federal control of education would be highly desirable, by which they mean that if the purpose of the aid is to achieve minimum standards and at least reasonable equalization then there must be some enforcement of those standards. This does not imply central dictation of what and how to teach. . . .[29]

A viewpoint less sympathetic to federal aid is reflected in comments by K. B. Watson, representing the Chamber of Commerce of the United States before the House Subcommittee on General Education:

Evidence shows remarkable, and increasingly remarkable, accomplishment in construction, relatively and actually, and in improving teachers' salaries and in improving education generally. This is a trend we would expect to continue and for which our educational people in the States and communities are to be congratulated.

We believe that any "massive infusion" of Federal funds would not stimulate but would, in the long run, actually deter local effort and local interest. . . .

If they have "X" million dollars coming from the Federal government to be used for education, certainly that money will be used for education. But their own money which might have been raised for education if they had to, would probably be diverted elsewhere. . . .

If the Federal Government is going to allocate taxpayers' money . . . it must assume responsibility, in our judgment, as to how it should be used. The inevitability of Federal control is one of the principal reasons why we opposed Federal financing of public education. This leads to control eventually, we believe, of the education process itself.[30]

Similar views were expressed to the subcommittee by representatives of the American Farm Bureau Federation and the American Legion.

---

[29] *Ibid.*, pp. 94–95.
[30] Quoted in the *Congressional Digest*, June–July 1959, p. 183.

The Study Committee on Federal Responsibility in the Field of Education of the Commission on Intergovernmental Relations presented a number of interesting observations and conclusions. A majority of the Committee recognized the importance of initiative and responsibility at the state and local level and then observed, "If there is a disturbing tendency of the Federal government to assume disproportionate powers, we feel there is an equally dangerous tendency of the States and communities to neglect, and even abandon, their proper roles."[31] The Committee felt that this situation was particularly regrettable because "We have not been able to find a State which cannot afford to make more money available to its schools or which is economically unable to support an adequate school system." According to the Committee, "Research does not sustain the contention that Federal funds are essential to support the elementary and secondary school system." Recognizing the existence of differences in fiscal ability among the states, the Committee suggested that "Efforts to narrow the gap should aim at raising the economic level and the capacity of the less wealthy States rather than to subsidize them." However, no program was outlined for accomplishing this goal.

HIGHER EDUCATION

"Higher education is the formally organized process whereby our society conserves, transmits, and advances its intellectual resources. Our concept of civilization, the wellsprings of our culture, the foundation of much of our physical and material well-being, the search for truth, and the worship of God—all of these are in one way or another in some measure dependent upon higher education."[32] All levels of government have shared in organizing and supporting institutions of higher education in the United States, but primary responsibility has rested with the states.

America's first college, Harvard, was established partly as the result of an appropriation in 1636 by the Massachusetts Colonial Assembly. Nine of the nation's 1900-odd institutions of higher learning were founded during the colonial period, and their names are illustrious.[33] In addition to Harvard, they are William and Mary,

---

[31] *Federal Responsibility in the Field of Education*, p. 6.

[32] John D. Millett, *Financing Higher Education in the United States*, Columbia University Press, New York, 1952, p. 3.

[33] The Council of State Governments, *Higher Education in the Forty-Eight States*, Chicago, 1952, p. 19.

Yale, Princeton, Brown, Rutgers, Dartmouth, King's College (later Columbia), and the University of Pennsylvania. All of these institutions, excepting the University of Pennsylvania, were sectarian when established. Although each was controlled by a religious group, they all admitted students without religious restrictions. Following the Revolution, the states began to organize colleges. The curricula of these early institutions stressed classical learning in philosophy, theology, mathematics, Greek, and Latin.

Changes occurred gradually in the pattern of higher education during the nineteenth century, and developments of revolutionary proportions began to appear about the time of the Civil War. According to John D. Millett, these developments may be "epitomized in a single sentence. The college lost ground to the university."[34] Animated by a "dual vision," the universities fastened their eyes on new intellectual horizons in the belief that scientific research would bring the world under the control of man. "The university, as distinct from the college, offered graduate study and awarded advanced degrees; it promoted research activities and published learned treatises. . . ."[35] The second part of the vision concerned emphasis on the creation of a center of learning where many varied subjects were taught. Increased stress was placed on professional training in such fields as law, medicine, agriculture, and engineering. A major factor in these shifts of emphasis was the Morrill Act of 1862, providing federal assistance to the states for the support of institutions "to teach such branches of learning as are related to agriculture and the mechanic arts." With the creation of land-grant colleges "began the era of modern development in American higher education."[36] At least one land-grant college is found in each state today, and in all but four states they are public institutions. In Massachusetts, New York, New Jersey, and Pennsylvania, arrangements have been made for private institutions to implement the Morrill Act.

The "new era" witnessed a sharp departure from the traditional emphasis on "liberal education." Science, technology, and professional training were stressed, and graduates were turned out in large numbers to "find their place" in society. John D. Millett has summed up the consequences as follows:

---

[34] Millett, *op. cit.*, pp. 5–6.
[35] *Ibid.*, p. 6.
[36] The Council of State Governments, *op. cit.*, p. 19.

The promise of professional education has been abundantly fulfilled in this country; it has educated large numbers of professionally competent lawyers, doctors, accountants, architects, social workers, foresters, statisticians, engineers, and school teachers. When the process was finished, our society had acquired trained technicians and the individual had obtained a passport to a specialized means of earning his livelihood. But the professional student has failed to obtain an education along the way; he remained a cultural illiterate. Suddenly the professional schools realized they must add "humanities" to their course of study. Liberal education has been called upon to redress an obvious imbalance.[37]

Unfortunately, the imbalance still has not been redressed in many institutions of higher education, but there is a heartening conviction among a significant group of educators that all senior college and university students should be exposed to a common core of liberal education.

Central Administration. Great variety characterizes the administrative arrangements provided by the states for the supervision and control of higher education. The earlier pattern called for the creation of a separate governing board for each institution. In recent times the practice has been to place two or more institutions under a single lay board. In about a dozen states all institutions of higher learning are administered by one board. Nationally, almost three-fourths of all board members are gubernatorial appointees, while the remainder are either elected or serve *ex officio*. Often members of a single board are chosen in a combination of ways. Board members usually serve rather long terms, averaging more than five years, and overlapping terms are common. Qualifications for serving on such boards are generally not high. Requirements most often relate to residence, political party affiliation, alumni status, sex, or occupation.[38]

The authority vested in boards of higher education varies appreciably from state to state. Nevertheless, major responsibilities are normally placed in their hands. Except where legislatures make determinations by statute, the governing boards usually exercise complete control over institutional curricula, admission requirements, degrees offered and requirements therefor, and extension

---

[37] Millet, *op. cit.*, p. 15.
[38] The Council of State Governments, *op. cit.*, pp. 126–131.

programs. Subject to a variety of controls by central fiscal agencies, these boards formulate budgets for institutions under their supervision and submit them to the governor and the legislature. Legislatures commonly make appropriations for higher education in such a manner that governing boards have some control over allocations. Authority to issue bonds for capital improvements, either with or without legislative approval, is generally vested in these boards. Of course, certain limits are regularly imposed on their bonding capacity. Often governing boards have responsibilities with regard to the purchase of supplies and equipment by institutions under their supervision.

All boards of higher education exercise control over aspects of personnel management. Some of the more important tasks pertain to setting salary and wage scales; authorization of new staff positions; determination of policies with regard to tenure, vacations, sabbaticals, and leaves; recruitment of personnel and approval of new staff members; approval of promotions; and supervision of retirement programs. These functions are sometimes shared with civil service or some other state agency such as a retirement board. Also, board control over matters like approval of new staff members and promotions is purely formal in that decisions are made at the institutional level and sent to the board for approval as a matter of routine.

Oklahoma in 1941, followed by New York in 1948 and New Mexico in 1951, inaugurated a new pattern of central administration of higher education. A board was established in each of these states to coordinate the activities of all institutions of higher learning, but each institution continued to operate under the direction of existing boards. Especially wide powers are granted to the Oklahoma State Regents for Higher Education to prescribe standards for each institution, to determine courses of study, to grant degrees, to set fees within legislative limits, and to submit a consolidated budget for higher education to the legislature and allocate appropriations among the institutions. Some dozen states have placed detailed supervision of all state institutions of higher education in a single board.

Junior and "Community" Colleges. A junior college is a two-year institution that provides terminal vocational and subprofessional training beyond the secondary level as well as college preparatory work for those who plan to continue their education at a four-year institution. A "community college" is defined as a junior college with a comprehensive program of adult education. Although a few junior colleges were established during the nineteenth century, the great majority are products of the twentieth. More than 600 such institutions are now in operation, of which about half are public.[39] The great majority of public junior colleges are locally controlled and supported with state assistance. Junior colleges "bring education to the people" in that they enable many persons to benefit from advanced education and training who otherwise would be unable to do so. They also reduce the over-all costs of higher education because the relatively expensive facilities and staff of four-year institutions are not employed to instruct many freshmen and sophomores who are either not seriously interested in advanced education or who for one reason or another are unable to pursue it for more than two years beyond high school.

Municipal Colleges and Universities. Much less numerous than other types of institutions of higher education, municipal colleges and universities are operated by cities primarily to bring senior college education to their residents. A number of small colleges have become municipal institutions when local authorities chose to take them over from private hands rather than allow them to cease operation. According to the Council of State Governments, only thirteen municipal colleges and universities were functioning in 1952.[40] The first municipal college in the United States, the College of Charleston in Charleston, South Carolina, changed from private to public hands in 1837. The second such institution is also the largest today: City College, the first of the four institutions that now comprise the College of the City of New York. Some of the larger municipal colleges are found in Akron, Cincinnati, and Toledo, Ohio; Louisville, Kentucky; Omaha, Nebraska; Wichita, Kansas; and Buffalo, New York.

Federal Assistance. Although chief responsibility for higher education rests with the states, considerable help has come from the national government, which has established well-known schools, particularly West Point, Annapolis, and the Air Force Academy. More important from the standpoint of impact on education nationally have been different types of assistance extended to other institutions, both public and private. Attention already has been directed briefly

---

[39] Cf. the Council of State Governments, *op. cit.*, p. 25.

[40] *Ibid.*, p. 18. Included in this number was Wayne University, Detroit, which since then has come under state control.

to results stemming from the Morrill Act.[41] Many federal programs have been inaugurated during the present century that advance higher education. By the Smith-Lever Act of 1914 Congress provided for "agricultural extension work" to be administered cooperatively by land-grant colleges and the United States Department of Agriculture. The basic purpose of the program was and is to provide agricultural information to the farmer.

During World War I a number of temporary programs were begun. The Student Army Training Corps, for example, enlisted the help of higher education in the war effort. The national government also sponsored a small number of research programs, particularly in aeronautics. Federal assistance was provided during the depression of the 1930's through the Civilian Conservation Corps, the Works Project Administration, the Public Works Administration, and the National Youth Administration. During World War II two major federal programs were inaugurated that have greatly affected higher education. One was the "G.I. Bill of Rights" which resulted in large payments to public and private institutions to defray the costs of veterans' education. The second consisted of federally sponsored research programs. In the long view, the research programs probably had the greater impact on higher education, as they have increased in scope since the war. With the exception of agricultural research, federally sponsored research was practically nonexistent in colleges and universities prior to World War II.

Expansion of research programs under federal sponsorship has not been an unmixed blessing for institutions of higher learning. At least two major problems have emerged. One concerns the relative impact of the projects on large and small institutions. Arrangements for the great bulk of federal research have been made with large colleges and universities. As noted by Dean Sidney French of Colgate, the absence of such programs at small schools may result in a tendency for their scientific work to atrophy.[42] A second and very serious implication concerns the relationship between research and teaching, both major concerns of higher learning. Although the value of research to teaching, especially at the graduate level, is obvious, increases in research activity do not necessarily strengthen

---

[41] For a good discussion of the effects of this act, see Richard G. Axt, *The Federal Government and Financing Higher Education,* Columbia University Press, New York, 1952, Chapters II and III.

[42] Reported in the *New York Times,* December 5, 1949, p. 18.

teaching. Indeed, a regrettable fact is that very highly qualified personnel are often diverted largely, if not entirely, from teaching. Apologists for this development occasionally seek to justify it on the ground that research is more important than teaching. A detailed refutation of this claim is beyond the scope of this chapter, but its proponents are unable to answer satisfactorily this simple question: Who is to train the researchers of tomorrow?

Interstate Agreements. A device only recently applied to education is the interstate compact or agreement, which has been used in essentially two ways. One approach has been to create regional arrangements whereby the states in a particular part of the country in a sense "pool" their resources in order to provide more adequate higher education facilities for their respective residents. The Southern Regional Education Compact of 1948 was the first of its type. The compact created a board with membership from each of the participating states.[43] In illustration of the way the plan works, a member state, unable to provide first quality professional training of all types, enters into an agreement with the board to place certain of its residents seeking specialized training in, for example, medicine or dentistry. A participating state accepts the students, and on the basis of a contractual agreement the first state agrees to pay a sum of money to help defray the costs of their training. Students from each participating state pay resident fees at the institutions of other member states. However, the compact does not enable students to attend an institution in another state on this favored basis if they are able to obtain the training they seek in their own state.

In 1951 the legislatures of Colorado, Montana, New Mexico, Oregon, and Utah ratified a compact providing for the Western Interstate Commission for Higher Education.[44] Although it has not functioned as effectively as its southern prototype, the Commission is designed to act as a clearinghouse for a contract program and to assess the resources of the West in higher education in relation to its present and future needs. Recently, the New England states have taken steps to establish a similar arrangement in that part of the country. Regional cooperation in higher education is definitely in

---

[43] The participating states include Alabama, Arkansas, Florida, Georgia, Kentucky, Louisiana, Maryland, Mississippi, North Carolina, Oklahoma South Carolina, Tennessee, Texas, and Virginia.

[44] Thirteen states have joined the Western Regional Education Compact: Alaska, Arizona, California, Colorado, Hawaii, Idaho, Montana, Nevada, New Mexico, Oregon, Utah, Washington, and Wyoming.

the experimental stage, but experience thus far indicates that it possesses a great deal of promise.

The second way in which the interstate agreement has been applied to higher education has been through agreements between two states for the use of specified facilities. In 1944 the University of West Virginia was authorized to contract with the Medical College of Virginia to admit a number of West Virginia students so that they might complete their medical studies. West Virginia agreed to pay a portion of the cost of training each student. Similarly, in 1950 Wyoming authorized the negotiation of contracts with out-of-state schools to provide Wyoming students with training in medicine, dentistry, veterinary medicine, and nursing. Such bilateral arrangements do not appear to be as satisfactory an approach to providing facilities for higher education as the regional compact.

PROBLEMS

Far too many problems face education today for them even to be catalogued in a few pages. However, attention should be called to a few major controversies relating to educational policy. Education shares with other governmental functions many difficulties pertaining to finances, organizational arrangements, political control, and relations among levels of government. These matters are considered at other places in the text.

Desegregation. Few, if any, persons in 1938 appreciated the portent for public education of the United States Supreme Court's decision in *Missouri ex rel. Gaines* v. *Canada*.[45] Lloyd Gaines was a resident of Missouri and a graduate of Lincoln University, an institution maintained by the state for the higher education of Negroes. Although academically qualified, Gaines was denied admission to the University of Missouri Law School simply because he was colored. Obtaining no relief from the courts of Missouri, Gaines appealed to the U.S. Supreme Court on the ground that the refusal of admission constituted a denial by the state of equal protection of the laws contrary to the Fourteenth Amendment of the U.S. Constitution. The Supreme Court ruled that the offer by Missouri to provide Gaines a legal education *outside* the state was not the equivalent of admitting him to the state's law school and concluded that he was entitled to be admitted "in the absence of other and proper provision for his legal

---

[45] 305 U.S. 337 (1938).

training within the State." It is important to note that this case and others dealing with similar circumstances did *not* outlaw segregation in education.[46] They merely held that in the field of higher education the states must provide equal or at least comparable facilities for the education of whites and Negroes.

Although these cases may in a sense have "foretold" the outlawing of segregation on the basis of race in public education, they did not soften the impact of *Brown* v. *Board of Education of Topeka, Kansas,* decided in 1954.[47] In an opinion dealing with public primary and secondary schools, the Supreme Court held that "in the field of public education the doctrine of 'separate but equal' has no place. Separate educational facilities are inherently unequal." Recognizing the tremendous implications of its decision, the Court directed gradual desegregation and turned the supervision of the process over to federal district courts in the states involved.

It is impossible to express in a few words the impact of the *Brown* case on the educational systems in the South.[48] Integration has proceeded gradually and calmly in the border states. In other places, like Little Rock, Arkansas, efforts by local school authorities to take steps toward desegregation have met with violent opposition. In still other states insignificant steps have been taken to comply with the Supreme Court's ruling. Instead, through constitutional amendments and legislative enactments, some states have declared a firm determination to postpone integration indefinitely. One thing is certain. Many years will pass before the schools in the South will be patterned after a declaration by the Supreme Court contrary to the deeply ingrained customs and fervent beliefs of dominant segments of the population.

Quantity and Quality. As noted earlier, there was a great increase in the proportion of the nation's youth in public schools during the first half of this century. A similar growth occurred in higher education. In 1900, only about four per cent of persons between eighteen and twenty-one years of age were enrolled in institutions of higher learning. In 1950, the number was around twenty per cent,

---

[46] *Sipuel* v. *Board of Regents,* 332 U.S. 631 (1948); *Sweatt* v. *Painter,* 339 U.S. 629 (1950).

[47] 347 U.S. 483.

[48] For detailed information see *Southern School News,* published monthly by the Southern Education Reporting Service; and *Race Relations Law Reporter,* published by Vanderbilt University School of Law.

and it has continued to increase.[49] There appears no reason to assume the upward trend will not continue. Many persons are asking, Are there limits? If so, what should they be?

Education must compete with other governmental services for the resources of the nation. Consequently, the quality of public education at all levels is largely determined at any one time by the proportion of resources that are allocated to it. Limits, both economic and political, exist. Decisions must be made as to the primary goals to be achieved. Thus in recent times the chief goal in primary and secondary education has been to get as many as possible of the young people under a certain age into school. The first concern has been for the provision of physical plants to house the multitudes, and the second has been for the acquisition of teachers. There are indications that a similar hierarchy of concerns has developed in higher education.

The President's Commission on Higher Education went on record in 1947 to the effect that education through the junior college level (sophomore year) should be made available in the same manner as high school education.[50] The Commission emphasized education for citizenship and democracy, but it did not face up to the implications of its suggestion that two years should be added to the twelve now considered standard for public schools. The costs in money and effort would be nothing short of staggering. Also, implementation of such a proposal would add impetus to the idea that every person, regardless of capacity and interest, is "entitled" to advanced education. It would blur even further any distinction between the functions of higher education and those of common schooling provided in the primary and secondary grades.

On the other hand, there are signs of an increasing recognition of the value of quality as well as quantity in public schools and in higher education. Arrangements are being made with increasing frequency for special classes and enriched curricula for superior students. If the nation is to make the best use of its most valuable resources, the talent of its citizens, such action is imperative. The problems associated with such a program are insignificant in comparison with the importance of the goal to be achieved. Without special treatment, the ablest youngsters become bored, stale, and

---

[49] See John D. Millett, *op. cit.,* pp. 38–39.
[50] *Higher Education for American Democracy,* vol. I.

disillusioned with education. They also become accustomed to functioning at a level far below their capacity.

Without selective admissions at the college level, numbers may become overwhelming, and then this characteristic may indeed be an apt description of higher education: "College tends to become a grand holiday, a pleasant resort, a kind of happy interlude in life. Any student seriously interested in his studies is a 'grind' and a 'bore.' In this kind of atmosphere the intellectual purposes of higher education are compromised and even abandoned."[51] If the task of higher education is to help the gifted and the interested students to develop their capacities to the greatest degree, available resources must not be absorbed in efforts to stimulate the uninterested and discover means of graduating the mediocre. Persons who reach college age unable to spell, unable to calculate, unable to read, and uninterested in what they would learn if they could, are a heavy burden upon those who wish to seek the truth and make it known to those interested in learning.

The Impact of Education. A study of the values of American college students concludes that "A dominant characteristic of students in the current generation is that they are *gloriously contented* both in regard to their present day-to-day activity and their outlook for the future."[52] This attitude exists in spite of the large number of problems with which the government is wrestling. Furthermore, international problems do not appear to interest them, and except for voting, "they are content to abdicate the citizen's role in the political process and to leave to others the effective power of governmental decision. They are politically irresponsible, and often politically illiterate as well."[53] Although not characteristic of all students, it appears that these attitudes are found among a very large proportion of them.

Clearly, if value is to be received for the vast sums of money and untold man-hours spent on education, much work is needed to define more accurately and consistently the immediate purposes and the long-range goals. Also, techniques for achievement must be more closely examined. Consideration needs to be given, for example, to the role of the teacher. If teaching is important, steps must be taken to rescue the profession from its "underdog" status. If students need

---

[51] John D. Millett, *op. cit.,* p. 44.
[52] Philip E. Jacob, *Changing Values in College,* Harper & Brothers, New York, 1957, p. 1.
[53] *Ibid.,* p. 3.

more freedom to pursue individual interests, they must be prepared to assume this responsibility. If, on the other hand, more rigid requirements in areas such as mathematics, languages, history, and government are needed, steps should be taken to inaugurate them. Education served cafeteria-style may be no better for the young mind than food served in the same manner before the youngster learns the ingredients of a balanced diet.

SELECTED REFERENCES

Books:

American Assembly, *The Federal Government and Higher Education,* Prentice-Hall, Englewood Cliffs, N.J., 1960.

American Association of School Administrators, *School District Organization,* Washington, D.C., 1958.

Axt, Richard G., *The Federal Government and Financing Higher Education,* Columbia University Press, New York, 1952.

Babbidge, Homer D., and Rosenzweig, Robert M., *Federal Interest in Education,* McGraw-Hill, New York, 1962.

Benson, Charles S., *The Economics of Public Education,* Houghton Mifflin, Boston, 1961.

Butts, R. Freeman, and Cremin, Lawrence A., *A History of Education in American Culture,* Holt and Co., New York, 1953.

Conant, James B., *Education and Liberty,* Harvard University Press, Cambridge, 1953.

Council of State Governments, *Higher Education in the Forty-Eight States,* Chicago, 1952.

Good, H. G., *A History of American Education,* Macmillan Co., New York, 1956.

Hagman, Harlan, *The Administration of American Public Schools,* McGraw-Hill, New York, 1951.

Hales, Dawson, *Federal Control of Public Education,* Teachers College, Columbia University, New York, 1954.

Keezer, Dexter M., editor, *Financing Higher Education, 1960–70,* McGraw-Hill, New York, 1959.

Knight, Douglas (ed.), *The Federal Government and Higher Education,* Prentice-Hall, Englewood Cliffs, N.J., 1960.

Lieberman, Myron, *The Future of Public Education,* University of Chicago Press, Chicago, 1960.

MacKinnon, Frank, *The Politics of Education,* University of Toronto Press, Toronto, 1960.

Millett, John D., *Financing Higher Education in the United States,* Columbia University Press, New York, 1952.

Moos, Malcolm, and Rourke, Francis E., *The Campus and the State,* Johns Hopkins University Press, Baltimore, 1959.

Morlan, Robert L., *Intergovernmental Relations in Education,* University of Minnesota Press, Minneapolis, 1950.

Nevins, Allan, *The State Universities and Democracy,* University of Illinois Press, Urbana, 1962.

Thurston, Lee M., and Roe, William H., *State School Administration,* Harper and Brothers, New York, 1957.

Articles:

Benton, E. Maxwell, "Better Schooling, Less Cost," *National Municipal Review,* November 1949.

Chisholm, Leslie L., "School District Reorganization Today," *State Government,* May 1956.

Cocking, Walter D., "The Role of the States in Education Since 1900," *State Government,* June 1950.

Freeman, Roger A., "Challenge: Education," *National Civic Review,* January 1959.

——, "State Aid and the Support of Our Public Schools," *State Government,* October 1953.

"Higher Education under Stress," Symposium, *The Annals,* September 1955.

Larsen, Roy E., "What Is Being Done About the School Building Crisis?" *State Government,* May 1955.

Wescoe, W. Clarke, "Expansion and Excellence: A Choice in Higher Education?" *State Government,* Autumn 1964.

CHAPTER 27

Agriculture and Natural Resources, Highways, and Planning

Some state activities may be classed as "developmental" in nature. These are the functions which, in contributing to the well-being of all citizens, deal with the physical character and capability of a state, particularly those activities that concern natural resources and the productivity of land. Development of a system of roads and highways is also included. A large and rapidly growing population has made increasing demands on the nation's resources. Consequently, government has been called upon to promote the intelligent use and development of natural resources. In accomplishing this important task, governments have found long-range planning to be an essential factor in conservation and development.

AGRICULTURE AND NATURAL RESOURCES

The blessings of mankind most likely to be taken for granted, and thus ignored, are those provided by nature. Throughout most of American history the usual practice has been to increase both quality and quantity of agricultural produce, but at the same time natural resources have been exploited with little thought for the future. Only since the turn of the twentieth century has anything like intelligent conservation of such resources as forests, soil, minerals, and water been practiced. During this period the nation and states alike have been active in promoting conservation.

The National Role. There is no doubt that national efforts overshadow those of the states in regard to agricultural and other resources. National programs are carried on primarily under the powers to regulate commerce, raise and spend money, and administer the public domain. In some instances national activities are conducted as purely national programs; others are cooperative ventures with state and local governments. Many national programs in these areas date well back into the nineteenth century, but many, particularly in the field of conservation, represent efforts undertaken after 1900.

The scope of federal activity is extremely broad and involves many different agencies. Within the Department of Agriculture, for example, various agencies conduct programs in agricultural marketing, price stabilization, extension of agricultural credit, and conservation. Programs relating to fish and wildlife, mineral resources, water and power development, and public land management are carried on in the Department of the Interior. Credit is made available to farmers and farm groups by the various lending agencies within the Farm Credit Administration. The Tennessee Valley Authority is active in developmental programs in the southeastern part of the country. Other agencies such as the Tariff Commission, Federal Trade Commission, and Federal Power Commission also influence developmental programs. The many federal agencies and their field organizations active in developmental programs affect virtually every aspect of agriculture and resource utilization.

State and Local Organization. State organization for the administration of programs in the fields of agriculture and natural resources is typically fragmented; that is, the functions performed by a state in these areas are usually scattered among various agencies. Even in states like Alaska, Hawaii, and New Jersey, which are organized according to the principles of "good" administration, not all functions pertaining to agriculture and natural resources are grouped in a single, integrated department.

The principal state agency in the general field of resource development is the department of agriculture, an agency known by a variety of titles across the nation.[1] It usually is headed by a single director appointed by the governor, although in some states the office is elective, and in others a board is used. The functions of departments of agriculture vary widely. Included in a usually long list of duties are enforcement of food inspection laws, control of plant and animal diseases, inspecting and grading farm produce, issuance of various licenses, conducting research programs, rendering advice, registering agricultural products, inspecting weights and

[1] See *Book of the States, 1964–65.* The section entitled "Natural Resources" is a survey of recent developments in agriculture and conservation of resources. The *Agricultural Yearbook,* published by the United States Department of Agriculture, provides much useful information in this field, as does the Department of Commerce's *Statistical Abstract of the United States,* which is also published annually.

measures, eradicating insect pests, conducting fairs, operating prisons and prison farms, and compiling market reports. Some of these responsibilities are performed in cooperation with the national government, but most are solely state functions.

In addition to the department of agriculture a state may have a large number of agencies that administer one or more functions that an integrated department might perform. Conservation activities, for example, are carried on by separate agencies in three-fourths of the states, and some states have separate conservation agencies for different resources. Among the states are found numerous commissions for licensing, inspecting, and grading agricultural products and natural resources—agencies such as livestock boards, plant commissions, fish commissions, and forestry boards.

Local organization in agriculture and natural resources is, for the most part, the result of state or federal programs. For example, about 2,950 local conservation districts have been formed under a cooperative federal program. County agents who act as consultants to local farmers are available as a result of federal-state-local cooperation. Counties, towns, and townships sometimes maintain fish wardens, forest fire watchers, and veterinarians. Also, special districts for the purpose of draining land, weed control, irrigation, and flood control are common.

Resource Programs. In general, the economic well-being of a nation depends upon its natural resources. Wasteful utilization of resources can lead to their depletion and thus contribute to dependency on other countries. To avoid this danger the national government and the states have inaugurated conservation programs, some of which are cooperative federal-state ventures. Through such efforts it is possible to achieve more intelligent use of nonrenewable resources such as metals, oil, and gas, and to avoid unnecessary waste of those that can be replaced.

Soil Conservation. One of the basic resources of any country is its soil, for from the earth comes practically all of man's food supply. For generations Americans paid little attention to soil conservation. The country was vast, the population relatively small, and the danger of soil depletion seemed remote. "Worn out" farms were abandoned. Erosion by wind and water took its toll. By the 1930's and the years of the "Dust Bowl" droughts, soil depletion had become a real problem. It has been estimated that 300 million acres of formerly useful land lay ruined as a result of erosion and misuse.

After detailed research and inquiries, Congress enacted the Soil Conservation Act of 1935.[2] Under the stimulus of this law all states have enacted legislation creating conservation agencies and permitting establishment of local soil conservation districts that work with the federal Soil Conservation Service. The local districts are created as a result of application to the state agency by interested farmers and a favorable vote in a public referendum in which affected farmers and ranchers cast ballots. Each district is headed by an elective board of three to five members. Today there are about 2,950 districts that include ninety-seven per cent of all farms and ranches in the United States.

The Soil Conservation Service works with local districts, aiding and instructing them in techniques of preserving and building up soil fertility and productivity. Federal personnel work not only with district officials, but also directly with individual farmers. The general program must be regarded as successful, even though it has been in operation only thirty years, much too short a period to repair the damages of generations of neglect.

Water. The importance of water resources is obvious, for water, like soil, is necessary to the existence of man. Throughout the history of the world, civilization has flourished only in fertile, well-watered areas. Until recent years water conservation was not a problem in the United States and still is not in some areas. However, in densely populated, heavily industrialized areas and in regions requiring irrigation, conservation of water has assumed urgent proportions.

Although the states are active in conservation of water resources, national efforts are definitely predominant. Through its power to regulate commerce among the states, the federal government exercises control over all navigable streams in the country.[3] Federal control over such streams has been implemented since 1920 largely by the Federal Power Commission. State projects involving navi-

---

[2] Other federal programs designed primarily for other purposes have direct effects upon soil conservation. For example, the 1957 soil bank program was intended as a method of reducing agricultural surpluses and was an essential feature of the agricultural price stabilization program. By the same token federal legislation pertaining to conservation of forests, water, and wild life affect soil conservation.

[3] Federal authority was held in *The Daniel Ball,* 10 Wall. 557 (1871), to include control over rivers used "or susceptible of being used, in their ordinary condition, as highways for commerce." Federal authority was expanded in *United States* v. *Appalachian Electric Power Company,* 211 U.S. 377 (1940), which held that a stream is navigable if by improvements it can be made so. Further, federal control was not limited to navigation, but was recognized as including flood control, watershed development, and development of hydroelectric facilities. For detailed discussion of state activities in conservation of water resources, see Council of State Governments, *State Administration of Water Resources,* Chicago, 1957.

gable waters must, therefore, be cleared through that agency. There have been few instances of conflict over the past forty years, and the national government has followed a policy of encouraging state action.

Paramount federal control has not caused the states to abandon the problem of water conservation. On the contrary, state action is both lively and comprehensive. The Federal Power Commission cooperates by issuing licenses for power projects only after state power agencies have given their approval. Much state effort is directed at insuring adequate supplies of water through construction of watersheds, determination of water rights, and regulation of water use. Problems of flood control and pollution of rivers and bodies of water are also of major concern to the states. These water problems are usually interrelated and are frequently associated with federal projects and programs. Regional water problems requiring interstate cooperation have been increasingly dealt with in recent years by means of interstate compacts. At present, about thirty such agreements, all but a half-dozen administered by permanent interstate commissions, are in effect.

Forests. Forests are one of America's most valuable resources. Not only do they provide building materials, fuel, and wood products, they also support wildlife and help to prevent floods, droughts, and soil erosion through their capacity to hold moisture. For years the nation's forests were cut without concern for depletion. Vast acreages were consumed by fire. Conservation efforts of the last half-century have checked the worst abuses, and forest acreage is slowly increasing. Today, the total area of forest lands in the United States is approximately 770,000,000 acres.[4]

Conservation of forest resources at the state level is largely a result of national efforts during the past fifty years. In performing the significant task of preserving and developing forest resources, practically every state has established some kind of agency to further forest conservation. Some states, especially those with large forests areas, are well organized for this function, while in others small independent agencies or departmental subdivisions do little more than attempt to prevent forest fires.

---

[4] The United States Forest Service classes 530 million acres of these forest lands as capable of producing usable crops of wood, and indicates that nearly 70 per cent of the commercial acreage is privately owned. See the *Statistical Abstract of the United States*, 1964, pp. 679–692, and William J. Stahl, "State Forestry Administration," *Book of the States, 1964–65*, pp. 510–515.

Beginning in 1911 and continuing down to the present, the national government has developed conservation programs in which forest owners, both public and private, may participate. Under federal grants-in-aid states are assisted in the prevention and control of forest fires, reforestation projects, extension of forestry education, controlling some plant diseases, and eradication of insect pests. Technical aid in these areas was extended in 1950 to private owners of forest lands and to processors of forest products. All but a few states cooperate with the U.S. Forest Service through which these programs are conducted.

Mineral Resources. The poorest conservation record of the states is in regard to minerals. Except for mineral deposits under lands owned or controlled by the national government, little has been done to check depletion of these non-renewable resources.[5] Conservation of oil and natural gas has received state attention, but they are the only mineral resources about which the states have done anything of note. Metal ores and coal have been largely ignored, although tax and safety laws have had incidental effects in the promotion of conservation.

Measures to curb waste of oil and gas appeared in the states as early as the 1880's. Pennsylvania and New York, followed soon by other states, enacted laws during that period to prohibit wasteful practices such as allowing seepage of water into wells, burning of gas, and crowding of wells.[6] Today virtually all oil-producing states have laws of this sort and cooperate with each other to conserve oil and gas resources. Thirty-three states now work together for this purpose under the Interstate Oil Compact Commission organized in 1935.

In 1914 Oklahoma introduced *proration*—a policy whereby oil production quotas are assigned to producers essentially on the basis of production capacity and market demand. Other states followed Oklahoma's example during the early years of the Depression,[7] and

---

[5] The national government reaches mineral operations on state and private lands through its powers to tax and to regulate interstate commerce. These powers have been used to regulate, to some extent, the extraction, processing, and transportation of minerals and mineral products. Even so, severe criticism of federal actions have been voiced, particularly in regard to the liberal depletion allowances permitted in taxation of mineral extraction—allowances that encourage rapid exploitation of resources.

[6] The power of the states to enact laws of this type was upheld by the United States Supreme Court in *Ohio Oil Company* v. *Indiana,* 177 U.S. 190 (1900).

[7] *Champlin Refining Company* v. *Corporation Commission of Oklahoma,* 286 U.S. 210 (1932), was the case in which prorationing was upheld by the United States Supreme Court.

Congress strengthened them by prohibiting oil produced in excess of state quotas—"hot oil"—from interstate commerce. Proration served during the depression to improve market prices, and many states were undoubtedly attracted to proration for that reason, but whatever the motivation for its adoption proration is an effective tool of conservation.

A development of more than usual interest was the "tidelands" oil controversy of a decade ago. The national government and the states disputed control of the oil under the lands of the three-mile coastal belt. In *United States* v. *California*,[8] decided in 1947, the Supreme Court held that paramount rights to the oil belonged to the federal government. In 1953, however, Congress returned jurisdiction over resources in the marginal seas to the states after two earlier attempts to do so, in 1946 and 1952, had been defeated by presidential vetoes. Today, petroleum resources in the controversial tidelands remain under state control.

Fish and Game. Of all state efforts in the conservation field probably none has been more successful than those devoted to the protection of wildlife. Fish and game laws date back to colonial days, but it was not until the last half of the nineteenth century that state agencies began to appear. New Hampshire's fish commission created during the Civil War and broadened to include game in 1878 was, in the modern sense, the first state wildlife protection agency. Other states adopted the New Hampshire approach and, stimulated by national activity from 1871 on, more than two-thirds of the states instituted active conservation agencies by the turn of the century. Fish and game agencies now exist in every state either as independent establishments or as divisions of departments. Some states maintain fish commissions and game commissions, and a few have two fish commissions, one for fresh water and another for salt water fish.

Basically the same conservation activities are followed in all states with differing emphases according to the nature of a state's resources. Variations are based, for example, on such factors as whether a state is large or small, inland or coastal, northern or southern, mountainous or level, heavily forested or barren. The principal methods used in fish and game conservation are requirements that licenses or per-

---

[8] 332 U.S. 19 (1947). Later suits involving oil lands off the coasts of Texas and Louisiana produced similar results. *United States* v. *Louisiana,* 339 U.S. 232 (1950); *United States* v. *Texas,* 339 U.S. 707 (1950). The struggle for control of the tidelands is related in Ernest R. Bartley, *The Tidelands Oil Controversy,* University of Texas Press, Austin, 1953.

mits be obtained by hunters and fishermen, restrictions on the length of hunting and fishing seasons, imposition of bag limits, maintenance of fish hatcheries, game farms and game refuges for wildlife propagation, destruction of predatory animals, and operation of research and public education programs. The success of these efforts over the past seventy-five years is indicated by the fact that in many states the wildlife population, or at least that of some species, is much greater than it was when active conservation programs were begun.

Education and Research. Each of the fifty states conducts programs of research and education to promote agriculture and conservation. A large number of pursuits are followed, ranging from making graduate study available in state universities to staging state agricultural fairs. The states themselves carry the burden of much of the work, but the main areas of activity are cooperative programs between the nation and the states. There are now about seventy land grant colleges and universities at which basic research is carried on. These institutions were originally established under the national Morrill Act of 1862 which granted to the states portions of federal land for support of the colleges on condition that instruction be offered in "agriculture and mechanic arts." Another federally assisted activity is the maintenance of an agricultural experiment station in each state. These installations are operated in conjunction with the land grant colleges and are a principal means by which the results of agricultural research are tested. A third cooperative state-federal program is the extension service found in each state. Under this program the results of research are taken to the farmer through home demonstrations and county agricultural agents.

HIGHWAYS

The United States today is webbed by a tremendous network of more than 3.5 million miles of public roads and streets. Every populated area or section of the nation is accessible by means of one or more modern, surfaced highways. In terms of both quality and quantity this system is unmatched by any other country. Perhaps the most remarkable facts concerning the American highway system are that it has been built largely by state and local governments and primarily within the last fifty years.

Early roads in the United States were little more than wagon ruts in the woods. The most impressive road project during the early nineteenth century was the Cumberland Road, or Great National Pike, a national effort begun in 1806 that extended from Cumberland, Maryland, westward to Vandalia, Illinois. Most long-distance travel was accomplished on the nation's waterways. With the coming of transcontinental railways the demand for overland highways subsided. The national government withdrew from roadbuilding,[9] while the states and local governments continued to provide only such local roads as were necessary or popularly demanded.

It was not until the advent of the motor vehicle that insistent demands for improved highways were heard. A curiosity at the beginning of the twentieth century, the automobile quickly became common. So rapidly did the automobile become the general means of private travel that roadbuilding could not keep up with popular demands. In 1916 the federal government re-entered the highway picture by making available $75 million in grants to the states over a five-year period to expedite construction. From that modest beginning a comprehensive grant-in-aid program has developed by which federal funds are employed in the construction and maintenance of virtually all major highways in the United States.

Highway Administration. Building and maintaining roads are responsibilities borne by the national, state, and local governments. The federal government actually builds roads only in areas that it administers directly or when such activity is essential to federal projects and installations. Federal participation in general highway building takes the form of grants-in-aid, with the states performing the task of road construction. Funds granted by the national government must be supplemented by state funds, and conditions as to state administrative organization, use of funds, inspection, and auditing, are imposed. Administration of the federal program is centered in the Bureau of Public Roads located in the Department of Commerce.

State organization for highway development dates from 1891 when New Jersey established a system of state aid to local units of government for road building. In less than thirty years, by 1917, every state had created a road agency. During that period most states began to build highway systems, and with the establishment of the

---

[9] Even today the national government itself builds very little highway mileage and directly controls slightly less than 100,000 miles of roads. This mileage consists of roads and streets in national forests, national parks, territorial possessions, the District of Columbia, and those essential to federal projects.

federal grant program state construction and control became standard practice. Today each state has a highway commission or department that cooperates with the Bureau of Public Roads and exercises some control over local efforts.

Local responsibility for rural road building rests in a majority
of states with counties, but in some it is divided between counties
and townships. In New England local road functions are performed
by towns. Traditionally, local governments maintain boards rather
than single officers for purposes of road administration. The importance of these local boards is attested by the fact that almost 2.5 million miles of rural roads are under local control. State supervision
ranges from advice and recommendations to relationships in which
local road boards do little more than carry out instructions of the
state agency. In only four states have local governments been divested of all control over roads. North Carolina, in 1931, placed
responsibility for building and maintaining *all* roads in its state
agency. Since then similar action has been taken in Delaware, Virginia, and West Virginia.

City streets, except those constituting extensions of highways, are
controlled by municipal authorities. Municipalities do not maintain
separate administrative boards for construction and maintenance of
streets. Instead, the governing body, the council or commission,
makes the decisions as to where and when new streets are built, subject in many instances to remonstrances by property owners. When
a highway goes through an incorporated place, control of the streets
over which it passes is shared by the municipal governing body and
the state highway agency.

Financing Highways and Streets. Raising money to finance highways is based, to a great extent, on the idea that those who use the
roads or are specifically benefited by them should bear the principal
responsibility of paying for them.[10] Thus states characteristically
impose a tax upon motor fuels and earmark the proceeds for highway
finance. Other income is realized from automobile tags and drivers'
licenses. Property taxes constitute a major source of revenue for
road construction and maintenance at the local level, with special
assessments the usual method of paying for streets in municipal corporations. State and local borrowing is also a common method of
raising funds for highway construction. In fact, a third of state long-

---

[10] See Chapter 15 for discussion of methods of raising money for road construction.

term debt—over two billion dollars—represents highway indebtedness.

In general, the manner in which a roadway is financed is deter-mined by its classification.[11] About a fifth of the nation's rural high-ways are included in the "federal aid system" and are constructed and maintained by the states in cooperation with the national gov-ernment under grant-in-aid programs. Other rural roads are paid for by the states and local governments. City streets, as noted above, are usually financed by means of special assessments. The cost of toll roads is met, at least in part, by the proceeds of fees paid by users.

The National System of Interstate and Defense Highways. In the Federal Aid Highway Act of 1956 Congress provided for a 41,000-mile network of superhighways to be constructed over a fifteen-year period. These multiple-laned, divided, limited-access highways eventually will connect forty-two state capitals and nine-tenths of the cities with populations in excess of 50,000. The cost of this system of superhighways will be approximately $50 billion and will be met by the national government and the states. The lion's share of the financial outlay is to be borne by the federal government, for under the grant-in-aid provisions now in effect the states assume responsi-bility for only ten per cent of the costs.

Primary Highways. That portion of the federally aided highways known as the primary system consists in each state of a network of connected main highways. These roads are designated by state high-way officials subject to the approval of the Secretary of Commerce, and their combined length in a state cannot exceed seven per cent of the state's total highway mileage. Primary highways may be located in urban as well as rural areas. Most states match federal funds dollar-for-dollar in financing primary highways although in states where there are large amounts of untaxed public lands the federal share is increased.

Secondary Highways. Included in the secondary system of fed-erally aided highways are more than a half-million miles of rural roads that interlace and interconnect the primary system. Selected by state highway officials with approval of the Secretary of Commerce, this system includes many farm-to-market roads, rural mail routes, and county and township roads. Federally assisted on a 50–50 basis,

---

[11] For purposes of convenience and uniformity, the designations of roads discussed here are those used in the administration of federal grants-in-aid as set forth in 23 U.S. C. 103. States may and do use their own systems of classification.

secondary highways are confined almost entirely to rural areas. Urban roads can be included only if a state has a population density of 200 per square mile and an urban extension of a secondary highway connects inside an urban area with an Interstate or primary highway.

Local Roads. Throughout the fifty states there are almost 2.5 million miles of rural roads that are not included in the federal aid system. These are county and township roads that trail through the countryside connecting farms and small rural communities with routes that lead to county seats. Many of these roads are surfaced, but hundreds of thousands of miles are merely graded dirt roads or covered perhaps by gravel or a film of oil. As already indicated, four states assume responsibility, including financial liability, for local roads. Elsewhere the basic responsibility for building and paying for local highways rests with counties and other units of rural local government.

Toll Roads. Modern state-operated toll roads made their appearance in Pennsylvania when, in 1940, the first section of a 400-mile turnpike was opened. Since then almost 2,300 miles of toll highways have been constructed and financed by appropriations from current tax revenues, by borrowing, sometimes partially with federal funds, or a combination of these. Tolls are charged to offset original costs. Since 1956 there have been no new authorizations of toll roads, and two states, Iowa and Washington, have cancelled projected toll roads. Disappointing yields from tolls, a possibility that Congress may eventually require reimbursement of federal funds used in toll road construction, and the effects of the 41,000-mile Interstate program are responsible for sagging interest in new toll roads.

City Streets. Special assessments ordinarily are employed by municipal corporations to pay for city streets. Charges are assessed against property adjacent to or near a street on the theory that such property is benefited or increased in value by construction of the roadway. Many variations are used throughout the country, with cities sometimes paying part of the cost in view of the fact that all municipal residents benefit from street improvements. Some city streets, such as those in public parks, zoos, and golf courses, are paid for out of general revenues. Occasionally, streets are built by private persons, usually in accordance with city specifications. Also, streets that double as urban highway extensions are financed in part by state and federal funds.

HIGHWAY SAFETY

Over the last decade about 40,000 persons have been killed and more than another million injured every year in motor vehicle accidents. In just two years more people are killed and injured on the nation's highways and streets than have been listed as casualties in all the wars in which America has fought! In their efforts to check this slaughter the states and local governments have adopted numerous restrictions upon drivers and vehicles.

State and local traffic regulations control almost every aspect of motor vehicle operation, especially the speed at which cars, trucks, and buses may be driven. Licensing requirements are enforced to keep inept drivers off the roads. Inspection laws are designed to bar mechanically deficient and overloaded vehicles from traffic. Safety campaigns and driver education programs are conducted. "Crackdowns" or periods of especially strict enforcement of traffic rules are occasionally undertaken to emphasize the need for highway safety. All states now have "financial responsibility" laws whereby drivers involved in accidents must show insurance coverage or post cash security against possible damage claims or lose their driving privileges. New highways are now being designed with a view to reducing the number of accidents by eliminating railway grade crossings, providing traffic separators, broadening shoulders, flattening hills, modifying curves, lighting dangerous areas, and similar refinements.

Despite the efforts of government, deaths, injuries, and property loss due to accidents remain high. Stricter laws and more assiduous enforcement of traffic regulations appear to afford only temporary reduction. The only effective way to bring about significant improvement lies in attacking the source—the driver. By instilling in him an awareness of the consequences of accidents, perhaps through better educational and instructional programs, the nation's traffic record can be improved.

PLANNING

State and local governments perform a great many functions in serving the interests and regulating the activities of their citizens. More than a half-million elected office holders and several million employees and appointed personnel are organized into thousands of boards, commissions, departments, offices, and agencies to administer numerous programs. The activities of some officers and agencies are integrated with, or by law are contingent upon, those of others, but many functions are carried out with little or no reference to other, associated programs. Under such circumstances important programs may work at cross purposes resulting in wasted effort, time, money, and resources. Consequently, governments need to devote attention to the task of outlining, from an over-all viewpoint, what should be done and how best to do it—in other words, to planning.[12]

Several factors are essential to successful planning. First, definite *goals* must be identified and defined. They must be realistic and determined in the light of available physical and human resources. Next, a plan must be *comprehensive*. Omission of some functions or agencies from consideration defeats the purpose of planning. Third, good planning is *long-range* in character. Finally, plans must be *adaptable,* for there are always developments that cannot be anticipated even by the most competent planner, including such things as technological advances, war, and election results.

Planning of a sort has always existed in government. In one sense, a statute is a plan. So is a program of work laid out by an administrative agency. Such "planning," however, is nothing more than the foresight needed to do a day's work or to see a single program through to completion.

State Planning. Planning as a state function enjoyed a few brief years of general acceptance during the depression of the 1930's and then faded into the limbo of forgotten functions. In 1931 only four states had planning agencies, but after the federal government established the National Resources Committee[13] and offered the states financial assistance in setting up planning bodies, every state except Delaware responded by 1936. The state agencies flourished until prosperity began to return and World War II diverted attention to matters of defense. Today, with modest federal financial assistance available for planning functions, most states have revived or strengthened their planning agencies.

The activities of a planning board include research and analysis,

---

[12] A sampling from various sources on planning is found in Albert Lepawsky, *Administration,* Alfred A. Knopf, New York, 1949, pp. 492–536.

[13] The name of the Committee was changed successively to National Resources Board, National Planning Board, and National Resources Planning Board. It ceased to function in 1943.

coordination of programs, promotion of state attractions, and advice and assistance to local planning groups. A planning body is essentially a staff arm whose basic purpose is to advise the executive and legislature. Despite its obvious value, planning has been regarded with suspicion during the past twenty-five years or so because of popular association with the dictatorial planning employed in totalitarian countries. Consequently, state planning agencies have been severely limited in the scope of their activities and in some cases have functioned primarily as state promotional agencies.

City Planning. In contrast to state planning, city planning is ancient. There is evidence that planners were at work over 5,000 years ago in the cities of Egypt and Mesopotamia.[14] Examples of early city planning in the United States include the laying out of Philadelphia by William Penn in 1682 and Pierre-Charles L'Enfant's plan for Washington, D.C., prepared in 1791.

City planning differs from state planning in that the local variety is concerned primarily with the physical aspects of development. City planners are interested not only in beautification of municipalities through use of boulevards, parks, and city centers, but also in the correction and prevention of problems of a practical nature. Coping with such problems as traffic congestion, promoting industry, planning for adequate water and sewage disposal systems, eliminating blighted areas, and contending with smog illustrate the array of matters considered by local planners. Today most cities over 10,000 population have established planning commissions and enacted ordinances designed to implement planning.

The usual pattern followed by municipalities in effectuating planning is establishment of a planning commission that recommends action to the governing body which in turn, at its discretion, enacts the necessary ordinances. Organization and procedures vary from city to city, but adequate planning at the municipal level always involves two essential features: a master plan and a zoning ordinance. A master plan is, as the name implies, a long-range plan providing for all aspects of municipal development. A zoning ordinance divides the municipality into land-use districts in accordance with the master plan. Zoning ordinances cannot eliminate existing inconsistencies

---

[14] Charles M. Kneier, *City Government in the United States*, 3rd ed., Harper & Brothers, New York, 1957, p. 571.

with master plans, but they do provide that future land-use must accord with them.

Metropolitan and Regional Planning. For all practical purposes, municipal authority to plan stops at the city limits, but frequently the need for planning extends far beyond them.[15] In fact, since most people in the United States live in metropolitan areas with millions residing in suburban areas around central cities, planning logically should transcend municipal boundaries. It is only within recent years that planning agencies have begun to emerge in these areas, and although now found in a large number of metropolitan centers, significant implementation of their findings and proposals has not yet been achieved.

One of the major stumbling blocks in metropolitan planning is the fact that each local government is a distinct legal entity and often jealous of its powers and status. Cooperation is necessary, yet the selfish interests of each unit of government must be given consideration. Consequently, the questions of how much authority a metropolitan planning body should have and how its recommendations should be implemented are difficult to resolve. County planning may work well in lieu of a metropolitan authority, particularly if a county contains all or most of the area in a metropolitan population center. Even more satisfactory as an alternative is a joint city-county planning agency, of which there are now some two dozen.

Regional planning ignores state boundaries. A true regional planning agency would plan for an area such as the Ohio Valley, the Missouri Valley, or the territory covered by the Great Plains states in much the same way that a state agency operates within its jurisdiction. Regional planning bodies obviously must be established either by the national government or by interstate agreements. There are no regional planning agencies in existence, but some bodies exercise functions that might be placed in the hands of regional planners. The developmental functions of the Tennessee Valley Authority, for example, fall into this category as do the activities of interstate commissions dealing with pollution of rivers and allocation of water resources.

---

[15] Municipalities are permitted the exercise of some authority beyond their boundaries. For detailed treatment of this subject see Russell W. Maddox, *Extraterritorial Powers of Municipalities in the United States,* Oregon State University Press, Corvallis, 1955.

SELECTED REFERENCES

Books:

Benedict, Murray R., *Farm Policies of the United States, 1790–1950,* Twentieth Century Fund, New York, 1953.

Ciriacy-Wantrup, S. V., *Resource Conservation: Economics and Policies,* University of California Press, Berkeley, 1952.

Clawson, Marion, Held, R. Burnell, and Stoddard, Charles H., *Land for the Future,* Johns Hopkins University Press, Baltimore, 1960.

Council of State Governments, *State Administration of Water Resources,* Chicago, 1957.

Netschert, Bruce C., *The Future Supply of Oil and Gas,* Johns Hopkins University Press, Baltimore, 1958.

Ordway, Samuel H., Jr., *Resources and the American Dream,* Ronald Press, New York, 1953.

Tyler, Poyntz, editor, *American Highways Today,* H. W. Wilson, New York, 1957.

Wengert, Norman, *Natural Resources and the Political Struggle,* Doubleday Co., Garden City, N.Y., 1955.

Articles:

Augur, Tracy B., "Planning Assistance: A Growing Service for Cities," *State Government,* June 1958.

Ball, Charles, "The States and Regional Planning," *State Government,* Summer 1959.

"Highway Safety and Traffic Control," Symposium, *The Annals,* November 1958.

McConnell, Grant, "The Conservation Movement—Past and Present," *Western Political Quarterly,* September 1954.

Meier, Richard L., "Systems and Principles for Metropolitan Planning," *Centennial Review,* Winter 1959.

"Perception and Natural Resources," Symposium, *Natural Resources Journal,* January 1964.

"The Poverty Problem in American Agriculture," Symposium, *Journal of Farm Economics,* May 1964.

"Public Power in the United States," Symposium, *Current History,* May 1958.

"United States Agriculture: Policy, Politics, and the Public Interest," Symposium, *The Annals,* September 1960.

"Water Resources," Symposium, *Law and Contemporary Problems,* Summer 1957.

CHAPTER 28

Business and Labor

Today hardly an activity in the business world escapes governmental regulation. Entrepreneurs and laborers alike are subject to numerous controls by the national, state, and local governments. While regulation is extensive, governments at all levels also perform a variety of services in the interests of business and labor.

Acting under its delegated powers, particularly its authority to tax and to regulate interstate commerce, the national government has enacted a broad range of laws that affect business and labor.[1] Within the limitations of superior federal law the states also have imposed numerous controls based most often upon the police power which permits regulation for the protection of the public health, safety, welfare, and morals. Local governments also impose regulations, basing their actions upon powers derived from the states.

Federal regulations and services present such a wide variety of actions that no recognizable general pattern can be identified. Included in the list of regulations are such activities as granting corporation charters, issuing licenses and permits, enacting tax laws that inhibit various business practices, prohibiting monopolies, proscribing unfair labor and trade practices, controlling the supply of raw materials through conservation programs, fixing postal rates, controlling transportation and communications, setting tariffs, enforcing patent and copyright laws, controlling exports, regulating the value of currency, affecting interest rates, policing the investment and banking field, defining rights of organized labor, imposing minimum wage standards, and limiting hours of work. Business and labor are affected by federal services such as compiling statistics and collecting data on prices, markets, and unemployment, paying subsidies and price supports, lending money, forecasting weather conditions, pro-

---

[1] In addition to its powers to tax and to regulate interstate commerce, the national government has made extensive use of the "war powers" particularly in times of emergency. Among other federal powers that have frequently been used as the basis of regulatory action are the postal, currency, patent and copyright, and bankruptcy powers.

tecting rights of inventors and authors, providing facilities for settling labor disputes, promoting foreign trade, and conducting employment service programs. Federal ownership and management of government corporations, control and sale of public lands, and construction and operation of dams and hydroelectric facilities also have a profound effect upon business and labor.

The multiplicity of federal activities suggests the impression that there is little if anything left for the states and local governments to regulate! It would be unrealistic to deny that federal regulation of economic pursuits predominates over that of the states. However broad the delegated powers of the federal government, they do not furnish legal basis for *all* necessary or desirable regulation. Interstate commerce does not include all economic activity. Nor does federal authority include a general police power. Consequently, state and local governments are quite active in the regulation of business and labor.

STATE REGULATION OF BUSINESS

Organization. Each state has a large number of departments, boards, commissions, and offices that are responsible for enforcement of regulations pertaining to designated aspects of business. No state maintains a central department in which are collected all such functions, nor would such an arrangement be desirable. There are so many different types of businesses and such a wide variety of business practices that a single agency could not hope to do a competent job. Consequently, state authority to regulate businesses and business practices is implemented by a profusion of administrative bodies.

Government Ownership. Although there are many examples of public ownership and operation of business enterprises, the practice is not prevalent.[2] Popular resistance to government competition with private enterprise serves as an effective check on proposals for governmental business activities. Nevertheless, states and local governments conduct various types of business enterprises, sometimes in direct competition with private firms and sometimes under conditions of monopoly. There are no discernible trends in public

---

[2] Some functions now considered properly governmental in character were at one time, and in some cases still are, performed by private concerns. During the early years of the Union road construction was commonly undertaken by private agencies. Postal service was rendered briefly by the famous "Pony Express." Today, garbage and waste disposal services in some municipalities are performed by private companies.

ownership either at the state or local level. No surge of expansion is apparent; neither is there strong demand for its contraction.

State business ventures are not numerous. Seventeen states exercise monopolies in the liquor business. Operation of toll roads, toll bridges, tunnels, and port facilities are common state enterprises. The best known state organization in this respect is the Port of New York Authority, a New York–New Jersey corporation that controls and administers docks, terminals, airports, and related facilities. Among the fifty states North Dakota is unique in terms of its commercial interests, operating a bank, a system of mills and grain elevators, a land-sales agency, and a casualty and bonding insurance business.

It is at the local level, particularly among municipalities, that public ownership is most apparent. Most cities today own and operate their water supply systems, and power utilities are public property in many municipalities. Other activities of a commercial nature that are undertaken by local governments include the operation of waste disposal facilities, airports, transit systems, wharves and docks, slaughterhouses, public markets, golf courses, auditoriums, stadiums, and swimming pools.

Public ownership has been subject to attack, especially by individuals and groups who must compete with government enterprises. A long list of arguments are cited, the major ones being that public ownership is destructive of the free enterprise system, it puts "politics" above good business practices, and it creates powerful pressure groups within government. Those who favor public ownership reply that it is undertaken in the public interest and ordinarily only when private enterprise fails to serve that interest. As in so many other problem areas neither viewpoint is wholly correct. It is, in fact, necessary to examine individual situations to determine the validity of claims and counterclaims.

REGULATION OF GENERAL BUSINESS PRACTICES

Each state has laws that regulate practices and procedures common to all business enterprises. Some are general laws that affect business as well as other elements of society; others are designed specifically to regulate business activities as such. In the first category, for example, are the laws on ownership, sale, and transfer of property; the laws that regulate the making of contracts; tax legislation of all descriptions; zoning ordinances; regulations promoting conservation of natural resources; and the general criminal law. The most important measures regulating business practices directly are those which (1) are designed to control entry into business, (2) prevent monopolies and unfair trade practices, and (3) prevent and punish dishonest and fraudulent business practices.

Entry into Business. Before a group of individuals can do business as a corporation they must obtain a *charter*. Charters conferred by states[3] are usually issued by the secretary of state although the function is sometimes lodged in a special administrative agency. The conditions under which a corporation must operate are set forth in its charter. Since charters are legally regarded as contracts that may not be impaired under the national Constitution,[4] the states are careful to see that they contain clauses permitting subsequent necessary modification. Intended as a means of controlling corporate activity, restrictions contained in charters are not as effective as they might be, and in some states they are quite lax. This is due primarily to a desire to attract new businesses and, in some states, to increase the yield of taxes placed on the privilege of doing business. A generation ago New Jersey's incorporation laws were such that numerous corporations sought charters there. Today new corporations tend to favor Delaware charters.

A corporation is referred to as a "domestic" corporation in the state in which it is incorporated. In all other states it is regarded as "foreign." This distinction is important since it affects business activities that cross state boundaries. As an artificial person a corporation does not enjoy the right of citizens to enter other states at will as guaranteed by Article IV, Section 1, of the national Constitution. A corporation engaged *solely* in interstate commerce may enter into business in any state, provided the business it conducts is not prohibited. Such a corporation can use the mails, advertise, send salesmen into various states, and utilize common carriers in carrying on its operations. However, should a foreign corporation do *local* (intrastate) business within a state, it is subject to whatever restrictions and conditions the state places on foreign corporations within

---

[3] Congress also has authority to grant charters to corporations. National banks and government-owned corporations, for example, are incorporated by Congress.

[4] Article I, Section 10. The contract nature of corporation charters was set forth in the early case of *Dartmouth College* v. *Woodward*, 4 Wheaton 518 (1819).

its borders. The line between interstate and local commerce is often hazy, but a business takes on "local" characteristics if it involves establishment of facilities such as local sales and service agencies and warehouses.

Going into business often involves procedures in addition to obtaining a charter, and, of course, when the corporate form is not used a charter is unnecessary. Some businesses such as power companies, banks, common carriers, and insurance firms may be incorporated only after receiving a permit or certificate from a special regulatory administrative agency. Partnerships, while regulated by state law, do not operate under charters. State and local governments alike regulate professions and occupations by means of licenses and permits. These matters relate to special business activities, however, and are discussed later in the chapter.

Regulation of Competition. Statutes and constitutional provisions designed to prevent monopolies exist in practically all states.[5] These regulations, some of which predate federal antimonopoly legislation, may be in the form of general prohibitions of all activities that tend to curtail competition, or they may be directed at specifically designated practices. State antimonopoly legislation has not been effective for two reasons. First, there are no special enforcement agencies. Attorney generals ordinarily are given responsibility for seeing that antimonopoly laws are obeyed although suits may also be instituted by private individuals. The second and principal reason stems from the interstate character of most modern, large businesses. Since most firms that are able to create monopolies operate in more than one state, and the power to regulate interstate and foreign commerce is vested in Congress, national leadership has dominated the field.

Since the early 1930's there has been a continuing controversy involving so-called *fair trade* laws. Such laws provide that agreements may be reached between manufacturers and retailers whereby the retail prices of the manufacturer's products may be fixed. Most contain a provision that when one or more dealers enter into such agreements the prices determined are binding upon *all* dealers who handle affected products. These "nonsigner" provisions make fair trade

---

[5] Not all monopolies are forbidden, nor would such a policy be wise. In some instances the public interest is most effectively served through legal monopolies, particularly in regard to utilities.

laws effective and at the same time stimulate controversy. At one time or another fair trade laws have been in force in forty-five states.

Congress removed the possibility of conflict of state fair trade laws with national power to regulate interstate commerce by approving the Miller-Tydings Act of 1937 specifically exempting fair trade agreements from federal anti-monopoly legislation. The 1937 act did not mention nonsigner provisions, however, and in 1951 the United States Supreme Court reversed the conviction of a New Orleans retailer who, as a nonsigner, had refused to be bound under Louisiana's fair trade law.[6] The following year Congress passed the McGuire Act which bound nonsigners in interstate commerce if by state law they were bound in intrastate commerce. In 1953 the Supreme Court refused to review a court of appeals decision in favor of the Act.[7]

Those who favor fair trade laws contend that they make it possible for small merchants to compete with larger ones. Opponents insist that they violate the idea of free enterprise and are, in fact, nothing more than *price-fixing* statutes. Controversy has resulted in litigation in many states. To date, about a fourth of the fair trade laws have either been declared void or the essential nonsigner provisions invalidated.

Prevention of Fraud. Most states now have laws designed to prevent and punish certain unethical business practices. False or misleading advertising, for example, is commonly prohibited. Labeling laws require that representations appearing on labels must be factual. Usury legislation regulates the maximum interest rates that may be charged, and the content of sales contracts is often fixed by state specification. New stock and security offerings are policed by the states. The effect of many such laws, although they are framed in general terms, is to regulate special businesses. In some instances they complement similar federal legislation. For example, the laws enforced by the Federal Trade Commission and the Securities and Exchange Commission affect interstate advertising and investment practices.

REGULATION OF SPECIAL BUSINESSES

Some business enterprises bear a more intimate relationship to the general well-being of society than do others. Obviously, provision

---

[6] *Schwegmann Brothers* v. *Calvert Distillers Corporation,* 341 U.S. 384 (1951).

[7] *Schwegmann Brothers* v. *Eli Lilly and Company,* 346 U.S. 856.

of electricity or transportation facilities is more important to the general public than manufacturing toys and paper clips. Business activities that are essential to general welfare are said to be "affected with a public interest" and thus subject to a greater degree of regulation than ordinary commercial ventures. The United States Supreme Court declared over three-quarters of a century ago that property is:

> clothed with a public interest when used in a manner to make it of public consequence, and affect the community at large. When, therefore, one devotes his property to a use in which the public has an interest, he, in effect, grants to the public an interest in that use, and must submit to be controlled by the public for the common good, to the extent of the interest he has thus created.[8]

A principal difficulty in applying such a criterion arises from the fact that some enterprises bear a closer relationship to the public interest than others. Utilities, banks, insurance companies, common carriers, and the like have been closely regulated on the basis of their obvious relation to the public welfare. The public interest rationale breaks down under analysis, however, for some enterprises that are extensively controlled do not exhibit intimate involvement with the public interest while others performing vital services escape detailed regulation. For example, the newspaper business is intimately associated with public well-being but is not legally regarded as "affected with a public interest." Conversely, the liquor trade, which is not vital or necessary, is subjected to more intense control than are most commercial ventures. By way of assessing the current utility of the public interest approach, it is probably accurate to say that "every business is affected with a public interest to whatever extent Congress or a state legislature chooses to make it so."[9]

Public Utilities. The type of business subjected to the most extensive regulation is probably the utility. Utilities provide necessary and essential services such as gas and electric power, public transportation, telephone service, water supply, and sewage disposal. They tend to be "natural monopolies," for effective competition in the

---

[8] *Munn* v. *Illinois*, 94 U.S. 113, 126 (1887).

[9] Kenneth C. Davis, *Administrative Law*, West Publishing Co., St. Paul, 1951, pp. 117–118.

utility field is uneconomical and, in most instances, physically undesirable, if not impossible. Utilities are frequently governmentally
owned and operated, especially for the provision of water and electricity, but most are in private hands. The national government
shares in the function of utility regulation when interstate commerce
or federal facilities are involved. Federal agencies of importance in
this area are the Interstate Commerce Commission, Federal Power
Commission, Federal Communications Commission, and Securities
and Exchange Commission.

Each state maintains an agency for utility regulation. A commission of three to seven members, usually appointed by the governor, performs this function except in Oregon and Rhode Island,
where single commissioners are used. The powers of utilities commissions are broad, including the authority to decide who shall provide what services, what the standards of service shall be, when and
under what conditions service may be expanded or contracted, and
the rates that may be charged. Private utilities operating in local
communities are subject to regulation by state utilities commissions.
Government-owned local utilities must observe various restrictions
imposed by state agencies, but are largely controlled by local governing bodies.

Although virtually every phase of utility operation is subject to
some degree of control, probably the most important regulatory task
—and also the chief problem—is setting rates. Utilities must be permitted a reasonable profit, but the rates must also be reasonable.
Balancing these two basic considerations is difficult. The problem is
compounded by various factors that detract from the technical
competency of regulation. Partisanship often leads to the appointment of personnel who are not qualified, and popular election leaves
competence largely to chance. Low salaries and uncertain tenure
discourage able persons who might otherwise be interested. Inadequate authority and small budgets also hinder effective regulation.
These shortcomings must be corrected before substantial improvement in the quality of regulation can be expected.

Securities Regulations. For many years the investment field was
a fertile and profitable hunting ground for swindlers and confidence
men. *Caveat emptor,* a common law principle meaning "let the buyer
beware," was the rule of the day. The appeal of quick profits in
speculative stocks made many investors unwary and resulted in the

enrichment of many unscrupulous promoters. "Blue-sky" laws designed to protect investors, or at least help them make wiser decisions, have been enacted in practically all states.[10] Rhode Island in 1910 and Kansas in 1911 enacted the first securities regulation statutes. Other adoptions came slowly but were accelerated by increased losses to swindlers during the prosperous 1920's. Today all states except Nevada and Delaware have blue-sky laws.

Blue-sky laws usually deal with three phases of security regulation. First, new issues of stocks and securities must be approved by state officers before being offered for sale. Second, dealers in securities must be registered or licensed. Third, fraud provisions prescribe penalties for various prohibited activities in the investment field. Enforcement is undertaken in some states by securities commissions, but in most the function is assigned to an agency or department performing a related function or to the secretary of state or attorney general. Results at the state level have not been impressive because of the interstate nature of many stock swindles. Since 1934 the federal Securities and Exchange Commission has enforced national securities regulation laws on an interstate basis. National and state agencies, acting cooperatively, have effectively reduced the volume of investors' losses to dishonest promoters.

Banking. Commercial banks in the United States may be chartered either by the states or national government.[11] Regardless of charter derivation, however, banks doing business within a state are subject to the state's banking regulations. National banks, in addition, are regulated under national law as are state banks that elect to affiliate with the Federal Reserve System and the Federal Deposit Insurance Corporation. In the event of conflicting regulations, national rules prevail.

Two-thirds of the states have banking departments headed by

---

[10] The term "blue sky" is attributed to a Kansas legislator who, in supporting the 1911 bill that became that state's securities regulation act, is supposed to have remarked that some brokers were so unethical that they would sell shares in "the bright blue sky."

[11] Commercial banks are the general purpose institutions that receive deposits, maintain savings accounts, extend trust and escrow services, make loans and investments, and other banking operations. They contrast to such specialized banking organizations as savings institutions, credit unions, small-loan companies, and mortgage associations. There are about 14,000 commercial banks in the United States, of which two-thirds are state incorporated. The easiest way to distinguish state and national banks is by their corporate titles, for the name of a national bank must include the word, "national."

single administrators known as commissioners, secretaries, or examiners. Arrangements in the remaining states present a variety of
administrative forms, including a few regulatory boards. The functions of a typical banking department range from issuing charters
to new banks to the enforcement of regulations that affect practically
every aspect of banking practice. One of the most effective tools of
banking regulation is the audit. Each state maintains a staff of bank
examiners whose job is to inspect the accounts of banks.

Although states exercise important functions in the regulation of
banks, national control has increased considerably over the last century. National banks were authorized by the National Banking Act
of 1863. The Federal Reserve System, created in 1913, extended
national authority. State failures with deposit insurance laws and the
large number of bank failures during the early years of the Great
Depression led to the establishment, in 1933 of the Federal Deposit
Insurance Corporation. Since most state banks have some connection
with these or other federal agencies and programs, national authority
over state banks is extensive.

Insurance. Virtually every phase of the insurance business is
strictly regulated by the states. In each state there is an administrative
agency, usually headed by an appointive commissioner, for the enforcement of the regulatory laws. Insurance companies must obtain
licenses to sell various types of insurance, and out-of-state companies
must deposit large reserves with the commissioner as a guarantee that
claims within the state can be met. Individual agents must also be
licensed. Investment of company assets is closely controlled by the
state. Rate-setting has not developed into a general practice, but
state agencies can order reduction of rates considered unreasonable
or discriminatory. In some instances, as in fire insurance, rates have
been governmentally fixed.[12]

The national government does not participate directly in regulating the insurance business. A Supreme Court decision in 1869
held that insurance was not interstate commerce even if sales were
made across state boundaries, and thus could not be regulated by
Congress.[13] This attitude prevailed until 1944 when, in an antimonopoly prosecution of a group of insurance companies, the seventy-

---

[12] The power to fix rates was upheld by the United States Supreme Court in *German Alliance Insurance Company* v. *Lewis,* 233 U.S. 389 (1914).

[13] *Paul* v. *Virginia,* 8 Wall. 168.

five year old doctrine was reversed.[14] Almost immediately, however, Congress enacted legislation exempting insurance firms from federal antimonopoly legislation. To date Congress has declined to authorize national regulation of the insurance business although it has the power to do so.

Small Loans. One aspect of moneylending that is attended by special problems is the small loan. Such loans involve small amounts and are usually secured by personal property such as furniture or automobiles and sometimes only by the promise of the borrower to repay. The high risks involved discourage conventional lending institutions, particularly since usury laws do not permit high enough interest charges to compensate for losses on bad loans. As a result borrowers may, in the absence of protective state laws, fall prey to "loan sharks," lenders willing to loan small amounts at exorbitant rates of interest. All but a few states now have laws which fix the maximum rates of interest that may be charged on small loans. There is a great deal of variation among the states, but a typical law provides for a descending scale of rates as the amount of a loan increases.

Liquor. Because of the relationship of alcoholic beverages to popular concepts of morality, the liquor trade is subjected to strict regulation. Three basic systems of control are used: (1) prohibition, (2) government monopoly, and (3) licensing. Prohibition, employed on a state-wide basis only in Mississippi, outlaws the manufacture, transportation, and sale of all beverages containing more than a specified amount of alcohol. National prohibition was effected in 1920 when the Eighteenth Amendment became a part of the United States Constitution. Approval of the Twenty-first Amendment in 1933 returned to the states the freedom to decide whether to continue prohibition. State monopolies exist in seventeen states, although in Wyoming it operates only at the wholesale level.[15] In North Carolina the state monopoly is operated through the counties. The licensing system involves sales by private persons operating under state licenses.

---

[14] *United States* v. *Southeastern Underwriters Association,* 322 U.S. 533.

[15] States exercising monopoly control of liquor are Alabama, Idaho, Iowa, Maine, Michigan, Montana, New Hampshire, North Carolina, Ohio, Oregon, Pennsylvania, Utah, Vermont, Virginia, Washington, West Virginia, and Wyoming.

None of these systems of control constitutes the only method of regulation within a state. Even in "dry" Mississippi, for example, beers and wines of low alcoholic content are sold by licensed dealers. The monopoly states generally license private clubs, hotels, and restaurants to sell liquor by the glass. In most states relying on the license system, and in some monopoly states as well, "local option" laws permit local governments to decide whether to adopt prohibition within their boundaries. Other regulatory actions include assessment of taxes, forbidding sales to minors, imposing closing hours, and limiting the number and types of liquor outlets.

REGULATION OF PROFESSIONS AND TRADES

In the interest of maintaining high standards of performance, many professions are subjected to more or less extensive control. There is no precise yardstick by which to determine the extent to which a given profession ought to be regulated, but the general criterion is the degree to which a profession is considered related to the general welfare. Thus medicine is virtually completely controlled with only slightly less attention paid to other aspects of the healing arts. Law, engineering, architecture, accounting, realty, and teaching are also regulated in considerable detail. Many states also exercise appreciable control over such occupations as plumbing, contracting, midwifery, funeral direction, barbering, and the like. The authority of a state to regulate professions in pursuance of its police powers is unquestioned so long as regulatory statutes are reasonable.

The usual pattern of administration in the regulation of professions and trades involves an examining and licensing board for the enforcement of applicable provisions of law. These boards are appointive and consist largely of active practitioners in the field regulated. Meetings may be held at regularly scheduled times, or as necessary, with routine administration handled by a full-time executive secretary. In two-thirds of the states such boards are independent agencies, while in the remainder the licensing function is centralized in a single licensing department containing specialized examining boards or committees. In some centralized licensing departments issuance of licenses is virtually automatic upon favorable recommendation of examining boards, an arrangement that approximates the usual decentralized practice.

The powers of examining and licensing boards are extensive. Within the context of enabling statutes they determine standards of admission and performance. They devise and administer examinations by which applicants must demonstrate their qualifications and then grant or refuse licenses. Should a licensed practitioner fail to perform on a par with established standards the board has authority to suspend or revoke his license.

Regulation at the local level is confined largely to the occupations known as "trades" as distinguished from "professions." Thus plumbers, electricians, masons, mechanics, and builders are often required to obtain occupational licenses. Local regulation is secondary to state provisions and must yield in the event of conflict. The extent of local regulation varies from place to place with the greatest incidence occurring in large cities.

STATE REGULATION OF LABOR

When America was primarily an agricultural nation there were no labor problems in the modern sense. Most industrial products were manufactured by self-employed craftsmen, and when factories existed they were small, with individual workers negotiating terms of employment. With the coming of industrialization, however, the small factory gave way to large plants, mass production became the rule, hordes of laborers moved to the cities to be near the factories, and labor problems became more important. Today both nation and states have enacted many statutes in quest of solutions to the problems of labor. These laws may be divided into two basic groups. One group relates to labor organization and activity; the second pertains to standards and conditions of labor.

Organization. State administrative organization for labor regulation takes many forms. In most states agencies responsible for the enforcement of labor statutes have been gathered into a department of labor. Such departments usually are headed by a single appointive administrator although some are elected, while in a few states boards are used. Some state labor departments contain only a few agencies and possess little or no jurisdiction over others. Thus agencies administering workmen's compensation laws or unemployment compensation statutes may operate independently of the department.

LABOR ORGANIZATION AND ACTIVITY

The history of organized labor in the United States goes back to the closing years of the eighteenth century. Local unions existed before 1800, but there was no appreciable growth of unionism before the Civil War. During these early years the growth of labor unions was impeded by judicial acceptance and application of the common law concept that such organizations were illegal conspiracies in restraint of trade. This ancient doctrine quickly faded, however, after the Massachusetts supreme court recognized the legality of labor unions in 1842.[16] The first labor organization to achieve national importance was the Knights of Labor, an organization begun as a secret society in 1869. Membership was open to all workers and by the mid-1880's exceeded 700,000. Failure to win key strikes and inability to attract strong political support led to the demise of the Knights, and by 1900 the union had lost its effectiveness.

Today's American Federation of Labor and Congress of Industrial Organizations began in 1881 as the Federation of Trades and Labor Unions. The Federation bitterly opposed the Knights of Labor and in 1886 rallied other unions to form the American Federation of Labor. The AFL was a federation of *craft* unions, each of which contained members skilled in the same trade. Over the years dissatisfaction arose among leaders of the federation over the question of taking in *industrial* unions—those composed of all workers, skilled and unskilled, in a single industry. Finally, in 1938, after expulsion from the AFL, a group of labor leaders established the Congress of Industrial Organizations. Almost twenty years later, in 1955, the rupture was healed and the two unions reunited as the AFL-CIO.

Nearly a fourth of the 75,000,000 persons who make up the American labor force are members of labor unions. About eighty-five per cent of these union members are in the AFL-CIO, with the remainder belonging to various independent unions. The percentage of union membership may seem low, but the effectiveness of unions does not depend upon numbers alone. Included are workers in all of the nation's basic crafts and industries, a fact that gives organized labor tremendous economic and political strength.

Collective Bargaining. The term "collective bargaining" refers to a method of negotiation whereby representatives of labor organi-

---

[16] *Commonwealth* v. *Hunt*, 45 Mass. 111.

zations and representatives of employers work out agreements in regard to terms and conditions of employment. This process relieves the individual laborer of the task of trying to win favorable terms of employment by his own efforts. Collective bargaining strengthens organized labor, for if a union can speak for all or at least a large number of an employer's workers, it is in a favorable bargaining position.

At the time when unions won general legal recognition they were not effective organizations. Rivalries and bickering within the ranks of labor deprived the over-all movement of the strength that comes with solidarity. Another important reason for union impotency was the fact that employers were not legally required to bargain collectively. The position of unions was further weakened by the practice of "blacklisting" union leaders, making it difficult for them to find employment. Many workers could find jobs only by signing "yellow-dog" contracts that made employment conditional upon not joining a union. It was common practice for employers to discriminate against union members in regard to wage, hiring, and firing policies. Frequently, employers operated company unions to prevent recruiting by labor unions. Labor's most effective weapon, the strike, was often negated or even prevented by resort to injunctions issued by courts of equity.

State efforts in behalf of labor during the first thirty years of the twentieth century were sporadic. It was not until the national government enacted a series of labor laws during the 1930's that state labor legislation began to accumulate. The Norris-LaGuardia Act of 1932 prohibited the use of injunctions as a means of enforcing yellow-dog contracts. The National Industrial Recovery Act of 1933 provided that workers "shall have the right to organize and bargain collectively," and similar language was included in the Guffey Coal Act of 1935, but both statutes were struck down by the Supreme Court.[17] The Wagner Act of 1935, sometimes referred to as the "Charter of American Labor," contained not only a solid guarantee of the right of collective bargaining but also prohibited a number of "unfair labor practices" including refusal by employers to bargain

---

[17] The N.I.R. Act was held unconstitutional in *Schechter Poultry Corporation* v. *United States*, 295 U.S. 495 (1935), and the Guffey Coal Act was set aside in *Carter* v. *Carter Coal Company*, 298 U.S. 238 (1936). An earlier federal law which guaranteed collective bargaining rights in the railroad industry, the Railway Labor Act of 1926, was upheld in *Texas and New Orleans Railway Company* v. *Brotherhood of Railway and Steamship Clerks*, 281 U.S. 548 (1930).

with the recognized representatives of organized employees. It also created the National Labor Relations Board, an independent agency before which disputes over alleged violations of the unfair practices provisions could be heard and decided. The national Wagner Act applies only to interstate commerce, of course, but about a fourth of the states have enacted "little Wagner Acts" applicable to intrastate labor-management relations. Most of the states without general legislation have enacted various provisions dealing with an assortment of "unfair labor practices."

The Right to Strike. The ultimate weapon at the disposal of organized labor is the strike. Labor's right to resort to this drastic measure is now generally recognized. However, unions are not altogether free to use the strike when, where, and however they please. Strikes may be carried out only for a legal purpose and in a lawful manner.

A strike, or threat to strike, is used most commonly to achieve higher wages, shorter hours, and improved working conditions. However, a strike called to gain these legitimate objectives may be halted if strikers indulge in threats or acts of violence, coercion, or intimidation. The strike may not be used in connection with forbidden labor practices. For example, a strike to force an employer to hire only union members is illegal in states that outlaw the "closed shop." Forcing an employer to refuse to do business with another employer, the "secondary boycott," is commonly prohibited. "Jurisdictional strikes" to compel an employer to accept a striking union as bargaining agent rather than another labor organization are frequently forbidden. In states that have imitated the "cooling off" provision of the national Taft-Hartley Act of 1947 strikes may not be called during a compulsory waiting period. Several states specifically forbid the "sit down" strike that flourished briefly during the 1930's.[18] Other areas in which strikes of any type are, or may be, generally forbidden relate to government employment and to essential industries, particularly during times of emergency.

Open, Closed, and Union Shops. Regulations pertaining to hiring practices determine whether a place of employment is an *open,*

---

[18] Sit-down strikes in which strikers refuse to vacate the premises on which they work were declared illegal as applied to industries subject to federal regulation in *National Labor Relations Board* v. *Fansteel Metallurgical Corporation*, 306 U.S. 240 (1939).

closed, or *union* shop. An open shop is one in which the employer is free to hire whomever he pleases regardless of prospective employees' union status. Furthermore, employees are not compelled at a later time to join a union. A closed shop exists when only union members may be hired. Jobs in a union shop are available to non-union members who must, as a condition of employment, join a recognized union within about thirty to sixty days.

The Taft-Hartley Act outlaws the closed shop in employment subject to federal regulation. Union shops are permitted if approved by a majority of workers in a place of employment, *except in states that prohibit union shops.* Today, nineteen states have statutes or provisions in their constitutions called "right to work" laws that prohibit agreements requiring union membership as a condition of employment.[19] A dozen such laws were in existence at the time the Taft-Hartley legislation was enacted.

Organized labor bitterly opposes "right to work" laws, contending that they are designed to weaken unions and that they have the effect of extending to nonunion members the benefits of collective bargaining that are made possible by union efforts. Proponents insist that "right to work" laws preserve the freedom of individual choice in regard to union membership and have the salutary effect of forcing unions to improve themselves in order to attract members. Popular reaction and legislative response to these arguments seems to correspond in rough approximation to the strength of organized labor in the respective states. Of the entire list of states with "right to work" laws Indiana is the only one that can be classed as heavily industrialized. In every other industrial state where "right to work" laws have been proposed, they have been defeated.

Mediation, Conciliation, and Arbitration. Practically all states provide means to facilitate the settlement of disputes between labor and management. In most instances assistance is offered in the form of *conciliation* and *mediation* whereby a neutral third party attempts, through suggestions, to help disputants to resolve their differences. No attempt is made to force a decision upon the parties in disagree-

---

[19] Right to work laws may also forbid *agency shop* agreements. Under these agreements employees are required to pay fees, equal in amount to union dues, to a union in return for the union's services as bargaining agent. The United States Supreme Court, in *Retail Clerks International Association* v. *Schermerhorn,* 375 U.S. 96 (1963), ruled unanimously that the Taft-Hartley Act permits states to outlaw union security agreements of the type represented by the so-called agency shop.

ment. Generally, conciliation and mediation are synonymous with the only practical difference, if indeed there is any, being that a conciliator takes a more active part in face-to-face conferences. *Arbitration,* on the other hand, is a process in which disputants agree before negotiations begin to accept as binding the decision reached by the arbitrator. Experience with these procedures has been disappointing, for only on infrequent occasions have they been employed successfully.

In 1920 Kansas enacted a statute imposing *compulsory* arbitration upon most essential industries. Two United States Supreme Court decisions within the next five years so narrowed the application of the act, however, that it was quickly repealed.[20] At present a few states have compulsory settlement laws that apply only to utilities. Doubt has been cast on their usefulness by a 1951 Supreme Court ruling that Wisconsin's statute was invalid because of conflict with national authority to regulate interstate commerce.[21] In view of the intense opposition of both organized labor and a great many employers to compulsory arbitration, it is doubtful that such laws are practicable.

LABOR STANDARDS

Bettering the lot of the working man is the principal goal of organized labor. Improvement of the conditions under which he works, the number of hours he must spend on the job, the wages he receives for his efforts, his welfare when injured or unemployed, and similar areas of concern comprise the immediate goals.

Safety and Health. All states have enacted laws designed to protect the health of workers and to reduce the likelihood of accidental injury. For example, moving parts of dangerous machinery ordinarily must be enclosed by some sort of guard. Fire escapes and exits must be provided. Inspection of buildings, mines, and machines is generally required. Occupations that involve dangerous materials such as explosives or radioactive substances are subjected to detailed safety regulations. Statutes and regulations dealing more directly with the health of workers include those excluding children from gainful occupations and limiting the types of jobs that women may hold. Adequate ventilation, rest periods, washrooms, and lunch

---

[20] *Wolf Packing Company* v. *Court of Industrial Relations,* 262 U.S. 522 (1923), and *ibid.,* 267 U.S. 552 (1925), held the act invalid as applied to nonutility enterprises.

[21] *Amalgamated Association* v. *Wisconsin Employment Relations Board,* 340 U.S. 383.

facilities must be provided by many employers. The danger of occupational diseases has resulted in requirements that respirators, special clothing, masks, and the like be used or be kept readily available. The pattern and extent of safety and health regulations varies among the states, of course, depending upon the character and range of occupational pursuits in each.

Hours and Wages. For many years attempts by states to limit the number of hours a job holder might be required to work were considered by state and federal courts to be in violation of the freedom of employers and employees to contract. It was not until the 1917 decision of *Bunting* v. *Oregon*[22] that the United States Supreme Court approved a state statute prescribing a maximum number of hours for industrial workers. Since then every state has enacted hours legislation applicable to at least a part of its labor force. All states strictly regulate the employment of minors, including the number of hours they may work. Over forty states also prescribe maximums for women. Adult males, however, are restricted by hours legislation in only a few states.

Minimum-wage laws did not receive the blessing of the nation's highest court until 1937, when it upheld a Washington statute setting minimum wages to be paid to women and minors.[23] Today, two-thirds of the states have minimum wage statutes although some of them apply only to women or to women and children. In a few instances minimum wages are fixed by statutory provisions, but in view of the hardships that an inflexible minimum may cause in some industries, the usual arrangement involves a wage board empowered to make adjustments among industries. Wage legislation also deals with such points as the times or intervals at which wages must be paid, payment of wages in legal tender, and payment of wages upon termination of employment. Each state also recognizes "mechanic's liens" by which designated classes of laborers such as mechanics and construction workers are permitted to secure unpaid wages in proceedings against the value of employers' property.

National wage and hour legislation applicable to all employers in interstate commerce was provided by Congress in 1938 in the Fair Labor Standards Act. Upheld by the Supreme Court in 1941,[24] the

---

[22] 243 U.S. 426.
[23] *West Coast Hotel* v. *Parrish,* 300 U.S. 379.
[24] *United States* v. *Darby Lumber Company,* 312 U.S. 100.

federal act, as amended to date, fixes $1.25 as the minimum hourly wage that must be paid, without discrimination on the basis of sex, by all employers engaged in interstate commerce. The act also limits hours of work to eight per day and forty per week, but "overtime" or work beyond these maximums is permitted if compensated at a rate of one and one-half times the hourly minimum. Similar laws are found in most states, although the limits as to hours and wages as well as coverage both of workers and employers present broad extremes from state to state.

Child Labor. Until recent years it was not uncommon to see boys and girls working long hours alongside adults. Early wage and hour legislation enacted in their behalf, as noted above, was not particularly successful in improving their lot. Organized labor, reform groups, and enlightened employers fought for measures to curb exploitation of children in industry. Congress responded with appropriate legislation, but in 1918 and again in 1922 the Supreme Court negated the acts.[25] In 1924 Congress proposed an amendment to the Constitution which would have delegated to the national government authority to regulate child labor. However, before the necessary number of ratifications could be secured the Supreme Court reversed its previous rulings, making the amendment unnecessary. In upholding the Fair Labor Standards Act, the Court approved provisions which forbade employers in interstate commerce to hire anyone under the age of sixteen or, in hazardous occupations, anyone under eighteen.[26]

Each of the fifty states has enacted laws strictly limiting the use of child labor in intrastate commerce. The minimum age requirement for employment is, depending upon the state, fourteen, fifteen, or sixteen. Hazardous jobs may not be held by persons under sixteen or eighteen. Many exceptions are made although only under circumstances of extreme necessity are minors permitted to work during hours they are required by law to be in school. Night work is limited in every state, with the hours of 7:00 P.M. to 7:00 A.M. generally forbidden although in some states certain types of labor may be extended to 11:00 P.M. or midnight. The principal problems remaining in regard to child labor are chiefly those associated with enforce-

---

[25] *Hammer* v. *Dagenhart,* 247 U.S. 251 (1918); and *Bailey* v. *Drexel Furniture Company,* 259 U.S. 20 (1922).

[26] *United States* v. *Darby Lumber Company,* 312 U.S. 100 (1941).

ment. Many state laws could be improved, particularly by eliminating exceptions, but greater advances could be realized by compelling stricter observation of existing laws.

Workmen's Compensation. Before the development of workmen's compensation programs, the worker who was disabled in industrial accidents was at extreme disadvantage. He could bring a suit for damages in a court of law, but prevailing common law doctrines favored the employers. The *assumption of risk* doctrine forbade awards of damages if injury resulted from the ordinary risks associated with an occupation. A worker injured as a result of his own negligence could not win damages because of the doctrine of *contributory negligence.* Similarly, the *fellow-servant rule* prevented collection by a worker injured in an accident resulting from the negligence of a co-worker. It was not until 1911 when California, New Jersey, Washington, and Wisconsin adopted workmen's compensation laws that the position of the injured worker began to improve. In increasing numbers states enacted similar laws on the theory that the costs of industrial accidents are legitimate costs of production. Such costs are eventually passed on to consumers in the prices they pay for goods and services. Today all states have such statutes covering all or some industrial workers.

Under a typical workmen's compensation program, a disabled worker is paid a percentage of his weekly salary, usually about two-thirds. In two-thirds of the states the period of weekly payments ranges from 208 to 500 weeks; in the remainder they continue throughout the entire period of disability. About half the states have set maximums on the total amount that may be paid to a worker as a result of a single accident, the limits varying among the states from $6,500 to $25,000. The costs are borne by employers who usually insure their risks with private insurance firms. A few states require employers to insure with a special state insurance fund. Most states have special boards or commissions to administer workmen's compensation programs, although in some a subordinate agency of the department of labor performs this function.

Workmen's compensation programs have undergone impressive development during the past half-century, but there is still room for much improvement. Not all occupations are covered by compensation laws, with agricultural workers, domestics, and casual laborers commonly excluded. Employers who hire only a few workers are usually exempt. All occupational diseases, or some of them, are commonly not compensable. In many states employers may elect not to accept coverage of the workmen's compensation law. This is not as serious a flaw as it may appear, however, for employers who decline participation are liable for damages, and the common law defenses discussed earlier are specifically denied to them.

Unemployment Compensation. Unemployment is a serious and continuing problem in an industrial society. In the American labor force of about 75,000,000 workers three or four million jobless are thought normal. Temporary fluctuations in the economy, technological advances that replace men with machines, seasonal variations, and changes in consumer preferences are among the important factors contributing to unemployment. Because of such developments many willing workers are forced into temporary idleness. For many of them these periods of unemployment are weeks, or months, of hardship and privation. Unemployment compensation programs, based on the idea that costs of unemployment, like disability, are legitimate production costs, are designed to ease the burden.

Early state programs, attempted during the first years of the Great Depression, were unsuccessful. The primary reasons for their failure were the reluctance of states to reduce the competitive position of home industries by placing additional taxes upon them and the deterrent effect of the added tax burden upon industrial recovery. As the Depression wore on, however, and a fourth of the labor force —over 12,000,000 workers—joined the ranks of the unemployed, action was necessary. After a period of stop-gap relief measures the national government responded with the Social Security Act of 1935 that established the cooperative state-federal program in effect today.

Under the Social Security Act, as amended, the national government levies a payroll tax of 3.1 per cent upon all employers of four or more persons. The tax is assessed against only that portion of a payroll equivalent to $3,000 per employee per year or less to the extent that one or more employees do not earn that amount. However, if a state enacts a tax for unemployment compensation purposes, the taxes paid to the state by an employer may be credited against his federal tax bill to the extent that the federal tax is reduced to 0.4 per cent. As a result of this feature, the taxes assessed by the states tend to be at about the 2.7 per cent level. The program is federally administered, with all tax collections paid into the United States treasury, credited to state accounts, and then released to the states as needed to meet claims. The funds collected by the federal government are used to pay the costs of administering the unemployment compensation program, including costs incurred by states that adhere to certain federally imposed conditions. These requirements include application of the merit principle in state programs, adequate administrative organization, provision of means for hearing complaints of persons denied benefits, keeping a minimum amount of funds in reserve, and paying collections into the federal treasury.

State laws vary considerably in detail. Most apply to employers of four or more, but six states include *all* employers while a dozen or so provide that some employers of one or more are covered. All states use an "experience rating" system whereby employers whose enterprises have low rates of unemployment are taxed at lower rates. Benefits are calculated by a variety of formulas, but all are based upon the same general principle: a percentage of wages earned weekly during a stipulated period of employment. Since unemployment compensation payments are intended only to help a jobless worker until he finds new employment, benefits are relatively low and of short duration. Weekly benefits can be as high as seventy dollars or as low as three, and for as many as twenty-two to thirty-nine weeks, but the average weekly payment for all states is about thirty-five dollars paid over a period of approximately thirteen weeks.

Employment Services. Finding a job is sometimes difficult, especially during times of economic recession or depression. Frequently, workers possessing special skills cannot locate employment in which their talents can be most effectively used. Private employment agencies that place workers in return for a fee have long existed. Unethical practices by some of them led a few states to establish public agencies during the 1890's. During the next thirty years many other states did so. A nationwide system of public employment agencies was not established, however, until the depression of the 1930's when the national government assisted the states financially.

The problem of unemployment had become so severe by 1933 that Congress established a grant-in-aid program to help states create more employment agencies. Within a few years every state was participating in the program. In 1942 the national government took over all such agencies as a means of contending with the wartime manpower shortage. Throughout World War II agencies were operated by the United States Employment Service, but in 1946, after the cessation of hostilities, they were returned to state control. Today the USES continues to coordinate state programs and to provide advice, information, and technical assistance, but the only agencies it operates directly are those for veterans, farm workers, and residents of the District of Columbia.

Discrimination in Employment. During the past twenty years impressive strides have been made in the states toward elimination of discrimination in employment. Since World War II half the states have enacted laws known as "fair employment practices" acts. New York was first to enact such legislation in 1945, followed the same year by New Jersey. Today the list includes all states, other than those of the southern and Gulf coast regions, which have large populations and in which large minority groups are found.[27] Also, for the first time in the history of the nation, a federal fair employment statute was enacted—as part of the Civil Rights Act of 1964.

FEP laws typically forbid employers to discriminate in hiring, promoting, and firing on the basis of race, creed, color, or national origin.[28] Similarly, labor unions may not deny membership on such grounds, and employment agencies must also refrain from discrimination. Enforcement is accomplished by a commission which is empowered to begin proceedings on its own initiative or on the basis of complaints lodged with it. After investigation, which may entail a public hearing, the commission may issue an order directing compliance with the provisions of the statute. Refusal to obey an order may lead to court action by the commission. Rarely, however, do such cases get into the courts and only infrequently are formal hearings necessary, for in most instances persuasion is adequate. As a rule employers prefer to comply rather than face the effects of the unfavorable publicity invariably associated with noncompliance.

The new federal law established an Equal Employment Opportunities Commission with powers similar to those of state FEP commissions. Its jurisdiction, of course, is much broader in that it may reach

---

[27] Alaska, California, Colorado, Connecticut, Delaware, Hawaii, Idaho, Illinois, Indiana, Iowa, Kansas, Massachusetts, Michigan, Minnesota, Missouri, New Jersey, New Mexico, New York, Ohio, Oregon, Pennsylvania, Rhode Island, Vermont, Washington, and Wisconsin. Note that the most heavily industrialized states are included.

[28] In most of the states noted above, as well as a few others, discrimination on the basis of age is also forbidden.

employers and labor organizations in all parts of the country. However, small enterprises are exempt from the processes of the EEOC,[29] and it is statutorily obliged to attempt settlements by persuasion. Unlike many state agencies the federal commission has no enforcement powers of its own. It must apply to a federal court for an order directing compliance, violation of which may be punished as a contempt of court. Whether the EEOC will be effective in the elimination of discrimination in employment is a question that cannot yet be answered in view of its recent establishment.

Opponents of FEP laws contend that they violate the rights of employers to operate their businesses as they think best, and that they stir up more antagonisms than they eliminate. Supporters maintain that discrimination, wherever found, is un-American and is an evil that government has a duty to prevent. To what degree existing laws have achieved their objectives cannot be accurately determined. Discrimination is difficult to prove, laws are easily evaded, many violations go unreported, and as a matter of record comparatively few charges have been heard in courts.

SELECTED REFERENCES

Books:

Bureau of Labor Standards, U.S. Department of Labor, *Federal Labor Laws and Programs,* Washington D.C., 1964.

Cotter, Cornelius P., *Government and Private Enterprise,* Holt, Rinehart and Winston, New York, 1960.

Dimock, Marshall E., *Business and Government,* 4th edition, Holt, Rinehart and Winston, New York, 1961.

Koontz, Harold, and Gable, Richard W., *Public Control of Economic Enterprise,* McGraw-Hill, New York, 1952.

Leek, John H., *Government and Labor in the United States,* Holt and Company, New York, 1952.

Somers, Herman M., and Somers, Anne R., *Workmen's Compensation,* John Wiley and Sons, New York, 1954.

Wilcox, Clair, *Public Policies Toward Business,* revised edition, Richard D. Irwin, Inc., Homewood, Ill., 1960.

---

[29] EEOC became operative in July 1965 with a jurisdiction limited to employers of 100 or more persons. Its jurisdiction is scheduled to broaden to include employers of twenty-five or more by 1970.

Articles:

"Arbitration and the Courts," Symposium, *Northwestern University Law Review,* September–October 1963.

Bates, Richard K., "Constitutionality of State Fair Trade Acts," *Indiana Law Journal,* Winter 1957.

Dempsey, J. R., S. J., "The Operation of the Right-to-Work Laws," *Labor Law Journal,* September 1959.

"Government and Labor in the United States," Symposium, *Current History,* September 1959.

Hayes, Edward R., " 'Blue Sky' and Federal Securities Laws," *Vanderbilt Law Review,* June 1958.

Katz, Harold A., "Two Decades of State Labor Legislation: 1937–1957," *Labor Law Journal,* November 1957.

Kovarsky, Irving, "A Review of State FEPC Laws," *Labor Law Journal,* July 1958.

Morgan, Chester A., "Unions and State Antitrust Laws," *Labor Law Journal,* July 1956.

"The Question of Extending Minimum Wage Coverage," Symposium, *Congressional Digest,* June–July 1957.

Samoff, Bernard, "Federal-State Relations: Enforcing Collective Bargaining Agreements," *Labor Law Journal,* June 1958.

Chapter 29

State and Local Government—
An Assessment

An astute foreign observer of American political institutions, James Bryce, writing toward the end of the nineteenth century, asserted that the states had "shrivelled up."[1] It was also his opinion that "The faults of the State governments are insignificant compared with the extravagance, corruption, and mismanagement which mark the administrations of most of the great cities."[2] Indeed, as Lord Bryce said, "There is no denying that the government of cities is the one conspicuous failure of the United States."[3] Regrettably, Bryce witnessed a low ebb in the performance of state and local governments during the post-Civil War period, which has been aptly characterized as an "era of greed, grab, and gain." Thus at the turn of the century commentators were much concerned about the vitality of state and local governmental institutions. Some still are gloomy. Writing in 1949, Robert S. Allen denounced state government generally as "the tawdriest, most incompetent, and most stultifying unit of the nation's political structure. . . . The whole system of state government is moribund, corrosive, and deadening."[4]

State and local governments have experienced good and bad times, periods of advance, and periods of retrogression. They grew in stature and improved in quality during the first quarter of the twentieth century. Then came the Great Depression of the 1930's, and states and localities proved unequal to the burdens cast upon them. At a time when increased governmental activity was necessary to minimize privations, even starvation, some local governments became bank-

---

[1] James Bryce, *The American Commonwealth,* The Commonwealth Publishing Co., New York, 1908, Vol. I, p. 604.

[2] *Ibid.,* p. 681.

[3] *Loc. cit.*

[4] Robert S. Allen (ed.), *Our Sovereign State,* Vanguard Press, New York, 1949, pp. vii and xi.

rupt, and states curtailed their expenditures. The story of how the federal government stepped into the breach is well known. With the advantage of hindsight, it is now possible to perceive ways in which the response to the demands of those times might have been better, but the important fact is that the national government *acted*. The states and localities functioned in part as a means of implementing federal programs.

Ever since the 1930's many criticisms have been made concerning federal encroachments upon "states' rights." Many state officials have been eager to take advantage of federal largesse and at the same time criticize expansion of federal power, but few of them have been willing to go on record with a statement so forthright as that of Governor J. M. Broughton of North Carolina in 1944:

> Those of us who believe in the fundamental principles of states' rights and local self-government may as well concede frankly that much of the almost terrifying expansion of federal encroachment upon the original domain of the states has come about because state governments failed to meet the challenge of the new day. . . .
>
> The best answer, indeed the only one, to the alarming and rapid spread of federal encroachment is to give the people a better government through state agencies. Conditions like these cannot be met either by harking back or moaning low.[5]

Whether federal expansion into areas of activity formerly reserved to the states has been "terrifying" or not is a matter of opinion. However, no one can challenge the *fact* of the expansion, and changes in federal-state relations continue apace. Fortunately or unfortunately, no clearly defined criteria exist by which to determine whether the developments of recent years are "good" or "bad." Considerable insight is reflected in the observation by Herbert O'Connor to the effect that "The one factor . . . in state-federal relations that has stood absolutely unchanged through all the years is their purpose. They are right when they serve best the welfare of the people; they are wrong when they interfere in any way with that welfare."[6]

Critics of federal expansion may argue that developments have not

---

[5] Quoted in Roy Victor Peel, *State Government Today*, University of New Mexico Press, Albuquerque, 1948, p. 138.

[6] Herbert R. O'Connor, "The Sovereign States," *State Government*, August 1945, pp. 126–128.

really promoted the welfare of the people. But, practically speaking, who is to judge? The people and their chosen representatives or some self-appointed theorist? Only one answer to such a query is at all consistent with democracy. All levels of government have shared in the appreciable increase in activity characteristic of modern times, and the expansion has occurred largely because major segments of the population, if not a majority of the people at any one time, have demanded more services. Streets have been paved, sewers built, and recreational facilities established because people wanted them. Highways have been improved, welfare programs strengthened, and facilities for public education expanded because of popular demands. Not everyone wants more paved streets, better highways, more welfare, or advances in education, but the bulk of the people do.

Certainly, the responsibilities of the states have grown appreciably in recent years. Contrary to some opinions, they are in no danger of atrophy. Instead, the states are growing continually in importance, a fact that is amply attested by an examination of expenditure trends. The American Assembly noted in 1955 that "The great increase in state expenditures has been devoted to meeting responsibilities that the states scarcely recognized as theirs at all 50 years ago."[7] No one can argue rationally that the states are less important to their residents than they were at the beginning of the century. It is extremely difficult to generalize concerning the efficiency of state governments, as there is no "typical" state. Some appear "well geared to handle their responsibilities," while others are "poorly prepared to meet the problems that press upon them."[8] The same may be said of local governments.

If the states are to function most effectively while shouldering the burdens imposed by future needs, some improvements need to be made. Probably no state will implement them all; some already have moved in the right direction. In 1955 the Commission on Intergovernmental Relations urged the states to modernize and strengthen their political institutions and practices. It noted that the Council of State Governments already had called upon the states "to revise their constitutions, to modernize their legislative processes and procedures, to reorganize their executive branches . . . to reorganize

---

[7] The American Assembly, *The Forty-Eight States: Their Tasks as Policy Makers and Administrators*, Graduate School of Business, Columbia University, New York, 1955, p. 23.

[8] *Ibid.*, p. 138.

their tax systems, to maintain adequate planning and resource agencies, and to extend home rule to their political subdivisions.["]9

Attention has been directed here to a few new state constitutions
and some halting steps toward improvements in legislative procedures. Much interest has been evidenced recently in administrative reorganization. Results, however, have not been commensurate
with the effort expended. A number of states have analyzed their
tax systems rather thoroughly, sometimes even calling in outside experts for advice and assistance. Less has been done in regard to
creation of agencies to study carefully the resources of individual
states and prepare plans for future development. Slightly more than
half of the states have granted home rule to certain units of local
government.

A necessary prerequisite to large-scale improvements in state and
local government is citizen support. "Citizens who fail to understand
the essential conditions of effective government in their home States
may unintentionally promote the centralization they deplore."[10]
Most citizens are much too occupied with other matters to be greatly
concerned or to become well informed about matters of state and
local government. Indifference and ignorance are fostered by the
curricula of secondary schools and institutions of higher learning because they permit young men and women to become "educated"
without requiring them even to take a look at the governmental institutions under which they live. "College graduates, whether they
have had a good political education or not, belong to the group of
the population to which society increasingly turns for leadership."[11]
It is no wonder that as a people Americans are not "greatly concerned
about the quality of our state and local governments."[12] In order to
experience intelligent concern, a person must first be informed.

Quantities of information are available, but its quality often
leaves much to be desired. Most citizens obtain the bulk of their
information about government through the press, radio, and television. Besides occasional personal contacts, the newspapers are
probably most influential in shaping the average citizen's impressions

---

[9] The Commission on Intergovernmental Relations, *A Report to the President for Transmittal to the Congress*, June 1955, p. 37. See also, John F. Kennedy, "The Shame of the States," *New York Times Magazine*, May 18, 1958.

[10] Commission on Intergovernmental Relations, *op. cit.*, p. 58.

[11] Earl Latham, Joseph P. Harris, and Austin Ranney, *College Standards for Political Education*, Citizenship Clearinghouse, 1959, p. 8.

[12] Robert S. Babcock, *State and Local Government and Politics*, Random House, Inc., New York, 1957, p. 377.

concerning his government. In general, their treatment of occurrences in governmental agencies emphasizes "scandals, crimes, and other misdeeds" as well as errors of judgment. The multitude of tasks handled daily in an honest and efficient manner are not newsworthy. "Accordingly the pictures of state affairs the voters have in their heads are mostly of strife and struggle among a lot of fools and crooks."[13] If true, this situation is most unfortunate. Fools and crooks are found in government as elsewhere, but their influence on public affairs does not appear disproportionate.

It is impossible to stress too strongly the importance of citizen interest and participation in state and local as well as national affairs. Indeed, interest and participation in governmental affairs by *informed* citizens is "the only final assurance of effective and responsive government."[14] Contrary to frequently heard clichés, participation by everyone, regardless of his interest or knowledge, is not a source of strength for democratic institutions. The hope for the future of these institutions at all levels of government lies in the ability of informed men and women to separate the true from the false, the wise from the unwise, and to make their influence felt in the councils of the nation.

---

[13] The American Assembly, *op. cit.*, p. 66.
[14] *Ibid.*, p. 141.

Table of Cases Cited

Index